PRACTITIONER'S PERSPECTIVE

PROBATION AND PAROLE OFFICER

Name: Dori Ege

Current Position: Arizona Deputy Compact Administrator for Adult Probation, Arizona Compact Commissioner for Parole and Probation

City, State: Phoenix, Arizona

College Attended/Academic Major: Bachelor of arts in criminal justice from St. Cloud State University, Minnesota

How long have you been a practitioner in a career relating to probation and parole? 13 years, 3 months.

The primary duties and responsibilities of a probation and parole officer: To ensure offender compliance with the conditions of supervision imposed by the court or paroling authority through required face-to-face contacts, reports from treatment providers, drug testing, residence searches, and providing or referring the offender to other resources as needed (e.g., employment skills training). In addition, officers must update the court or compliance through either m behavior return h and par status o complia

range from hearings to determine early termination of supervision or hearings to revoke supervision and return the offender to custody. In many, officers are also required to update victims who are associated with an offender's case in accordance with local victim notification requirements.

The qualities/characteristics that are most helpful in this career: Resilience, integrity, confidence, reliability, excellent writing skills, excellent communication skills, leadership skills, and fairness and consistency.

In general, this is what a *typical day* looks like for a practitioner in this career: Conducting office and field visits with offenders to or compliance with condition sed by a cou or paroling aut y wr other compliance or n c of condi s; testifying at or attending court hearings regaring assigned offenders; and fielding phone calls and email correspondence from offenders, their families, employers, treatment providers, attorneys, and other members of the criminal justice system regarding cases assigned to the officer's caseload.

My advice to someone either wishing to study,

You Be the... JUDGE

Within a few weeks of initiating a six-month pilot program to equip officers with body cameras, the city received the following request by an anonymous citizen:

> Public disclosure requests for all body-cam videos since police begin using them; every 911 dispatch on which Seattle police officers were sent; all videos from patrol-car cameras; all of the reports officers write; and the details of all computer searches by officers for persons' names, addresses, or license plate numbers were expected to financially cripple the city of Seattle, Washington, and result in the demise of a plan to equip Seattle police officers with body cameras.[32]

Washington state law allows such anonymous requests, and public agencies cannot deny records on the grounds that a request is overbroad, as long as the materials are identifiable.[33] In one such case, a request for all emails received and sent by city employees could have cost the city $110 million in salary and

taken 1,376 years for one full-time employee to fulfill. The city of course argues that the administrative costs relating to such requests make honoring them cost-prohibitive.[34]

Some people argue, however, that public officials should not complain that the "sky is falling" in regard to such requests, and that public officials can address these large requests through such means as delivering materials in installments and collecting copy fees with each release to make sure the requester is serious. It is also argued that city officials sometimes exaggerate the time and technical requirements required to produce records, and look for horror stories to persuade legislators of the need to change the law.

1. Should the public be allowed to make such broad requests for body-camera videos? If so, should there be a limit on the number, kinds, and costs of such requests?

2. How can the whole field of police body camera use be made fair to all parties concerned?

PRACT ESSONS

- New *Practitioner's Perspectives* allow students to hear from a wide array of criminal justice professions from lice, court, and corrections professiona ance abuse counselors and cyberse nts, covering the nature of th eparation, and the decisions ake e ◀◀

- New *You Be the _____* boxes offer a broad range of perspectives for students to take on, such as judge, sentencing commissioner, and policy maker. ◀◀◀

LEARNING TOOLS TO SUCCEED IN THE COURSE AND BEYOND

- Chapter-opening *Assess Your Awareness* quiz allows students to determine what they do and don't know about the chapter's contents and sharpen their focus as they read.

- *New real-life, crime-related case studies* open each chapter to increase student interest and engagement.

- End-of-chapter *summaries, key terms,* and *review questions* enhance student mastery and help them prepare for exams.

- *Learn by Doing* exercises at the end of each chapter give students an opportunity to apply what they learn to real-life scenarios. ▼▼▼

LEARN BY DOING

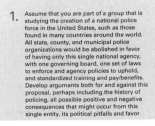

1. Assume that you are part of a group that is studying the creation of a national police force in the United States, such as those found in many countries around the world. All state, county, and municipal police organizations would be abolished in favor of having only this single national agency, with one governing board, one set of laws to enforce and agency policies to uphold, and standardized training and pay/benefits. Develop arguments both for and against this proposal, perhaps including the history of policing, all possible positive and negative consequences that might occur from this single entity, its political pitfalls and favor

with the general public, and whether or not you would support this proposal.

2. Describe the duties of the four policing offices that originated in England (if they exist in your area): sheriff, constable, justice of the peace, and coroner.

3. You have been assigned to describe federal and state law enforcement agencies for a class presentation. Prepare a lecture outline covering the major agencies—including their functions—that compose both the Department of Justice and the Department of Homeland Security; include the complementary roles of Interpol.

RESOURCES

Interactive eBook

An Interactive eBook includes all of the pages from the printed text in an easy-to-use electronic format, plus video and audio links, full-text SAGE Journal articles, links to helpful learning tools from the student study site, and interactive study features such as highlighting, roll-over terms definitions, note-taking, and more.

SAGE Video

An extensive video package, available in the SAGE edge online resources and within the Interactive eBook, includes original SAGE videos, including:

- Chapter-related insights and perspectives directly from the authors Kenneth J. Peak and Pamela M. Everett
- Interviews with Los Angeles County Lieutenant Brian D. Fitch
- Student interviews highlighting misconceptions on key CJ concepts with author responses

SAGE Market Research Shows:

- **87%** of instructors said they use video in lecture.
- **More than 75%** of instructors said they use video to increase student engagement, incorporating current events into class discussion and to illustrate key concepts.
- **Over 90%** of instructors said they use documentaries, films, and YouTube as their primary sources for video.
- **Over 60%** of instructors would use videos of students being interviewed by an expert or author to clarify misconceptions around the course, key concepts from the text, and real-world implications.

> *"This text provides a clear and interesting format through which students may understand often difficult criminal justice concepts. Peak provides students with an interactive format for learning, complete with up-to-date supplementary information. The text is concise, informative, and interesting."*
>
> —Tameka Samuels-Jones,
> University of Florida

SAGE edge for Instructors supports your teaching by making it easy to integrate quality content and create a rich learning environment for students.

- **Test banks** built on Bloom's Taxonomy to provide a diverse range of pre-written options as well as the opportunity to edit any question and/or insert your own personalized questions to effectively assess students' progress and understanding.

- **Sample course syllabi** for semester and quarter courses provide suggested models for structuring your courses.

- Editable, chapter-specific **PowerPoint®** **slides** offer complete flexibility for creating a multimedia presentation for your course.

- EXCLUSIVE! Access to full-text **SAGE** **journal articles** that have been carefully selected to support and expand on the concepts presented in each chapter is included.

- **SAGE Original Video** created for the text enable students to gain a deeper understanding of the material

- **Video and multimedia content** includes original SAGE videos that appeal to students with different learning styles.

- **Lecture notes** summarize key concepts by chapter to help you prepare for lectures and class discussions.

- **Course cartridge** for easy LMS integration.

- **Chapter-specific discussion questions** help launch classroom interaction by prompting students to engage with the material and by reinforcing important content.

SAGE edge for Students provides a personalized approach to help students accomplish their coursework goals in an easy-to-use learning environment.

- Mobile-friendly **eFlashcards** strengthen understanding of key terms and concepts.

- Mobile-friendly practice **quizzes** allow for independent assessment by students of their mastery of course material.

- A customized online **action plan** includes tips and feedback on progress through the course and materials, which allows students to individualize their learning experience.

- **Chapter summaries** with **learning objectives** reinforce the most important material.

- EXCLUSIVE! Access to full-text **SAGE** **journal articles** that have been carefully selected to support and expand on the concepts presented in each chapter is included.

- **SAGE Original Video** created for the text enable students to gain a deeper understanding of the material.

- **Video and multimedia content** includes original SAGE videos that appeal to students with different learning styles.

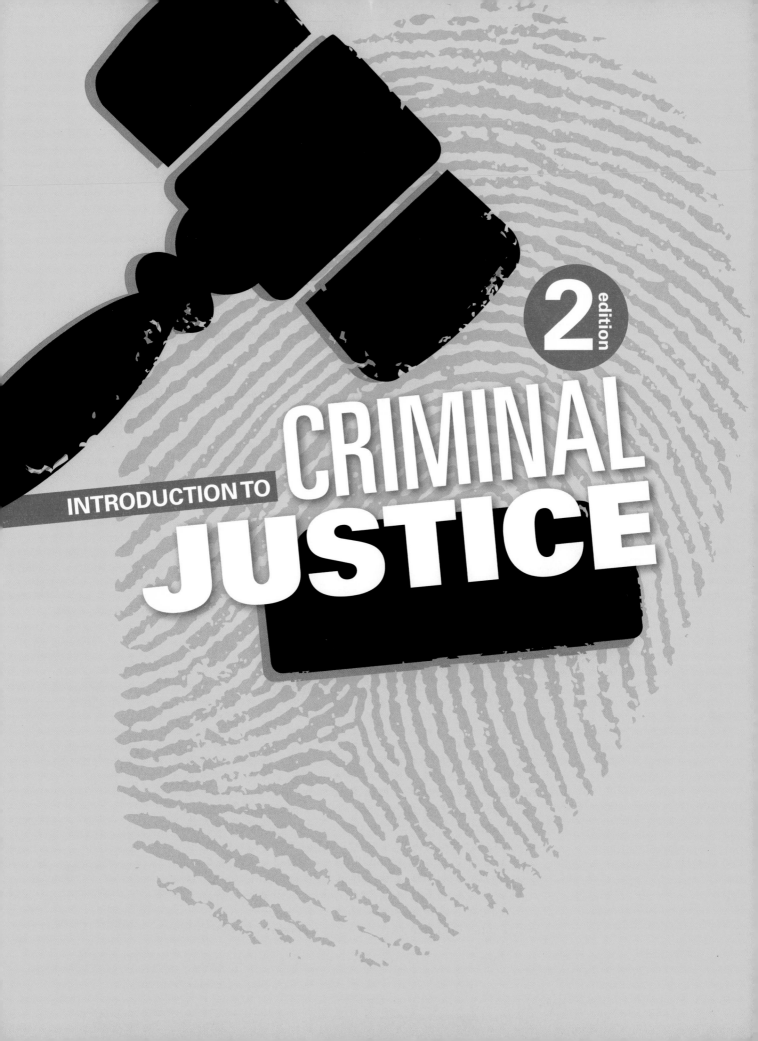

2 edition

INTRODUCTION TO **CRIMINAL JUSTICE**

To Kathy—Glad we were "still speaking in the spring."

—K. J. P.

For my students—past, present, and future—thank you for making it all worthwhile.

—P. M. E.

SAGE was founded in 1965 by Sara Miller McCune to support the dissemination of usable knowledge by publishing innovative and high-quality research and teaching content. Today, we publish over 900 journals, including those of more than 400 learned societies, more than 800 new books per year, and a growing range of library products including archives, data, case studies, reports, and video. SAGE remains majority-owned by our founder, and after Sara's lifetime will become owned by a charitable trust that secures our continued independence.

Los Angeles | London | New Delhi | Singapore | Washington DC

INTRODUCTION TO **CRIMINAL JUSTICE**

PRACTICE AND PROCESS

2 edition

KENNETH J. PEAK • **PAMELA M. EVERETT**
UNIVERSITY OF NEVADA, RENO
UNIVERSITY OF NEVADA, RENO

**SAGE**

Los Angeles | London | New Delhi
Singapore | Washington DC

Los Angeles | London | New Delhi
Singapore | Washington DC

FOR INFORMATION:

SAGE Publications, Inc.
2455 Teller Road
Thousand Oaks, California 91320
E-mail: order@sagepub.com

SAGE Publications Ltd.
1 Oliver's Yard
55 City Road
London EC1Y 1SP
United Kingdom

SAGE Publications India Pvt. Ltd.
B 1/I 1 Mohan Cooperative Industrial Area
Mathura Road, New Delhi 110 044
India

SAGE Publications Asia-Pacific Pte. Ltd.
3 Church Street
#10-04 Samsung Hub
Singapore 049483

Publisher: Jerry Westby
Associate Editor: Jessica Miller
eLearning Editor: Nicole Mangona
Editorial Assistant: Laura Kirkhuff
Production Editor: David C. Felts
Copy Editor: Amy Marks
Typesetter: C&M Digitals (P) Ltd.
Proofreader: Gretchen Treadwell
Indexer: Naomi Linzer
Cover Designer: Scott Van Atta
Marketing Manager: Amy Lammers

Printed in Canada.

ISBN 978-1-5063-0592-9

This book is printed on acid-free paper.

16 17 18 19 20 10 9 8 7 6 5 4 3 2

BRIEF CONTENTS

DETAILED CONTENTS

©iStockphoto.com/mcmenomy

Part I. Criminal Justice as a System: The Basics   1

©iStockphoto.com/Vilches

Part II. The Police   105

© istockphoto.com/wdstock

Part III. The Courts 213

9. COURT ORGANIZATION: STRUCTURE, FUNCTIONS, AND THE TRIAL PROCESS 214

10. THE BENCH AND THE BAR: THOSE WHO JUDGE, PROSECUTE, AND DEFEND 244

©Joseph Sohm/Visions of America/Corbis

Part IV. Corrections   289

13. THE INMATES' WORLD: THE "KEEPERS" AND THE "KEPT" — 316

14. CORRECTIONS IN THE COMMUNITY: PROBATION, PAROLE, AND OTHER ALTERNATIVES TO INCARCERATION — 344

©iStockphoto.com/Robert Ingelhart

Part V. Spanning the System: Methods and Issues 371

15. JUVENILE JUSTICE: PHILOSOPHY, LAW, AND PRACTICES 372

16. ON THE CRIME POLICY AND PREVENTION AGENDA: TERRORISM, THE MENTALLY ILL IN THE CRIMINAL JUSTICE SYSTEM, AND THE CHANGING WAR ON DRUGS 396

PREFACE

A Unique Approach

Famed educator John Dewey advocated the "learning by doing" approach to education, or problem-based learning. This book is written, from start to finish, with that philosophy in mind. Its approach also comports with the popular learning method espoused by Benjamin Bloom, known as "Bloom's Taxonomy," in which he called for "higher-order thinking skills"—critical and creative thinking that involves analysis, synthesis, and evaluation.

This book also benefits from the authors having many years of combined practitioners' and academic experience, to include several positions in criminal justice administration, policing, corrections, and the practice of law. Therefore, its chapters contain a palpable, real-world flavor that is typically missing for college and university criminal justice students.

It is hoped that readers will put to use the several features of the book that are intended to help them accomplish this overall goal. In addition to chapter opening questions (which allow students to assess their knowledge of the chapter materials), learning objectives, and a chapter summary, each chapter also contains a number of boxed features such as case studies, "Investigating Further," "Learn by Doing," "You Be the Judge" (or prosecutor, defense attorney, and so on, as the case may require), and "Going Global" exhibits and exercises. Also provided are "Practitioner's Perspectives" (with people in the field describing their criminal justice occupation) as well as brief glimpses into comparative criminal justice systems, law, and practice in selected foreign venues. Taken together, these supplemental materials should also greatly enhance readers' critical analysis, problem-solving, and communication capabilities, and allow them to experience the kind of decisions that must be made in the field.

In today's competitive job market, students who possess these kinds of knowledge, skills, and abilities will have better opportunities for obtaining employment as a criminal justice practitioner and succeeding therein. Although the book certainly delves into some theoretical, political, and sociological subject matter, it attempts to remain true to its *practical*, applied focus throughout and to the extent possible.

Distinctive Chapter Contents

This book also contains chapters devoted to topics not typically found in introductory criminal justice textbooks. For example, Chapter 4 is devoted to criminal justice ethics. Certainly ethics is always a timely topic for our society, and especially for today's criminal justice students and practitioners. Chapter 16 also describes three unique and contemporary issues on the U.S. criminal justice policy-making agenda: terrorism, the mentally ill in the criminal justice system, and the changing war on drugs. Finally, several chapters also discuss the technologies employed in the system.

In sum, this book introduces the student to the primary individuals, theorists, practitioners, processes, concepts, technologies, and terminologies as they work within or are applied to our criminal justice system. Furthermore, the concepts and terms learned in this introductory textbook will serve as the basis for more complex criminal justice studies of police, courts, and corrections in later course work.

Chapter Organization

To facilitate the above goals, we first need to place the study of criminal justice within the big picture, which is accomplished in the four chapters composing Part I. **Chapter 1** discusses the major theme and organization of this book, foundations and politics of criminal justice, an overview of the criminal justice process and the offender's flow through the system, and how discretion and ethics apply to the field. **Chapter 2** defines many legal terms and concepts as they apply to crime, and includes the sources and nature of law (including substantive and procedural law, common law, and criminal and civil law), the elements of criminal acts, felonies and misdemeanors, offense definitions and categories, and legal defenses allowed under the law. **Chapter 3** reviews some of the prevailing explanations concerning why people commit crimes, and the three methods now used for trying to measure how many crimes are committed in the United States. **Chapter 4** concerns ethics and includes definitions and problems, with emphases on the kinds of ethical problems that confront the police, the courtroom work group, and corrections staff. Included are an ethical decision-making process, legislative enactments, and judicial decisions involving ethics at the federal, state, and local levels.

Part II consists of four chapters that address federal law enforcement and state and local policing in the United States. **Chapter 5** discusses the organization and operation of law enforcement agencies at the federal, state, and local (city and county) levels. Included are discussions of their English and colonial roots, the three eras of U.S. policing, and brief considerations of INTERPOL and the field of private security. **Chapter 6** focuses on the roles and tasks of policing, particularly with respect to the broad areas of patrolling and investigating. After beginning with recruitment, training (including higher education for police), and stressors in policing, we consider patrol and traffic functions, use of discretion, community policing, and the work of criminal investigators. **Chapter 7** broadly examines several policing issues. First we consider the recent incidents of lethal use of force and military equipment against citizens in Ferguson, Missouri, and elsewhere; some historical aspects of police-minority relations; and what might be some "lessons learned" and solutions to such problems in the future. Also discussed are police corruption, civil liability, and use of selected technologies. **Chapter 8** examines the constitutional rights of the accused (as per U.S. Supreme Court decisions) as well as limitations placed on the police under the Fourth, Fifth, and Sixth Amendments; the focus is on arrest, search and seizure, the right to remain silent, and the right to counsel.

Part III consists of three chapters that generally examine the courts. **Chapter 9** looks at court organization and functions in the local trial court, state court, and federal court systems. Included in the chapter are discussions of the courts as hallowed places in our society, their use of the adversarial process, the trial process (including pretrial motions and activities), and the jury system. **Chapter 10** considers the roles and functions of those persons who compose the courtroom work group: judges, prosecutors, and defense attorneys. Finally, **Chapter 11** discusses sentencing, punishment, and appeals. Included are the types and purposes of punishment, types of sentences convicted persons may receive, federal sentencing guidelines, victim impact statements, capital punishment, and selected technologies in the courts.

Part IV includes three chapters and examines many aspects of correctional organizations and operations. **Chapter 12** examines federal and state prisons and local jails generally, in terms of their mission, evolution, and organization; included are discussions of factors contributing to inmate populations (including what some observers have termed today's mass incarceration of minorities), prison life, inmate classification, supermax prisons, and selected technologies. **Chapter 13** considers the lives led and challenges faced by both correctional personnel and the inmates. Included are the underground economy, solitary confinement, the work of personnel in prisons and jails, administrative challenges (e.g., overseeing executions, inmate litigation, drugs, women and gangs in prison, preparing inmates for reentry), and selected constitutional rights of inmates. **Chapter 14** reviews community corrections and alternatives to incarceration: probation, parole, and several other diversionary approaches. Included are discussions of the origins of probation and parole, functions of probation and parole offices, several intermediate sanctions (e.g., house arrest, electronic monitoring), a model for addressing recidivism, and restorative justice.

Finally, Part V contains two chapters that consider methods and issues that span the criminal justice system. **Chapter 15** examines juvenile justice—an area where the treatment of offenders is quite different in terms of its overall philosophy, legal bases, and judicial process. Included are the history and extent of juvenile crime, the case flow of juvenile courts, labeling, whether there is a school-to-prison pipeline, youth gangs, and juveniles' legal rights. **Chapter 16** provides an in-depth view of three particularly challenging problems and policy issues confronting today's criminal justice system: terrorism (including related topics of congressional legislation and government use of unmanned aerial vehicles), mentally ill persons who become involved with the criminal justice system, and the changing nature of the war on drugs.

New Topics in This Second Edition

In addition to updated information included throughout the book, the following substantively new materials have been added to this revised second edition:

- Chapter-opening vignettes in each chapter aim to increase student interest and engagement.

- Nine new career profile boxes now cover an even broader array of criminal justice professions, such as substance abuse counselor, juvenile probation officer, and cybersecurity consultant.

- Twenty new "Investigating Further" boxes (formerly called "Focus On") explore current issues in criminal justice and help students dig deeper into the material.

- New "You Be the . . . " boxes offer a broader range of perspectives for students to take on, such as those of sentencing commissioners and policy makers.

Following are additional chapter-by-chapter additions:

Chapter 1:   Expanded discussion of discretion; more explanation about the interplay between the crime control/due process models and discretion; and more detailed coverage of the criminal justice system process.

Chapter 2:   Expanded treatment of *mens rea* with more examples from actual cases; a table summarizing murder and manslaughter and the required *mens rea* for each (with examples); fully updated treatment of sexual assault; expanded treatment of justification defenses; updated exploration of the insanity defense; and new exercises using recent cases on sexual assault, homicide, and self-defense.

Chapter 3:   An explanation of the importance of studying criminology and how research can affect public policy with new "from theory to policy to practice" questions regarding the major schools of thought; balanced treatment of the various criminological theories; and an updated summary chart to help students distinguish between classical and positivist approaches. "From Theory to Policy to Practice" boxes display the relevance of theory and help students make the connection between theory, policy, and practice in criminal justice.

Chapter 4:   The ethical decision-making process (for helping one arrive at a choice in a situation where there is no clear right or wrong answer).

Chapter 5:   Contributions of August Vollmer to advancing police practices; selected federal law enforcement agencies' organization and functions and related career information; and a "Going Global" exhibit on criminal justice challenges in India.

Chapter 6:   Police hiring of immigrants with work permits; higher education and police; and effects and management of police stress.

Chapter 7:   Brief history of police-minority relations; lessons of Ferguson, Missouri; a new transparency with police shootings; uses and costs of police body cameras; a "Going Global" exhibit on the struggle for democracy in Hong Kong; and the role of local police in homeland security.

Chapter 8:   Expanded treatment of stop-and-frisk and racial profiling, including NYPD's controversial program and its demise; further exploration of lineups and eyewitness misidentifications in general; and police agency reforms.

Chapter 9:   Expanded coverage of grand juries, including the Ferguson, Missouri, case; more detailed treatment of the dual court system and a new table showing state and federal courts from trial to last resort; a new feature with examples of circuit court law-making; a brief review of a 2015 study on bail discrimination; and new, expanded material on specialty "problem-solving" courts.

Chapter 10:   Prosecutorial misconduct/immunity and expanded coverage of prosecutorial discretion and power; and a new discussion of victim advocates as part of the courtroom workgroup.

Chapter 11:   Updates on death penalty issues, botched executions, and state responses to DNA exonerations of death row inmates; and expanded coverage of DNA exonerations generally.

Chapter 12:   Mass incarceration; jail rehabilitation and reintegration programs; a career with the Federal Bureau of Prisons; and how drones and cellphones affect prison security.

Chapter 13:   Zimbardo's mock prison experiment; becoming prisonized; underground economy; conditions of confinement; use and effects of solitary confinement; an inmate's perspective on prison; riots in prisons and jails; women in prison (effects on, rights of); preparation for reentry and aftercare; inmates' right to marry.

Chapter 14:   Terms and conditions commonly applied to persons on probation/parole; and the risk-needs-responsivity model for addressing reoffending.

Chapter 15:   The problem of labeling; the "school-to-prison pipeline"; secure and nonsecure custodial options for juvenile offenders; a "Going Global" exhibit concerning juvenile detention in Panama; youth gangs; and providing aftercare and reentry services.

Chapter 16:   Concerns with "homegrown" and "lone wolf" terrorists; the ISIS threat; USA Freedom Act; the mentally ill in the criminal justice system; the changing war on drugs, and the "national epidemic" of prescription painkiller abuse.

ANCILLARIES

$SAGE edge™

edge.sagepub.com/peak2e

SAGE edge offers a robust online environment featuring an impressive array of tools and resources for review, study, and further exploration, keeping both instructors and students on the cutting edge of teaching and learning. SAGE edge content is open access and available on demand. Learning and teaching has never been easier!

SAGE edge for Instructors supports teaching by making it easy to integrate quality content and create a rich learning environment for students.

- **Test banks** provide a diverse range of pre-written options as well as the opportunity to edit any question and/or insert personalized questions to effectively assess students' progress and understanding

- **Sample course syllabi** for semester and quarter courses provide suggested models for structuring one's course

- Editable, chapter-specific **PowerPoint**® **slides** offer complete flexibility for creating a multimedia presentation for the course

- EXCLUSIVE! Access to full-text **SAGE journal articles** have been carefully selected to support and expand on the concepts presented in each chapter to encourage students to think critically

- **Multimedia content** includes original SAGE videos that appeal to students with different learning styles

- **Lecture notes** summarize key concepts by chapter to ease preparation for lectures and class discussions

- A **Course cartridge** provides easy LMS integration

SAGE edge for Students provides a personalized approach to help students accomplish their coursework goals in an easy-to-use learning environment.

- Mobile-friendly **eFlashcards** strengthen understanding of key terms and concepts

- Mobile-friendly practice **quizzes** allow for independent assessment by students of their mastery of course material

- Carefully selected chapter-by-chapter **video links** and **multimedia content** which enhanced classroom-based explorations of key topics

- A customized online **action plan** includes tips and feedback on progress through the course and materials, which allows students to individualize their learning experience

- **Chapter summaries** with **learning objectives** reinforce the most important material

- EXCLUSIVE! Access to full-text **SAGE journal articles** that have been carefully selected to support and expand on the concepts presented in each chapter

ACKNOWLEDGMENTS

This second edition, like its predecessor, is the culmination of dedicated efforts on the part of several key individuals at SAGE Publications, Inc.; they should be recognized. First, this team effort was led by Jerry Westby, Publisher and Acquisitions Editor; we greatly appreciate his ongoing commitment to this publishing effort and rendering his astute experience and assistance toward that end. Also providing stellar performances in their roles were: Jessica Miller, Associate Editor; Laura Kirkhuff, Editorial Assistant; Amy Marks, Copy Editor; and David C. Felts, Production Editor.

The authors also wish to acknowledge the invaluable assistance of the reviewers of the first and second edition, whose reviews of this text resulted in many beneficial additions and modifications. We are grateful for their attention to detail and dedication to criminal justice education.

—K. J. P. and P. M. E.

REVIEWERS OF THE SECOND EDITION

Sami Abdel-Salam, West Chester University

Dianne Berger-Hill, M.A.S., Old Dominion University

Dr. Michele P. Bratina, Shippensburg University of Pennsylvania

Kevin D. Cannon, SIU Edwardsville

Mr. Chris Chaney, William Jessup University

Professor Johnston, NCC Arizona State University

Tameka Samuels-Jones, University of Florida

Margaret A. Schmuhl, John Jay College

Michele Stacey, Ph.D., East Carolina University

Richard J. Stringer, Old Dominion University

Jacqueline van Wormer, Ph.D., Washington State University

Thomas H. Williams, Community College of Denver

Dominic D. Yin, MS., JD., City College of San Francisco

REVIEWERS OF THE FIRST EDITION

George Ackerman
Palm Beach State College

Rosemary Arway
Hodges University

John Augustine
Triton College

Ken Ayers
Kentucky Wesleyan College

Lee Ayers
Southern Oregon University

James Beeks
Piedmont College

Dianne Berger-Hill
Old Dominion University

Joanne Black
Salem College

Heidi Bonner
East Carolina University

Patrick Bradley
University of Maryland University
College

Kathryn Branch
University of Tampa

Christine Broeker
Seminole State College

James Chapman
Wake Technical Community College

Amy Cook
Virginia State University

Michael Cretacci
Buffalo State College

Patrick Cundiff
East Carolina University

Melchor de Guzman
The College at Brockport

Steven Egger
University of Houston–Clear Lake

Mary Beth Finn
Herzing University

Charlene Freyberg
Bellevue College

Julie Globokar
Kent State University

Jill Gordon
Virginia Commonwealth University

Ginny Hatch
Boise State University

Vincent Hunter
Texas A&M Commerce

Joe Kuhns
University of North Carolina at Charlotte

Rebecca Loftus
Arizona State University

David Mackey
Plymouth State University

Jon Maskaly
East Carolina University

Henry Meade
University of Texas at San Antonio

Robert Mellin
University of Maryland

Eric Metchik
Salem State University

Patricia Millhoff
University of Akron

Robert Morin
Western Nevada Community College

Jacqueline Mullany
Triton College

James Ness
University of Phoenix

Christopher O'Connor
University of Wisconsin–Superior

Patrick Patterson
Eastfield College

Nicole Piquero
University of Texas at Dallas

Michael Ramon
Missouri State University

Cassandra Reyes
West Chester University

Melissa Ryan
Sam Houston State University

Shannon Santana
University of North Carolina at
Wilmington

Kim Schnurbush
Hodges University

Cindy Stewart
College of Mount Saint Joseph

Jerry Stinson
Southwest Virginia Community College

Richard Stringer
Old Dominion University

Jason Waller
Tyler Junior College

Franzi Walsh
University of Phoenix

ABOUT THE AUTHORS

Kenneth J. Peak is emeritus professor and former chair of the Department of Criminal Justice, University of Nevada, Reno, where he was named "Teacher of the Year" by the university's Honor Society. Following four years as a municipal police officer in Kansas, he subsequently held positions as a nine-county criminal justice planner for southeast Kansas; director of a four-state technical assistance institute for the Law Enforcement Assistance Administration (based at Washburn University in Topeka); director of university police at Pittsburg State University (Kansas); acting director of public safety, University of Nevada, Reno; and assistant professor of criminal justice at Wichita State University. He has authored or coauthored 28 textbooks (relating to general policing, community policing, criminal justice administration, police supervision and management, and women in law enforcement), two historical books (on Kansas temperance and bootlegging), and more than 60 journal articles and invited book chapters. He is past chair of the Police Section of the Academy of Criminal Justice Sciences and president of the Western and Pacific Association of Criminal Justice Educators. He received two gubernatorial appointments to statewide criminal justice committees while residing in Kansas and holds a doctorate from the University of Kansas.

Pamela M. Everett is a lecturer in the Department of Criminal Justice, University of Nevada, Reno. She earned her undergraduate degree in criminal justice at the University of Nevada, Reno, where she was the top graduating senior in the College of Arts and Sciences. She then earned her Juris Doctorate from the University of San Diego School of Law, where she wrote for the University of San Diego Law Review, garnered first-place honors in the Appellate Moot Court competition, and earned the Best Brief/Best Oralist award for first-year law students. Everett began her teaching career as an adjunct instructor of criminal justice at the University of Nevada, Reno, and then served as an assistant/associate professor of criminal justice at Wayne State College in Nebraska. During her tenure at Wayne State College, she focused her research and publishing efforts on wrongful convictions, community policing, and the mentally ill in the criminal justice system, including serving as assistant editor and a contributor for SAGE's *Encyclopedia of Community Policing and Problem Solving.* She also served as a features/opinion columnist for the Omaha *World-Herald* and an opinion columnist for the Wayne *Stater.* She is a member of the California Bar Association, a volunteer attorney with the California Innocence Project, and a member of the Academy of Criminal Justice Sciences/Law and Policy Section.

PART I

CRIMINAL JUSTICE AS A SYSTEM: THE BASICS

This part consists of four chapters. **Chapter 1** briefly examines why it is important to study criminal justice, the foundations and politics of criminal justice, an overview of the criminal justice process and the offender's flow through the system, and how discretion and ethics apply to the field.

Chapter 2 considers the sources and nature of law (including substantive and procedural, and criminal and civil), the elements of criminal acts, felonies and misdemeanors, offense definitions and categories, and legal constructs and defenses that are allowed under the law.

Chapter 3 examines some of the attempts to explain why people commit crimes (including the classical, positivist, biological, psychological, and sociocultural theories) as well as prevailing methods in use for trying to measure how many crimes are committed.

Chapter 4 looks at definitions and types of ethics in general, and then examines ethical dilemmas that confront the police, the courtroom work group, and correctional staff. Included are legislative enactments and judicial decisions involving ethics at the federal, state, and local levels.

FUNDAMENTALS OF CRIMINAL JUSTICE

Essential Themes and Practices

LEARNING OBJECTIVES

As a result of reading this chapter, you will be able to:

1 Explain the importance of studying and understanding our criminal justice system

2 Describe the foundations of our criminal justice system, including its legal and historical bases

3 Review the influence of politics on our criminal justice system, as well as what can constitute "good" politics and "bad" politics

4 Define the crime control and due process models of criminal justice

5 Describe the importance of discretion throughout the justice system

6 Describe the fundamentals of the criminal justice process—the offender's flow through the police, courts, and corrections components, and the functions of each component

7 Explain the wedding cake model of criminal justice

8 Discuss the importance of ethics and character in criminal justice

ASSESS YOUR AWARENESS

Test your knowledge of criminal justice fundamentals by responding to the following six true-false items; check your answers after reading this chapter's materials.

1 Under the U.S. system of justice, people basically join together, form governments (thus surrendering their rights of self-protection), and receive governmental protection in return.

2 Very little if any political or discretionary behavior or authority exists in the field of criminal justice; its fixed laws and procedures prevent such influences.

3 All prosecutions for crimes begin with a grand jury indictment.

4 Police make the final decisions concerning the actual crimes with which a suspect will be charged.

5 *Parolee* is the term used to describe one who has been granted early release from prison.

6 The U.S. system of criminal justice is intended to function, and indeed does function in all respects, like a "well-oiled machine."

The true administration of justice is the firmest pillar of good government.

—Inscription on the New York State Supreme Court, Foley Square, Manhattan, New York

When we pull back the layers of government services, the most fundamental and indispensable virtues are public safety and social order.

—Hon. David A. Hardy, Washoe County District Court, Reno, Nevada

<< Answers can be found on page 424.

Polly Klaas was 12 years old when she was abducted from her home in Petaluma, CA in 1993. Her body was found several weeks later; she had been sexually assaulted and murdered.

In October 1993, 12-year-old Polly Klaas was having a slumber party at her home in Petaluma, California, when a strange man appeared in her bedroom. He had a knife, and he tied up all the girls and put pillowcases over their heads. He then disappeared into the night with Polly. Law enforcement investigators would learn two months later that the man was Richard Allen Davis. He had been released from prison early—paroled—just a couple of months before the kidnapping. When he was released, he had served only half of a 16-year sentence for another kidnapping, the latest in a long line of violent felonies he had committed over four decades. After a lengthy and complex investigation, Davis finally confessed to kidnapping and murdering Polly, and he led investigators to a shallow grave where he had buried her. Davis had sexually assaulted her and strangled her to death.

Richard Allen Davis was convicted in 1996 of kidnapping and murdering Polly Klaas. Davis remains on death row at San Quentin State Prison in northern California.

When the story made headlines, Americans began asking how someone like Davis, with such a long and horrific criminal record, could have been set free, and more important, how could we keep repeat offenders like Davis from committing more crimes? Like most issues raised in our criminal justice system, the solution would have to begin with a change in the law.

As you read this chapter, think about how the criminal law is influenced, and how new laws are made and ultimately changed, as society and its norms change. What kind of solution would you propose to prevent the next Richard Allen Davis from being set free to kidnap and murder? What political pressures would lawmakers feel in crafting such a law, and what are the risks that societal and political reactions could be extreme in the wake of a heinous crime like the Polly Klaas murder?

INTRODUCTION

The criminal justice system as we know it has existed for more than a century and a half. Yet, even though most Americans have watched countless fictional "cops-and-robbers" programs since childhood, they remain unable to read or watch actual crime news stories and understand what is taking place. Our justice system is a mystery to many, as are the reasons people commit crimes, the purposes of punishment, and our protections under the Bill of Rights. Yet, our system is a critical part of our free, democratic society, and for that reason alone, we need to study and understand it.

Another reason for understanding the criminal justice system is the precarious situation in which Americans find themselves in the aftermath of September 11, 2001. Since that fateful day, we can no longer take domestic well-being for granted. Americans also learned on 9/11 that crime is an international problem. Crime now easily transcends national borders, and the manner in which our federal, state, and local criminal justice agencies must organize and plan in order to deal with crime has also changed in many ways, as later chapters will show.

In addition, odds are that you and most Americans will be affected by crime during your lifetime. About 10.2 million Part I offenses are reported to the Federal Bureau of Investigation (FBI) each year, with about 1.2 million of them being violent and 9 million involving property (Part I offenses are defined and discussed in Chapter 3).[1] Also occurring are millions more offenses that are less serious in nature as well as those that go unreported. Americans thus also need to understand the flow of the offender through the police, courts, and corrections processes, as well as their legal rights in a democracy.

Finally, your tax dollars will support criminal justice in federal, state, and local governments (which now spend about $228 billion annually and employ approximately 2.5 million persons).[2] The resources required to support our criminal justice system are staggering. But as the French novelist Alain-René Lesage stated several centuries ago, "Justice is such a fine thing that we cannot pay too dearly for it."[3]

This chapter looks at the underpinnings of our criminal justice system—the "big picture"—including the foundations of criminal justice (legal and historical bases), two models of crime, the politics of criminal justice, an overview of one's flow through the criminal justice process, and how discretion and ethics permeate the system.

FOUNDATIONS OF CRIMINAL JUSTICE: LEGAL AND HISTORICAL BASES

The foundation of our criminal justice system is the criminal law: laws that define criminal acts and how such acts will be punished. Indeed, enforcing these laws is what sets in motion the entire criminal justice process. But like most things in our dynamic society, the law is not static. Enactment of new criminal laws and changes to those laws are almost always triggered by social, political, and economic changes. New ways to commit crimes are discovered, new illegal drugs make their way to the marketplace, new weapons and technology (for criminals and police alike) come on the scene, and suddenly, lawmakers and law enforcement officials find themselves needing new tools to prevent and prosecute crimes. We turn first to how the law changes and the historic principles that still guide—and sometimes challenge—that process.

Three-strikes law: a crime control strategy whereby an offender who commits three or more violent offenses will be sentenced to a lengthy term in prison, usually 25 years to life.

Three-strikes laws, while differing in content somewhat from state to state, all have a simple premise: making violent offenders with three qualifying convictions serve lengthy prison sentences.

The Criminal Law: How It Changes and How It Changes the System

In the wake of the Polly Klaas case (outlined at the beginning of the chapter), California lawmakers—like most politicians—understandably wanted to appear tough on crime and on offenders like Richard Allen Davis. They responded just months after the Klaas case by proposing the nation's first **three-strikes law**—a seemingly simple solution giving

Video:
Three-strikes law

violent offenders only two chances to turn themselves around. If they did not, and they committed another crime, the third crime would be the final "strike" and the state could lock them up and throw away the key for 25 years to life.[4] California voters overwhelmingly approved the measure, and within two years more than 20 states and the federal government had done the same.[5]

Supporters predicted the new law would curb crime and protect society by incapacitating the worst offenders for a long period of time, while opponents argued that offenders facing their third strike would demand trials (rather than plea bargain) and send prison populations skyrocketing.[6]

The law that was finally enacted in California was vastly different from what was originally intended—and with many negative and unanticipated repercussions.[7] According to the *New York Times*, the law was unfairly punitive and

> created a cruel, Kafkaesque criminal justice system that lost all sense of proportion, doling out life sentences disproportionately to black defendants. Under the statute, the third offense that could result in a life sentence could be any number of low-level felony convictions, like stealing a jack from the back of a tow truck, shoplifting a pair of work gloves from a department store, pilfering small change from a parked car or passing a bad check.[8]

Other studies of the California law found that prisoners added to the prison system in one decade's time would cost taxpayers an additional $8.1 billion in prison and jail expenditures.[9] Furthermore, three-strikes inmates sentenced for nonviolent offenses would serve 143,439 more years behind bars than if they had been convicted prior to the law's passage.[10]

Some nineteen years later, in November 2012, Californians voted to soften the sentencing law, to impose a life sentence only when the third felony offense is serious or violent, as defined in state law. The law also authorizes the courts to resentence thousands of people who were sent away for low-level third offenses and who present no danger to the public,[11] and provides redress to mentally ill inmates—who were estimated to compose up to 40 percent of those inmates with life sentences under the three-strikes rule.[12]

The Polly Klaas murder, as cruel and senseless as it was, and the events in its aftermath nevertheless provide an excellent illustration of the national impact of crime, the legislative process, and the democratic system of criminal justice that exists to deal with offenders. California's experience with "three strikes" also allows us an opportunity to consider questions about the interaction of government and the justice system: What is the source of such legislative and law enforcement powers? How can governments presume to maintain a system of laws that effectively governs its people and, moreover, a legal system that exists to punish persons who willfully violate those laws? On what basis can states legally construct prisons to restrain anyone—and especially the high numbers of individuals who will no doubt be incarcerated as a result of tough new laws? We now consider those questions.

The Consensus-Versus-Conflict Debate

First we look at the role of the criminal justice system in our democratic society. We enact criminal laws to maintain order and to punish those who violate the democratically decided rules. But is order maintained through consensus—agreement—or is it preserved through conflict, the exercise of power by certain groups over others? This debate is important because it forces us to look at the competing views of humankind toward its ruling group and to examine our justice system (or process) in light of those views.

Consensus

Our society contains innumerable lawbreakers—many of whom are more violent than Richard Allen Davis. Most of them consent to police power in a cooperative manner, without challenging the legitimacy of the law if arrested and incarcerated. Nor do they challenge the system of government that enacts the laws or the justice agencies that carry them out. The stability of our government for more than 200 years is a testimony to the existence of a fair degree of consensus as to its legitimacy.[13] Thomas Jefferson's statements in the Declaration of Independence are as true today as the day when he wrote them and are accepted as common sense:

Video: Richard Allen Davis sentencing

> We hold these truths to be self-evident, that all men are created equal, that they are endowed by their Creator with certain inalienable Rights, that among these are Life, Liberty and the pursuit of Happiness—That to secure these rights, Governments are instituted among Men, deriving their just powers from the consent of the governed. That whenever any Form of Government becomes destructive of these ends, it is the Right of the People to alter or abolish it.

The principles of the Declaration are almost a paraphrase of John Locke's Second Treatise on Civil Government, which justifies the acts of government on the basis of Locke's social contract theory. In the state of nature, people, according to Locke, were created by God to be free, equal, and independent, and to have inherent inalienable rights to life, liberty, and property. Each person had the right of self-protection against those who would infringe on these liberties. In Locke's view, although most people were good, some would be likely to prey on their fellows, who in turn would constantly have to be on guard against such evildoers. To avoid this brutish existence, people joined together, forming governments to which they surrendered their rights of self-protection. In return, they received governmental protection of their lives, property, and liberty. As with any contract, each side has benefits and considerations; people give up their rights to protect themselves and receive protection in return. Governments give protection and receive loyalty and obedience in return.[14]

Author Video: The Sovereign Citizen Movement

Locke believed that the chief purpose of government was the protection of property. Properties would be joined together to form a commonwealth. Once the people unite into a commonwealth, they cannot withdraw from it, nor can their lands be removed from it. Property holders become members of that commonwealth only with their express consent to submit to its government. This is Locke's famous theory of tacit consent: "Every Man . . . doth hereby give his tacit consent, and is as far forth obliged to Obedience to the Laws of the Government."[15] Locke's theory essentially describes an association of landowners.[16]

Another theorist connected with the social contract theory is Thomas Hobbes, who argued that all people were essentially irrational and selfish. He maintained that people had just enough rationality to recognize their situation and to come together to form governments for self-protection, agreeing "amongst themselves

John Locke, an English philosopher and physician and one of the most influential thinkers of his day, developed two influential theories concerning government and natural law: social contract and tacit consent. Another English philosopher and social contract theorist, Thomas Hobbes, believed in individual rights and representative government.

Sir Godfrey Kneller

John Michael Wright

You Be the... JUDGE

Shawn Rice, a 50-year-old Arizona man who rejects government authority as a member of the "sovereign citizen movement," was sentenced to 98 months in a federal prison and ordered to forfeit more than $1.29 million in assets. Rice was convicted on 1 count of conspiracy to commit money laundering, 13 counts of money laundering, and 4 counts of failure to appear, and ordered to pay $98,782 in restitution once he leaves prison.[17]

Rice and other members of this movement believe that the U.S. government is illegitimate and that they should not have to pay taxes or be subject to federal laws. Most of them have their own constitution, bill of rights, and government officials.

Members of the group often commit financial fraud crimes, or "paper terrorism." However, they are

extremely dangerous and violent, and have been tied to a number of shootouts with, and killings of, police officers.[18]

It is estimated that "hundreds of thousands" of sovereign citizens currently live throughout the United States.[19] They are such a threat that the FBI maintains a website on these citizens.[20]

1. Looking only at their beliefs, and not the violent acts that are committed by some members of the sovereign citizen movement, do you think such people are truly U.S. "citizens"?
2. Do their beliefs have any redeemable merit?
3. What types and amounts of punishment, if any, do you believe are justified for sovereign citizens?

Maurice Quentin de La Tour

Jean-Jacques Rousseau, a Genevan conflict theorist, argued that while the coexistence of human beings in equality and freedom is possible, it is unlikely that humanity can escape alienation, oppression, and lack of freedom: "Everywhere he is in chains."

Consensus theory: said to exist where a society functions as a result of a group's common interests and values, which have been developed largely because the people have experienced similar socialization.

to submit to some Man, or Assembly of men, voluntarily, on confidence to be protected by him against all others."[21] Therefore, they existed in a state of consensus with their governments.

Conflict

Jean-Jacques Rousseau, a conflict theorist, differed substantively from both Hobbes and Locke, arguing that "man is born free, but everywhere he is in chains."[22] Like Plato, Rousseau associated the loss of freedom and the creation of conflict in modern societies with the development of private property and the unequal distribution of resources. Rousseau described conflict between the ruling group and the other groups in society, whereas Locke described consensus within the ruling group and the need to use force and other means to ensure the compliance of the other groups.[23]

Thus, the primary difference between the consensus and conflict theorists with respect to government's relation to the governed is how they view the legitimacy of the actions of ruling groups in contemporary societies. The systems approach is part of **consensus theory**, which assumes that all parts of the system work toward a common goal.[24] **Conflict theory**, holding that agency interests tend to make actors within the system self-serving, provides the other approach. This view notes the pressures for success, promotion, and general accountability, which together result in fragmented efforts of the system as a whole, leading to a criminal justice nonsystem.[25]

POLITICS AND CRIMINAL JUSTICE

As the preceding discussion of California's three-strikes law demonstrates, and as with society in general, politics permeates the field of criminal justice. Governing boards and politicians appropriate laws and budgets to cover policy making, the construction of new police stations, courthouses, jails, and prisons, and other operations of police, courts, and corrections organizations at the national, state, and local levels of government. Certainly politics and policy making are intrinsic to our form of government and affect every aspect of our lives.

Permeating the Field

No doubt many politicians want to do what is right and proper for society as well as the justice system; however, many times their coming out forcefully against crime may be prompted more by a desire to grandstand for votes or as a "knee-jerk" response to a high-profile criminal event. Politicians may react out of anger or political expediency, or with limited information about a problem (see the three-strikes law, discussed earlier).

With regard to the police, where chiefs of police serve at the pleasure of their city councils and sheriffs must run for election, the potential for political patronage and influence is obvious. Indeed, as will be seen in Chapter 5, the history of policing is so replete with politics that it even experienced a formal political "era." Perhaps because society perceives the police as a powerful entity, this aspect of policing is often overlooked.

Our courts are certainly bound closely to the laws and budgets that politicians put in force. And while it is generally believed that the federal courts (where judges receive life appointments) are, or at least can be, removed from local political influence, state and local judges (like police chiefs and sheriffs) are often appointed by city councils or elected. The latter issue—judges having to run for election and thus being compelled to accept campaign contributions and run under a political party label—has led many states to opt for a merit selection plan for judges, which is discussed in Chapter 10. Certainly the same can be said for directors of state correctional systems and their prison wardens, both of whom may be appointed by, and serve at the pleasure of, their governors.

Good Politics, Bad Politics

There can be "good" politics as well as "bad" politics. **Political influence** can range from major beneficial policy, personnel, and budgetary decisions to the overzealous city manager or city council member who wants to micromanage the police department and even appears unexpectedly at night at a crime scene (overheard on his or her police scanner) to "help" the officers. Norm Stamper, former chief of police in Seattle, Washington, provided a succinct yet excellent example of how politics can be good or bad; although he speaks in the context of policing, his comments are certainly applicable in other criminal justice systems—and in society-at-large:

> *Everything* about policing is ultimately political. Who gets which office: political. Which services are cut when there's a budget freeze: political. Who gets hired, fired, promoted: political, political, political. I hire my brother-in-law's cousin, a certifiable doofus, because he's got a bass boat I wouldn't mind borrowing—bad politics. I promote a drinking buddy—bad politics. I pick an individual because he or she will add value to the organization and will serve the community honorably—good politics.[26]

CRIME CONTROL AND DUE PROCESS: DO ENDS JUSTIFY MEANS?

Before learning about the specifics of the criminal justice process, it is important to consider how our system can serve the two seemingly competing goals of crime control and due process. How do we operate a system that is tough on crime and criminals

Video: Norm Stamper lecture

Conflict theory: said to exist in societies where the worker class is exploited by the ruling class, which owns and controls the means of production and thus maintains a constant state of conflict between the two classes.

Political influence: matters taken into account for developing public policies, allocating funds and other resources, and choosing among preferred alternatives.

while preserving the constitutional rights of those being accused? Crime control is an obvious and understandable goal for any society, but in a country founded on the ideals of freedom, liberty, and equality, we must be concerned about trampling on individual rights in our quest to do justice—we must ask whether the ends justify the means. For example, if the police illegally search a house and find clear evidence of several crimes, should the state be able to use that evidence to convict someone or should the evidence be excluded because the police violated the defendant's constitutional rights in the pursuit of crime control?

Questions like these will become clearer as you learn about the criminal process, the law that governs police actions, and ethics, but even at this early stage one can see the competing interests. And by considering these two different approaches to our criminal justice system, we can better understand how different offenders and criminal justice players move through the system and the different results—intended and otherwise—we might expect. In 1968, Herbert Packer described the two now-classic models of the criminal justice process in terms of these two competing value systems: crime control and due process (see Table 1.1).[27] The **due process model**—likened to an "obstacle course" by some authors—focuses on fairness as its primary goal. In this model, criminal defendants should be presumed innocent, the courts' first priority is protecting the constitutional rights of the accused, and law enforcement officials—the police and prosecutors—must be held in check to preserve freedom and civil liberties for all Americans. As such, this model is designed to present "obstacles" for government actors at every stage, slowing down the process and affording an opportunity to uncover mistakes or overreaching in the pursuit of justice. This view also stresses that crime is not a result of individual moral failure, but is driven by social influences (such as unemployment, racial discrimination, and other factors that disadvantage the poor); thus, courts that do not follow this philosophy are fundamentally unfair to these defendants. Furthermore, rehabilitation aimed at individual problems will prevent further crime.

In contrast, the **crime control model** is a much more traditional philosophy that Packer likened to an "assembly line." The primary goal of this model is repressing criminal conduct and thus protecting society. The accused is presumed guilty, police and prosecutors should have extensive freedom to exercise their own discretion (judgment) in the interest of crime control, legal loopholes should be eliminated, and offenders swiftly punished. This model views crime as a breakdown of individual responsibility, and as such, only swift and certain punishment will deter and control crime.

Although Packer indicated that neither of these models would be found to completely dominate a particular community or control U.S. crime policy,[28] even to say that one of these models is superior to the other requires an individual to make a value judgment. Again, we must ask how much leeway should be given to the police?

Due process model: Packer's view that criminal defendants should be presumed innocent, courts must protect suspects' rights, and some limits must be placed on police powers.

Crime control model: a model by Packer that emphasizes law and order and argues that every effort must be made to suppress crime, and to try, convict, and incarcerate offenders.

TABLE 1.1   Packer's Crime Control and Due Process Models

	CRIME CONTROL MODEL	DUE PROCESS MODEL
Views criminal justice system as an . . .	Assembly line	Obstacle course
Goal of criminal justice system	Controlling crime	Protecting rights of defendants
Values emphasized	Efficiency, speed, finality	Reliability
Process of adjudication	Informal screening by police and prosecutor	Formal, adversarial procedures
Focuses on . . .	Factual guilt	Legal guilt

Should they be allowed to "bend" the laws just a little bit in order to get criminals off the streets? Do the ends justify the means?

> **The Polly Klaas Case:** Think about California's three-strikes law, enacted after the Polly Klaas kidnapping and murder and designed to stop repeat offenders like Richard Allen Davis. Can you characterize it under the crime control model or the due process model, and what arguments would you make about why it falls under either category? What types of laws—those focused on crime control or on due process—are more likely to be attractive to both the public and politicians after a crime like the Klaas case?

DISCRETION: MAKING AND APPLYING THE LAW

After considering the two competing criminal justice models, you may wonder why the two models are even possible—in other words, how can criminal justice professionals follow different procedures in different situations when ours is a nation under the rule of law and due process? The answer is that players throughout the system exercise **discretion**, making decisions based on their own judgments in particular situations, and as you consider the processes and cases throughout this book, you will see discretion at work in many different ways.

Video: Police discretion

For example, lawmakers understand they cannot anticipate the range of circumstances surrounding each crime, or local attitudes and priorities concerning crime control, and they cannot possibly enact laws that clearly cover all conduct that is criminal and all that is not. The report of the President's Commission on Law Enforcement and Administration of Justice (published in 1967) made a pertinent comment in this regard:

> Crime does not look the same on the street as it does in a legislative chamber. How much noise or profanity makes conduct "disorderly" within the meaning of the law? When must a quarrel be treated as a criminal assault: at the first threat, or at the first shove, or at the first blow, or after blood is drawn, or when a serious injury is inflicted? How suspicious must conduct be before there is "probable cause," the constitutional basis for an arrest? Every [officer], however sketchy or incomplete his education, is an interpreter of the law.[29]

Student on the Street Video: Arrest for every violation

Accordingly, enacting laws is just a first step, and persons charged with the day-to-day response to crime must exercise their own judgment within the limits set by those laws. Basically, they must decide whether to take action, which official response is appropriate, and how the community's attitude toward specific types of criminal acts should influence decisions. For example:

- Police officers exercise extensive discretion in deciding whether to stop, search, or arrest someone (Chapter 6).

- **Prosecuting attorneys** decide whether to bring criminal charges against an arrestee, thus making one of the most important judgment calls in the system (Chapter 10).

- Judges exercise discretion in setting or denying bail, and in imposing sentences (even with sentencing guidelines, discussed in Chapter 11).

- Corrections officials decide key issues of where to house convicted criminals, how to discipline them for rules violations on the inside, and whether to grant them early release on parole (Chapters 12–14).

Discretion: authority to make decisions in enforcing the law based on one's observations and judgment ("spirit of the law") rather than the letter of the law.

Prosecuting attorney: a federal, state, or local prosecutor who represents the people, particularly victims.

The Polly Klaas Case: How does a law like the three-strikes sentencing scheme affect a judge's discretion in sentencing offenders? How does it affect a parole board's discretion in reviewing offenders who are seeking early release? If either of these criminal justice players loses the ability to exercise discretion under such a sentencing model, with whom does the discretion lie?

THE CRIMINAL JUSTICE PROCESS: AN OVERVIEW OF FLOW AND FUNCTIONS

What follows is a brief description of the **criminal justice flow and process** in the United States. Figure 1.1 shows a flowchart of that system and summarizes the major events, including entry into the criminal justice system, prosecution and pretrial services, adjudication, sentencing and sanctions, and corrections. Note that *all* of the discussions in the following chapters of this book are based on the *people* and *processes* included in this concise sequence of events.

The Offender's Pathway Through the Process

As we follow the path of the offender through the process, note that Figure 1.1 also depicts vertical pathways out of the criminal justice system. That is because many crimes fall out of the system for one of a variety of reasons: The crime is not discovered or reported to the police (the so-called shadow of crime); no perpetrator is identified or apprehended; or, in some instances, a suspect is arrested, but later the police determine that no crime was committed, and he or she is released from custody.

Law Enforcement: Investigation/Arrest

The flowchart in Figure 1.1 begins with "reported and observed crime." Law enforcement agencies learn about crime from the reports of victims or other citizens, from discovery by a police officer in the field, from informants, or from investigative and intelligence work. Once a law enforcement agency has established that a crime has been committed, the perpetrator must be identified and apprehended in order for the case to proceed through the system. Sometimes, the offender is apprehended at the scene but in other cases, the police must conduct an investigation to find their perpetrator. Either way, the first formal step for most offenders in the criminal justice system is when the police take a suspect into custody for purposes of charging that person with a crime, known as an **arrest**.

Prosecution and Pretrial Activities

Next we enter the **prosecution** and pretrial services phase of the process—and the realm of the powerful individuals who "control the floodgates" of the courts process. After an arrest, law enforcement agencies present information concerning the case and the accused (typically in the form of an official offense/arrest report) to the prosecutor, who will decide—at his or her discretion—if formal charges will be filed with the court. If no charges are filed, the accused must be released. The prosecutor can also elect, after initially filing charges, to drop charges (*nolle prosequi*) if he or she determines that the probable cause and/or evidence in the matter is weak. (Probable cause, discussed more fully in Chapter 8, is a legal term that basically refers to information that would lead a reasonable person to believe that a person has committed, is committing, or is about to commit a crime.) Furthermore, in some jurisdictions, defendants, often those without a prior criminal record, may be eligible for diversion from prosecution subject to the completion of

Criminal justice flow and process: the horizontal movement of defendants and cases through the criminal justice process, beginning with the commission of a crime, investigation, arrest, initial appearance, arraignment, trial, verdict, sentencing, and appeal (to include vertical movement, as when a case is dropped or leaves the system for some other reason).

Arrest: the taking into custody or detaining of one who is suspected of committing a crime, to answer the charges against him or her.

Prosecution: the bringing of charges against an individual, based on probable cause, so as to cause the matter to go to court.

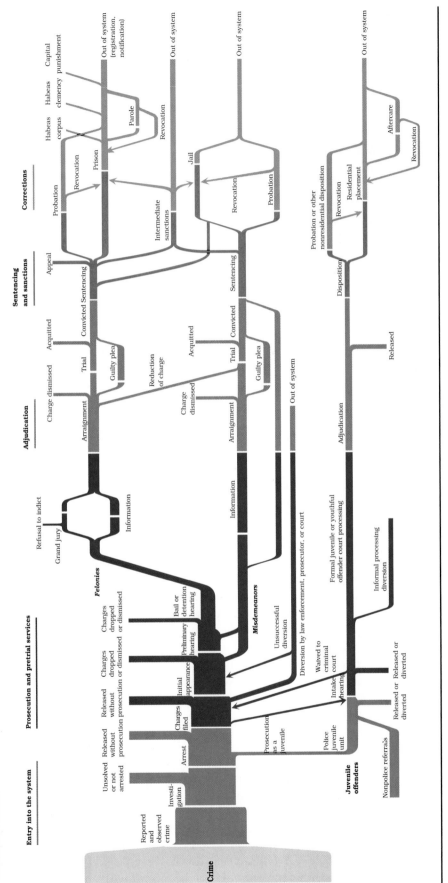

FIGURE 1.1 The Sequence of Events in the Criminal Justice System

Source: Adapted from President's Commission on Law Enforcement and Administration of Justice, *The Challenge of Crime in a Free Society* (Washington, D.C.: U.S. Government Printing Office, 1967). This revision, a result of the Symposium on the 30th Anniversary of the President's Commission, was prepared by the Bureau of Justice Statistics in 1997.

Note: This chart gives a simplified view of caseflow through the criminal justice system. Procedures vary among jurisdictions. The weights of lines are not intended to show actual size of caseloads.

©REUTERS/Alex Gallardo

Scott Dekraai (L), sits next to his attorney, Assistant Public Defender Scott Sanders, at Orange County Superior Court in Santa Ana, California. The former tugboat worker pleaded guilty to first-degree murder for killing eight people in a Southern California hair salon where his ex-wife worked. Under the United States' system of justice, all criminal defendants prosecuted for serious crimes have the right to be represented by an attorney.

specific conditions such as drug treatment. Successful completion of the conditions may result in charges being dropped or the record of the crime being expunged (meaning to legally strike or erase).

Initial Appearance

Persons charged with a crime must be taken for an initial appearance before a judge or magistrate without unnecessary delay (the amount of time is typically specified in the state's statutes or in municipal ordinances). There, the judge will inform the accused of the charges and decide whether there is probable cause to detain him or her. If the offense is not very serious, the determination of guilt and assessment of a penalty may also occur at this stage.

Often, a defense attorney is also assigned at the initial appearance. All defendants who are prosecuted for serious crimes have a right to be represented by an attorney. If the court determines the defendant is indigent and cannot afford such representation, the court will assign counsel at the public's expense.

A decision about whether to release the defendant on bail or some other conditional release may also be made at this initial appearance. The court considers factors such as the seriousness of the charge; whether the defendant is a flight risk; and if he or she has a permanent residence, a job, and family ties. If the accused is likely to appear at trial, the court may decide that he or she should be released on recognizance (often termed "ROR," meaning that the defendant is released without having to provide bail, upon promising to appear and answer the criminal charge) or into the custody of a third party after the posting of a financial bond.

Preliminary Hearing or Grand Jury

The next step is to determine whether there is probable cause to believe the accused committed the crime and whether he or she should be tried. Depending on the jurisdiction and the case, this determination is made in one of two ways: through a preliminary hearing or through a grand jury. In a preliminary hearing, a judge determines if there is probable cause to believe that the accused committed the crime. If so, the case moves forward to trial, also known as "binding the defendant over" for trial. If the judge does not find probable cause, the case is dismissed.

In other jurisdictions and cases, the prosecutor presents evidence to a grand jury, which decides if there is sufficient evidence to bring the accused to trial. If the grand jury finds sufficient evidence, it submits to the court an indictment, a written statement of the essential facts of the offense charged against the accused. Misdemeanor cases and some felony cases proceed by the issuance of an "information," which is a formal, written accusation submitted to the court by a prosecutor (rather than an indictment from the grand jury). In some jurisdictions, indictments may be required in felony cases. Grand juries are discussed more in Chapter 9.

Adjudication

Next, in the middle of the flowchart shown in Figure 1.1, is the **adjudication** process. Once an indictment or information has been filed with the trial court, the accused is scheduled for arraignment.

Adjudication: the legal resolution of a dispute—for example, when one is declared guilty, or a juvenile is declared to be dependent and neglected—by a judge or jury.

Arraignment

At the arraignment, the accused is informed of the charges, advised of the rights of criminal defendants, and asked to enter a plea to the charges. Generally, defendants enter a plea of guilty, not guilty, or *nolo contendere.*

If the accused pleads guilty or *nolo contendere* (accepts penalty without admitting guilt), the judge may accept or reject the plea. If the plea is accepted, the defendant has in effect given up his or her constitutional right to a trial, no trial is held, and sentencing occurs at this proceeding or at a later date. But contrary to popular media depictions, not guilty pleas and trials are very rare; approximately 95 percent of criminal defendants plead guilty as a result of plea bargaining between the prosecutor and the defendant.

Gary Leon Ridgway and his attorneys look over the plea agreement allowing him to escape the death penalty by pleading guilty to 48 counts of aggravated first degree murder in the Green River serial killing cases.

Trial

If the accused pleads not guilty or not guilty by reason of insanity, he or she is basically forcing the government to prove its case—to prove the defendant's guilt beyond a reasonable doubt. A person accused of a serious crime is guaranteed a trial by jury but may request a bench trial where the judge alone, rather than a jury, will hear both sides of the case. In both instances the prosecution and the defense present physical evidence and question witnesses, while the judge decides on issues of law. The trial results in an **acquittal** (not guilty) or a **conviction** (guilty) on the original charges or on lesser included offenses.

Sentencing and Sanctions, Generally

After a conviction, a sentence is imposed. With the exception of capital cases where the death penalty is being sought and the jury decides the punishment, the judge determines the sentence.

In arriving at an appropriate sentence, a sentencing hearing may be held at which time evidence of **aggravating** or **mitigating circumstances** is considered (aggravators are elements that tend to increase the offender's blame, such as use of torture; mitigators tend to reduce blame, such as youthfulness and lack of prior criminal record; these are discussed more in Chapter 11). Here the court may rely on presentence investigations by probation agencies and consider victim impact statements (a written or oral statement by the victim concerning the pain, anguish, and financial devastation the crime has caused).

The sentencing choices that may be available to judges and juries include one or more of the following:

- Death penalty (only in first-degree murder cases and only in certain states)

- Incarceration in a prison (for sentences of a year or longer), a jail (for sentences of a year or less), or another confinement facility

- Probation—allowing the convicted person to remain at liberty but subject to certain conditions and restrictions such as drug testing or drug treatment

- Fine—applied primarily as penalties in minor offenses

Acquittal: a court or jury's judgment or verdict of not guilty of the offenses charged.

Conviction: the legal finding, by a jury or judge, or through a guilty plea, that a criminal defendant is guilty.

Aggravating circumstances: elements of a crime that enhance its seriousness, such as the infliction of torture, killing of a police or corrections officer, and so on.

Mitigating circumstances: circumstances that would tend to lessen the severity of the sentence, such as one's youthfulness, mental instability, not having a prior criminal record, and so on.

The United States Supreme Court has held that trial juries may hear and consider victim impact statements (concerning such factors as the pain, anguish, and suffering the defendant's crime has caused) when making sentencing decisions.

- Restitution—requiring the offender to pay compensation to the victim

- Intermediate **sanction** (used in some jurisdictions)—an alternative to incarceration that is considered more severe than straight probation but less severe than a prison term (e.g., boot camps, intense supervision often with drug treatment and testing, house arrest and electronic monitoring, and community service)

Sentences and punishment are discussed in Chapter 11, whereas intermediate sanctions, probation, and parole are examined in Chapter 14.

Appellate Review

Following trial and sentencing, a defendant may appeal his or her conviction or sentence by requesting that a higher court review the arrest and trial (a process known as appellate review). The appellate process provides checks on the criminal justice system by ensuring that errors at trial (except for those considered to be "harmless") did not adversely affect the fairness of trial processes and the defendant's constitutional rights. In death penalty cases, appeals of convictions are automatic. In other cases, the appellate court has sole discretion over whether to review the case.

Corrections

The next phase into which the offender enters is corrections, as shown in Figure 1.1. Offenders sentenced to incarceration usually serve time in a local jail or a state prison. Offenders sentenced to less than one year generally go to jail; those sentenced to more than one year go to prison.

A prisoner may become eligible for parole after serving a portion of his or her **indeterminate sentence** (a range, such as 5–10 years). **Parole** is the conditional release of a prisoner before the prisoner's full sentence has been served. The decision to grant parole is made by an authority such as a parole board, which has power to grant or revoke parole (i.e., return the parolee to prison) or to discharge a parolee altogether. In some jurisdictions, offenders serving what is termed a **determinate sentence**—a fixed number of years in prison—will not come before a paroling authority, because each offender is required to serve out the full sentence prior to release, less any earned "good time credits" (a reduction in the time served in jail or prison due to good behavior, participation in programs, and other activities).

If released by a parole board or through mandatory release, the parolee will be under the supervision of a parole officer in the community for the balance of his or her unexpired sentence. This supervision is governed by specific conditions of release, and the parolee may be returned to prison ("parole revocation") for violations of such conditions.

Once a person who is suspected of committing a crime is released from the jurisdiction of a criminal justice agency, he or she may commit a new crime (recidivate) and

---

Sanction: a penalty or punishment.

Indeterminate sentence: a scheme whereby one is sentenced for a flexible time period (e.g., 5–10 years) so as to be released when rehabilitated or when the opportunity for rehabilitation is presented.

Parole: early release from prison, with conditions attached and under supervision of a parole agency.

Determinate sentence: a specific, fixed-period sentence ordered by a court.

AP Photo/Press of Atlantic City, Danny Drake

thus need to be processed again through the criminal justice system. Studies show that individuals with prior criminal histories are more likely to be rearrested.

The Juvenile Justice System

Juvenile courts usually have jurisdiction over matters concerning children, including delinquency, neglect, and adoption. They also handle "status offenses" such as truancy and running away, which are not applicable to adults. State statutes define which persons are under the original jurisdiction of the juvenile court. The maximum age of original juvenile court jurisdiction in delinquency matters is 17 in most states.[30] Chapter 15 examines the juvenile justice system.

THE WEDDING CAKE MODEL OF CRIMINAL JUSTICE

The criminal justice system flowchart shown in Figure 1.1 makes it easy to see the steps through which the offender moves through the process horizontally. It is also helpful to see how the system treats cases differently by viewing it vertically, as shown in the "wedding cake" model, which was developed by Samuel Walker (see Figure 1.2).[31]

This approach begins with the premise that not all criminal cases are viewed or handled in the same manner—by either the police or the judiciary. The type of treatment given to a particular case, including its outcome, may well be determined in large measure by factors such as the seriousness of the charge, the current policy implications, and the defendant's celebrity and resources. In other words, some cases are run-of-the-mill, and will be treated as such, as opposed to more high-profile crimes and/or criminals, which command much more attention.

As shown in Figure 1.2, the wedding cake model divides the proceedings in the criminal justice system into four different categories: celebrated cases, serious felonies, lesser felonies, and misdemeanors. This partitioning of cases allows for a closer analysis of how the criminal justice system deals with them.

Layer 1: Celebrated Cases

The top layer of the **wedding cake model** includes the "celebrated cases." These cases command a great deal of media attention because the crimes are unusual (such as Andrea Yates, the Texas woman who drowned her five children) or because the defendants are celebrities or high-ranking officials (consider Michael Jackson; O. J. Simpson, the celebrated athlete and actor whose "trial of the century" is discussed in Chapter 2; and Bernie Madoff, the operator of a Ponzi scheme who bilked investors out of billions of dollars). The legal process for these types of cases is not different from that of the "usual" case, but because of their complexity or high-profile nature, many more resources will be devoted in the form of forensic tests, use of expert witnesses, jury sequestering (seclusion), cameras in the courtroom, and crowd control. At the same time, extra care will be taken to ensure that the defendant's rights are protected—and, it is hoped, because these cases are so public in nature and used as examples of U.S. justice in action, that the accused is not being given preferential treatment.

©iStockphoto.com/wsmahar

Convicted offenders who are to be incarcerated will either serve time in a local jail (typically for misdemeanants serving less than one year) or a federal or state prison (for felons, and usually for more than one year).

Video: Andrea Yates

Wedding cake model of criminal justice: a model of the criminal justice process whereby a four-tiered hierarchy exists, with a few celebrated cases at the top, and lower tiers increasing in size as the severity of cases become less.

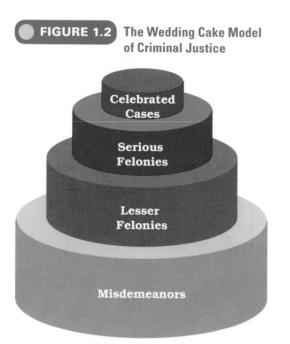

FIGURE 1.2 The Wedding Cake Model of Criminal Justice

Celebrated Cases

Serious Felonies

Lesser Felonies

Misdemeanors

Layer 2: Serious Felonies

The second layer of the wedding cake includes serious felonies, which are violent crimes committed by people with lengthy criminal records and who often prey on people they do not know. These are viewed by the police and prosecutors as the cases that are most deserving of "heavy" treatment and punishment, and there is not as great a chance that the defendant will be allowed to enter into a plea agreement before trial.

Layer 3: Lesser Felonies

On the third layer of the wedding cake are the lesser felonies, which tend to be nonviolent and typically viewed as less important than the felonies in Layer 2. Here, the offender may have no criminal record, may have had a prior relationship with the victim, and may be charged with drug-related, financial, or other such crimes. A good portion of these cases will be filtered out of the system prior to trial and end in plea agreements.

Layer 4: Misdemeanors

Layer 4 consists of misdemeanor cases, which make up about 90 percent of all criminal matters. They include the so-called junk crimes: public drunkenness, minor theft, disturbing the peace, and so on. Police may deal with them informally, and when arrests are made, they will be handled by the lower courts—where speed is of the essence and thus trials are rare. Many misdemeanor cases are resolved with plea agreements and penalties that involve fines, probation, or short-term jail sentences.[32]

ETHICS THROUGHOUT THE CRIMINAL JUSTICE SYSTEM

Robert F. Kennedy, in his 1960 book, *The Enemy Within: The McClellan Committee's Crusade Against Jimmy Hoffa and Corrupt Labor Unions*, stated that

> in the fall of 1959 I spoke at one of the country's most respected law schools. The professor in charge of teaching ethics told me the big question up for discussion among his students was whether, as a lawyer, you could lie to a judge. I told the professor . . . that I thought we had all been taught the answer to that question when we were six years old.[33]

As Kennedy, the late U.S. attorney general and U.S. senator, implied, by the time they reach the point of being college or university students, it is hoped that everyone—in particular, those studying the field of criminal justice—will have had deeply ingrained in them the need to practice exemplary and ethical behavior. Ethical behavior is often emphasized in postsecondary education in the form of instructors explaining the need for academic honesty. Later, it is typically emphasized in terms of how people conduct themselves when dealing with others as well as perhaps how they are to handle property and responsibility with which they have been entrusted.

Character in the criminal justice arena is of utmost importance. Without it, nothing else matters. Character, it might be said, is who we are when no one is watching. Having character means that people would never betray their fellow human beings or violate oaths of office or public trust. Unfortunately, character of mind and actions cannot be inculcated in someone in a college or university classroom, nor can it be implanted in a doctor's office, administered intravenously, or ingested as a pill.

Prior to commencing your journey into the field of criminal justice (and, later, reading Chapter 4, concerning ethics), you might do well to first ask yourself these questions: Should police officers receive free coffee from restaurants and quick-stop establishments? Free or half-priced meals? What about judges? Prison wardens? If we do not "reward" judges, wardens, schoolteachers, plumbers, pizza delivery persons, or others with "freebies," then should establishments compensate police officers in such a manner? On what grounds do many police officers expect such favored treatment? And can this lead to ethical problems with respect to their work?

At its root, the field of criminal justice is about people and their activities; and in the end, the primary responsibilities of people engaged in this field is to ensure that they be of the highest ethical character and treat everyone with dignity and respect. Therefore, as indicated earlier, this textbook, unlike most or all others of its kind, devotes an entire chapter to the subject of **ethics**—or what essentially constitutes "correct" behavior in criminal justice.

Video: Criminal justice ethics

Ethics: a set of rules or values that spell out appropriate human conduct.

You Be the... JUDGE

Nancy Black, a California marine biologist, also captains a whale-watching ship. She was with some watchers when a member of her crew whistled at a nearby humpback whale, hoping the whale would linger. Meanwhile, on land, one of Black's employees contacted a national oceanographic organization to see if the whistling was in fact harassment of a marine mammal—an environmental crime. Black provided a videotape of the incident, edited slightly to show the whistling; for the editing, she was charged with a felony under the 1863 False Claims Act. She was also charged with a federal crime involving the feeding of killer whales (orcas)—having rigged an apparatus that would stabilize a slab of blubber so that the orca could be better photographed while feeding on a dead gray whale. After the charges were filed, Black spent more than $100,000 in legal fees and faced a sentence of up to 20 years in prison. In January 2014, Black pleaded guilty to one misdemeanor violation of the Marine Mammal Protection Act; she was fined $12,500

and was sentenced to three years' probation and 300 hours of community service. Additionally, the judge ordered Black to stay 100 yards from the whales.

1. Does this case represent the conflict or consensus model of justice?

2. Assume Black were to be convicted: Would the end justify the means? Conversely, would the means justify the end result (i.e., having such federal laws, compelling such exorbitant legal fees)?

3. Do you believe politics played a part in this case?

4. Where would this type of case fit on the wedding cake model of criminal justice?

5. Should the prosecutor have had the discretion to drop all charges in this case?

Source: For more information, see Jason Wells, "Biologist Pleads Guilty to Feeding Killer Whales in Monterey Bay," *Los Angeles Times,* January 14, 2014, http://touch.latimes.com/#section/-1/article/p2p-78891109/.

IN A NUTSHELL

- It is important to study criminal justice because we need to understand crime and criminal justice generally, and because all of us are potential victims, witnesses, and taxpaying supporters of our justice system. Particularly since 9/11, we have also learned that we are no longer safe within our borders. Furthermore, we need to be able to

understand the processing of criminals and the rights we enjoy under law in a democracy.

- The consensus-versus-conflict debate concerns challenges to the legitimacy of the law, the system of government that enacts the laws, and the justice agencies that carry them out. The stability of our government for more than 200 years is a testimony to the existence of consensus as to its legitimacy, although some theorists described long ago the conflicts between the ruling group and the other groups in society, and the need to use force and other means to ensure the compliance of the other groups.

- The due process model of criminal justice basically holds that criminal defendants should be presumed innocent and constitutional rights of the accused should be upheld. Conversely, the crime control model, likened to an "assembly line," emphasizes repressing criminal conduct and protecting society; legal loopholes should be eliminated and offenders swiftly punished, and the police and prosecutors should be given a high degree of discretion. Neither of these models, however, completely dominates a particular community or U.S. crime policy.

- Politics permeates the field of criminal justice, from governing boards and politicians to enactment of laws and budgets; everything—who is hired and elected as officeholders; the construction of new police stations, courthouses, jails, and prisons; and other operations at the national, state, and local levels of government—is driven by politics.

- Discretion is exercised throughout the criminal justice system, because violations of laws vary in their seriousness, and there are not enough human and financial resources to enforce all laws equally. Therefore, persons charged with enforcing laws, adjudicating cases, and punishing offenders exercise considerable judgment in terms of deciding whether to take action, which official response is appropriate, and to what extent the community's attitude toward specific types of criminal acts should affect such decisions.

- Although the offender's path through the criminal justice process may be viewed as horizontal in nature, there are many points through which an offender can take a vertical pathway out of the system.

- The wedding cake model of criminal justice argues that not all criminal cases are viewed or handled in the same manner by either the police or the courts. The type of treatment given to a particular case is determined by factors such as the seriousness of the charge, the current policy implications, and the defendant's celebrity and resources. The processing of cases by the criminal justice system is divided into four categories: celebrated cases, serious felonies, lesser felonies, and misdemeanors.

- Ethical considerations are also at the root of criminal justice. The people engaged in this field must be of the highest ethical character and treat everyone with dignity and respect.

KEY TERMS & CONCEPTS

► Review key terms with eFlashcards. $SAGE edge™

$ SAGE edge™ Test your understanding of chapter content. Take the practice quiz. ◄

1. Having read the chapter, do you believe it is important for you to study the structure and function of our criminal justice system? Why or why not?

2. How would you describe the crime control and due process models of criminal justice? What indicators might be present in your local community for determining which particular model is apparently dominant?

3. How would you characterize the influence of politics on our criminal justice system? What might be examples of "good" politics and "bad" politics?

4. What are the major points at which an offender is dealt with in the criminal justice process, as he or she moves through the police, courts, and corrections components?

5. Do you believe there exists a true criminal justice "system"? Explain your answer.

6. How would you characterize the importance of discretion and ethics throughout the justice system?

 LEARN BY DOING

As indicated in this textbook's preface, this "Learn by Doing'" section, as well as those at the end of each chapter, is an outgrowth of teachings by famed educator John Dewey, who advocated the "learning by doing" or problem-based approach to education. It also follows the popular learning method espoused by Benjamin Bloom in 1956, known as Bloom's Taxonomy, in which he called for "higher-order thinking skills"—critical and creative thinking that involves analysis, synthesis, and evaluation.[34]

The following scenarios and activities will shift your attention from textbook-centered instruction and move the emphasis to student-centered projects. By being placed in these hypothetical situations, you can thus learn—and apply—some of the concepts covered in this chapter, develop skills in communication and self-management, at times become a problem solver, and learn about and address current community issues.

1. Assume that you are an officer in your campus criminal justice honor society and are invited to speak at the society's monthly meeting concerning your view of how crime is perceived and dealt with in your community. You opt to approach the question from Packer's crime control and due process perspectives. Given what you know about crime and criminal justice in your community, what will you say in your presentation?

2. As a member of your campus criminal justice honor society, you are asked to speak at a meeting of your local police department's Citizens' Police Academy, focusing on the general need for citizens to "become involved" in addressing crime. What will you say?

3. Your criminal justice professor asks you to prepare your own succinct diagram of the criminal justice process, including brief descriptions of each of the major stages (arrest, initial appearance, and so on) as a case flows through the process. What will your final product look like?

4. As part of a class group project concerning the nature of crime and punishment, you are asked by your fellow group members to develop a 10-minute presentation on the wedding cake model of crime. How will you describe it?

STUDY SITE

$ SAGE edge™

Review → Practice → Improve

Sharpen your skills with **SAGE edge** at edge.sagepub.com/peak2e

SAGE edge for students provides a personalized approach to help you accomplish your coursework goals in an easy-to-use learning environment. Access the videos, audio clips, quizzes, and SAGE journal articles that are noted in this chapter.

CHAPTER 02

FOUNDATIONS OF LAW AND CRIME
Nature, Elements, and Defenses

LEARNING OBJECTIVES

As a result of reading this chapter, you will be able to:

1 Explain how modern-day law evolved from English common law

2 Describe the three sources of law in the U.S. legal system

3 Identify the differences between criminal and civil law

4 Explain the difference between substantive and procedural law

5 Review two critical elements of the criminal law—criminal intent (*mens rea*) and the physical commission of the criminal act (*actus reus*)

6 Delineate the definitions of, and distinctions between, felonies and misdemeanors, crimes against persons and property, and the different degrees of homicide and sexual assault

7 Discuss the various defenses that criminal defendants may offer to reduce or eliminate their criminal liability

ASSESS YOUR AWARENESS

Test your knowledge of the nature of law and crime by responding to the following seven true-false items; check your answers after reading this chapter's materials.

1 The U.S. legal system is based on English common law.

2 A person who, upon returning home, discovers that her premises have been illegally entered and valuables removed, will correctly tell police, "I've been robbed."

3 Under current U.S. law, one can be charged only with criminal acts he or she actually performs, and not for failure to act or perform in some manner.

4 As opposed to the situation under English common law, today one may use force, even deadly force, if he or she reasonably believes that an attack against him or her is imminent.

5 Intoxication will generally always be a successful defense and excuse one from guilt.

6 No particular amount of time is necessary for one to legally premeditate a murder.

7 An individual can use one of only two defenses against being charged with a crime: "I didn't know it was a crime," and/or "I was too intoxicated to know what I was doing."

The Constitution of the United States was made not merely for the generation that then existed, but for posterity—unlimited, undefined, endless, perpetual posterity.

—Henry Clay

<< Answers can be found on page 424.

Yeardley Love, a 22-year-old lacrosse player with the University of Virginia, was found dead in her apartment in 2010. The medical examiner found that Love had been beaten with such force her right eye was caved in and her brain was bruised.

©ZUMA Press, Inc. / Alamy

Love's estranged boyfried George Huguely, 22, a University of VA men's lacrosse player, was convicted in 2012 of second-degree murder for Love's death.

©AP Photo/The Daily Progress via Charlottesville Police Department

In May 2010, police found 22-year-old Yeardley Love dead in her apartment. The University of Virginia lacrosse player had died of blunt force trauma. Evidence quickly led investigators to focus on Love's former boyfriend, 22-year-old George Huguely, also a lacrosse player with UVA. Huguely had some history of committing domestic violence against Love, and the two had recently broken up. Prosecutors said Huguely killed the UVA women's lacrosse player after a day of golf and binge drinking, incensed that she had had a relationship with a North Carolina lacrosse player. Love's right eye was bashed in and she was hit with such power that her brain was bruised. Huguely's defense attorneys admitted that Huguely had been in Love's apartment before her death and that the two had argued, but they claimed the death was unintentional, a tragic accident resulting from a fight that spiraled out of control.

Ultimately the jurors would have to decide among several different scenarios:

- Did Huguely batter Love to death intentionally? Did he plan it?

- Did Huguely batter Love to death intentionally but without planning it?

- Did Huguely kill Love in a burst of jealous rage?

- Or did the former lovers' discussion lead to physical contact and an accidental blunt force trauma to Love?

As you will learn in this chapter, these different scenarios contain the elements of very different crimes with different corresponding levels of punishment. Think about why the different facts of each scenario should lead to a different crime and punishment. What facts are important to us in defining crimes and why? Why should these facts matter? What other facts might help you to decide more easily what really happened and what type of crime Huguely might have committed?

The answers to these questions are at the very heart of the criminal law and of our system of justice, which holds people criminally responsible only when the state can prove beyond a reasonable doubt that the accused committed each and every element of a crime without a valid defense.

INTRODUCTION

John Adams famously said we have a "government of laws and not of men," meaning that our democracy is not ruled at the whim of kings or rulers or demagogues. As explained in Chapter 1, Americans willingly give up some of their rights to their elected governments to create laws and to receive protection for their persons and property.

It thus becomes important that Americans possess at least a fundamental knowledge of the rule of law; however, most of us probably fall quite short of having such knowledge.

As an example, we often hear someone screaming, "I've been robbed!" on television or in the movies after returning home and discovering the home has been entered and ransacked (he or she was not robbed). Or, someone discovers a dead body and states, "He's been murdered!" (a person may have indeed been killed, but many killings are not criminal in nature; only a judge or jury can decide). Another common error is when a news reporter states, "John Jones, a convicted murderer, was sentenced to jail today" (Jones will serve his sentence in a prison, not a jail). As French philosopher Voltaire wrote, "If you wish to converse with me, define your terms." That statement represents the major purpose of this chapter.

The reader should bear in mind, however, that several important components of the rule of law are not discussed here, either because they go beyond the reach of an introductory textbook or because of space limitations. Persons wishing to inquire more deeply into the law—for example, in such areas as conspiracies, attempted crimes, omissions, and causation—would be wise to enroll in criminal law and procedure courses.

COMMON LAW AND ITS PROGENY

Rules were laid out in ancient societies. The law can be traced back to the reign of Hammurabi (1792–1750 B.C.E.), the sixth king of the ancient empire of Babylon. The Code of Hammurabi set out crimes and punishments based on *lex talionis*—"an eye for an eye, a tooth for a tooth." A more recent source of law is found in the Mosaic Code of the Israelites (1200 B.C.E.), in which, according to tradition, Moses—acting as an intermediary for God—passed on the law to the tribes of Israel.

But the system of law as we know it today (except for Louisiana's, which is based on the French civil code) is based on the common law: collections of rules, customs, and traditions of medieval England, created during the reign of Henry II (1154–1189 C.E.), who began the process of unifying the law. Henry established a permanent body of professional judges who traveled a "circuit" and sat as tribunals in shires throughout the Crown's realm; these judges eventually gave the Crown jurisdiction over all major crimes and sowed the seeds of the trial by jury and the doctrine of *stare decisis.*[1]

The latter doctrine, *stare decisis* (Latin for "to stand by things settled"), is perhaps the most distinctive aspect of Anglo-American common law. According to the simple definition in *Black's Law Dictionary*, *stare decisis* is the doctrine stating that, when a court has once laid down a principle of law as applicable to a certain state of facts, it will adhere to that principle—and apply it in the same manner to all future cases where facts are substantially the same.[2] This doctrine binds courts of equal or lower status or levels in a given jurisdiction to the principles established by the higher appellate courts within the same jurisdiction.

For example, a federal district court in Maryland is required to follow the decisions of

Lex talionis: "eye for eye, tooth for tooth"; retaliation or revenge that dates back to the Bible and Middle Ages.

Stare decisis: "to stand by a decision" (Latin)—a doctrine referring to court precedent, whereby lower courts must follow (and render the same) decisions of higher courts when the same legal issues and questions come before them, thereby not disturbing settled points of law.

©iStockphoto.com/jsp

The Code of Hammurabi, written in about 1780 B.C.E., set out crimes and punishments based on *lex talionis*—"an eye for an eye, a tooth for a tooth." It is the earliest-known example of a ruler's setting forth a body of laws arranged in orderly groupings.

the Fourth Circuit Court of Appeals, of which it is a part, as well as those of the U.S. Supreme Court, but it is not bound by the decisions of other district courts or by the Maryland state courts.[3] Note, however, that our system of law still must remain flexible and capable of change, and thus courts can also revisit earlier decisions and set new precedents.

MODERN-DAY SOURCES AND HIERARCHY OF LAW

In addition to the two primary types of law—criminal and civil (discussed in the next section)—the U.S. legal system features different sources of law and jurisdictions where those laws are enforced and administered. As you would expect to find in our federal system of government, we have federal and state laws with corresponding federal and state courts to preside over such cases. Within those two legal arenas, laws—criminal and civil—are organized hierarchically, with different priorities and legal effects depending on their source and application.

Again, terminology is critical to understanding law. Generally speaking, a *statute* is a law enacted by Congress (a federal law) or by a state legislature (a state law). Statutes are also known as *statutory law*. A *code* or *ordinance* typically refers to a law enacted by a local lawmaking body—a county board or a city council, for example (municipal laws). These and other types of laws are prioritized as follows:

Federal Law

1. The U.S. Constitution—"the supreme law of the land," which takes precedence over state constitutions and law even if they conflict

2. Federal statutes—civil and criminal laws enacted by Congress

3. Administrative laws—orders, directives, and regulations for federal agencies, such as workplace laws promulgated by the Occupational Safety and Health Administration (OSHA)

4. Federal common law—published decisions from the U.S. Supreme Court and the U.S. Circuit Courts of Appeal, which, like the common law from England (discussed earlier), establish legal "precedence" and must be followed by lower courts in the federal and state systems. (Chapter 9 describes how the Supreme Court decides to hear cases and render its decisions.)

Sources of federal law include the U.S. Constitution, the U.S. Supreme Court, and those laws enacted by Congress.

State Law

1. State constitutional law—state constitutional rulings (from a state's highest court) that may give greater protection or rights than the federal constitution but may not give less, and that contain protections similar to the U.S. Constitution—civil rights and liberties, separation of powers, and checks and balances[4]

2. State statutes—laws enacted by state legislatures, including criminal laws like statutes prohibiting murder or robbery

3. State common law—precedent established in published opinions by state appellate judges when deciding civil or criminal cases

City/County Law

Municipal ordinances or codes govern many aspects of our daily lives, including the following:

- Building and construction standards
- Rent control
- Noise and nuisance regulations
- Public health and safety
- Business licenses
- Civil rights and antidiscrimination

CRIMINAL AND CIVIL LAW

Simply put, **criminal law** applies to criminal matters, for example, when someone breaks a law against committing robbery. **Civil law** applies to civil matters, for example, when two parties have a property dispute or want to get divorced. These two distinct types of law differ in several critical ways.

First, each type involves different parties. When someone commits a crime, the state or government—through the prosecutor or district attorney—prosecutes the person on behalf of the people (because the criminal law represents what we as a people have decided is criminal behavior and crimes are considered harmful to all of us, as a society). A typical criminal case name is something like *U.S. v. Jones* or *State of Nevada v. Smith*. In a civil matter, two individuals (or business entities like a corporation) are on either side. In a property dispute, such as when A erects a fence over the property line of B, one neighbor brings a lawsuit against the other so that the court can referee their dispute. Or, if a person is injured using a product like a hairdryer, that person can bring a civil case against the manufacturer, probably a corporation. A typical civil law case name is something like *Jones v. Smith* or *Jones v. ABC Corporation*. In the former example, Jones is the party bringing the suit—the **plaintiff**—and Smith is the party defending against the suit—the **defendant**.

Not surprisingly, these two types of cases are heard in different courts, and most courthouses have separate criminal and civil "divisions," where judges are more experienced in either of these particular type of cases.

Another important difference involves how these cases are decided. In a criminal case, the prosecutor or the state has the burden of proving—the **burden of proof**—the defendant's guilt "beyond a reasonable doubt." This sometimes-heavy burden is designed

Criminal law: the body of law that defines criminal offenses and prescribes punishments for their infractions.

Civil law: a generic term for all noncriminal law, usually related to settling disputes between private citizens, governmental, and/or business entities.

Plaintiff: the party bringing a lawsuit or initiating a legal action against someone else.

Defendant: a person against whom a criminal charge is pending; one charged with a crime.

Burden of proof: the requirement that the state must meet to introduce evidence or establish facts.

to force the government—the prosecutor—to prove its case because, again, underlying our rule of law in the United States is the all-important concept that one is innocent until proven guilty (technically, one is innocent until the prosecution proves him or her guilty). Sometimes the burden shifts to the defense to prove something, as with self-defense claims, discussed later. In a civil case, the burden on the party seeking damages or a remedy is less than in a criminal matter—those representing this party must prove their case by a "preponderance of the evidence." These two terms can be hard to distinguish, even for experienced lawyers.

Reasonable doubt can be difficult to explain; in fact, several courts prefer not to attempt to give the jury any explanation at all. However, in most cases reasonable doubt means that, after hearing all of the evidence, jurors do not possess an abiding conviction—to a moral certainty—that the charges brought against the defendant are true. This does not necessarily mean absolute certainty—there can still be some doubt, but only to the extent that it would *not* affect a "reasonable person's" belief that the defendant is guilty. By contrast, if such doubt *does* affect a reasonable person's belief that the defendant is guilty, then the prosecution has not met its burden of proof, and the judge or jury must acquit—find the defendant not guilty.

The civil standard of a preponderance of the evidence is a much less difficult burden to meet and is often referred to as the "50 percent plus a feather" test. It asks jurors to decide which way the evidence causes the scales of justice to tip, toward guilt or innocence, and to decide the case on that basis.

The major difference between civil and criminal matters is the penalty. In a criminal case, the state or prosecutor seeks to punish a defendant with prison or jail time, a monetary fine, or both (or perhaps a community-based punishment such as probation, discussed in Chapter 14). In a civil matter, one party is seeking "damages" (money or some legal remedy) from the other party rather than trying to send him or her to jail or prison. In the property dispute example, A would be required to tear down or move the fence and perhaps pay for the legal fees B incurred in bringing the suit. And in the hairdryer example, the corporation could be ordered to pay the consumer's medical expenses and legal fees.

Some conduct can give rise to both a criminal and a civil matter as the cases of O. J. Simpson and others illustrate (see "Investigating Further").

A few examples might serve to explain the difference—and how the two types of cases can cause problems for the police and misunderstanding by the public. Assume that Jane calls the police to her home and tells the officer that she and her husband, Bill, recently separated and he recently went to their home and removed some furniture and other goods that she does not believe he should have taken. The officer must inform Jane that there is nothing he can do—at this point, this is a *civil*, not a criminal, matter. Jane may be upset with the officer, but legally the police have no jurisdiction in such disputes. Assume, however, that Bill goes to the home and makes serious threats of injury toward Jane, and she then goes to court and obtains a temporary protection order (TPO) commanding Bill to avoid any form of contact with her; Bill disregards the TPO and stalks Jane at her place of employment. Because he violated the court's order, this has now become a *criminal* matter, and the police may arrest Bill.

Or, look again at the example of someone erecting a fence that cuts across his neighbor's property by five feet. The neighbor refuses to move or tear down the fence, so the matter is taken to court. This is a civil cause of action. Both sides have a dispute that the courts will resolve if the parties cannot reach an agreement. Assume further that the neighbors cannot resolve the fence matter, and one day while one

Reasonable doubt: the standard used by jurors to arrive at a verdict—whether or not the government (prosecutor) has established guilt beyond a reasonable doubt.

of them is working in his yard the other attacks him with a club. Now the attacking neighbor could face a criminal charge from the state (assault with a deadly weapon) and a civil lawsuit by the injured neighbor (for medical expenses and emotional trauma).

Table 2.1 shows the primary differences between civil and criminal law.

TABLE 2.1 Differences Between Civil and Criminal Law

	CIVIL	CRIMINAL
Burden of proof	"Preponderance of evidence"	"Beyond a reasonable doubt"
Nature of crime	A private wrong	A public wrong
Parties	Case is filed by an individual party	Some level of government files charges against the individual
Punishment	Usually in the form of monetary compensation for damages caused; no incarceration	Jail, fine, prison, probation, possibly death
Examples	Landlord/tenant dispute, divorce proceeding, child custody proceeding, property dispute, auto accident	Person accused of committing some crime (or, perhaps, neglecting a duty to act)

INVESTIGATING FURTHER

CRIMINAL AND CIVIL LAW—THE O.J. SIMPSON CASE

O. J. Simpson was once a wealthy and admired college and professional football player as well as a movie and television personality. But in 1994 he was charged with stabbing to death his estranged wife, Nicole, and her friend, Ron Goldman. The media covered the trial live as California prosecutors presented evidence of Simpson's history of domestic abuse and damning DNA evidence from the crime scene, while Simpson's "Dream Team" of high-caliber defense attorneys cross-examined the state's witnesses and dissected their evidence in hopes of creating reasonable doubt about Simpson's guilt. After the nearly yearlong trial, the jury deliberated only four hours before returning not-guilty verdicts on all charges. One year later, the victims' parents filed a civil suit against Simpson, alleging that he caused the victims' wrongful deaths and seeking millions of dollars in damages for those deaths. Many people wondered how the families could hope to win when Simpson had been found not guilty in the criminal trial. The answer lies in the differences between the criminal and civil cases. In the civil case, the burden of proof on the families was less than the burden on the prosecutors in the criminal case. The families needed to show only by a preponderance of the evidence—rather than beyond a reasonable doubt—that Simpson killed the victims. The civil jurors needed to decide only which way the scales of justice tipped, toward guilt or innocence, not whether the state had proven Simpson's guilt beyond a reasonable doubt. Indeed, the civil jury found Simpson responsible for the deaths and awarded the families $33.5 million in damages. So while Simpson was acquitted in the criminal trial and did not serve any prison time, he was adjudged responsible in the civil trial and ordered to pay money damages for his conduct.

Source: For a complete analysis of the Simpson case, see, for example, Jeffrey Toobin, *The Run of His Life: The People v. O. J. Simpson* (New York: Random House, 1998); Lawrence Schiller and James Willwerth, *American Tragedy: The Uncensored Story of the O. J. Simpson Defense* (New York: Random House, 1996); Joseph Bosco, *A Problem of Evidence: How the Prosecution Freed O. J. Simpson* (New York: William Morrow, 1996); CNN.com, *O. J. Simpson Main Page,* http://www.cnn.com/US/OJ/.

SUBSTANTIVE AND PROCEDURAL LAW

Substantive law is the written law that defines criminal acts—the very "substance" of the criminal law. Examples are laws that define and prohibit murder and robbery. **Procedural law** (discussed in detail in Chapter 8) sets forth the procedures and mechanisms for processing criminal cases. The Fourth Amendment (requiring police officers to obtain search and arrest warrants, except in certain situations) is procedural law, as is the requirement that officers give the *Miranda* warning before a suspect is interrogated while in custody (Fifth and Sixth Amendments) and the right to an attorney at key junctures during processing through the criminal justice system. (Note that these requirements are not criminal laws in the way the law prohibits robbery or murder, but rather these laws govern how police officers, lawyers, judges, corrections officers, and a host of others do their work in the justice system.) Procedural law also prescribes rules concerning jurisdiction, jury selection, appeal, evidence presented to a jury, order of conducting a trial, and representation of counsel.

ESSENTIAL ELEMENTS: *MENS REA* AND *ACTUS REUS*

The Latin term for criminal intent is *mens rea*, or "guilty mind," and its importance cannot be overstated. Our entire legal system and criminal laws are designed to punish only those actors who intend to commit their acts, and as will be seen later in the discussion of homicide, acts that are clearly intentional and premeditated (e.g., murder in the first degree) are punished most severely, while those acts that are less intentional and/or accidental are punished less harshly. For example, assume Bill, while hunting deer, shoots another hunter while out in the woods. If the prosecutor has evidence to show the shooting was purely accidental in nature (the other hunter was out of position, or Bill's gun malfunctioned), the prosecutor will not charge Bill with unlawful killing. If, by contrast, the evidence shows that Bill intended to shoot the other hunter (again, considering evidence of the position of the two men, the number of shots, or proof of Bill's planning), the prosecutor will charge Bill with homicide.

Mens Rea: Intent Versus Motive to Commit Crime

An important distinction to be made concerns the difference between *intent* and *motive*. One's specific **intent** concerns what he or she is seeking to do and is connected to a purpose or goal; **motive** refers to one's reason for doing something. For example, when a poverty-stricken woman steals milk for her child, her intention is to steal, but her motive is to provide for her child. Therefore, motive (the "why" someone is stirred to perform an action) is grounded primarily in psychology; intent, conversely, is the result of one's motive, is grounded in law, and carries a higher degree of blameworthiness because a harmful act was committed. Anyone who watches crime movies will agree that much ado is often made of one's possible motive for committing a particular crime. However, as one law professor put it, "As any first year law student will tell you, motive is irrelevant in determining criminal liability. Unlike in the television show . . . in the perceived real world of criminal liability, motive is just a bit player, appearing only in

Substantive law: the body of law that spells out the elements of criminal acts.

Procedural law: rules that set forth how substantive laws are to be enforced, such as those covering arrest, search, and seizure.

Intent, specific: a purposeful act or state of mind to commit a crime.

Motive: the reason for committing a crime.

One's criminal intent is a major consideration in our legal system; for example, one who intentionally kills someone during a robbery may well be charged with premeditated murder, while a hunter who accidentally (without intent) shoots and kills another typically would not.

limited circumstances, usually as a consideration in certain defenses. Ordinarily, the only real questions at trial are (1) did the defendant commit the illegal act and (2) did she have the necessary mental state (*mens rea*)?"[5]

To determine the requisite *mens rea* for a specific crime, we look to the criminal statute that defines the offense. But you will not find the term "*mens rea*" as part of any criminal law. Instead, this element is expressed through a variety of terms that differ from state to state. For example, an intentional crime might be defined as an act committed "intentionally," "willfully," or "maliciously," while a less serious crime—an accidental crime—can be expressed as an act committed "negligently," "recklessly," or "without due caution." The terms used to express *mens rea* are not uniform, so criminal justice professionals must learn to identify these terms and understand how they operate within a criminal statute (see the discussion of homicide and related exercises later in this chapter).

One's intent while committing a crime is not always easy to prove. As is discussed later, regarding the crime of homicide, when A shoots B, there are a variety of possible outcomes, and the prosecutor will "look behind the act" to determine what was going on in the mind of the killer, and whether to reduce what appears to be a charge of murder in the first degree (an intentional killing) to one of manslaughter (an accidental killing).

Actus Reus: The Act

Another critical feature of the U.S. criminal justice system is that we do not punish people for merely thinking about committing criminal acts; rather, the law generally requires a voluntary, overt act—killing, injuring, threatening, or breaking and entering, for example. The intentional *failure* to act (an "omission") can also be criminal but only when there is a legal duty to do something, such as when a parent fails to feed a child or give him or her medical attention.

The rule for establishing criminal liability is to prove that the defendant committed the ***actus reus*** element (the criminal act) with the ***mens rea*** ("guilty mind") set forth in the particular criminal law. When these two critical elements are present, it is known as "concurrence." For example, a man in a ski mask breaking into a locked home might seem to be committing the *actus reus* element for burglary (see "Crimes Against Property," below). But what if he is doing so to save himself from a terrible snowstorm after

Actus reus: "guilty deed" (Latin)—an act that accompanies one's intent to commit a crime, such as pulling out a knife and then stabbing someone.

Mens rea: a necessary element of a crime; the evil intent.

You Be the... POLICE OFFICER

The Nebraska Revised Statutes set forth the following statutory provisions. Read them carefully and then respond to the questions posed.

28-306. Motor vehicle homicide; penalty.

(1) A person who causes the death of another unintentionally while engaged in the operation of a motor vehicle in violation of the law of the State of Nebraska or in violation of any city or village ordinance commits motor vehicle homicide.

60-6,213. Reckless driving, defined.

Any person who drives any motor vehicle in such a manner as to indicate an indifferent or wanton disregard for the safety of persons or property shall be guilty of reckless driving.

60-6,214. Willful reckless driving, defined.

Any person who drives any motor vehicle in such a manner as to indicate a willful disregard for the safety of persons or property shall be guilty of willful reckless driving.

1. What is the *mens rea* element under Section 1 of the motor vehicle homicide statute (and what words define the *mens rea* element)? What is the *actus reus* element?

2. Provide an example of what would qualify as motor vehicle homicide under Section 1.

3. A woman who is texting while driving strikes and kills a pedestrian who is crossing the street. The woman was not speeding. Can she be charged for a violation of Section 1? Why or why not?

4. Which words supply the *mens rea* element under Section 60-6,213 (reckless driving)? Define and provide examples. Which words identify the *actus reus* element under this section?

5. Answer the questions in item 4 for Section 60-6,214.

his car broke down? The all-important *mens rea* element is missing and there is no concurrence. Accordingly, the prosecutor must prove both elements beyond a reasonable doubt—a question of fact for the jury to decide.

FELONIES AND MISDEMEANORS

Crimes are also classified into two broad categories based on the severity of the criminal act and the corresponding punishment. **Felonies** are offenses punishable by death or that have a possible sentence of more than one year of incarceration in prison. Many states further divide their felonies into different classes; for example, under Arizona's laws, first-degree murder is a Class 1 felony and is punishable by death or life imprisonment; rape is a Class 2 felony (the number of years for which one may be sentenced to prison for this and other offenses will differ, depending on an offender's prior record); aggravated robbery (the offender has an accomplice) is a Class 3 felony; and forgery is a Class 4 felony.[6]

A **misdemeanor** is a less serious offense and is typically punishable by incarceration for less than one year in a local jail. Like felonies, misdemeanors are often classified under state laws. In Arizona, shoplifting is a Class 1 misdemeanor (if the value of items taken is less than $250); reckless driving is a Class 2 misdemeanor; a vehicle driver who leaves the scene of an accident is guilty of a Class 3 misdemeanor; and so on.[7]

OFFENSE DEFINITIONS AND CATEGORIES

Crimes Against Persons

Crimes against persons are what most people consider "violent crime" or "street crime," such as certain homicides, sexual assault, robbery, and aggravated assault.

Felony: a serious offense with a possible sentence of more than a year in prison.

Misdemeanor: a lesser offense, typically punishable by a fine or up to one year in a local jail.

Crime against persons: a violent crime, to include murder, rape, robbery, and assault.

As you will learn more in Chapter 3, the Federal Bureau of Investigation (FBI) defines these crimes as offenses that involve force or threat of force. Reviewing homicide and sexual assault will help you understand this class of crimes against persons.

Homicide

The taking of a human life—homicide—is obviously the most serious act that one can perpetrate against another person. But not every killing is criminal in nature, as the following examples demonstrate:

AP Photo/Joshua Polson, The Greeley Tribune

Excusable killings include those that are accidental in nature, such as when a driver strikes and kills a toddler who darts out into the street; in such cases the driver will not be deemed culpable (blameworthy).

- Justifiable homicide—acts of war, self-defense, legal state or federal executions, or when a police officer uses lawful lethal force

- Excusable homicide—killings that are wholly accidental, such as when a person who is driving the speed limit and paying full attention but who hits a small child who darts into the street from behind a large RV, where no reasonable person could have known that such a risk was possible or preventable

- Criminal homicides fall into two categories: murder (intentional killings) and manslaughter (accidental killings). Within these two categories, offenses are ranked in seriousness by degrees. As mentioned earlier, under our system of justice, the premise underlying homicide is that "when A shoots B, there are a variety of possible outcomes." The prosecutor must attempt to determine the shooter's intent, which can result in criminal charges ranging from murder in the first degree to involuntary manslaughter. A useful way to think of the universe of possible homicide charges is as a "ladder of offenses," going from the least serious up to the most serious (see Table 2.2).

Murder

The term *murder* includes only intentional killings, which are categorized by degrees.

- *Murder in the first degree* (sometimes termed "murder one") is the unlawful, intentional killing of a human being with *premeditation and deliberation* (often termed "P&D") and *malice aforethought* (as noted earlier, federal and state statutes define murder and its elements differently, but generally they all require the elements of intent, P&D, and malice aforethought). P&D means the defendant thought about committing the act before doing so. Courts generally look at the following factors to determine P&D: evidence of planning, the manner of killing, and the prior relationship between the defendant and the victim.[8] Courts also look at the *time* a defendant may have contemplated or planned, in order to determine whether premeditation existed, but courts differ on this issue. The federal courts have held that *no* minimum time period is necessary, and a jury can determine from the facts whether or not a defendant premeditated murder.[9]

- Malice aforethought is often said to be shown when someone acts with "a depraved heart," evidenced by one's shooting a gun, or stabbing with a knife.

• Dangerous conduct can also be prosecuted as first-degree murder under the **felony-murder rule**, which provides that if a death occurs during the commission of a felony, the defendant will be charged with murder in the first degree, regardless of his or her intent (a crime that does not require a *mens rea* element is known as a "strict liability" crime—see also the discussion of statutory rape, later). The classic example involves multiple defendants robbing a bank and during the robbery the bank security guard dies from a heart attack. In that case, all the defendants may be charged with first-degree murder under the felony-murder rule. Likewise, if one of the bank robbers panics and shoots a security guard, all of the defendants will be charged with first-degree murder even though the robbers intended only to rob, not to kill anyone. The felony-murder rule is designed to deter those who might otherwise commit dangerous felonies. If a would-be bank robber knows the penalty for an accidental death during his or her crime might be a charge of first-degree murder, perhaps the robber will think twice about committing the crime.

• *Murder in the second degree* ("murder two") is distinguished from first-degree murder in that it is also intentional—with malice—yet *impulsive*, without P&D. An

Felony-murder rule: the legal doctrine that says that, if a death occurs during the commission of a felony, the perpetrator of the crime may be charged with murder in the first degree.

INVESTIGATING FURTHER

ARIEL CASTRO—THE CLEVELAND "MONSTER"

Between 2002–2004, Ariel Castro kidnapped three young women and then held them captive in his Cleveland, OH, home, where he raped and tortured them for a decade. In 2013, he pleaded guilty to nearly 1,000 charges of kidnapping, sexual assault, and other offenses, and was sentenced to life in prison plus 1,000 years.

Some people are thought to be purely evil, such as Ariel Castro, who abducted three young women— Amanda Berry, Michelle Knight, and Gina DeJesus— over the course of several years and then imprisoned them in his home in urban Cleveland, Ohio, for more than a decade. He raped, abused, and starved them, while depriving them of simple needs like sunlight, a working bathroom, regular showers, and the ability to see the outside (windows were boarded).

He fathered a child with Berry, and threatened to kill Knight, if she didn't deliver the baby safely. Berry was able to escape one day when Castro made the uncharacteristic mistake of leaving an interior door unlocked and going out allowing Berry to go to the front door to bang and scream for help. Castro pleaded guilty to 937 criminal counts including kidnapping, sexual assault, and aggravated murder (for killing at least one unborn child by beating Knight when she was pregnant with Castro's child). At his sentencing, Castro told the courtroom he was not a monster, but he was "sick" because he was addicted to pornography. Judge Michael Russo responded with a classic statement of *mens rea* by observing, "You were acquainted with the kidnap victims and that was a factor in your abduction strategy. You had an outwardly normal relationship with your girlfriend—it's clear you are able to choose who you wished to victimize." In August 2013, Castro was sentenced to life plus 1,000 years, but within a month of his sentencing, he committed suicide by hanging himself in his prison cell. His "house of horrors" was demolished shortly after his sentencing.

Source: Eliott C. McLaughlin and Pamela Brown, "Judge Sentences Cleveland Kidnapper Ariel Castro to Life, Plus 1,000 Years," CNN, August 1, 2013, http://www.cnn.com/2013/08/01/justice/ohio-castro/.

example would be when two men get into an argument at a bar, and one pulls a knife and stabs the other to death. He intended to stab the other man, but the killing did not involve premeditation. Furthermore, although the intent to kill is an essential element of both first- and second-degree murder, a defendant can also be found guilty of second-degree murder if his or her actions show gross recklessness and a disregard for human life is high, and there is extreme risk of death. Although it will depend on the jury's views, acts such as allowing a dangerous dog to run at large (which then bites and kills a child), intentionally shooting a gun into a crowd of people, throwing a heavy object off of a roof onto a crowded street below, and playing Russian roulette (loading a gun and intentionally firing it at another person) have been found to lead to conviction for second-degree murder (as you will see later, these actions could also qualify as involuntary manslaughter).[10]

Manslaughter

The term *manslaughter* refers to accidental killings, categorized as voluntary (intentional but without malice) and involuntary (unintentional).

- *Voluntary manslaughter* is an intentional killing, but it involves (at least in the eyes of the law) no malice. Instead, there is "heat of passion" to a degree that a "reasonable person" might have been provoked into killing someone. The best example is when a person comes home early in the day and finds his or her significant other in the arms of another person, becomes enraged, grabs a gun, and kills one or both of them. The killer acted in the heat of passion rather than intentionally. A killing can be downgraded on the homicide ladder, from murder to voluntary manslaughter, only if the actor was adequately provoked (generally, words alone—as in an argument—are not enough to provoke, but seeing something like a cheating spouse is), and the actor must not have had time to "cool off." The person discovering his cheating spouse cannot leave, go to a bar and drink a few beers, and then return to the scene and kill the offending couple (this would be first-degree murder, as explained earlier). The "passion" that aroused the person to kill must have arisen contemporaneously—at the same time of the provocation—and continued until the time of the criminal act.

- The circumstances of a killing might cause a prosecutor to look at both second-degree murder and voluntary manslaughter as possible charges. When a perpetrator clearly killed with intent but without P&D (e.g., two people fighting with weapons), a second-degree murder charge is appropriate. But when that same actor is fighting with weapons because the victim provoked her and she did not have time to "cool off" after that provocation, the charge could be downgraded to voluntary manslaughter. A prosecutor will consider all of the evidence to determine the right homicide charge, up or down the "ladder."

- *Involuntary manslaughter* is typically established in one of two ways: (1) acts of negligence, such as when one is driving too fast on a slick road and kills a pedestrian, or (2) the misdemeanor-manslaughter rule—similar to the felony-murder rule, but the crime involved is a misdemeanor. For example, a man enters a convenience store and shoplifts a six-pack of beer; the clerk chases him out the door but slips and falls, striking his head on the sidewalk and dying from the force of the impact. The shoplifter may be charged with involuntary manslaughter, as his actions caused the clerk's death.

Video: George
Huguely Trial

The George Huguely Case: Now that you have learned the different types of homicide and how the critical element of *mens rea* determines the degree and punishment, consider the scenarios (from the beginning of the chapter) under which the jury could have convicted Huguely and how *mens rea* was a part of each of them:

- First-degree murder: Huguely battered Love to death intentionally, and he planned it.

- Second-degree murder: Huguely battered Love to death intentionally but did not plan it.

- Voluntary manslaughter: Huguely killed Love in a burst of jealous rage.

- Involuntary manslaughter: The former lovers' discussion led to physical contact and an accidental, unintentional blunt force trauma to Love.

Further, consider that the prosecution presented evidence that Huguely had emailed Love about a week before her death, writing, "I should have killed you" (when he learned about her relationship with another man). The jury also convicted Huguely of grand larceny because Love's laptop and other items from her apartment were found in his apartment after the altercation; how might those facts affect the homicide case? Finally, jurors saw videotapes of police interrogating Huguely after arrest and the prosecution was able to show that Huguely lied on multiple occasions during questioning. Decide the correct homicide conviction and check your answer in the Notes section at the end of the book.[11]

TABLE 2.2 The "Ladder" OF HOMICIDE CRIMES AND THE REQUIRED MENS REA

MURDER (INTENTIONAL KILLINGS)		
Charge	*Mens Rea*	**Example**
First-Degree Murder	Premeditated, with malice aforethought	Planning to kill your wife's boyfriend by waiting at his home one evening and killing him when he arrives
Second-Degree Murder	Intentional but not premeditated	Unexpectedly seeing your wife's boyfriend several days after you discover their affair, grabbing a gun you keep in your car, and killing him
MANSLAUGHTER (ACCIDENTAL KILLINGS)		
Voluntary Manslaughter	Committed in the "heat of passion"; being adequately provoked and not having time to cool off	Arriving home and finding your wife and her boyfriend together, immediately grabbing a nearby weapon, and killing the boyfriend in a blind rage
Involuntary Manslaughter	Unintentional/accidental; causing a death while breaking the law (typically a misdemeanor criminal law) or while being negligent	Texting while driving and accidentally hitting a child who darts out into the street
FELONY MURDER (STRICT LIABILITY)		
Felony/First-Degree Murder	Unintentionally causing a death while intentionally committing a dangerous felony; no *mens rea* required = strict liability	Burglarizing your wife's office to find evidence of her affair and causing her death because she has a heart attack when she arrives and finds you there

You Be the... PROSECUTOR

A 19-year-old college student drinks heavily at a friend's house one night. When he tries to leave, his friends take his car keys and tell him he is too drunk to drive. He retrieves the keys, leaves anyway, and drives the wrong way on a New York highway, slamming head-on at high speed into a limousine carrying a family coming from a wedding (ironically, the family hired the limo to avoid drinking and driving after the wedding reception). The limo driver and a 7-year-old passenger are both killed instantly, and the other passengers are critically injured. The college student's blood alcohol level is more than three times the legal limit. The relevant laws in New York are as follows:

New York Penal Law § 125.25: A person is guilty of *murder in the second degree* when . . . under circumstances evincing a depraved indifference to human life, he recklessly engages in conduct which creates a grave risk of death to another person, and thereby causes the death of another person (penalty: 15 years to life).

New York Penal Law § 125.13: A person is guilty of vehicular *manslaughter* . . . when he or she [causes the death of another person] . . . while operating a motor vehicle while [intoxicated] . . . (penalty: 3 to 15 years).

1. What are the *actus reus* and *mens rea* elements for second-degree murder? For vehicular manslaughter?

2. How would you argue as the prosecutor that the driver should be convicted of second-degree murder? Remember, you will have to prove *mens rea*, so what facts would you use to tie into the second-degree murder statute's definition of *mens rea*?

3. How could the defense attorney argue that the driver should be convicted only of manslaughter, that second-degree murder is not appropriate? (See "Excuse Defenses: Intoxication" later in this chapter.)[12]

Sexual Assault ("rape" or "forcible rape" under some older state laws): Sexual assault was historically defined as the carnal knowledge of a female forcibly and against her will, and most criminal laws did not recognize rape of men, same-sex rape, or rape between spouses. Today, most states have adopted the modern definition of "sexual assault"—sexual contact without the victim's consent, but with no limitations on gender or relationship of perpetrator and victim. Most states have also recognized that sexual assault occurs when someone has sexual contact with a person who is incapable of consenting (someone who is intoxicated, under anesthesia, or mentally challenged). In such cases, the "perpetrator" knows or should know that the victim cannot consent to the act.

Like other crimes, sexual assault is categorized by degrees depending on the type of contact, from sexual penetration without the consent of the victim (first degree, the most serious) to unwanted sexual contact that does not result in physical injury (often third degree). Like homicide, sexual assault includes a "strict liability" crime with no *mens rea* element, also known as "statutory rape." This crime is defined as sexual contact between a "victim" of a certain age, typically between ages 12 and 16, and a "perpetrator" who is older, typically 19 and above.

Robbery: Robbery is the taking of or attempt to take anything of value from the care, custody, or control of a person or persons by force or threat of force or violence and/or by putting the victim in fear. About 350,000 robberies are reported to the police annually in the United

©moodboard / Alamy

Robbery involves the taking, or attempting to take, anything of value from another person by force or threat of force or violence, where the victim is in fear of injury or death.

INVESTIGATING FURTHER

SEXUAL ASSAULT ON COLLEGE CAMPUSES—YES MEANS YES

Sexual assault on college campuses has garnered a lot of media attention in recent years, particularly when athletes from high-profile sports programs are involved and when cell phone cameras have provided a clear record of offenses. Although media attention has increased, the Bureau of Justice reports that student sexual assaults are actually less likely than nonstudent assaults (6.1 per 1,000 students, or 0.61 percent versus 7.6 per 1,000 nonstudents).[13]

Nevertheless, when these cases are reported to police, the offenses fall under criminal laws that define the crime as sexual contact without the victim's consent. The prosecution need not prove the perpetrator acted with any specific *mens rea*, only that he or she acted without the victim's consent. Of course, this issue often boils down to competing testimony—"he said, she said"—about the often-confusing communication of yes and no.

In 2014, the California legislature addressed this issue by passing the "Yes Means Yes" law, which requires that universities receiving public funding must require students to get "affirmative, conscious, and voluntary agreement to engage in sexual activity." Under the new law, consent for sex has to be explicit—neither lack of resistance nor silence can mean consent. While the new California law is not a criminal statute and applies only to public universities (which must incorporate the consent requirement into their student conduct policies), it may mark a new trend in more clearly defining consent in the criminal law as well.[14]

Check your college or university's policies and standards on sexual assault. How is the offense defined? How is consent defined? Compare it to your state's criminal statutes on sexual assault and their definitions of *mens rea* and consent.

States.[15] As stated earlier in this chapter, many times people who come home to find their houses have been broken into claim they have been "robbed" when they obviously have not been (they have been burglarized), given that robbery requires a face-to-face taking—a combination of theft and assault.

Aggravated Assault: Aggravated assault is an unlawful attack upon another for the purpose of inflicting severe or aggravated bodily injury. This offense is usually accompanied by the use of a weapon or by other means likely to produce death or great bodily harm. When aggravated assault (or even regular assault, as long as there is a threat) and larceny-theft occur together, the offense falls under the category of robbery. Each year about 750,000 aggravated assaults are reported in the United States.[16]

As is the case with homicide crimes, criminal justice students often have difficulty understanding the "ladder" of assault crimes. A few examples will help to clarify the differences.

- First, the mere placing of someone in fear for their safety is an assault. If Joe yells at Jack threateningly, "I'm going to beat your brains out," this is an assault. An *assault*, then, occurs when one person makes threatening gestures that alarm someone and makes that person feel under attack; actual physical contact is not necessary.

- But if Joe intentionally strikes Jack on his cheek, the intentional physical contact intended to harm raises this conduct to the crime of *assault and battery*.

- Finally, if Joe gets a lug wrench out of his car and strikes Jack with it several times, inflicting severe injury, Joe has now committed an *aggravated assault*.

Crimes Against Property

Crimes against property are offenses where no violence is involved, only the taking of property—crimes such as burglary, larceny-theft, motor vehicle theft, and arson.

Burglary: Burglary is the unlawful entry of a structure to commit a felony or theft. To classify an offense as a burglary, the use of force to gain entry need not have occurred, nor does anything of value have to have been stolen. The FBI, in its *Uniform Crime Reports* (detailed in Chapter 3), defines "structure" as an apartment, a barn, a house trailer or houseboat when used as a permanent dwelling, an office, a railroad car (but not an automobile), a stable, and a vessel (i.e., ship). Annually, about 2.2 million burglaries are reported in the United States.[17]

Larceny-Theft: Larceny-theft is the unlawful taking, carrying, leading, or riding away of property from the possession of another; it includes attempted thefts as well as thefts of bicycles, motor vehicle parts and accessories, shoplifting, pocket-picking, or the stealing of any property or article that is not taken by force and violence or by fraud. The value of the item stolen is significant, and in all states the monetary worth will determine whether the larceny-theft is a felony or a misdemeanor; each state's statutes will set forth its limits. Using Nevada statutes as examples, if the item is worth more than $250, it is a felony; Iowa, however, has several classifications: It is a "serious misdemeanor" if the item stolen is valued between $200 and $500, an "aggravated misdemeanor" if worth between $500 and $1,000, and a felony if worth more than $1,000.[18] Each year about 6.26 million larceny-thefts are reported to the police in the United States.[19]

Arson: Arson is any willful or malicious burning of or attempting to burn, with or without intent to defraud, a dwelling house, a public building, a motor vehicle or aircraft, personal property of another, and so forth. There are different types of arsonists, with very different motives for setting fires. Each year about 43,500 arsons are reported to police, with an average dollar loss per event of about $13,000. About half (45.9 percent) of all arsons involve structures (residential, storage, public, and so on).[20]

DEFENSES

In the U.S. system of justice, criminal defendants have the opportunity to defend their actions by asserting **affirmative defenses**, in which the defendant admits to the criminal conduct but offers his or her reasons for acting. Because the defendant asserts such defenses, he or she typically has the burden to prove them. These **defenses** fall under two categories, justifications and excuses. In the former case, defendants argue they were justified in acting because, for example, they were defending themselves or others. A police officer who had to injure a fleeing felon could claim a justification defense. In the latter case, defendants admit to the criminal act but claim they are not legally responsible—they are excused—because they are too young or insane, for example.

Learning about defenses is really another way to learn about the critically important element of *mens rea*. Most defenses are designed to negate or reduce criminal liability by showing that the accused did not act with the required criminal intent. The prosecution may be able to easily show that the criminal act—the *actus reus*—was committed (e.g., the killing, the assault, the breaking and entering), but the defense can then defeat the criminal charges by showing that the required *mens rea* simply was not present (killing

Crime against property: a crime during which no violence is perpetrated against a person, such as burglary, theft, and arson.

Affirmative defense: the defendant admits he or she committed the act charged but argues that for some mitigating reason he or she should not be held criminally responsible under the law.

Defense: the response by a defendant to a criminal charge, to include denial of the criminal allegations in an attempt to negate or overcome the charges.

INVESTIGATING FURTHER

"STAND YOUR GROUND" LAWS

The fatal shooting of Trayvon Martin by George Zimmerman in Sanford, Florida, generated tremendous controversy because of its racial overtones and the state's "stand your ground" law. In July 2013, Zimmerman was acquitted of second-degree murder.

When George Zimmerman shot and killed an unarmed teen named Trayvon Martin in February 2012, a major controversy erupted calling into question the entire criminal justice system and a controversial law that binds police and prosecutors. The "stand your ground"

law essentially sets forth the common law "castle doctrine" that allows a homeowner to use deadly force against an intruder and then expands the right to defend beyond the home, to any place someone has a right to be. Under the law, an accused killer may argue he or she acted in self-defense because the killer believed he or she was facing the threat of seriously bodily injury or death. The burden then shifts to the prosecutor, who must prove *beyond a reasonable doubt* (the highest legal standard) that the killer was not facing such a threat of serious bodily harm or death, that the killer did not act in self-defense. The laws were originally intended to give citizens a presumption of innocence when defending themselves, while also generally banning police from detaining someone if they have evidence that the shooter was attacked "in a place he had a right to be." Prosecutors largely despise the law because of the aforementioned burden of proof, whereas defense attorneys have found it to be a means of defending people who claim they had a right to meet force with force. "Stand your ground" became law in Florida in 2005, and at least 25 states have since enacted some version.

Source: John Arnold, "The Law Heard Round the World," *Time,* April 9, 2012, http://www.time.com/time/magazine/article/0,9171,2110471,00.html; also see "Trayvon Martin Case (George Zimmerman)," *New York Times,* July 19, 2012, http://topics.nytimes.com/top/reference/timestopics/people/m/trayvon_martin/index.html.

Author Video: Stand your ground law

in self-defense is not the same as killing intentionally because you are trying to save yourself, and breaking and entering to save yourself from freezing to death is not the same as burglarizing a home to steal things). As a result, examining these defenses helps us understand how *mens rea* operates in real cases.

Justification Defenses

Self-defense is a justification defense rooted in necessity, where the defendant argues that he or she had to commit the act because it was necessary to avoid some greater harm. Under early common law of England, people had a "duty to retreat," also known as "retreat to the wall," prior to using force to defend themselves. In effect, a person could not respond to an attacker until he or she was "cornered" and had no other retreat option available. Today, most state laws do not impose a duty to retreat and, in fact, provide in many situations that people may "stand their ground" (see discussion in the "Investigating Further" box).

Under modern laws, one may use force, even deadly force, without first "retreating to the wall" against another person if he or she reasonably believes that an attack against him or her is imminent, but defensive actions must be proportionate to the threatened harm and not unreasonable for the circumstances. One cannot respond to an attack with a tree branch by using a shotgun.

Other justification defenses include defense of others, law enforcement actions (e.g., justifiable homicide in killing a fleeing felon), and necessity, which involves breaking the law to preserve life or to avoid injury (e.g., breaking into a home to escape a life-threatening storm or driving at a reckless speed to get a pregnant woman to the hospital).

Excuse Defenses

Age

The infancy defense excuses the acts of children ages 7 and under because they are too young to be criminally responsible for their actions—they are too young to form the requisite *mens rea*. Minors between ages 7 and 14 are presumed incapable of committing a crime, but prosecutors may challenge that assumption in certain cases. Minors over age 14 have no infancy defense, but those under 16 at the time of the crime are typically tried in juvenile court. Under some state statutes, however, serious felony cases are automatically transferred to adult court, or the prosecutor has the option to seek such a transfer if the juvenile is not a suitable candidate for the more lenient and protective philosophy and law of the juvenile court (see Chapter 15).

Entrapment

If the police induced a person to commit a crime that he or she would otherwise not have attempted, the defendant can claim the defense of **entrapment**.[21] But it is not always clear what constitutes entrapment. A state supreme court deemed that police officers posing as homeless persons with cash sticking out of their pockets was entrapment because it could tempt even honest persons who were not otherwise predisposed to committing theft. But the U.S. Supreme Court did not find entrapment where undercover drug agents provided an essential chemical to defendants who were already planning to manufacture illegal drugs.[22] Nor is it entrapment when a drug agent sells drugs to a suspected drug dealer, who then sells it to government agents. The defense of entrapment will fail where the government has merely set the scene for people to commit a crime they are predisposed to commit anyway, such as where a police officer positions himself on the route of a known working prostitute and offers her money for sex when she comes by.

Intoxication

The intoxication defense is rooted in the concept of *mens rea*, and defendants must show that they were operating under such "diminished capacity" that they could not know what they were doing and cannot be held responsible. The defense is not available in cases of voluntary intoxication (except in some cases of severe alcoholism where *mens rea* is permanently impaired) and is only successful—albeit rarely—in cases of involuntary intoxication (the spiked drink or slipped drug), where the intoxicant was ingested without awareness of its intoxicating nature or where the consumption was coerced. The burden on the defendant is high in these cases, and defense attorneys generally have a difficult time convincing juries that defendants should be excused (although diminished capacity can be useful for defense attorneys to seek reduced charges or punishment).

Student on the Street Video: Intoxication and crime

Duress

The duress defense is an excuse where defendants claim they committed the act only because they were not acting of their own free will. For example, the wife of a bank president calls her husband and informs him that someone has broken into their home and put a gun to her head, and if he does not bring money home immediately, she will be killed. The husband then removes the money from his bank in order to supply the ransom. The husband could claim that he acted under duress, only to save his wife. Other actual cases include a person who was forced by gangsters to commit certain criminal acts or be killed, a drug smuggler who argued that his family would have been killed if he did not do what he was told,[23] and a Texas prison inmate whose three cellmates planned an escape

Entrapment: police tactics that unduly encourage or induce an individual to commit a crime he or she typically would not commit.

PRACTITIONER'S PERSPECTIVE

SUBSTANCE ABUSE COUNSELOR

Name: Jessica Richards

Current Position: Outpatient Mental Health Counselor

City, State: Orlando, Florida

College Attended/Academic Major: Bachelor of science in psychology from the University of Central Florida; master's degree in mental health counseling from NOVA Southeastern University

How long have you been a practitioner in this criminal justice position? Since October 2013

My primary duties and responsibilities as a practitioner in this position: To provide, as an outpatient therapist, intensive clinical therapeutic services to children, adolescents, and adults with identified mental health or substance abuse diagnoses. This service is designed to meet the specific mental health needs of the identified client as they relate to their diagnosis and can be provided in home, in office, in school, or in another approved/appropriate community setting. Outpatient therapy includes psychoeducational activities/interventions designed to assist the client in the reduction of dysfunction. Services are provided with client-centered and family-centered approaches and are delivered through intensive, time-limited, goal-specific interventions.

The qualities/characteristics that are most helpful in this career: Empathy; active listening; boundary setting; social and communication skills; critical thinking; abilities in business management, organizational management, and time management; and an ability to balance one's own emotions and manage self-care appropriately to avoid burnout.

In general, this is what a *typical day* looks like for a practitioner in this career: First, the ability to structure your time and make your own hours. Some therapists prefer to devote their mornings to providing counseling services within schools and within the community, while spending the evening hours catching up on paperwork and documentation. Other therapists prefer to spend the morning hours catching up on documentation and phone calls while spending the evening hours providing in-home and in-the-community services to clients. Each day presents different challenges, so no one day is exactly the same as the next. For example, one day I might work 5 hours seeing clients, driving 3 hours to and from counseling locations within the community to meet with clients, and another 4 hours completing documentation and paperwork. The following day I might spend 4 hours working with clients, 2 hours driving, and 3 hours completing documentation. Then, the following two days might include devoting 3 hours per day providing services, an hour driving between clients, and no time spent on documentation. Normally, one day per week is reserved for making phone calls, preparing administrative paperwork and documentation, and catching up on backlogged work. Occasionally, I will spend a few hours on Saturdays seeing clients within the community as well.

My advice to someone either wishing to study, or now studying, criminal justice and wanting to become a practitioner in this career: Obtain a mentor—someone in the field—who will provide guidance and expertise while you are navigating the processes involved to become a practitioner. Also, interview a number of practitioners who are already in the field and ask a lot of questions; obtain their feedback on what they would have done differently, do the same, or change about the field if they had the chance.

and threatened to slit his throat if he did not accompany them.[24] Again, the burden will be on the accused to convince the jury that he or she committed the act under duress.

Double Jeopardy

Double jeopardy: subjecting an accused person to be tried twice for the same offense; prohibited by the Fifth Amendment.

The Fifth Amendment to the U.S. Constitution states that no person shall be "subject for the same offense to be twice put in jeopardy of life or limb," prohibiting the government from prosecuting someone for the same offense more than once (**double jeopardy**). Other than some specific exceptions (a mistrial, a reversal on appeal, or a situation in which the crime violates laws of separate jurisdictions such as civilian/ military or federal/state), the government has only one attempt to obtain a conviction. If a defendant is acquitted, the prosecution may not appeal that conviction or retry the defendant.

Mental Illness/Insanity

The insanity defense is perhaps the most misunderstood area of the criminal law. Ask anyone on the street, and most people will say that the insanity defense is a way for criminals to "get off" by arguing that they were "crazy" at the time of the crime. Some crimes by their very nature seem to indicate that the perpetrator was indeed not thinking straight, and many people believe that those who commit especially gruesome crimes will, by default, plead insanity. These are just a few of the common misconceptions about this defense.

Several notorious trials in recent decades have contributed to the confusion. Most notably, in 1981, John Hinckley Jr. attempted to assassinate President Ronald Reagan but was found not guilty by reason of insanity after he claimed he had done so in an effort to impress actress Jodie Foster and after psychiatrists testified at length about his childhood.[25]

Then, in 1986, Steve Roth hired two men who slashed model Marla Hanson's face with razors after Hanson rejected Roth's sexual advances. Her injuries required more than 100 stitches. Roth's insanity defense—based on the psychiatric effects of his short stature—failed, and all three men were convicted.[26]

More recently, the 2008 movie *Milk* recalled the so-called Twinkie defense from the trial of Dan White, who in 1978 murdered Harvey Milk, a San Francisco gay rights activist and politician. Although the defense never even mentioned Twinkies during White's trial, the media coined the term following psychiatric testimony that White had been depressed and consuming junk food and sugar-laden soft drinks— allegedly "blasting sugar through his arteries and driving him into a murderous frenzy."[27]

Despite these high-profile cases, the insanity defense is raised in less than 1 percent of felony cases and is successful in only a fraction of those.[28] The defense is really quite simple if you think of it as another way of examining the critical element of *mens rea:* A defendant must prove that he or she has a recognized, diagnosable mental illness—a disease of the brain (e.g., schizophrenia, bipolar disorder, psychosis)—and that because of that mental illness, he or she cannot be held criminally responsible for his or her actions.

State laws set forth the applicable test for legal insanity. Most states use the M'Naghten Rule, also known as the **right-wrong test**. Under this test, it must be "proved that, at the time of the committing of the act, the defendant suffered from a mental illness and because of that disease of the mind, was laboring under such a defect of reason that he did not know the nature and quality of the act he was doing, or if he did know it, that he did not understand what he was doing was wrong."[29]

Another test is the "irresistible impulse test," requiring a showing that the defendant, because of a mental illness, could not control his or her impulses or volition. Also known as "the policeman at your elbow" test, this standard for legal insanity requires a showing that the defendant would have committed the crime even if a police officer had been on the scene, literally at the accused's elbow, thereby evidencing that the defendant had no impulse control.[30]

Contrary to another popular misconception, a finding of legal insanity does not mean the defendant walks free. Instead, the defendant will be committed to a psychiatric facility. In some states, in reaction to the Hinckley verdict, the jury can

Right-wrong test: the test of legal insanity, asking whether the defendant understood the nature and quality of his or her act and, if so, if he or she understood it was wrong.

reach a "guilty but mentally ill" verdict, allowing mentally ill defendants to be found guilty but to receive psychiatric treatment while incarcerated or to be placed in a mental hospital until well enough to be moved to a prison to serve their sentences.[31]

After John Hinckley's trial, many states shifted the burden of proving insanity to the defense, requiring them to show either clear and convincing evidence or a preponderance of the evidence that the defendant was legally insane at the time of the crime. Consider the following notorious post-Hinckley cases in which the insanity defense failed:

- Jeffrey L. Dahmer, the serial killer who claimed that necrophilia drove him to murder and dismember/cannibalize 15 men and boys, was convicted in 1992.[32]

- David Berkowitz, known as the "Son of Sam" killer (he reported receiving messages from the devil through a neighbor's dog, Sam), murdered six people in New York in the mid-1970s and was deemed fit by the trial court to stand trial (despite a psychiatric report that found him paranoid and delusional).[33]

- John Wayne Gacy, the Chicago-area so-called Killer Clown who murdered more than 30 youths, pleaded not guilty by reason of insanity but was convicted and executed in 1994.[34]

INVESTIGATING FURTHER

JAMES HOLMES—THE "BATMAN" SHOOTER

©RJ SANGOSTI/UPI/Newscom

When James Holmes made his first appearance in court, accused of turning a Colorado movie theater into a shooting gallery, killing 12 and injuring more than 50, many people assumed he must be "crazy," but the question of his guilt and mental state is much more complicated under the criminal law.

In July 2013, James Holmes went to the midnight viewing of the new Batman movie, *The Dark Knight Rises*. He had dyed his hair orange like the Joker character in the movie, but otherwise, Holmes seemed like any other Batman fan. While the movie got under way, Holmes slipped out an exit door, propped it open, went to his car and picked up SWAT gear, firearms, and ammunition,

and then went back to the theater and opened fire, killing 12 and injuring more than 50. When law enforcement officers later caught Holmes outside the theater, he was quickly subdued and told officers he'd booby-trapped his apartment with bombs and other weapons. There would seem to be no clearer case of someone acting with *mens rea* and premeditation, but questions quickly arose regarding Holmes's psychiatric condition in the months leading up to the shooting. His attorneys ultimately entered a plea of not guilty by reason of insanity, and the world watched to see if this apparently evil, plotting killer would be convicted and sentenced to death. But the insanity defense in Colorado requires that the prosecution—not the defense—show that Holmes understood right from wrong (the M'Naghten test) and that he was not acting on impulses he could not control (the irresistible impulse test). The defense countered with evidence of Holmes's mental illness to lay the foundation for a finding that he could not have fully understood or controlled what he was doing. In July 2015, a jury decided Holmes was not insane and convicted him of 24 counts of first-degree murder, 140 counts of attempted murder, and one explosives count. Despite the prosecution's arguments that Holmes deserved to die for his crimes, the jury sentenced him to life in prison without parole.

Source:.Colo. Rev. Stats §16-8; see also *Denver Post* Editorial Board, "Shining a Light on Insanity Plea," *Denver Post,* June 9, 2013, **http://www.denverpost. com/ci_23406862/shining-light-james-holmes-insanity-plea.**

IN A NUTSHELL

- Our legal system is based on the English common law: collections of rules, customs, and traditions. At its core is the doctrine of *stare decisis*, meaning that when a court has decided a case based on a set of facts, it will adhere to that principle, and other courts will apply that decision in the same manner to all future cases where facts are substantially the same.

- There are both civil and criminal laws at the federal, state, and local levels. Many more laws are enacted each year by the U.S. Congress, state legislatures, and city councils.

- Substantive law is the written law that defines or regulates our rights and duties. Procedural law sets forth the procedures and mechanisms for processing criminal cases.

- Two essential elements that underlie our system of law are *mens rea* (criminal intent) and *actus reus* (a criminal act or a failure to act where there is a legal duty).

- Criminal laws define crimes by specifying the *actus reus* (such as killing for homicide and the taking of property for robbery) and the *mens rea* (intentionally, recklessly, by force, unintentional, etc.). Most crimes are categorized by degrees depending on the seriousness of the physical contact or threat (threatening versus physical contact) and the perpetrator's *mens rea* (intentional versus accidental), or based on the value of items stolen or damaged in crimes against property.

- Our system of justice allows for persons charged with crimes to offer defenses for their behavior; one can argue that his or her acts were justified (self-defense, or when a police officer injures a suspect during a lawful arrest); or the accused can admit wrongdoing but argue that he or she is not deserving of blame due to circumstances surrounding the offense (e.g., entrapment, intoxication, mental illness).

$SAGE edge™ Review key terms with eFlashcards. ◀

KEY TERMS & CONCEPTS

Actus reus, 31
Affirmative defense, 39
Burden of proof, 27
Civil law, 27
Crimes against persons, 32
Crimes against property, 39
Criminal law, 27
Defendant, 27

Defense, 39
Double jeopardy, 42
Entrapment, 41
Felony, 32
Felony-murder rule, 34
Intent, specific, 30
Lex talionis, 25
Mens rea, 31

Misdemeanor, 32
Motive, 30
Plaintiff, 27
Procedural law, 30
Reasonable doubt, 28
Right-wrong test, 43
Stare decisis, 25
Substantive law, 30

$SAGE edge™ Test your understanding of chapter content. Take the practice quiz. ◀

REVIEW QUESTIONS

1. What are the differences between criminal law and civil law?

2. How would you define and explain the importance and contributions of *mens rea* and *actus rea* as they operate in our legal system?

3. What is the difference between one's motive and one's intent to commit a crime, and which is the most important in our legal system?

4. A Nebraska law states the following: "Any person who knowingly or intentionally causes or permits a child or vulnerable adult to ingest methamphetamine, a chemical substance used in manufacturing methamphetamine, or paraphernalia is guilty of a Class I misdemeanor." The *mens rea* for this crime is _____; the *actus reus* element of this crime is _____.

5. What is double jeopardy, why does this constitutional protection from the Fifth Amendment exist, and what are some examples of exceptions to the rule? Many years after O. J. Simpson was acquitted of murdering his ex-wife and her friend, he finalized a contract to publish a book entitled *If I Did It,* which detailed how he "could have" committed the murders.[35] Could prosecutors retry Simpson for the murders based on this new "evidence?"

6. How can age, entrapment, intoxication, and duress each be used as a criminal defense?

Below are several additional case studies, all of which are grounded in actual case facts and chapter materials (concerning sexual assault, self-defense, and homicide, respectively). While studying each scenario, first assume that you are the *prosecuting* attorney and decide which charge(s), if any, should be brought against the accused on the basis of the facts. Next, assume the role of the *defense* attorney and explain, given the facts, what defenses should legitimately be made against the crime(s) charged. Remember that the Sixth Amendment entitles every defendant to the "guiding hand" of effective counsel, whose job it is to ensure that all legal protections are afforded. Answers and/or outcomes for each case are provided in the Notes section. For purposes of discussion, however, approach all of them as if there are no absolute, totally correct answers.

A high school principal threatens a graduating senior that if she does not have sex with him, he will prevent her from graduating. She submits against her will and then reports the incident to police after she is able to graduate. The state prosecutes the man under a first-degree sexual assault statute that reads as follows:

A person who knowingly has sexual intercourse without consent with a person of the opposite sex commits the offense of sexual intercourse without consent. "Without consent" shall mean the victim is compelled to submit by force or by threat of force.

1. What is the prosecution's best argument that this is precisely the type of situation the law seeks to prevent and that the defendant is guilty of first-degree sexual assault? What facts would you want to know in your capacity as a prosecutor to bolster your case?

2. What is the defense attorney's best argument that this statute does not apply in this case? What other facts would you want to know to strengthen your argument?

3. You are a state lawmaker—how would you revise this statute to better address this case and ones like it? Be specific and rewrite the law as necessary.[36]

A woman is at home with her two children when her estranged husband arrives and begins threatening and assaulting her, following a pattern of alleged past conduct with this woman and prior women. Fearing for her and her children's safety, she flees to the garage but later claims she was unable to open the garage door.

Instead, she gets a gun out of her car and returns to the house. Her husband tells her he will kill her, and their young son witnesses the threat. The woman fires a warning shot that hits the wall behind the husband and then deflects into the ceiling, injuring no one. The woman is charged with aggravated assault with a deadly weapon, but she lives in a "stand your ground" jurisdiction and argues that she acted in self-defense.

1. How can the prosecutor argue that the woman had no right to "stand her ground" and exercise her self-defense rights? What other options did she have in the situation?

2. How can the defense argue that this is precisely the type of case in which the wife should be able to argue self-defense? What other facts would you want to know about the husband-wife relationship?

3. What are the dangers if the wife is successful at using this defense? What are the dangers if she fails and is convicted of attempted murder? Think about broader social policy issues.[37]

Peterson is relaxing at home when he hears noises in the alley behind his house; he looks in that direction and sees three men who are removing parts from his parked vehicle. Peterson approaches the men and tells them to stop what they are doing; he then runs inside his home, obtains a pistol, and returns to the alley. By now the three men are back in their vehicle and preparing to drive away. Peterson approaches them and tells them not to move, or he will shoot. The driver exits the car and, with a wrench in his hand, begins advancing toward Peterson. Peterson then warns the driver not to come any closer. Still carrying the wrench, the man continues to move toward Peterson, who then shoots and kills him (see *U.S. v. Peterson*, 1973).[38]

1. What is the *primary* legal issue here?

2. Also consider:

   ○ What charge should the prosecutor bring against Peterson: Murder in the first degree? Second degree? Manslaughter?

   ○ Did Peterson act in self-defense?

   ○ What other options might have been available to Peterson, aside from obtaining a gun and returning to the alley? Besides shooting the driver?

$SAGE edge™

Review → Practice → Improve

Sharpen your skills with **SAGE edge** at **edge.sagepub.com/peak2e**

SAGE edge for students provides a personalized approach to help you accomplish your coursework goals in an easy-to-use learning environment. Access the videos, audio clips, quizzes, and SAGE journal articles that are noted in this chapter.

CHAPTER 03

THEORIES OF CRIME AND MEASURING VICTIMIZATION

©REUTERS/Zachary Fagenson

LEARNING OBJECTIVES

As a result of reading this chapter, you will be able to:

1 Explain the importance of criminology and how research contributes to public policy

2 Distinguish between the classical and positivist schools of criminology and their explanations for criminality

3 Delineate the various biological theories of crime, to include Lombroso's "born criminal," the "criminal" chromosome, and studies of body types

4 Review the psychological explanations of crime

5 Discuss the several social and cultural explanations of crime—generally how living in social groups might shape people's behavior

6 Review the fundamental aspects of feminist theory—the explanation for women becoming much more engaged in criminal activities since the 1970s

7 Describe the nature and types of white-collar crime

8 Explain the three primary methods for measuring crime and advantages and disadvantages of each

ASSESS YOUR AWARENESS

Test your knowledge of crime theories and measurement by responding to the following eight true-false items; check your answers after reading this chapter's materials.

1 Studies show that the "root" of all crime lies in one's biological makeup.

2 Research shows that nearly all male offenders carry an extra Y chromosome—the "criminal" chromosome.

3 Scholarly studies have revealed that identical twins have a greater likelihood than fraternal twins of having criminal records.

4 The term *white-collar crime* was introduced in 1939, when a criminologist discovered many crimes were committed by persons of respectability and high social status.

5 The best, most widely used, and most accurate reporting of crimes in the United States is published by the Federal Bureau of Investigation (FBI) in the *Uniform Crime Reports*.

6 Increases in labor force participation of women are related to their significantly higher crime rates.

7 If a burglar enters a premises and also commits an aggravated assault and a murder while inside, the police are required to report to the FBI only the crime of murder.

8 Carjacking is now one of the FBI's eight Part I crimes on which it thoroughly reports annually.

Children will watch anything, and when a broadcaster uses crime and violence and other shoddy devices to monopolize a child's attention, it's worse than taking candy from a baby.

—Newton N. Minow, Chair, Federal Communications Commission

Crimes are not to be measured by the issue of events, but by the bad intentions of men.

—Marcus Tullius Cicero

<< Answers can be found on page 424.

Video: Tsarnaev
sentencing

Convicted Boston Marathon Bomber Dzhokhar Tsarnaev was Rolling Stone's cover story in July of 2013, as the nation and the world asked how a 19-year-old American college student could have committed such a heinous crime.

He was born in a war-torn area of Russia, arriving in the United States when he was eight years old. He did well in school and sports and went on to college at Dartmouth. By all accounts, he was a typical American kid—into sports, cars, friends, and social media—and most people described him as polite, respectful, and the last person they'd expect to commit any type of crime. On September 11, 2012, he became an American citizen. Then something went terribly wrong. He started getting behind in classes and spending more time with his older brother, who was a follower of radical Islam. In April 2013, the brothers detonated two pressure cooker bombs near the Boston Marathon finish line, killing three and wounding nearly 300, many of them critically and with life-changing losses of limbs. After several days, law enforcement identified the two from surveillance videos and the manhunt was on. The brothers then killed an MIT police officer in his squad car, hijacked a man who had stopped in his car to read a text, and ultimately engaged with multiple law enforcement agencies in a nighttime street battle using more pressure cooker bombs, homemade grenades, and guns. The older brother, Tamerlan Tsarnaev, died at the scene, but Dzhokhar Tsarnaev escaped. He was found the next day hiding in a nearby backyard, in a stored boat, where he wrote a note saying that he and his brother acted to avenge Muslim deaths caused by the U.S. wars in Iraq and Afghanistan.

Tsarnaev was convicted in May 2015 of multiple crimes for his role in the Boston Marathon bombing. In June 2015, he was sentenced to death, and at his sentencing hearing he admitted he and his brother were the bombers and that he was "sorry for the lives that I've taken, for the suffering that I've caused you, for the damage that I've done. Irreparable damage."

Terrorism experts agree that typical terrorist recruits—young Middle Eastern men who have little hope of prospering in economically challenged areas—commit terrorist acts precisely because they have so little opportunity and are fueled by radical religious beliefs. But Dzhokhar Tsarnaev had a seemingly successful "American" life with a promising future. In the wake of this horrific attack, most people wondered what could have gone wrong to lead someone down such a criminal path.

These are the important questions that criminologists ask and answer, and their work is a critical part of criminal justice study. As you consider the criminological theories discussed in this chapter, try to answer this question: What went wrong, and how can we prevent the next Marathon Bomber who may be among us?[1] Check Tsarnaev's Twitter account for Tweets from before and after the bombings for clues and more information: @J_tsar.

INTRODUCTION

What causes some people to devote much or most of their lives to preying on and harming others? Is it their "nature" or how they were "nurtured"? How could someone enter an elementary school and kill 26 children and teachers? Or shoot up a movie theater, leaving 12 dead and more than 50 wounded?[2] Are such people just base and cruel? Is crime a product of poverty and need? Congenital defects? Greed? Vengeance?

We humans have always sought to better understand the world around us, and so we seek answers to such questions—what amounts to seeking the Rosetta Stone of crime.[3]

We have long sought to unravel the mysteries of human behavior and nature, and the authors of many books have attempted to explain these mysteries. This chapter briefly addresses some of these explanations.

This chapter looks first at the two major, original schools of criminological thought: classical and positivist. It then provides an overview of the biological, psychological, and sociocultural theories put forth to explain criminal behavior, followed by a consideration of the unique role played by women in criminality. After looking at theorists' efforts over the past two and a half centuries to explain crime, the chapter briefly reviews offenders' motivations (in their own words) for selected crimes—sexual assault, armed robbery, burglary, and carjacking. Following that is a discussion of a companion concept: how crimes are measured, including three primary approaches to measuring crime, and the advantages and shortcomings of each.

Criminology

Before delving into the world of criminology, students should ask why this field of study—and its findings—are important to the criminal justice system. An obvious answer is that we can perhaps learn how to better deter and stop crime from happening in the first place. But crime continues to occur and, given human nature, probably always will, so criminology findings are useful to policy makers all along the criminal justice spectrum—from juvenile courts seeking to stop would-be criminals early in life, to lawmakers and judges deciding on appropriate sentencing schemes, to corrections officials seeking to manage probationers, inmates, and parolees in hopes of reducing recidivism. For example, if sociocultural criminologists determine that nonviolent drug offenders labeled as criminals through the typical criminal court process are more likely to reoffend, lawmakers may decide to provide funding for alternative drug courts, where "offenders" are provided a path to rehabilitation with the opportunity to "graduate" from a drug treatment program, rather than simply doing time in prison or on probation.

Video: California solitary confinement

CLASSICAL AND POSITIVIST THEORIES

Until the 18th century, criminal behavior was explained by most Europeans in supernatural or quasi-religious terms. Criminal behavior was caused by forces outside the individual, and people who committed criminal acts were deemed "possessed" by the devil. In an effort to rid society of such evil, the accused was not allowed to put forth a defense, confessions could be obtained through the use of torture, and the penalty for most offenses was some form of physical punishment or death.

All that changed in the mid-18th century, when the classical school of criminology emerged and focused criminal responsibility away from outside evil forces and onto the individual. Criminality was attributed to an individual's free will—criminals made a rational choice to commit crimes. Then in the 19th century, new theorists, the positivists, would seek criminal responsibility more outside the individual, pointing instead to scientific explanations—biological, psychological, and sociological—as forces that affect free will and decision making.

Understanding the development and evolution of criminology can seem daunting, with all its studies and theories, but this field of research is fairly simple if you begin by distinguishing between the two major schools and understanding their major tenets and ideas. Table 3.1 should help guide your review of these important schools of thought.

⬤ TABLE 3.1   Classical and Positivist Theories of Criminology

CLASSICAL	POSITIVIST
Rational Choice Theory	**Scientific Theories: Biology, Psychology, Sociology**

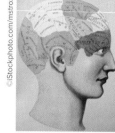

CLASSICAL

Rational Choice: Everyone is capable of criminal acts; individuals weigh the risks and benefits (Beccaria, Bentham).

Deterrence: Fear of punishment—swift and certain—deters crimes; criminal justice system must have predictable laws and punishments; punishments should fit the crime, not the offender.

Neoclassical: Law must account for differences in individuals; criminal responsibility based on level of free will.

POSITIVIST

Biology: Criminals are born—criminal "types" (body types, heredity, chromosomes) (Comte, Lombroso, Sheldon, Fox).

Psychology: Free will/decision making is affected by mental conditions and processes (Freud, Sutherland).

Sociology: Criminals are "made, not born"—sociocultural influences affect criminality.

- Social Structure Theory: Class divisions cause crime as people strive to achieve despite obstacles (Merton, Durkheim).
- Social Process Theory: Justice system causes crime through disparate treatment of offenders.
- Learning Theory: Criminal behavior is learned (Sutherland, Cressey).
- Control Theory: Criminal behavior occurs when social controls like family break down (Reckless, Hirschi).
- Labeling Theory: Offenders once labeled cannot escape their criminal identity (Becker).
- Critical Theory: More powerful social groups use the law to serve their needs and to oppress less powerful groups (Vold).

The Classical School

In 1764 the first attempt was put forth to explain crime in more rational terms. Cesare Beccaria published his classic *Essays on Crime and Punishments*, in which he bemoaned that potential criminals had no way of anticipating the whimsical nature of the criminal law; attempted to expose the injustices in, and arbitrariness of, the administration of law and punishment; and encouraged reform in the way law was enforced to be more consistent and rational. The **classical school** of criminology evolved from this movement, the main principles of which were as follows:

Classical school (of criminology): a perspective indicating that people have free will to choose between criminal and lawful behavior, and that crime can be controlled by sanctions and should be proportionate to the offense.

- Criminal behavior is rational, and most people have the potential to engage in such behavior.
- People may choose to commit a crime after weighing the costs and benefits of their actions.
- Fear of punishment is what keeps most people law-abiding; therefore, the severity, certainty, and speed of punishment affect the crime rate.

- The punishment should fit the crime rather than the offender.

- The criminal justice system must be predictable, with laws and punishments known to the public.

Beccaria's contemporary, Jeremy Bentham, who argued that the laws should provide "the greatest good for the greatest number," saw the purpose of punishment to be deterrence, rather than vengeance, and emphasized the certainty of punishment over its severity.[4]

Although classical criminology laid the cornerstone of modern western criminal law as it was formulated from 1770 to 1812,[5] its influence began to decline in the 19th century, largely because of the rise of science and in part because its principles did not take into account differences among individuals or the manner in which crimes were committed.[6]

Cesare Beccaria, an Italian jurist, philosopher, and politician who is best known for his essays on crime and punishment, believed that punishment should be proportional to the crime, that it is better to prevent crimes than to punish them, and that crimes are prevented more effectively by the *certainty* rather than the *severity* of punishment.

Neoclassical Criminology

Classical ideas began to take on new life in the 1980s, when scholars again began arguing that crimes may result from the rational choice of people who have weighed the benefits to be gained from the crime against the costs of being caught and punished (**neoclassical criminology**). They also argued that the criminal law must take into account the differences among individuals. To a large extent, sentencing reform, criticisms of rehabilitation, and greater use of incarceration sprung from this renewed interest in classical ideas. However, the **positivist school** of thought (positivist criminology) has dominated U.S. criminology since the beginning of the 20th century.

Positivist Criminology

By the middle of the 19th century, the classical school seemed to be out of date, in large part because of the expansion of science. In its place emerged positivist criminology—a philosophical approach proposed by French sociologist Auguste Comte—emphasizing the criminal actor rather than the criminal act,[7] and using science to study the offender's body, mind, and environment. Positivists seek to uncover the basic cause of crime, relying heavily on scientific experts, and believing in rehabilitating "sick" offenders rather than punishing them.[8] Following are some of the tenets of this viewpoint:

Video: Injustice

- Human behavior is controlled by physical, mental, and social factors, not by free will.

- Criminals are different from noncriminals.

- Science can be used to discover the true causes of crime and to treat offenders.[9]

What also became evident was that possessing an understanding of the causes of crime is important, because that will affect how laws are enforced, how guilt is determined, and how punishment is meted out.

The major types of positivism—biological and psychological—are discussed next. As both theories are described, consider their potential to affect public policy making with respect to crime.

Neoclassical criminology: views the accused as exempted from conviction if circumstances prevented the exercise of free will.

Positivist school: a school of thought arguing that science can be used to discover the true causes of crime, which are a result of social, biological, psychological, and economic factors.

©Marmaduke St. John / Alamy

Positivists seek to find the basic cause of one's crimes and believe in rehabilitating offenders rather than punishing them. Prison therapy groups focus on rehabilitation.

Video: Anatomy and violence

XYY chromosome: the so-called criminal chromosome, where criminal behavior is felt to be caused in some offenders who possess an extra Y chromosome—believed to cause agitation, aggression, and greater criminal tendencies—as opposed to the "passive" X chromosome.

BIOLOGICAL DETERMINISM

Biological theories of crime have persisted over time. These theories have their foundation in the belief that the causes of crime are found in the biological determinants—or "original nature"—of the offender and are the result of some biological element or defect, and that criminals are *born* and not *made* by their home or social environment.

A Throwback?

In the 19th century, Italian criminologist Cesare Lombroso gave life to the anthropological study of crime and criminals, believing that offenders were a product of their physical stigmata—or "atavism," a throwback to some earlier stage in the evolution of humans or to an apelike ancestor, and the "born criminal." Having been influenced by the evolutionary doctrines of Charles Darwin, Lombroso saw in criminals some of the same characteristics that were found in "savages" or "prehuman people": a slanting forehead, abnormal teeth, excessively long arms and dimensions of the jaw and cheekbones, ears of unusual size, a sparse beard, a twisted nose, woolly hair, recessed eyes (and pronounced supraorbital ridges, or bony structures surrounding the eye sockets), fleshy and swollen lips, excessive vanity, or the presence of tattoos.[10]

Lombroso's theories, however, failed to explain crime fully—obviously, many offenders did not possess any, much less all, of these "born criminal" characteristics—so over time these "revelations" fell out of favor. Nonetheless, for his groundbreaking work that forced people to consider the makeup of the criminal in addition to his or her offense, Lombroso is today known as "the father of criminology."[11]

Related to Lombroso's views are those of Charles Goring and Henry Goddard, both of whom began publishing their theories in the early 1900s. Goring compared "criminals" and "noncriminals" and determined that criminals were, in general, shorter; they weighed less; and, more important, they were "mentally defective" or "feebleminded." Goddard compared offspring of a Revolutionary War militiaman who had fathered children with two wives, one a "barwench" and the other a "respectable" woman. He found the children of the former to be feebleminded and deviant, while children of the latter were moral and relatively intelligent. He thus deemed that crime was caused by feeblemindedness, and was the first to coin the term *moron*.[12]

Aberrant or "Criminal" Chromosomes

During the second half of the 20th century, advances in the field of molecular biology led to the belief that a link might exist between chromosomal abnormality and criminal behavior. Most females have two X chromosomes, and the majority of males have an XY set. Much speculation and research has been done with respect to males carrying an extra Y chromosome (**XYY chromosome**), or the "criminal" chromosome. Some scientists have hypothesized that the extra male chromosome produces tall men, generally with below-average intelligence, who behave aggressively or antisocially.

Italian criminologist Cesare Lombroso saw in criminals a pattern of physical characteristics that were found in "savages" or "prehuman people."

William H. Sheldon believed that human beings can be separated into three distinct body types, and that more serious offenders tended to be athletically built, or mesomorphic.

However, a number of studies—including an international review of relevant research by R. G. Fox—failed to be conclusive regarding differences between XYY and XY males.[13] Fox stated that "the information gleaned from research so far provides . . . a flimsy suggestion that an XYY constitution produces a disposition toward deviant behavior." Fox called for "some form of longitudinal study of XYY persons" that, "with the aid of computers, could ascertain and record the chromosome structure of all new-born infants in a large hospital over a period of time and subsequently check police records to determine the significance of any criminal patterns that may develop in the population."[14]

Other Biological Studies

Other theories grounded in biocriminology have resulted from research into body types, heredity, twins, and adopted children. But none of this research has yielded conclusive results.

William Sheldon, for example, focused his studies primarily on juvenile delinquents, and believed that human beings can be separated into several body types, or somatotypes (with varying degrees for each).[15] He determined, in examining 200 Boston delinquents, that the more serious offenders tended to be athletically built, with a "mesomorphic" body type. Later studies of Sheldon's work confirmed the relationship between mesomorphy and delinquency.

However, Sheldon's body type or constitutionalist theories in criminology have largely been discredited because they have little value in predicting criminal behavior. If indeed a relationship exists between body type and crime, it is more likely a result of social factors that are involved—for example, more muscular (mesomorphic) individuals might well be recruited into gangs.

Adoption studies have also revealed that identical twins have a greater tendency for criminal behavior than fraternal (nonidentical) twins, but researchers have not been able to isolate environmental influences (identical twins tend to spend more time together, be treated more alike by families and friends, and share more of a common identity than do fraternal twins) as an equally possible explanation.[16]

Likewise, research on adopted children has yielded limited results. Although the percentage of adoptees who are criminal is greater when the biological father has a criminal record than when the adoptive father has one, certain environmental influences cannot be ruled out. For instance, children who are adopted may be placed in environments that are similar to those from which they were adopted; many children are adopted months or years after birth, and early life experiences may have contributed to their criminality.[17]

→ **From Theory to Policy to Practice:** If biological explanations for crime are true, what public policy decisions should lawmakers and criminal justice professionals make in response? For example, when scientists identified certain hereditary patterns of criminality, lawmakers in Oklahoma required that repeat offenders be sterilized to stop the chain of criminality. These laws were constitutional in the United States until 1942.[18] How would you respond to the following findings? Consider all the potential risks and benefits.[19]

✓ Children with a criminal biological father will have criminal tendencies.

✓ Childhood attention-deficit disorders may be linked to criminality.[20]

PSYCHOLOGICAL RATIONALES

Video: Raising Adam Lanza

Adoption studies: criminological research that looks at whether adopted children share criminal tendencies with their natural or adoptive parents.

Psychological rationales for crime: explanations of crime that link it to mental states or antisocial personality.

The **psychological rationale** for criminal behavior focuses on mental conditions and processing—personality disorders or limited intellect. Sigmund Freud, who is credited with the development of psychoanalytic theory, argued that all humans have criminal tendencies influenced by natural drives and urges repressed in the unconscious. Using case studies, Freudians document examples of the Oedipus complex, the death wish, the inferiority complex, birth trauma, castration fears, and penis envy, and they believe that crime represents a substitute response to goals that are blocked or repressed during childhood as well as hostility to male authority symbols.[21] Through the process of socialization, however, these tendencies are curbed by the development of inner controls that are learned through childhood experience. Freud hypothesized that the most common element that contributed to criminal behavior was faulty identification by a child with her or his parents. The improperly socialized child may develop a personality disturbance that causes her or him to direct antisocial impulses inward or outward. The child who directs them outward becomes a criminal, and the child who directs them inward becomes a neurotic.[22]

In 1931, Edwin Sutherland examined approximately 350 studies of the relationship between intelligence and delinquency and criminality. He concluded from this review that, although intelligence may play a role in individual cases, the distribution of the intelligence scores of criminals was roughly the same as the distribution of such scores for the general population. In other words, intelligence was not a predictor of crime.[23]

The 1970s saw a resurgence of interest in the debate, however, and several studies reported that there was such a relationship—that IQ was as important a predictor of juvenile delinquency as race or social class. The studies found an eight-point difference in IQ levels between delinquent and nondelinquent youths.[24] Of note—and what these studies failed to point out—however, is the fact that both IQs were within the normal range.

→ **From Theory to Policy to Practice:** If psychological explanations for crime are true, what public policy decisions should lawmakers and criminal justice professionals make in response?

  ✓ Researchers find a high incidence of antisocial personality disorder among inmates in U.S. prisons.[25]
  ✓ What if scientists find that sexual predators tend to have poor parental relationships and a lack of empathy?

SOCIOCULTURAL EXPLANATIONS

Sigmund Freud argued that all humans have natural drives and urges repressed in the unconscious as well as criminal tendencies.

Whereas the psychological approaches to studying crime, as laid out by Freud, focus on one's mental condition, the sociocultural explanations look at how people's living in social groups might shape their behavior. Sociologists argue that criminality is not innate in one's biological makeup but instead is caused by external social factors. They believe that one's contact with the world—and such related factors as poverty, age, race, gender, family, problems faced by immigrants, and so on—will foster crime; in sum, criminals are made, not born.

Next we discuss three of the many theories that stress the influence of social factors on crime: social structure theory, social process theory, and critical theory.

Social Structure Theory

Robert Merton is perhaps the primary proponent of **social structure theories**, which maintain that criminal behavior is related to culture and social class—and provides, he wrote, a "basis for determining the nonbiological conditions which induce deviations from prescribed patterns of conduct."[26] Merton built on the concept of anomie—a state of normlessness, in which the existing rules and values of society have little impact—which was first introduced by the famed French sociologist Émile Durkheim in the late 19th century. Merton argued that social change often leads to anomie, when rules are unclear or people cannot achieve their goals. Criminologists who have incorporated the concept of anomie into theories of criminal behavior are known as "strain theorists." They believe that crime is caused by the strain (frustration, hopelessness, anger, and so on) that comes from living in disadvantaged, dysfunctional, and generally normless families and/or communities where legitimate opportunities for success and prosperity are nearly if not altogether out of reach. Therefore, Merton argued, the individual in such an environment will turn to crime as a means of alleviating this strain and to reach his or her goals.[27] Furthermore, the anger caused by strain—as well as the child abuse, unemployment, victimization, and family problems—can lead to crime and delinquency. Merton believed that

> the extreme emphasis upon the accumulation of wealth as a symbol of success in our own society militates against the completely effective control of institutionally regulated modes of acquiring a fortune. Fraud, corruption, vice, crime, in short, the entire catalogue of proscribed behavior, becomes increasingly common.[28]

Social structure theory: generally attempts to explain criminality as a result of the creation of a lower-class culture based on poverty and deprivations, and the subsequent response of the poor to the situation

©Lawrence Bryant/UPI/Newscom

Strain theorists argue that crime is caused by frustration, hopelessness, and anger resulting from living in disadvantaged and dysfunctional families and/or communities, where opportunities for success and prosperity are largely nonexistent.

→ **From Theory to Policy to Practice:** If the following social structure theory explanations for crime are true, what public policy decisions should lawmakers and criminal justice professionals make in response?

✓ Crime is grounded in social conditions like unemployment.

✓ Inmates who participate in vocational training in prison are less likely to reoffend and more likely to find jobs after they are released.[29]

Social Process Theories

Many criminologists believe that the aforementioned social structure theory places too much responsibility for crime on the shoulders of the poor, and too much emphasis on the offender's being in a state of poverty. Subsequently, they do not believe that social structure theory adequately explains crime that is committed by more affluent, middle- or upper-class people. Therefore, **social process theories** argue that any person, regardless of social class, education, or nature of the family, neighborhood, or community, can learn to become a criminal.

There are three primary social process theories: learning theory, control theory, and labeling theory.

Learning Theories

In 1934, Edwin Sutherland first put forth in his book *Criminology* his theory of differential association. When Sutherland died in 1950, Donald Cressey continued to popularize the theory. The existence of white-collar crime and professional theft led them to believe that there were social learning processes that could turn anyone into a criminal, anytime or anywhere. Following are some of the major points of **learning theory**:

- Criminal behavior is learned, in interaction with others, in a process of communication.

- Learning criminal behavior occurs within primary groups (family, friends, peers, one's most intimate, personal companions) and involves learning their techniques, motives, drives, rationalizations, and attitudes.

- A person becomes a criminal when there is an excess of definitions favorable to violation of law over definitions unfavorable to violation of law (this is the principle of differential association).

- Differential associations vary in frequency, duration, priority, and intensity (frequent contacts, long contacts, age at first contact, important or prestigious contacts).[30]

Sutherland's theory was tested mainly on juveniles because delinquents tend to act in groups. One of the problems with such research is in determining which comes first, the delinquency or delinquent friends. It may be that "birds of a feather flock together" and delinquency "causes" delinquent friends, but delinquent friends do not

Social process theory: argues that criminality is a normal behavior and that everyone has the potential to commit crime, depending on the influences that compel them toward or away from crime and on how they are viewed by others.

Learning theory (of crime): any school of thought that suggests criminal behaviors are learned from associating with others and from social interactions and social experiences.

cause delinquency. Another problem is that the theory does not explain, nor does it even attempt to explain, the point at which, or cause for which, the initial inclination to commit a crime occurred.

Control Theories

In the 1960s, Walter Reckless and Travis Hirschi began proposing a new theory of criminality known as **social control theory**—also known as containment theory—in which it is argued that people are essentially rational beings but that they also are motivated by a desire to maximize pleasure and minimize pain. Therefore, external pressures (poor living conditions or economy, lack of legitimate opportunities), sensitivity to the opinions of others, and belief in the values expressed by friends and relatives will influence one to either obey or disobey the law. Lawbreaking occurs due to the weakness, breakdown, or absence of these social bonds or socialization processes that are presumed to encourage law-abiding conduct.[31]

Video:
Travis Hirschi

Labeling Theory

Howard Becker observed that society creates deviance, and thus criminality, "by making the rules whose infraction constitutes deviance and by applying those rules to particular people and labeling them outsiders."[32] In simpler terms, **labeling theory** means in the extreme that no act that we deem to be criminal in and of itself is deviant; rather, it is deviant—and labeled as a crime—only because some group has determined that the behavior is different and should be criminalized.

Why is the possession of cocaine labeled a criminal act, while possession and even home manufacturing of alcohol is not? Why is a corporate executive who commits a white-collar crime less likely to receive a prison term than one who is caught in the act of committing a burglary? Why is it that one who shoots a bald eagle is guilty of committing a felony federal offense (with maximum penalties of up to $100,000 and/or one year in federal prison)[33] while the same man who, the day before, killed a large elk might well be labeled a skilled "sportsman" and praised for his marksmanship? Such questions underscore labeling theory and compel us to consider how different acts may be labeled as criminal, be applied to individuals, and result in their losing their freedom.

A companion issue that arises in labeling theory is the notion that being labeled as a criminal *promotes* individuals' identification with their stigmatized status. When they have been labeled, they begin to believe the label is true, and then they may adopt a deviant identity and begin acting in deviant ways—a self-fulfilling prophecy of sorts.

→ **From Theory to Policy to Practice:** If the social process theory explanations for crime are true, what public policy decisions should lawmakers and criminal justice professionals make in response?

  ✓ How can the criminal justice system avoid labeling of both adults and juveniles?

  ✓ How would you apply social process theories to gangs, and what public policies might help prevent gang membership and proliferation?[34]

The Boston Marathon Bomber: While the younger Tsarnaev brother seemingly had so many of the assets that help someone to be a success in our society—education, accomplishments, friends, and the support of teachers and other professionals—the rest of his family did not. His parents returned to Russia after not being able to "make it" in the United States, and his brother was increasingly frustrated because he could not be on the Olympic boxing team without being a U.S. citizen. Did the younger Tsarnaev anticipate similar frustrations and turn to crime? Or did he take on a criminal "label" after seeing his parents' failures and while spending time with his brother?

Social control theory: argues that deviant behavior results when social controls are weakened or break down, so that people are not motivated to conform to them.

Labeling theory (of crime): holds that persons acquire labels or defined characteristics that are deviant or criminal; thus, perceiving themselves as criminals, they follow through and commit crimes.

Critical Theory

In the mid-1960s, the biological, psychological, and sociological theories described earlier were challenged by scholars whose theories became known as **critical theory**. These theorists argued that crime is defined in terms of the concept of oppression.

Critical theorists maintain, perhaps first and foremost, that the criminal justice system acts in the interests of the dominant groups and classes of a society, and that the police can do nothing more than act repressively against potential and real challenges to the established order.[35] Conversely, the working class—women (particularly those who are single heads of household and are socially isolated) and ethnic minorities (those from non-English-speaking backgrounds and refugees, in particular)—are the most likely to suffer oppressive treatment based on class division, sexism, and racism. In other words, the criminal laws are designed by those who are in power, and the laws are intended to oppress those who are not in power. These theorists argue that people of means commit as many crimes as do the oppressed, but the latter groups are more likely to be apprehended and punished.

A theory that can be said to be within the critical criminology arena is the social conflict theory, which maintains that crime is the result of conflict between competing interest groups: rich against poor, management against labor, whites against minorities, men against women, adults against children, and so on. In many of these conflicts, the competing interest groups are not equal in power and resources, so one group will be dominant, the other subordinate. One of the earliest conflict theorists was George B. Vold, who believed that many behaviors are defined as crimes because it is in the best interest of the dominant groups to do so.[36]

To these theorists, in order to understand crime, one must view it as a product of group struggle. Humans are by nature social beings, forming groups out of shared interests and needs. The criminal law serves the goals of the dominant group—which is successful in achieving control of the legislative process—and contains the "crime norms," inappropriate behavior and its punishment. At the same time, the "conduct norms" of the subordinate groups often come into conflict with the crime norms; this in turn leads to the production of deviant or criminal definitions surrounding the everyday behavior of the individual members of these less powerful groups.[37]

→ **From Theory to Policy to Practice:** If the critical theory explanations for crime are true, what public policy decisions should lawmakers and criminal justice professionals make in response?

- ✓ How might government funding for prosecutors' offices in comparison to public defenders' offices contribute to crime, and how can lawmakers fix the disparity?[38]
- ✓ How would critical theorists explain the differences between sentences for possession of crack cocaine and powder cocaine, and how would you recommend reforming other sentencing differences?[39]

Critical theory: a school of thought in criminology arguing that crime is largely a product of capitalism, that laws are created to separate haves and have-nots and are wielded by those in power.

Of course, there are many more theories that attempt to explain criminality than are discussed here, and the number and thrust of such theories continue to expand and broaden. It is probably beneficial that such is the case, for no one theory has yet been found that can explain all forms of criminal behavior. Some criminologists still believe that aspects of the biological theories have merit, while others argue that elements of the psychological or sociocultural theories have some basis in fact. In truth, each of these theories may explain in part why someone commits a criminal act.

WOMEN AND CRIME

Although it has often been said that "crime is a young man's game,"[40] and women commit far fewer crimes (especially violent crimes) than their male counterparts, women are not to be overlooked in our consideration of theories of crime. This area of criminality, sometimes termed **feminist theory**, is felt to be a part of the broader area of the aforementioned critical theory. Freda Adler, criminologist and author of *Sisters in Crime*, wrote the following in 1975:

©Andrew Aitchison / Alamy

The study of crime has historically focused on male offenders, but the recent extent and nature of female criminality—more predatory and violent—has brought them more attention from criminologists as well.

> Women are no longer indentured to the kitchens, baby carriages, or bedrooms of America. There will be no turning back to the days when women found it necessary to justify their existence by producing babies or cleaning houses. Women have chosen to desert those kitchens and plunge exuberantly into the formerly all-male quarters of the working world.[41]

At about the time Adler wrote those words, women were indeed beginning to "desert those kitchens" and enter the labor force in large numbers. With passage of the Equal Employment Opportunity Act in 1972,[42] women were given the right to compete with men for jobs and promotions, and to receive the same compensation upon being hired. Later, the Pregnancy Discrimination Act of 1978,[43] which required employers to treat pregnancy, childbirth, and related medical conditions in the same manner as any other temporary disability, and the Family and Medical Leave Act of 1993,[44] which allowed employees to take 12 weeks of unpaid leave for the birth or adoption of a child, helped women to enter the labor force. By extension, these increases in labor force participation of women would become related to their significantly higher crime rates.[45]

Adler also believed that the arrival of a wave of feminism during the 1970s consequently coincided with a "dramatic" upsurge in women's criminal activity. She claimed that while

> women have demanded equal opportunity in the fields of legitimate endeavors, a similar number of determined women have forced their way into the world of major crime such as white collar crime, murder and robbery.[46]

That women criminals today represent a "new breed" can be demonstrated, according to Adler, by evidence of the changing nature of female involvement in a wide variety of crimes. This "new female criminal" engaged in predatory crimes of violence and corporate fraud has broken into a man's world.[47] For example, female white-collar crime increased following the "liberation" of women. Adler also suggested that as women were "climbing up the corporate business ladder," they were making use of their "vocational liberation" to pursue careers in white-collar crime (discussed in the next section).[48] Adler's theory has invited much criticism from other feminist writers, who argue instead that feminism has made female crime more visible through increased reporting, policing, and sentencing of female offenders.[49]

Feminist theory: emphasizes gender involvement in crime.

Irrespective of how women became engaged in crime, as a result of these and many studies of women and their criminality, feminist theory is among the newest in criminology. With gender as its central focus, it recognizes that the study of crime has historically focused on male offenders; as a result, criminal behavior by women and young girls tended to be ignored. Adler's work, as well as Rita Simon's *Women and Crime*,[50] proposed that the emancipation of women and increased economic opportunities for women allowed women to be as crime-prone as men. Again, there is disagreement on the emancipation or liberation thesis, and some scholars argue that absolutely no empirical evidence supports it.[51]

Two important questions have yet to be answered. First, do the traditionally male-centered theories of crime that apply to men apply to women as well? Second, what explains the long-standing fact that women commit far fewer crimes than men? It might be argued that, if women were socialized in the same manner as men, then one would also expect their rates of criminal offending to be about the same. Another criticism of feminist criminology is that it fails to take into account differences between the experiences of white women and women of color. A number of scholars are now attempting to address these questions and omissions.[52]

Table 3.2 shows a five-year arrest trend for women for selected crimes. The table shows that, as with the nation at large, arrests of women have declined overall—with the exception of slight increases in property crimes (largely as a result of increased arrests for larceny-theft), rape (due to reporting issues as noted), and drug abuse violations.

WHITE-COLLAR CRIME

Today it seems inconceivable that anyone would attempt to rob a bank or burglarize a home—possibly to be met with fortified premises that include guard dogs, security patrols, and/or video cameras—when he or she could engage in any of several dozen if not hundreds of less hazardous forms of illegal activity. These approaches—under the broad umbrella of property crimes—are termed white-collar or **corporate crimes**, which can and do make some people financially comfortable if not wildly rich for their efforts.

Theoretical Foundation

Certainly the social control theory discussed earlier—in which it is argued that people are essentially rational beings but motivated by a desire to maximize pleasure and minimize pain—would appear to explain this type of unlawful behavior. White-collar crime also challenges many of the traditional assumptions concerning criminality—that is, that it occurs in the streets and is mostly committed by criminals who are lower class and uneducated. White-collar crime is also the largest and most costly type of crime in the United States. As criminologist Frank Hagan put it, "All the other forms of criminal behavior together do not equal the costs of occupational and organizational (corporate) crime."[53]

Perhaps John D. Rockefeller, the famed industrialist, explained the nature of the white-collar criminal well in a lecture he reportedly gave often to his Sunday school classes:

> The growth of a large business is merely the survival of the fittest. The American Beauty rose can be produced in the splendor and fragrance which bring cheer to its beholder only by sacrificing the early buds which grow up around it.[54]

Corporate crime: crimes committed by wealthy or powerful individuals in the course of their professions or occupations; includes price-fixing, insider trading, and other white-collar crimes.

TABLE 3.2 Five-Year Arrest Trend for Women

OFFENSE CHARGED	2009	2013	PERCENT CHANGE
TOTAL[1]	**2,241,403**	**2,023,477**	**−9.7**
Violent crime[3]	73,173	66,663	−8.9
Property crime[3]	422,637	397,656	−5.9
Murder and nonnegligent manslaughter	853	806	−5.5
Rape[2]	174	190	+9.2
Robbery	9,782	8,683	−11.2
Aggravated assault	62,364	56,984	−8.6
Burglary	31,617	30,507	−3.5
Larceny-theft	380,279	356,864	−6.2
Motor vehicle theft	9,485	8,866	−6.5
Arson	1,256	1,419	+13.0
Other assaults	223,016	207,857	−6.8
Forgery and counterfeiting	21,066	15,309	−27.3
Fraud	61,189	37,663	−38.4
Embezzlement	6,591	5,349	−18.8
Stolen property; buying, receiving, possessing	12,242	13,626	+11.3
Vandalism	32,043	27,697	−13.6
Weapons; carrying, possessing, etc.	9,048	8,337	−7.9
Prostitution and commercialized vice	34,891	25,380	−27.3
Sex offenses (except rape and prostitution)	4,709	3,055	−35.1
Drug abuse violations	210,496	219,834	+4.4
Gambling	746	614	−17.7
Offenses against the family and children	18,330	17,213	−6.1
Driving under the influence	214,178	188,557	−12.0
Liquor laws	100,049	63,309	−36.7
Drunkenness	70,222	59,787	−14.9
Disorderly conduct	104,023	78,895	−24.2
Vagrancy	5,335	4,008	−24.9
All other offenses (except traffic)	598,130	574,106	−4.0
Suspicion	316	127	−59.8
Curfew and loitering law violations	19,289	8,562	−55.6

[1] Does not include suspicion.

[2] The rape figures in this table are based on the legacy definition of rape only. The rape figures shown include converted National Incident-Based Reporting System rape data and those states/agencies that reported the legacy definition of rape for both years.

[3] Violent crimes in this table are offenses of murder and nonnegligent manslaughter, rape (legacy definition), robbery, and aggravated assault. Property crimes are offenses of burglary, larceny-theft, motor vehicle theft, and arson.

Source: Adapted from Federal Bureau of Investigation, "Table 35. Five-Year Arrest Trends, by Sex, 2009–2013," *Crime in the United States—2013* (Washington, D.C.: Uniform Crime Reporting Program), https://www.fbi.gov/about-us/cjis/ucr/crime-in-the-u.s/2013/crime-in-the-u.s.-2013/tables/table-35/table_35_five_year_arrest_trends_by_sex_2013.xls.

But Rockefeller could not have envisioned how that would have led to the many forms of criminality that occur today in the "suites" of the corporate world. Table 3.3 provides an often-cited typology of such crimes, as developed by Herbert Edelhertz in 1970.

TABLE 3.3 Edelhertz's (1970) Typology of White-Collar Crime

EDELHERTZ'S TYPOLOGY OF WHITE-COLLAR CRIME DETAILS A VARIETY OF OFFENSES

Crimes committed in the course of their occupations by those operating inside business, government, or other establishments in violation of their duty of loyalty and fidelity to employer or client

1. Commercial bribery and kickbacks (i.e., by and to buyers, insurance adjusters, contracting officers, quality inspectors, government inspectors, and auditors)
2. Bank violations by bank officers, employees, and directors
3. Embezzlement or self-dealing by business or union officers and employees
4. Securities fraud by insiders trading to their advantage by the use of special knowledge
5. Employee petty larceny and expense account fraud
6. Frauds by computer, causing unauthorized payments
7. "Sweetheart contracts" entered into by union officers
8. Embezzlement or self-dealing by attorneys, trustees, and fiduciaries
9. Fraud against the government:
   a. Padding of payrolls
   b. Conflict of interest
   c. False travel, expense, or per diem claims

Crimes incidental to and in furtherance of business operations, but not the central purpose of the business

1. Tax violations
2. Antitrust violations
3. Commercial bribery of another's employee, officer, or fiduciary (including union officers)
4. Food and drug violations
5. False weights and measures by retailers
6. Violations of Truth in Lending Act by misrepresentation of credit terms and prices
7. Submission or publication of false financial statements to obtain credit
8. Use of fictitious or overvalued collateral
9. Check kiting to obtain operating capital on short-term financing
10. Securities Act violations (i.e., sale of nonregistered securities to obtain operating capital, false proxy statements, manipulation of market to support corporate credit or access to capital markets)
11. Collusion between physicians and pharmacists to cause the writing of unnecessary prescriptions
12. Dispensing by pharmacists in violation of law, excluding narcotics trafficking
13. Immigration fraud in support of employment agency operations to provide domestics
14. Housing code violations by landlords
15. Deceptive advertising
16. Fraud against the government:
    a. False claims
    b. False statements
    c. Moving contracts in urban renewal
17. Labor violations (Davis-Bacon Act)
18. Commercial espionage

Origin and Measurement Problems

The concept of white-collar crime was introduced in 1939 in an address to the American Sociological Association by Edwin Sutherland, who defined it as "a crime committed by a person of respectability and high social status in the course of his occupation."[55] Sutherland, after examining 40 years of records held by regulatory agencies, courts, and commissions, reported that of the 70 largest industrial and mercantile corporations, each of them violated at least one law and had an adverse decision lodged against it for false advertising, patent abuse, wartime trade violations, price fixing, fraud, or intended manufacturing and sale of faulty goods. Many of them were recidivists, and those that were recidivists averaged eight such violations apiece.[56]

Although today we recognize and frequently hear of white-collar criminals, for several reasons the actual extent of white-collar crime remains shrouded in darkness. First, collecting accurate data is difficult, and official statistics of the *Uniform Crime Reports* (discussed later in this chapter) and victim surveys generally do not include much information concerning this type of crime. And, for obvious reasons, corporations zealously guard their public image and thus prefer to regulate themselves and maintain a code of silence. In addition, the police, social scientists, and members of the media are often inexperienced in the ways of corporate crime, which itself is made even more complicated by the very web of complex corporations that exist. Furthermore, although the Sherman Antitrust Act (1890) and hundreds of laws and regulatory agencies exist to keep white-collar crime in check and to police corporations—through recalls, warnings, consent agreements, injunctions, fines, and criminal proceedings—but guilty companies often maintain legions of attorneys and accountants who possess considerable expertise in seeing their bosses are seldom if ever punished.[57]

Author Video: White-collar criminality

Types

Most people have heard of Bernie Madoff's $50 billion fraudulent Ponzi scheme (where one basically uses new investors' funds to pay early investors, rather than using profits earned by the individual or organization running the operation); Madoff was sentenced to 150 years in prison for his crimes.[58] Or they know that businesswoman/author/television personality Martha Stewart was convicted of committing and lying about insider trading, in which she sold stock that she knew was likely to plunge in price.[59] These celebrated cases will go down in the annals of white-collar crime, but white-collar crime can take many more forms, including the following:

- A Swiss pharmaceutical company pleaded guilty and paid a record $500 million in fines for price fixing on vitamins.

- Medical quackery and unnecessary surgical procedures victimize more than 2 million Americans, cost $4 billion, and result in 12,000 deaths per year. Fee splitting and "ping-ponging" (in which doctors refer patients to other doctors in the same office) also occur.

- A major auto manufacturing company, aware that a defect (which would cost $11 to repair) in one of its vehicles could result in a fiery explosion during a rear-end collision (even at low speeds), decided it would be cheaper not to recall the vehicles and make repairs, but instead to pay drivers' injury and death claims.[60]

Bernie Madoff, a former stockbroker and financial advisor, was convicted of operating a Ponzi scheme that is considered to be the largest of its kind in U.S. history.

Video:
Martha Stewart

- Lawyers engage in "ambulance-chasing," file unnecessary lawsuits, and falsify evidence.
- Corporations dump or release toxic chemicals and hazardous materials into the environment to cut costs and avoid regulatory laws.
- Companies steal secrets and patents from one another and thus commit corporate espionage.

You Be the... U.S. SENTENCING COMMISSIONER

Many Americans believe that white-collar criminals are treated far too leniently, particularly given the huge sums of money such offenders often obtain and the harm done to their victims. Part of the problem, however, is the inconsistent sentencing system that exists for such offenses.

For example, someone convicted of racketeering (a form of criminal activity that is to benefit a crime syndicate, such as money laundering or loan sharking) in the federal court of the District of Columbia faces about 13 years in prison, while that same person might walk free after only 5 years for the same charges in other federal circuit courts. Forgery or counterfeiting might earn someone 9 months in prison in Washington, D.C., and 23 months if sentenced in the Seventh Circuit.

In fact, such disparity in punishments has become so problematic that in mid-2015 the U.S. Sentencing Commission stated that it would place high priority on resolving the matter in the near future. The commission understands that the current system does not work simply because, although sentences for white-collar criminal offenses have been increased several times, in 2005 the U.S. Supreme Court held that these guidelines were only "advisory," and

so sentencing decisions are ultimately left to the discretion of the judges.[61]

Therefore, society's determination of a just sentence in such cases depends on which judge happens to be doing the sentencing. If Judge A follows the federal guidelines, the offender will receive an extraordinarily high sentence. Conversely, if the sentencing judge feels the guidelines are too harsh, then a much more lax sentence will follow. So, when two people commit similar crimes, they may receive wildly different sentences, and such disparity is what troubles the sentencing commission and is prompting it to adjust the guidelines.

1. What do you think? Should judges rely on the more rigid, strict guidelines? Or, alternatively should judges be permitted to exercise discretion in such cases?

2. What are advantages and disadvantages of each approach with regard to punishing white-collar criminals (e.g., deterring others from committing such crimes, allowing judges to try to tailor the punishment to fit the crime, and so on)?

Related Fraudulent Acts

Social control theorists would nod their heads knowingly when told of other such schemes people have concocted over time, motivated by a desire to maximize pleasure and minimize pain and committing what might be said to be "cousins" of white-collar crimes.

First is the broad category of identity theft, wherein the offender assumes someone else's identity, uses the other person's stolen credit cards, steals his or her login credentials, and performs countless other such acts. Identity theft costs some 40.5 million Americans about $1.5 billion per year in total losses.[62]

Other fraudulent acts, all of which would fit within Edelhertz's typology, including the following:

- Postal schemes: These widespread schemes involve everything from leaving town with payments for orders, to offering to arrange a "guaranteed" business loan or employment in exchange for an "advance fee," to chain letters, to work-at-home schemes, to fraudulent sales of property.

- Religious cons: Here, religious cults, televangelists, or organizers skam money from the church.

- Phony accident claims: In this one of many forms of insurance fraud, people fake accidents or forge accident claims.

- Nigerian letter scams: Often emailed, these are pleas to help transfer money from Nigeria or some other part of the world, for which the recipients will be rewarded handsomely (after providing their banking information).[63]

- Paper hanging: This includes passing bad checks, forgery, and other such fraudulent acts.

- Phony fund-raising: Offenders may target victims of natural disasters or other types of victims.

- Cons: These are offenses involving nonexistent home electrical or plumbing repairs, fortune tellers who persuade people to bury their money in a cemetery so as to lift its "curse," and so on.

- Hundreds of other assorted swindles: These can include schemes, frauds, deceptions, stings, rip-offs, hoaxes, and rackets.

INVESTIGATING FURTHER

THE GREAT SAVINGS AND LOAN SCANDAL

The biggest, most costly white-collar crime in U.S. history, costing an estimated $500 billion, was the scandal involving the savings and loan industry during the 1980s. To simplify the matter in very basic terms, the scandal had its genesis in the 1930s when the federal government, seeking to protect banking and savings and loan (S&L) customers, began guaranteeing their deposits (eventually up to $100,000). At the same time, the government strictly limited S&Ls to financing home mortgages and smaller loans. By the 1970s, double-digit inflation wreaked havoc on the S&L industry, which was strapped with 6 percent, 30-year mortgages when inflation was 14 to 16 percent. In 1982, the government decided to deregulate these institutions, allowing them to charge more competitive interest rates and invest in other commercial and banking enterprises. Still, more than 300 federally insured S&Ls collapsed from 1980 to 1986, leaving the government holding the bag. Meanwhile, Congress and Washington were distracted by a presidential election, so the deregulation of S&Ls created a climate of criminal opportunity—a "junk bond" (high-risk) speculative environment with federal depositors' insurance money. Criminals such as Charles Keating and Michael Milken robbed the S&Ls and were aided by some of the best and brightest financial and legal talent in the United States (80 law firms represented Keating), which were described as a "financial mafia of swindlers, mobsters, greedy SL executives and con men [who] capitalized on regulatory weaknesses and thoroughly fleeced the thrift industry."[64]

IN THEIR OWN WORDS: OFFENDERS SPEAK

With a background in some of the major criminological theories for why men and women commit crimes, this is a good opportunity to consider the motives and methods that offenders themselves offer to explain their criminal behavior. Using a variety of field-research methods (including interviews with active offenders, incarcerated individuals, and probationers and parolees), researchers have allowed us to learn from actual criminals—armed robbers, burglars, and carjackers—and thus narrow the "distance" between students and their criminal subjects.

Armed Robbery

Certainly the motive underlying the crime of armed robbery is clear: financial gain (and another long-standing dynamic—temptation; discussed in Chapter 4). Unlike perpetrators of most forms of street crime, armed robbers are never secret or ambiguous. And, like the crime of carjacking, discussed in the next section, the crime of robbery bridges property and violent crimes.[65] The armed robber must also create the illusion of impending death in the victim's mind.

By announcing their intentions to rob, armed robbers believe they are committing themselves irrevocably to the offense; that is the "make or break" moment, and they must establish dominance over the victims and convince them they are not in a position to resist, and displaying a weapon usually precludes the need to do much talking.[66]

The most difficult aspect of armed robberies, according to those who commit them, is the transfer of goods. Here, robbers must keep their victims under strict control while attempting to make sure they have obtained everything of value; it must be done quickly, lest the police or a passerby discover the act.[67] Finally, robbers must escape—another difficult stage of the robbery. Armed robbers must maintain their control over their victims while increasing their distance from them. Robbers can either flee—possibly bringing attention to themselves or allowing their victims to raise an alarm—or force their victims to flee. The latter allows offenders to leave the scene in a leisurely manner.[68]

INVESTIGATING FURTHER

APPLICATION OF CRIME THEORIES

For each of the following scenarios, determine which of the theories described in this chapter might be applied in order to understand the person's motivation for engaging in criminal behavior:

- An employee in a county treasurer's office has developed a means of "juggling the books" and circumventing expenditure controls in such a way as to embezzle county funds. She examines the risks of doing so (i.e., engaging in unethical behavior, getting arrested) against the benefits that would be derived from committing the crimes (i.e., converting to her possession perhaps hundreds of thousands of dollars in a very short period of time). She has also determined that punishment for such crimes is not "swift and certain" because her methods would be difficult to detect (and, to her knowledge, embezzlers receive relatively light punishments). She also perceives that she lives in a society that values people who are financially successful and that the legal means for attaining such success are otherwise unavailable to her. She thus embezzles the funds.

- A young girl attending college desires to complete her education and enter into a successful career. With financial obstacles in the way, she weighs the benefits and drawbacks of employment with a local "dating service," which she has learned is actually a cover for girls to engage in acts of prostitution. One deterrent, however, is that if arrested, she would be deemed a less-than-acceptable member of society; however, she also perceives that degrees of punishment in such cases are typically light. At the same time, she is aware that society reveres those who become educated, obtain a good position, and live comfortably. To do so, however, she must somehow find the means to afford her tuition and living expenses. In the end, she opts to take the position with the "dating service," thus risking being arrested and labeled as an outcast, in order to achieve her goals.

- A 16-year-old boy is contemplating whether or not to drop out of school and join a local gang. He knows that to do so he will have to suffer painful initiation rites and that the lifestyle poses considerable dangers. Conversely, he is also aware that his city's policing of gangs is relatively lax, punishment is not certain, and financial rewards are promising. His legal options for obtaining lucrative employment and financial comfort are limited if not altogether blocked, given his likewise limited (i.e., below-average) education and training. After considering his options and looking at both the benefits and the potential disadvantages, he decides the benefits outweigh the deterrents, and he joins the gang.

Burglary

Burglars, like armed robbers, are motivated primarily by money in order to maintain their "high-living" lifestyle; however, they may also be motivated by noneconomic reasons, including the "thrill" of the act, as well as by revenge.[69] Burglars, then, while usually being prompted by a perceived need for cash, may also derive psychic rewards as a secondary benefit, finding the crime to be exciting. Some also commit residential burglaries to get even with someone for a real or imagined wrong—an attack on one's status, identity, or self-esteem. For example, a burglar can have an argument over a traffic or parking matter, and then follow the victim home; later, after learning the victim's routine, he or she may burglarize the person's home to settle the "grudge"—possibly even destroying more goods than are removed.[70]

Carjacking

According to one study,[71] with the exception of homicide, "probably no offense is more symbolic of contemporary urban violence than carjacking." Indeed, following the 1992 murder of a woman when two men commandeered her car in Washington, D.C., carjacking was made a federal crime punishable by up to 25 years in prison.[72] Unlike most robberies, carjacking is directed at an object rather than a person; still, weapons are used in two-thirds to three-fourths of carjackings.[73]

Carjackers are motivated by two primary objectives: opportunity (i.e., weighing potential risks and rewards) and situational inducements (peer pressure, need for cash or drugs, or revenge). They typically have a precarious day-to-day existence, exacerbated by "boom or bust" cycles, and are always under some degree of financial pressure. The sale of stolen vehicles and parts can be very lucrative, with carjackers either selling the car parts or delivering the car to a "chop shop," where it will be stripped; items of value include tire rims, hubcaps, and stereos—for which the average carjacker will be paid about $1,750 per car.[74]

MEASURING CRIME AND VICTIMIZATION

Criminological theories can help us to understand on the "front end" why crimes may occur, whereas data about actual crime rates—incidents, offenders, location, and so on—help us more fully understand after the fact just how prevalent crime and offenders are, which can then guide scholars and researchers to seek explanations for rates that are spiking or falling. Criminology and crime measurement work together to answer the questions of "why" and "how much" with respect to crime in the United States, arming both criminal justice professionals and policy makers with critically important information to run this complex, human system.

How Much Crime in the United States? Depends on Whom You Ask

Mark Twain once said, rather famously, that there are "lies, damn lies, and statistics."[75] Unfortunately, that assessment of statistics is somewhat (if not significantly) accurate with respect to U.S. reported crime figures. One example that will make the point is two different data sets reporting hate crimes. Specifically, in a recent year, the Federal Bureau of Investigation's (FBI's) *Uniform Crime Reports* (discussed in the next section) reported a total of 6,222 hate crimes (with 7,713 victims).[76] However, the National Crime Victimization Survey (NCVS, also discussed later in this chapter) reported an annual average of *169,000* violent hate crime victimizations. This significant

Video: What is the National Crime Victimization Survey?

Student on the
Street Video:
How many murders
were committed
in the U.S. in 2013?

discrepancy is largely due to the fact that about 54 percent of victims in the NCVS did not report their crimes to the police. Furthermore, in the NCVS, hate-related victimizations are based on victims' suspicion of the offenders' motivation, rather than on the suspicion of the police.[77] Thus, crime figures must be viewed with more than a hint of suspicion.

Errors and variations notwithstanding, to comprehend the impact of crime on our society, criminologists, victimologists, sociologists, psychologists, and members of other related disciplines need such information for their research and for making recommendations concerning planning and policy making. Knowing the nature and extent of crime also aids in one's understanding of the social forces that are driving those offenses and aggregated trends. Furthermore, measuring crime is one of the best ways of attempting to determine the policies and effectiveness of our agencies of criminal justice. We can better examine the structure and functions of the police (by looking at reported crimes and the proportion of crimes solved by arrest or other means), the courts (to determine the types of punishment and treatment that offenders are receiving), and corrections organizations (to ascertain, among other things, whether or not our offenders are being returned to prisons and jails).

Having crime data also allows for calculations of a national *crime rate* (discussed later), which in turn provides us with a "victim risk rate" of sorts—the odds that we (or relatives and friends) will become a victim of a serious crime.

Discussed first is the FBI's *Uniform Crime Reports*, and following is a review of a more in-depth method of capturing and analyzing reported crimes: the National Incident-Based Reporting System; finally, the National Crime Victimization Survey is examined. Unfortunately, as just discussed, these three sources of crime information are very different in their approaches and findings.

Uniform Crime Reports:
published annually by the FBI, each report describes the nature of crime as reported by law enforcement agencies; includes analyses of Part I crimes.

The FBI's *Uniform Crime Reports*

The Federal Bureau of Investigation's Uniform Crime Reporting Program publishes annual crime data for selected crimes as reported to the police in the United States.

The Uniform Crime Reporting (UCR) Program was conceived in 1929 by the International Association of Chiefs of Police to meet a need for reliable, uniform crime statistics for the nation. In 1930, the FBI was tasked with collecting, publishing, and archiving those statistics. Today, several annual statistical publications, such as the comprehensive *Crime in the United States*, are produced from data provided by nearly 17,000 law enforcement agencies across the United States.

Other annual publications, such as *Hate Crime Statistics* and *Law Enforcement Officers Killed and Assaulted*, address specialized facets of crime such as hate crime or the murder and assault of law enforcement officers.[78] Special studies, reports, and monographs prepared using data mined from the UCR Program's large database are published each year as well. In addition to these reports, information about the National Incident-Based Reporting System, answers to general UCR questions, and answers to specific UCR questions are available on this site.

For the purposes of the *Uniform Crime Reports*, the FBI divides offenses into two groups, Part I and Part II crimes. Each month, contributing agencies voluntarily submit information to the FBI concerning the number of Part I offenses reported to them, as well as those offenses that were cleared by arrest, and the age, sex, and race of persons arrested for each of the offenses.

Crime Rate

A fundamental aspect of calculating and understanding crime concerns how the FBI calculates the **crime rate**. The formula used is not complicated in nature. It is as follows: number of crimes reported, divided by the population of the jurisdiction in question, then multiplied by 100,000; this renders the number of crimes reported for each 100,000 population. It is depicted as follows:

Student on the Street Video: Violent crime over the past 20 years

$$\frac{\text{Number of offenses}}{\text{Population of the jurisdiction}} \times 100,0000 = \text{Number of offenses per 100,000 population}$$

As an example, assume, as in a recent year, that about 1,203,000 violent crimes were reported to the police in the United States; also for that year the nation's reported population was 311,600,000. Using this formula, the resulting crime rate for that year was 386 violent crimes per 100,000 population.[79]

The crime rate formula can also be considered a "victim risk rate," or the chances of one's becoming a victim; therefore, the chances of one's being a victim of a violent Part I offense for that recent year were about 386 in 100,000.

Part I Offenses

Part I or "index" crimes are composed of eight serious felonies—murder, forcible rape, robbery, aggravated assault, burglary, larceny-theft, motor vehicle theft, and arson. About 10.2 million such crimes are reported each year (about 1.2 million being violent and 9 million, property).[80] The first four of these eight offenses are deemed crimes against persons and are defined in the UCR Program as offenses that involve force or threat of force.

Each year, about 14,000 homicides are reported to the police in the United States.[81] As seen in Table 3.4, however, crimes of murder have been declining since 2009.

TABLE 3.4 Declining Rates of Murder Committed in the United States

YEAR	POPULATION	MURDER AND NONNEGLIGENT MANSLAUGHTER	MURDER AND NONNEGLIGENT MANSLAUGHTER RATE
2009	307,006,550	15,399	5.0
2010	309,330,219	14,722	4.8
2011	311,587,816	14,661	4.7
2012	313,873,685	14,856	4.7
2013	316,128,839	14,196	4.5
2014	318,857,056	14,249	4.5

Source: Adapted from Federal Bureau of Investigation, "Table 1. Volume and Rate per 100,000 Inhabitants, 1994–2013," Crime in the United States—2013 (Washington, D.C.: Uniform Crime Reporting Program).

Crime rate: the number of reported crimes divided by the population of the jurisdiction, and multiplied by 100,000 persons; developed and used by the FBI *Uniform Crime Reports.*

FIGURE 3.1 FBI's UCR "Crime Clock"

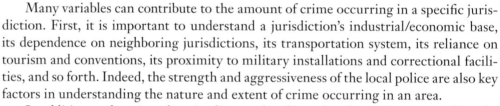

2014 CRIME CLOCK STATISTICS

A Violent Crime occurred every	26.3 seconds
One Murder every	36.9 minutes
One Rape every	4.5 minutes
One Robbery every	1.6 minutes
One Aggravated Assault every	42.5 seconds
A Property Crime occurred every	3.8 seconds
One Burglary every	18.2 seconds
One Larceny-theft every	5.4 seconds
One Motor Vehicle Theft every	45.7 seconds

The FBI's annual *Uniform Crime Reports* contain a "Crime Clock" that depicts the average time intervals between Part I crimes; a sample Crime Clock is shown in Figure 3.1.

Part II Offenses

In addition to information concerning the eight Part I offenses, the FBI provides arrest-only data for about 20 Part II offenses—simple assaults, forgery, embezzlement, prostitution, vandalism, drug violations, and so forth.[82]

Cautions and Criticisms of UCR Data

Each year when the FBI's *Crime in the United States* is published, many people and groups with an interest in crime rush to use the crime figures in attempts to rank and compare crimes in cities and counties. The FBI is quick to point out each year in its *Uniform Crime Reports* that making such comparisons is ill advised, due to the variety of characteristics of different states, counties, and communities.

Many variables can contribute to the amount of crime occurring in a specific jurisdiction. First, it is important to understand a jurisdiction's industrial/economic base, its dependence on neighboring jurisdictions, its transportation system, its reliance on tourism and conventions, its proximity to military installations and correctional facilities, and so forth. Indeed, the strength and aggressiveness of the local police are also key factors in understanding the nature and extent of crime occurring in an area.

In addition to the crime theories discussed earlier, other factors known to affect the volume and type of crime are largely outside the control of the criminal justice system:

- Population density and degree of urbanization
- Variations in composition of the population, particularly youth concentration
- Stability of the population with respect to residents' mobility, commuting patterns, and transient factors
- Modes of transportation and highway system
- Economic conditions, including median income, poverty level, and job availability
- Cultural factors and educational, recreational, and religious characteristics[83]

Critics of UCR data—who include any person engaged in serious research into crime, criminology, victimology, and so on—commonly note the shortcomings of these data (see Table 3.5).[84]

The Hierarchy Rule: Definition and Application

In tabulating how many crimes occur each year, law enforcement agencies are instructed by the FBI to use what is known as the **hierarchy rule**, which basically says that when more than one Part I offense is committed during a criminal event, the law enforcement agency must identify and report only the offense that is highest on the hierarchy list.[85]

Student on the Street Video: Burglary, assault, and murder

Hierarchy rule: in the FBI *Uniform Crime Reports* reporting scheme, the practice whereby only the most serious offense of several that are committed during a criminal act is reported by the police.

TABLE 3.5 Limitations of the *Uniform Crime Reports*

Although the FBI's *Uniform Crime Reports* include several unique publications such as special reports providing statistics on hate crimes and law enforcement officers killed and assaulted, it has some limitations.

UCR Limitations

- offense data are available only for a small number (8) of all crimes committed in the United States;

- the UCR data only list crimes reported to law enforcement agencies (not all crimes that occur are known to the police);

- reporting of citizens' reports of crime by the police is voluntary, and therefore police may choose to not report or might report inaccurately (thus UCR data may be affected by the reporting practices of local law enforcement);

- the hierarchy rule (discussed below) is employed, meaning that where a number of crimes are committed as part of a single criminal act, only the most serious offense of all of them is reported to the UCR;

- attempted crimes are combined with completed crimes;

- when computing crime rates, the UCR counts incidents involving all kinds of targets (for example, crimes of burglary are against businesses and residents, not against "populations"); and

- UCR includes very little information concerning crime victims.

Source: A complete UCR handbook may be viewed at http://www.fbi.gov/about-us/cjis/ucr/additional-ucr-publications/ucr_handbook.pdf/view.

Put another way, the hierarchy rule requires counting only the most serious offense and ignoring all others. Note, however, that this rule applies only to the crime reporting process; it does *not* affect the number of charges for which the defendant may be prosecuted in the courts.

INVESTIGATING FURTHER

THE HIERARCHY RULE

To better understand the hierarchy rule in these exercises, you may wish to first revisit the Part I offenses listed earlier in this chapter, ranked in terms of their severity.

1. Assume that Doe, during the daytime hours, enters Smith's home through an unlocked back door and removes furniture that is valued at about $10,000. If Doe is apprehended, under the hierarchy rule the *only* crime that the police will report to the FBI is

    a. burglary   c. robbery

    b. theft   d. felony theft

2. Further assume that Smith returns home and finds Doe inside; after scuffling briefly, Doe strikes Smith sharply with a candlestick holder, rendering Smith unconscious and near death. Then Doe, fearing he will be caught and returned to prison if Smith testifies against him, picks up a nearby vase and strikes enough blows to end Smith's life.

What crime(s) has Doe committed? Under the UCR Program's hierarchy rule, which crime(s) will be reported by the police to the FBI?

The National Incident-Based Reporting System

Being aware of the criticisms leveled over time against the UCR Program, the U.S. Department of Justice in 1988 launched the **National Incident-Based Reporting System** (NIBRS). Although the UCR Program collects and analyzes data for eight Part I offenses, the NIBRS furnishes crime data provided by nearly 6,500 participating federal, state, and local law enforcement agencies for 46 specific crimes (called Group A offenses) in the following major crime categories: terrorism, white-collar crime, weapons offenses, missing children where criminality is involved, drug/narcotics offenses, drug involvement in all offenses, hate crimes, spousal abuse, abuse of the elderly, child abuse, domestic violence, juvenile crime/gangs, parental abduction, organized crime, pornography/child pornography, driving under the influence, and alcohol-related offenses.[86]

Furthermore, with the NIBRS, legislators, municipal planners/administrators, academicians, sociologists, and the public will have access to more comprehensive, detailed, accurate, and meaningful crime information than the traditional UCR system can provide. Furthermore, with such information, law enforcement can better make a case to acquire the resources needed to fight crime. The NIBRS also enables agencies to locate similarities in crime-fighting problems so that agencies can work together to develop solutions or discover strategies for addressing the issues. Several NIBRS manuals, studies, and papers are available on the UCR Program's website at www.fbi.gov/about-us/cjis/ucr/ucr.

Another change is that the "hierarchy rule" (discussed earlier) does not apply in the NIBRS. If more than one crime was committed by the same person or group of persons and the time and space intervals were insignificant, then all of the crimes would be reported as offenses within the same incident.

In addition to having the UCR Program's two crime categories—crimes against persons (e.g., murder, rape, and aggravated assault) and crimes against property (e.g., robbery, burglary, and larceny-theft), the NIBRS includes a third crime category, crimes against society, to represent society's prohibitions against certain types of activities (e.g., drug or narcotic offenses).

The National Crime Victimization Survey

The **National Crime Victimization Survey** (NCVS), created to address some of the shortcomings with the UCR Program, has been collecting data on personal and household victimization since 1973. The NCVS claims on its website to be "the nation's primary source of information on criminal victimization." Each year, data are obtained from a nationally representative sample of about 40,000 households comprising nearly 75,000 persons on the frequency, characteristics, and consequences of criminal victimization in the United States. Each household is interviewed twice during the year. The survey enables the Bureau of Justice Statistics to estimate the likelihood of victimization by rape, sexual assault, robbery, assault, theft, household burglary, and motor vehicle theft for the population as a whole as well as for segments of the population such as women, the elderly, members of various racial groups, city dwellers, or other groups. The NCVS provides the largest national forum for victims to describe the impact of crime and characteristics of violent offenders.[87]

The survey—which asks respondents to report crime experiences occurring in the past six months—is administered by the U.S. Census Bureau (under the U.S. Department of Commerce) on behalf of the Bureau of Justice Statistics (under the U.S. Department of Justice).

National Incident-Based Reporting System: a crime reporting system in which police describe each offense in a crime as well as describing the offender.

National Crime Victimization Survey: a random survey of households that measures crimes committed against victims; includes crimes not reported to police.

The four primary objectives of the NCVS are to:

- Develop detailed information about the victims and consequences of crime

- Estimate the number and types of crimes not reported to the police

- Provide uniform measures of selected types of crimes

- Permit comparisons over time and types of areas[88]

The NCVS categorizes crimes as "personal" or "property." Personal crimes cover rape and sexual attack, robbery, aggravated and simple assault, and purse-snatching/pocket-picking, whereas property crimes cover burglary, theft, motor vehicle theft, and vandalism.

A potential problem with the NCVS is that it estimates crime based on a representative sample; therefore, it is subject to sampling error. There is also the possibility of nonsampling error, such as with respondents' inability to recall in detail the crimes that occurred during the six months prior to the interview, when the crimes occurred, and other details of the crimes.[89]

IN A NUTSHELL

- The classical and neoclassical schools of criminology were the first attempt to explain crime in rational terms. They postulated that criminal behavior is rational, and most people have the potential to engage in such behavior; that punishment should fit the crime rather than fit the offender; and that justice must be predictable. To a large extent, sentencing reform, criticisms of rehabilitation, and greater use of incarceration sprung from these classical ideas.

- Later, the positivist school of thought, which has dominated U.S. criminology since the beginning of the 20th century, used science to study the body, mind, and environment of offenders and how they could be rehabilitated. Human behavior is controlled by physical, mental, and social factors, not by free will.

- Biological theories of crime offer that the causes of crime are found in the biological determinants—or "original nature"—of the offender and are the result of some biological element or defect; criminals are *born* and not *made* by their home or social environment. Included here are studies of the influence of chromosomes, body types, twins, and adopted children.

- Psychological rationales for crime argue that mental conditions—a personality disorder or limited intellect—are the reason for criminal behavior. The improperly socialized child may develop a personality disturbance that causes her or him to have antisocial and criminal impulses.

- Social and cultural explanations for crime argue that living in social groups might shape criminal behavior; criminality is not innate in one's biological makeup, but instead is caused by external social factors through one's contact with the world. Factors such as poverty, age, race, gender, family, problems faced by immigrants, and so on will foster crime. Theories that stress the influence of social factors on crime are social structure theory, social process theory, and critical theory.

- The wave of feminism during the 1970s consequently gave women equal opportunity and brought female involvement in a wide variety of crimes—sometimes termed *feminist theory*—as well as new studies and questions of that involvement: Do the traditionally male-centered theories of crime apply to women as well? And what explains the long-standing fact that women commit far fewer crimes than men?

- Corporate crime is committed by individuals in the course of their employment, typically in the white-collar professions. These crimes are the most costly type in the United States, difficult to track using traditional crime-reporting techniques, and often the most difficult to explain because the perpetrators are often already wealthy and successful. Social control theorists posit that white-collar criminals are merely motivated by a desire to maximize pleasure and minimize pain by making even more money with little risk of detection.

- In their own words, criminals explain and rationalize their acts in a variety of ways, including financial gain, the need to maintain street status and a partying lifestyle, revenge, and "thrill seeking."

- Crimes in the United States are measured and reported in three primary ways: the FBI's *Uniform Crime Reports*, the National Incident-Based Reporting System, and the National Crime Victimization Survey. Each has its unique approaches as well as advantages and disadvantages.

KEY TERMS & CONCEPTS

▶ Review key terms with eFlashcards. **⑤SAGE** edge™

Adoption studies, 56
Classical school
  (for criminology), 52
Corporate crime, 62
Crime rate, 71
Critical theory, 60
Feminist theory, 61
Hierarchy rule, 72

Labeling theory (of crime), 59
Learning theory (of crime), 58
National Crime
  Victimization Survey, 74
National Incident-Based
  Reporting System, 74
Neoclassical criminology, 53
Positivist school, 53

Psychological rationales
  for crime, 56
Social control theory, 59
Social process theory, 58
Social structure theory, 57
Uniform Crime Reports, 70
XYY chromosome, 54

REVIEW QUESTIONS ?

▶ Test your understanding of chapter content. Take the practice quiz. **⑤SAGE** edge™

1. What were the prevailing beliefs concerning the causes of crime prior to the mid-1700s?

2. How did Cesare Beccaria and the classical school form the foundation for explaining crime in more rational terms?

3. What were the major contributions of the positivist school of criminology in attempting to explain criminality?

4. How would you describe the tenets of the biological theories of crime, including the "born criminal," the "criminal" chromosome, and studies of body type, twins, and adopted children?

5. What were the central psychological explanations of crime as explained by personality disorder and limited intellect?

6. What, in your opinion, are the most compelling of the several social and cultural explanations of crime?

7. What explanations have been offered for women becoming much more engaged in criminal activities since the 1970s?

8. What is white-collar crime, and how/why does it function and persist?

9. What are the three primary methods of measuring the extent of crime, and what have been offered as disadvantages for some of them?

1. Assume that our legal system is neoclassical: People make a rational choice to commit crimes after weighing the benefits to be gained against the costs of being caught and punished, but the criminal law must take into account differences among individuals. You are engaged in a class debate concerning the following resolution: "Our legal system has struck an excellent balance between holding people responsible for their crimes and allowing them to be excused for their crimes." Choose a side, and stake out your argument.

2. Your criminal justice professor hands out the following scenario: John, aged 14 years, is on an errand for his parents (who are in a lower socioeconomic class) when he decides to stop at a crafts shop and look at model cars and airplanes—a hobby he greatly enjoys. While in the store, he puts two small bottles of model paint in his pockets and leaves, but he is quickly stopped by a clerk as he attempts his escape. Explain the possible reasons for John's actions in view of the biological, psychological, and sociocultural theories of crime discussed in this chapter.

3. As part of a criminal justice honor society paper to be presented at a local conference, you are asked to use the Internet and determine how many crimes were reported for your city, your county, your state, and the United States during the past calendar year. How will you proceed?

4. Ellen believes Sally prevented her from receiving a Best Citizen Award and is extremely upset. Ellen confronts Sally on the street and verbally threatens her, saying, "I'm going to beat you within an inch of your life." Ellen then hits Sally with her purse, causing a bloody nose. Ellen then grabs a sharp nail file from the bottom of her purse, and after briefly contemplating whether or not to stab Sally with it, decides not to do so and then runs away. Sally goes to the district attorney's office to file charges. As the prosecutor, what crime(s) do you believe Ellen has actually committed?

5. Your criminal justice professor is working on a journal article concerning the dangers of police work, and she asks you to obtain some information on police deaths and assaults. Using the FBI's UCR website and its supplemental report, *Law Enforcement Officers Killed and Assaulted* (at www.fbi.gov/about-us/cjis/ucr/ucr#leoka), what would you report?

STUDY SITE

$SAGE edge™

Review → Practice → Improve

Sharpen your skills with **SAGE edge** at **edge.sagepub.com/peak2e**

SAGE edge for students provides a personalized approach to help you accomplish your coursework goals in an easy-to-use learning environment. Access the videos, audio clips, quizzes, and SAGE journal articles that are noted in this chapter.

ETHICAL ESSENTIALS
"Doing Right When No One Is Watching"

LEARNING OBJECTIVES

As a result of reading this chapter, you will be able to:

1 Articulate legitimate ethical dilemmas that arise with police, courts, and corrections practitioners

2 Explain the philosophical foundations that underlie and mold modern ethical behavior

3 Discuss the need for, and application of, ethical standards as they concern police

4 Explain the importance of ethics in the court system

5 Delineate the unique ethical considerations and obligations that exist with federal employees

6 Explain the interplay of ethics with the subculture and job-related stress in corrections practitioners

7 Evaluate the ethical decision-making process using a scenario

8 Apply ethical tests to decide what is and is not ethical behavior

ASSESS YOUR AWARENESS

Test your knowledge of ethics by responding to the following seven true-false items; check your answers after reading this chapter's materials.

1 The term *ethics* is rooted in the ancient Greek idea of *character*.

2 The "ends justify the means" philosophy is typically a good, safe philosophy for the police and judges to follow.

3 Communities sometimes seem to tolerate questionable police behavior, if it is carried out to benefit the greater public good (such as dealing with violent gang members).

4 During an oral interview, applicants for policing jobs should *never* indicate a willingness to "snitch" on another officer whom they observe doing something wrong.

5 The receipt of gratuities by criminal justice personnel is a universally accepted practice.

6 Whistleblowers who expose improper acts of their coworkers now have no legal protection.

7 Because of their constitutional obligations, prosecutors and defense attorneys are not bound to the same ethical standards as other criminal justice employees.

Watch your thoughts, for they become words. Watch your words, for they become actions. Watch your actions, for they become habits. Watch your habits, for they become character. Watch your character, for it becomes your destiny.

—Unknown

<< **Answers can be found on page 424.**

A South Hackensack, New Jersey, municipal court judge held a unique part-time job—as a stand-up comedian on a major network's hidden-camera program. But the judge was informed by the state's judicial advisory committee that this part-time job conflicted with his judicial work and violated rules that judges are to follow. He appealed his case to the state's supreme court. One of the ethical questions raised was whether or not people understand that the judge's comedy program—which includes portraying racist and homophobic characters—is an act; in addition, the judge could meet defendants who are familiar with his comic routine and might not believe he's a serious judge. The state also argued that municipal court judges are the face of the judiciary for most citizens, and it is vital that such judges maintain the confidence of the public and the impartiality, dignity, and integrity of the court.

This situation raised several issues: Should the judge have been allowed to work as a comedian during his own time? Or, alternatively, for the reasons stated above was it unethical for him to do so? Must judges at all times "appear to do justice"? (The outcome is provided in endnote #1.)

INTRODUCTION

As regular practice is essential to being a renowned musician, and a perfect cake is essential to having a beautiful wedding, so too is ethics essential to being a criminal justice practitioner. A Latin term that might be used to describe this relationship is *sine qua non*—"without which, nothing." A fundamental knowledge of ethics, as well as some guideposts concerning what constitutes unethical behavior, is an important topic in today's society and for all criminal justice students—not only to guide their own behavior but also because unethical behavior at times appears to permeate contemporary U.S. politics/government, business, and sports.

What specific behaviors are clearly unethical for criminal justice employees? What criteria should guide these employees in their work? To what extent, if any, should the public allow criminal justice employees to violate citizens' rights in order to maintain public order?

This chapter attempts to address these questions and examines many types of ethical problems that can and do arise in police departments, courts, and corrections agencies. The focus is necessarily on the police, who find themselves in many more situations where corruption and brutality can occur than do judges and corrections personnel.

This is not a black-and-white area of study; in fact, there are definitely "shades of gray" for many people where ethics is called into question. Also problematic is that some people who are hired into criminal justice positions simply are not of good character. Furthermore, as stated in Chapter 1, we cannot *train* people to have high ethical standards, nor can we infuse ethics intravenously. In sum, character and ethics are largely something that someone either has or does not have.

GOOD EXAMPLES OF BAD EXAMPLES

To frame the concept of ethics and demonstrate how one's value system can easily be challenged in criminal justice work, consider the following scenarios, all of which are based on true events, and what might be an appropriate punishment (if any) for each:

- *Police*: Upon seeing a vehicle weaving across the center line of the highway, Officer A stops the car, approaches the driver's door, and immediately detects a strong odor of alcohol. The motorist is removed from the car and joins Officer A and a backup, Officer B, on the roadside. Officer A decides to use a portable breath test device to confirm his suspicions of driving under the influence, or DUI, and he gives a sterile

Video:
Unique ethical
considerations

plastic mouthpiece to the driver to blow into. The driver attempts to thwart the test by appearing (but failing) to blow into the mouthpiece. Irritated by this attempt, Officer A yanks the mouthpiece away, throws it on the ground, and arrests the driver for DUI. At trial, the driver claims the mouthpiece was flawed (blocked) so he was unable to blow through it. Officer A testifies under oath that it was not blocked, and as "evidence," he takes a mouthpiece out of his pocket, stating it is the mouthpiece he used for the test that night. Officer B, sitting in the room, hears this testimony and knows differently, having seen Officer A impatiently throw the mouthpiece on the ground and leave it at the scene.[2]

- *Courts*: For several weeks, a wealthy divorcée receives menacing telephone calls that demand dates and sexual favors. The caller's voice is electronically disguised. The suspect also begins stalking the woman. After working some clues and tailing a suspect, a federal agent finally makes contact with a suspect, determining that he is the chief judge of the state's supreme court. Upon confronting him, the agent is told by the judge to "forget about it, or you'll be checking passports in a remote embassy."[3]

- *Corrections*: A correctional officer in a minimum-security facility for young offenders is working the night shift when a youth is admitted. The youth is frightened because this is his first time in custody, and the officer places him in isolation because the youth told the staff he is feeling suicidal. Over the next several days, the officer develops a friendship with the youth. Looking through the youth's file, the officer learns that the boy does not wish to remain male; rather, he wants to become a female. One day while doing a routine cell search, the officer observes the youth stuffing women's panties into his pillowcase. With a terrified and pleading look, the youth explains that he prefers them to boxer shorts and begs the officer not to mention this incident to other staff or youths in the facility. The officer ponders what to do; surely the boy would be seriously ridiculed (or possibly physically assaulted) if others knew of the panties, and it does not seem to be a "big deal." On the other hand, if the officer does not report the event and the boy's choice of underwear is revealed later, the officer knows he will be accused of being lax and not watching over the youths as he should have, and at the very least will lose credibility with other staff and the administration.[4]

PHILOSOPHICAL FOUNDATIONS

Video:
Ethical theories

The term *ethics* is rooted in the ancient Greek idea of *character*. Ethics involves doing what is right or correct and is generally used to refer to how people should behave in a professional capacity. Many people would argue, however, that no difference should exist between one's professional and personal behavior. Ethical rules of conduct should apply to everything a person does.

A central problem with understanding ethics concerns the questions of "whose ethics" and "which right." This becomes evident when one examines controversial issues such as the death penalty, abortion, use of deadly force, and gun control. How individuals view a particular controversy depends largely on their values, character, or ethics. Both sides of controversies such as these believe they are morally right. These issues demonstrate that to understand behavior, the most basic values must be examined and understood.

Another area for examination is **deontological ethics**, which does not consider consequences but instead examines one's duty to act. The word *deontology* comes from two Greek roots, *deos*, meaning "duty," and *logos*, meaning "study." Thus, deontology means the study of duty. When police officers observe a violation of law, they have a duty to act. Officers frequently use this as an excuse when they issue traffic citations

Deontological ethics: one's duty to act.

that appear to have little utility and do not produce any great benefit for the rest of society. For example, when an officer writes a traffic citation for a prohibited left turn made at two o'clock in the morning when no traffic is around, the officer is fulfilling a departmental duty to enforce the law. From a utilitarian standpoint (where we judge an action by its consequences), however, little if any good was served. Here, duty and not good consequences was the primary motivator.

Immanuel Kant, an 18th-century philosopher, expanded the ethics of duty by including the idea of "good will."[5] People's actions must be guided by good intent. In the previous example, the officer who wrote the traffic citation for an improper left turn would be acting unethically if the ticket was a response to a quota or some irrelevant motive. However, if the citation was issued because the officer truly believed that it would result in some good outcome, it would have been an ethical action.

Some people have expanded this argument even further. Richard Kania argued that police officers should be allowed to freely accept gratuities because such actions would constitute the building blocks of positive social relationships between the police and the public.[6] In this case, duty is used to justify what under normal circumstances would be considered unethical. Conversely, if officers take gratuities for self-gratification rather than to form positive community relationships, then the action would be considered unethical by many.

Types of Ethics

Ethics usually involves standards of fair and honest conduct; what we call conscience, the ability to recognize right from wrong; and actions that are good and proper. There are absolute ethics and relative ethics. **Absolute ethics** has only two sides—something is either good or bad, black or white. Some examples in police ethics would be unethical behaviors such as bribery, extortion, excessive force, and perjury, which nearly everyone would agree are unacceptable behaviors by the police.

Relative ethics is more complicated and can have a multitude of sides with varying shades of gray. What one person considers to be ethical behavior may be deemed highly unethical by someone else. Not all ethical issues are clear-cut, however, and communities *do* seem willing at times to tolerate extralegal behavior if there is a greater public good, especially in dealing with problems such as gangs and the homeless. This willingness on the part of the community can be conveyed to the police. Ethical relativism can be said to form an essential part of the community policing movement, discussed more fully in Chapter 6.

A community's acceptance of relative ethics as part of criminal justice may send the wrong message: that few boundaries are placed on justice system employee behaviors and that, at times, "anything goes" in their fight against crime. As John Kleinig pointed out, giving false testimony to ensure that a public menace is "put away" or illegally wiretapping an organized crime figure's telephone might sometimes be viewed as "necessary" and "justified," though illegal.[7] This is the essence of the crime control model of criminal justice (discussed in Chapter 1). Another example is that many police believe they are compelled to

Absolute ethics: the type of ethics where there are only two sides—good or bad, black or white; some examples would be unethical behaviors such as bribery, extortion, excessive force, and perjury, which nearly everyone would agree are unacceptable for criminal justice personnel.

Relative ethics: the gray area of ethics that is not so clear-cut, such as releasing a serious offender in order to use him later as an informant.

Relative ethics involves gray areas that are not clear-cut, such as how the criminal justice system should deal with citizens in terms of mass incarceration, immigration, homelessness, police use of force, and so on.

skirt along the edges of the law—or even violate it—in order to arrest drug traffickers. The ethical problem here is that even if the action could be justified as morally proper, it remains illegal. For many persons, however, the protection of society overrides other concerns.

This viewpoint—the "principle of double effect"—holds that when one commits an act to achieve a good end and an inevitable but intended effect is negative, then the act might be justified. A long-standing debate has occurred about balancing the rights of individuals against the community's interest in calm and order.

These special areas of ethics can become problematic and controversial when police officers use deadly force or lie and deceive others in their work. Police could justify a whole range of activities that others may deem unethical simply because the consequences resulted in the greatest good for the greatest number—the *utilitarian* approach (or **utilitarianism**). If the ends justified the means, perjury would be ethical when committed to prevent a serial killer from being set free to prey on society. In our democratic society, however, the means are just as important as, if not more important than, the desired end.

One of the ethical responsibilities of police officers is to testify truthfully in court concerning what they saw, heard, and did during the performance of their duties.

As examples, citizens in some jurisdictions may not object to the police "hassling" suspected gang members—pulling them over in their cars, say, and doing a field interview—or telling homeless people who are loitering in front of a heavy tourism area or public park to "move along."

It is no less important today than in the past for criminal justice employees to appreciate and come to grips with ethical essentials. Indeed, ethical issues in policing have been affected by three critical factors:[8] (1) the growing level of temptation stemming from the illicit drug trade; (2) the potentially compromising nature of the organizational culture—a culture that can exalt loyalty over integrity, with a "code of silence" that protects unethical employees; and (3) the challenges posed by decentralization (flattening the organization and pushing officers' decision making downward) through the advent of community-oriented policing and problem solving (the community era of policing is discussed in Chapter 5).

Video: Law and Disorder: Hurricane Katrina

Noble Cause Corruption

When the police practice relative ethics and the principle of double effect, described earlier, it is known as **noble cause corruption**—what Thomas Martinelli, perhaps gratuitously, defined as "corruption committed in the name of good ends, corruption that happens when police officers care too much about their work."[9] It basically holds that when an act is committed to achieve a good end (such as an illegal search) but its outcome is negative (the person who is searched eventually goes to prison), the act might still be justified.

Although noble cause corruption can occur anywhere in the criminal justice system, we might look at the police for examples. Officers might bend the rules, such as not reading a drunk person his rights or performing a field sobriety test; planting evidence; issuing "sewer" tickets—writing a person a ticket but not giving it to her, resulting in a warrant issued for failure to appear in court; "testilying," or "using the magic pencil," whereby police officers write up an incident in a way that criminalizes a suspect—this

Utilitarianism: in ethics, as articulated by John Stuart Mill, a belief that the proper course of action is that which maximizes utility—usually defined as that which maximizes happiness and minimizes suffering.

Noble cause corruption: a situation in which one commits an unethical act but for the greater good; for example, a police officer violates the Constitution in order to capture a serious offender.

is a powerful tool for punishment. Noble cause corruption carries with it a different way of thinking about the police relationship with the law. Here, officers operate on a standard that places personal morality above the law, becoming legislators *of* the law and acting as if they *are* the law.[10] Some officers rationalize such activities; as a Philadelphia police officer put it, "When you're shoveling society's garbage, you gotta be indulged a little bit."[11]

Obviously the kinds of noble cause behaviors mentioned here often involve arrogance on the part of the police and ignore the basic constitutional guidelines the occupation demands. Administrators and middle managers must be careful to take a hardline view that their subordinates always tell the truth and follow the law. A supervisory philosophy of discipline based on due process, fairness, and equity, combined with intelligent, informed, and comprehensive decision making, is best for the department, its employees, and the community.[12]

ETHICS IN POLICING

Having defined the types of ethics and some dilemmas, next we discuss in greater detail some of the ethical issues faced by police leaders and their subordinates.

A Primer: The Oral Job Interview

During oral interviews for a position in policing, applicants are often placed in a hypothetical situation that tests their ethical beliefs and character. For example, they may be asked to assume the role of Officer Brown, who is checking on foot an office supplies retail store that was found to have an unlocked door during early morning hours. On leaving the building, Brown observes another officer, Smith, removing a $100 writing pen from a display case and placing it in his uniform pocket. What should Officer Brown do?

This kind of question commonly befuddles the applicant: "Should I rat on my fellow officer? Overlook the matter? Merely tell Smith never to do that again?" Unfortunately, applicants may do a lot of "how am I *supposed* to respond" soul searching and second-guessing with these kinds of questions.

Bear in mind that criminal justice agencies do not wish to hire someone who possesses ethical shortcomings; it is simply too potentially dangerous and expensive, from both legal and moral standpoints, to take the chance of bringing into an agency someone who is corrupt. That is the reason for such questioning and a thorough background investigation of applicants.

Before responding to a scenario like the one concerning Officers Brown and Smith, the applicant should consider the following issues: Is this likely to be the first time that Smith has stolen something? Don't the police arrest and jail people for this same kind of behavior?

In short, police administrators should *never* want an applicant to respond that it is acceptable for an officer to steal. Furthermore, it would be incorrect for an applicant to believe that police do not want an officer to "rat out" another officer. Applicants should never acknowledge that stealing or other such activities are to be overlooked.

Police Corruption

"For as long as there have been police, there has been police corruption."[13] Thus observed Lawrence Sherman about one of the oldest problems in U.S. policing. Indeed, the Knapp Commission investigated police corruption in the early 1970s, finding that there are two primary types of corrupt police officers: the "meat-eaters" and the

Video: Law enforcement and corruption

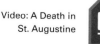
Video: A Death in St. Augustine

"grass-eaters." Meat-eaters spend a good deal of their working hours aggressively seeking out situations that they can exploit for financial gain, including gambling, narcotics, and other lucrative enterprises.

Grass-eaters, the commission noted, constitute the overwhelming majority of those officers who accept payoffs; they are not aggressive but will accept gratuities from contractors, tow-truck operators, gamblers, and the like. Although such officers probably constitute a small percentage of the field, any such activity is to be identified and dealt with sternly.

Police corruption can be defined broadly, from major forms of police wrongdoing to the pettiest forms of improper behavior. Another definition is "the misuse of authority by a police officer in a manner designed to produce personal gain for the officer or for others."[14] Police corruption is not limited to monetary gain, however. Gains may be made through the acceptance of services received, status, influence, prestige, or future support for the officer or someone else.[15]

Police executives typically address the public in the aftermath of officer-involved shootings. Here, St. Louis County Police Chief Jon Belmar comments on issues surrounding the shooting of Michael Brown, in August 2014.

To Inform or Not to Inform: The Code of Silence

Let's continue with the earlier scenario. Remember that Officer Brown witnessed Officer Smith putting an expensive ink pen in his pocket after they found an unlocked office supplies retail business on the graveyard shift. If reported, the misconduct will ruin Smith, but if not reported, the behavior could eventually cause enormous harm. To outsiders, this is not a moral dilemma for Brown at all; the only proper path is for her to report the misconduct. However, arguments exist both for and against Brown's informing on her partner. Reasons for informing include the fact that the harm caused by a scandal would be outweighed by the public's knowing that the police department is free of corruption; also, individual episodes of corruption would be brought to a halt. Brown, moreover, has a sworn duty to uphold the law. Reasons against informing include the fact that, at least in Brown's mind, the other officer is a member of the "family," as well as that a skilled police officer is a valuable asset whose social value far outweighs the damage done by moderate corruption.[16]

Author Video: Ethical dilemmas

Student on the Street Video: Blue wall of silence

A person who is in charge of investigating police corruption would no doubt take a punitive view, because police are not supposed to steal, and they arrest people for the same kinds of acts every day. Still, the issue—and a common question during an oral interview when citizens are being tested for police positions—is whether or not Brown would come forth and inform on her fellow officer.

It is necessary to train police recruits on the need for a corruption-free department. The creation and maintenance of an internal affairs unit and the vigorous prosecution of lawbreaking police officers are also critical to maintaining the integrity of officers.

The Law Enforcement Code of Ethics and Oath of Honor

The Law Enforcement Code of Ethics (LECE) was adopted by the International Association of Chiefs of Police (IACP) in 1957, and it has been revised several times since then. It is a powerful proclamation, and tens of thousands of police officers across the nation have sworn to uphold this code upon graduating from their academies. Unfortunately, the LECE is also quite lengthy, covering rather broadly the following topics as they relate to police officers: primary responsibilities, performance of one's duties, discretion, use of force, confidentiality, integrity, cooperation with other officers and agencies, personal/professional capabilities, and private life.

Police corruption: misconduct by police officers that can involve but is not limited to illegal activities for economic gain, gratuities, favors, and so on.

Recently the IACP adopted a separate, shorter code that would be mutually supportive of the LECE but also easier for officers to remember and call to mind when they come face-to-face with an ethical dilemma. It is the Law Enforcement Oath of Honor, and the IACP is hoping the oath will be implemented in all police agencies and by all individual officers. It may be used at swearing-in ceremonies, graduation ceremonies, promotion ceremonies, beginnings of training sessions, police meetings and conferences, and so forth.[17] The Law Enforcement Oath of Honor is as follows:

On my honor,

I will never betray my badge,

my integrity, my character,

or the public trust.

I will always have

the courage to hold myself

and others accountable for our actions.

I will always uphold the constitution,

my community and the agency I serve.[18]

going GLOBAL

IN MEXICO, POLICE "ETHICS" MATTERS LITTLE

©REUTERS/Henry Romero

Mexican police have long been known to engage in crime, graft, and corruption. In March 2015 relatives of 43 missing students demand justice in Mexico City; officials believe they were abducted by corrupt police officers and handed over to a local drug gang.

Mexico has long been involved in fighting an epidemic of corruption as drug cartels bribe poorly paid police officers and state officials.

Massive firings of police for corruption is not uncommon: In mid-2010 more than 3,200 Mexican federal police were fired for failing to do their work or being linked to corruption; of those, 465 were charged with crimes, and more than 1,000 officers faced disciplinary proceedings for failing confidence exams.[19] Another 500 officers were dismissed in late 2012 after failing tests specifically targeted at weeding out corrupt officials.[20]

The problem is real and goes beyond involvement in drug crime: Municipal officers have killed their own mayors, state jailers have assisted inmates who escape, federal agents are forced to rise up against corrupt commanders, and officers themselves have been murdered because they work for gangster rivals.[21]

Nor have substantial amounts of U.S. aid and training under the Mérida Initiative (a cooperative agreement between the governments of the United States and Mexico to combat drug trafficking, organized crime, and money laundering) worked; Mexico's 32,000 federal police remain understaffed and replete with graft.

Accepted and Deviant Lying

In many cases, no clear line separates acceptable from unacceptable behavior in policing. The two are separated by an expansive gray area that comes under relative ethics. Some observers have referred to such illegal behavior as a **"slippery slope,"** meaning that people tread on solid or legal ground but at some point slip beyond the acceptable into illegal or unacceptable behavior.

Criminal justice employees lie or deceive for different purposes and under varying circumstances. In some cases, their misrepresentations are accepted as an essential part of a criminal investigation, whereas in other cases they are viewed as violations of law. David Carter examined police lying and perjury and found a distinction between accepted lying and deviant lying.[22] **Accepted lying** includes police activities intended

Lying and deception have long been used by the police to identify and arrest criminals; this undercover DEA agent is posing as a student as part of a drug investigation.

to apprehend or entrap suspects. This type of lying is generally considered to be trickery. **Deviant lying**, by contrast, refers to occasions when officers commit perjury to convict suspects or are deceptive about some activity that is illegal or unacceptable to the department or public in general.

Deception has long been practiced by the police to ensnare violators and suspects. For many years, it was the principal method used by detectives and police officers to secure confessions and convictions. *Accepted lying* is allowed by law, and to a great extent, it is expected by the public. Gary Marx identified three methods police use to trick a suspect: (1) performing the illegal action as part of a larger, socially acceptable, and legal goal; (2) disguising the illegal action so that the suspect does not know it is illegal; and (3) morally weakening the suspect so that the suspect voluntarily becomes involved.[23] The courts have long accepted deception as an investigative tool. For example, in *Illinois v. Perkins*,[24] the U.S. Supreme Court ruled that police undercover agents are not required to administer the *Miranda* warning to incarcerated inmates when investigating crimes. Lying, although acceptable by the courts and the public in certain circumstances, does result in an ethical dilemma. It is a dirty means to accomplish a good end—the police using untruths to gain the truth relative to some event.

In their examination of lying, Thomas Barker and David Carter identified two types of *deviant lying*: lying that serves legitimate purposes and lying that conceals or promotes crimes or illegitimate ends.[25] Lying that serves legitimate goals occurs when officers lie to secure a conviction, obtain a search warrant, or conceal omissions during an investigation. Barker found that police officers believe that almost one-fourth of their agency would commit perjury to secure a conviction or to obtain a search warrant.[26] Lying becomes an effective, routine way to sidestep legal impediments. When left unchecked by supervisors, managers, and administrators, lying can become organizationally accepted as an effective means to nullify legal entanglements and remove obstacles that stand in the way of convictions. Examples include using the services of nonexistent confidential informants to secure search warrants, concealing

"Slippery slope": the idea that a small first step can lead to more serious behaviors, such as the receipt of minor gratuities by police officers believed to eventually cause them to desire or demand receipt of items of greater value.

Accepted lying: police activities intended to apprehend or entrap suspects. This type of lying is generally considered to be trickery.

Deviant lying: occasions when officers commit perjury to convict suspects or are deceptive about some activity that is illegal or unacceptable to the department or public in general.

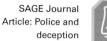

SAGE Journal Article: Police and deception

that an interrogator went too far, coercing a confession, or perjuring oneself to gain a conviction.

Lying to conceal or promote criminality is the most distressing form of deception. Examples range from when the police lie to conceal their use of excessive force when arresting a suspect to obscuring the commission of a criminal act.

Accepting Gratuities

Gratuities are commonly accepted by many police officers as a part of their job. Restaurants frequently give officers free or half-price meals and drinks, and other businesses routinely give officers discounts for services or merchandise. While some officers and their departments accept the receipt of such gratuities as a legitimate part of their job, other agencies prohibit such gifts and discounts but seldom attempt to enforce any relevant policy or regulation. Finally, some departments attempt to ensure that officers do not accept free or discounted services or merchandise and routinely enforce policies or regulations against such behavior.[27]

Video: Banning gratuities

There are two basic arguments *against* police acceptance of gratuities. First is the slippery slope argument, discussed earlier, which proposes that gratuities are the first step in police corruption. This argument holds that once gratuities are received, police officers' ethics are subverted and they are open to additional breaches of their integrity. In addition, officers who accept minor gifts or gratuities are then obligated to provide the donors with some special service or accommodation. Furthermore, some critics propose that receiving a gratuity is wrong because officers are receiving rewards for services that they are obligated to provide as part of their employment. That is, officers have no legitimate right to accept compensation in the form of a gratuity. If the police ever hope to be accepted as members of a full-fledged profession, then they must address whether the acceptance of gratuities is professional behavior.

Former New York police commissioner Patrick V. Murphy was one of those who believed that "except for your pay check, there is no such thing as a clean buck."[28] He also noted that judges, teachers, doctors, and other professionals do not accept special consideration from restaurants, convenience stores, movie theaters, and so on.

Gratuities: the receipt of some benefit (a meal, gift, or some other favor) either for free or for a reduced price.

You Be the... POLICE OFFICER

Assume the county sheriff's department prohibits personnel from soliciting or accepting gifts. A deputy sheriff has been using a variety of problem-solving approaches to address problems at a shopping mall where juveniles have been loitering, engaging in acts of vandalism, dumping trash, and generally causing traffic problems after hours in the parking lot. Now the mall manager, Mr. Chang, feels morally obligated to express his appreciation to the deputy. Mr. Chang has made arrangements for the deputy and his family to receive a 15 percent discount while shopping at any store in the mall. Also, as part owner of a toy store in the mall, Mr. Chang offers the deputy a bicycle for his young daughter. Knowing that the agency policy requires that such offers be declined, the deputy is also aware that Mr. Chang will be very hurt or upset if the proffered gifts are refused.

1. Are Mr. Chang's motives honorable?
2. Should the deputy accept the offered discount? The bicycle?
3. Do you believe the department's policy should be modified to accommodate such situations?

INVESTIGATING FURTHER

YIELDING TO LYING AND TEMPTATION: ENGRAINED?

Certainly a related aspect of crime that should not be overlooked in discussions of greed, opportunity for crime, and so on, concerns two other long-standing human traits: lying and succumbing to temptation. First, regarding lying, experts note that we humans begin lying at around age 4 or 5, when we gain an awareness of the use and power of language. This early lying is not malicious, but rather to find out, or test, what can be manipulated in the child's environment. As this lying continues, rightly or wrongly, it leads to cynicism about the criminal justice system.[29] For example, as noted police researchers Carl Klockars and Stephen Mastrofski observed, although traffic violators frequently offer what they feel are very good reasons for the officer to overlook their offense, "every police officer knows that, if doing so will allow them to escape punishment, most people are prepared to lie through their teeth."[30] Regarding temptation, researchers have long known that the best way to establish a causal relationship is through setting up an experiment; however, it would be unethical to create new opportunities for burglary or robbery, then sit back to see what happens. But some researchers have undertaken such experiments using more minor transgressions. For example, in the 1920s, researchers gave schoolchildren the opportunity to cheat on tests, to lie about cheating, and to steal coins from puzzles that were used. What they discovered was that only a few children resisted all these temptations. In fact, most behaved dishonestly some of the time, supporting the idea that opportunities cause crime. In another experiment, researchers disseminated stamped and addressed letters in the streets to see whether people would pick them up and mail them. It was found that people were less likely to mail the letters they found that contained money, again showing their response to opportunity. Furthermore, people were more likely to place in the mail letters that were addressed to males rather than females, indicating that a person gives some thought and makes a conscious decision whether to respond to temptation.[31]

Below is an example of a policy developed by a sheriff's office concerning gratuities.

1. Without the express permission of the Sheriff, members shall not solicit or accept any gift, gratuity, loan, present, or fee where there is any direct or indirect connection between this solicitation or acceptance of such gift and their employment by this office.

2. Members shall not accept, either directly or indirectly, any gift, gratuity, loan, fee, or thing of value, the acceptance of which might tend to improperly influence their actions, or that of any other member, in any matter of police business, or which might tend to cast an adverse reflection on the Sheriff's Office.

3. Any unauthorized gift, gratuity, loan, fee, reward, or other thing falling into any of these categories coming into the possession of any member shall be forwarded to the member's commander, together with a written report explaining the circumstances connected therewith. The commander will decide the disposition of the gift.

Greed and Temptation

Edward Tully underscored the vast amount of temptation that confronts today's police officers and what police leaders must do toward combating it:

> Socrates, Mother Teresa, or other revered individuals in our society never had to face the constant stream of ethical problems of a busy cop on the beat.

One of the roles of [police leaders] is to create an environment that will help the officer resist the temptations that may lead to misconduct, corruption, or abuse of power. The executive cannot construct a work environment that will completely insulate the officers from the forces which lead to misconduct. The ultimate responsibility for an officer's ethical and moral welfare rests squarely with the officer.[32]

Most citizens have no way of comprehending the amount of temptation that confronts today's police officers. They frequently find themselves alone inside retail businesses after normal business hours, clearing the building after finding an open door or window. A swing or graveyard shift officer could easily obtain considerable plunder during these occasions, acquiring everything from clothing to tires for a personal vehicle. At the other end of the spectrum is the potential for huge payoffs from drug traffickers or other big-money offenders who will gladly pay the officer to look away from their crimes. Some officers, like the general public, find this temptation impossible to overcome.

The organization's culture is also important in this regard. The police culture often exalts loyalty over integrity. Given the stress usually generated more from within the organization than from outside and the nature of life-and-death decisions they must make daily, even the best officers who simply want to catch criminals may become frustrated and vulnerable to bending the rules for what they view as the greater good of society.

ETHICS IN THE COURTS

Although the public tends to think of criminal justice ethics primarily in terms of the police, certainly other criminal justice professionals—including the court work group—have expectations in this regard as well. The ethical standards and expectations—and some examples of failings—of those individuals are discussed next.

Evolving Standards of Conduct

The first call during the 20th century for formalized standards of conduct in the legal profession came in 1906, with Roscoe Pound's speech "The Causes of Popular Dissatisfaction With the Administration of Justice."[33] However, the first canons of judicial ethics probably grew out of a professional baseball scandal in 1919, in which the World Series was "thrown" to the Chicago White Sox by the Cincinnati Reds. Baseball officials turned to the judiciary for leadership and hired U.S. District Court Judge Kenesaw Mountain Landis as baseball commissioner—a position for which Landis was paid $42,500, compared to his $7,500 earnings per year as a judge. This affair prompted the 1921 American Bar Association (ABA) convention to pass a resolution of censure against the judge and appoint a committee to propose standards of judicial ethics.[34]

Model Code of Judicial Conduct: adopted by the House of Delegates of the American Bar Association in 1990, it provides a set of ethical principles and guidelines for judges.

In 1924, the ABA approved the Canons of Judicial Ethics under the leadership of Chief Justice William Howard Taft, and in 1972, the ABA approved a new **Model Code of Judicial Conduct**; in 1990, the same body adopted a revised model code. Nearly all states and the District of Columbia have promulgated standards based on the code. In 1974, the United States Judicial Conference adopted a Code of Conduct for United States Judges, and Congress over the years enacted legislation regulating judicial conduct, including the Ethics Reform Act of 1989.

PRACTITIONER'S PERSPECTIVE

POLICE INTERNAL AFFAIRS INVESTIGATOR

Name: David Schofield, Police Officer/Detective

Current Position: Investigator, Professional Standards Section

City, State: Cincinnati, Ohio

College Attended/Academic Major: Bachelor of arts in economics from the University of Cincinnati; master of science degree in criminal justice from the University of Cincinnati

How long have you been a practitioner in this criminal justice position? Since May 2006

My primary duties and responsibilities as a practitioner in this position: I investigate allegations of criminal conduct, sexual misconduct, serious misconduct, excessive use of force, unnecessary pointing of firearms, improper searches and seizures, and discrimination by sworn and nonsworn department members of the Cincinnati Police Department.

The qualities/characteristics that are most helpful in this career: Honesty/integrity; high moral values; confidence; professionalism; accountability; strong work ethic; ability to perform well during dangerous situations; high level of physical fitness; ability to read and write well; ability to speak well in front of others; ability to be readily available for various shifts; ability to work long, often stressful hours.

In general, this is what a *typical day* looks like for a practitioner in this career: Interviewing citizens and police officers regarding allegations of officer misconduct. Decisions must be made on which investigative leads ought to be given priority and how best to pursue those leads. Investigators are given considerable freedom to pursue their investigation how he or she deems necessary. This requires self-motivation to stay on task and complete the assignment properly. Investigators also must find and develop witnesses for further investigation, while some investigative techniques require covert operations investigating fellow police officers. Other investigative techniques may involve hours of mundane fact-finding. Honesty and integrity are crucial to conduct fair investigations and gain the public trust.

Investigators must be able to put the police department's mission first, even when it involves sustaining serious allegations of misconduct by fellow officers. Investigators must also be able to present their findings in court, disciplinary hearings, the media, and other venues using verbal and written communication. Oftentimes, long hours are spent documenting the findings of an investigation. Information gathered must be documented fairly and concisely. Considerable time is also spent investigating erroneous complaints; however, investigations can be as important as legitimate complaints when the integrity of a police employee is called into question.

My advice to someone either wishing to study, or now studying, criminal justice and wanting to become a practitioner in this career: Research what type of employment you desire. Once that is determined, candidates ought to determine what actual practitioners did in order to get there. Uniform patrol is the backbone of policing. Most local sworn law enforcement positions require candidates to perform exceptionally well as patrol officers prior to attaining other duties such as investigations, canine, or special operations. If a candidate must be a patrol officer for several years before attaining the position of an investigator, the candidate must be willing to fulfill that requirement.

Prior to gaining employment with a police agency, candidates must protect their reputation and abstain from questionable behavior. Many dreams are lost due to a bad, single decision.

Candidates must also do well in high school and college, as one's academic standing is a strong reflection of his or her work ethic. The lack of a quality education and strong academic background can prevent candidates from achieving their goals.

The Judge

Judges are discussed generally in Chapter 10; however, here the focus is on their ethical responsibilities. Ideally, our judges are flawless, not allowing emotion or personal biases to creep into their work, treating all cases and individual litigants with an even hand,

and employing "justice tempered with mercy." The perfect judge has been described as follows:

> The good judge takes equal pains with every case no matter how humble; he knows that important cases and unimportant cases do not exist, for injustice is not one of those poisons which . . . when taken in small doses may produce a salutary effect. Injustice is a dangerous poison even in doses of homeopathic proportions.[35]

Not all judges, of course, can attain this lofty status. Judges can become embroiled in improper conduct or overstep their bounds in many ways: abuse of judicial power (against attorneys or litigants); inappropriate sanctions and dispositions (including showing favoritism or bias); not meeting the standards of impartiality and competence (discourteous behavior, gender bias and harassment, incompetence); conflict of interest (bias; conflicting financial interests or business, social, or family relationships); and personal conduct (criminal or sexual misconduct, prejudice, statements of opinion).[36]

Following are examples of some true-to-life ethical dilemmas involving the courts:[37]

- A judge convinces jailers to release his son on a nonbondable offense.
- A judge is indicted on charges that he used his office for a racketeering enterprise.

INVESTIGATING FURTHER

JUDGES' ETHICAL MISCONDUCT

©AP Photo/Scranton Times-Tribune, Michael J. Mullen

Former Pennsylvania judge Mark Ciavarella Jr., convicted of racketeering, was sentenced to a federal prison for 28 years.

A former county juvenile court judge in Pennsylvania was sentenced to prison for 28 years after being convicted on federal racketeering charges—specifically, sentencing juveniles to a detention facility for minor crimes while accepting more than $1 million in kickbacks from the private company that built and maintained the facility.[42]

One-fourth of this judge's juvenile defendants were sentenced to detention centers, as he routinely ignored requests for leniency made by prosecutors and probation officers. Some of the nearly 5,000 sentenced juveniles were as young as 10. One girl, who described the experience as a "surreal nightmare," was sentenced to three months of "hard time" for posting spoofs about an assistant school principal on the Internet. Some juveniles even committed suicide following their commitment.[40] The judge was said to have maintained a culture of intimidation in which no one was willing to speak up about the sentences he was handing down. Although he pleaded guilty to the charges, he denied sentencing juveniles who did not deserve it or receiving remuneration from the detention centers.[43]

The matter also raised concerns about whether juveniles should be required to have counsel either before or during their appearances in court: It was revealed that more than 500 juveniles had appeared before the judge without representation. Although juveniles have long had a right to counsel,[44] Pennsylvania, like at least 20 other states, allows children to waive counsel, and about half of these Pennsylvania youths had chosen to do so.[45]

You Be the...

ETHICS COMMITTEE MEMBER

A U.S. District Court judge in Alabama was controversial even before he was arrested on allegations of beating his wife. He was criticized for hearing government cases while his aviation company was getting hundreds of thousands of dollars in government business. He was also infamous for having an extramarital affair with his courtroom assistant, as well as for his messy public divorce.

In May 2015, Judge Mark Fuller resigned because of a fight he had with the same former courtroom assistant—now his wife—who is heard yelling, "He's beating on me! Please help me" to a police dispatcher.

A five-judge review panel investigated Fuller's behavior, and a U.S. House of Representatives committee considered conducting impeachment hearings against him.

However, because of his lifetime appointment to the bench, the judge could not be forced off the bench; he could only be reprimanded and asked to resign, and the congressional committee could have recommended impeachment.

1. Should judges with lifetime appointments receive such protections while sitting on the bench?

2. If not, what would kind of system would you propose?

- Two judges attend the governor's $500-per-person inaugural ball.

- A judge is accused of acting with bias in giving a convicted murderer a less severe sentence because the victims were homosexual.

- A judge whose car bears the bumper sticker "I am a pro-life Democrat" acquits six pro-life demonstrators of trespassing at an abortion clinic on the grounds of necessity to protect human life.

Such incidents certainly do little to bolster public confidence in the justice system. People expect more from judges, who are "the most highly visible symbol of justice."[38]

Unfortunately, codes of ethical conduct have not eradicated these problems or allayed concerns about judges' behavior. Indeed, one judge who teaches judicial ethics at the National Judicial College in Reno, Nevada, stated that most judges attending the college admit never having read the Model Code of Judicial Conduct before seeking judicial office.[39]

According to the American Judicature Society, during one year 25 judges were suspended from office, and more than 80 judges resigned or retired either before or after formal charges were filed against them; 120 judges also received private censure, admonition, or reprimand.[40]

The key to judicial ethics is to identify the troublesome issues and to create an "ethical alarm system" that responds.[41] Perhaps the most important tenet in the code and the one that is most difficult to apply is that judges should avoid the *appearance* of impropriety—in other words, it is not enough that judges *do* what is just; they must also avoid conduct that would create in the public's mind a perception that their ability to carry out responsibilities with integrity, impartiality, and competence is impaired.

Ethical requirements for the federal judiciary and other federal employees are discussed later in this chapter.

Prosecutors

Given their power and authority to decide which cases are to be prosecuted, prosecuting attorneys must closely guard their ethical behavior. It was decided over 75 years ago (in *Berger v. United States*, 1935) that the primary duty of a prosecutor is "not that he shall win a case, but that justice shall be done."[46]

Instances of prosecutorial misconduct were reported as early as 1897[47] and are still reported today. One of the leading examples of unethical conduct by a prosecutor is *Miller v. Pate*,[48] in which the prosecutor concealed from the jury in a murder trial the fact that a pair of undershorts with red stains contained not blood but red paint.

According to Elliot Cohen, misconduct works:[49] Oral advocacy is important in the courtroom and can have a powerful effect. Another significant reason for such conduct is the harmless error doctrine, in which an appellate court can affirm a conviction despite the presence of serious misconduct during the trial. Only when appellate courts take a stricter, more consistent approach to this problem will it end.[50]

Defense Attorneys

Defense attorneys, too, must be legally and morally bound to ethical principles as agents of the courts. Cohen suggested the following moral principles for defense attorneys:[51]

- Treat others as ends in themselves and not as mere means to winning cases.

- Treat clients and other professional relations in a similar fashion.

- Do not deliberately engage in behavior apt to deceive the court as to truth.

- Be willing, if necessary, to make reasonable personal sacrifices of time, money, and popularity for what you believe to be a morally good cause.

- Do not give money to, or accept money from, clients for wrongful purposes or in wrongful amounts.

- Avoid harming others in the course of representing your client.

- Be loyal to your client, and do not betray his or her confidence.

Other Court Employees

Other court employees have ethical responsibilities as well. For example, an appellate court judge's secretary is asked by a good friend who is a lawyer whether the judge will be writing the opinion in a certain case. The lawyer may be wishing to attempt to influence the judge through his secretary, renegotiate with an opposing party, or engage in some other improper activity designed to alter the case outcome.[52] Bailiffs, court administrators, court reporters, courtroom clerks, and law clerks all fit into this category. It would be improper, say, for a bailiff who is accompanying jurors back from a break in a criminal trial to mention that the judge "sure seems annoyed at the defense attorney" or for a law clerk to tell an attorney friend that the judge she works for prefers reading short bench memos.[53]

ETHICAL CONDUCT OF FEDERAL EMPLOYEES

The laws governing the ethical conduct of federal employees are contained in a variety of statutes, the two major sources of which are Title 18 of the U.S. Code and the Ethics in Government Act of 1978 (enacted following the Watergate scandals of the early

1970s to promote public confidence in government). The latter act has been amended a number of times, with its most significant revision occurring in the Ethics Reform Act of 1989 (Public Law 101-194). A brief general description of that law, as well as expectations of the federal judiciary, is provided next.

The Ethics Reform Act

The Ethics Reform Act addresses a number of areas of ethical concern, including the receipt of gifts, financial conflicts involving employees' position, personal conflicts that may affect their impartiality, misuse of position (for private gain), and outside activities or employment that conflicts with their federal duties (such as an expert witness, payment for speaking, writing, and teaching).

SAGE Journal Article: Whistle-blowing and government

In 1989 the **Whistleblower Protection Act** (Public Law 101-12) strengthened the protections provided in the Ethics Reform Act. These whistleblower protection laws prohibit reprisal against federal employees who reasonably believe that their disclosures show "a violation of law, rule, or regulation, gross mismanagement, a gross waste of funds, an abuse of authority, or a specific and substantial danger to public health and safety."

The Federal Judiciary

Federal judges have the authority to resolve significant public and private disputes. Occasionally, however, a matter assigned to them may involve them or their families personally, or affect individuals or organizations with which they have associations outside of their official duties. In these situations, if their impartiality might be compromised, they must disqualify (or recuse) themselves from the proceeding.

Whistleblower Protection Act: a federal law prohibiting reprisal against employees who reveal information concerning a violation of law, rules, or regulations; gross mismanagement or waste of funds; an abuse of authority; and so on.

INVESTIGATING FURTHER

WHISTLEBLOWER OR TRAITOR?

In mid-2013, people around the globe began learning of the vast reach of the U.S. National Security Agency's (NSA's) collection of data from hundreds of millions of people via their phone calls, their email messages, their friends, email contacts, even how they spend their days and nights. The agency even broke into the communications links of major data centers around the world, spying on hundreds of millions of user accounts. In doing so, the NSA had exceeded its mandate and abused its authority, all of which prompted outrage among citizens and politicians; even a panel appointed by President Barack Obama strongly condemned the agency's invasions of privacy and called for a major overhaul of its operations. These revelations came to light because of information provided to journalists by Edward Snowden, then an NSA contractor who, after becoming disillusioned with the agency's activities, became a whistleblower and soon left for Russia in order to escape U.S. charges of espionage and theft.

The question in the minds of many people became whether Snowden was a saint or sinner, dissident or patriot. On the one hand, the information he revealed exposed many abuses—and did his country a great service in the process; on the other hand, he committed several violations of the Espionage Act, punishable by up to 30 years in prison.

Snowden still resides in an undisclosed location in Russia and is seeking asylum in the European Union. He has since been awarded a number of whistleblower awards from both foreign and domestic organizations, typical of which was one in Germany that noted his "bold efforts to expose the massive and unsuspecting monitoring and storage of communication data, which cannot be accepted in democratic societies."

Source: Edward Snowden, "Whistle-blower," *New York Times* Editorial Board, January 1, 2014, http://www.nytimes.com/2014/01/02/opinion/edward-snowden-whistle-blower.html; TASS, "Snowden Says He Feels Very Secure in Russia," December 10, 2014, http://tass.ru/en/world/766293/; "Snowden Wins Whistleblower Award in Germany," September 3, 2013, http://rt.com/news/snowden-prize-whistleblower-germany-255.

Disqualification is required under Canon 3C(1) of the Code of Conduct for United States Judges of the ABA if the judge

- has personal knowledge of disputed facts;

- was employed in a law firm that handled the same matter while he or she was there;

- has a close relative who is a party or attorney;

- personally owns, or has an immediate family member who owns, a financial interest in a party; or

- as a government official, served as a counsel in the case.

The next "Investigating Further" box shows the canons of ethical conduct for federal judges as set forth by the Administrative Office of the United States Courts.

INVESTIGATING FURTHER

CANONS OF ETHICS FOR THE FEDERAL JUDICIARY

Following are the canons of the Code of Conduct for United States Judges:

Canon 1: A judge should uphold the integrity and independence of the judiciary.

Canon 2: A judge should avoid impropriety and the appearance of impropriety in all activities.

Canon 3: A judge should perform the duties of the office impartially and diligently.

Canon 4: A judge may engage in extrajudicial activities that are consistent with the obligations of judicial office.

Canon 5: A judge should refrain from political activity.

Implicit in these canons are restrictions on judges' soliciting or accepting gifts, outside employment, and payment for appearances, speeches, or written articles.

Source: Administrative Office of the United States Courts, *Code of Conduct for United States Judges*, http://www.uscourts.gov/RulesAndPolicies/ CodesOfConduct/CodeConductUnitedStatesJudges.aspx; further guidance appears in Federal Judicial Center, *Guide to Judiciary Policies and Procedures: Volume 2. Maintaining the Public Trust: Ethics for Federal Judicial Law Clerks* (Washington, D.C.: Author, 2002).

ETHICS IN CORRECTIONS

SAGE Journal Article: Correctional officer deviance

Corrections personnel confront many of the same ethical dilemmas as police personnel. Thus, prison and jail administrators, like their counterparts in the police realm, would do well to understand their occupational subculture and its effect on ethical decision making.

The strength of the corrections subculture correlates with the security level of a correctional facility and is strongest in maximum-security institutions. Powerful forces within the correctional system have a stronger influence over the behavior of correctional officers than the administrators of the institution, legislative decrees, or agency policies.[54] Indeed, it has been known for several decades that the exposure to external danger in the workplace creates a remarkable increase in group solidarity.[55]

Some of the job-related stressors for correctional officers are similar to those the police face: the ever-present potential for physical danger, hostility directed at officers by inmates and even by the public, unreasonable role demands, a tedious and unrewarding work environment, and dependence on one another to effectively and safely work in their environment.[56] For these reasons, several norms of corrections work have been identified: Always go to the aid of an officer in distress; do not "rat"; never make another officer look bad in front of inmates; always support an officer in a dispute with an inmate; always support officer sanctions against inmates; and do not wear a "white hat" (participate in behavior that suggests sympathy or identification with inmates).[57]

Security issues and the way in which individual correctional officers have to rely on each other for their safety make loyalty to one another a key norm. The proscription against ratting out a colleague is strong. In one documented instance, two officers in the Corcoran, California, state prison blew the whistle on what they considered to be unethical conduct by their colleagues. Officers were alleged to have staged a gladiator-style fight among inmates from different groups in a small exercise yard. The two officers claimed that their colleagues would even place bets on the outcome of the fights, and when the fights got out of hand, the officers would fire shots at the inmates. Since

Like police officers, correctional officers in jails and prisons at times must exercise force—which raises ethical considerations and concerns for them as well.

the institution had opened in 1988, eight inmates had been shot dead by officers, and numerous others had been wounded. The two officers who reported these activities were labeled by colleagues as "rats" and "no-goods" and had their lives threatened; even though they were transferred to other institutions, the labels traveled with them. Four correctional officers were indicted for their alleged involvement in these activities, but all were acquitted in a state prosecution in 2001.[58]

In another case, a female correctional officer at a medium-security institution reported some of her colleagues for sleeping on the night shift. She had first approached them and expressed concern for her safety when they were asleep and told them that if they did not refrain from sleeping, she would have to report them to the superintendent. They continued sleeping, and she reported them. The consequences were severe: Graffiti was written about her on the walls, she received harassing phone calls and letters, her car was vandalized, and some bricks were thrown through the windows of her home.[59] Obviously, she deserved better, both in terms of protection during these acts, and with the investigation and prosecution of the parties involved.

It would be unfair to suggest that the kind of behavior depicted here reflects the behavior of correctional officers in all places and at all times. The case studies do demonstrate, however, the power and loyalty of the group, and correctional administrators must be cognizant of that power. It is also noteworthy that the corrections subculture, like its police counterpart, provides several positive qualities, particularly in crisis situations, including mutual support and protection, which is essential to the emotional and psychological health of officers involved; there is always the "family" to support you.

You Be the... CORRECTIONAL OFFICER

Correctional Officer Ben Jones has worked for one year in a medium-security housing unit in a state prison and has gotten on friendly terms with an inmate, Stevens. Known to have been violent, manipulative, and associating with a similarly rough crowd while on the outside, now Stevens appears to be a model inmate; in fact, Officer Jones relies heavily on Stevens to keep him informed of the goings-on in the unit as well as to maintain its overall cleanliness and general appearance. Over time, the two address each other on a first-name basis and increasingly discuss personal matters; Jones occasionally allows Stevens to get by with minor infractions of prison rules (e.g., being in an unauthorized area or entering another inmate's cell). Today Stevens mentions that he is having problems with his fiancé—specifically, that he has received a "Dear John" letter from her, stating that she is dating other men and is "moving on." Upon arriving home from work that evening, Jones finds a case of wine on his porch. There is no card left on the case of wine, but at work the next morning Stevens winks at Jones and asks if he "ventured into the vineyard last night."

1. Should Officer Jones report the incident?
2. Has Jones's behavior thus far violated any standards of ethics for correctional officers? If so, what form of punishment (if any) would be appropriate?
3. What should be the relationship between Jones and Stevens in the future?
4. What could Jones have done differently, if anything?

THE ETHICAL DECISION-MAKING PROCESS

Sometimes criminal justice practitioners are confronted with a situation—a dilemma—where he or she simply does not know the right course of action to follow. The situation may not even be covered in the agency policy or procedures/general orders manuals. Or perhaps the course of action that appears to be the proper one is simply difficult (or even painful) to carry out, or some improper course of action is very tempting or would seem to be the easiest and most trouble-free approach to take.

In such cases, the following **ethical decision-making process** may be used to work through an ethical quandary. After reading the process, consider the ethical problem presented in the next "You Be the Police Officer" box.

Assume you perceive that an ethical problem has surfaced:

1. *Consider your alternatives:* What are existing options in the situation you are facing? Try to devise three or more options, even some that may not appear, on the surface, to be the best courses of action.

2. *List the stakeholders:* Which people and organizations will be affected by your decision and your actions? Including yourself, also consider your coworkers, supervisors, agency, any affected neighborhoods, and the community-at-large (some options may even involve a criminal justice agency internal affairs investigation or explanation).

3. *Consider the consequences of each alternative:* What are the potential pros and cons of pursuing each option? Which people and organizations will likely favor and oppose each option, and why? Remember that the best option is not always the one with the best or fewest negative outcomes. Also remember that for each action, there is a reaction. After thinking through the consequences, choose an alternative that appears best suited for the situation.

Ethical decision-making process: a series of steps for addressing an ethical dilemma; includes looking at alternatives, considering stakeholders and consequences, and explaining the decision to others.

4. Finally, after selecting an option, consider how would you feel about explaining your ethical decision to the aforementioned stakeholders. How will your decision be received when you are forced to defend it to the public? The media? The internal affairs office? To your family? Is this an action that you will be proud of or one you will be ashamed to talk about?[60]

ALTERNATIVES?	STAKEHOLDERS INVOLVED IN EACH ALTERNATIVE?	CONSEQUENCES OF EACH ALTERNATIVE?	CONSEQUENCES OF TELLING THE STORY?
#1			
#2			
#3			
#4			

You Be the... POLICE OFFICER

The following case study involved one of the authors: Assume that you are a small-town police officer and it is summertime. You are driving your patrol car one evening when a vehicle suddenly pulls up beside you, and the woman driver yells, "Officer, my baby's dying!" You have her drive her car to the curb, and she then carries the child to your patrol car. You note that the infant is about eight months of age, her face has a blue tinge to it, her eyes are rolled back, and she does not appear to be breathing. You quickly check her airway and resolve the situation (the baby's airway had become obstructed by her tongue during a seizure). Three months later, the same woman comes to your home one morning. Sobbing, she says, "Officer, my husband is in jail for shoplifting, I'm broke, and my kids have no food or milk. I need money to bail him out of jail and get back to work and pay for groceries. You gave me help once—can you help me now?" Her husband, well-known to your police agency, does not enjoy a good reputation in town.

1. Will you do something to assist the woman financially? If not, explain.
2. If yes, will you loan her grocery money only, or enough for her to also bail her husband out of jail?
3. Assume you recently received a large income tax refund and thus decide to loan her the money to get her husband out of jail so that he can return to his job. Is this ethical? Why or why not?

ETHICS TESTS FOR THE CRIMINAL JUSTICE STUDENT

Following are some tests to help guide you, the criminal justice student, to decide what is and is not ethical behavior:[61]

- *Test of common sense.* Does the act make sense, or would someone look askance at it?

- *Test of publicity.* Would you be willing to see what you did highlighted on the front page of the local newspaper?

- *Test of one's best self.* Will the act fit the concept of oneself at one's best?

"The bell, the book, and the candle" test can be used as a guide against making unethical decisions.

- *Test of one's most admired personality.* What would one's parents or minister do in this situation?

- *Test of hurting someone else.* Will it cause pain for someone?

- *Test of foresight.* What is the long-term likely result?

Other questions that a criminal justice practitioner might ask are "Is it worth my job and career?" and "Is my decision legal?"

Another tool is that of "the bell, the book, and the candle." Ask yourself these questions: Do bells or warning buzzers go off as I consider my choice of actions? Does it violate any laws or codes in the statute or ordinance books? Will my decision withstand the light of day or spotlight of publicity (the candle)?[62]

In sum, all we can do is seek to make the best decisions we can and be a good person and a good justice system employee, one who is consistent and fair. We need to apply the law, the policy, the guidelines, or whatever it is we dispense in our occupation without bias or fear and to the best of our ability, being mindful along the way that others around us may have lost their moral compass and attempt to drag us down with them. To paraphrase Franklin Delano Roosevelt, "Be the best you can, wherever you are, with what you have."

In closing, it might be good to mention that ethics is important to all criminal justice students and practitioners, not only because of the moral/ethical issues and dilemmas they confront each day, but also because they have a lot of discretion with the people with whom they are involved—such as the discretion to arrest or not arrest, to charge or not charge, to punish or not punish, and even to shoot or not shoot.

IN A NUTSHELL

- Ethics involves doing what is right or correct in a professional capacity. Deontological ethics considers one's duty to act. Immanuel Kant expanded the ethics of duty by including the idea of "good will." People's actions must be guided by good intent.

- There are two types of ethics: absolute and relative. Absolute ethics has only two sides—something is either good or bad. Relative ethics is more complicated and can have varying shades of gray. What is considered ethical behavior by one person may be deemed highly unethical by someone else.

- The "principle of double effect"—also known as noble cause—refers to the commission of an unethical act in order to achieve a good outcome.

- The Knapp Commission identified two types of corrupt police officers: the "meat-eaters" and the "grass-eaters." The branch of the department and the type of assignment affect opportunities for corruption. Officers' code of silence can interfere with the efforts of police leadership to uncover police corruption.

- The Law Enforcement Code of Ethics (LECE) was adopted in 1957; recently a separate, shorter code was adopted, which is easier for officers to remember when they come face-to-face with an ethical dilemma; it is the Law Enforcement Oath of Honor.

- *Accepted lying* includes police activities intended to apprehend or entrap suspects. This type of lying is generally considered to be trickery. *Deviant lying* occurs when officers commit perjury to convict suspects or are deceptive about some activity that is illegal or unacceptable.

- There are two basic arguments *against* police acceptance of gratuities. First is the slippery slope argument, which proposes that gratuities are the first step in police corruption. In addition, when officers accept minor gifts or gratuities, they may then be obligated to provide the donors with some special service or accommodation.

- The first call for formalized standards of conduct in the legal profession came in 1906, with Roscoe Pound's speech "The Causes of Popular Dissatisfaction with the Administration of Justice." In 1924, the ABA approved the Canons of Judicial Ethics, and in 1972 the ABA approved a new Model Code of Judicial Conduct; in 1990, the same body adopted a revised model code. Nearly all states and the District of Columbia have established standards based on the code.

- In 1974, the United States Judicial Conference adopted a Code of Conduct for federal judges, and Congress over the years has enacted legislation regulating judicial conduct.

- Judges can engage in several types of abuses of judicial power, such as showing favoritism or bias, not being impartial, engaging in conflicts of interest, and being unethical in their personal conduct.

- Prosecutors and defense attorneys, too, must be legally and morally bound to ethical principles as agents of the courts.

- Federal employees are governed by the Ethics Reform Act of 1989, which addresses the receipt of gifts, financial and personal conflicts, and outside activities or employment that conflicts with their federal duties.

- Corrections personnel confront many of the same ethical dilemmas as police personnel.

- The strength of the corrections subculture correlates with the security level of a correctional facility and is strongest in maximum-security institutions.

- The ethical decision-making process can assist criminal justice practitioners in analyzing and working through an ethical quandary.

SAGE edge™   Review key terms with eFlashcards. ◄

KEY
TERMS
•••• & ••••
CONCEPTS

SAGE edge™   Test your understanding of chapter content. Take the practice quiz. ◄

REVIEW
QUESTIONS
?

1. How would you define *ethics*?

2. What are examples of relative and absolute ethics?

3. What specific examples of legitimate ethical dilemmas arise with police, courts, and corrections practitioners in the course of their work?

4. How would you describe the codes and canons of ethics that exist in police departments, courts, and corrections? What elements do they have in common?

5. How does the principle of double effect pose problems for criminal justice and society?

6. Why was the Law Enforcement Oath of Honor developed recently, and how does it differ from the Code of Ethics?

7. What constitutes police corruption? What are its types, and what are the most difficult ethical dilemmas presented in this chapter? Consider the issues presented in each.

8. Do you believe criminal justice employees should be allowed to accept minor gratuities? Explain your reasoning.

9. In what ways can judges, defense attorneys, and prosecutors engage in unethical behaviors?

10. What forms of behavior by correctional officers in prisons or jails may be unethical?

11. What are the steps of the ethical decision-making process?

12. What are some of the ethics "tests" for criminal justice students?

LEARN BY DOING

Following are several brief case studies (based on real events) involving criminal justice employees. Having read this chapter's materials, determine for each case the ethical dilemmas involved and what you believe is the appropriate outcome.

1. You are sitting next to a police officer in a restaurant. When the officer attempts to pay for the meal, the waiter says, "Your money is no good here. An officer just visited my son's school and made quite an impression. Plus, I feel safer having cops around." Again the officer offers to pay, but the waiter refuses to accept payment. The police department has a policy prohibiting the acceptance of free meals or gifts.

2. A municipal court judge borrows money from court employees, publicly endorses and campaigns for a candidate for judicial office, conducts personal business from chambers (displaying and selling antiques), directs other court employees to perform personal errands for him during court hours, suggests that persons appearing before him contribute to certain charities in lieu of paying fines, and uses court employees to perform translating services at his mother's nursery business.

3. A judge often makes inappropriate sidebar comments and uses sexist remarks or jokes in court. For example, a woman was assaulted by her husband who beat her with a telephone; from the bench the judge said, "What's wrong with that? You've got to keep her in line once in a while." He begins to address female lawyers in a demeaning manner, using such terms as *sweetie, little lady lawyer,* and *pretty eyes.*[61]

4. (a) An associate warden and "rising star" in the local prison system has just been stopped and arrested for driving while intoxicated in his personal vehicle and while off-duty. There are no damages or injuries involved, he is very remorseful, and he has just been released from jail. His wife calls you, the warden, pleading for you to allow him to keep his job. (b) One week later, this same associate warden stops at a local convenience store after work; as he leaves the store, a clerk stops him and summons the police—the individual has just been caught shoplifting a package of cigarettes. You have just been informed of this latest arrest.

STUDY SITE

⑤SAGE edge™

Review → Practice → Improve

Sharpen your skills with **SAGE edge** at **edge.sagepub.com/peak2e**

SAGE edge for students provides a personalized approach to help you accomplish your coursework goals in an easy-to-use learning environment. Access the videos, audio clips, quizzes, and SAGE journal articles that are noted in this chapter.

PRACTICE AND APPLY WHAT YOU'VE LEARNED

▶ edge.sagepub.com/peak2e

$SAGE edge™

THINK YOU'VE MASTERED THE CONTENT?

Check your comprehension on the study site with:

- An online **action plan** that includes tips and feedback on progress through the course and materials, allowing you to individualize your learning experience

- **Chapter summaries with learning objectives** that reinforce the key concepts in each chapter

PART II

THE POLICE

This part consists of four chapters. **Chapter 5** discusses the organization and operation of selected federal law enforcement agencies as well as the roles and operations of state and local (municipal police and county sheriffs) agencies. Included are discussions of the English and colonial roots of policing, the three eras of policing after arrival in the United States, and brief considerations of INTERPOL and private police (security).

Chapter 6 focuses on the kinds of work that police do; after looking at their recruitment and training, considered next are the patrol and investigative functions, to include the dangers of the job, the traffic function, and the use of police discretion, as well as the work of criminal investigators.

Chapter 7 broadly examines several policing issues that exist today: use of force, corruption, civil liability, stress, some police technologies, and women and minorities in the field.

Chapter 8 examines the constitutional rights of the accused as well as limitations placed on the police under the Fourth, Fifth, and Sixth Amendments; the focus is on arrest, search and seizure, the right to remain silent, and the right to counsel.

CHAPTER 05

POLICE ORGANIZATION
Structure and Functions

LEARNING OBJECTIVES

As a result of reading this chapter, you will be able to:

1 Describe how policing began in England, to include the four major police-related offices that evolved and came to America

2 Discuss the three eras of policing and August Vollmer's major contributions to advancing early policing

3 Explain the duties and functions of selected federal law enforcement agencies, the departments into which they are organized, and the basic qualifications and working conditions for a career in these agencies

4 Delineate the various types of specialized functions that are found in state law enforcement agencies

5 Distinguish between, and diagram, the functions of municipal police and county sheriff's agencies

6 Explain how and why private policing was developed, and the contemporary purposes and issues of the private police

ASSESS YOUR AWARENESS

Test your knowledge of police structure and functions by responding to the following nine true-false items; check your answers after reading this chapter's materials.

1 The four primary criminal justice officials of early England—sheriff, constable, coroner, and justice of the peace—remain in existence today.

2 The "architect" and "crib" of policing—the person and agency where most initial practices were developed—were J. Edgar Hoover, in the Philadelphia Police Department.

3 The creation of the Department of Homeland Security in 2002 (and the concurrent reorganization of several major federal law enforcement departments and agencies) was the most significant transformation of the U.S. government in over a half-century.

4 Full-time professional policing, as it is generally known today, began in the early 1900s in New York City.

5 The patrol function may be said to represent the backbone of policing.

6 State law enforcement agencies typically perform only one function: patrolling state highways.

7 INTERPOL is the oldest, best-known, and probably only truly international crime-fighting organization.

8 The officers of the federal Transportation Security Administration are not armed (except for air marshals) and do not possess law enforcement authority.

9 The Central Intelligence Agency (CIA) is a part of, and reports to, the U.S. Department of Homeland Security.

We are born in organizations, educated by organizations, and most of us spend much of our lives working for organizations. We spend much of our leisure time paying, playing, and praying in organizations. Most of us will die in an organization, and when the time comes for burial, the largest organization of all—the state—must grant official permission.

—Amitai Etzioni

<< Answers can be found on page 424.

©MICHAEL REYNOLDS/epa/Corbis

The police have always been paramilitary in nature. However, many people are concerned about what is perceived as the excessive militarization, as seen in several communities in the aftermath of officer-involved shootings.

In a recent five-year period, the federal government provided state and local law enforcement agencies with $18 billion worth of tactical military vehicles and weapons—equipment that was recently blamed for stoking tensions between protesters and authorities in Ferguson, Missouri (discussed in Chapter 7). In total, the federal government provided about 460,000 military-grade items. A recent White House report noted the overall lack of police training in using the equipment and observed that a lack of oversight with such programs can "facilitate excessive uses of force and serve as a highly visible barrier between police and the communities they serve."[1] The police have always been paramilitary, with ranks, uniforms, chain of command, and so on. But many people believe it is not only dehumanizing for the police officers themselves (who need to be able to meld with the public under the current community policing era), but can also lead to abuse of power and misconduct. However, a competing argument is that there may not be alternative organizational structures available to the police, particularly during critical incidents when chain of command and rank are very important. So as you read this chapter, consider the extent to which you believe the police should be militarized; whether there should be federal, state, and local law enforcement collaboration in crime control efforts; and consider the pros and cons of having a single, national police force (as is found in many other countries).

INTRODUCTION

How did the police come into being? How are they "designed" and organized to accomplish their mission? These are legitimate questions.

This chapter's primary aims are (1) to look at the early development of policing and (2) to inform the reader about the role and functions of contemporary federal, state, and local agencies, as well as the private police.

The chapter begins with a brief history of the evolution of four primary criminal justice officers—sheriff, constable, coroner, and justice of the peace—from their roots in early England to their coming to America. Following is an overview of the three eras of policing in the United States, and the events and shortcomings that were a part of the first two eras, thus leading to today's *community era*. Discussed next are the structures and functions of selected major federal law enforcement agencies and **organizations** that compose the Department of Homeland Security and Department of Justice (as well as general information for related careers). After a discussion of the primary duties of state-level law enforcement organizations, next is a review of local law enforcement—municipal police and county sheriff's agencies. Then brief examinations are provided of the world's premier international crime-fighting organization, INTERPOL, as well as of private policing.

Organization: an entity of two or more people who cooperate to achieve an objective(s).

ENGLISH AND COLONIAL ROOTS: AN OVERVIEW

All four of the primary criminal justice officials of early England—sheriff, constable, coroner, and justice of the peace—either still exist or existed until recently in the United States. Accordingly, it is important to grasp a basic understanding of these offices, including their early functions in England and, later, in America.

Sheriff

The word **sheriff** is derived from *shire-reeve*—*shire* meaning "county" and *reeve* meaning "agent of the king." The shire-reeve appeared in England before the Norman Conquest of 1066. His job was to maintain law and order in the tithings (groupings of ten households). At the present time in England, a sheriff's only duties are to act as an officer of the court, to summon juries, and to enforce civil judgments.[2]

The first sheriffs in America appeared in the early colonial period. Today, the American sheriff remains the basic source of rural crime control.

Sheriff's offices are discussed more later.

Constable

Like the sheriff, the **constable** can be traced back to Anglo-Saxon times. The office began during the reign of Edward I, when every parish or township had a constable. As the county militia turned more and more to matters of defense, only the constable pursued felons. Hence the ancient custom of citizens raising a loud "hue and cry" and joining in pursuit of criminals lapsed into disuse. The constable had a variety of duties, including collecting taxes, supervising highways, and serving as magistrate. The office soon became subject to election and was conferred upon local men of prominence. However, the creation of the office of justice of the peace around 1200 quickly changed this trend forever; soon the constable was limited to making arrests only with warrants issued by a justice of the peace. As a result, the office, deprived of social and civic prestige, was no longer attractive. It carried no salary, and the duties were often dangerous.[3] In the American colonies, the position fell into disfavor largely because most constables were untrained and believed to be wholly inadequate as officials of the law.[4]

Coroner

The office of **coroner** has been used to fulfill many different roles throughout its history and has changed steadily over the centuries since it began functioning by the end of the 12th century. From the beginning, the coroner was elected; his duties included oversight of the interests of the Crown, including criminal matters. In felony cases, the coroner could conduct a preliminary hearing, and the sheriff often came to the coroner's court to preside over the coroner's jury. This "coroner's inquest" determined the cause of death and the party responsible for it. Initially, coroners were given no compensation, yet they were elected for life. Soon, however, they were given the right to charge fees for their work.[5] The office was slow in gaining recognition in America, as many of the coroners' duties were already being performed by the sheriffs and justices of the peace. By 1933, the coroner was recognized as a separate office in two-thirds of the states. By then, however, the office had been stripped of many of its original functions. Today, in many states, the coroner legally serves as sheriff when the elected sheriff is disabled or disqualified. However, since the early part of the 21st century, the coroner has basically performed a single function: determining the causes of all deaths by violence or under suspicious circumstances.[6]

Sheriff: the chief law enforcement officer of a county, typically elected and frequently operating the jail as well as law enforcement functions.

Constable: in England, favored noblemen who were forerunners of modern-day U.S. criminal justice functionaries; largely disappearing in the United States by the 1970s.

Coroner: an early English court officer; today one (usually a physician) in the United States whose duty it is to determine cause of death.

PRACTITIONER'S PERSPECTIVE

SHERIFF

Name: Scott R. Jones

Current Position: Sheriff

City, State: Sacramento County, California

College Attended/ Academic Major: Juris doctorate (J.D.) from Lincoln Law School, Sacramento, California; bachelor of science degree in criminal justice from California State University, Sacramento

How long have you been a practitioner in this criminal justice position? I was first elected as sheriff in November 2010.

My primary duties and responsibilities in this position: Chief executive officer of a very large sheriff's department with nearly 1,300 sworn officers, 2,000 total employees, and an annual budget over $400 million. My agency also provides first-responder public safety to more than 580,000 persons, while also overseeing corrections and other county-wide services for the entire county of 1.4 million people.

My three greatest challenges in this administrative role: (1) trying to bring about change in an agency having a large, decentralized, and diverse workforce; (2) creating "growth" without utilizing additional resources; (3) looking internally for growth opportunities through better technologies, strategies, deployment of resources, and partnerships; and (4) Trying to be available to all the myriad of stakeholders in the community, with limited time to do so.

Personal qualities/characteristics that have proven most helpful to me in this position: First, the ability to seek input on decisions when possible, while being able to make decisions quickly and decisively when necessary; having a diminished ego; recognizing as a personal mantra that "there is no best, only better"; and having a vision and striving for innovation, while eschewing the status quo.

Personal accomplishments during my administrative career about which I am most proud: Creating the first dedicated youth services unit in the history of the organization, to better foster early relationships with our youth; creating an annual strategic planning process that establishes our priorities year by year, being the primary impetus for driving our department forward despite external budgetary and other types of challenges; creating a multi-jurisdictional team to combat youth and gang violence that is truly intelligence-led and unique in U.S. law enforcement; protecting our employees from layoffs and rehiring all personnel who were laid off during our downsizing; and creating and maintaining an air of transparency and trust for our department with the public and the media.

My advice to someone either wishing to study, or now studying, criminal justice and wanting to become a practitioner in this career: [Do] not be too concerned with where you want your agency to be in the long-term; instead, focus on where you and the agency are at present, and base your decisions and guide your actions on how best to accomplish your current role, not some future role. Never be satisfied that anything you do or see is the best it can be; once you adopt a mindset that ANYTHING can be improved, you'll be surprised at the vision that comes from yourself AND others. Avoid having an oversized ego about who or what you are; remember that you are the same person now that you were before you became an organizational leader. Finally, always be human; you are not dealing with automatons or robots, but rather human beings with their own limitations, challenges, motivations, priorities, etc.

Justice of the Peace

Justice of the peace (JP): a minor justice official who oversees lesser criminal trials; one of the early English judicial functionaries.

The **justice of the peace (JP)** can be traced back as far as 1195 in England. Early JPs were wealthy landholders. The duties of JPs eventually included the granting of bail to felons, which led to corruption and criticism as the justices bailed out people who clearly should not have been released into the community. By the 16th century, the office came under criticism again because of the caliber of the people holding it (wealthy landowners who bought their way into office).[7] By the early 20th century, England had abolished the property-holding requirement, and many of the medieval functions of the JP's office were removed. Thereafter, the office possessed strictly extensive criminal jurisdiction but no civil jurisdiction whatsoever. This contrasts with the American system, which gives JPs limited jurisdiction in both criminal and civil cases. By 1930, the office had constitutional status in all of the states. JPs have long been allowed to collect fees for their services. As in England, it is typically not necessary to hold a law degree or to have pursued legal studies in order to be a JP in the United States.[8]

Police Reform in England, 1829

In England, after the end of the Napoleonic Wars in 1815, workers protested against new machines, food riots, and an ongoing increase in crime. The British army, traditionally used to disperse rioters, was becoming less effective as people began resisting its commands. In 1822, England's ruling party, the Tories, moved to consider new alternatives. The prime minister appointed Sir Robert Peel to establish a police force to combat the problems. Peel, a wealthy member of Parliament,[9] finally succeeded in 1829 when Parliament passed the Metropolitan Police Act. The London police are nicknamed "bobbies" after Sir Robert Peel.[10] Peel's remark that "the police are the public, and the public are the police" emphasized his belief that the police are first and foremost members of the larger society.[11]

Sir Robert Peel's "bobbies" were established in London in 1829.

POLICING COMES TO THE UNITED STATES

The following section provides an overview of the three eras of U.S. policing—political, reform, and community—that were shaped and defined by the varying goals and philosophies of each over time.

Video: Changes in law

The Political Era, 1840s–1930s

In 1844, the New York state legislature passed a law establishing a full-time preventive police force for New York City. However, this new body came into being in a very different form than in Europe. The American version, as begun in New York City, was deliberately placed under the control of the city government and city politicians. The American plan required that each ward in the city be a separate patrol district, unlike the European model, which divided the districts along the lines of criminal activity. The process for selecting officers was also different. The mayor chose the recruits from a list of names submitted by the aldermen and tax assessors of each ward; the mayor then submitted his choices to the city council for approval. This system resulted in most of the power over the police going to the ward aldermen, who were seldom concerned about selecting the best people for the job. Instead, the system allowed and even encouraged political patronage and rewards for friends.[12]

Video: A history of policing in America

This was the **political era** of policing, from the 1840s to the 1930s. Politics were played to such an extent that even nonranking patrol officers used political backers to obtain promotions, desired assignments, and transfers.

Police corruption also surfaced at this time. Corrupt officers wanted beats close to the gamblers, saloonkeepers, madams, and pimps—people who could not operate if the officers were "untouchable" or "100 percent coppers."[13] Political pull for corrupt

Political era: from the 1840s to the 1930s, the period of time when police were tied closely to politics and politicians, dependent on them for being hired, promoted, and assignments—all of which raised the potential for corruption.

officers could work for or against them; the officer who incurred the wrath of his superiors could be transferred to the outposts, where he would have no chance for financial advancement.

Still, it did not take long for other cities to adopt the general model of the New York City police force. New Orleans and Cincinnati adopted plans for a new police force in 1852, Boston and Philadelphia followed in 1854, Chicago in 1855, and Baltimore and Newark in 1857.[14] By 1880, virtually every major American city had a police force based on Peel's model.

The Reform Era, 1930s–1980s

During the early 20th century, reformers sought to reject political involvement by the police, and civil service systems were created to eliminate patronage and ward influences in hiring and firing police officers. In some cities, officers were not permitted to live in the same beat they patrolled in order to isolate them as completely as possible from political influences.[15] However, policing also became a matter viewed as best left to the discretion of police executives. Any noncrime activities required of police were considered "social work." The **reform era** (also termed the professional era) of policing would soon be in full bloom.

The policing career of August Vollmer has been established as a major factor in the shaping and development of police professionalism, or the reform era (see Figure 5.1). In April 1905, at age 29, Vollmer became the town marshal in Berkeley, California; as indicated earlier, this was a time when police departments were notorious for their corruption and politics.

Vollmer commanded a force of only 3 deputies; his first act as town marshal was to request an increase in his force from 3 to 12 deputies in order to form day and night patrols.[16] Obtaining that, he soon won national publicity for being the first chief to order his men to patrol on bicycles (his research demonstrated that officers on bicycles would be able to respond three times more quickly to calls for service than men on foot). Vollmer then persuaded the Berkeley City Council to purchase a system of red lights. The lights, hung at each street intersection, served as an emergency notification system for police officers—the first such signal system in the country.[17]

In 1906, Vollmer began to question the suspects he arrested, finding that nearly all criminals used their own peculiar method of operation, or modus operandi. In 1907, he sought the advice of a professor of biology at the University of California, becoming convinced of the value of scientific knowledge in criminal investigation.[18]

Vollmer's most daring innovation, however, came in 1908 with the idea of a formal police school that drew on the expertise of university professors and included courses on police methods and procedures, fingerprinting, first aid, criminal law, anthropometry, photography, and public health. In 1916, he persuaded a professor of pharmacology and bacteriology to become a full-time criminalist supervising the department's criminal investigation laboratory. By 1917, Vollmer had his entire patrol force operating out of automobiles; it was the first completely mobile patrol force in the country.[19]

In 1918, to improve the quality of police recruits in his department, Vollmer began to hire college students as part-time officers and to administer a set of intelligence, psychiatric, and neurological tests to all applicants (out of this group of "college cops" came several outstanding and influential police leaders across the United States). Finally, in 1921, in addition to experimenting with the lie

Reform era: also the professional era, from the 1930s to 1980s, when police sought to extricate themselves from the shackles of politicians, and leading to the crime-fighter era—with greater emphases being placed on *numbers*—arrests, citations, response times, and so on.

©Bettmann/CORBIS

Chief August Vollmer developed many "firsts" in the Berkley, California, police department during the professional (reform) era of policing.

detector, two of Vollmer's officers installed a crystal set and earphones in a Model T touring car, thus creating the first radio car.[20]

The crime-fighter image gained popularity under the reform model of policing, when officers were to remain in their "rolling fortresses," going from one call to the next with all due haste. Much of police work was driven by *numbers*—numbers of arrests and calls for service, response time to calls for service, numbers of tickets written and miles driven by a patrol officer during a duty shift, and so on. For many people, like Los Angeles Chief of Police William Parker, the police were the "thin blue line," protecting society from barbarism. He viewed urban society as a jungle, needing the restraining hand of the police; the police had to enforce the law without fear or favor. Parker opposed any restrictions on police methods. The law, he believed, should give the police wide latitude to use wiretaps and to conduct search and seizure.[21]

The Community Era, 1980s–Present

Today, policing is in the **community era**, practicing community policing and problem solving. This strategy was born because of the problems that overwhelmed the reform era, beginning in the 1960s. During the reform era, officers had little long-term effect in dealing with crime and disorder; they were neither trained nor encouraged to consider the underlying causes of problems on their beats.[22]

In addition, several studies struck at the very heart of traditional police methods. For example, it was learned that response time had very little to do with whether or not an arrest was made

FIGURE 5.1 The Crib of Modern Law Enforcement: August Vollmer and the Berkeley Police Department

1905 — Vollmer is elected Berkeley town marshal.

1906 — Trustees create detective rank. Vollmer initiates a red light signal system to reach beat officers from headquarters; telephones are installed in boxes. A police records system is created.

1908 — Two motorcycles are added to the department. Vollmer begins a police school.
©Hulton-Deutsch Collection/CORBIS

1909 — Trustees approve the appointment of a Bertillon expert and the purchase of fingerprinting equipment. A modus operandi file is created, modeled on the British system.

1911 — All patrol officers are using bicycles.

1914 — Three privately owned autos are authorized for patrol use.

1915 — A central office is established for police reports.

1916 — Vollmer urges Congress to establish a national fingerprint bureau (later created by the FBI in Washington, D.C.), begins annual lectures on police procedures, and persuades a biochemist to install and direct a crime laboratory at police headquarters.

1917 — Vollmer has the first completely motorized force; officers furnish their own automobiles. Vollmer recruits college students for part-time police jobs.
©Corbis

1918 — Entrance examinations are initiated to measure the mental, physical, and emotional fitness of recruits; a part-time police psychiatrist is employed.

1919 — Vollmer begins testing delinquents and using psychology to anticipate criminal behavior. He implements a juvenile program to reduce child delinquency.

1921 — Vollmer guides the development of the first lie detector and begins developing radio communications between patrol cars, handwriting analysis, and use of business machine equipment (a Hollerith tabulator).
©Bettmann/CORBIS

at the scene; detectives were greatly overrated in their ability to solve crimes;[23] less than 50 percent of an officer's time was committed to calls for service (CFS); and of those calls handled, over 80 percent were noncriminal incidents.[24] As a result, a new "common wisdom" of policing came into being. The police were trained to work with the community to solve problems by looking at their underlying causes and developing tailored responses to them. Community policing and problem solving are discussed more thoroughly in Chapter 6.

Community era: beginning in about 1980, a time when the police retrained to work with the community to solve problems by looking at their underlying causes and developing tailored responses to them.

TABLE 5.1 Federal Law Enforcement Agencies

Department of Homeland Security

- Citizenship and Immigration Services
- Customs and Border Protection (CBP)
- Immigration and Customs Enforcement (ICE)
- Secret Service
- Transportation Security Administration (Air Marshals)
- United States Coast Guard

Department of Justice

- Federal Bureau of Investigation (FBI)
- Bureau of Alcohol, Tobacco, Firearms and Explosives (ATF)
- United States Marshals Service
- Drug Enforcement Administration

Department of the Interior

- Bureau of Safety and Environmental Enforcement
- National Park Service
- United States Fish and Wildlife Service

Department of Agriculture

- United States Forest Service

Federal law enforcement agencies: federal organizations that, for example, are charged with protecting the homeland (DHS); investigating crimes (FBI) and enforcing particular laws, such as those pertaining to drugs (DEA) or alcohol/tobacco/firearms/explosives (ATF); and guarding the courts and transporting prisoners (USMS).

FEDERAL LAW ENFORCEMENT

Agencies and Employment in General: What Preapplicants Need to Know

For those aspiring to a career in a federal law enforcement agency, it would be helpful to know about the basic organization, kinds of qualifications, job requirements, benefits, and potentially undesirable elements of **federal law enforcement agencies** and positions.

Federal law enforcement jobs are organized under a few, centralized agencies (see Table 5.1).[25] Most of these agencies are found within the Department of Homeland Security and the Department of Justice. Note that the Central Intelligence Agency (CIA) works as an independent agency.

In addition to the agencies listed in Table 5.1, a number of other federal agencies employ sworn, armed enforcement personnel. Table 5.2 shows many of those agencies and the numbers of sworn employees. By a wide margin, U.S. Customs and Border Protection employs the most sworn agents and officers.

Some fundamental requirements, qualifications, benefits, and working conditions are generally common to all federal law enforcement agencies. An applicant must be a U.S. citizen, have a valid driver's license, be able to pass the agency's physical abilities testing, and be at least 21 years of age (federal law requires that one not be hired after age 37, or after age 40 if a military veteran). Other typical demands for federal agencies include passing a rigorous entrance exam, interviews, and background/character investigation; working long hours; traveling from home for extended periods; carrying a firearm; relocating to duty stations throughout the United States and abroad as needed; and working undercover as requested.[26]

Agents are generally hired at a GS-07 or GS-09 level, depending on educational and skills levels. Some agencies require only a high school diploma, while others require, at a minimum, a bachelor's degree. Grade-point-average requirements can vary; a Superior

Homeland Security is actually composed of multiple law enforcement agencies, including officers performing both customs and border protection duties.

James R. Tourtellotte, U.S. Customs and Border Protection – U.S. Department of Homeland Security

TSGT STEVE FAULISI, USAF

Academic Achievement pay bonus is available to those with higher GPAs, and some agencies also provide a Foreign Language Award Program, which provides cash awards for persons qualifying. For reasons relating to travel and mobility, a Law Enforcement Availability Pay bonus is provided to agents that is an additional 25 percent of their annual base pay. Generally, uniforms and equipment are provided at no cost, and annual leave, sick leave, holiday pay, and moving expenses are generous. Some agencies prohibit employees from having visible body markings (tattoos, body art, branding) on the head, face, neck, and extremities.[27]

Some of the steps used by the FBI for hiring special agents are described in more detail later in the chapter.

Department of Homeland Security

Within one month of the terrorist attack on U.S. soil on September 11, 2001, President George W. Bush issued a proposal to create a new Department of Homeland Security (DHS)—which was established in November 2002 and became the most significant transformation of the U.S. government in over a half-century. All or parts of 22 different federal departments and agencies were combined, beginning in January 2003, and 80,000 new federal employees were immediately put to work.[28] Congress committed $32 billion toward safeguarding the nation, developing vaccines to protect against biological or chemical threats, training and equipping first responders (local police, firefighters, and medical personnel), and funding science and technology projects to counter the use of biological weapons and assess vulnerabilities. Since 2003, three-fourths of a trillion dollars has been appropriated by the federal government to support homeland security.[29] Figure 5.2 shows the current organizational structure of the DHS.

Following are brief descriptions of the major law enforcement agencies that are organizationally located within the DHS; all of them have full law enforcement authority:

• *Customs and Border Protection (CBP)* is one of the largest federal law enforcement agencies, with more than 60,000 agents. CBP is responsible for preventing terrorists and terrorist weapons from entering the United States while facilitating the flow of legitimate trade and travel. The CBP protects nearly 7,000 miles of border with Canada and Mexico and 95,000 miles of shoreline.[30]

• *Immigration and Customs Enforcement (ICE)* is the largest investigative arm of the DHS with about 12,500 sworn employees in more than 40 offices worldwide. ICE is responsible for identifying and shutting down vulnerabilities both in the nation's borders and in economic, transportation, and infrastructure security.[31] In

TABLE 5.2 Federal Agencies Employing 250 or More Full-Time Personnel With Arrest and Firearm Authority

AGENCY	NUMBER OF FULL-TIME OFFICERS
U.S. Customs and Border Protection	36,863
Federal Bureau of Prisons	16,835
Federal Bureau of Investigation	12,760
U.S. Immigration and Customs Enforcement	12,446
U.S. Secret Service	5,213
Drug Enforcement Administration	4,308
U.S. Marshals Service	3,313
Veterans Health Administration	3,128
Internal Revenue Service, Criminal Investigation	2,636
Bureau of Alcohol, Tobacco, Firearms and Explosives	2,541
U.S. Postal Inspection Service	2,288
U.S. Capitol Police	1,637
National Park Service—Rangers	1,404
Bureau of Diplomatic Security	1,049
Pentagon Force Protection Agency	725
U.S. Forest Service	644
U.S. Fish and Wildlife Service	598
National Park Service—U.S. Park Police	547
National Nuclear Security Administration	363
U.S. Mint Police	316
Amtrak Police	305
Bureau of Indian Affairs	277
Bureau of Land Management	255

Source: Adapted from U.S. Department of Justice, Bureau of Justice Statistics, Federal Law Enforcement Officers, 2008 (June 2012), p. 2.

Note: Most current data available.

FIGURE 5.2   Department of Homeland Security Organizational Structure

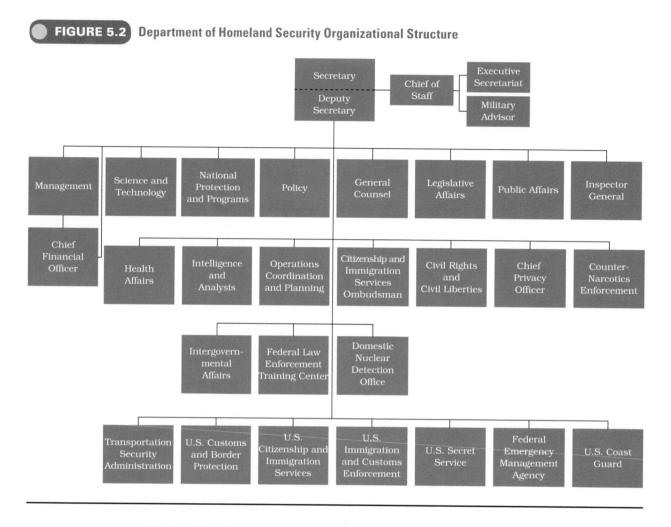

2010, a Homeland Security Investigations agency was formed within ICE to investigate financial crimes, money laundering and smuggling, intellectual property theft, cybercrimes, human trafficking and other rights violations, narcotics and weapons smuggling/trafficking, international gang activity, and international art and antiquity theft; the agency has 26 U.S. field offices as well as offices in 47 other countries.[32]

- The *Transportation Security Administration (TSA)* protects the nation's transportation systems. TSA employs 48,000 personnel at 457 airports who screen approximately two million people per day to ensure travel safety. Agents also inspect air carrier operations to the United States, assess security of airports overseas, fly air marshal missions, and train overseas security personnel.[33] TSA personnel hold the title of "officer" in name only; they neither carry guns nor have law enforcement powers (TSA's federal air marshals are armed, however).[34]

- The *Coast Guard* is the nation's leading maritime law enforcement agency; it has broad police power to enforce, or assist in enforcing, federal laws and treaties on waters under U.S. jurisdiction and other international agreements on the high seas. Its officers possess the civil authority to board any vessel subject to U.S. jurisdiction; once aboard, they can inspect, search, inquire, and arrest.[35]

- The *Secret Service* protects the president and other high-level officials and investigates counterfeiting and other financial crimes, including financial institution fraud, identity theft, computer fraud, and computer-based attacks on our nation's financial, banking, and telecommunications infrastructure. The Secret Service's Uniformed Division protects the White House complex and the vice president's residence as well as foreign embassies and missions in the Washington, D.C., area. The Secret Service has agents assigned to approximately 125 offices located in cities throughout the United States and in select foreign cities.[36]

- The *Federal Protective Service* within the DHS employs about 900 law enforcement police officers, criminal investigators, security officers, and support personnel (as well as 14,000 contract security personnel) to protect buildings and critical infrastructure (e.g., power plants, dams) in the United States.[37] Because its roles and purpose are closely related to the protection of the United States against terrorism and other crimes, a discussion of **INTERPOL** is provided in the next "Investigating Further" box.

 Video: INTERPOL

INVESTIGATING FURTHER

INTERPOL

INTERPOL is the oldest, the best-known, and probably the only truly international crime-fighting organization for crimes committed on an international scale, such as drug trafficking, bank fraud, money laundering, and counterfeiting. INTERPOL agents do not patrol the globe, nor do they make arrests or engage in shootouts. They are basically intelligence gatherers who have helped many nations work together in attacking international crime since 1923.

Lyon, France, serves as the headquarters for INTERPOL's crime-fighting tasks and its 190 member countries. Today, INTERPOL has six priority crime areas: corruption, drugs and organized crime, financial and high-tech crime, fugitives, public safety and terrorism, and trafficking in human beings. It also manages a range of databases with information on names and photographs of known criminals, wanted persons, fingerprints, DNA profiles, stolen or lost travel documents, stolen motor vehicles, child sex abuse images, and stolen works of art. INTERPOL also disseminates critical crime-related data through its system of international notices. There are seven kinds of notices, of which the most well known is the Red

Notice, an international request for an individual's arrest.

INTERPOL has one cardinal rule: It deals only with common criminals; it does not become involved with political, racial, or religious matters. It has a basic three-step formula for offenses that all nations must follow for success: (1) pass laws specifying the offense is a crime, (2) prosecute offenders and cooperate in other countries' prosecutions, and (3) furnish INTERPOL with and exchange information about crime and its perpetrators. This formula could reverse the trend that is forecast for the world at present: an increasing capability by criminals for violence and destruction. The following crimes, because they are recognized as crimes by other countries, are covered by almost all U.S. treaties of extradition: murder, rape, bigamy, arson, robbery, burglary, forgery, counterfeiting, embezzlement, larceny, fraud, perjury, and kidnapping.[38]

Source: "INTERPOL: Global Crackdown on Illicit Online Pharmacies," October 4, 2012, http://www.interpol.int/news-and-media/news-media-releases/2012/PR077; also see INTERPOL, "Overview," http://www.interpol.int/about-interpol/overview.

Department of Justice

The Department of Justice is headed by the attorney general, who is appointed by the U.S. president and approved by the Senate. The president also appoints the attorney general's assistants and the U.S. attorneys for each of the judicial districts. The U.S. attorneys in each judicial district control and supervise all federal criminal prosecutions and represent the government in legal suits in which it is a party. These attorneys may appoint committees to investigate other governmental agencies or offices when questions of wrongdoing are raised or when possible violations of federal law are suspected or detected.

The Department of Justice is the official legal arm of the U.S. government. Within the Justice Department are several law enforcement organizations that investigate violations of federal laws; we discuss the Federal Bureau of Investigation; Bureau of Alcohol, Tobacco, Firearms and Explosives; Drug Enforcement Administration; and U.S. Marshals Service. Figure 5.3 shows the organizational chart for the Department of Justice.

INTERPOL: the only international crime-fighting organization, it collects intelligence information, issues alerts, and assists in capturing world criminals; it has nearly 200 member countries.

FIGURE 5.3 Department of Justice Organizational Chart

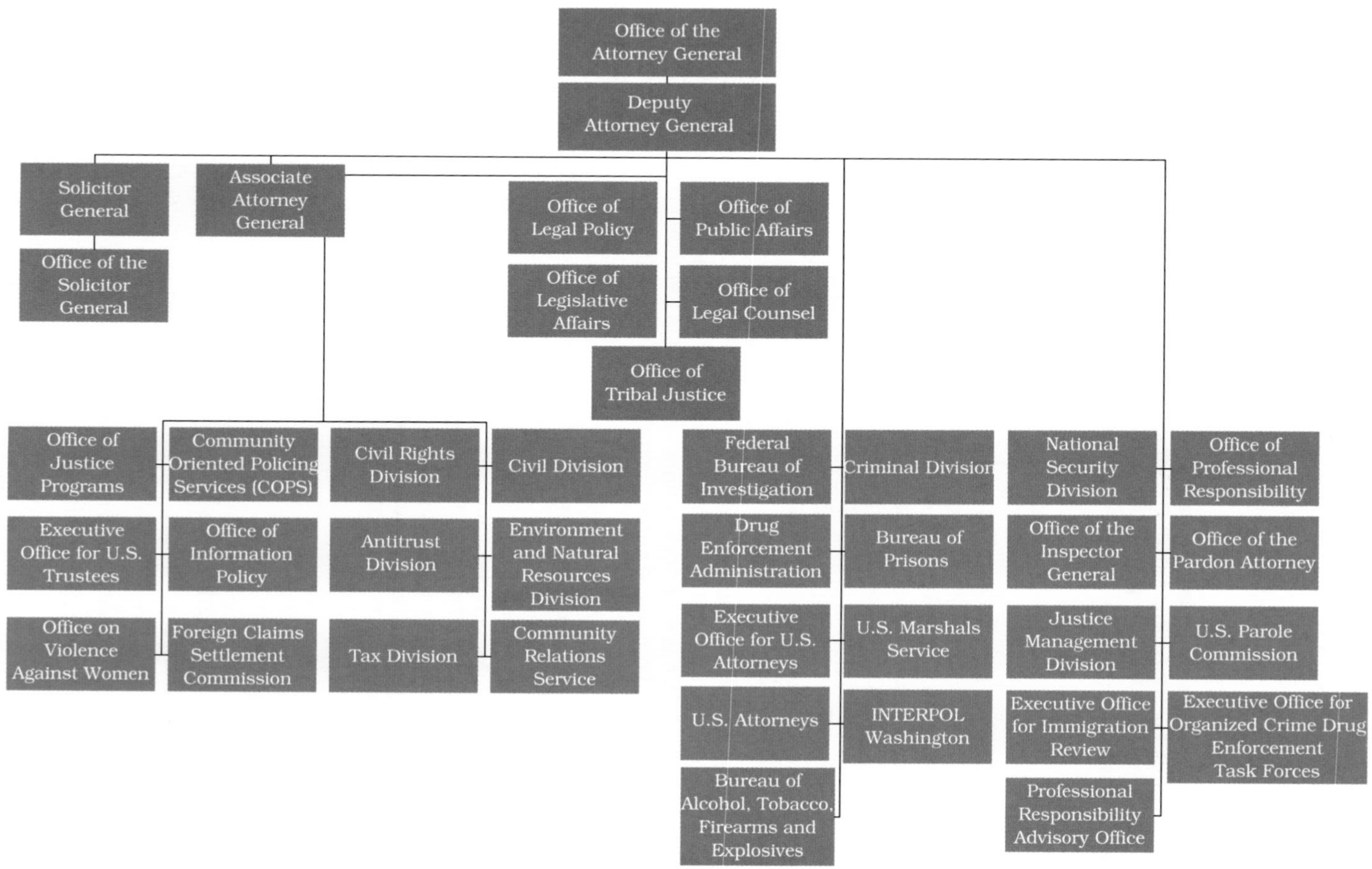

Federal Bureau of Investigation

The Federal Bureau of Investigation (FBI) was created and funded through the Department of Justice Appropriation Act of 1908. A new era was begun for the FBI in 1924 with the appointment of J. Edgar Hoover, who was determined to professionalize the organization, as director. Special agents were college graduates, preferably with degrees in law or accounting. During Hoover's tenure in office, many notorious criminals, such as Bonnie Parker, Clyde Barrow, and John Dillinger, were tracked and captured or killed.[39] The bureau's top three priority areas are as follows:[40]

1. Protect the United States from terrorist attack

2. Protect the United States against foreign intelligence operations and espionage

3. Protect the United States against cyber-based attacks and high-technology crimes

Figure 5.4 shows an organizational chart for the FBI.

To combat terrorism, the bureau can now monitor Internet sites, libraries, churches, and political organizations. In addition, under revamped guidelines, agents can attend public meetings for the purpose of preventing terrorism.[41] The FBI's laboratory examines blood,

Library of Congress Prints and Photographs Division, Harris & Ewing

J. Edgar Hoover was the first director of the Federal Bureau of Investigation and served in that capacity from 1924 until his death in 1972, at age 77.

FIGURE 5.4 **FBI Organizational Chart**

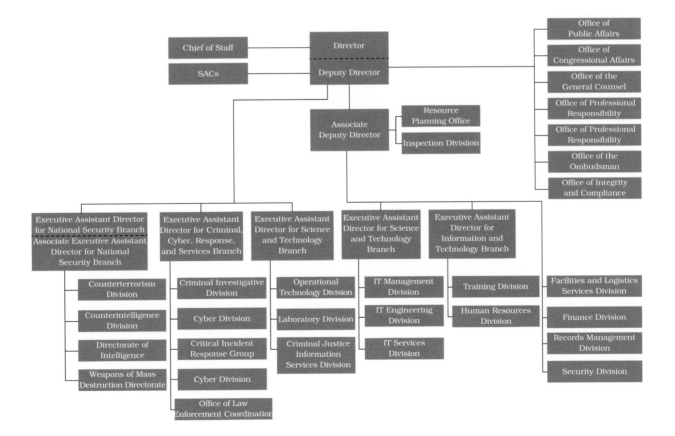

Video: FBI
Director speaks on
law enforcement
and race

hair, firearms, paint, handwriting, typewriters, and other types of evidence—at no charge to state police and local police agencies. The FBI also operates the National Crime Information Center (NCIC), through which millions of records—including wanted persons as well as stolen vehicles and all kinds of property items or any object with an identifying number—are entered.

A synopsis of the hiring process of the FBI is shown in Table 5.3. Although simplistic in its appearance, the process involves a number of individual activities by applicants and FBI personnel at each phase.

Bureau of Alcohol, Tobacco, Firearms and Explosives

The Bureau of Alcohol, Tobacco, Firearms and Explosives (ATF) originated as a unit within the Internal Revenue Service in 1862, when certain alcohol and tobacco tax statutes were created. Like the FBI and several other federal agencies, the ATF has a rich and colorful history, much of which has involved capturing bootleggers and disposing of illegal whiskey stills during Prohibition. The ATF administers the U.S. criminal code provisions concerning alcohol and tobacco smuggling and diversion. ATF also maintains a U.S. Bomb Data Center (to collect information on arson- and explosives-related incidents) and a Bomb and Arson Tracking System, which allows local, state, and other federal agencies to share information about bomb and arson cases.[42]

TABLE 5.3 The FBI Special Agent Selection System (SASS)

STAGE	DESCRIPTION	TIME FRAME
Phase I Test	Consists of three (3) sections—Biodata Inventory, Logical Reasoning, and Situational Judgment—that are designed to assess the competencies that successful Special Agents possess. Invited candidates complete the computerized test in a proctored environment. Candidates who pass Phase I are required to submit a PFT self-evaluation [see below] within 30 days of passing the test.	Candidates receive pass/fail notification within one hour of completing the test.
Meet and Greet	The Applicant Coordinator or other HR staff in your processing field office reviews online applications and evaluates applicant qualifications in person. Those deemed most competitive will be selected for Phase II testing.	Approximately 4–6 weeks after passing Phase I.
Phase II Test	Phase II consists of a structured interview conducted by a panel of three (3) Special Agents. Phase II also consists of a written exercise.	Approximately 4–6 weeks after passing Phase I. *(Note: Phase II testing occurs on an as-needed basis.)*
Conditional Appointment Offer (CAO)	Candidates who pass Phase II will receive a Conditional Appointment Offer (CAO). Actual hiring is contingent on the successful completion of the remaining SASS components (medical, background investigation, polygraph etc.).	Approximately 2 weeks after passing Phase II.
Physical Fitness Test (PFT)	The PFT assesses a candidate's physical fitness level relative to the essential tasks performed by FBI Special Agents. An official PFT will be conducted at your local field office by trained FBI personnel.	Within approximately 2 weeks of issuance of a CAO.
Background Investigation (BI)	The BI consists of a Personnel Security Interview, polygraph examination, and medical examination, followed by a thorough background investigation.	The BI process generally takes 4 months to complete.
New Agent Training (NAT)	Candidates who successfully complete the entire SASS, as described above, are eligible to be scheduled for New Agents Training at the FBI Academy in Quantico, VA. Assignment to NAT is based on the needs of the bureau.	NAT training is 20 weeks in duration.

Source: Federal Bureau of Investigation, *Candidate Information* Packet (revised 8/2011), p. 7, https://www.fbijobs.gov/1121.asp.

Some agencies operate mobile forensic crime laboratories in addition to those that are fixed.

Drug Enforcement Administration

Today's Drug Enforcement Administration (DEA) had its origin with the passage of the Harrison Narcotics Tax Act, signed into law on December 17, 1914, by President Woodrow Wilson.[43] It was created as the DEA by President Richard Nixon in July 1973 in order to create a single federal agency to coordinate and enforce the federal drug laws. In 1982, the organization was given primary responsibility for drug and narcotics enforcement, sharing this jurisdiction with the FBI.

U.S. Marshals Service

The U.S. Marshals Service (USMS) is one of the oldest federal law enforcement agencies, established under the Judiciary Act of 1789. Today, the USMS has 94 U.S. marshals, one for each federal court district. Deputy U.S. Marshals transport federal prisoners and track fugitives, while also protecting federal judges, prosecutors, and witnesses; they also conduct courthouse threat analyses and investigations, and perform security, rescue, and recovery activities for natural disasters and civil disturbances. Each district headquarters office is managed by a politically appointed U.S. marshal and a chief deputy U.S. marshal, who direct a staff of supervisors, investigators, deputy marshals, and administrative personnel. The USMS also operates the Witness Security Program. Federal witnesses are sometimes threatened by defendants or their associates; if certain criteria are met, the USMS will provide a complete change of identity for witnesses and their families, including new Social Security numbers, residences, and employment.[44]

Other Federal Agencies

Two other significant federal agencies outside of the Department of Justice with unique missions and contributions to the enforcement of the U.S. Code are the Central Intelligence Agency and the Internal Revenue Service.

Central Intelligence Agency

Although not a law enforcement agency, the Central Intelligence Agency (CIA) is of significance at the federal level to the nation's security and warrants a brief discussion. The National Security Act of 1947 established the National Security Council, which in 1949 created a subordinate organization, the CIA. Considered the most clandestine government service, the CIA participates in undercover and covert operations around the world for the purposes of managing crises and providing intelligence during the conduct of war.[45]

You Be the... JUDGE

Most European and many Asian countries have police organizations that are centralized into one national police force. On a smaller scale, centralizing or combining some police functions is not new in the United States: Since the 1960s, many police and sheriff's departments located in the same county have consolidated their units into one, thus avoiding the duplication of several expensive functions (e.g., records, communications, and jail).

The idea of a national police force is attractive to some Americans who believe that the nation is already drifting in that direction given the creation of the Department of Homeland Security and with local police devoting more and more energy to protecting the nation's borders, scanning the Internet for cybercrimes, engaging in searches and seizures at seaports, and enforcing immigration laws. They argue that the current decentralization of law enforcement into federal, state, municipal, county, and even private police (or security) entities is inefficient and fragmented, and that a single, national police force would be better able to train their personnel, have fewer laws to uphold, be more accountable, and realize considerable cost savings if eliminating the current duplication of effort.

In the other camp are those who see such centralization as a huge danger to democracy as well as personal freedom. They believe a national force would be more disengaged from the community, involve a loss of local control and oversight over the police, and be vulnerable to abuse by the central government.

1. Would implementing a single, national police force such as that found in many other countries work in the United States? Why or why not?

2. Would you have any concerns about or issues with having a single entity providing all law enforcement in the United States? If so, what are they?

Author
Video: National
Police Force

Internal Revenue Service

The Internal Revenue Service (IRS) has as its main function the monitoring and collection of federal income taxes from American individuals and businesses. Since 1919, the IRS has had a Criminal Investigation (CI) division employing "accountants with a badge." While other federal agencies also have investigative jurisdiction for money laundering and some bank secrecy act violations, the IRS is the only federal agency that can investigate potential criminal violations of the Internal Revenue Code.[46]

STATE AGENCIES

Student on
the Street Video:
County sheriffs and
traffic violations

As with federal law enforcement organizations, a variety of organizations, duties, and specialization can be found in the 50 states—although, generally, state troopers and highway patrol officers perform a lot of the same functions as their county and municipal counterparts: enforcing state statutes, investigating criminal and traffic offenses (and, by virtue of those roles, knowing and applying laws of arrest, search, and seizure), making arrests, testifying in court, communicating effectively in both oral and written contexts, using firearms and self-defense tactics proficiently, and effectively performing pursuit driving, self-defense, and lifesaving techniques until a patient can be transported to a hospital. Such agencies also maintain a wide array of special functions, including special weapons and tactics (SWAT) teams, drug units and task forces, marine and horse patrol, and so on.[47]

Patrol, Police, and Investigative Organizations

Perhaps the first distinction that might be made at the state level is between state police or highway patrol organizations and the state bureaus of investigation. Each state's statutes—and, often, the agency's name—will indicate the types of functions their agencies are authorized to perform. For example, a state's *highway patrol* division typically patrols and investigates crashes on the state highway system, while an agency that is officially named a **state police** organization typically performs a broader array of law enforcement functions in addition to those related to traffic. As an example, although the Missouri State Highway Patrol states on its website that its troopers provide assistance to motorists and "investigate highway traffic crashes and other roadway emergencies," it also states that "other responsibilities include assisting local peace officers upon request, investigating crimes, and enforcing criminal laws."[48]

Some agencies are even designated as *public safety* organizations and often encompass several agencies or divisions. For example, the Hawaii Department of Public Safety, by statute, includes a law enforcement division (with general arrest duties, narcotics division, sheriff division, and executive protection unit), a corrections division (inmate intake, incarceration, paroling authority, and industries), and a victim compensation commission.[49]

While many state troopers are, by statute, authorized to provide traffic control on their state's highways, others can conduct criminal investigations. Here, Georgia troopers investigate a shooting.

©John Spink/Atlanta Journal-Constitution via AP)

State bureaus of investigation (SBIs), as their name implies, are investigative in nature and might be considered a state's equivalent to the FBI; they investigate all manner of cases assigned to them by their state's laws and usually report to the state's attorney general. SBI investigators are plainclothes agents who usually investigate both criminal and civil cases involving the state and/or multiple jurisdictions. They also provide technical support to local agencies in the form of laboratory or record services and may be asked by the city and county agencies to assist in investigating more serious crimes (e.g., homicide).

Other Special-Purpose State Agencies

In addition to the traffic, investigative, and other units mentioned earlier, several other **special-purpose state agencies**, including police and other law enforcement organizations, have developed over time to meet particular needs. For example, many state attorney general's offices have units and investigators that investigate white-collar crimes; fraud against or by consumers, Medicare providers, and food stamp recipients; and crimes against children and seniors.[50]

States may also have limited-purpose units devoted to enforcing the following:

- Alcoholic beverage laws (regarding the distribution and sale of such beverages, monitoring bars and liquor stores, and so on)

- Fish and game laws (relating to hunting and fishing, to ensure that persons who engage in these activities have proper licenses and do not poach, hunt, or fish out of season, exceed their limit, and so on)

- State statutes and local ordinances on college and university campuses

- Agricultural laws, to include cattle brand inspection and enforcement

State police: a state agency responsible for highway patrol and other duties as delineated in the state's statutes; some states require their police to investigate crimes against persons and property.

State bureau of investigation: a state agency that is responsible for enforcing state highway laws and investigating crimes involving state statutes; they may also be called in to assist police agencies in serious criminal matters, and often publish state crime reports.

Special-purpose state agencies: specially trained units for particular investigative needs, such as those for violations of alcoholic beverage laws, fish and game laws, organized crime, and so on.

CRIMINAL JUSTICE CHALLENGES IN INDIA

©REUTERS/Andrew Biraj

A victim of an acid attack in India.

Today, the Indian criminal justice system faces many challenges. First, public confidence in the police in investigation of crimes and maintenance of law and order is at its lowest ebb. Perhaps related to this problem is the fact that India has one of the lowest police-population ratios: 131.1 officers per 100,000 population (compared with the United Nations members' norm of 222/100,000). This low ratio may also contribute to the estimate that, according to Transparency International, about 62 percent of citizens reported paying bribes during their interactions with the police; with such understaffing, there will be less direct supervision of officers. Widespread corruption of India's police officers is also widely documented.[51]

Another unique and problematic aspect of the Indian criminal justice system involves pretrial detention of arrestees. More than two-thirds of India's inmates of local jails are awaiting trial—more than twice the global average of 32 percent. Several thousand of these detainees have been awaiting trial for more than five years. This problem also leads to overcrowding, which is known to cause inmate stress, illness, and violence.[52]

As with India's police, the nation's prosecutors, judges, and prison officials are often overworked, understaffed, and underpaid, which leads to corruption in courts and corrections. Prosecutors lack basic facilities, such as access to legal databases, research, and administrative assistants.[53]

As a result of the shortcomings in India's criminal justice system, it is unable to deal with many crimes against persons. For example, 90 percent of Indians surveyed agree that the crime of rape is a "very big problem." Furthermore, about 80 percent say the problem is growing. Three in four Indians say the country's rape laws are too lax, and they criticize the police for not aggressively investigating rape cases. As a result, the federal government has enacted legislation increasing prison terms for rapists and criminalizing voyeurism, stalking, acid attacks, and the trafficking of women.[54]

An estimated 1,000 acid attacks take place in India every year; about 80 percent of them involve young women as victims. As in many other South Asian male-dominated societies, quite often the attacks are perpetrated by jealous boyfriends.[55]

- Commercial vehicle laws, such as those federal and state laws pertaining to weights and permits of interstate carriers (i.e., tractor-trailer rigs) and ordinances applying to taxicabs

- Airport laws—in addition to TSA employees (discussed earlier), airport police provide support for the local city/county police by enforcing statutes and ordinances; patrolling (foot and vehicle); monitoring threats to people, property, and aircraft; and generally providing information and service to the traveling public.

Most of these organizations have their own training academies, but some—campus police officers and fish and game agents, for example—may attend the regular police academies that train county deputies and local police officers.

LOCAL AGENCIES: MUNICIPAL POLICE AND SHERIFF'S DEPARTMENTS

Today, Sir Robert Peel (discussed earlier in this chapter) would be amazed because there are about 17,000 general-purpose municipal police departments and county sheriff's departments in the United States.[56] The municipal agencies are composed of about 463,000 sworn full-time police officers,[57] and sheriff's offices employ about 183,000 sworn full-time deputies.[58] Next we focus on the organization and functions of these local agencies.

Basic Operations

Municipal police departments employ an average of 2.3 officers per 1,000 population; about 1 in 8 of these sworn employees is a woman, and 1 in 4 is a member of a racial or ethnic minority. For recruiting qualified personnel, 86 percent of these agencies use physical agility tests, 82 percent use written aptitude tests, and two-thirds employ personality inventories. On average, these officers receive 760 hours of recruit training in their academies. Significantly, about half of local police agencies employ fewer than 10 sworn personnel. Two-thirds of these agencies require their officers to wear protective body armor at all times while on duty; 61 percent use video cameras in patrol cars, three-fourths authorize the use of electronic control devices (such as a Taser), and more than 90 percent of agencies serving 25,000 or more residents use in-car computers. More information concerning municipal police agencies may be obtained from the Bureau of Justice Statistics.[59]

In county sheriff's departments, about 1 in 8 sworn employees is a woman, and 19 percent are members of a racial or ethnic minority. For recruiting qualified personnel, 74 percent of these agencies use physical agility tests, 68 percent use written aptitude tests, and 52 percent employ personality inventories. On average, new deputy recruits receive about 580 hours of academy training. About three-fifths of sheriff's departments employ fewer than 25 sworn personnel. Fifty-seven percent of these agencies require their officers to wear protective body armor at all times while on duty; two-thirds use video cameras in patrol cars, 79 percent authorize the use of electronic control devices (such as a Taser), and about 80 percent of agencies use in-car computers. More information concerning county sheriff's departments may be obtained from the Bureau of Justice Statistics.[60]

For those persons interested in a police career, Figure 6.1 and Table 6.1, in Chapter 6, describe the kinds of screening methods that tend to be used in hiring new officers, as well as typical topics covered in basic recruit academies.

Organization

Every police agency, no matter what its size, has an **organizational structure or chart**, which is often prominently displayed for all to see in the agency's facility—or it may not even be written down at all. Even a community with only a town marshal has an organizational structure, although the structure will be very horizontal, with the marshal performing all of the functions displayed in Figure 5.5, the basic organizational chart for a small agency.

Operations, or the line-element, personnel are engaged in active police functions in the field. They may be subdivided into primary and secondary operations elements. The patrol function—often called the backbone of policing—is the primary operational element because of its major responsibility for policing. (The patrol function is examined in Chapter 6.) In most small police agencies, patrol forces are responsible

Student on the Street Video: Police behavior and physical violence

Municipal police department: a police force that enforces laws and maintains peace within a specified city or municipality.

Organizational structure or chart: a diagram of the vertical and horizontal parts of an organization, showing its chain of command, lines of communication, division of labor, and so on.

FIGURE 5.5 A Basic Police Organizational Structure

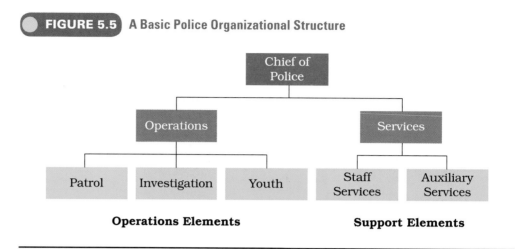

An example of a police organization's auxiliary services is the work done by crime laboratory services.

Video: Houston PD outreach

for all operational activities: providing routine patrols, conducting traffic and criminal investigations, making arrests, and functioning as generalists. The investigative and youth functions are the secondary operations elements. (The investigative function is discussed in Chapter 6, and juvenile rights in Chapter 15.) The support (or nonline) functions and activities can become quite numerous, especially in a large agency. These functions fall within two broad categories: staff (or administrative) services and auxiliary (or technical) services. The staff services usually involve personnel and include such matters as recruitment, training, promotion, planning and research, community relations, and public information services. Auxiliary services are the kinds of functions that civilians rarely see. They include jail management, property and evidence, crime laboratory services, communications, and records and identification. Many career opportunities exist for those who are interested in police-related work but who cannot or do not want to be a field officer.

Obviously, the larger the agency, the greater the need for specialization and the more vertical the organizational chart will become. With greater specialization comes the need and opportunity for officers to be assigned to different tasks, often rotating from one assignment to another after a fixed interval. For example, in a medium-sized department serving a community of 100,000 or more, it would be possible for a police officer with 10 years of police experience to have been a dog handler, a motorcycle officer, a detective, and a traffic officer while simultaneously holding a slot on the special-weapons or hostage-negotiation team.

Consider the organizational structure for a larger police organization, such as the Portland, Oregon, Police Bureau (PPB) (see Figure 5.6). This structure not only shows the various components of the organization, but also does the following:

- Apportions the workload among members and units according to a logical plan

- Ensures that lines of authority and responsibility are as definite and direct as possible

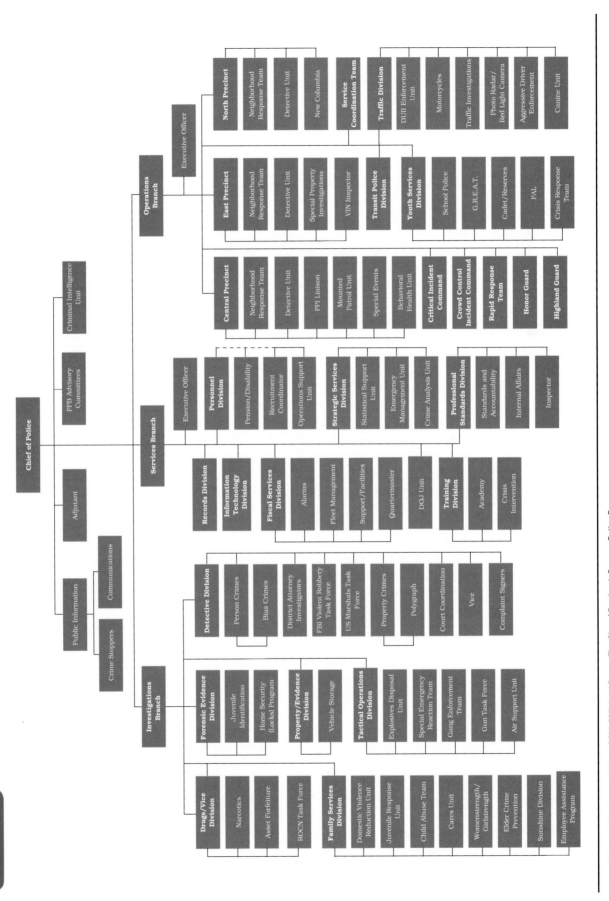

FIGURE 5.6 Portland Police Bureau Organizational Chart

Source: Printed with the permission of Chief Michael Reese, The City of Portland, Oregon, Police Bureau.

Note: DOJ = Department of Justice; DUII = driving under the influence of intoxicants; PPI = Portland Patrol Inc.

- Places responsibility and authority and, if responsibility is delegated, holds the delegator responsible

- Coordinates the efforts of members so that all will work harmoniously to accomplish the mission

In sum, this structure establishes the **chain of command** and determines lines of communication and responsibility.

ON GUARD: THE PRIVATE POLICE

SAGE Journal Article: Private security

Much has changed in society and the private security industry since 1851, when Allan Pinkerton initiated the Pinkerton National Detective Agency, specializing in railroad security. Pinkerton established the first private security contract operation in the United States. His motto was "We Never Sleep," and his logo, an open eye, was probably the genesis of the term "private eye."

Today, according to the late loss-prevention expert Saul Astor, "We are a nation of thieves"[61]—and, it might be added, a nation that needs to be protected against would-be terrorists, rapists, robbers, and other dangerous people. According to the National Crime Victimization Survey, there are about 6.1 million violent-crime victimizations and 16.8 million property-crime victimizations each year in this nation.[62] As a result, and especially since 9/11, the United States has become highly security minded concerning its computers, lotteries, celebrities, college campuses, casinos, nuclear plants, airports, shopping centers, mass transit systems, hospitals, and railroads. Such businesses, industries, and institutions have recognized the need to conscientiously protect their assets against threats of crime and other disasters—as well as the limited capabilities of the nation's full-time sworn officers and agents to protect them—and have increasingly turned to the "other police"—those of the **private police security**—for protection.

In-house security services, directly hired and controlled by the company or organization, are called **proprietary services. Contract services** are those outside firms or individuals hired by the individual or company to provide security services for a fee. The most common security services provided include contract guards, alarm services, private investigators, locksmith services, armored-car services, and security consultants.

Although some of the duties of the security officer are similar to those of the public police officer, their overall powers are entirely different. First, because security officers are not police officers, court decisions have stated that the security officer is not bound by the *Miranda* decision concerning suspects' rights. Furthermore, security officers generally possess only the same authority to effect an arrest as does the common citizen (the exact extent of citizen's arrest power varies, however, depending on the type of crime, the jurisdiction, and the status of the citizen). In most states, warrantless arrests by private citizens are allowed when a felony has been committed and reasonable grounds exist for believing that the person arrested committed it. Most states also allow citizen's arrests for misdemeanors committed in the arrester's presence.

The tasks of the private police are similar to those of their public counterparts: protecting executives and employees, tracking and forecasting security threats, monitoring alarms, preventing and detecting fraud, conducting investigations, providing crisis management and prevention, and responding to substance abuse.[63]

Still, there are concerns about the field. As one author noted, "Of those individuals involved in private security, some are uniformed, some are not; some carry guns, some are unarmed; some guard nuclear energy installations, some guard golf courses; some are trained, some are not; some have college degrees, some are virtually

Chain of command: vertical and horizontal power relations within an organization, showing how one position relates to others.

Private police/ security: all nonpublic officers, including guards, watchmen, private detectives, and investigators; they have limited powers and only the same arrest powers as regular citizens.

Proprietary services: in-house security services, whose personnel are hired, trained, and supervised by the company or organization.

Contract services: a for-profit firm or individuals hired by an individual or company to provide security services.

uneducated."[64] Studies have shown that security officer recruits often have minimal education and training; because the pay is usually quite low, the jobs often attract only those people who cannot find other jobs or who are seeking temporary work. Thus, much of the work is done by the young and the retired, and the recruitment and training of lower-level private security personnel can present a real concern.[65] Clearly, today's security officer needs to be highly trained and competent.

Another long-standing issue that concerns private police is whether or not they should be armed. In the past, much has been made about security officers who have received little or no prior training or have undergone no checks on their criminal history records but are carrying a weapon. Training is recommended for all security personnel, including 23 hours of firearms instruction and another 24 hours on general matters and proper legal training.[66]

Our society has increasingly turned to the "other police"—those of the private sector—for protection.

IN A NUTSHELL

- All four of the primary criminal justice officials of early England—sheriff, constable, coroner, and justice of the peace—either still exist or existed until recently in the United States.

- In 1829, Sir Robert Peel established professional policing as it is known today, under the Metropolitan Police Act of 1829. Later, in 1844, the New York state legislature passed a law establishing a full-time preventive police force for New York City. However, this new body took a very different form than in Europe. The U.S. version was placed under the control of the city government and city politicians, thus launching the first era of policing, the political era, from the 1840s to the 1930s.

- The reform (also known as the professional) era of policing, from the 1930s to the 1980s, sought to remove police from political control. August Vollmer was a major contributor to this era, being the architect of many developments in policing that paved the way for today's practices. Civil service systems were created, and soon the crime-fighter image was projected; much of police work was driven by *numbers*—arrests, calls for service, response time to calls for service, number of tickets written, and so on. The police were the "thin blue line," but crimes continued to increase, and the police

were becoming increasingly removed from their communities.

- The community era of policing, 1980s to present, was born because of the problems that overwhelmed the reform era. The police were trained to work with the community to solve problems by looking at their underlying causes and developing tailored responses to them.

- At the federal level, agencies of the Department of Homeland Security were formed in 2003 to combat terrorism; agencies of the Department of Justice and other federal agencies support that and other efforts as well.

- State law enforcement agencies are of two primary types: general law enforcement agencies engaged in patrol and related functions, and state bureaus of investigation.

- Today there are approximately 17,000 police agencies, each with an organizational structure divided into a number of operations and support functions.

- INTERPOL is the oldest, the best-known, and probably the only truly international crime-fighting organization for crimes committed on an international scale; its agents do not patrol the globe, nor do they make arrests or engage in shootouts. They are basically intelligence gatherers who have helped many nations work together in attacking international crime since 1923.

- The field of private policing or security is much larger than public policing, and is divided into in-house security services, called *proprietary services,* and *contract services,* where outside firms or individuals are hired by the individual or company to provide security services for a fee. Private security officers are not bound by court decisions that govern the public police, but security officers generally possess the same authority to make an arrest as a private citizen. Issues with this industry involve training, the carrying of weapons, and criminal background checks of personnel.

► Review key terms with eFlashcards. ⑤SAGE edge™

KEY TERMS & CONCEPTS

Chain of command, 128
Community era, 113
Constable, 109
Contract services, 128
Coroner, 109
Federal law enforcement
   agencies, 114
INTERPOL, 117

Justice of the peace (JP), 110
Municipal police
   department, 125
Organization, 108
Organizational
   structure or chart, 125
Political era, 111
Private police/security, 128

Proprietary services, 128
Reform era, 112
Sheriff, 109
Special-purpose
   state agencies, 123
State bureau of
   investigation, 123
State police, 123

► Test your understanding of chapter content. Take the practice quiz. ⑤SAGE edge™

REVIEW QUESTIONS

1. What were the four major police-related offices and their functions during the early English and colonial periods?

2. What are the three eras of local policing, what are August Vollmer's contributions to policing's reform era, and what primary problems of the two initial eras led to the development of the current community era?

3. What are the major agencies within the Department of Homeland Security and the Department of Justice, and what are their primary functions?

4. What general qualifications, job requirements, and benefits are involved in careers in federal law enforcement agencies?

5. How would you describe the primary differences between federal and state law enforcement agencies?

6. What functions do the Central Intelligence Agency and the Internal Revenue Service perform?

7. How does INTERPOL function, and what are its primary contributions to crime fighting?

8. What are some of the differences between municipal police agencies and county sheriff's departments?

9. Using a simple organizational structure that you have drawn, how would you describe the major functions of a local (i.e., municipal or county) police agency?

10. Why were the private police organizations developed, and what are their contemporary purposes and issues?

1. Assume that you are part of a group that is studying the creation of a national police force in the United States, such as those found in many countries around the world. All state, county, and municipal police organizations would be abolished in favor of having only this single national agency, with one governing board, one set of laws to enforce and agency policies to uphold, and standardized training and pay/benefits. Develop arguments both for and against this proposal, perhaps including the history of policing, all possible positive and negative consequences that might occur from this single entity, its political pitfalls and favor with the general public, and whether or not you would support this proposal.

2. Describe the duties of the four policing offices that originated in England (if they exist in your area): sheriff, constable, justice of the peace, and coroner.

3. You have been assigned to describe federal and state law enforcement agencies for a class presentation. Prepare a lecture outline covering the major agencies—including their functions—that compose both the Department of Justice and the Department of Homeland Security; include the complementary roles of Interpol.

$SAGE edge™

Review → Practice → Improve

Sharpen your skills with **SAGE edge** at **edge.sagepub.com/peak2e**

SAGE edge for students provides a personalized approach to help you accomplish your coursework goals in an easy-to-use learning environment. Access the videos, audio clips, quizzes, and SAGE journal articles that are noted in this chapter.

LEARNING OBJECTIVES

As a result of reading this chapter, you will be able to:

1 Explain the kinds of topics that are taught in the recruit academy and overall methods for preparing recruits for a career in policing

2 Describe the ideal traits typically sought among people who are hired into policing

3 Explain what is meant by a police working personality, including how it is developed and how it operates

4 Describe the several basic tasks and distinctive styles of patrol

5 Identify potential stressors and perils in policing

6 Discuss the nature of the police traffic function

7 Define police discretion, how and why it is allowed to function, and some of its advantages and disadvantages

8 Explain the current era of policing, the community era, and the prevailing philosophy and strategies of community policing and problem solving

9 Review the qualities, myths, and methods that involve investigative personnel

ASSESS YOUR AWARENESS

Test your current knowledge of police patrol and investigations by responding to the following seven true-false items; check your answers after reading this chapter's materials.

1 Studies show that a police officer who has a college degree is no better in terms of overall performance than one who is without a degree.

2 The terms *forensic science* and *criminalistics* are often used interchangeably, but they have quite different meanings.

3 As typically shown in movie and television portrayals, detective work is primarily action packed and involves a successful search for offenders.

4 The four basic tasks of policing that involve the public include patrolling, tracking, arresting, and appearing in court.

5 What is termed the "CSI effect" has actually helped jurors to become much more knowledgeable about law and jurisprudence, and thus widely improved the quality of justice in the United States.

6 DNA is the most sophisticated and reliable type of physical evidence.

7 Police officers, being governed by laws and procedure manuals, actually have very little discretion.

[P]roper recruitment and selection of officers is paramountly important. If police organizations cannot recruit, select, and retain quality individuals, the citizens they are sworn to serve and protect will ultimately endure substandard police service.

—Albert Antony Pearsall III and Kim Kohlhepp[1]

Murder, though it have no tongue, will speak.

—Shakespeare, *Hamlet*, Act II, Scene 2

<< Answers can be found on page 424.

Consider the following statement by Bernard Parks, former chief of the Los Angeles Police Department and an African American: "We have an issue of violent crime against jewelry salespeople. The predominant suspects are Colombians. We don't find Mexican-Americans, or blacks or other immigrants. It's a collection of several hundred Colombians who commit this crime. If you see six in a car in front of the Jewelry Mart, and they're waiting and watching people with briefcases, should we play the percentages and follow them? It's common sense."[2]

Do you believe that following, stopping, and questioning these six men would be racist in nature? Or would it represent good police work? Where does proactive policing such as this case cross the line and become racial profiling?

Police officers are largely unsupervised in the field and can often apply the law and policy to such situations as they deem necessary: to stop someone or not, to question them or not, to search or not, to arrest or cite or not, to use force or not, and so on. This exercise of discretion is nearly inevitable for several reasons: Some police options are not covered by law or policy, some laws are outdated or unpopular, the community at times demands enforcement of selected crimes, and there is simply not enough time and resources to enforce all of the laws all of the time.

As you read through this chapter concerning the work of policing—particularly the section on discretion—remember that this ability to use discretionary authority can come into play and will thus cut across all aspects of officers' duties, to include minority relations, the perception of fairness and impartiality, the application of force, and even (in the minds of some people) opportunities for corruption.

INTRODUCTION

How do I become a police officer? A detective? A criminal profiler? How do I qualify to work in forensics? Do police have to arrest everyone they see breaking the law?

These are all legitimate, oft-heard questions as posed by university students. Unfortunately, owing in large measure to Hollywood's portrayals of police work and investigations, there are many misperceptions about the field. First, the odds of one's becoming a criminal profiler are virtually nil—as are the odds of some federal agent academy trainee being brought out to help investigate a serial killer case (as was the plot in a major movie starring Jodie Foster). Second, one who wishes to work in a forensics lab must have a background in chemistry, biology, or a related natural science field (e.g., biochemistry or microbiology). Finally, to become a detective, one must typically begin as a regular officer; then, with years of training, experience, and often testing or at least an oral examination, one might be deemed worthy of being an investigator. This chapter hopes to remedy those misperceptions, at least in part, by looking at some of the primary roles and functions of the individuals who work in police organizations. Beginning with the kinds of knowledge, skills, and abilities sought at the point of their recruitment, we then consider how they are trained and eventually begin working either as officers on patrol or as criminal investigators.

First is a review of the types of persons who are sought for and hired into policing, as well as their initial training at the academy; included is a consideration of the benefits of higher education for police and how one's occupational personality is formed—the subculture of the "cop's world." The roles and tasks of the police are discussed, as is their discretionary use of authority in enforcing the law. Finally, those who investigate crimes, the detectives, are examined; included is a review of the nature of their work, some myths and attributes, and how advances in DNA have assisted in achieving their goals.

FROM CITIZEN TO PATROL OFFICER

The idea of a police subculture was first proposed by William Westley in his 1950 study of the Gary, Indiana, Police Department, where he found, among many other things, a high degree of secrecy and violence.[3] The police develop traditions, skills, and attitudes that are unique to their occupation because of their duties and responsibilities. In this section, we consider how citizens are brought into, and socialized within, the police world.

Video: The hiring process

Recruiting the Best

Recruiting an adequate pool of applicants is an extremely important facet of the police hiring process. August Vollmer, the renowned Berkeley, California, police innovator and administrator, said that law enforcement candidates should

SAGE Journal Article: Recruiting the best

> have the wisdom of Solomon, the courage of David, the patience of Job and leadership of Moses, the kindness of the Good Samaritan, the diplomacy of Lincoln, the tolerance of the Carpenter of Nazareth, and, finally, an intimate knowledge of every branch of the natural, biological and social sciences.[4]

Police officers are solitary workers, spending most of their time on the job unsupervised. At all times they must be able to make sound decisions and adjust quickly to changing situations during periods that are unpredictable and unstable, chaotic, or high-stress—all the while acting ethically and in keeping with the U.S. Constitution, their state statutes, and their agency's policy and procedures manual. For these reasons, police agencies must attempt to attract the best individuals possible.

Figure 6.1 shows the general kinds of screening and testing methods used with new police recruits in the United States. Even after a person meets the minimum

FIGURE 6.1 Local Police Officers' Selected Screening Methods in the Hiring Process, 2003 and 2007

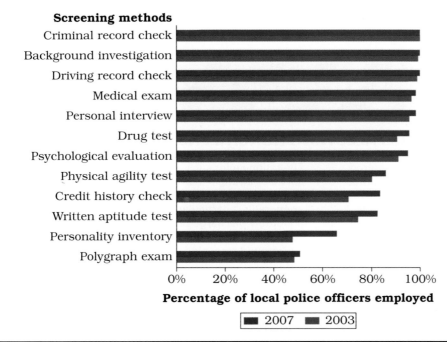

Source: Brian A. Reaves, *Local Police Departments, 2007* (Washington, D.C.: U.S. Department of Justice, Bureau of Justice Statistics, December 2010), p. 11, http://bjs.ojp.usdoj.gov/content/pub/pdf/lpd07.pdf.

*Note: Most current data available.

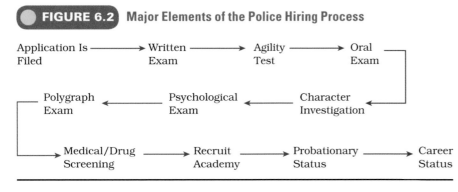

FIGURE 6.2 Major Elements of the Police Hiring Process

qualifications for being a police officer (age, education, no disqualifying criminal record), and is recruited into the testing process, much work and testing remains before he or she is ready to be sent to the streets as a police officer. This so-called hurdle process is shown in Figure 6.2. Certainly not all types of tests shown in the figure are employed by all of the 17,000 local police agencies and sheriff's offices in America; nor are these tests necessarily given in the sequence shown. Furthermore, this gamut of testing can easily require several months to complete, depending on the number and types of tests used and the ease of scheduling and performing them.

An example of an agency's hiring process is provided in the accompanying "Investigating Further" box, setting forth the components of the hiring process as used by the Kansas City, Missouri, Police Department.

Does a College Degree Matter?

To interact with an educated public, enforce the rule of law, investigate crimes, testify in court, write cogent and accurate reports, and perform the myriad other duties for which we call upon the police, one would assume that all officers must obtain a two- or four-year college degree prior to assuming the role. Such, however, is not even close to being the case. Indeed, only 1 percent of all police agencies require a minimum of a four-year degree for new officers, and fewer than 10 percent require a two-year degree.[6]

In 1973, the National Advisory Commission on Criminal Justice Standards and Goals, recognizing the need for college-educated police officers, recommended that all police officers have a four-year college education by 1982.[7] Indeed, from 1967 to 1986, every national commission that studied crime, violence, and police in America

INVESTIGATING FURTHER

CITIES, STATES, AND COUNTIES ALLOWING NONCITIZENS TO WEAR A BADGE

Although historically police agencies have required their new officers to be U.S. citizens, today a number of agencies are allowing green-card holders and legal immigrants with work permits to wear their badge.

Some agencies, such as the Chicago and Hawaii police departments, allow any immigrant with a work authorization from U.S. Citizenship and Immigration Services to become an officer. This means that even people in the country on temporary visas or who are applying for green cards can join. For other agencies, such as the Cincinnati Police Department and the Los Angeles County Sheriff's Department, officers must at least have applied for citizenship with the federal government. Still others require that officers be legal permanent residents, or green-card holders.

The rationale for such hires is clear: At a time when agencies struggle to diversify their ranks or to find people who will do the kinds of work policing requires, immigrants—particularly those who have been honorably discharged from the military in their home country and thus have already undergone a thorough background screening process—are becoming more attractive as employees.

There are some concerns about such hires, however. Some people see security risks in allowing an immigrant with a work permit to become an officer, given that the Obama administration gave hundreds of thousands of undocumented immigrants work permits. As one person put it, "We're handing over a gun and a badge to somebody whose background we don't really know a lot about."[5]

maintained that a college education could help the police to do their jobs better.[8] Obviously, the recommendations of all those commissions have gone unmet.

Abundant empirical evidence indicates that college-educated police officers are better officers. For example, compared to non-college-educated officers, college-educated officers have significantly fewer founded citizen complaints;[9] have better peer relationships;[10] are likelier to take a leadership role in the organization;[11] tend to be more flexible;[12] are less dogmatic and less authoritarian;[13] take fewer leave days, receive fewer injuries, have less injury time, have lower rates of absenteeism, use fewer sick days, and are involved in fewer traffic accidents;[14] have greater ability to analyze situations and make judicious decisions; and have a more desirable system of personal values.[15] Furthermore, college graduates are accused of negligent use of a firearm significantly less often than are officers who lack a college degree.[16]

A strong endorsement for police higher education came in 1985, when a lawsuit challenged the Dallas, Texas, Police Department's requirement that all applicants for police officer positions possess 45 credit hours and at least a C average at an accredited college or university. The Fifth Circuit Court of Appeals and, eventually, the U.S. Supreme Court upheld the educational requirement. According to the circuit court,

Many studies have indicated that college-educated persons make better officers; yet relatively few agencies require a college degree for hiring

> A significant part of a police officer's function involves his ability to function effectively as a crisis intervenor, in family fights, teen-age rumbles, bar brawls, street corner altercations, racial disturbances, riots and similar situations. Few professionals are so peculiarly charged with individual responsibilities as police officers. Mistakes of judgment could cause irreparable harm to citizens or even to the community. The educational requirement bears a manifest relationship to the position of police officer. We conclude that the district court's findings . . . are not erroneous.[17]

Finally, Norm Stamper, former police chief in Seattle, Washington, observed that not only do the degree and college credits matter, but so does

> getting up in the morning for classes or attending at night after work, reading dense texts, writing term papers, questioning professors, associating with people and ideas that force you to think, [and] taking midterms and finals. The politics of higher education, the discipline of learning *how* to learn—that was the most useful thing about higher ed.[18]

Recruit Training

Once hired into an agency, police recruits are taught a variety of subjects in **academy training** (see Table 6.1). They are taught to nurture a **"sixth sense"**: suspicion. A suspicious nature is as important to the street officer as a fine touch is to a surgeon. The officer should be able to visually recognize when something is wrong or out of the ordinary. As a Chicago Police Department bulletin stated,

> Actions, dress, or location of a person often classify him as suspicious in the mind of a police officer. Men loitering near schools, public toilets, playgrounds

Academy training: where police and corrections personnel are trained in the basic functions, laws, and skills required for their positions

"Sixth sense": in policing, the notion that an officer can "sense" or feel when something is not right, as in the way a person acts, talks, and so on.

and swimming pools may be sex perverts. Men loitering near . . . any business at closing time may be robbery suspects. Men or youths walking along looking into cars may be car thieves or looking for something to steal.[19]

Table 6.1 displays the predominant topics included in training new officers and the median length of training for each. A considerably high percentage of police agencies use physical agility tests, perform psychological evaluations, and provide educational incentive pay to officers; and municipal police officers receive about 55 additional hours of initial (i.e., academy and field) training.

TABLE 6.1 Topics Included in Basic Training of State and Local Law Enforcement Training Academies

TOPICS	PERCENTAGE OF ACADEMIES WITH TRAINING	MEDIAN NUMBER OF HOURS OF INSTRUCTION
Operations		
Report writing	100	20
Patrol	99	40
Investigations	99	40
Basic first aid/CPR	99	24
Emergency vehicle operations	97	40
Computers/information systems	58	8
Weapons/self-defense		
Self-defense	99	51
Firearms skills	98	60
Nonlethal weapons	98	12
Legal		
Criminal law	100	36
Constitutional law	98	12
History of law enforcement	84	4
Self-improvement		
Ethics and integrity	100	8
Health and fitness	96	46
Stress prevention/management	87	5
Basic foreign language	36	16
Community policing		
Cultural diversity/human relations	98	11
Basic strategies	92	8
Mediation/conflict management	88	8
Special topics		
Domestic violence	99	14
Juveniles	99	8
Domestic preparedness	88	8
Hate crimes/bias crimes	87	4

Source: Brian A. Reaves, *State and Local Law Enforcement Training Academies, 2006* (Washington, D.C.: U.S. Department of Justice, Bureau of Justice Statistics, February 2009), p. 6, http://bjs.ojp.usdoj.gov/content/pub/pdf/slleta06.pdf.

Note: Most current data available.

Police recruits undergo training in a variety of subjects during their many weeks in the academy.

INVESTIGATING FURTHER

THE POLICE HIRING PROCESS IN KANSAS CITY, MISSOURI

Following are the types of examinations and activities involved in the hiring process for the Kansas City, Missouri, Police Department (KCPD) (as well as many other police agencies). The entire process, which includes a substance abuse questionnaire (not shown), may require several months to complete.

- *Written Examination:* All applicants begin with and must take the Police Officer Selection Test (POST). A review for this exam is generally given within one month prior to the written examination, and a sample test is available upon request.

- *Physical Abilities Test:* This is an obstacle course designed to simulate challenges that could be encountered during an officer's tour of duty. Applicants must demonstrate their ability to maneuver through the course with minimal errors.

- *Preemployment Polygraph Examination:* The polygraph examination is administered by a qualified polygraph examiner and covers criminal activity, drug usage, integrity, truthfulness, and employment history.

- *Background Investigation:* The background investigation will cover pertinent facts regarding the applicant's character, his or her work history, and any criminal or traffic records.

- *Ride-Along:* To expose applicants to the actual duties performed by KCPD officers, during the background investigation, the applicant will be required to ride with an officer on a weekend for a full tour of duty during the evening or night shift.

- *Oral Board:* This interview consists of questions designed to allow the KCPD to assess an applicant's overall abilities as they relate to the field of law enforcement.

- *Psychological Examination:* This interview is conducted by a certified psychologist, after a job offer has been made.

- *Physical Examination:* Applicants undergo a complete medical and eye examination performed by a licensed physician, after a job offer has been made.

Source: Kansas City, Missouri, Police Department, "Hiring Process," http://www.kcmo.org/police/AboutUs/Departments/Administration/Human Resources/EmploymentSection/HiringProcess/index.htm.

Field Training Officer

Once the recruits leave the academy, they are not merely thrown to the streets to fend for themselves in terms of upholding the law and maintaining order. Another important part of this acquisition process is being assigned to a veteran officer for initial field instruction and observation. This veteran is sometimes called a **field training officer (FTO)**.[20] This training program provides recruits with an opportunity to make the

Field training officer (FTO): one who is to oversee and evaluate the new police officer's performance as he or she transitions from the training academy to patrolling the streets.

©AP Photo/Matt Rourke

To assist in their transition from the training academy to the street, new officers are typically assigned to work with a veteran field training officer for a period of time before being released to act on their own.

transition from the academy to the streets under the protective arm of a veteran officer. Recruits are on probationary status, typically ranging from six months to one year; their employment may be terminated immediately if their overall performance is unsatisfactory during that period.

Most FTO programs consist of three identifiable phases:

1. An introductory phase (the recruit learns agency policies and local laws)

2. Training and evaluation phases (the recruit is introduced to more complicated tasks that patrol officers confront)

3. A final phase (the FTO acts strictly as an observer and evaluator while the recruit performs all the functions of a patrol officer)[21]

Video: FTO training

The length of time rookies are assigned to FTOs will vary. A formal FTO program might require close supervision for a range of 1–12 weeks.

Most police officers also receive in-service training throughout their careers, because their states require a minimum number of hours of such training. News items, court decisions, and other relevant information can also be covered at roll call before the beginning of each shift. Short courses ranging from a few hours to several weeks are available for in-service officers through several means such as videos and nationally televised training programs.

HAVING THE "RIGHT STUFF": A WORKING PERSONALITY

Since the publication of Westley's aforementioned examination of police subculture in 1950, the notion of a police personality has become a popular area of study. In 1966, Jerome Skolnick described what he termed the working personality of the police.[22] He determined that the police role contained two important variables: danger and authority. Danger is a constant feature of police work. Police officers, constantly facing potential violence, are warned at the academy to be cautious. They are told many war stories of officers shot and killed at domestic disturbances or traffic stops. Consequently, they develop "perceptual shorthand," Skolnick said, that they use to identify certain kinds of people as "symbolic assailants"—individuals whom the officer has come to recognize as potentially violent based on their gestures, language, and attire.

It is not too difficult to identify bad police officers through their unethical or criminal behavior. But what are the traits of good officers? Dennis Nowicki, who served twice as a police chief, acknowledged that although certain characteristics form the foundation of a police officer—honesty, ethics, and moral character—no scientific formula can be used to create a highly effective officer.[23] However, he compiled a list of 12 qualities that he believes are imperative for entry-level police officers (see Table 6.2).

DEFINING THE ROLE

What are the police supposed to do? Often this question is given such oversimplified answers as "They enforce the law" or "They 'serve and protect.'"[24] But policing is much more complex, and most Americans probably do not have an accurate idea of what the police really do. In reality, the police are called on to perform an almost countless number of tasks.

One of the greatest obstacles to understanding the American police is the crime-fighter image. Because of film and media portrayals, many people believe that the role of the police is confined to the apprehension of criminals.[25] However, only about 20 percent of the police officer's typical day is devoted to fighting crime per se.[26] And, as Jerome Skolnick and David Bayley point out, the crimes that terrify Americans the

A sense of humor, the ability to communicate, and job enthusiasm even for routine duties are some of the crucial traits required for police officers to be successful.

TABLE 6.2 Traits That Make a "Good" Officer

Enthusiasm	Believing in what one is doing and going about even routine duties with a certain vigor that is almost contagious
Good communication skills	Having highly developed speaking and listening skills and the ability to interact equally well with a wealthy person or someone lower on the socioeconomic ladder
Good judgment	Having wisdom and the ability to make good analytic decisions based on an understanding of the problem
Sense of humor	Being able to laugh and smile, to help oneself cope with regular exposure to human pain and suffering
Creativity	Using creative techniques to place oneself in the mind of the criminal and accomplish legal arrests
Self-motivation	Making things happen, proactively solving difficult cases, and creating one's own luck
Knowing the job and the system	Understanding the role of a police officer, the intricacies of the justice system, and what the administration requires; using both formal and informal channels to be effective
Ego	Believing one is a good officer; having self-confidence that enables one to solve difficult crimes
Courage	Being able to meet physical and psychological challenges; thinking clearly during times of high stress; admitting when one is wrong; standing up for what is right
Understanding discretion	Enforcing the spirit of the law, not the letter of the law; not being hard-nosed, hardheaded, or hard-hearted; giving people a break; showing empathy
Tenacity	Staying focused; seeing challenges, not obstacles; viewing failure not as a setback but as an experience
A thirst for knowledge	Being aware of new laws and court decisions; always learning (from the classroom but also through informal discussions with other officers)

most—robbery, rape, burglary, and homicide—are rarely encountered by police on patrol. In their words:

> Only "Dirty Harry" has his lunch disturbed by a bank robbery in progress. Patrol officers individually make few important arrests. The "good collar" is a rare event. Cops spend most of their time passively patrolling and providing emergency services.[27]

Also, many individuals enter police work expecting it to be exciting and rewarding, as depicted on television and in the movies. Later they discover that much of their time is spent with boring, mundane, and trivial tasks—and that paperwork is seldom stimulating.

Four Basic Tasks

Video: Police functions and duties

Patrol officers may be said to perform four basic **tasks of policing:**

1. *Enforce the laws:* Although this is a primary function of the police, as we saw earlier, they actually devote a very small portion of their time to "chasing bad guys."

2. *Perform welfare tasks:* Throughout history, the police have probably done much more of this type of work than the public (or the police themselves) realize; following are some of them:

   o "Check the welfare of" kinds of calls, where someone has not been seen or heard from for some time and may be deceased, ill, missing, or in distress

   o "Be on the lookout" (BOLO) calls, where someone has wandered away from a nursing or an assisted living home, is a juvenile runaway, and so forth

   o Delivering death messages

   o Delivering blood to hospitals (particularly in more rural areas where blood banks are not available)

   o Assisting firefighters and animal control units

   o Reporting burned-out street lights or damaged traffic signs

   o Performing all manner of errands simply because they are available—locking and unlocking municipal parking lots, collecting receipts from municipal entities such as golf courses, delivering agendas to city/county commissioners, and so forth

3. *Prevent crime:* This function of police involves engaging in random patrol and providing the public with crime prevention information.

4. *Protect the innocent:* By investigating crimes, police are systematically removing innocent people from consideration as crime suspects.

Tasks of policing (four basic): enforce the law, prevent crime, protect the innocent, and perform welfare tasks.

Policing styles: James Q. Wilson argued that there are three styles of policing: watchman, legalistic, and service.

Three Distinctive Styles

James Q. Wilson also attempted to clarify what it is that the police are supposed to do; Wilson maintained that there are three distinctive **policing styles:**[28]

- The *watchman* style involves the officer as a "neighbor." Here, officers act as if order maintenance (rather than law enforcement) is their primary function. The emphasis is on using the law as a means of maintaining order rather than regulating conduct through arrests. Police ignore many common minor violations, such as traffic and juvenile offenses. These violations and so-called victimless crimes, such as gambling and prostitution, are tolerated; they will often be handled informally. Thus the individual officer has wide latitude concerning whether to enforce the letter or the spirit of the law; the emphasis is on using the law to give people what they "deserve."

- The *legalistic* style casts the officer as a "soldier." This style takes a much harsher view of law violations. Police officers issue large numbers of traffic citations, detain a high volume of

As opposed to Hollywood's portrayals, very little police work is action packed; these officers are, by their mere presence, preventing crime and assisting with crowd control at a street fair.

juvenile offenders, and act vigorously against illicit activities. Large numbers of other kinds of arrests occur as well. Chief administrators want high arrest and ticketing rates not only because violators should be punished but also because it reduces the opportunity for their officers to engage in corrupt behavior. This style of policing assumes that the purpose of the law is to punish.

Video: James Q. Wilson

- The *service* style views the officer as a "teacher." This style falls in between the watchman and legalistic styles. The police take seriously all requests for either law enforcement or order maintenance (unlike in the watchman-style department) but are less likely to respond by making an arrest or otherwise imposing formal sanctions. Police officers see their primary responsibility as protecting public order against the minor and occasional threats posed by unruly teenagers and "outsiders" (tramps, derelicts, out-of-town visitors). The citizenry expects its service-style officers to display the same qualities as its department store salespeople: They should be courteous, neat, and deferential. The police will frequently use informal sanctions instead of making arrests.

Perils of Patrol

Although several occupations—commercial fishing, logging, piloting airplanes, farming, and ranching in particular—have workers dying at much higher rates than policing,[29] police officers' lives are still rife with occupational hazards. Each year, 25 to 50 police officers die through felonious means; on average, the slain officer was in his or her late 30s, and he or she had worked in law enforcement about a dozen years. Another 50 or so officers die through accidental means.[30]

Student on the Street Video: High-risk occupations

Officers seldom know for certain whether a citizen whom they are about to confront is armed, high on drugs or alcohol, or perhaps even planning to die at the hands of the police using a technique known as "suicide by cop." This danger is heightened during the graveyard (night) shift, when patrol officers encounter burglars looking to invade homes and businesses, people who are intoxicated from a night of partying, and so on, all under cover of darkness.

SAUDI ARABIA: LITTLE TO DO ON PATROL

The police in Saudi Arabia assist with enforcing the very cruel (by Western standards) Islamic law, which is governed by the Koran and can include amputations of limbs, which are conducted in many cities and with some frequency on the Justice Square in Riyadh. Believing that public beheadings and amputations deter other prospective offenders, the police encourage people in the vicinity of the square to witness these events. When a thief's right hand is cut off in public, a string is tied to the middle finger and the hand is hung from a hook high on a streetlight pole on Justice Square for all to see. Because there is a near total absence on Saudi Arabian streets of gangs, drive-by shootings, purse snatchings, and contraband, the police patrol the streets in Chevrolets, BMWs, and Volvos, looking for minor infractions of the law.[31]

Owing to the aforementioned harsh criminal code, there is little for the Saudi police to do in terms of crime prevention or investigation. The religious police—the *Mutawin*—patrol and stroll in their white cotton robes and sandals and look, as one writer observed, like "desert nomads who have stumbled unexpectedly into the 20th century." They look for people who are improperly dressed or women who have a loose strand of hair falling across their face or who need to adjust their *tarhas* (head coverings). Around-the-clock patrols ensure that shops are closed in time for daily prayers and that only married couples are sitting in family sections of restaurants. The patrols often follow persons suspected of being involved in what is deemed immoral behavior, such as drug use, homosexuality, gambling, and begging. Teams of religious police will also destroy home satellite dishes, which bring uncensored Western television broadcasts into Saudi homes.[32]

● FIGURE 6.3 Schematic Representation of the Kansas City Preventive Patrol Experiment

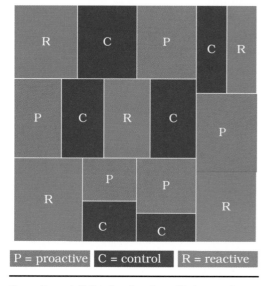

P = proactive   C = control   R = reactive

Source: George L. Kelling, Tony Pate, Duane Dieckman, and Charles E. Brown, *The Kansas City Preventative Patrol Experiment: A Summary Report* (Washington, D.C.: Police Foundation, 1974). Reprinted with permission of the Police Foundation.

A Study of Patrol Effectiveness

The best known study of patrol effectiveness, the **Kansas City Preventive Patrol Experiment**, was conducted in Kansas City, Missouri, in 1973. Researchers—wanting to know if random patrol had any significant effect on crime, police response rates to crime, or citizen fear of crime—divided the city into 15 beats, which were then categorized into 5 groups of 3 matched beats each. Each group consisted of neighborhoods that were similar in terms of population, crime characteristics, and calls for police services. In one beat area, there was no preventive patrol (police only responded to calls for service); another beat area had increased patrol activity (two or three times the usual amount of patrolling); in the third beat there was the usual level of patrol service. Citizens were interviewed and crime rates were measured during the year the experiment was conducted.

The study found that the deterrent effect of policing was not reduced by the elimination of routine patrolling; nor were citizens' fear of crime, their attitudes toward the police, or the ability of the police to respond to calls reduced. The Kansas City Preventive Patrol Experiment (depicted in Figure 6.3) indicated that the traditional assumption of "Give me more cars and more money, and we'll get there faster and fight crime" was probably not a viable argument.[33]

STRESSORS OF POLICE WORK

There is an aspect of police work that officers would prefer to ignore but that must be acknowledged: the stress induced by the job. Indeed, Sir W. S. Gilbert observed that "When constabulary duty's to be done, the policeman's lot is not a happy one."[34] But if, as the saying goes, "knowledge is power," those persons either working in the field or contemplating doing so must know of the challenges of stress and how to cope with them. The job of policing has never been easy, as many of the people they confront are armed and dangerous; but the dangers of the job have been made worse by the recent drug war as well as the "fishbowl" effect of the work, given the close scrutiny, videotaping, and accountability of today's police.

By its nature, policing carries a high potential for danger. This funeral procession escorts one of two officers shot dead in New York in December 2014.

Sources of Stress

Stress can come from a number of directions, so police officers can experience job stress as the result of a wide range of problems and situations. The four general sources of stress are (1) organizational and administrative practices, (2) the criminal justice system, (3) the public, and (4) stress intrinsic to police work itself.

Organizational and Administrative Practices

A primary source of stress is the police organization itself. Police departments typically are highly bureaucratic and possibly authoritarian in nature, which creates stress for individual officers in at least two ways. First, police departments follow strict policies and procedures, general orders, and rules and regulations that are dictated by top management. Street officers and first-line supervisors seldom have direct input into their formulation, resulting in officers feeling powerless and alienated about the decisions that directly affect their jobs. Second, these rules dictate how officers specifically perform many of their duties and responsibilities. They are created to provide officers with guidance and direction. Police officers, however, sometimes view them as mechanisms used by management to restrict their freedom and discretion or to use in order to punish them when they make incorrect decisions or errors.

Female and minority police officers also face unique problems. Because policing has traditionally been a male- and white-dominated occupation, in many agencies female and minority officers do not always have the same standing or career options as their counterparts. In addition, female officers might confront sexual harassment,[35] whereas minority officers might feel they are ostracized by people of their own race for being "traitors" against them and their neighborhoods.

The Criminal Justice System

Each component of the criminal justice system affects the other components. For example, judges have openly displayed hostile attitudes toward the police, or prosecutors have not displayed proper respect to officers, arbitrarily dismissing cases, having them appear in court during regularly scheduled days off, and advocating rulings restricting police procedures. Another example occurs when parole officers and probation officers do an inadequate job of supervising parolees, which results in their being involved in an inordinate amount of crime. The courts have the most direct impact on police officers and probably are the greatest source of stress from the criminal justice system.

Kansas City Preventive Patrol Experiment: in the early 1970s, a study of the effects of different types of patrolling on crime—patrolling as usual in one area, saturated patrol in another, and very limited patrol in a third area; the results showed no significant differences.

©JOSH EDELSON/AFP/Getty Images

Recently, incidents involving police use of force have become a flashpoint for the public. Here, citizens express their concerns at an anti-police brutality march in Oakland in January 2015.

The Public

When police officers perform community services, they also become involved in conflicts or negative situations. They arrest citizens, they write tickets, and they give citizens orders when intervening in domestic violence or disorder situations. Often, to resolve problems, they make half of the participants happy, but the other half are unhappy. The problem is that police officers develop unrealistic or inaccurate ideas about citizens as a result of their negative encounters. Officers must keep their relationship with citizens in proper perspective. This is achieved by open, straightforward discussions of public attitudes and encounters with citizens. It also means that managers must emphasize the importance of good police-public relations and of the majority of citizens supporting and respecting the police.

Stressors Intrinsic to Police Work

Police work is fraught with situations that pose physical danger to officers. Domestic violence, felonies in progress, and fight calls often require officers to physically confront suspects. It would seem that police work itself, since it includes dealing with dangerous police activities and people, would be the most stressful part of police work. Certainly traumatic incidents can require long-term follow-up support for law enforcement personnel.

Coping With Stress

If officers do not relieve the pressure of the job, they eventually may suffer heart attacks, nervous breakdowns, back problems, headaches, psychosomatic illnesses, or alcoholism. They may also experience excessive weight gain or loss; combativeness or irritability; excessive perspiration; excessive use of sick leave; excessive use of alcohol, tobacco, or drugs; marital or family disorders; inability to complete an assignment; loss of interest in work, hobbies, and people in general; more than the usual number of "accidents," including vehicular and other types; and shooting incidents. It is imperative that officers learn to manage their stress before it causes deep physical and/or emotional harm. One means is to engage in hobbies or activities that provide legitimate means of relaxing and venting. Exercise, proper nutrition, and positive lifestyle choices (such as not smoking and using alcohol only in moderation) are also essential for good health.

Police agencies need a comprehensive wellness program to assist officers in coping with stress, but if that fails or is absent, an employee assistance program (EAP) should be available to help officers to cope with alcohol and substance abuse, psychological problems such as depression, or family management problems.

THE TRAFFIC FUNCTION

No one enjoys being on the receiving end of a traffic citation, but traffic hazards (especially drunk or texting drivers and those with "road rage") pose a major problem. Thus, traffic control is part of the police role. Indeed, traffic stops account for about half (52 percent) of the contact Americans have with the police.[36] Citizens are often unhappy about having to pay a traffic fine or possibly go to court, and may verbally express their displeasure: "You should be out catching bank robbers," "I'm a taxpayer, and I pay your salary," or "I know the police chief!" Because this traffic encounter may be the citizen's one and only contact with a police officer, the officer's display of a professional and courteous demeanor may well have long-term significance for community policing, and strict traffic enforcement policies can also negatively impact police-community relations.[37]

PRACTITIONER'S PERSPECTIVE

PATROL OFFICER

Name: Tony Moore

Current Position: Drug Interdiction Task Force Detective

City, State: Reno, Nevada

College Attended/Academic Major: Bachelor of arts in criminal justice from the University of Nevada

Most significant career achievement: Selected by peers for the distinguished rank of Master Police Officer

How long have you been a practitioner in this criminal justice position? 17 years (6 years as patrol officer, 10 years as gang officer and detective, 1 year as drug interdiction detective)

My primary duties and responsibilities as a practitioner in this position: Generally, providing safety for the public. As a citizen, I expect the same from my police. Also, the patrol officer is the first responder to every emergency, ranging from something very minor (such as a stalled vehicle) to rescuing children and adults from violent attacks, in-progress felonies, or burning buildings and vehicles.

With every response or arrest comes responsibility for making the right decisions. The patrol officer must know applicable laws and procedures so the correct actions are taken and decisions made. Bad decisions or inappropriate actions can lead to civil liability, departmental discipline, or the officer or another person being injured or killed.

Proactive policing is another aspect of the patrol officer's role. The officer must address problems and crime trends in his or her area, including traffic enforcement, drug activity, warrant arrests, gang activity, or investigations that extend beyond merely taking a crime report.

In addition, problem solving is the patrol officer's responsibility. Arrests are not the only solutions to neighborhood problems, so officers must understand crime theories and study crime trends, environmental factors leading to crime, and so on—while also using community resources such as residents, businesses, schools, hospitals, the news media, and treatment programs.

Although about one-third of my career has been as a patrol officer, that was my most influential assignment. The patrol function is where officers learn a style of policing; accumulate the basic skills to be a safe, productive, and effective officer; and develop the skills for accomplishing the above tasks as well as for more specialized assignments. Even interviewing skills are learned while working the street.

The qualities/characteristics that are most helpful in this career: Integrity, good decision-making skills, the desire to work, and the physical ability to perform. Integrity is absolutely essential, as it guides the officer to make good decisions, especially under difficult circumstances.

Good decision-making skills are necessary for making dozens or hundreds of critical decisions daily. These decisions affect people, and involve criminal procedures and laws, safety concerns, civil liability, and departmental guidelines. Not every situation and decision the patrol officer is faced with is covered by clearly defined standards or laws, so the ability to effectively use discretion is an essential element of good decision making.

Anyone can learn a skill or information, but the desire and drive to work is far more valuable. A very knowledgeable officer who chooses not to fully apply his or her skills is far less effective and productive and useful than a less skilled officer who works hard.

Remaining physically fit will also prepare one for a long career in law enforcement. This is essential because, inevitably, the officer will be involved in fights with suspects, foot pursuits, climbing over fences, lifting arrestees, and performing searches.

(Continued)

(Continued)

In general, this is what a *typical day* looks like for a practitioner in this career: A shift briefing at the outset, where the previous day's or shift's significant events are discussed, and might include short training segments, discussions of crime trends and persons of interest, and departmental business. Once the patrol officer is in service, he or she will first respond to any high-priority calls for service (e.g., a traffic accident with injuries, an escalating domestic disturbance, a burglary in progress, a bank robbery, a fight, a shooting, a missing child, or a suicidal subject), and then may assist the officers still on calls from the previous shift. Then the officer will respond to lower-priority calls, such as "cold" burglary or larceny reports, traffic problems, graffiti reports, tenant/landlord civil disputes, or shoplifting cases. From there, a wide variety of occurrences is possible (i.e., there is no "typical" day): The day may begin in a calm and structured manner, and then become very chaotic. For example, while completing a crime report, the officer might be sent across town to assist other officers in a fight, then immediately go to another area for a violent domestic dispute, and then go assist the fire department—all in the span of an hour or so.

As indicated above, the patrol officer must also designate time for proactive policing and problem solving. Patrol officers are also expected to be extremely familiar with their assigned areas and the people within them.

Developing communication skills is also important, as most reported crimes or significant actions taken by the patrol officer will be documented through official reporting. Paperwork is often a very unpopular, time-consuming task, and reports are plentiful, but they are important, are expected to be accurate and detailed, and must typically be completed before the end of the shift.

My advice to someone either wishing to study, or now studying, criminal justice and wanting to become a practitioner in this career: Be certain that you want to be a police officer and are willing to begin working in patrol. While very rewarding, the patrol officer's role is inherently dangerous, is at times quite stressful and difficult, and involves great successes and terrible tragedies. If you cannot function in this environment, then you may want to consider a different career.

Also, you should become familiar with every aspect of policing and patrol assignments. My education was instrumental in preparing me for employment with my department. In addition to providing me with an overall education and view into the criminal justice system, I took opportunities for internships at different agencies that afforded firsthand experience, and also helped me to identify the department that was most desirable to me. This is a good means of preparing for patrol work and policing prior to entering the academy. The educational resources, literature, and training opportunities that you can use prior to being hired are endless.

Finally, identify those patrol officers and law enforcement practitioners who are successful, and apply the traits and skills that make them successful. Surround yourself with others like you who want to have a successful career. Be a positive example for your peers, and know that your actions and attitudes are contagious. And never compromise your integrity.

Video: Chicago Police Traffic Stop Guidelines

Traffic function: the aggregate of motor vehicles, pedestrians, streets, and highways, for which police must investigate and apply laws to provide safe travels for citizens in their jurisdictions.

By trying to enforce traffic laws and investigating traffic collisions, the police endeavor to reduce traffic deaths and injuries and generally make vehicular travel safer; on its face, this is a noble undertaking. In this era of accountability and litigation—and the vast amounts of damage done to people and property each year as a result of traffic accidents—it is essential that officers competently investigate traffic collisions and cite the guilty party, not only from a law enforcement standpoint but also in the event that the matter is taken to civil court.

One of the **traffic functions** for which the police receive public support is in their efforts to identify, apprehend, and convict the hit-and-run (or "phantom") driver. No one thinks highly of these offenders—who are often intoxicated—who collide with another innocent party's vehicle or strike a pedestrian and then leave the scene. In fact, this matter quickly becomes more of a criminal investigation than a mere collision investigation for the police. In most states, the killing of a human being by someone driving under the influence (DUI) is a felony. Physical evidence and witness statements must be collected in the same fashion as in a conventional criminal investigation; paint samples and automobile parts left at the scene are sent to crime laboratories for examination. The problem for the police is that unless the driver of the vehicle is identified—by physical evidence, an eyewitness, or a confession—the case can be lost.

As will be seen in Chapter 7, the police traffic function also carries tremendous potential for liability, particularly in the area of high-speed pursuits; examples are provided in that chapter.

POLICE DISCRETION

The power to use discretion in performing one's role is at the very core of policing. However, as is discussed in this section, this power can be controversial—and used for both good and bad.

SAGE Journal Article: Police discretion

Author Video: Discretion

The Myth of Full Enforcement

The law is written in black and white; however, the manner in which most laws are enforced by the police can be said to be colored gray. Noted police scholar Herman Goldstein wrote in 1963 that the police should be "Enforcing the law without fear or favor."[38] However, the truth is anything but (except for laws or policies related to domestic violence and driving under the influence, for example, where the police are given no discretion but to arrest).

Consider this scenario: The municipal police chief or county sheriff is asked during a civic club luncheon speech which laws are and are not enforced by his or her agency. The official response will inevitably be that *all* of the laws are enforced equally, all of the time. Yet the chief or sheriff knows that full enforcement of the laws is a myth— that there are neither the resources nor the desire to enforce them all, nor are all laws enforced impartially. There are legal concerns as well. For example, releasing some offenders (to get information about other crimes, because of a good excuse, etc.) cannot be the official policy of the agency (and letting an offender go is a form of discretion as well); however, the chief or sheriff cannot broadcast that fact to the public. Indeed, it has been stated that "the single most astonishing fact of police behavior is the extent to which police do *not* enforce the law when they have every legal right to do so."[39]

Attempts to Define Discretion

The way police make arrest decisions is largely unknown (see possible determining factors, described in the next section). What *is* known, however, is that when police observe something of a suspicious or an illegal nature, two important decisions must be made: (1) whether to intervene in the situation and (2) how to intervene. The kinds, number, and possible combinations of interventions are virtually limitless. What kinds of decisions are available for an officer who makes a routine traffic stop? David Bayley and Egon Bittner observed long ago that officers have as many as 10 actions to select from at the initial stop (for example, order the driver out of the car), 7 strategies appropriate during the stop (such as a roadside sobriety test), and 11 exit strategies (for instance, releasing the driver with a warning), representing a total of *770* different combinations of actions that might be taken![40]

Criminal law has two sides—the formality and the reality. The formality is found in the statute books and opinions of appellate courts. The reality is found in the practices of enforcement officers. In some circumstances, the choice of action to be taken is relatively easy, such as arresting a bank robbery suspect. In other situations, such as quelling a dispute between neighbors or determining how much party noise is too much, the choice is more difficult.[41]

Our system tends to treat people as individuals. One person who commits a robbery is not the same as another person who commits a robbery. Our system also takes into account why and how a person committed a crime (his or her intent, or *mens rea*, discussed in Chapter 2). The most important decisions take place on the streets, day or night, generally without the opportunity for the officer to consult with others or to carefully consider all the facts.

Determinants of Discretionary Actions

The power of discretionary policing can be awe-inspiring. Kenneth Culp Davis, an authority on police discretion, writes, "The police are among the most important policy makers of our entire society. And they make far more discretionary determinations in individual cases than does any other class of administrators; I know of no close second."[42]

What determines whether the officer will take a stern approach (enforcing the letter of the law with an arrest) or will be lenient (issuing a verbal warning or some other outcome short of arrest)? Several variables enter into the officer's decision:

1. The *law* is indeed a factor. For example, many state statutes and local ordinances now mandate that the police arrest for certain suspected offenses, such as driving under the influence or domestic violence.

2. The *officer's attitude* can also be a factor. First, some officers are more willing to empathize with offenders who feel they deserve a break than others. Furthermore, police, being human, can bring to work either a happy or an unhappy disposition. Personal viewpoints can play a role, such as when, for example, the officer is fed up with juvenile crimes that have been occurring of late and thus will not give any leniency to youths that he or she encounters. Also, as Carl Klockars and Stephen Mastrofski observed, although violators frequently offer what they feel are very good reasons for the officer to overlook their offense, "every police officer knows that, if doing so will allow them to escape punishment, most people are prepared to lie through their teeth."[43]

3. Another major consideration in the officer's choice among options is the *citizen's attitude*. If the offender is rude and condescending, denies having done anything wrong, or uses some of the standard clichés that are almost guaranteed to rankle the officer—such as "You don't know who I am" (someone who is obviously very important in the community), "I'll have your job," "I know the chief of police," or "I'm a taxpayer, and I pay your salary"—the probable outcome is obvious. On the other hand, the person who is honest with the officer, avoids attempts at intimidation and sarcasm, and does not try to "beat the rap" may fare better.

In addition to these considerations, other factors that an officer may take into account when deciding whether or not to arrest might include injury to and preference of the victim; prior criminal record of the offender; amount and strength of evidence; peer and agency pressure regarding certain kinds of crimes; media coverage of this and other related crimes; and availability and credibility of witnesses. The officer's specific assignment will also come into play. For example, homicide investigators would care little about a driver's tendency to disobey traffic laws, whereas one who is assigned and dedicated to traffic work will probably not let such offenders off with a warning.

Pros and Cons of Discretion

Having discretionary authority carries several advantages for the police officer: First, because the law cannot (and should not) cover every sort of situation the officer encounters, discretion allows the officer to have the flexibility to treat different situations in accordance with humanitarian and practical goals. For example, assume an officer pulls over a speeding motorist, only to learn that the car is en route to the hospital with a woman who is about to deliver a baby. While the agitated driver is endangering everyone in the vehicle as well as other motorists on the roadway, discretion allows the officer to be compassionate and empathetic, giving the car a safe escort to the hospital rather than issuing a citation for speeding. In short, discretionary use of authority allows the police to employ a philosophy of "justice tempered with mercy."

One disadvantage of discretionary authority is that those officers who are the least trained and experienced have the greatest amount of discretion to exercise. In other words, as the rank of the officer *increases*, the amount of discretion that he or she can employ typically *decreases*. The patrol officer or deputy, being loosely supervised on the streets, makes many discretionary decisions about whether or not to arrest, search, frisk, and so forth. Conversely, the chief of police or sheriff will be highly constrained by department policies and procedures, union agreements, affirmative action laws, and/or governing board guidelines and policies. Another disadvantage is that allowing police to exercise such discretion belies their need to appear impartial—treating people differently for committing essentially the same offense. Critics of discretion also argue that such wide latitude in decision making may serve as a breeding ground for police corruption; for example, an officer may be offered a bribe to overlook an offense.

See the case study in the accompanying "You Be the Officer" box and respond to the questions posed.

You Be the... POLICE OFFICER

Assume a police officer pulls over a vehicle for swerving across the center line. The driver, a 17-year-old college student who is an elementary education major, admits she's been drinking at a party. The breathalyzer test reveals a .07 blood alcohol concentration. In this state, .07 can result in a charge of either "driving after having consumed alcohol" or a more serious "driving while ability is impaired." There are two other girls in the car: One has a badly swollen jaw after having fallen at the party; the driver is attempting to get her to the urgent care facility. Another girl, the older sister of the driver, is visibly pregnant.

1. What discretionary issues are presented?
2. Given all of the facts at hand, how do you believe the officer should deal with the driver?

COMMUNITY POLICING AND PROBLEM SOLVING

Chapter 5 discussed the three eras of policing, which led to today's "community era." Following is a brief description of policing in terms of how it moved from the political and reform eras—both of which experienced problems in terms of recognizing and working with the community. The seeds of community policing and problem solving were sown in London in 1829, when the architect of London's police force, Sir Robert Peel, offered that "the police are the public and . . . the public are the police," and that by establishing patrol beats, officers could get to know their citizens and thus be better able to gather information about neighborhood crime and disorder. As was seen in Chapter 5, however, in the United States that close police-public association over time often led to powerful political influences and corruption in terms of who was hired, who was promoted, and who could bring elected officials the most votes. This led to the onset of the reform era in the 1930s. Reforms included the removal of police from the influence of the community and politics through the creation of civil

As part of their community-policing and problem-solving efforts, many agencies use bicycle patrols to focus on crime prevention and greater interaction with the community.

©HERB SWANSON/epa/Corbis

Video: Problem-oriented policing

service systems. The community era of policing recognized that the public has a vested interest in addressing—as well as vital information concerning—neighborhood crime and disorder, and thus a return to Peel's principles were needed and the two entities should work hand in glove to resolve problems.

Problem-oriented policing, which began to develop in the mid-1980s, was grounded in principles different from, but complementary to, those of community-oriented policing. Problem-oriented policing is a strategy that puts the community policing philosophy into practice. It advocates that police examine the underlying causes of recurring incidents of crime and disorder. The problem-solving process helps officers to identify problems, analyze them completely, develop response strategies, and assess the results. Police must be equipped to define more clearly and to understand more fully the problems they are expected to handle. They must recognize the relationships between and among incidents—for example, incidents involving the same behavior, the same address, or the same people. The police must therefore develop a commitment to analyzing problems—gathering information from police files, the minds of experienced officers, other agencies of government, and private sources as well. It can also require conducting house-to-house surveys and talking with victims, complainants, and offenders. It includes an uninhibited search for the most effective response to each problem, looking beyond just the criminal justice system to a wide range of alternatives; in sum, police must try to design a customized response that holds the greatest potential for dealing effectively with a specific problem in a specific place under specific conditions.

Thousands of police agencies have thus broken away from their reactive, incident-driven methods that characterized the reform era—where police would race from call to call, take an offense report, and leave the scene without seeking any resolution to problems or achieving any long-term benefits. This change in philosophy and strategies goes far beyond merely creating a "crime prevention specialist" position, a "community relations unit," a foot or bicycle patrol, or a neighborhood mini-station. Today, community-oriented policing and problem solving involves radical changes in police organizational culture and structures, management styles, and external relationships. It requires a cultural transformation within the entire police agency, involving changes in recruiting, training, awards systems, evaluation, and promotions. New technologies have also been designed to help effect this transition, while personnel training, evaluation, and reward systems have been altered to fit this philosophy. At its core, this approach fosters more long-term, thoughtful crime control and prevention strategies.

Finally, what every criminal justice employee knows is that there are three elements that must exist in order for a crime to occur: an offender, a

● **FIGURE 6.4** **Problem Analysis Triangle**

Offender   Problem   Victim

Place

Source: John E. Eck and William Spelman, Problem-Solving: *Problem-Oriented Policing in Newport News* (Washington, D.C.: U.S. Department of Justice, National Institute of Justice, 1987), p. 43.

victim, and a location, as shown in Figure 6.4. The problem analysis triangle helps officers visualize the problem and understand the relationships among these three elements. Additionally, it helps officers to analyze problems, it suggests where more information is needed, and it assists with crime control and prevention. Simply put, if there is a victim and he or she is in a place where crimes occur but there is no offender, no crime occurs. If there is an offender and he or she is in a place where crimes occur but there is nothing or no one to be victimized, then no crime will occur. If an offender and a victim are not in the same place, there will be no crime. Part of the analysis phase involves finding out as much as possible about the victims, offenders, and locations where problems exist in order to understand what is prompting the problem and what can be done about it.

INVESTIGATING FURTHER

COMMUNITY POLICING AND PROBLEM SOLVING

In the scenario presented below, consider how the police would have handled the problem using traditional, reactive patrol methods versus the contemporary community-oriented policing and problem-solving approach. In the problem-solving approach, the police use what is termed the SARA problem-solving process, which is composed of the following four steps: scanning (officers first identify a problem and look for a pattern or persistent repeat incidents), analysis (here, officers thoroughly examine the nature and causes of the problem in order to identify possible responses), response (the officer develops creative solutions that will address the problem), and assessment (later, officers look at the problem and neighborhood to see if their responses were effective, examining such indicators as numbers of reported crimes, calls for service to the area, and citizen fear of crime).

In a relatively quiet neighborhood, police have recently had to respond to a series of disturbances. All of the disturbances—loud music, fighting, screeching tires, people displaying lewd behavior on and near the premises—appear to be related to a recently opened live-music dance club. In a month's time, police officers have been sent to the club to restore order on more than 50 occasions. Under the traditional policing model, typically the swing (evening) shift officers would respond to the club and restore order for a short period of time; later, graveyard (night) shift officers often would have to return to the club to again restore calm. Usually when officers arrive, however, the offenders are already gone, so a report is taken, and the officer leaves. This problem—with police basically showing up, taking a disturbance or noise complaint report, and leaving—persists for months on end.

Under the community-policing and problem-solving approach, however, following are examples of activities that might be used to resolve the problem. First, information is gathered concerning possible zoning and health department violations. Officers

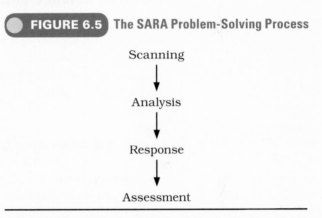

FIGURE 6.5 The SARA Problem-Solving Process

Scanning

↓

Analysis

↓

Response

↓

Assessment

Source: John E. Eck and William Spelman, Problem-Solving: *Problem-Oriented Policing in Newport News* (Washington, D.C.: U.S. Department of Justice, National Institute of Justice, 1987), p. 43.

arrange a meeting with the club manager/operator and representatives from the city's business licensing division, during which the consequences for continued problems are explained. This also results in the manager's removal of an unsavory employee and his "following" of drug users and other undesirable characters at the club. The hours of the club's live music are limited, and the manager and employees are trained in relevant sections of the municipal code covering disturbing the peace, minors in liquor establishments, trespassing laws, disorderly behaviors, and so on. The officers also arrange a meeting with the club's landlord, who agrees to install more lights in the parking lots and a "sound wall" around the business to buffer the area residents. A later assessment reveals that a reduction in calls for service in the area was realized, and area residents, although not entirely happy with the continuing existence of the business, acknowledged satisfaction from their complaints; no further newspaper stories appeared regarding the noise and disorder in the neighborhood.

THE WORK OF FORENSICS AND DETECTIVES

The challenges involved with investigating crimes may well be characterized by a quote from Ludwig Wittgenstein: "How hard I find it to see what is right in front of my eyes!"[44] Certainly the art of sleuthing has long fascinated the American public, and news reports on the expanding uses of DNA and television series such as *CSI: Crime Scene Investigation* have done much to capture the public's fascination with criminal investigation and forensic science in the 21st century. This interest in "sleuthing" is not a recent phenomenon. For decades, Americans have feasted on the exploits of dozens of fictional masterminds, like Sherlock Holmes, Agatha Christie's Hercule Poirot and Miss Marple, Clint Eastwood's portrayal of Detective "Dirty Harry" Callahan, and Peter Falk's Columbo, to name a few.

In reality, investigative work is largely misunderstood, often boring, and generally overrated; it results in arrests only a fraction of the time, and it relies strongly on the assistance of witnesses and even some luck.

Forensic Science and Criminalistics: Defining the Terms

The terms *forensic science* and *criminalistics* are often used interchangeably. **Forensic science** is the broader term; it is that part of science used to answer legal questions. It is the examination, evaluation, and explanation of physical evidence in law. Forensic science encompasses pathology, toxicology, physical anthropology, odontology (development of dental structure and dental diseases), psychiatry, questioned documents, ballistics, tool work comparison, and serology (the reactions and properties of serums), among other fields.[45]

Criminalistics is one branch of forensic science; it deals with the study of physical evidence related to crime. From such a study, a crime may be reconstructed. Criminalistics is interdisciplinary, drawing on mathematics, physics, chemistry, biology, anthropology, and many other scientific fields.[46]

Basically, the analysis of physical evidence is concerned with identifying traces of evidence, reconstructing criminal acts, and establishing a common origin of samples of evidence. The types of information that physical evidence can provide are as follows:[47]

- Information on the *corpus delicti* (or "body of the crime") is physical evidence showing that a crime was committed, such as tool marks, a broken door or window, a ransacked home, and missing valuables in a burglary or a victim's blood, a weapon, and torn clothing in an assault.

- Information on the *modus operandi* (or method of operation) is physical evidence showing means used by the criminal to gain entry, tools that were used, types of items taken, and other signs—items left at the scene, an accelerant used at an arson scene, the way crimes are committed, and so forth.

- *Linking a suspect with a victim* is one of the most important linkages, particularly with violent crimes. It includes hair, blood, clothing fibers, and cosmetics that may be transferred from victim to perpetrator. Items found in a suspect's possession, such as bullets or a bloody knife, can also be linked to a victim.

- *Linking a person to a crime scene* is also a common and significant linkage. It includes fingerprints, glove prints, blood, semen, hairs, fibers, soil, bullets, cartridge cases, tool marks, footprints or shoeprints, tire tracks, and objects that belonged to the criminal. Stolen property is the most obvious example.

Forensic science: the study of causes of crimes, deaths, and crime scenes.

Criminalistics: the interdisciplinary study of physical evidence related to crime; drawing on mathematics, physics, chemistry, biology, anthropology, and many other scientific fields.

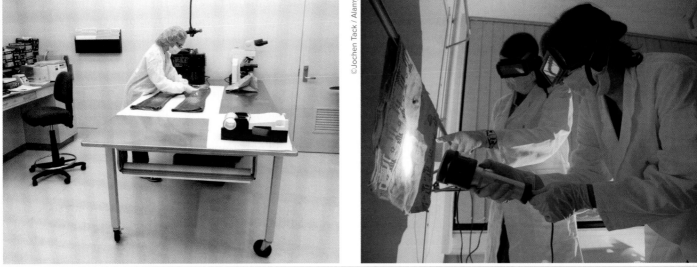

Forensic scientists examine of all kinds of articles and substances in their search for physical evidence that will link persons to their crimes.

- In terms of *disproving or supporting a witness's testimony*, evidence can indicate whether or not a person's version of events is true. An example is a driver whose car matches the description of a hit-and-run vehicle. If blood is found on the underside of the car and the driver claims that he hit a dog, tests on the blood can determine whether the blood is from an animal or from a human.

- One of the best forms of evidence for *identification of a suspect* is DNA evidence, which proves "individualization." Without a doubt, that person was at the crime scene.

Investigative Stages and Activities

The police, more specifically investigators and criminalists, operate on the age-old theory that there is no such thing as a perfect crime; criminals either leave a bit of themselves or take something away from the crime scene. This is termed **Locard's exchange principle,** which asserts that when any person comes into contact with an object or another person, a cross-transfer of evidence—in the form of fingerprints, hairs, fibers, and all manner of residue or other materials—will occur.[48] An example is when a victim is strangled to death (by an assailant who is not wearing gloves); the suspect may well have the victim's skin cells under his nails, the victim's hair on his clothing, and other such residual material on his person. In the apprehension process, when a crime is reported or discovered, police officers respond, conduct a search for the offender, and check out suspects. If the search is successful, evidence for charging the suspect is assembled, and the suspect is apprehended.[49] Cases not solved in the initial phase of the apprehension process are assigned either to an investigative specialist or, in smaller police agencies, to an experienced uniformed officer who functions as a part-time investigator. Following are the basic investigative stages:[50]

- *The preliminary investigation:* Duties include establishing whether a crime has been committed; securing from any witnesses a description of the perpetrator and his or her vehicle; locating and interviewing the victim and all witnesses; protecting the crime scene (and searching for and collecting all items of

Locard's exchange principle: the notion that offenders both leave something at the crime scene and take something from it; the crime scene analyst or investigator's job is to locate that evidence and use it in the investigation.

possible physical evidence); determining how the crime was committed and what the resulting injuries were, as well as the nature of property taken; recording in field notes and sketches all data about the crime; and arranging for photographs of the crime scene.

- *The continuing investigation:* This stage includes follow-up interviews; developing a theory of the crime; analyzing the significance of information and evidence; continuing the search for witnesses; beginning to contact crime lab technicians and assessing their analyses of the evidence; conducting surveillances, interrogations, and polygraph tests, as appropriate; and preparing the case for the prosecutor.

- *Reconstructing the crime:* The investigator seeks a rational theory of the crime. Most often, inductive reasoning is used: The collected information and evidence are analyzed carefully to develop a theory. One of the major traits of criminals is vanity; their belief in their own cleverness, not chance, is the key factor in their leaving a vital clue. Investigators look for mistakes.

- *Focusing the investigation:* When this stage is reached, all investigative efforts are directed toward proving that one suspect (perhaps with accomplices) is guilty of the crime. This decision is based on the investigator's analysis of the relationships among the crime, the investigation, and the habits and attitudes of the suspect.

Myths and Attributes of Detectives

SAGE Journal Article: Homicide detectives

Detectives/investigators are members of police agencies who investigate crimes by obtaining evidence and information relating to illegal activities; furthermore, by extension—and what is often overlooked in their role—they ultimately present in court the findings of their investigation. To be effective, detectives must be trained in general areas such as the laws of arrest, search, and seizure; investigative principles and practices; judicial proceedings; and oral and written communications. More specialized training will often be required if individuals are specializing in areas such as sex crimes, family crimes, homicide investigation, and gang and drug enforcement.

Several myths surround police detectives, who are often portrayed in movies as rugged, confident (sometimes overbearing), independent, streetwise individualists who bask in glory, are rewarded with big arrests, and are surrounded by beautiful women (movie detectives are almost always men). In reality, detective work is seldom glamorous or exciting. Investigators, like their bureaucratic cousins, often wade in

Detective/investigator: a police officer who is assigned to investigate reported crimes, to include gathering evidence, completing case reports, testifying in court, and so on.

You Be the... DETECTIVE

As the coach opened the door to the locker room, the only light that shone was from the players' large shower area. Upon flipping the light switch, he saw the body of his once-"ace" pitcher, Hines, lying on the floor in the shower. In his pale left hand he held a gun. There was a bullet wound in his left temple. Under his tanned right hand was a note saying, "My pitching days are gone, my debts and humiliation more than I can bear. Sorry." His nearby locker contained a half-empty bottle of beer, his uniform, an uneaten stadium hot dog, a picture of his two children, and his Acme-brand ball glove with "RH" stamped in the webbing. Wet footprints were observed walking in and out of the shower. Upon surveying the scene, the responding detective said, "I do not believe this was a suicide."

1. Was this a suicide or a murder?
2. What fact(s) led you to this conclusion?

paperwork and spend many hours on the telephone. Furthermore, studies have not been kind to detectives, showing that their vaunted productivity is overrated. Not all cases have a good or even a 50-50 chance of being cleared by an arrest. Indeed, in a study of over 150 large police departments, a RAND research team learned that only about 20 percent of their crimes could have been solved by detective work.[51] Another study, involving the Kansas City Police Department, found that fewer than 50 percent of all reported crimes received more than a minimal half-hour's investigation by detectives. In many of these cases, detectives merely reported the facts discovered by the patrol officers during the preliminary investigations.[52]

Yet the importance and role of detectives should not be understated. Detectives know that a criminal is more than a criminal. As Paul Weston and Kenneth Wells said,

> John, Jane and Richard are not just burglar, prostitute and killer. John is a hostile burglar and is willing to enter a premises that might be occupied. Jane is a prostitute who wants a little more than pay for services rendered and is suspected of working with a robbery gang and enticing her customers to secluded areas. Richard is an accidental, a person who, in a fit of rage, killed the girl who rejected him.[53]

Student on the Street Video: The "CSI Effect"

INVESTIGATING FURTHER

THE "CSI EFFECT"

Television programs focusing on criminal investigations and forensic techniques may be creating unrealistic courtroom expectations among jurors that cannot be achieved in real life. This phenomenon has been labeled the "CSI effect." Some court officers believe this "effect" is truly present: Prosecutors indicate that jurors want to see all evidence subjected to substantial forensic examination, whether warranted in a specific case or not; conversely, some defense attorneys believe that jurors deem all scientific evidence to be flawless and thus establish their client's/defendant's guilt. The *voir dire* jury selection process may also be altered to ensure that those jurors who are unduly influenced by shows like *CSI* are screened from jury service. Such modifications to the usual process could result in longer trials and increased use of expert witnesses to aid the jury in understanding the presence or absence of physical evidence.[54]

A survey of Kentucky circuit court judges found that the impact has been strong—but not in areas where one

might expect. First, three-fourths of the judges indicated that jurors have come to expect more forensic evidence; furthermore, 82 percent of the judges believed that "shows like *CSI* have distorted the public's perception of time needed to obtain forensic results." In that same connection, a slight majority (53.4 percent) believed that the popularity of shows like *CSI* has made it harder to convict defendants. The responding judges also perceived that these television programs create unrealistic representations concerning the state of the forensic art in their jurisdiction, as well as the speed of forensic testing.[55]

In one Illinois case, jurors acquitted the defendant of a rape charge—even when presented with DNA evidence and strong testimony from the victim and an emergency room nurse—because no test was performed to see if "debris" found in the victim matched soil from the park where the crime occurred.[56]

To be successful, the investigator must possess four personal attributes to enhance the detection of crime: an unusual capability for observation and recall; extensive knowledge of the law, rules of evidence, scientific aids, and laboratory services; power of imagination; and a working knowledge of social psychology.[57] Successful detectives (and even patrol officers) also appear to empathize with the suspect; if a detective can appear to understand why a criminal did what he or she did, a rapport is often established that results in the suspect's telling the officer his or her life history—including how and why he or she committed the crime in question. Perhaps first and foremost, however, detectives need logical skills—the ability to exercise deductive reasoning—to assist in their investigative work.

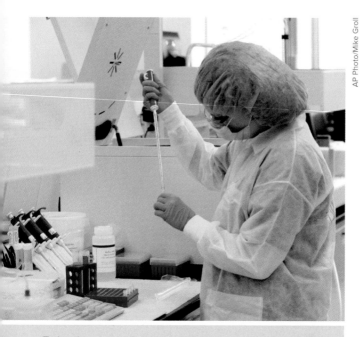

Today the power of what can be done with DNA, as well its variety of uses, is incredible.

Using DNA Analysis

Today, **DNA** is the most sophisticated and reliable type of physical evidence (see Figure 6.6). Police are now able to submit to laboratories work that until recently was not even possible to examine in recent years. For example, "touch" DNA evidence can now be examined and requires very small amounts of skin cells left on an object after it has been touched or handled; it can be used to determine whether a defendant merely touched a weapon, or whose hand threw drugs to the floor of a room.[58]

A testimonial to DNA's promise in investigations is offered by a former supervising criminalist of the Los Angeles County Sheriff's Department:

> The power of what we can look for and analyze now is incredible. It's like magic. Every day we discover evidence where we never thought it would be. You almost can't do anything without leaving some DNA around. DNA takes longer than fingerprints to analyze, but you get a really big bang for your buck.[59]

Furthermore, DNA has allowed investigative personnel to exonerate people who were convicted in the past for crimes they did not commit. Indeed, in April 2007 it was reported that the 200th person—a former Army cook who spent nearly 25 years in prison for a rape he did not commit—was exonerated by DNA evidence (the 100th exoneration since January 2002).[60]

FIGURE 6.6   "What Is DNA?"

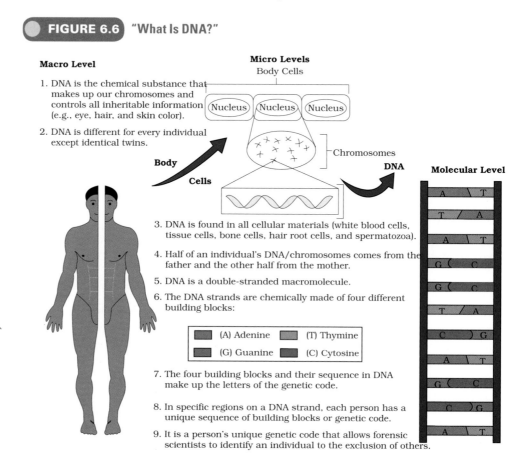

Macro Level

1. DNA is the chemical substance that makes up our chromosomes and controls all inheritable information (e.g., eye, hair, and skin color).

2. DNA is different for every individual except identical twins.

3. DNA is found in all cellular materials (white blood cells, tissue cells, bone cells, hair root cells, and spermatozoa).

4. Half of an individual's DNA/chromosomes comes from the father and the other half from the mother.

5. DNA is a double-stranded macromolecule.

6. The DNA strands are chemically made of four different building blocks:

| (A) Adenine | (T) Thymine |
| (G) Guanine | (C) Cytosine |

7. The four building blocks and their sequence in DNA make up the letters of the genetic code.

8. In specific regions on a DNA strand, each person has a unique sequence of building blocks or genetic code.

9. It is a person's unique genetic code that allows forensic scientists to identify an individual to the exclusion of others.

DNA: deoxyribonucleic acid, which is found in all cells; used in forensics to match evidence (hair, semen) left at a crime scene with a particular perpetrator.

Police at Work: Patrolling and Investigating • CHAPTER 6   159

PRACTITIONER'S PERSPECTIVE

FORENSIC SCIENTIST (CRIMINALIST)

Name: Renee Romero

Current position: Director, Forensic Science Division, Washoe County Sheriff's Office

City, state: Reno, Nevada

College attended/academic major: Bachelor of arts degree in chemistry, forensic science from Michigan State University; master of science degree in cell and molecular biology from University of Nevada, Reno

How long have you been a practitioner in this criminal justice position? Since 1989

My primary duties and responsibilities as a practitioner in this position: Being responsible for the management of the Forensic Science Division at the Sheriff's Office. This entails managing budgets, planning for future forensic technology changes, and ensuring we are meeting our accreditation standards. Prior to becoming the director in 2008, I was a practicing forensic scientist (criminalist). While I have limited controlled substances experience, the majority of my experience is in the DNA field. The primary duty of a forensic scientist is to examine evidence from criminal cases. This evidence can range from drugs, firearms, toxicology, and DNA to shoe prints, tire tracks impressions, and latent fingerprints. A forensic scientist usually specializes in one specific discipline. After examining the evidence, the forensic scientist must issue the findings to the investigating agency and then work with the district attorney's office to prepare for expert testimony when the cases go to trial.

The qualities/characteristics that are most helpful in this career: Attention to detail, organization, and excellent communication skills.

In general, this is what a *typical day* looks like for a practitioner in this career: Spending time in the laboratory examining evidence, reviewing findings, and writing reports. The day may be interrupted with changing priorities based on the investigative needs of new cases as they arise.

My advice to someone either wishing to study, or now studying, criminal justice and wanting to become a practitioner in this career: Obtain a scientific degree. If you believe you are interested in toxicology or controlled substances, then work toward a chemistry degree. If you think you are interested in the DNA field, then work toward a molecular biology degree—and you must also earn college credits in genetics and biochemistry. The field of forensic science is getting more competitive, so obtaining a master's degree would be beneficial as well.

IN A NUTSHELL

- The idea of a police subculture was first proposed in 1950 by William Westley, who found a high degree of secrecy and violence.

- Recruit academy training covers a variety of subjects; neophyte officers learn how to use lethal and less lethal weapons, and how to deal with criminal suspects, offenders, victims, and witnesses; hands-on training and simulated situations are also employed.

- Studies show that higher education is important for police officers, in order to interact with an educated public, enforce the rule of law, investigate crimes, testify in court, write cogent and accurate reports, and perform myriad other duties. From 1967 to 1986, every national commission that studied crime, violence, and police in America maintained that a college education could help the police to do their jobs better.

- After leaving the academy, new officers are assigned to a veteran officer—a field training officer—for initial field instruction and observation; this phase of training helps recruits to make the transition from the academy to the streets under the protective arm of a veteran officer, while on probationary status.

- Jerome Skolnick said officers develop a working personality, and that the police role contains two important variables: danger and authority. Consequently, they develop a "perceptual shorthand" to identify certain kinds of people as "symbolic assailants"—those who pose a physical threat to them.

- Police have four basic tasks: enforcing the laws, performing welfare tasks, preventing crimes, and protecting the innocent.

- James Q. Wilson maintained that there are three distinctive policing styles: the watchman style, the legalistic style, and the service style.

- Although workers in several other occupations die at much higher rates than those in policing, this occupation still has many occupational hazards.

- There are several stressors for police, both within and outside of their employing agency. It is important that officers take appropriate measures to reduce or eliminate stress.

- The traffic function is an important part of policing; as officers enforce traffic laws and investigate traffic collisions, they attempt to reduce traffic deaths and injuries.

- Full enforcement of the laws by police is a myth; they typically have considerable discretion in whether or not to arrest someone. Determining factors include the law (e.g., some ordinances mandate arrest for certain offenses, such as domestic violence), the officer's attitude (concerning the law that is violated, as well as toward the offender), and the citizen's attitude toward the officer.

- Today, under the community-policing philosophy, officers are trained to examine the underlying causes of problems in the neighborhoods on their beats and to involve citizens in the long-term resolution of neighborhood problems.

- The fields of forensic science and criminalistics are the most rapidly developing areas in policing—and probably in all of criminal justice.

- Several myths surround police detectives, who often perform mundane duties and are often unsuccessful in their search for the offender.

- DNA is the most sophisticated and reliable type of physical evidence and has resulted in hundreds of arrestees being exonerated.

KEY TERMS & CONCEPTS

▶ Review key terms with eFlashcards. ⑤SAGE edge™

Academy training, 137
Criminalistics, 154
Detective/investigator, 156
DNA, 158
Field training officer (FTO), 139

Forensic science, 154
Kansas City Preventive Patrol Experiment, 144
Locard's exchange principle, 155
Policing styles, 142

"Sixth sense," 137
Tasks of policing (four basic), 142
Traffic function, 148

REVIEW QUESTIONS

▶ Test your understanding of chapter content. Take the practice quiz. ⑤SAGE edge™

1. What ideal traits are sought among those persons wishing to enter policing?

2. How are police recruits socialized into the police subculture while in academy training, and what are some topics that trainees study while attending the academy?

3. What are the methods and purposes of the FTO concept?

4. What is meant by the working personality, how was the concept developed, and how does it function?

5. What traits or qualities are said to make a "good" officer?

6. What are the primary tasks and styles of policing?

7. What are the primary causes of stress among police officers?

8. How would you describe the activities that are involved in the police traffic function?

9. What examples can you provide of police use of discretion? What are some pros and cons of police use of discretionary authority?

10. What are the qualities, myths, and methods that tend to revolve around investigative personnel?

LEARN BY DOING

1. You are a patrol sergeant lecturing to your agency's Citizens' Police Academy about the patrol function. Someone asks, "Sergeant, your officers obviously can't enforce all of the laws all of the time. Which laws are always enforced, and which ones are not?" How do you respond to her (without saying something absurd like "We enforce all of the laws, all of the time," which of course would be untrue)? How would you fully explain police discretion to the group?

2. The "Crime & Investigation Network," based in the United Kingdom, advertises on its website that it "investigates the darker corners of human life" and "offers viewers stories of real life crime" that "open the door to real crime labs, police archives and courtrooms, allowing viewers to join detectives as they examine evidence and piece together clues." You can access and participate in solving a number of different crimes at www.crimeandinvestigation.co.uk/games/solve-the-murder.html.

3. For a practical view of traffic problems and solutions, visit www.popcenter.org/problems/street_racing/ or www.popcenter.org/problems/drunk_driving/. These are guides published by the federal Center for Problem-Oriented Policing. Read and describe the kinds of problems that are caused by illegal street racing and/or drunk driving. Also, consider the efforts described in the guides that police are using to successfully address these problems.

STUDY SITE

$SAGE edge™

Review → Practice → Improve

Sharpen your skills with **SAGE edge** at **edge.sagepub.com/peak2e**

SAGE edge for students provides a personalized approach to help you accomplish your coursework goals in an easy-to-use learning environment. Access the videos, audio clips, quizzes, and SAGE journal articles that are noted in this chapter.

POLICING METHODS AND CHALLENGES

LEARNING OBJECTIVES

As a result of reading this chapter, you will be able to:

1 Describe how the police shooting in Ferguson, Missouri, and encounters with citizens in other states have raised serious concerns about such actions and led to calls for reforms

2 Delineate the functions that local police can perform to assist with homeland security

3 Explain the types of police actions that are vulnerable to lawsuits and how police officers—and their supervisors—might be held criminally liable for their misconduct

4 Explain the status and advantages of women and minorities in policing

5 Delineate several types of technologies that are assisting police in their duties, but that also raise privacy concerns

ASSESS YOUR AWARENESS

Check your current knowledge of police methods and challenges by responding to the following eight true-false items; check your answers after reading this chapter's materials.

1 Recent deaths involving police and minority citizens in the United States, and the ensuing unrest, demonstrate that the public wants less police militarization and more body cameras to be employed.

2 Police behavior can be described as "brutal" in only one way: when they use physical violence toward a citizen.

3 The preferred police role in homeland security can be stated in a single sentence: "Stay out of the way and let the federal agencies handle it."

4 Although the police can be sued, the fear of civil liability is of minor concern to those who administer or perform police work.

5 Currently the only legal means of being compensated when police violate someone's rights is to take the matter to a criminal trial.

6 The decision by a police officer to pursue a citizen in a motor vehicle is among the most critical that can be made.

7 Due to legal challenges, today only a small fraction of police officers are authorized to use handheld electronic control devices.

8 The Fourth Amendment does not protect citizens' electronically stored information, as there is no legal "reasonable expectation of privacy" in an online context.

But justice is inverted when those engines of the law,

Instead of pinching vicious men, keep honest ones in awe.

—Daniel Defoe (1660–1731)

<< Answers can be found on page 424.

AP Photo/The Enterprise, Wayne Tilcock

The University of California at Davis agreed to pay about $1 million to settle a lawsuit filed by students who were pepper sprayed by campus police during an nonviolent protest on campus in November 2011.

In late 2011, a group of Occupy protesters were seated on a paved path on the University of California at Davis campus quad. After asking the protesters to leave, university police used pepper spray on a group. A video of a police lieutenant spraying protesters immediately went viral around the world. The lieutenant was later fired.

The incident was the latest in a string of such episodes. In fact, University of California system police have been accused of aggressively attacking students for years, and many people believe there is a repeated pattern of excessive force against nonviolent protests.[1] As examples:

- In November 2009, 40 students occupying a campus building were beaten with batons and shot with rubber bullets; at least 100 students and faculty members were arrested.

- UCLA police used a Taser on a student in a library in 2010 for refusing to show his student ID (the school settled a lawsuit for $220,000).

- When UC Berkeley students climbed trees in 2007 to prevent them from being destroyed, campus police cut the ropes being used to transport food and water to the students.

- When 300 people showed up at a November 2010 Board of Regents meeting in San Francisco to protest tuition hikes, authorities pepper sprayed at least 15 students and arrested 13. One officer pulled a loaded gun on a crowd of protesters surrounding him in a parking garage.

The University of California system announced in September 2012 that it would pay $30,000 in damages to each of the 21 UC Davis students and alumni who were pepper sprayed. The total settlement was nearly $1 million, to include $250,000 in attorneys' fees and a $100,000 set-aside of funds for anyone else who could prove they were harmed during the event. An attorney deemed the incident as "among the worst examples of police violence against student demonstrators that we've seen in a generation. The settlement should be a wake-up call for other universities and police departments."[2]

As you read this chapter, consider recent events across the United States involving police and deaths of minorities, the power and authority that is possessed by the police and the need to restrain that power so that it is meted out judiciously, the great expense in taxpayers' dollars when the police abuse their power, and citizens' ability to be "made whole" again through the use of the courts and civil litigation.

INTRODUCTION

How much force can the police use in performing their duties? What can local police do to prepare for and cope with a terrorist attack in their community? What constitutes police liability? How have technologies affected policing? This chapter addresses such questions, as well as others that often arise today.

The topics covered in this chapter strike at the very heart of policing today. They concern police behaviors that can greatly affect all Americans. Following a discussion of police use of force, next are discussions of police civil liability, the need for greater racial and ethnic diversity in agencies, and selected uses—and serious concerns—regarding police use of technologies. (A major related issue, police corruption, was discussed in Chapter 4.)

USE OF FORCE: A SACRED TRUST

Given the unusually high number of police shootings—often involving unarmed minorities—that occurred in the United States in 2014 (and would continue into 2015), an unusual measure was taken in December 2014 to examine the problem: the creation of a presidential task force on contemporary policing. The task force noted that "recent events…have exposed rifts in the relationships between local police and the communities they protect and serve," and had the mission of determining "how to foster strong, collaborative relationships between local law enforcement and the communities they protect and to make recommendations to the President on how policing practices can promote effective crime reduction while building public trust."[3]

This chapter section discusses some of the problems that exist between the police and citizens they serve, as well as some ideas for bridging those rifts that exist in police-community relations.

Lessons From History and Ferguson

Britain's Benjamin Disraeli observed more than a century ago, "No man will treat with indifference the principle of race. It is the key of history." Certainly the riotous events that unfolded in Ferguson, Missouri, in August 2014, following the shooting death of Michael Brown by a white police officer, as well as the in-custody death of Freddie Gray in Baltimore in April 2015 (where six police officers were charged with murder and/or assault) would prove that statement rings true today.[4]

Problems of police-minority relations are certainly not a recent phenomenon. Indeed, in March 2015, thousands of people—including President Barack Obama—commemorated the 50th anniversary of "Bloody Sunday" in Selma, Alabama—when state troopers met Dr. Martin Luther King and 25,000 peaceful civil rights marchers at the Edmund Pettus Bridge with batons and tear gas. This peaceful demonstration led to the Voting Rights Act of 1965.[5]

However, not all such protests were as peaceful: During the 1960s, major race riots occurred in Harlem, New York; Watts, California; Newark, New Jersey; and Detroit (often fomented by such violent militant groups as the Black Panthers). There were 75 civil disorders involving African Americans and the police in 1967 alone, with at least 83 people killed. A number of presidential commissions were created to study riots, campus disorder, and minority relations in general. One such commission, the National Advisory Commission on Civil Disorders (also known as the Kerner Commission), stated in 1968 that "our nation is moving toward two societies, one black, one white—separate and unequal."[6] Then, in the late 1980s and early 1990s, police-community relations appeared to worsen again, with major riots, looting, and burning in Miami, Florida; Los Angeles; Atlanta; Las Vegas; Washington, D.C.; and St. Petersburg, Florida, as

Problems of police-minority relations are long-standing in nature. Here, a 17-year-old civil rights demonstrator is attacked by a police dog in Birmingham, Alabama, in May 1963.

©AP Photo/Bill Hudson

A crowd of protesters faced Alabama state troopers during one of three Selma-to- Montgomery marches in 1965.

well as in other cities. Race riots during the 1960s, such as the one in Watts, California, often pitted police against protesting members of the community.

James Baldwin, the African American sociologist, was moved to write in 1960 (about Harlem):

> None of the Police Commissioner's men, even with the best will in the world, have any way of understanding the lives led by the people they swagger about in twos and threes controlling. Their very presence is an insult, and it would be, even if they spent their entire day feeding gumdrops to children.[7]

Then the new millennium arrived, and bias-based policing—also known as racial profiling or "driving while black or brown"—became a hot-button issue. A 2007 study released by the Bureau of Justice Statistics found that although black, Hispanic, and white drivers were equally likely to be pulled over by the police, black and Hispanic drivers were much more likely to be searched and arrested, and police were much more likely to threaten or use force against black and Hispanic drivers than against white drivers in any encounter. Even though some police executives lost their jobs because of their officers' racial profiling, the Bureau of Justice Statistics report warned that the findings do not prove that police treat people differently along racial lines and that the differences could be explained by driver conduct or other circumstances.[8]

Indeed, for many minorities, the four words that are inscribed over the entrance to the U.S. Supreme Court building in Washington, D.C.—Equal Justice Under Law—ring hollow; for them, justice is neither equal nor blind. The widespread discontent following the April 2015 police shooting of unarmed African American Walter Scott in North Charleston, South Carolina, as well as the shooting of 12-year-old Tamir Rice in Cleveland, the chokehold death of Eric Garner in New York City, and the aforementioned death of Freddie Gray led to thousands of demonstrators marching and staging "die-ins" near the White House and across the country (as well as federal lawsuits against the officers' employing agencies).[9] "Black lives matter" became their rallying cry, and even a new university course by that name was launched at Dartmouth College in Hanover, New Hampshire.[10] Other widely publicized incidents would follow, such as the police shooting deaths involving an unarmed black teenager in the city of Madison, Wisconsin, in March 2015,[11] and a 50-year-old black man (unarmed and running away from the officer) in Charleston, South Carolina, in April 2015.[12]

After Michael Brown's death, the city of Ferguson raged for a week, gas and rubber bullets were used, the National Guard was deployed, and a police officer was shot (two officers were also shot during a protest in March 2014).[13] Ultimately, five Ferguson officials resigned (including the police chief, city manager, municipal judge, and two police supervisors), and the U.S. Department of Justice issued a scathing report about the widespread racially biased abuses by police, who routinely targeted African Americans for arrests and ticketing.[14] Much controversy was also raised concerning the use of

Video: Preventing abuse of authority

the state's National Guard and military equipment and tactics in Ferguson and across the nation. The Justice Department report points to the millions of pieces of surplus military equipment that have been given to local police departments across the country, including military-grade semi-automatic weapons, armored personnel vehicles, tanks, helicopters, and airplanes. Of course, a competing viewpoint is that the public wants the police to utilize whatever tools and resources are required to keep them safe.

To make matters worse, it was reported in August 2015 that during the year following Michael Brown's death, 29 additional unarmed black men were killed by police. These killings certainly raised new questions for many Americans concerning how police hire and train, as well as the existence of police brutality, racial profiling, and the relationship between police officers and people of color.[15]

How to Develop Harmony, Justice, and Policy?

What is the solution for cities such as Ferguson and Baltimore—cities that are vastly different in their demographics but quite similar in attitudes and emotions? If someone had the perfect answer to that question, he or she would probably be very wealthy. Although it takes years if not decades for the many underlying social problems in such communities to reach a boiling point, a priority is to seriously examine these cities' relationships with and understanding of their minority communities. In a community such as Ferguson—where 67 percent of the population but only 5 percent of police officers were African American—and in a nation where many people see discrimination and prejudice when blacks are arrested at nearly three times the rate of people of other races,[16] a good starting point is to diversify the agency, thus giving people a voice. As one witness told the President's Task Force on 21st Century Policing concerning youth in poor communities:

Video: Police force

> By the time you are 17 you have been stopped and frisked a dozen times. That does not make that 17-year-old want to become a police officer. The challenge is to transform the idea of policing in communities among young people into something they see as honorable. They have to see people at local events, as the person who lives across the street, not someone who comes in and knows nothing about my community.[17]

A task force member questioned why today's police seem to have gotten away from their central mission:

> Why are we training police officers like soldiers? Although police officers wear uniforms and carry weapons, the similarity ends there. The missions and rules of engagement are completely different. The soldier's mission is that of a warrior: to conquer. The police officer's mission is that of a guardian: to protect. Soldiers come into communities as an outside, occupying force. Guardians are members of the community, protecting from within.[18]

More than 1000 people gathered in New York City's Union Square in April 2015 to demand justice for Freddie Gray, who died in Baltimore while in police custody. Over 100 people were arrested.

©Giorgio Savona/Demotix/Corbis

Ray Kelly, former NYPD police commissioner, believes that in such cases the state must step in as an outside force, and a new police chief (preferably one of color) must be hired. Others (such as former Philadelphia mayor Ed Rendell, and mayors of Baltimore and Gary, Indiana) suggested that city officials and police must reach out to community leaders, meet with civic associations, add African Americans to the administration, and add an advisory committee on community relations that is composed of people of all colors.[19]

Other reform ideas in the aftermath of Ferguson included that police stop blurring the lines with the military (**militarization**) and begin wearing body cameras (discussed later in this chapter), and even that drugs be legalized (it is asserted that African Americans distrust the police because so many young black men are sent to prison for nonviolent drug offenses).[20] Also recommended was that the U.S. Department of Justice investigate such shootings to determine whether any civil rights violations occurred; other recommendations included implementing training on racial profiling and creating programs to address vestiges of segregation, dehumanization, and stereotyping in our society.[21]

In response to Freddie Gray's death in April 2015, newly appointed U.S. attorney general Loretta Lynch announced that the Justice Department's Civil Rights Division and the Federal Bureau of Investigation (FBI) would investigate the case—which is the normal approach. However, what many people wish to see are not more platitudes (like "What is needed is a national discussion on race relations"), but actual *policy* changes such as those mentioned here, as well as a review of accountability standards for officers and, as one African American minister in Baltimore put it, the use of warnings rather than a "shoot first" policy when dealing with potential suspects.[22] Certainly one form of public policy that might be examined is a requirement for police officers to possess a college degree. As discussed in Chapter 6, a long line of research—including a 2015 study at Michigan State University—has found that college-educated officers are less likely to use force on citizens; and, as researcher William Terrill stated, "If you use less force on individuals, your police department is going to be viewed as more legitimate and trustworthy and you're not going to have all the protests we're having across the country."[23]

Militarization: the use of military equipment and tactics by local police.

INVESTIGATING FURTHER

DALLAS POLICE DEPARTMENT'S POSTINGS OF INFORMATION CONCERNING OFFICER-INVOLVED SHOOTINGS

On Monday, December 9, 2013, at approximately 3:11 p.m., plain clothes deployment officers were conducting surveillance on a vehicle at 9524 Military Parkway that had been taken in a robbery offense. The vehicle became occupied by two individuals and a felony traffic stop supported by uniformed officers in marked vehicles was attempted outside the apartment complex. The vehicle did not stop and turned back into the complex. The driver fled on foot and the passenger remained in the vehicle. One officer approached the vehicle, pulled her weapon and fired one time at the B/M/19 suspect striking him. The suspect was injured and transported to Baylor Hospital.

Suspect was unarmed. The officer was terminated for violation of departmental policy and later indicted by a Dallas County Grand Jury for Aggravated Assault. No officer was injured.

One officer fired 1 round. Involved Officer: W/F 12 years, 3 months service.[24]

Some Police Responses: Greater Transparency Using Websites and Databases

Some police agencies now demonstrate complete openness regarding officer-involved shootings. An example is provided in the "Investigating Further" box, which shows facts and outcomes of one such shooting as provided by the Dallas, Texas, Police Department's website.

Also coming to light is the near total lack of national information concerning such shootings. Although one seven-year study ending in 2012 concluded that a white police officer killed a black person nearly two times a week in the United States, such information has long been considered flawed and largely incomplete (only about 750 agencies of 17,000 contribute such information, and doing so is voluntary).[25] In the wake of the police shooting death of Michael Brown in Ferguson, Missouri, measures were put in place to initiate a national database tracking such shootings in the United States. The 2014 presidential task force mentioned earlier recommended that all police agencies be required to "collect, maintain, and report data to the Federal Government on all officer-involved shootings, whether fatal or nonfatal, as well as any in-custody death."[26] The U.S. Senate passed the Death in Custody Reporting Act in December 2014, mandating that all states do so, or risk losing millions of dollars in federal grants.[27]

Throughout our history, police agencies have faced allegations of brutality and corruption. In the late 19th century, New York police sergeant Alexander "Clubber" Williams epitomized police brutality; he spoke openly of using his nightstick to knock a man unconscious, batter him to pieces, or even kill him. Williams supposedly coined the term *tenderloin* when he commented, "I've had nothing but chuck steaks for a long time, and now I'm going to have me a little tenderloin."[28] Williams was referring to opportunities for graft in an area in downtown New York that was the heart of vice and nightlife, often termed Satan's Circus. This was Williams's beat, where his reputation for using force and brutality became legendary.[29] Next we look at its permissible use, restrictions, and types.

PRACTITIONER'S PERSPECTIVE

POLICE CHIEF

Name: Michael A. Davis

Current Position: Chief of Police

City, State: Brooklyn Park, Minnesota

College Attended/ Academic Major: Bachelor of arts in criminal justice and master of arts in organizational management from Concordia University, St. Paul, Minnesota

How long have you been a practitioner in this criminal justice position? 5 years as a police chief, 21 years in law enforcement.

My primary duties and responsibilities as a practitioner in this position: To create and then lead the police department towards a cogent vision of outcomes in the community related to public safety and service. As a police chief, I also have a vital role in the community as a leader, facilitator, and expert on issues related to community livability, social fabric, and crime control. With a community of just under 80,000 residents, I also work quite closely with other department heads to ensure that the whole organization is moving in lock-step in service to our community members.

(Continued)

(Continued)

The qualities/characteristics that are most helpful in this career: Based on what my earlier career as a major in the United States Army taught me: the most important trait of an effective leader was vision. At that time, I didn't perceive "vision" as being all that important because, as a supervisor, my job (so I thought) was to execute my duties in accordance with the paradigm set by others of much higher rank. As police chief, however, vision has everything to do with my success. In this context, vision is the ability not only to project measurable outcomes for an organization but also having the knowledge and intuition to lead people towards that vision. As a police chief, I also must possess the ability to distill problems down to their root cause and coalesce the talents of those around me to come up with the best possible solution. My success depends on me effectively leveraging the strengths, capacities, passions, and skills of all stakeholders to achieve the vision. Finally, a person in my position must have an unwavering moral compass, both personally and professionally, along with an intense passion for bettering the community you serve.

In general, this is what a *typical day* looks like for a practitioner in this career: First, far from being an 8-hour day or a set schedule, spending considerable time engaged in personal development activities. These activities include reading, research, and communicating with my professional network of fellows chiefs, scholars, and experts in various fields related to community building. A typical day for me consists of first reviewing all the significant activity from the night before. This task is typically done from home early in the morning. Here I'm looking for not only what events occurred but more importantly how we as an organization responded to those events. My expectation is that not only do we consistently demonstrate competence and compassion in our work but also the ability to challenge those conditions that led to the event in the first place. I encourage each member of our department to take ownership of not just their tasks but the outcomes that we are collectively seeking in the community. Upon my arrival at work I spend much of time in communication with police staff, community members, and other stakeholders. While there are a number of formal meetings on my calendar, perhaps my most productive time is spent in the hallways, doorways, and common spaces talking to people. Much of my work is the confluence of effective task management and relationship building. Both are critical to my success as a police chief.

My advice to someone either wishing to study, or now studying, criminal justice and wanting to become a practitioner in this career: Anyone seeking a career in criminal justice must first have an understanding of what their "telos" (or purpose/goal) is for seeking a career of this type. The question one should ask is: How do my passions, capacities, and strengths fit into the work I seek to do? Oftentimes a person's perception of the work they seek and the real outcomes of that work are incongruous. People often forget that the criminal justice system is just that—a "system" designed to produce the exact results that it produces. My satisfaction is derived from the way in which I do my work within the construct of the criminal justice system. It is the autonomy that I exercise in how my work is done that creates a sense of purpose for me. I understand that my work is slow and incremental and often stalled with unexpected challenges, but it is the process of creating a future for both the department and the community that is distinct from the past that drives me in this work. If a person is not driven for outcomes they control within the criminal justice system, then I suggest they find other work, as there are some practitioners in the field that have not found their "telos" and thus satisfaction in their careers. The work of the criminal justice system is to protect our democracy and requires that all who work within it to have an intense passion for this work.

Calls for Police Use of Body Cameras

Another outgrowth of the police shootings in Ferguson, Baltimore, and other cities is the emphasis on greater police transparency—and the calls for officers to wear body cameras. With cell phones recording what appear to be a number of questionable if not criminal cases of police **use of force**—and what also appears for many people to be misrepresentation or cover-up of facts by police in the aftermath—many politicians and activists argue that all officers should be compelled to do so. But having such a policy would raise at least two important questions: (1) When, specifically, should the cameras be used; and (2) who should be allowed to view which kinds of footage?

Use of force: the type and amount of effort required to compel compliance by an unwilling suspect.

Regarding the first issue, cameras cannot be activated all of the time; officers have a reasonable right to privacy (e.g., during bathroom breaks or in private conversations), just as citizens do. Also, many people—such as confidential informants, crime victims, or witnesses—would understandably not come forward if they knew they would be recorded. There are similar problems concerning the second question, of who should view the videos: Publicly embarrassing videos of people who are being arrested or are intoxicated raise privacy concerns, and the public would also deem the recording of innocent bystanders, witnesses, victims, children, and people in their homes to be an egregious invasion of privacy.

Finally, as one expert put it, there is an "800-pound gorilla in the room" that needs to be discussed: Unless state laws are changed, it would be extremely challenging, if not impossible, for police to dedicate personnel and equipment to store, redact, and provide videos for all open-records requests (to include those by defense attorneys).[30] Body cameras can carry tremendous costs—not from the equipment itself (ranging from a few hundred to a few thousand dollars per camera), but from the time required to store and edit the videos, as well as the impact of public disclosure or open records requests under the Freedom of Information Act (FOIA). A related issue is that such FOIA requests are often from individuals or companies wishing to generate income by posting police activity on YouTube and selling advertising space.[31] The "You Be the Judge" box addresses body-camera use.

An outgrowth of recent officer-involved shootings across the U.S. is an emphasis on greater police transparency – and calls for officers to wear body cameras.

You Be the... JUDGE

Within a few weeks of initiating a 6-month pilot program to equip officers with body cameras, the city received the following request by an anonymous citizen:

> Public disclosure requests for all body-cam videos since police begin using them; every 911 dispatch on which Seattle police officers were sent; all videos from patrol-car cameras; all of the reports officers write; and the details of all computer searches by officers for persons' names, addresses, or license plate numbers were expected to financially cripple the city of Seattle, Washington, and result in the demise of a plan to equip Seattle police officers with body cameras.[32]

Washington state law allows such anonymous requests, and public agencies cannot deny records on the grounds that a request is overbroad, as long as the materials are identifiable.[33] In one such case, a request for all emails received and sent by city employees could have cost the city $110 million in salary and taken 1,376 years for one full-time employee to fulfill. The city of course argues that the administrative costs relating to such requests make honoring them cost-prohibitive.[34]

Some people argue, however, that public officials should not complain that the "sky is falling" in regard to such requests, and that public officials can address these large requests through such means as delivering materials in installments and collecting copy fees with each release to make sure the requester is serious. It is also argued that city officials sometimes exaggerate the time and technical requirements required to produce records, and look for horror stories to persuade legislators of the need to change the law.[35]

1. Should the public be allowed to make such broad requests for body-camera videos? If so, should there be a limit on the number, kinds, and costs of such requests?

2. How can the whole field of police body camera use be made fair to all parties concerned?

STUDENTS BATTLE FOR DEMOCRACY IN HONG KONG

Hong Kong police officers clashed with hundreds of pro-democracy protesters who tried to surround government headquarters in November 2013.

Under a 1984 agreement between China and Britain, the British colony of Hong Kong was returned to the People's Republic of China on July 1, 1997. Hong Kong retained its British common-law-based political system and independent judiciary.[36] At the time of the handover, Hong Kong was to have a high degree of autonomy with guaranteed rights and freedoms for its people for at least 50 years, as set forth in the Hong Kong Basic Law.

In August 2014, however, a new method for electing Hong Kong's chief executive was proposed by the mainland government. Pro-democracy activists in Hong Kong—many of them university students—feared that Beijing would eventually control all elections and Hong Kong's suffrage.[37] At an initial protest, police broke up a group of about 100 demonstrators and arrested 19 people for illegal assembly.[38] More student boycotts and rallies ensued in an "Occupy" fashion, and in September 2014 the police used pepper spray and injured several protesters during their arrests.[39]

Thus began in late 2014 a string of many such student protests—and arrests and injuries—continuing into 2015, with hundreds of protesters being arrested and injured. Seven police officers were arrested for kicking and beating a pro-democracy protester.[40] Police have used a variety of tactics and less-lethal weapons to address the protestors, which at times have numbered more than 100,000.[41] These tactics are viewed widely as heavy-handed and have included the use of tear gas on peaceful protesters.[42]

By the beginning of 2015, police had fired tear gas nearly 100 times and reported that a total of 955 individuals had been arrested and 130 police officers had received light injuries.[43] The general public on the mainland and those in Hong Kong have little direct knowledge of activities by their police or the students, however, because the Chinese government forces all websites to remove protest information and posts, and blocks all social media.

In October 2014, the United Nations Human Rights Committee urged China to allow free elections in Hong Kong.[44] Meanwhile, political leaders around the world supported the protest and suffrage, and rallies in support of the protestors have occurred in over 64 cities.[45] The protesters claim that they will end their activities only if the government offers a detailed timeline or roadmap to allow universal suffrage.

The Force Prerogative

SAGE Journal Article: Police discretion and force

Our society recognizes three legitimate and responsive forms of force: the right of self-defense (including the use of lethal force in order to protect oneself from harm), the power to control those for whom one is responsible (such as a prisoner or a patient in a mental hospital), and the relatively unrestricted authority of police to use force as required. Police work is dangerous; a routine arrest may result in a violent confrontation, sometimes triggered by drugs, alcohol, or mental illness. To confront those situations, police officers are given the unique right to use force, even deadly force, against others. There are, of course, limitations on when an officer may exercise deadly and nondeadly force; they are discussed later in this chapter.

Police Brutality

Many people contend that there are actually three means by which the police can be "brutal." There is the literal sense of the term, which involves the physical abuse of others. There is the verbal abuse of citizens, exemplified by slurs or epithets. Finally, for many who feel downtrodden, the police symbolize brutality because the officers represent the majority group's law, which serves to keep the minority groups in their place. It is perhaps this last form of **police brutality** that is of the greatest concern for anyone who is interested in improving community relations; because it is a philosophy or frame of mind, however, it is probably the most difficult to overcome.

Citizen use of the term *police brutality* encompasses a wide range of practices, from the use of profane and abusive language to the actual use of physical force or violence.[46] Although no one can deny that some police officers use brutal practices, it is impossible to know with any degree of accuracy how often and to what extent these incidents occur. They are low-visibility acts, and many victims decline to report them. It is doubtful that police brutality will ever disappear forever. There are always going to be, in the words of A. C. Germann, Frank Day, and Robert Gallati, "Neanderthals" who enjoy their absolute control over others and become tyrannical in their arbitrary application of power.[47]

THE ROLE OF LOCAL POLICE IN HOMELAND SECURITY

In March 2015, firefighters in a western city responded to a report of a firebomb at a fast food restaurant. Upon arrival, they observed a broken window, a flammable material inside, and the initials "ALF" written on a drive-through sign. Recognizing the signs of possible domestic terrorism (ALF are the initials of the Animal Liberation Front, a group that is at times violent in its opposition to anything they suspect to involve animal cruelty), the firefighters immediately secured the scene and contacted the FBI.[48]

This incident clearly demonstrates the need for all public-safety first responders—police, fire, medical, military, health, and so on—to be vigilant in identifying the signs of terrorism in today's post-9/11 society. Although the role of the federal Department of Homeland Security was discussed in Chapter 5, and terrorism *per se* is reviewed in Chapter 16, here we briefly examine the role of local (municipal police and county sheriff's) personnel in **homeland security**—a daunting task for a nation with 3.79 million square miles, about 3,000 counties, and 2,500 cities with 10,000 or more people.[49]

Since September 11, 2001, there have been more than 50 terrorist attacks in the United States. Some are well-known and highly publicized, such as the attack involving two bombs at the Boston Marathon in April 2013. Most, however, involve lesser-known violent acts in which a single extremist (often an Islamic person engaged in jihad) uses a gun or knife; others are foiled, such as attempts to place bombs near public facilities or to send harmful chemicals through the mail; some involve people protesting against perceived animal abuses, abortion clinics, or the armed forces.[50]

Local police are widely recognized as being the eyes and ears in the U.S. counterterrorism effort. New York City police chief William Bratton argues that local police also know which targets are more at risk and are best equipped to coordinate the

Police brutality: unnecessary use of force by police against citizens, resulting in injury.

Homeland security (police role in): local police working with federal agencies to obtain the tools, information, and resources necessary for understanding tactics, behaviors, and other indicators of terrorist activity.

©JIM BOURG/Reuters/Corbis

Local police have had to assume an increasingly important role in homeland security. Here, officers search for Dzhokhar Tsarnaev, the surviving suspect in the Boston Marathon bombings in April 2013.

SAGE Journal Article: Police and homeland security

first response to attacks. Furthermore, because they are experienced in conducting investigations, well-schooled in community policing and problem solving, and thus possess a vast network of contacts in the community, local police are well positioned to deal with terrorist networks.[51]

Today's police agencies must assume that it is not a question of *if* another terrorist attack will occur on U.S. soil, but *when* it will occur. They must consider the possibility of attacks using weapons of mass destruction, including biological, nuclear, or radioactive devices. Depending on their location, agencies must plan for the possibility that the risk of attack is high—for example, if their community has historically significant assets (e.g., Independence Hall in Philadelphia, the Alamo in San Antonio, Texas); is a center of tourism (Las Vegas); is a state capital or a major commercial, manufacturing, or financial center (Wall Street); is near a port of entry; is the site of animal research facilities; is near a large military base; or is a major site for petroleum refineries, nuclear facilities, or a transportation hub.[52]

Particularly in such locations, police agencies should have plans in place for addressing a terrorist threat. They also might create a counterterrorism unit; reassign officers to assess and protect the kinds of critical infrastructure described previously; send officers to receive training in new skills relating to terrorism; shift staffing from lower priority programs, such as DARE (Drug Abuse Resistance Education) or foot patrols; and attempt to obtain federal grants to help cover these additional tasks. In addition, police executive staff should ensure that intelligence data are collected and analyzed, limit access to and parking near critical facilities, have personnel and the community be alert for suspicious packages, monitor all municipal reservoirs and wastewater treatment plants, and ensure that related assets such as command posts, public information, officer shift modification and family assistance, and equipment are in place.[53]

Finally, when an attack does occur, local police must ensure that

- Ingress and egress from the attack site are managed, so that emergency vehicles can get to and from the scene and victims can be evacuated

- Community policing remains in place, not only so that officers can take the lead in coordinating efforts against vigilantism, but also to reach out to involved communities (for example, Islamic and Arabic communities in the case of terrorism by Islamic militants) for information or help in developing informants.

- Manage and share information (not only with the public, but also with assisting police, fire, military, and medical units), and give accurate instructions.[54]

WHEN FAILING THE PUBLIC TRUST: CIVIL LIABILITY

The specter of **civil liability** looms large every workday for people engaged in police work. With the possible exception of professionals working in the medical field, no group of workers is more susceptible to litigation and liability than police (and prison) employees. Frequently cast into confrontational situations, and given the complex nature of their work and its requisite training needs, they will from time to time act in a manner that evokes public scrutiny, complaints, and financial remuneration to persons who have suffered as a result (see next section). As we will see, the price of failure among public servants can be quite high, in both human and financial terms.

Following are recent examples, as reported by ABC News, of the kinds of police actions that lead to liability; none of these cases were tried by a jury, being settled out of court instead:

- Two women mistakenly shot by Los Angeles police during a manhunt in early 2013 reached a $4.2 million settlement. A woman and her daughter were delivering newspapers when police officers fired about 100 bullets at their pickup truck—which did not match the suspect's vehicle. The city attorney opined that the settlement allowed the city to get out "pretty cheaply all things considered."

- A dancer on a boat chartered for a gay pride party in San Diego jumped into the San Diego Bay and was shot and killed by Harbor Police during an altercation as they tried to get him out of the water. Police said the man fought with an officer and tried to grab his gun, but the man's parents argued he was unarmed and shot in the back; they settled the case for $2.5 million.

- In 2011, a 37-year-old homeless man with schizophrenia was stopped by two Fullerton, California, officers for allegedly trying to break in to cars at a bus depot. Officers beat the man and used a Taser several times; he died five days later. The city awarded $1 million to the victim's mother.

- Heavily armed police entered a home in Connecticut with guns drawn and flash grenades exploding, and then shot and killed a man who was watching television at the time. The raid reportedly occurred because police were under pressure to "do something" about the man, who entertained exotic dancers in his home and was considered a blot on the neighborhood. His family settled their lawsuit for $3.5 million in early 2013.[55]

Student on the Street Video: Police officers and civil rights

Civil liability: in tort law, the basis for which a cause of action (e.g., fine) is made to recover damages; in criminal justice, where a police or corrections officer, for example, violates someone's civil rights.

Torts and Negligence

A **tort** is the infliction of some injury on one person by another. Three categories of torts generally cover most of the lawsuits filed against criminal justice practitioners: negligence, intentional torts, and constitutional torts.

Negligence can arise when a criminal justice employee's conduct creates a danger to others. In other words, the employee did not conduct his or her affairs in a manner so as to avoid subjecting others to a risk of harm and may be held liable for the injuries caused to others.[56]

Intentional torts occur when an employee engages in a voluntary act that has a substantial likelihood of resulting in injury to another; examples are assault and battery, false arrest and imprisonment, malicious prosecution, and abuse of process. *Constitutional torts* involve employees' duty to recognize and uphold the constitutional rights, privileges, and immunities of others; violations of these guarantees may subject the employee to a civil suit, most frequently brought in federal court under 42 U.S. Code Section 1983, discussed in the next section.[57]

Assault, battery, false imprisonment, false arrest, invasion of privacy, negligence, defamation, and malicious prosecution are examples of torts that are commonly brought against police officers. **False arrest** is the arrest of a person without probable cause. False imprisonment is the intentional illegal detention of a person; this can occur not only in jail, but also whenever someone is confined to a specified area. For example, the police may fail to release an arrested person after a proper bail or bond has been posted, they can delay the arraignment of an arrested person unreasonably, or authorities can fail to release a prisoner after they no longer have authority to hold him or her.

A single act may also be a crime as well as a tort. For example, if Officer Smith, in an unprovoked attack, injures Jones, the state will attempt to punish Smith in a criminal action by sending him to jail or prison, fining him, or both. The state would have the burden of proof at criminal trial, having to prove Smith guilty "beyond a reasonable doubt." Furthermore, Jones may sue Smith for money damages in a civil action for the personal injury he suffered. In this civil suit, Jones would have the burden of proving Smith's acts were tortious by a "preponderance of the evidence"—a lower standard than that in a criminal court and thus easier to satisfy.

Section 1983 Legislation

The primary civil instrument that can be used against the police is **Section 1983**. Following the Civil War and in reaction to the activities of the Ku Klux Klan, Congress enacted the Ku Klux Klan Act of 1871, later codified as U.S. Code, Title 42, Section 1983. It states that:

> Every person who, under color of any statute, ordinance, regulation, custom, or usage of any State or Territory, subjects, or causes to be subjected, any citizen of the United States or any other person within the jurisdiction thereof to the deprivation of any rights, privileges, or immunities secured by the Constitution and laws, shall be liable to the party injured in an action at law, suit in equity, or other proper proceeding for redress.

A trend is for such litigants to cast a wide net in their lawsuits, suing not only the principal actors in the incident, but agency administrators and supervisors as well. This breadth of suing represents the notion of **vicarious liability**, or the doctrine of *respondeat superior*, an old legal maxim meaning, "let the master answer." In sum, an employer can be found liable in certain instances for wrongful acts of the employee.

Tort: a civil wrong or infraction; the remedy will be damages awarded in civil trial.

Negligence: failure to perform a duty owed.

False arrest: unlawful physical restraint by a police officer, for no valid reason.

Section 1983: a portion of the U.S. Code that allows a legal action to be brought against a police officer or other person in position of authority who, it is believed, used his or her position ("acted under color of law") to violate one's civil rights.

Vicarious liability: a legal doctrine whereby a person is responsible for the actions of another and is to exercise reasonable and prudent care in supervising that person.

Respondeat superior: "let the master answer" (Latin)—a doctrine in liability that establishes a duty of supervisors to control their employees and be considered liable for their actions.

An example is the 1991 case of Rodney King, who, following a vehicle pursuit, was kicked, stomped, and beaten with batons (totaling 56 blows, all of which was caught on an 81-second videotape) by three Los Angeles police officers.[58] King sued the officers and the city under Section 1983 and was awarded $3.8 million for his injuries.[59]

Police *supervisors* have also been found liable for injuries arising out of an official policy or custom of their department. Injuries resulting from a chief's verbal or written support of heavy-handed behavior resulting in the use of excessive force by officers have resulted in such liability.[60]

General Areas of Liability

To help readers to conceptualize what is meant by police civil liability, following are some general areas in which police liability may be found.

Proximate Cause

Proximate cause is basically something that causes an event, particularly an injury due to negligence or an intentional wrongful act. In other words, the injury caused would not have occurred but for the cause. As an example, it is established by asking, "But for the officer's conduct, would someone have been injured or killed?" If the answer to this question is no, then proximate cause is established, and the officer can be held liable for the damage or injury. An example is where an officer is inappropriately and negligently involved in a high-speed chase and the fleeing driver strikes an innocent third party.[61] Proximate cause also may be found when an officer who leaves the scene of an accident is aware of dangerous conditions (e.g., spilled oil, smoke, vehicle debris, stray animals) and does not give proper warning to motorists.[62]

Persons in Custody and Safe Facilities

Courts generally rule that police officers have a **duty of care** to persons in their custody, including a legal responsibility to take reasonable precautions to keep detainees free from harm, to render medical assistance when necessary, and to treat detainees humanely.[63] This duty, however, typically does not include self-inflicted injury or suicide, because these acts are generally considered to result from the detainee's own intentional conduct.[64] However, if a prisoner's suicide is "reasonably foreseeable" from his or her actions or statements, then the jailer has a duty of care to help prevent that suicide.

Police also need to provide safe facilities. For example, the construction of a Detroit jail's holding cell did not allow officers to observe detainees' movements; there were no electronic monitoring devices for observing detainees, and there was an absence of detoxification cells required under state department of corrections rules. Therefore, following a suicide in this facility, the court held that these building defects contributed to the detainee's death.[65]

Failure to Protect

This form of negligence may occur if a police officer fails to protect a person from a known and foreseeable danger. Claims of **failure to protect** most often involve battered women. However, police informants, witnesses, and other people dependent on the police can be a source of police liability if an officer fails to take reasonable action to prevent them from being victimized. (See the "You Be the Judge" box.)

The 1991 beating of Rodney King by Los Angeles police officers resulted in King's being awarded $3.8 million for his injuries.

Charles Steiner/Image Works/Time Life Pictures/Getty Images

Video: Seattle Police lawsuit

Proximate cause: a factor that contributed heavily to an event, such as an auto crash or death.

Duty of care: a legal obligation imposed on someone; in the case of the police, they have a legal responsibility to see that persons in their custody are free from harm, given necessary medical assistance when necessary, and treated humanely.

Failure to protect: a situation where police place someone in jeopardy, such as giving out the location of a battered spouse or names of victims or witnesses.

Vehicle Pursuits

Vehicle pursuits are of great concern because they involve tremendous potential for injury, property damage, and liability. As one police manual describes it, "The decision by a police officer to pursue a citizen in a motor vehicle is among the most critical that can be made,"[66] putting innocent third parties—other drivers and bystanders—at risk. Police policy and procedure manuals are very thorough where pursuits are concerned, and they typically order the supervisor to shut down the pursuit unless there is probable cause to believe the suspect presents a clear and immediate threat to the safety of others, or has committed or is attempting to commit a violent felony.

Two cases explain the law of high-speed pursuits. The first involves two Sacramento County, California, deputies who pursued a motorcyclist for a traffic violation at speeds greater than 100 miles per hour; the motorcycle crashed, and the deputies' vehicle could not stop in time, striking and killing the motorcycle's passenger. The passenger's family claimed in a civil suit that the pursuit violated the crash victim's due process rights under the Fourteenth Amendment. The U.S. Supreme Court, in *County of Sacramento v. Lewis* (1998),[68] held that the proper standard in such cases is whether the officer's conduct "shocks the conscience." That is, was the conduct offensive to a reasonable person's sense of moral goodness? The Court felt that, in this case, deputies had no intent to harm the suspects and thus their behavior did not "shock the conscience." In 2007, the Supreme Court heard another case involving the level of force used by police in such pursuits. A deputy's pursuit of a 19-year-old Georgia youth, driving at speeds up to 90 miles per hour for 9 miles, ended in a violent crash that left the youth a quadriplegic. His lawyers argued that the Fourth Amendment protects against the use of excessive force—and that when high-speed drivers have their cars stopped in pursuits, a "seizure" occurs for Fourth Amendment purposes. The Supreme Court held that an officer's attempt to terminate a dangerous high-speed car chase that threatens the lives of innocent bystanders "does not violate the Fourth Amendment, even when it places the fleeing motorist at risk of serious injury or death."[69]

Still, it is important to remember that a police pursuit is justified only when the necessity of apprehension outweighs the degree of danger created by the pursuit.

You Be the... POLICE OFFICER

What, if any, legal obligation is held by the police to protect someone from his or her estranged spouse who has been served with a legal restraining order? That question was at the crux of a lawsuit from Castle Rock, Colorado, which was ultimately heard by the U.S. Supreme Court. Jessica Gonzales's restraining order required her husband to remain at least 100 yards from her and their three daughters except during specified visitation times. One evening the husband took possession of the three children in violation of the order; Mrs. Gonzales repeatedly urged the police to search for and arrest her husband, but they took no immediate action (due to Jessica's allowing her husband to take the children at various hours). At approximately 3:20 a.m., the husband appeared at the city police station and instigated a shoot-out with the police (he died). A search of his vehicle revealed the corpses of the three daughters, whom the husband had killed prior to his arrival. U.S. cities are generally immune from lawsuits, so in this case the Supreme Court was asked to decide whether Jessica Gonzales could sue the city because of inaction by its police officers.

1. Were the police *morally* responsible for the deaths of the three girls?
2. Were the police *legally* responsible for their deaths?
3. If you believe Jessica should be allowed to sue the city, and the police were liable, how much financial compensation should Jessica receive?

See the Notes section at the end of the book for the outcome and whether or not the city was deemed as liable for its police department's actions.[67]

NEEDED: MORE WOMEN AND MINORITIES

Although this chapter section could have been included in the discussion of recruitment in Chapter 6, certainly a *challenge* for today's police in our increasingly diverse society is for the police to be represented by women and minorities. But practically since its beginning, as reflected by the numbers, policing has been a predominantly male- and non-minority-dominated occupation.

Gains and Obstacles for Women

Over the past 30 years, the proportion of women police officers has grown steadily. During the 1970s, some formal barriers to hiring women were eliminated, such as height requirements; in addition, subjective physical agility tests and oral interviews were modified. Some job discrimination suits further expanded women's opportunities. Women now represent about 12 percent of the sworn personnel in local (municipal and county) police agencies.[70] State agencies as a whole have a much lower percentage of female officers (6.5 percent) than either local or federal law enforcement agencies.[71] Women account for about 15 percent of all federal sworn officers, which is a bit higher than local agencies.[72]

In addition to helping to diversify the police labor force, there are certainly practical advantages to having women in uniform; according to a report by the National Center for Women and Policing:

Certainly one of the challenges facing police agencies today is greater representation by female and minority police officers.

• Female officers are proven to be as competent as their male counterparts. The center notes that several evaluations of the effectiveness of female officers in a number of work-related areas in several large cities (e.g., Washington, D.C., St. Louis, New York City, Denver, Philadelphia) concluded that men and women were equally capable of successful performance as patrol officers.

Author Video: Women and minorities in policing

• Female officers are less likely to use excessive force. Research both in the United States and in international venues demonstrates that, compared to male officers, female officers use a less authoritarian style of policing that relies less on physical force—and their communication skills allow them to defuse situations.

• Female officers implement "community-oriented policing." Community policing and problem solving emphasize communication and cooperation with citizens as well as informal problem solving. The center believes that, in addition to their communication skills, women officers demonstrate empathy toward others and interact in a way that is not designed to "prove" something.

• More female officers will improve law enforcement's response to violence against women. It is critical that the police respond properly to problems of sexual and physical assaults against women; the price of failure is high, not only in terms of crimes against the victims, but also in terms of the risk of litigation (particularly in domestic violence cases). The center cites studies indicating that female officers have

SAGE Journal Article: Female policing

long been viewed as more effective than their male counterparts in responding to crimes against women.

- Increasing the presence of female officers reduces problems of sex discrimination and harassment within a law enforcement agency.

Video: Women and minorities in policing

A primary challenge to seeing more women in policing begins with the fact that most women never consider such a career to begin with, perhaps owing to their misunderstanding of the nature of the job and the macho image portrayed in the media. Then, if hired, women may face discrimination, sexual harassment, or even peer intimidation, and possibly enter an agency where there might be few women role models or mentors to help them adjust and to move up the ranks.[73] Certainly these are issues that must be addressed before women are fully represented and provide the aforementioned benefits to the field.

Greater Racial and Ethnic Diversity Needed as Well

Today, about 12 percent of local police officers are African American; about 12 percent are Hispanic; and 3 percent are Asian, American Indian, or other races or ethnicities. In communities of fewer than 50,000 people, however, less than 6 percent of local police officers are either African American or Hispanic, and fewer than 2 percent are Asian or American Indian.[74] Obviously, in these smaller communities (particularly in those such as the aforementioned Ferguson, Missouri, where only 5.6 percent of police officers were African American, compared with 67 percent of the general population),[75] diversification of the police force to reflect the community's demographics is of major importance. The President's Task Force on 21st Century Policing stated that "law enforcement agencies should strive to create a workforce that contains a broad range of diversity including race, gender, language, life experience, and cultural background to improve understanding and effectiveness in dealing with all communities."[76]

L3 Communications

Police agencies are equipped with many forms of high-technology. This device uses a computer to scan license plate numbers and locate stolen vehicles or persons who have outstanding arrest warrants.

POLICE TECHNOLOGIES

New Uses, New Concerns

In addition to the new emphasis on police use of body cameras, discussed earlier in this chapter, there are other concerns and pressures for reform in the area of police technologies. Historically, technologies have had a tremendous impact on policing, greatly expanding and changing the work of patrol officers, criminal investigators, forensics, and other specialized assignments (e.g., bomb disposal). With those technologies—now including the use of video cameras on light poles, satellites and drones to observe from the skies, smartphones that relay all sorts of information to sentinel towers, and license-plate cameras tracking people's movements—come a number of concerns, however. For example, in January 2015, the U.S. Senate Judiciary Committee indicated "privacy concerns of the highest order" with at least 50 federal and local law enforcement agencies using radar devices to effectively see inside suspects' homes. Like sophisticated motion detectors, the devices can detect movement as slight as someone breathing. Civil rights organizations and even several federal judges have indicated strong concerns about using the devices without a search warrant.[77]

This chapter section provides a sampling of other, less controversial police technologies for addressing old crime and security problems. What is becoming clear, however, is that the greater the sophistication of a piece of technology, the greater the likelihood it will be challenged on Fourth Amendment grounds.

Many U.S. police departments, including small agencies, are using laptop computers with wireless connections to access crime and motor vehicle databases. These systems are believed to pay for themselves in increased fines and officer safety. Officers can access court documents, in-house police department records, and a system of computer-aided dispatching and can enter license numbers into their computers. Through a national network of motor vehicle and criminal history databases, they can locate drivers with outstanding warrants, expired or suspended licenses, and so on. Furthermore, rather than using open radio communications, police officers use their computers to communicate with one another via email.[78]

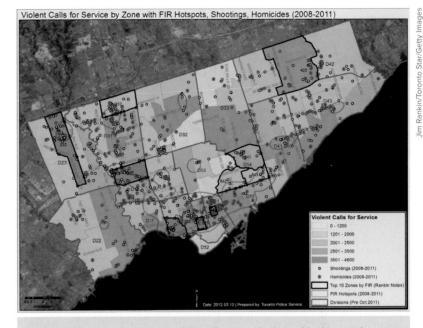

Using computerized crime mapping, police can obtain a wide perspective on crime. (FIR stands for field information reports.)

Crime Mapping

Computerized **crime mapping** combines geographic information from Global Positioning System (GPS) devices with crime statistics gathered by a department's computer-aided dispatching system and demographic data provided by private companies or the U.S. Census Bureau. The result is a picture that combines disparate sets of data for a whole new perspective on crime. For example, maps of crimes can be overlaid with maps or layers of causative data: unemployment rates in the areas of high crime, locations of abandoned houses, population density, reports of drug activity, or geographic features (such as alleys, canals, or open fields) that might be contributing factors.[79] Furthermore, the hardware and software are now available to nearly all police agencies for a few thousand dollars. In 1997, the national Crime Mapping Research Conference was established to promote research, evaluation, development, and dissemination of geographic information systems technology for criminal justice research and practice.[80]

Video: Recording the police

Locating Serial Offenders

Most offenders operate close to home and tend to operate in target-rich environments to "hunt" for their prey. Geographic profiling analyzes the geography of such locations and the sites of the victim encounters—the attacks, the murders, and the body dumps—and maps the most probable location of the suspect's home.[81] Washington state uses a homicide investigation and tracking system (HITS) that links crime-related databases to vice and gang files, sex offender registries, corrections and parole records, and department of motor vehicle databases. Then, when a major crime occurs, a central system scans every database to compare eyewitness descriptions of a suspect and vehicle, and then builds a data set containing profiles of the offender, the victims, and the incidents. The data set then goes into a geographic information system, where the program selects and maps the names and addresses of those suspects whose method of operation fits the crimes being investigated.[82]

Crime mapping: plotting of crimes on maps so as to show patterns of location, time, day, and so on.

Smartphones

Video: Technology and policing

Unquestionably, social media are changing the way police operate as well (see "Investigating Further"). One smartphone app now allows officers responding to calls for service to determine instantly if previously reported incidents and convicted criminals are associated with a particular address. Officers can point their phone at a particular location and, using the phone's GPS, check the arrest history or officer safety hazard information of the address in question. When looking for a missing child, an icon appears if any sex offenders are living nearby. The app can also track the location of police units, allowing the officer to determine distances of backup units.[83]

INVESTIGATING FURTHER

SOCIAL MEDIA AND CRIME FIGHTING

Minutes after a shooting near the Oakland Airport (which killed seven people), the gunman was on the loose. A police sergeant quickly fired off a flurry of text alerts to thousands of nearby residents through a social media tool for law enforcement agencies, warning them to stay out of the area and, eventually, informing them the danger had passed and the shooter was in custody.

Across the country, police agencies are using social media as crime-fighting tools, providing residents with real-time alerts on crimes in progress, traffic messes, and missing children. And it works: Police in Amarillo, Texas, captured a fugitive wanted for aggravated

robbery, and a robbery suspect in Fayetteville, North Carolina, was caught after an alert was sent out.

A survey found that about 9 of 10 agencies use some form of social media; some, like Nixle, have security features that make them less susceptible to hacking than some social media. This tool allows police to send out alerts and advisories to its subscribers either citywide or just to a specific neighborhood within a quarter-mile radius. Subscriptions typically spike when populaces suffer crises such as tornadoes, wildfires, and major violent crimes.

Source: Adapted from Terry Collins, "Police Embrace Emerging Social Media Tool," *Associated Press*, August 11, 2012, http://news.yahoo.com/police-embrace-emerging-social-media-tool-150141734.html.

Electronic control devices: less-lethal tools used by police to incapacitate noncompliant suspects by stimulating the motor neurons, thus causing temporary motor skill dysfunction.

Robotics: technology for designing, building, and operating robots.

Stored Communications Act: an act allowing law enforcement access to electronic messages greater than 180 days old without a warrant (but with a court order or subpoena, such access may be obtained for messages less than 180 days old).

Electronic Control Devices

A federal survey found that about 60 percent of local police departments, employing 75 percent of all officers, and 30 percent of sheriff's offices, authorized their officers to use handheld **electronic control devices** (ECDs, also known as conducted energy devices, or CEDs), such as a Taser or stun gun.[84] These ECDs have become smaller and easier for police to carry, and more effective to use (including a range of up to 35 feet). A new Taser Cam has been introduced, which allows the Taser ECD's deployment to be recorded with full audio and video, even in zero light conditions. Also new is the Taser X3, a multishot ECD that can engage multiple targets and display warning arcs while loaded.

Robotics

Recent advances in **robotics** ("bots" in tech-speak) have allowed policing (and soldiering) to become safer. Robots are now fitted with odor sensors; video capability, including night vision; a camera (also useful for photographing crime scenes); a Taser ECD; and even the ability to engage in two-way communications.[89] Robots with seven-foot arms (that scan the inside and undercarriage of vehicles for bombs), lights, video cameras (that zoom and swivel), obstacle-hurling flippers, and jointed arms (that have hand-like grippers to disable or destroy bombs) are even relatively commonplace. A recent application of such a robot for policing is discussed in the next "Investigating Further" box.

You Be the... JUDGE

In February 2001, a businessman was gunned down in Fort Lauderdale, Florida; four years later the prosecutor charged three men with the murder. The three suspects awaited trial for over five years, and the evidence to be used turned on the admissibility of two of the suspects' cell phone records—specifically, an analysis of the location data contained in them (which placed two of the men within 500 feet of the murder as it occurred). The defense argued that the use of such evidence violated the defendants' constitutional rights, but the judge refused to suppress the cell phone records on grounds that cell phone users have no reasonable expectation of privacy in location information gathered by the police.[85]

One survey found that there are now about 1.3 million such requests for cell phone tracking data each year. The potential for tracking data to assist police investigations is undeniable. However, the issue is whether or not law enforcement agencies, phone manufacturers, cell carriers, and software makers should be exploiting users' personal privacy data without their knowledge.[86]

The **Stored Communications Act**,[87] enacted in 1986, speaks to these issues. Essentially, whereas the Fourth Amendment to the U.S. Constitution protects people's right to be secure against unreasonable searches and seizures in their houses, papers, and effects, the amendment's protections do not apply to electronically stored information in part because Americans do not have a "reasonable expectation of privacy" in an online context. Furthermore, users of such devices generally entrust the security of online information to a third party, an Internet service provider (ISP), and many courts have held that, in doing so, users relinquish any expectation of privacy.

At present, the Stored Communications Act allows law enforcement access to electronic messages greater than 180 days old without a warrant (or, with a court order or subpoena, such access may be obtained for messages less than 180 days old). The government does not need to establish probable cause but must only offer facts showing that the information sought is material to an ongoing criminal investigation.[88]

1. Which side do you believe makes the most compelling argument: people have a right to privacy, or law enforcement agencies need to use such technologies to identify and arrest offenders?

2. Would it alter or reinforce your opinion to know that in *Katz v. U.S.* (1967), the U.S. Supreme Court ruled that police violate one's right to privacy when electronically listening to and recording, without a warrant, one's conversation inside a public telephone booth?

Traffic Functions

A multicar traffic collision (also termed a traffic crash) can turn a street or highway into a parking lot for many hours, sometimes even days. The police must collect evidence related to the collision, including measurements and sketches of the scene, vehicle and body positions, skid marks, street or highway elevations, intersections, and curves. Some police agencies have begun using GPS devices to determine details such as vehicle location and damage, elevation, grade, radii of curves, and critical speed. A transmitter takes a series of "shots" to find the exact locations and measurements of collision details like skid marks, area of impact, and debris. That information is then downloaded into the system, and the coordinates are plotted on an aerial shot of the intersection or roadway. Using computer technology, investigators then superimpose the details on the aerial shot, thus re-creating the collision scene to scale. Digital photos of the collision are incorporated into the final product, resulting in a highly accurate depiction of the collision.[90]

Computer technologies now assist police in investigating traffic crashes; this officer is using collision reconstruction software.

AP Photo/The Gazette, Cliff Jette

INVESTIGATING FURTHER

USING ROBOTS FOR A MASS SHOOTER

James Holmes committed one of the worst mass shootings in American history: killing 12 people and wounding more than 50 at an Aurora, Colorado, movie theater on July 20, 2012, during a late-night screening of a *Batman* movie. After being arrested, Holmes informed police that his apartment was booby-trapped, so local, state, and federal police officers; firefighters; and bomb-squad experts converged on Holmes's apartment to evacuate neighbors and search for additional evidence.

The officers' first action was to send in a bomb-removal robot to disarm a tripwire guarding the apartment's front door. The robot then neutralized potential explosive devices, incendiary devices, and fuel found near the door. Next, the robot's camera—which revealed numerous containers with accelerants and trigger mechanisms—searched for computers or any other evidence to be removed before

attempting to disarm additional explosives. Eventually, 30 aerial shells filled with gunpowder, two containers filled with liquid accelerants, and numerous bullets left to explode in the resulting fire were found in the apartment. Evidence was collected and sent to the FBI laboratory's Terrorist Explosive Device Analytical Center in Quantico, Virginia. Later, another bomb-disposal robot was sent to a potentially related threat on the University of Colorado at Denver's medical campus in Aurora, where Holmes could have shipped some of the items used in the attack.

Source: John Ingold, "James Holmes Faces 142 Counts, Including 24 of First-Degree Murder," *Denver Post*, July 30, 2012, http://www.denverpost .com/breakingnews/ci_21191265/hearing-underway-man-suspected-killing-12-aurora-theater; also see Larry Greenmeier, "Bomb-Disarming Robot Was First to Enter Alleged Aurora Shooter's Apartment, " *Scientific American*, July 25, 2012, http://blogs.scientificamerican.com/observations/2012/07/25/bomb-disarming-robot-was-first-to-enter-alleged-aurora-shooters-apartment/.

Databases for Fingerprints and Mug Shots

Though perhaps not as exotic as DNA identification, fingerprints are still a reliable means of positively identifying someone, and advances continue to be made in the field. Throughout the country, filing cabinets are filled with ink-smeared cards that hold the keys to countless unsolved crimes if only the data could be located. An automated fingerprint identification system (AFIS) allows this legacy of data to be shared rapidly. One such system is the Western Identification Network (www.winid.org), established by nine states as a way to share their 17 million fingerprint records. These states were later joined by local agencies and the FBI, the Internal Revenue Service, the Secret Service, and the Drug Enforcement Administration. The system can generally provide a match within a few hours and has helped solve more than 5,000 crimes. A digital photo exchange facility known as WinPho is now being added to supplement fingerprint data.[91]

IN A NUTSHELL

- The exceptionally high—and well-publicized—number of police shootings involving unarmed minorities in recent years has resulted in a national task-force study, calls for better record-keeping of such shootings, greater demands for transparency and less militarization of police, and the use of body cameras.

- Our society recognizes three legitimate and responsive forms of force: the right of self-defense, the power to control those for whom one is responsible, and the relatively unrestricted authority of police to use

force as required. Police officers are given the unique right to use force, even deadly force, against others; however, limitations are placed on when an officer may exercise force.

- Historically, three forms of police brutality have been recognized: the physical abuse of others, the verbal abuse of citizens, and officers representing the majority group's law.

- The role of local police in homeland security is key to identifying and investigating terrorist attacks. Comprehensive plans should be in place for addressing such attacks before, while, and after they occur.

- The specter of civil liability looms large over police work. Often being in confrontational situations, police officers may from time to time act in a manner that evokes public scrutiny and complaints. They and their superiors may be sued for a variety of reasons if a citizen believes his or her rights were violated; the primary civil instrument that can be used against the police is Section 1983.

- High-speed vehicle pursuits by police are legally permissible but are to be used only when certain conditions are met.

- Although women and minority representation in policing has grown over the past decades, these groups are still underrepresented overall; greater numbers of both women and minorities are needed—as is greater accommodation—if the police are to become diversified like the rest of society.

- Technology has improved the capabilities of nearly every aspect of police patrol and investigations—bringing with it some concerns about citizens' right to privacy.

⑤SAGE edge™ Review key terms with eFlashcards. ◀

KEY TERMS & CONCEPTS

Civil liability, 175
Crime mapping, 181
Duty of care, 177
Electronic control devices, 182
Failure to protect, 177
False arrest, 176

Homeland security (police role in), 173
Militarization, 168
Negligence, 176
Police brutality, 173
Proximate cause, 177
Respondeat superior, 176

Robotics, 182
Section 1983, 176
Stored Communications Act, 183
Tort, 176
Use of force, 170
Vicarious liability, 176

⑤SAGE edge™ Test your understanding of chapter content. Take the practice quiz. ◀

REVIEW QUESTIONS?

1. What national concerns were raised with police use of deadly force and other practices as an outgrowth of events in Ferguson, Missouri, and other cities? What might other similarly situated cities do in order to prevent future problems of this nature?

2. What are the types of police brutality? Which one is most problematic for the police?

3. What do you believe constitutes inappropriate use of force by the police?

4. What functions can the local police perform in coping with a terrorist attack?

5. What kinds of police behaviors are deemed to be corrupt in nature?

6. How would you define U.S. Code, Title 42, Section 1983?

7. What is meant by duty of care and failure to protect, and what are some examples as these concepts apply to police supervisors and officers?

8. How might the police be deemed liable if they are involved in vehicle pursuits?

9. What challenges have made it difficult to bring more women and minorities into the field?

10. How have technologies assisted police investigative functions? Patrol operations?

11. What types of technologies have led to privacy concerns among legislators, civil rights organizations, and federal judges?

LEARN BY DOING

1. In the past six months, there has been a spike in the number of citizen complaints in your community alleging inappropriate use of force by police against minorities. Local interest groups and churches are demanding data concerning police use of force as well as a review of policies regarding same. As your police department's community liaison, you are asked to respond to these demands. What approaches will you take?

2. Your criminal justice professor assigns your class a group project wherein you are to argue which technologies are the most useful in crime fighting. How will you respond, and why?

3. Your police chief assigns you the task of developing a new method for recruiting both women and minority police officers. Money is no object, because the mayor has made agency diversity a top priority for the coming year. What will you recommend in terms of how to reach individuals in markets from which officers are not typically recruited?

STUDY SITE

⑤SAGE edge™

Review → Practice → Improve

Sharpen your skills with **SAGE edge** at **edge.sagepub.com/peak2e**

SAGE edge for students provides a personalized approach to help you accomplish your coursework goals in an easy-to-use learning environment. Access the videos, audio clips, quizzes, and SAGE journal articles that are noted in this chapter.

PRACTICE AND APPLY WHAT YOU'VE LEARNED

▶ edge.sagepub.com/peak2e

$SAGE edge™

THINK YOU'VE MASTERED THE CONTENT?

Check your comprehension on the study site with:

- An online **action plan** that includes tips and feedback on progress through the course and materials, allowing you to individualize your learning experience

- **Chapter summaries with learning objectives** that reinforce the key concepts in each chapter

EXPOUNDING THE CONSTITUTION
Laws of Arrest, Search, and Seizure

LEARNING OBJECTIVES

As a result of reading this chapter, you will be able to:

1 Outline the general protections enjoyed by citizens under the Fourth, Fifth, and Sixth Amendments

2 Define and provide examples of probable cause

3 Explain the rationale for, ramifications of, and exceptions to the exclusionary rule

4 Distinguish between arrests and searches and seizures with and without a warrant

5 Explain the rights of—and limitations on—the police with regard to searching a person's home, immediate area, body, and vehicle

6 Discuss some significant ways in which the *Miranda* decision has been eroded

7 Review what is meant by "stop and frisk"

8 Explain generally to what extent the police may use electronic devices in order to obtain information from members of the public

9 Describe what rights are held by criminal defendants regarding the right to counsel, for both felony and misdemeanor arrests

ASSESS YOUR AWARENESS

Test your knowledge of your constitutional rights regarding arrest, search, and seizure by responding to the following seven true-false items; check your answers after reading this chapter's materials.

1 The standard for a legal arrest, search, and seizure is probable cause.

2 The exclusionary rule requires that evidence obtained by police in violation of the Fourth Amendment may *not* be used against the defendant in a criminal trial.

3 There are essentially two ways for the police to make an arrest: with a warrant and without a warrant.

4 The courts grant police greater latitude in searching automobiles, which can be used to help make a getaway and to hide evidence.

5 The *Miranda* warning remains intact from its original version; no deviations in its explanation or practice by police are permitted.

6 Generally, police do not have to "search" for things they see in plain view.

7 Nowhere is the law harsher than in the Middle East, particularly in Saudi Arabia.

We must never forget that it is a constitution we are expounding.

—John Marshall, *McCulloch v. Maryland* (1819)[1]

<< Answers can be found on page 424.

Cell phones have changed everything, including the law that governs police officers when they arrest someone

In August 2009, a San Diego police officer pulled over David Riley for expired registrations tags. The officer then found that Riley's driver's license was suspended, and, following department policy for such cases, he searched the car before having it towed and impounded. He found two illegal handguns under the hood and arrested Riley. As is standard practice during a lawful arrest, the officer searched Riley and found his cell phone in a pocket. The phone contained evidence—pictures, cell phone contacts, texts messages, and video clips—indicating Riley's membership in a local gang. The cell phone also included a picture of a different vehicle that Riley owned and that was involved in a gang shooting a few days earlier. Ballistics tests would later show that the handguns found in Riley's car were also linked to the earlier shooting. Based in part on the evidence recovered from Riley's cell phone, Riley was charged in connection with a gang shooting.

Like most people around the world today, David Riley's cell phone contained many private details about his life—pictures, contacts, communications with other people, and even videos. In Riley's case, some of those details were evidence of criminal activity, but surely other "evidence" on his phone was simply the typical private, personal information we all carry with us wherever we go.

The Fourth Amendment to the U.S. Constitution protects us from unreasonable police searches and seizures, and the long line of U.S. Supreme Court cases interpreting the Fourth Amendment repeatedly recognize that we have reasonable expectations of privacy in certain circumstances. Sometimes, that expectation of privacy requires police to get a warrant before they can search people and places.

Did David Riley have an expectation of privacy in the contents of his cell phone? Did his contact with San Diego police change that expectation? Did the police have a legitimate, overriding interest in seizing evidence from his phone? Should the government be able to use that evidence against Riley in a criminal trial?

Think about these questions and about the contents on your own cell phone as you read further and learn about the critically important area of constitutional law in the criminal justice system.

Student on the Street Video: Can the police search your cell phone?

INTRODUCTION

What constitutional rights do Americans possess regarding arrest, search, and seizure? How are the police constrained by those rights? If the police have a search warrant for a friend you are accompanying, can they search you as well? If the police knock on your apartment door, must you allow them to enter if you do not see a search warrant in their possession? And if they arrest you, should they be able to search your person, your car, your apartment—your cell phone? These are certainly challenging questions if someone is not familiar with the Bill of Rights; after you read this chapter, however, the answers should be clear.

Most college and university students probably have few opportunities to witness police actions that concern the U.S. Constitution. Although they may become directly and innocently involved with arrest, search, and seizure by being present at parties, in friends' vehicles, or at their places of employment, most Americans' knowledge of the Bill of Rights probably comes from movies and television crime shows—which are questionable at best in terms of how they portray police conduct. This chapter will clarify any such confusion.

We focus in this chapter on three of the ten amendments that constitute the Bill of Rights: the Fourth Amendment (probable cause, the exclusionary rule, arrest, search and seizure, electronic surveillance, and lineups), the Fifth Amendment (confessions and interrogations), and the Sixth Amendment (right to counsel and interrogation). (*Note:* The Eighth Amendment, prohibiting cruel and unusual punishment, applies to jails and prisons; furthermore, the Fourteenth Amendment states that we are entitled to due process, as spelled out in the criminal justice system flow in Chapter 1. These two amendments are not examined in detail in this chapter, however.) Also note that the law as it pertains to juvenile offenders is quite different from that for adults; juvenile law is covered in Chapter 15.

Some Caveats

Students of criminal justice might do well to remember the classic words of John Adams, who said in 1774 that a republic is "a government of laws, and not of men."[2] The Bill of Rights was enacted largely to protect all citizens from excessive governmental power.

As was seen in previous chapters of this book, criminal justice practitioners have far-reaching powers. Furthermore, agencies of criminal justice have the added benefit of using expert witnesses, forensic crime laboratories, undercover agents, informants, and so forth. Therefore, the Bill of Rights serves as an important means of "balancing the scales"—controlling the police and others so that they conduct themselves in a manner suited to a democratic society. Criminal justice professionals must conform their behavior to the rule of law as set forth not only in the U.S. Constitution but also in the state constitutions, statutes enacted by state legislatures, municipal ordinances, and the precedent of prior interpretations by the courts.

Remember also that the law is *dynamic*—that is, constantly changing—by virtue of acts by federal and state courts as well as their legislative bodies. Therefore, criminal justice practitioners must keep abreast of such changes and have formal mechanisms for imparting these legal changes to their employees. In the best case, agencies will have an in-house assistant district attorney—or, at the least, one who is on call—to render advice concerning legal matters.

A final note: Anyone who believes our legal system to be unduly harsh and restrictive might wish to read the brief discussion of Islamic law in the "Going Global" feature toward the end of this chapter. Remember that governments—through their criminal justice systems (and, too often, their military forces)—may employ many methods to maintain order and attempt to maintain "justice." In China or Saudi Arabia, however, the methods used would be far different from those in the United States. But would "justice" really result? And would many Americans want to *live* in one of those venues?

THE FOURTH AMENDMENT

> The right of the people to be secure in their persons, papers, and effects, against unreasonable searches and seizures, shall not be violated, and no Warrants shall issue, but upon probable cause, supported by Oath or affirmation, and particularly describing the place to be searched, and the persons or things to be seized.

The **Fourth Amendment** is intended to limit overzealous behavior by the police. Its primary protection is the requirement that a neutral, detached magistrate, rather than a police officer, issue **warrants for arrest and search**. The all-important

---

Video: Fourth Amendment

Fourth Amendment: in the Bill of Rights, it contains the protection against unreasonable searches and seizures and protects people's homes, property, and effects.

Warrant, arrest: a document issued by a judge directing police to immediately arrest a person accused of a crime.

Warrant, search: a document issued by a judge, based on probable cause, directing police to immediately search a person, a premises, an automobile, or a building for the purpose of finding illegal contraband felt to be located therein and as stated in the warrant.

AP Photo/Greg Barnette/Record Searchlight

The exclusionary rule requires that evidence obtained improperly by the police may not be used in a criminal trial. These two officers wait outside a jewelry store for a search warrant to be signed by a judge so that they may then search the property for stolen goods.

principle of separation of powers in our American government demands that the legal right to search be decided by someone other than an agent for the police, because the police are not expected to be neutral or objective with respect to police matters. Instead, a neutral judicial officer oversees this important police function—the judicial branch oversees the executive branch to ensure law enforcement actions are constitutional.[3]

Probable Cause

The standard for a legal arrest, as well as for **search and seizure**, is **probable cause**. This important concept is elusive at best; it is often quite difficult for professors to explain and even more difficult for students to understand. One way to define probable cause is to say that for an officer to make an arrest or conduct a search of someone's person or effects, he or she must have a reasonable basis to believe that a crime has been or is about to be committed by that individual (which, in the case of a search, can include the individual's mere possession of some form of illegal contraband).

That definition still may not help much to explain this concept. However, if you read carefully the example provided in the next "Investigating Further" box (which is an actual case), you should have a better understanding of this concept—and how it is applied in the field.

Of course, the facts of each case and the probable cause indicators present are different; the court will examine the type and amount of probable cause that the officer had at the time of the arrest. Note that a police officer cannot add to the probable cause used to make the arrest after making the arrest; the judge will then determine whether or not sufficient probable cause existed to arrest the individual based on the officer's knowledge of the facts at the time of the arrest.

The U.S. Supreme Court has upheld convictions when probable cause was provided by a reliable informant,[4] when it came in an anonymous letter,[5] and when a suspect fit a Drug Enforcement Administration profile of a drug courier.[6]

The Exclusionary Rule

As observed in Chapter 7, the Fourth Amendment protects people's right to be secure against unreasonable searches and seizures in their houses, papers, and effects. However, simple as that may sound, the manner in which the amendment is applied on the street is more complicated. First of all, not *all* searches are prohibited—only those that are unreasonable. Another issue has to do with how to handle evidence that is obtained illegally. Should murderers be released, Justice Benjamin Cardozo asked, simply because "the constable blundered"?[7] The Fourth Amendment says nothing about how it is to be enforced; this is a problem that has stirred a good amount of debate for a number of years. Most of this debate has focused on the constitutional necessity for the **exclusionary rule**, which basically requires that all evidence obtained in violation of the Fourth Amendment must be excluded from government use in a criminal trial.

SAGE Journal Article: Warrantless searches and probable cause

Search and seizure: in the Fourth Amendment, the term refers to an officer's searching for and taking away evidence of a crime.

Probable cause: a reasonable basis to believe that a crime has been, or is about to be, committed by a particular person.

Exclusionary rule: the rule (see *Mapp v. Ohio,* 1961) providing that evidence obtained improperly cannot be used against the accused at trial.

INVESTIGATING FURTHER

PROBABLE CAUSE

At midnight, a 55-year-old woman, having spent several hours at a city bar, wished to leave the bar and go to a nightclub in a rural part of the county. A man offered her a ride, but rather than driving directly to the nightclub, he drove to a remote place and parked the car. There he raped the woman and forced her to sodomize him. She fought him and later told the police she thought she had broken the stems (side pieces) of his black glasses. After the assault, he drove her back to town; when she got out of the car, she saw the license plate number and thought that the hood of the car was colored red. Her account of the crime and her physical description of the rapist led the officers to have a suspect in mind, so they immediately conducted a photograph lineup with the victim. A known rape/sodomy suspect's picture was shown to her (along with those of several other men who were of similar physical description). She tentatively identified the suspect in the mug shot, but she was not absolutely certain (the suspect's mug shot had been taken several years earlier).

With this information and without an arrest or search warrant, two police officers hurried to the suspect's home to question him. Upon entering the suspect's driveway, the officers observed a beige car—but it had a red hood; next the officers noted that the vehicle's license number matched the one given by the victim; finally, as the suspect came out of the home, the officers observed that the front of his eyeglasses frame was black plastic, but the side pieces were gold aluminum.

1. Upon entering the suspect's driveway, what observations did the officers make that might lead "a reasonable person" to believe that the suspect had committed the offenses?

2. Do the officers have enough probable cause to make a warrantless arrest of the individual?

3. Is there anything else they could legally do to further establish the suspect's guilt?

The exclusionary rule first appeared in the federal criminal justice system when the U.S. Supreme Court ruled in *Weeks v. United States* (1914) that all illegally obtained evidence was barred from use in federal prosecutions.[8] Then, in *Mapp v. Ohio* (1961),[9] the Court applied the doctrine to the states' courts (see the next "Investigating Further" box).

SAGE Journal Article: Exclusionary rule

INVESTIGATING FURTHER

THE EXCLUSIONARY RULE

In May 1957, three Cleveland police officers went to the home of Dollree Mapp to follow up on an informant's tip that a suspect in a recent bombing was hiding there. They also had information that a large amount of materials for operating a numbers game would be found. Upon arrival at the house, officers knocked on the door and demanded entrance, but Mapp, after telephoning her lawyer, refused them entry without a search warrant.

Three hours later, the officers again attempted to enter Mapp's home, and again she refused them entry. They then forcibly entered the home. Mapp confronted the officers, demanding to see a search warrant; an officer waved a piece of paper at her, which she grabbed and placed in her bosom. The officers struggled with Mapp to retrieve the piece of paper, at which time Mapp's attorney arrived at the scene. The attorney was not allowed to enter the house or to see his client. Mapp was forcibly taken upstairs to her bedroom, where her belongings were searched. One officer found a brown paper bag containing books that he deemed to be obscene.

Mapp was charged with possession of obscene, lewd, or lascivious materials. At the trial, the prosecution attempted to prove that the materials belonged to Mapp; the defense contended that the books were the property of a former boarder who had left his belongings behind. The jury convicted Mapp, and she was sentenced to an indefinite term in prison.

In June 1961, the U.S. Supreme Court overturned the conviction, holding that the Fourth Amendment's prohibition against unreasonable search and seizure had been violated and that as

> the right to be secure against rude invasions of privacy by state officers is . . . constitutional in origin, we can no longer permit that right to remain an empty promise. We can no longer permit it to be revocable at the whim of any police officer who, in the name of law enforcement itself, chooses to suspend its enjoyment.

The David Riley Case: Now that you understand the Fourth Amendment, expectations of privacy, and the landmark *Mapp* case, reconsider David Riley's cell phone and how police obtained "evidence" from his phone. Was the police action an invasion of his privacy? Did officers have time or a legal obligation to obtain a warrant first? Riley's attorneys argued that the cell phone evidence was obtained illegally and that, under the exclusionary rule established in the *Mapp* case, the government should not have been able to use it against Riley in his trial. How do you think the case came out? We revisit the *Riley* case later in this chapter.

Police officers may perform warrantless arrests and searches under certain circumstances if they have probable cause to do so.

Affidavit: any written document in which the signer swears under oath that the statements in the document are true.

Exigent circumstance: an instance where quick, emergency action is required, such as searching for drugs before they are removed or destroyed.

Arrests With and Without a Warrant

It is always best for a police officer to arrest someone with a warrant, because that means a neutral magistrate—rather than a police officer—has examined the facts and determined that the individual should be arrested in order to make an accounting of the charge(s). An arrest made with a valid warrant will be presumed constitutional or legal, so an officer will always opt to act with a warrant when possible.

To obtain an arrest warrant, the officer or a citizen swears in an **affidavit** (as an "affiant") that he or she possesses certain knowledge that a particular person has committed an offense. This person might be, as an example, a private citizen who informs police or the district attorney that he or she attended a party at a residence where drugs or stolen articles were present. Or, as is often the case, a detective gathers physical evidence or interviews witnesses or victims and determines that probable cause exists to believe that a particular person committed a specific crime. In either case, the affidavit is presented to a judge, and if the judge finds that probable cause exists, he or she will issue the arrest warrant. Officers will execute the warrant, taking the suspect into custody to answer the charges.

However, when a making a routine felony arrest in a home, where no exigent circumstances exist, the Supreme Court has ruled that a police officer must first obtain a warrant.[10] **Exigent circumstances** means that immediate action is required—to prevent danger to life or serious damage to property, the escape of a suspect, or the destruction of evidence—and that the officer possesses probable cause. Patrol officers, unlike detectives, rarely have the time or opportunity to perform an arrest with a warrant in hand because the suspect is generally trying to escape, dispose of evidence, and so on. Although the situation described in the "You Be the Officer" box involves consent to search, it serves as a good example.

Police may not randomly stop a single vehicle to check the driver's license and registration; there must be probable cause for stopping the driver.[11] However, in 1990, the Supreme Court ruled that the stopping of all vehicles passing through sobriety checkpoints—a form of seizure—did not violate the Constitution, although singling out individual vehicles for random stops without probable cause is not authorized.[12] Several days later, it ruled that police were not required to give drunk-driving suspects a *Miranda* warning and could videotape their responses.[13]

The Supreme Court held also that police may arrest *everyone* in a vehicle in which drugs are found,[14] and that police may set up roadblocks to collect information from motorists about crime. Short stops, "a very few minutes at most," are not too intrusive considering the value in crime solving, the Court noted.[15]

PRACTITIONER'S PERSPECTIVE

Name: Ronald "Mark" Kendrick

Current Position: Senior Special Agent, Kansas Bureau of Investigation (KBI)

City, State: Colby, KS

College Attended/ Academic Major: Washburn University, BA Criminal Justice; Washburn School of Law, JD

How long have you been a practitioner in this criminal justice position? I have been with the KBI for over 27 years. I started in a sheriff's office and was there for 11 years part-time while I was in school.

My primary duties and responsibilities as a practitioner in this position are:

To assist local agencies in the investigation of the major crimes occurring in Kansas. In my case, this consists mostly of child-related crimes, death investigations, and sex crimes; however, there are all sort of other crimes mixed in.

The qualities/characteristics that are most helpful for one in this career are:

Honesty and integrity are of the utmost importance, followed by the notion that you want to help or be of service to others without becoming rich. You must have the knowledge to do the job and be able to apply this knowledge to a situation. That includes being able to think for yourself and sometimes to think outside the box to find a solution. You must then be able to communicate with all types of people to get the information you need and then be able to write about these encounters in reports and to testify professionally in court.

In general, a *typical* day for a practitioner in this career would include:

This job really has no typical day. You don't just come to the office and do the same thing day in and day out. One moment I could be writing reports; the next I could be headed to a murder scene or a hostage situation. You just never know. I spend a lot of time writing reports about the people I've spoken to and the information I have gathered. There have been many times when I have been called out, both day and night, in any weather, to investigate a crime or deal with a situation.

Additionally, I am one of KBI's High Risk Warrant Team Negotiators. In that position, you must able to think on your feet and talk with angry and upset individuals, calm them down, and get them to do what you need them to. Most of the time it works out.

My advice to someone either wishing to study, or now studying, criminal justice to become a practitioner in this career field would be:

First, learn the basics of the job. Then make yourself more proficient in that job. Always remember you are never too old to learn. You must be able to communicate with the worst of society, and then also be able communicate professionally when speaking with colleagues, attorneys, judges, and the public in both written and oral communication. That means not only taking courses for your chosen profession, but also communication courses like English and public speaking. Always try to avoid "tunnel vision."

Search and Seizure in General

An old saying holds that "a person's home is his castle," and the police are held to a high Fourth Amendment standard when wanting to enter and search someone's domicile. Regarding what have become known as "knock and announce" cases, the U.S. Supreme Court has determined that the Fourth Amendment does require the police to first knock and announce their presence before entering a person's home for the purpose of executing a warrant; the Court allows exceptions, however, if knocking and announcing would be likely to endanger the officers or lead to the destruction of evidence. In mid-2011, the Supreme Court expanded the ability of police to enter a home without a warrant—but under exigent circumstances. In *Kentucky v. King*, police in Lexington were pursuing a drug suspect and banged on the door of an apartment where they thought they smelled marijuana.[16] After identifying themselves, the officers heard movement inside the apartment and, suspecting that evidence was being destroyed, kicked in the door and found King smoking marijuana. King, convicted of multiple drug crimes,

You Be the... OFFICER

One spring afternoon a police officer was dispatched to the residence of several university students, who were hosting a keg party for about 20 guests. They reported that three unknown men (two white, one African American) entered the home, had a few beers, and quickly left. Soon thereafter, a party guest also left, and discovered that the stereo had been taken from his car, parked in the back yard. A description of the men and their vehicle was given to the officer, who soon (within 20 minutes and a mile from the crime scene) observed a vehicle and three men, all of whom matched the description that was given. The officer stopped the vehicle, informed the dispatcher of the stop and location, and approached the vehicle.

1. Are exigent circumstances and probable cause sufficient for the officer to search the vehicle without a warrant or the men's consent? If you believe not, how do you propose the three men be handled while a warrant is being sought from a judge?

2. Assume the officer asks the vehicle's driver for permission to search the vehicle, and consent is given; what is the officer's next move? Instead, assume the driver of the vehicle refuses to give the officer permission to search the vehicle; what action(s) do you believe the officer can then legally take?

3. Assume the officer, with or without a warrant, locates the stolen stereo equipment inside the vehicle under the driver's seat. Can the officer then arrest only the vehicle's driver, or should all other occupants be arrested as well?

4. Following the arrest of one or more of the occupants, can they then be searched (if necessary, see the section below, "Searches Incident to Lawful Arrest")?

5. What other issues arise for the officer (e.g., his or her safety) once an arrest is made of one or more of the occupants?

The U.S. Supreme Court has ruled that the stopping of all vehicles passing through sobriety checkpoints—a form of seizure—does not violate the Constitution.

©David Bro/ZUMA Press/Corbis

appealed, and Kentucky's highest court ruled there were no "emergency circumstances" present and thus the drugs were inadmissible as police should have sought a search warrant. The Supreme Court disagreed, saying that the police acted reasonably: When police knock on a door and there is no response, and then hear movement inside that suggests evidence is being destroyed, they are justified in breaking in.

In other Fourth Amendment cases, the Court has upheld a warrantless search and seizure of garbage in bags outside the defendant's home,[17] as well as approaching seated bus passengers and asking permission to search their luggage for drugs (because, they reasoned, such persons should feel free to refuse the officer's request).[18] The Court also decided that no "seizure" occurs (and therefore the Fourth Amendment does not apply) when a police officer is in a foot pursuit (here, a juvenile being chased by an officer threw down an object, later determined to be crack cocaine).[19]

Searches and Seizures With and Without a Warrant

As with arrests, the best means by which the police can search a person or premises is with a search warrant that has been issued by a neutral magistrate. A warrant will be issued only if

You Be the... JUDGE

In early 2013, the U.S. Supreme Court considered two Florida cases that involved the constitutionality of police using trained drug-sniffing dogs. *Florida v. Jardines* involved the use of a dog outside of a home to determine the presence of drugs within.[20] After receiving a tip that marijuana was being grown in a house, officers from the Miami-Dade Police Department approached the premises with a drug dog. The Labrador retriever alerted officers to the presence of marijuana in the house; subsequently, officers obtained a search warrant and discovered the plants inside.

The second such case heard by the Court, *Florida v. Harris,* concerned a traffic stop during which a trained

police dog alerted, which gave officers probable cause to further search the occupant's vehicle; the search uncovered methamphetamine ingredients inside.[21]

1. Does the use of a drug-sniffing dog near one's home violate the Fourth Amendment (and thus require a search warrant before doing so)?

2. Can a drug-sniffing dog be used in traffic stops without a warrant?

The Supreme Court's decisions for both cases are provided in the Notes section at the end of the book.

---

a judge finds, after reviewing a police officer's sworn affidavit, that there is probable cause to believe the named person possesses sought-after evidence (e.g., a weapon or stolen goods), or that the evidence is present at a particular location. Again, as with an arrest with a warrant, typically it is the detectives who have the "luxury" of searching and seizing with a warrant after interviewing victims and witnesses, perhaps obtaining analyses at a forensics laboratory, and gathering enough available evidence to request a search warrant. Patrol officers rarely have the opportunity to perform such a search, as the flow of events typically requires quick action to prevent escape and to prevent the evidence from being destroyed or hidden.

Figure 8.1 shows the pertinent parts of a search and seizure warrant form for persons or property that is used by the U.S. district courts, for execution by agents of the federal government.

Five types of searches may be conducted without a warrant: (1) searches incident to lawful arrest, (2) searches during field interrogation (stop-and-frisk searches), (3) searches of automobiles under special conditions, (4) seizures of evidence that is in "plain view," and (5) searches when consent is given.

Searches Incident to Lawful Arrest

In *Chimel v. California* (1969), officers arrested Chimel without a warrant in one room of his house and then searched his entire three-bedroom house, including the garage, attic, and workshop. The U.S. Supreme Court said that searches incident to a lawful arrest are limited to the area within the arrestee's immediate control or that area from which he or she might obtain a weapon, emphasizing that such searches are justified in large part to ensure officer safety. Therefore, if the police are holding a person in one room of the house, they cannot search and seize property in another part of the house, away from the arrestee's immediate physical presence.[22]

Another advantage given the police was the Court's allowing a warrantless, in-home "protective sweep" of the area in which a suspect is arrested to reveal the presence of anyone else who might pose a danger. Such a search, if justified by the circumstances, is not a full search of the premises and may only include a cursory inspection of those spaces where a person could be hiding.[23]

In April 2009, the Supreme Court held in *Arizona v. Gant* that, when an individual has been arrested and is in police custody away from his or her vehicle, unable to access the vehicle, officers may not then search the vehicle without a warrant. Here, the officers did so, and discovered a handgun and a plastic bag of cocaine; the Court overturned nearly three decades of such a police practice, saying it is a violation of

FIGURE 8.1 Federal Court Search and Seizure Warrant Form, U.S. District Courts

AO 93 (Rev. 12/09) Search and Seizure Warrant

UNITED STATES DISTRICT COURT
for the

In the Matter of the Search of   )
(Briefly describe the property to be searched   )
or identify the person by name and address)   ) Case No.
)
)
)

SEARCH AND SEIZURE WARRANT

To: Any authorized law enforcement officer

An application by a federal law enforcement officer or an attorney for the government requests the search
of the following person or property located in the _____ District of _____
(identify the person or describe the property to be searched and give its location):

The person or property to be searched, described above, is believed to conceal *(identify the person or describe the*
property to be seized):

I find that the affidavit(s), or any recorded testimony, establish probable cause to search and seize the person or
property.

YOU ARE COMMANDED to execute this warrant on or before _____
                                                                      (not to exceed 14 days)

❏ in the daytime 6:00 a.m. to 10 p.m.   ❏ at any time in the day or night as I find reasonable cause has been
                                                    established.

Unless delayed notice is authorized below, you must give a copy of the warrant and a receipt for the property
taken to the person from whom, or from whose premises, the property was taken, or leave the copy and receipt at the
place where the property was taken.

The officer executing this warrant, or an officer present during the execution of the warrant, must prepare an
inventory as required by law and promptly return this warrant and inventory to United States Magistrate Judge

_____ .
            (name)

❏ I find that immediate notification may have an adverse result listed in 18 U.S.C. § 2705 (except for delay
of trial), and authorize the officer executing this warrant to delay notice to the person who, or whose property, will be
searched or seized *(check the appropriate box)* ❏ for _____ days *(not to exceed 30)*.
                                                  ❏ until, the facts justifying, the later specific date of _____ .

Date and time issued: _____   _____
                                                                  Judge's signature

City and state: _____   _____
                                                                  Printed name and title

(Continued)

(Continued)

AO 93 (Rev. 12/09) Search and Seizure Warrant (Page 2)

Return		
Case No.:	*Date and time warrant executed:*	*Copy of warrant and inventory left with:*
Inventory made in the presence of :		
Inventory of the property taken and name of any person(s) seized:		

Certification
I declare under penalty of perjury that this inventory is correct and was returned along with the original warrant to the designated judge.

Date: _____

_____
Executing officer's signature

_____
Printed name and title

the Fourth Amendment's protection against unreasonable searches and seizures.[24] In essence, the Court is saying that police may search the passenger compartment of a vehicle incident to a recent occupant's arrest only if it is reasonable to believe that the arrestee might access the vehicle at the time of the search or that the vehicle contains evidence of the offense of arrest.

Finally, in mid-2013, in a decision that Justice Samuel Alito described as "the most important criminal procedure case this court has heard in decades," the Supreme Court held in *Maryland v. King* that police can collect DNA from people arrested but not yet convicted. The majority compared taking a DNA swab to fingerprinting, viewing it as a reasonable search that can be considered a routine part of a booking procedure.[25]

The David Riley Case: If you find yourself thinking about the David Riley case from the beginning of this chapter, you are exactly right. The San Diego police officer searched Riley's cell phone "incident to a lawful arrest," almost as an extension of Riley's person—like his wallet or a bag he may have been carrying. Was the search as invasive as taking a cheek swab for DNA? Or is it more like looking for weapons or contraband on an arrestee?

In 2014, the U.S. Supreme Court agreed with Riley's attorneys that the police search of Riley's cell phone was illegal. Speaking for the majority, Chief Justice John Roberts wrote:

Digital data stored on a cell phone cannot itself be used as a weapon to harm an arresting officer or to effectuate the arrestee's escape. Law enforcement officers

Video: The scars of stop and frisk

remain free to examine the physical aspects of a phone to ensure that it will not be used as a weapon—say, to determine whether there is a razor blade hidden between the phone and its case. Once an officer has secured a phone and eliminated any potential physical threats, however, data on the phone can endanger no one.[26]

Roberts also confirmed the realities of our modern digital lives and how the Court must interpret the Constitution with contemporary issues in mind, especially when reviewing police power:

> Modern cell phones are not just another technological convenience. With all they contain and all they may reveal, they hold for many Americans "the privacies of life." The fact that technology now allows an individual to carry such information in his hand does not make the information any less worthy of the protection for which the Founders fought.

Stop and Frisk

In 1963, Cleveland Detective McFadden, a veteran of 19 years of police service, first noticed Terry and another man who appeared to be "casing" a retail store. McFadden observed the suspects making several trips down the street, stopping at a store window, walking about a half-block, turning around and walking back again, pausing to look inside the same store window. At one point they were joined by a third party, who spoke with them and then moved on. McFadden claimed that he followed them because he believed it was his duty as a police officer to investigate the matter further.

Soon the two rejoined the third man; at that point McFadden decided the situation demanded direct action. The officer approached the subjects and identified himself, then requested that the men identify themselves as well. When Terry said something inaudible, McFadden "spun him around so that they were facing the other two, with Terry between McFadden and the others, and patted down the outside of his clothing." In a breast pocket of Terry's overcoat, the officer felt a pistol. McFadden found another pistol on one of the other men. The two men were arrested and ultimately convicted for concealing deadly weapons. Terry appealed on the grounds that the search was illegal and that the evidence should have been suppressed at trial.

The U.S. Supreme Court disagreed with Terry, holding in *Terry v. Ohio* that the police have the authority to detain a person briefly for questioning even without probable cause if they have "**reasonable suspicion**" that the person has committed a crime or is about to commit a crime. Reasonable suspicion is a lower standard than probable cause but more than a mere hunch that someone may be involved in criminal activity. Officers must be able to articulate a reasonable factual basis for a stop. Such detention—known as a **Terry Stop**—does not constitute an arrest, and a person may be frisked for a weapon if an officer reasonably suspects the person is carrying one and fears for his or her life. The *Terry* decision ushered in a new era for police officers, allowing them to stop and frisk suspects based only on reasonable suspicion, and not the higher threshold of suspicion required under a probable cause standard.[27]

Despite officers being trained in mock scenarios as seen here in the Bronx, the NYPD's aggressive stop-and-frisk program was abandoned after being deemed unconstitutional.

Reasonable suspicion: suspicion that is less than probable cause but more than a mere hunch that a person may be involved in criminal activity.

INVESTIGATING FURTHER

NYPD—STOP AND FRISK OR RACIAL PROFILING?

In the early 1990s, the New York Police Department (NYPD), like most large, metropolitan forces, began taking a proactive approach to fighting crime. A centerpiece of their approach was an aggressive stop-and-frisk policy by which officers targeted high-crime areas and the people in them, often developing suspicion from the mere fact that a person was in such an area. Officers focused on persons who, for example, made "furtive movements," such as a hand going for something in a waistband or someone who seemed nervous. Others targeted people who appeared to be coming and going from certain buildings associated with illegal activity. The result of this approach was an unprecedented number of stops: 175,000 during a 15-month period in 1998 and 1999. But the demographic breakdown of those stops was troubling to many: blacks (26 percent of the city's population) accounted for 51 percent of the total, Hispanics (24 percent of the population) accounted for 33 percent, and whites (43 percent of the population) accounted for only 13 percent.

Civil libertarians claimed the NYPD was engaged in illegal racial profiling. The NYPD responded by touting significantly lower rates for index crimes during the stop-and-frisk era.

Ultimately, in August 2013, the U.S. District Court for the Southern District of New York ruled that NYPD's stop-and-frisk practices were unconstitutional, violating the civil rights of racial minorities. The law enforcement community responded that the decision would dramatically change policing—and likely crime rates. In a move that seemed to signal the beginning of the end of stop-and-frisk, the NYPD in March 2015 issued new stop-and-frisk guidelines, requiring officers to be able to articulate facts establishing an objective justification for making the stop. Officers can no longer stop and frisk simply because suspects are making furtive movements in a high-crime area or because they fit a generalized description of a suspect, such as an African American male in a certain age group.[30]

An important extension of the *Terry* doctrine—known as the "plain feel" doctrine—was handed down in 1993 in *Minnesota v. Dickerson*, in which a police officer observed a man leave a notorious crack house and then try to evade the officer.[28] The man was eventually stopped and patted down, or frisked, during which time the officer felt a small lump in the man's front pocket that was suspected to be drugs. The officer removed the object—crack cocaine wrapped in a cellophane container—from the man's pocket. Although the arrest and conviction were later thrown out as not being allowed under *Terry*, the Court also allowed such seizures in the future when officers' probable cause is established by the sense of touch.

Another important Supreme Court decision in February 1997 took officer safety into account. In *Maryland v. Wilson*, the Court held that police may order passengers out of vehicles they stop, regardless of any suspicion of wrongdoing or threat to the officer's safety.[29] Citing statistics showing officer assaults and murders during traffic stops, the Court noted that the "weighty interest" in officer safety is present whether a vehicle occupant is a driver or a passenger.

Terry Stop: also known as a "stop and frisk"; when a police officer briefly detains a person for questioning and then frisks ("pats down") the person if the officer reasonably believes he or she is carrying a weapon.

Searches of Automobiles

The third general circumstance allowing a warrantless search is when an officer has

The courts have held that motorists have no expectation of privacy during a traffic stop if contraband hidden in a vehicle is detected by a drug-sniffing dog.

probable cause to believe that an automobile contains criminal evidence. The U.S. Supreme Court gives the police greater latitude in searching automobiles, because a vehicle can be used to effect a getaway and to hide evidence. In *Carroll v. United States* (1925), officers searched the vehicle of a known bootlegger without a warrant but with probable cause, finding 68 bottles of illegal booze. On appeal, the Court ruled that the seizure was justified. *Carroll* established two rules, however: First, to invoke the *Carroll* doctrine, the police must have enough probable cause that if there had been enough time, a search warrant would have been issued; second, urgent circumstances must exist that require immediate action.[31]

The Court also allows the police the right to enter an impounded vehicle following a lawful arrest in order to inventory its contents,[32] and has stated that a person's general consent to a search of the interior of an automobile also justifies a search of any closed container found inside the car that might reasonably hold the object of the search.[33] And, when an officer has probable cause to search a vehicle, the officer may search objects belonging to a passenger in the vehicle, provided the item the officer is looking for could reasonably be in the passenger's belongings[34] (such as finding drugs in a passenger's purse). Finally, motorists have no expectation of privacy during a traffic stop if contraband is hidden in a vehicle and detected by a drug-sniffing dog.[35]

MEASURING THE RULE OF LAW AROUND THE WORLD

The rule of law consists of a framework of rules and rights that provide for a fair society in which no one person or government is above the law, fundamental rights are protected, and justice is accessible to all.[36]

The World Justice Project (WJP), based in Washington, D.C., works to advance and enhance the rule of law worldwide, develop programs at the community level, and increase public awareness about the concept. One of its primary contributions is to score countries' practice of rule of law on the following eight factors: (1) limited government powers (e.g., government powers are limited by the legislature and judiciary; government officials are punished for corruption); (2) absence of corruption (e.g., government officials do not use office for public or private gain); (3) order and security (e.g., crime is effectively controlled); (4) fundamental rights (e.g., equal treatment, due process of law, freedom of belief and religion); (5) open government (e.g., laws are publicized and stable); (6) regulatory enforcement

(e.g., regulations are enforced without influence); (7) civil justice (e.g., affordable, free of corruption and influence); and (8) criminal justice (investigation, adjudication are effective; impartial, free of corruption, due process). Then each is scored (using an independent assessment conducted by the European Commission Joint Research Centre) on each of the factors and subfactors of the index.

The WJP Rule of Law Index is a quantitative assessment tool offering a detailed and comprehensive picture of the extent to which countries adhere to the rule of law in practice. Viewers can click on any of the 97 countries shown on the map to see the rule of law score.

More information is available at http://worldjusticeproject.org/rule-law-index-map.

Source: World Justice Project, *Rule of Law Index Map,* http://world justiceproject.org/rule-law-index-map.

In 2012, the Supreme Court ruled in *U.S. v. Jones* that police violated the Constitution when they attached a Global Positioning System (GPS) device to a suspect's vehicle without a search warrant.[37] Police had followed a drug trafficking suspect for a month and eventually found nearly 100 kilograms of cocaine and $1 million in cash when raiding the suspect's home in Maryland. Justice Antonin Scalia noted that the Fourth Amendment's protection of "persons, houses, papers, and effects, against unreasonable searches and seizures" extends to automobiles as well, and that even a small trespass, if committed in "an attempt to find something or to obtain information," constitutes a "search" under the Fourth Amendment. This decision is anticipated to affect primarily major narcotics investigations.

Plain-View and Open-Field Searches

Essentially, police do not have to search for items that are seen in plain view. If police are lawfully on the premises and the plain-view discovery is inadvertent, then they may seize the contraband. For example, if an officer has been admitted into a home with an arrest or search warrant and sees drugs and paraphernalia on a living-room table, he or she may arrest the occupants on drug charges as well as the earlier ones. Or, if an officer during a traffic stop observes drugs in the backseat of the car, he or she may arrest for that as well. Furthermore, fences and the posting of "No Trespassing" signs afford no expectation of privacy and do not prevent officers from viewing open fields without a search warrant.[38] Nor are police prevented from making a naked-eye aerial observation of a suspect's backyard or other curtilage (the grounds around a house or building).[39] Finally, where an officer found a gun under a car seat while looking for the vehicle identification number, the Court upheld the search and the resulting arrest as being a plain-view discovery.[40]

Consent to Search

Another permissible warrantless search involves situations where citizens consent to a search of their persons or effects—provided that the defendant's consent is given voluntarily (see the next "Investigating Further" box). However, police cannot deceive people into believing they have a search warrant when they in fact do not.[41] Nor can a hotel clerk give a valid consent to a warrantless search of the room of one of the occupants; hotel guests have a reasonable expectation of privacy, and that right cannot be waived by hotel management.[42]

Looking at the plain-view doctrine, assume police officers are lawfully inside a home to execute an arrest warrant on a suspected bank robber. If, by chance, they happen to observe this illegal marijuana operation, the officers could then also arrest the occupant on drug charges.

What if one occupant of a home consents to a search while the other occupant refuses? In a recent case, a wife gave police permission to search for her husband's drugs, but the husband refused to give such permission; the officers went ahead and searched and found cocaine. The Supreme Court reversed the husband's conviction, saying the Constitution does not ignore the privacy rights of an individual who is present and asserting his rights.[43] However, in a feature of the law that should be important to college students with roommates, an occupant may still give police permission to search when the other resident is absent or does not protest. In fact, in 2014, the Supreme Court expanded police powers to seek consent from a co-occupant, ruling that even after an occupant has refused consent to search and the police then legally arrest that occupant for some other reason, the police may return and seek consent from a co-occupant who then has the right to voluntarily consent to a search of the entire premises.[44]

Student on the Street Video: Can police officers search your entire apartment?

Electronic Surveillance

Katz v. United States (1967) held that any form of electronic surveillance, including wiretapping, is a search and violates a reasonable expectation of privacy.[45] The case involved a public telephone booth, deemed by the Court to be a constitutionally protected area where the user has a reasonable expectation of privacy. This decision expressed the view that the Constitution protects people, not places. Thus, the Court has required

Video: Rewriting *Miranda* rights

You Be the... JUDGE

In January 2013, the U.S. Supreme Court heard arguments in a landmark Fourth Amendment case involving nearly 50 years of uncertainty over whether or not police securing blood tests (for people who might be driving under the influence) without a suspect's consent is constitutional. Because of the frequency of drunk-driving stops, this decision is felt to have far-reaching effects.

The case involves Tyler McNeely, of Cape Girardeau, Missouri, who was pulled over for speeding. McNeely refused an on-scene breath test, so the trooper took him to a hospital, where McNeely again refused a test. The trooper told the lab technician to take a blood sample anyway, without a warrant. McNeely's blood-alcohol level was almost double the legal limit. Complicating the case is the fact that, earlier in 2010,

the Missouri legislature changed the state's "implied consent" law to say that when people drive on Missouri's roads, they automatically consent to take a sobriety test.

1. What do you believe should be the outcome in this case?
2. Why?

The Supreme Court's decision for this case is provided in the Notes section at the end of the book.[48]

Source: Adapted from M. Alex Johnson, "Supreme Court to Decide Whether Police Can Take Your Blood Without Your Permission," *U.S. News,* January 8, 2013, http://usnews.nbcnews.com/_news/2013/01/08/16416051-supreme-court-to-decide-whether-police-can-take-your-blood-without-your-permission?lite.

---

that warrants for electronic surveillance be based on probable cause, describe the conversations that are to be overheard, be for a limited period of time, name subjects to be overheard, and be terminated when the desired information is obtained.[46] However, the Court has also held that electronic eavesdropping (i.e., when an informant wears a "bug," or hidden microphone) does not violate the Fourth Amendment.[47]

THE FIFTH AMENDMENT

Video: Living in a surveillance state

No person shall be held to answer for a capital, or otherwise infamous crime, unless on a presentment or indictment of a Grand Jury, except in cases arising in the land or naval forces, or in the Militia, when in actual service in time of war or public danger; nor shall any person be subject for the same offense to be twice put in jeopardy of life or limb; nor shall be compelled in any criminal case to be a witness against himself, nor be deprived of life, liberty, or property, without due process of law; nor shall private property be taken for public use, without just compensation.

Application

Fifth Amendment: in the Bill of Rights, among other protections, it guards against self-incrimination and double jeopardy.

Interrogation: police questioning of a suspect about a particular crime(s); the suspect may have an attorney present if he or she desires (see *Escobedo v. Illinois,* 1964).

Today, the **Fifth Amendment** applies not only to criminal defendants but also to any witness in a civil or criminal case and anyone testifying before an administrative body, a grand jury, or a congressional committee. However, the privilege does not extend to blood samples, handwriting exemplars, and other such items not considered as testimony.[49]

The right against self-incrimination is one of the most significant provisions in the Bill of Rights. Basically it states that no criminal defendant shall be compelled to take the witness stand and/or give evidence against himself or herself. See the next "Investigating Further" box.

There are two legal triggers for the *Miranda* warning: custody and interrogation. Once a suspect has been placed under arrest, the police must give the suspect the *Miranda* warning before **interrogation** for any offense, be it a felony or a misdemeanor. Of course, if an officer does not give the warning when required, a defense attorney will have to ask the court to exclude the suspect's confession or statements—it does not happen automatically. In other words, there are no "eyes in the sky" monitoring police conduct, so plenty of suspects may and do talk with police without getting their *Miranda* warning, but they later plead guilty or their attorney does not question the police practices. Once a "Mirandized" suspect invokes his or her right to silence, however, interrogation must cease. The police also may not readminister *Miranda* and interrogate the suspect later unless the suspect's attorney is present. If, however, the suspect initiates further conversation, any confession he or she provides is admissible.[50] Moreover, after an accused has invoked the right to counsel, the police may not interrogate the same suspect about a different crime.[51]

An exception to the *Miranda* requirement is the brief, routine traffic stop, but a custodial interrogation of a DUI (driving under the influence) suspect requires the *Miranda* warning.[52] And the police may question a suspect who poses a public-safety threat—known as the "public-safety exception." For example, when a clearly armed suspect runs into a public place and hides the gun, officers can legally ask the suspect about the location of the gun without violating *Miranda*.[53] In a more extreme example under the same exception, police were able to question Boston Marathon bomber Dzhokhar Tsarnaev for 16 hours without a *Miranda* warning because of the potential threat of co-conspirators and more planned bombings.[54]

Gerald L. Nino, CBP, U.S. Dept. of Homeland Security

The Fifth Amendment does not apply to criminal defendants' handwriting exemplars, blood samples, and other such items not considered to be testimony.

INVESTIGATING FURTHER

THE *MIRANDA* WARNING

While walking to a Phoenix, Arizona, bus stop on the night of March 2, 1963, 18-year-old Barbara Ann Johnson was accosted by a man who shoved her into his car, tied her hands and ankles, and drove her to the edge of the city, where he raped her. He then drove Johnson to a street near her home, letting her out of the car and asking that she pray for him. The Phoenix police subsequently picked up Ernesto Miranda for investigation of Johnson's rape and included him in a lineup at the police station. Miranda was identified by several women; one identified him as the man who had robbed her at knifepoint a few months earlier, and Johnson thought he was the rapist.

Miranda was a 23-year-old eighth-grade dropout with a police record dating back to age 14, and he had also served time in prison for driving a stolen car across a state line. During questioning, the police told Miranda that he had been identified by the women; Miranda then made a statement in writing that described the rape incident. He also noted that he was making the confession voluntarily and with full knowledge of his

legal rights. He was soon charged with rape, kidnapping, and robbery.

At trial, officers admitted that during the interrogation the defendant was not informed of his right to have counsel present and that no counsel was present. Nonetheless, Miranda's confession was admitted into evidence. He was convicted and sentenced to serve 20 to 30 years for kidnapping and rape.

On appeal, the U.S. Supreme Court overturned Miranda's conviction, stating that

> the current practice of incommunicado interrogation is at odds with one of our Nation's most cherished principles—that the individual may not be compelled to incriminate himself. Unless adequate protective devices are employed to dispel the compulsion inherent in custodial surroundings, no statement obtained from the defendant can truly be the product of free choice.

See *Miranda v. Arizona,* 384 U.S. 436 (1966).

©Mikael Karlsson / Alamy

Photo-lineups, known as a "six-pack," are considered less likely to lead to misidentifications than live lineups.

Poole   Cotton

Explore the case of Ronald Cotton (right), who served 11 years in prison for a sexual assault he did not commit. Despite studying her attacker closely, the victim misidentified Cotton in live and photo lineups, mistaking him for the real perpetrator, Bobby Poole (left).

Lineup: a procedure in which police ask suspects to submit to a viewing by witnesses to determine the guilty party, based on personal and physical characteristics; information obtained may be used later in court.

Decisions Eroding *Miranda*

It has been held that a second interrogation session held after the suspect had initially refused to make a statement did not violate *Miranda*.[55] The Court also decided that when a suspect waived his or her *Miranda* rights, believing the interrogation would focus on minor crimes, but the police shifted their questioning to a more serious crime, the confession was valid; there was no police deception or misrepresentation.[56] And when a suspect invoked his or her right to assistance of counsel and refused to make written statements, then voluntarily gave oral statements to police, the statements were admissible.[57] Finally, a suspect need not be given the *Miranda* warning in the exact form as it was outlined in *Miranda v. Arizona*. In one case, the waiver form said the suspect would have an attorney appointed "if and when you go to court." The Court held that as long as the warnings on the form reasonably convey the suspect's rights, they need not be given verbatim.[58] Further, a suspect must clearly invoke the *Miranda* right. The Supreme Court has ruled that even where a suspect remained silent during three continuous hours of police questioning, the suspect had not invoked his rights under *Miranda*—suspects must specifically say that they are choosing to remain silent.[59]

Lineups and Other Pretrial Identification Procedures

A police **lineup** or other face-to-face confrontation after the accused has been arrested is considered a critical stage of criminal proceedings; therefore, the accused has a right to have an attorney present. If counsel is not present, the evidence obtained is inadmissible.[60] However, the suspect is not entitled to the presence and advice of a lawyer before being formally charged, or when the police are using the more typical modern technique of a photo lineup, by showing a witness individual photos or a group of several photos typically referred to as a "six-pack."[61]

Faulty eyewitness identifications are the leading cause of wrongful convictions, and as a result, the law regarding their use has changed significantly in recent years (see Chapter 11 for more on wrongful convictions). Lineups—whether in-person or through photos—must be fair and cannot be unreasonably suggestive, for example, by the suspect's being much taller than the others in the lineup or being the only person wearing a leather jacket similar to that worn by the suspect.[62] If identification procedures violate a suspect's due process rights to fairness, police risk having identifications made during these procedures excluded from evidence at trial. Further, in light of extensive social science research on faulty eyewitness identifications, many law enforcement agencies have changed their identification practices to include safeguards such as informing the witness that the suspect may or may not be in the lineup or photo set, preventing detectives working the case from being present to avoid inadvertent

THE MIDDLE EAST: THE LAW OF SHARIA

Nowhere in the Middle East is the law harsher than in Saudi Arabia. To describe Saudi law is to speak of the country's religion, culture, and customs, all of which are bound closely together. Islam means complete submission to the will of God, and to provide a well-ordered society. Alcohol is forbidden in Saudi Arabia, and possession of even small amounts of hashish or marijuana can carry a punishment of two years' imprisonment or deportation.

The law of Islam (the Sharia) is the fundamental code in Saudi Arabia. For the crime of theft, even for the first offense, the penalty may be amputation of the left hand at the wrist. The penalty for slander is flogging, usually with 80 lashes, and the same penalty may be applied for consuming alcohol. The penalty for adultery is flogging 100 times. A woman who engages in adultery is liable to flogging or burial to the waist in a pit; stoning may follow. Highway robbery is punishable by execution or crucifixion, the amputation of opposite hands and feet, or exile from the land. Transgression will be confronted by the Saudi armed forces until the foes of the imam are defeated, and apostasy carries the death penalty. Public executions are commonplace in Saudi Arabia. Hundreds of worshippers, including children and women, often gather to observe these and other punishments. The crowd usually applauds after the execution, and some bystanders spit on the blood of the dead persons and curse them.

Source: See Saudi Arabian International Schools, "An Introduction to the Kingdom of Saudi Arabia" (Debbie Cross, personal correspondence, October 19, 1985), p. 17; Adel Mohammed el Fikey, "Crimes and Penalties in Islamic Criminal Legislation," *CJ International* 2 (July–August 1986), p. 13.

supportive or other cues to witnesses, and having witnesses record their level of certainty at the time of identification.[63] Some courts have instituted much stricter legal standards for admitting eyewitness evidence.[64]

Student on the Street Video: Efforts to force a guilty plea

THE SIXTH AMENDMENT

> In all criminal prosecutions the accused shall enjoy the right to a speedy and public trial, by an impartial jury of the State and district wherein the crime shall have been committed, which district shall have been previously ascertained by law, and to be informed of the nature and cause of the accusation; to be confronted with the witnesses against him; to have compulsory process for obtaining witnesses in his favor, and to have the assistance of counsel for his defense.

Many people believe that the **Sixth Amendment** right of the accused to have the assistance of counsel before and during trial is the greatest right we enjoy in a democracy.

More than 80 years ago, in *Powell v. Alabama* (1932), it was established that in a capital case, when the accused is poor and illiterate, he or she enjoys the right to assistance of counsel for his or her defense and due process.[65] In *Gideon v. Wainwright* (1963), the Supreme Court mandated that all indigent people charged with felonies in state courts be provided counsel.[66] *Gideon* applied only to felony defendants, however; but in 1973, *Argersinger v. Hamlin* extended the right to counsel to indigent people charged with *misdemeanor* crimes if they face the possibility of incarceration (however short the incarceration may be).[67]

Another landmark decision concerning the right to counsel is *Escobedo v. Illinois* (1964).[68] Danny Escobedo's brother-in-law was fatally shot in 1960; Escobedo was

Video: Clarence Earl Gideon

Sixth Amendment: in the Bill of Rights, it guarantees the right to a speedy and public trial by an impartial jury, the right to effective counsel at trial, and other protections.

Many people believe our greatest protection is the right to have the "guiding hand" of legal counsel, not only when facing felony charges but also in certain cases involving misdemeanor charges.

arrested and questioned at police headquarters; and his request to confer with his lawyer was denied, even after the lawyer arrived and asked to see his client. The questioning of Escobedo lasted several hours, during which time he was handcuffed and forced to remain standing. Eventually, he admitted being an accomplice to murder. At no point was Escobedo advised of his rights to remain silent or to confer with his attorney. Escobedo's conviction was ultimately reversed by the U.S. Supreme Court, based on a violation of his right to counsel. However, the real thrust of the decision was his Fifth Amendment right not to incriminate himself and to be informed of his rights; when a defendant is scared, flustered, ignorant, alone, and bewildered, he or she is often unable to effectively make use of protections granted under the Fifth Amendment without the advice of an attorney. Note that *Miranda*, decided two years later, simply established the guidelines for the police to inform suspects of all of these rights.

The Sixth Amendment's provision for a speedy and public trial is discussed in Chapter 9.

IN A NUTSHELL

- The Fourth Amendment protects the right of the people to be secure in their persons, papers, and effects, against unreasonable searches and seizures; and no search or arrest warrants shall be issued without probable cause, describing the place to be searched and disclosing the persons or things to be seized.

- The standard for a legal arrest, search, and seizure is probable cause, meaning that for an officer to make an arrest or conduct a search of someone's person or effects, he or she must have a reasonable suspicion that a crime has been or is about to be committed by that individual (which, in the case of a search, can include his or her merely possessing some form of illegal contraband).

- The exclusionary rule requires that all evidence obtained in violation of the Fourth Amendment may not be used against the defendant in a criminal trial.

- There are two ways for the police to make an arrest: with a warrant, and without a warrant. It is always best for a police officer to arrest someone with a warrant, because a neutral magistrate has examined the facts and determined that the individual should be arrested in order to make an accounting of the charge(s).

- Police officers must obtain a warrant when making a felony arrest, unless exigent circumstances are present (immediate action being required) and the officer possesses probable cause to make the arrest.

- As with arrests, the best means by which the police can search a person or premises is with a search warrant issued by a neutral magistrate. The process for obtaining a search warrant is the same as for an arrest warrant; in this case, a determination is made, after hearing evidence from an affiant, about whether probable cause exists to believe a person possesses evidence of a crime, such as stolen property or a weapon believed to have been used in committing the crime.

- The police may detain a person briefly for questioning, even without probable cause, if they believe that the person has committed a crime or is about to commit a crime, and the person may be frisked for a weapon if an officer reasonably suspects the person is carrying one and fears for his or her life. An extension of that rule involves the "plain feel" doctrine, where police, having reasonable cause to believe a person possesses drugs and feels what resembles such an object on his or her person, may remove the object and make an arrest.

- The police have greater latitude in searching automobiles, because they can be used to effect a getaway and to hide evidence.

- The police may search incident to lawful arrest, and do not need a search warrant for items that are seen in plain view or when citizens gives police consent. The police must, however, obtain a search warrant to search a suspect's cell phone.

- Police may use drug-sniffing dogs at traffic stops but not near homes without a warrant; they may also collect DNA swabs from arrestees as part of a routine booking procedure.

- The right against self-incrimination, under the Fifth Amendment, states that no criminal defendant shall be compelled to take the witness stand and give evidence against himself or herself. Once a suspect is arrested, the *Miranda* warning must be given before he or she is interrogated for any offense, be it a felony or a misdemeanor.

- The Sixth Amendment guarantees the accused the right to have the assistance of counsel during custodial interrogation and during trial.

KEY TERMS & CONCEPTS

Affidavit, 194	Interrogation, 204	Sixth Amendment, 207
Exclusionary rule, 192	Lineup, 206	Terry Stop, 200
Exigent circumstance, 194	Probable cause, 192	Warrant, arrest, 191
Fifth Amendment, 204	Reasonable suspicion, 200	Warrant, search, 191
Fourth Amendment, 191	Search and seizure, 192	

REVIEW QUESTIONS

1. What protections are afforded citizens by the Fourth, Fifth, and Sixth Amendments?

2. What is an example of probable cause?

3. What, from both police and community perspectives, are the ramifications of having and not having the exclusionary rule?

4. How would you distinguish between arrests and searches and seizures with and without a warrant? Which method for arresting or searching is always best?

5. In what significant ways has the *Miranda* decision been eroded, and what future challenges might arise given the continuing tension between law enforcement powers and individual civil rights?

6. What limitations are placed on the police in their ability to use high-tech electronic equipment in order to listen in on conversations? Search for drugs?

7. What are two major court decisions concerning right to counsel, and how do they apply in everyday life?

LEARN BY DOING

1. Your criminal justice professor has assigned a class project wherein class members are to determine which amendment to the Bill of Rights—the Fourth, Fifth, or Sixth—contains the most important rights that are protected by citizens under a democracy. You are to analyze the three and present your findings as to which one is the most important.

2. As part of a criminal justice honor society exercise, you are debating which period of legal history was the most important: the so-called due process revolution of the Warren Court (when the Supreme Court granted many additional rights to the accused through *Gideon*, *Miranda*, *Escobedo*, and so forth), or the more conservative era that followed under the Rehnquist Court (during which time many Warren Court decisions were eroded, and more rights were given to the police). Choose a side, and defend your opinion.

3. From the time of his confirmation in 1969, Chief Justice Warren Burger viewed the exclusionary rule as an unnecessary and unreasonable intrusion on law enforcement. Assume that as part of a group project, you are to prepare a pro-con paper that examines why there should and should not be an exclusionary rule as a part of our system of justice. What will be your arguments, pro and con?

STUDY SITE

ⓈSAGE edge™

Review → Practice → Improve

Sharpen your skills with **SAGE edge** at **edge.sagepub.com/peak2e**

SAGE edge for students provides a personalized approach to help you accomplish your coursework goals in an easy-to-use learning environment. Access the videos, audio clips, quizzes, and SAGE journal articles that are noted in this chapter.

PRACTICE AND APPLY WHAT YOU'VE LEARNED

▶ edge.sagepub.com/peak2e

$SAGE edge™

THINK YOU'VE MASTERED THE CONTENT?

Check your comprehension on the study site with:

- An online **action plan** that includes tips and feedback on progress through the course and materials, allowing you to individualize your learning experience

- **Chapter summaries with learning objectives** that reinforce the key concepts in each chapter

PART III

THE COURTS

This part consists of three chapters. **Chapter 9** examines court structure and functions at the federal, state, and trial court levels; included are discussions of pretrial preparations, the actual trial process, the jury system, and some court technologies.

Chapter 10 looks at the courtroom work group: the judges, prosecutors, and defense attorneys.

Chapter 11 discusses sentencing, punishment, and appeals. Included are the types and purposes of punishment, types of sentences convicted persons may receive, federal sentencing guidelines, victim impact statements, and capital punishment.

COURT ORGANIZATION
Structure, Functions, and the Trial Process

LEARNING OBJECTIVES

As a result of reading this chapter, you will be able to:

1 Explain the methods and purposes of the adversarial court system

2 Explain court jurisdiction and how it is determined

3 Describe trial courts of general and limited jurisdictions

4 Identify the purpose and process of appeals courts

5 List the functions of the various tiers of the federal court system

6 Relate the activities that occur during the pretrial process as attorneys prepare for trial

7 Delineate the trial process, from opening statements through conviction and appeal

8 Discuss the impact of new technologies on the courts

ASSESS YOUR AWARENESS

Test your knowledge of court structure and functions as well as the trial process and jury system by responding to the following six true-false items; check your answers after reading this chapter's materials.

1 America's court system relies on the adversarial system, which includes, among other things, the cross-examination of witnesses.

2 America's court system consists of a national system of federal courts as well as 50 state court systems, plus those in the District of Columbia and U.S. territories.

3 Federal judges are nominated by the president and confirmed by the Senate, and they have a lifetime appointment.

4 All courts generally have unlimited jurisdiction to hear civil and criminal trials as well as appeals.

5 The Sixth Amendment gives the accused the right to a trial by an impartial jury of peers—meaning 12 people who are "similar in nearly all regards" to the defendant.

6 A convicted person may quickly and easily—and at any time—leave the state court appellate system and appeal in a federal court.

The place of justice is a hallowed place.

—Francis Bacon

Courts are at the center of life's important moments.

—Howard Conyers, former Washoe County, Nevada, district court administrator

<< Answers can be found on page 424.

Former NFL star Michael Vick's infamous criminal dog-fighting case in 2007 highlighted multiple facets of our criminal justice system, including the dual court system and the challenges of bail, plea bargaining, and sentencing.

In 2001, Michael Vick rose to national fame as a star quarterback with the NFL's Atlanta Falcons—the first African American player to be selected in the first round of the NFL draft. Vick then had six successful seasons with the Falcons, going to the playoffs twice and being selected to three Pro Bowls. But in 2007, Vick was implicated in an illegal dog-fighting operation in his home state of Virginia. Federal and state law enforcement authorities found evidence of an extensive dog-fighting venue at Vick's sprawling rural compound, along with evidence of illegal interstate activities, including dog trafficking, online betting, and drug sales. Authorities also found evidence of dog torture and killings, and Vick was soon charged with breaking a host of both Virginia state laws and federal laws.[1]

With his NFL career in shambles, Vick faced prosecution in both venues of our dual court system, and many observers asked where Vick would first answer for his alleged crimes and would he—could he—be brought to justice twice, raising questions of double jeopardy under the Fifth Amendment to the U.S. Constitution. Other questions followed: If convicted, could Vick appeal his case through both court systems, or was there a mechanism in place so that justice could be sought in one venue, thus avoiding the lengthy, complex appeals process—and saving time and taxpayer dollars? Would Vick's case be like any other criminal case—would he be granted bail, would a judge or a grand jury decide whether to charge him, would he enter into a plea bargain or go to trial, and what would a fair sentence be for such varied and unique crimes?

As you read this chapter, consider these questions and our nation's courts, which deal not only with high-profile cases like Vick's, but also with the much more minor and numerous cases that overload our state trial courts.

INTRODUCTION

Courts have existed in some form for thousands of years. The court system has survived the dark eras of the Inquisition and the Star Chamber (which enforced unpopular political policies in England during the 1500s and 1600s and, without a jury or public view, meted out severe punishment, including whipping, branding, and mutilation). The U.S. court system developed rapidly after the American Revolution and led to the establishment of law and justice on the western frontier.

We first consider the adversarial system the courts employ, and how the courts influence our lives as policy-making bodies. Then the focus shifts to the several levels of courts found in the United States. Your attention is drawn to the case of Barry Kibbe, presented near the chapter's end, which provides a rare look at the entire criminal trial and appeals process, all the way to the U.S. Supreme Court.

Colonial Courts: An Overview

Our nation's colonial courts began modestly. Thomas Olive, deputy governor of West Jersey in 1684, described the prevailing court system when he wrote that he was "in the habit of dispensing justice sitting in his meadow."[2] As the population of the colonies grew, however, formal courts of law appeared in Virginia, Massachusetts, Maryland, Rhode Island, and Connecticut, among other venues. The colonies drew on the example set by the English Parliament in that the colonial legislatures became the highest courts.[3]

Beneath the legislatures were the superior courts, which heard both civil and criminal cases. Over time, some colonies established trial courts headed by a chief justice and several associate justices. Appeals from the trial courts were heard by the governor and his council in what were often called "courts of appeals."[4]

Courts established at the county level played a key role in both the government and the social life of the colonies. In addition to having jurisdiction in both civil and criminal cases, county courts fulfilled many administrative duties, including setting and collecting taxes, supervising the building of roads, and licensing taverns.

Eventually, however, the founders of the new republic had profound concerns about the distribution of power between courts and legislatures, and between the states and the federal government. Coming from the experience of living under English rule, they feared the tyranny that could flow from the concentration of governmental power. At the same time, they were living with the problems associated with a weak centralized government. This conflict prompted the delegates to the Constitutional Convention of 1787 to create a federal judiciary that was separate from the legislative branch of government. As a result, today we have the **dual court system**—one implemented by the **state court system** (inherited directly from the Crown of England) and the other created by Congress and entrusted to the **federal court system**.[5]

Video: Rule of law

Dual court system: the state and federal court systems of the United States.

State court system: civil or criminal courts in which cases are decided through an adversarial process; typically including a court of last resort, an appellate court, trial courts, and lower courts.

Federal court system: the four-tiered federal system that includes supreme courts, circuit courts of appeal, district courts, and magistrate courts.

OUR ADVERSARIAL SYSTEM

Adversarial system: a legal system wherein there is a contest between two opposing sides, with a judge (and possibly jury) sitting as an impartial arbiter, seeking truth.

Ralph Waldo Emerson stated that "every violation of truth . . . is a stab at the health of human society."[6] Certainly, most people would agree that the traditional, primary purpose of our courts is to provide a forum for seeking and obtaining the truth. Indeed, the U.S. Supreme Court declared in 1966 in *Tehan v. United States ex rel. Shott* that "the basic purpose of a trial is the determination of truth."[7]

Our American court system relies on the **adversarial system**, which uses several means to get at the truth. First, evidence is tested under this approach through cross-examination of witnesses. Second, power is lodged with several different people; each courtroom actor is granted limited powers to counteract those of the others. If, for example, the judge is biased or unfair, the jury can disregard the judge and reach a fair verdict. If the judge believes the jury has acted improperly, he or she can set aside the jury's verdict and order a new trial. Furthermore, both the prosecuting and defense attorneys have certain rights and authority under each state's constitution. This series of checks and balances is aimed at curbing misuse of the criminal courts.

The American court system relies on the adversarial system of justice in attempting to discern the truth; this includes the questioning (examination) and cross-examination of witnesses.

PRACTITIONER'S PERSPECTIVE

PROSECUTING ATTORNEY

Name: Katherine Elizabeth Pridemore

Current Position: Assistant Prosecuting Attorney/ Division Chief, Juvenile Division, Hamilton County, Ohio

City, State: Cincinnati, Ohio

College Attended/Academic Major: Bachelor's degree in political science/pre-law from University of Cincinnati; Juris Doctorate (J.D.) from University of Cincinnati College of Law

How long have you been a practitioner in this criminal justice position? Since March 2001; from 1998 to 2001, assistant attorney general for the state of Ohio in the Non-Capital Crimes/Habeas Corpus/1983 Actions Section

My primary duties and responsibilities as a practitioner in this position: First, as felony prosecutor, I prosecute high-level felonies including homicides; sexual assaults; child endangerings; shootings and other felonious assaults; and media cases. Also, as felony assistant supervisor, I teach younger assistant prosecutors the fundamentals of felony prosecutions, trial work, the art of plea bargaining, and how to interview victims/witnesses/ police officers and effectively prosecute and resolve felony cases. I also cover the offices of other assistant prosecutors when they are out of the office in all of the above, plus going to trial on any and all felonies (drug trafficking, drug possession, burglaries, robberies, domestic violence, gun charges, etc.)

The qualities/characteristics that are most helpful in this career: In no particular order, to possess the following abilities: (1) to communicate in a meaningful manner with people from "all walks of life"—victims, witnesses, officers, business owners, the homeless, lower economics, higher economics, different ethnicities, races, genders, sexual orientations; (2) to analyze a felony case and determine the best resolution for the case; (3) to keep work life and personal life separate (because felony work can be extremely difficult and frustrating, and you don't want to take that home with you), and thus maintain a good balance between work and home; (4) to think on your feet, using reason and common sense; (5) to use good interpersonal skills when dealing with the public, the judges, the defense bar, and the court staff; and (6) the ability to remain ethical and professional at all points in time!

In general, this is what a *typical day* looks like for a practitioner in this career: (1) Going to court and addressing a docket that consists of a variety of cases that include different charges, settings, and actions, such as sentencings, jury trials, bench trials, plea or trial settings, initial case settings, reports; (2) interacting with the public, the court staff, the judges, the defense bar, and possibly the media; (3) possibly going to trial; if no trial, then office tasks include returning phone calls from witnesses, victims, defense attorneys, and officers; (4) responding to email from the same groups, doing paperwork (including requests for additional evidence, follow-ups on investigations, discovery, issuing subpoenas); (5) devoting time to prepare for upcoming trials; and (6) meetings with witnesses for upcoming trials.

My advice to someone either wishing to study, or now studying, criminal justice and wanting to become a practitioner in this career: Be prepared to take a vow of poverty! Honestly, though, be prepared for the fact that employment in the public sector yields very little money unless you are an elected public official. Sometimes the work can be very hard on one's home life, especially if you really care about the cases and are gearing up for, or are in, trial. Be prepared to experience much of the public (at least in urban settings) resenting you, distrusting you, ignoring subpoenas, and being hostile toward you—and know that the prosecution of criminal defendants rarely, if ever, results in anyone thanking you.

THE INFLUENCE OF COURTS IN POLICY MAKING

Determining what the law says and providing a public forum involve the courts in policy making. **Policy making** can be defined as choosing among alternative choices of action. The policy decisions of the courts affect virtually all of us in our daily living. In recent decades, the courts have been asked to deal with issues that previously were within the purview of the legislative and executive branches. Because many of the Constitution's limitations on government are couched in vague language, the judicial branch must eventually deal with potentially volatile social issues, such as those involving prisons, abortion, and schools.[8]

U.S. Supreme Court decisions have also dramatically changed race relations, resulted in the overhaul of juvenile courts, increased the rights of the accused, prohibited prayer and segregation in public schools, legalized abortion, and allowed for destruction of the U.S. flag. State and federal courts have together overturned minimum residency requirements for welfare recipients, equalized school expenditures, and prevented road and highway construction from damaging the environment. They have eliminated the requirement of a high school diploma for a firefighter's job and ordered increased property taxes to desegregate public schools. The only governmental area that has not witnessed judicial policy making since the Civil War is foreign affairs. Cases in which courts make policy determinations usually involve government, the Fourteenth Amendment, and the need for equity—the remedy most often used against governmental violations of law. Recent policy-making decisions by the judicial branch have been based not on the Constitution, but rather on federal statutes concerning the rights of the disadvantaged and consumers and the environment.[9]

Perhaps nowhere have the nation's courts had more of an impact than in the prisons—from which about 52,000 prisoner petitions are filed each year in the U.S. district courts (approximately 80 percent of them filed by state prisoners).[10] Among these accomplishments of judicial intervention have been extending recognized constitutional rights of free speech, religion, and due process to prisoners; abolishing the South's plantation model of prisons; accelerating the professionalization of U.S. correctional managers; encouraging a new generation of correctional administrators more amenable to reform; reinforcing the adoption of national standards for prisons; and promoting increased accountability and efficiency of prisons. The only failure of judicial intervention has been its inability to prevent the explosion in prison populations and costs.[11]

It may appear that the courts are overbroad in their review of issues. However, judges "cannot impose their views . . . until someone brings a case to court, often as a last resort after complaints to unresponsive legislators and executives."[12] Plaintiffs must be truly aggrieved and have a legal right to bring their case to court. The independence of the judicial branch, particularly at the federal court level, where judges enjoy lifetime appointments, allows the courts to champion the causes of the underclasses: those with fewer financial resources or votes (by virtue of, say, being a minority group) or without a positive public profile.[13] Also, the judiciary is considered to be the "least dangerous branch," having no enforcement powers. Moreover, the decisions of the courts can be overturned by legislative action. Thus, the judicial branch depends on a perception of legitimacy surrounding its decisions.[14]

AMERICAN COURTS: A DUAL COURT SYSTEM

In order to better understand the U.S. court system, it is first important to know that this country has a dual court system: both a national system of federal courts and 50 state courts systems. Although often sharing similar names, they operate under different constitutions and laws, as outlined in the sections that follow.

Before exploring these different courts, we take up the critical issue of **jurisdiction**, which is best defined as a court's legal authority to hear and decide a particular type of case. Jurisdiction is set forth in state and federal law, and it is typically based on geography (i.e., where the case is physically located) and subject matter (what the

Student on the Street Video: Who is Antonin Scalia?

Policy making: the act of creating laws or setting standards to govern the activities of government; the U.S. Supreme Court, for example, has engaged in policy making in several areas, such as affirmative action, voting, and freedom of communication and expression.

Jurisdiction, court: the authority of a court to hear a particular type of case, based on geography (city, state, or federal) and subject matter (e.g., criminal, civil, probate).

case is about: criminal, civil, juvenile, etc.). Courts hear only cases that fall under their jurisdiction and authority, and as such, our courts are organized along state and federal lines, and then further along subject matter lines (see Table 9.1). At the lower end are the limited jurisdiction state trial courts, handling traffic, misdemeanors, and juvenile matters, for example. At the highest level is the U.S. Supreme Court, which hears a limited number of appeals on federal and constitutional legal issues. The great majority of the nation's judicial business occurs at the state—not the federal—level and our discussion begins there.

TABLE 9.1   State and Federal Courts

STATE COURTS	FEDERAL COURTS
Appellate Jurisdiction—Courts of Last Resort	
State Supreme Court	U.S. Supreme Court
Appellate Jurisdiction—Intermediate Appeals Courts (IAC)	
State Courts of Appeals	Circuit Courts of Appeal
Trial Courts	
State Trial Courts	U.S. District Courts
Limited Jurisdiction Trial Courts	
Traffic, Juvenile, Justice of the Peace (for example)	Tax, Admiralty, Bankruptcy (for example)

STATE COURTS

Where Most Cases Begin: State Trial Courts

At the lowest level of state courts are trial courts of limited jurisdiction, also known as inferior courts or lower courts. There are more than 13,500 trial courts of limited jurisdiction in the United States, staffed by about 18,000 judicial officers. The lower courts constitute 85 percent of all judicial bodies in the United States.[15]

Variously called district, justice, justice of the peace, city, magistrate, or municipal courts, the lower courts decide a restricted range of cases. These courts are created and maintained by city or county governments and therefore are not part of the state judiciary. The caseload of the lower courts is staggering—more than 61 million a year, an overwhelming number of which are traffic cases (more than 41 million in any given year).[16]

The workload of the lower courts can be divided into felony criminal cases, nonfelony criminal cases, and civil cases. In the felony arena, lower court jurisdiction typically includes the preliminary stages of felony cases. Therefore, after an arrest, a judge in a trial court of limited jurisdiction will hold the initial appearance, appoint counsel for indigents, and conduct the preliminary hearing. Later, the case will be transferred to a trial court of general jurisdiction for trial (or plea) and sentencing.[17]

General Jurisdiction: Major Trial Courts

State trial courts of general jurisdiction are usually referred to as the major trial courts. There are an estimated 2,000 major state trial courts, staffed by more than 11,000 judges.

Each court has its own support staff consisting of a clerk of the court, a sheriff, and others. In most states, the trial courts of general jurisdiction are also grouped into judicial districts or circuits. In rural areas, these districts or circuits encompass several adjoining counties, and the judges are true generalists who hear a variety of cases and literally ride the circuit; conversely, larger counties have only one circuit or district for the area, and the judges are often specialists assigned to hear only certain types of cases.[18]

The term *general jurisdiction* means that these courts have the legal authority to decide all matters not specifically delegated by state law to the lower courts of limited jurisdiction. The most common names for these courts are district, circuit, and superior.[19] On the criminal justice front, most serious criminal violations, including a rising number of drug-related offenses, are

Major court complexes like this one in San Diego, CA, are common in bigger cities where a variety of courts—state and federal—handle sometimes overwhelming case loads.

heard in these trial courts of general jurisdiction. Although the courts are overburdened with heavy case filings, most criminal cases do not go to trial, and the dominant issue in the courts of general jurisdiction is not guilt or innocence, but what penalty to apply to someone who has entered a guilty plea through plea bargaining (described later in this chapter). Figure 9.1 shows an organizational structure for a county district court serving a population of 300,000. Note the variety of functions and programs that exist, in addition to the basic court role of hearing trials and rendering dispositions.

FIGURE 9.1 Organizational Structure for a District Court Serving a Population of 300,000

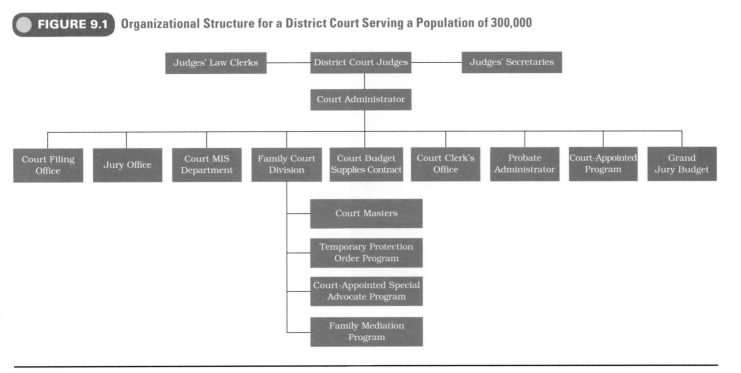

Note: MIS = Management Information Systems.

Within the state trial court system, a number of specialty courts or problem-solving courts, such as drug, family, mental health, veterans, and domestic violence courts, have become more common. They are used to divert criminal defendants into treatment programs rather than jail or prison (see "Diversion Programs/Problem-Solving Courts," later in this chapter).

Figure 9.2 shows the caseload trends for state criminal trial courts in the United States. As with crime in general, caseloads are declining in the trial courts.

Appeals Courts

After a conviction in a criminal case or a judgment in a civil case, the first stop for an appeal in the state courts is known as an **intermediate court of appeal** (ICA). These courts stand between trial courts and courts of last resort (state supreme courts), and they typically have appellate jurisdiction only; that is, they hear only appeals.

State courts have experienced a significant growth in appellate cases that would overwhelm a single appellate court such as a state's supreme court (see below). To alleviate the caseload burden on courts of last resort, state officials have responded by creating ICAs, which must hear all properly filed appeals. As of 2011, 40 states had established permanent ICAs.[20] The only states not having an ICA are sparsely populated with low volumes of appeals. Nevada was one such state until populations and caseloads grew in recent years, prompting voters in 2014 to approve the creation of an ICA, which began hearing its first cases in early 2015.[21]

The structure of the ICA varies. In most states these bodies hear both civil and criminal appeals, and these courts typically use rotating three-judge panels. Also, the state ICAs' workload is demanding: According to the National Center for State Courts, state ICAs report that more than 269,000 are cases filed annually.[22] ICAs engage primarily in error corrections; they review trials to make sure that the law was followed and the overall standard is one of fairness. The ICAs represent the final stage of the process for most litigants. Very few cases make it to the appellate court in the first place, and of those cases, only a small proportion will be heard by the state's court of last resort.[23]

State **courts of last resort** are usually referred to as the state supreme court. The specific names differ from state to state, as do the number of judges (from a low of five to as many as nine). Unlike the ICAs, these courts do not use panels in making decisions;

Intermediate courts of appeal: state courts that stand between trial courts and courts of last resort; they typically have appellate jurisdiction only.

Court of last resort: the last court that may hear a case at the state or federal level.

FIGURE 9.2 State Court Criminal Caseloads, 2003–2012

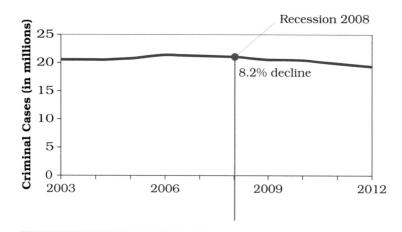

Source: R. LaFountain, R. Schauffler, S. Strickland, K. Holt, and K. Lewis. *Examining the Work of State Courts: An Analysis of 2012 State Court Caseloads* (Williamsburg, VA: National Center for State Courts, 2014).

Appellate court judges, Sandra Sgroi, left, John Leventhal, center, Mark Dillon, right, three members of a four-judge panel, listen to oral arguments from attorneys appealing for the public release of records from the grand jury in the videotaped chokehold death of Eric Garner, Tuesday, June 16, 2015, in New York.

rather, the entire court sits to decide each case. All state supreme courts have a limited amount of original jurisdiction in dealing with matters such as disciplining lawyers and judges.[24] Nowhere is the policy-making role of state supreme courts more apparent than in deciding death penalty cases—which, in most states, are appealed automatically to the state's highest court, thus bypassing the ICAs. The state supreme courts are also the ultimate review board for matters involving interpretation of state law.[25]

In states not having ICAs, the state supreme court has no power to choose which cases will be placed on its docket. However, the ability of most state supreme courts to choose which cases to hear makes them important policy-making bodies. Whereas ICAs review thousands of cases each year, looking for errors, state supreme courts handle a hundred or so cases that present the most challenging legal issues arising in that state.

FEDERAL COURTS

The next "You Be the Judge" box describes a case that uniquely demonstrates the entire appellate process through the dual state and federal court systems, going through the state courts and all the way to the U.S. Supreme Court.

Causation: a link between one's act and the injurious act or crime, such as one tossing a match in a forest and igniting a deadly fire.

You Be the... JUDGE

On a very cold night in Rochester, New York, Barry Kibbe and a friend met Stafford at a bar. Stafford had been drinking so heavily that the bartender refused to serve him more alcohol, so Kibbe offered to take him barhopping elsewhere. They visited other bars, and at about 9:30 p.m., Kibbe and his friend drove Stafford to a remote point on a highway and demanded his money. They also forced Stafford to lower his trousers and remove his boots to show he had no money hidden. Stafford was then abandoned on the highway, in the cold. A half-hour later, a man driving his truck down the highway saw Stafford standing in the highway, waving his arms for him to stop. The driver saw Stafford too late, and he was struck and killed. Even though the driver of the truck killed Stafford, Kibbe was arrested and charged with robbery and second-degree murder, raising a challenging question of **causation**—a necessary element in holding someone criminally responsible for a death.

State Court Actions: In *State v. Kibbe*, Kibbe was tried and convicted of robbery and murder in the second degree. At trial, the judge did *not* instruct the jury on the subject of causation (e.g., that the government had to prove Kibbe had actually caused Stafford's death). On appeal to New York's appeals court, in *Kibbe v. Henderson*, Kibbe argued that the judge *should* have given the jury such an instruction so that they would have to determine whether the state had proved this element beyond a reasonable doubt, but the appellate court affirmed his conviction. Then, on appeal to New York's supreme court, the conviction was also

affirmed. Both courts found that the judge did not err in failing to instruct the jury about causation.

Federal Court Actions: Having exhausted all possible state remedies, Kibbe then sought redress in the federal court, filing a *writ of habeas* corpus with the U.S. district court having jurisdiction and arguing that the trial judge had violated his due process rights by not giving the jury instructions regarding causation. The district court denied the *habeas* petition, saying that no constitutional question had been raised.

Next, Kibbe appealed to the Second U.S. Circuit Court of Appeals, making the same argument. This court, however, reversed his conviction, saying that Kibbe had been deprived of due process because of the trial judge's failure to instruct the jury on causation. Next, the government appealed, this time to the U.S. Supreme Court; in *Henderson v. Kibbe*, the Supreme Court, issuing a *writ of certiorari* (defined later in this chapter) to the lower court, decided to hear the case.

1. How do you believe the U.S. Supreme Court should rule—for or against Kibbe? Why?

2. Who was Henderson (Kibbe's adversary) in this case?

3. What is meant by "exhausting all possible state remedies"?

4. What is meant by habeas corpus?

Answers to these questions are provided in the Notes section at the end of the book.[26]

Federal Trial Courts: U.S. District Courts

The U.S. **district courts**, like their counterparts in the state court system, may be fairly described as the "workhorses" of the federal judiciary, because nearly all civil or criminal cases heard in the federal courts are initiated at the district court level.

The locations of the U.S. district courts are outlined in Figure 9.3 (sometimes designated by region—"northern" or "eastern," for example). Congress created 94 U.S. district courts, 89 of which are located within the 50 states. There is at least one district court in each state (some states have more, such as California, New York, and Texas, each of which has four). Congress has created 678 district court judgeships for the 94 districts. The president nominates district judges, who must then be confirmed by the Senate; they then serve for life unless removed for cause. In the federal system, the U.S. district courts are the federal trial courts of original jurisdiction for all major violations of federal criminal law (some 500 full-time magistrate judges hear minor violations).[27]

District court judges are assisted by an elaborate supporting cast of clerks, secretaries, law clerks, court reporters, probations officers, pretrial services officers, and U.S. marshals. The larger districts also have a public defender. Another important actor at the district court level is the U.S. attorney—the federal prosecutor. There is one U.S. attorney in each district. The work of district judges is significantly assisted by 352 bankruptcy judges, who are appointed for 14-year terms by the court of appeals in which the district is located.

Video:
Change of venue

District courts: trial courts at the county, state, or federal level with general and original jurisdiction.

FIGURE 9.3 Geographic Boundaries of U.S. Courts of Appeals and District Courts

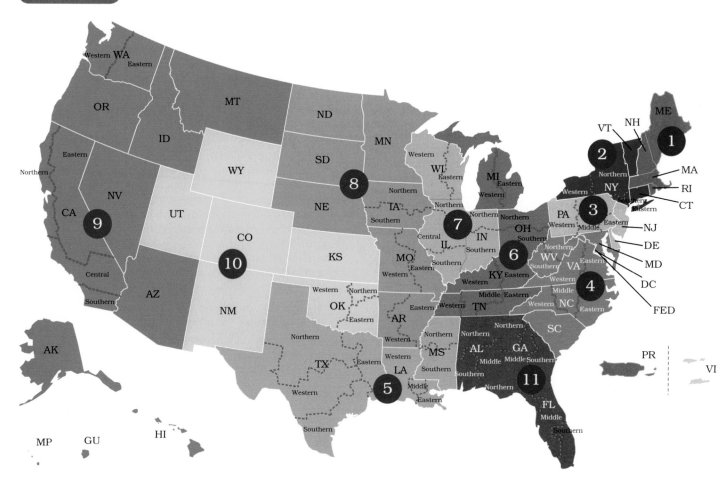

The Michael Vick Case: Michael Vick's dog-fighting case, outlined at the beginning of this chapter, began with an indictment (see the discussion of grand juries later in this chapter) in the U.S. District Court for the Eastern District of Virginia—the federal trial court with jurisdiction over federal criminal cases where Vick's home and operations were located.

IN THE UNITED STATES DISTRICT COURT FOR THE

EASTERN DISTRICT OF VIRGINIA

Richmond Division

FILED
IN OPEN COURT

JUL 17 2007

CLERK, U.S. DISTRICT COURT
RICHMOND, VA

UNITED STATES OF AMERICA	)	**Criminal No. 3:07CR 274**
	)	
	)	18 U.S.C. § 371
v.	)	Conspiracy to Travel in Interstate
	)	Commerce in Aid of Unlawful
	)	Activities and to Sponsor a Dog in an
PURNELL A. PEACE,	)	Animal Fighting Venture
a/k/a "P-Funk" and "Funk,"	)	(Count 1)
QUANIS L. PHILLIPS,	)	
a/k/a "Q,"	)	
TONY TAYLOR.	)	
a/k/a "T,"	)	
MICHAEL VICK,	)	
a/k/a "Ookie,"	)	
	)	
Defendants.	)	

INDICTMENT
JULY 2007 TERM - At Richmond, Virginia

COUNT ONE
(Conspiracy to Travel in Interstate Commerce in Aid of Unlawful Activities
and to Sponsor a Dog in an Animal Fighting Venture)

THE GRAND JURY CHARGES THAT:

1.   Beginning in or about early 2001 and continuing through on or about April 25,

2007, in the Eastern District of Virginia and elsewhere, defendants, PURNELL A. PEACE, also

known as "P-Funk" and "Funk," QUANIS L. PHILLIPS, also known as "Q," TONY TAYLOR,

also known as "T," and MICHAEL VICK, also known as "Ookie," did knowingly and willfully

combine, conspire, confederate and agree with each other, and with persons known and unknown

to the Grand Jury, to commit the following offenses against the United States, to wit:

The front page of this grand jury indictment against former NFL star Michael Vick shows that Vick was prosecuted in United States District Court - federal court - for multiple violations of federal criminal laws. An indictment is one method by which a criminal case can move forward to trial or a plea deal.

U.S. Courts of Appeals: Circuit Courts

Video: U.S. Supreme Court and crime

Much like the state court system, the federal system provides an intermediate appeals court—intermediate between the U.S. district courts and the U.S. Supreme Court. These courts are known as the **circuit courts** of appeals, referring to the 13 geographic areas—or circuits—where these courts are seated and over which they exercise jurisdiction. Eleven of the circuits are identified by number, and two others are called the D.C. Circuit and the Federal Circuit (see Figure 9.3). A court of appeals hears appeals from the U.S. district courts located within its circuit, as well as appeals from decisions of federal administrative agencies. These courts are the last stop for an appeal before it reaches the U.S. Supreme Court.

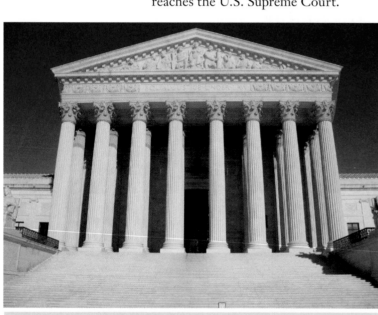

The judges who sit on the circuit courts of appeals are nominated by the president and confirmed by the Senate. As with the U.S. district courts, the number of judges in each circuit varies, from 6 in the First Circuit to 28 in the Ninth, depending on the volume and complexity of the caseload. Each circuit has a chief judge (chosen by seniority) who has supervisory responsibilities. Several staff positions aid the judges in conducting the work of the courts of appeals. A circuit executive assists the chief judge in administering the circuit. The clerk's office maintains the records. Each judge is also allowed to hire three law clerks. In deciding cases, the courts of appeals may use rotating three-judge panels. Or, by majority vote, all the judges in the circuit may sit together to decide a case or reconsider a panel's decision. Such *en banc* hearings are rare, however.[28]

The U.S. Supreme Court, in Washington, D.C., is where the court's nine justices meet, deliberate, and render the law of the land.

Because the U.S. Supreme Court hears so few cases (see next section), the U.S. circuit court decisions are very often the last word on legal issues and, as such, their decisions have great impact in setting legal precedent and in shaping the law for the many people who live within a circuit court's geographic jurisdiction.

U.S. Supreme Court

Circuit courts: originally courts wherein judges traveled a circuit to hear appeals, now courts with several counties or districts in their jurisdiction; the federal court system contains 11 circuit courts of appeals (plus the District of Columbia and territories), which hear appeals from district courts.

The **U.S. Supreme Court**, as the highest court in the nation, has ultimate jurisdiction over all federal courts, as well as over state courts in cases involving issues of federal law; it is the final interpreter of federal constitutional law. Also briefly discussed are its jurisdiction, practices, workload, and administration.

Judges and Advocacy

The Supreme Court, formed in 1790, and other federal courts have their basis in Article III, Section 1, of the Constitution, which provides that "the judicial Power of the United States, shall be vested in one supreme Court, and in such inferior Courts as the Congress may from time to time ordain and establish."[29] The Supreme Court is composed of nine justices: one chief justice and eight associate justices. As with other federal judges appointed under Article III, they are nominated to their post by the president and confirmed by the Senate, and they serve for life.[30] Each new term of the Supreme Court begins, by statute, on the first Monday in October.

U.S. Supreme Court: the court of last resort in the United States, also the highest appellate court; it consists of nine justices who are appointed for life.

INVESTIGATING FURTHER

CRIMINAL LAW FROM THE U.S. CIRCUIT COURTS

In 2010, the U.S. Court of Appeals for the Ninth Circuit (the largest circuit in the country, which includes the heavily populated state of California) heard an appeal from a criminal defendant who was convicted based on evidence the police obtained after placing a GPS tracking device on his car without first obtaining a search warrant. The police placed the device by going to the defendant's house in the early morning hours and sneaking up the defendant's rather long driveway to his car parked just outside his garage. They then tracked his vehicular movements, which provided evidence of his marijuana-growing activities. He was convicted and later appealed, claiming the police action was a violation of his Fourth Amendment protections. The Ninth Circuit justices disagreed and ruled the police action was constitutional, enabling law enforcement agencies in similar cases to use GPS tracking without a warrant.

That same year, on the other side of the country, the U.S. Court of Appeals for the D.C. Circuit ruled in a similar case that the use of a GPS tracking device was a search under the Fourth Amendment. The ruling stemmed from a case in which, in 2005, federal officers obtained a search warrant to attach a GPS tracking device to the car of a Washington, D.C., nightclub owner and suspected drug dealer, Antoine Jones. But officers attached the device a day later than the warrant required and they did so in Maryland, rather than in the D.C. jurisdiction the warrant specified. Nonetheless, they tracked Jones for

nearly a month and ultimately brought criminal charges against him based on the GPS evidence. Jones was tried in the U.S. District Court for the D.C. Circuit, where his attorneys argued that the GPS tracking violated Jones's Fourth Amendment protections because the GPS tracking was a "search" and the device was installed in violation of the warrant's requirements. The court disagreed with respect to Jones's movements tracked on public streets and areas outside his driveway and home. The GPS evidence was admitted, and Jones was convicted. But the D.C. Circuit reversed, and the effect was a new rule that governed law enforcement in the D.C. Circuit's jurisdiction: Get a warrant before using GPS tracking, or risk having tracking evidence thrown out at trial.

After these decisions, the "law of the land" in the Ninth Circuit governed police actions in the states within that circuit, and officers were able to use GPS tracking devices without first obtaining a warrant, whereas in states within the D.C. Circuit, officers were required to get a warrant. The U.S. Supreme Court then heard the *Jones* case and ruled in 2012 that law enforcement must first obtain a warrant to use GPS tracking devices on vehicles. But until that ruling was issued, these different circuit court decisions affected millions of people and law enforcement officers in their jurisdiction.

Source: See United States v. Jones, 565 U.S. ____ (2012) and United States v. Pineda-Moreno 617 F.3d 1120 (9th Cir. 2010).

Not just any lawyer may advocate a cause before the high court; all who wish to do so must first secure admission to the Supreme Court bar. Applicants must submit an application form that requires applicants to have been admitted to practice in the highest court of their state for a period of at least three years (during which time they must not have been the subject of any adverse disciplinary action), and they must appear to the Court to be of good moral and professional character. Applicants must also swear or affirm to act "uprightly and according to law, and . . . support the Constitution of the United States."[31]

Conferences and Workload

The Supreme Court does not meet continuously in formal sessions during its nine-month term. Instead, the Court divides its time into four separate but related activities. First, some amount of time is allocated to reading through the thousands of petitions for review of cases that come annually to the Court—usually during the summer and when the Court is not sitting to hear cases. Second, the Court allocates blocks of time for oral arguments—the live discussion in which lawyers for both sides present their clients' positions to the justices. During the weeks of oral arguments, the Court sets aside its third allotment of time, for private discussions of how each justice will vote on the cases they have just heard. Time is also allowed for the justices to discuss which additional cases to hear. These private discussions are usually held on Wednesday afternoons and Fridays during the weeks of oral arguments. The justices set aside a fourth block of time to work on writing their opinions.[32]

The Court has complete discretion to control the nature and number of the cases it reviews by means of the *writ* (order) *of certiorari*—an order from a higher court directing a lower court to send the record of a case for review. The Court considers requests for *writs of certiorari* according to the *rule of four*. If four justices decide to review a case—to "grant cert," the Court will hear the case. Several criteria are used to decide if a case requires action: First, does the case concern an issue of constitutional or legal importance? Does it fall within the Court's jurisdiction (the Court can only hear cases that are mandated by Congress or the Constitution)? Does the party bringing a case have **standing**—a strong vested interest in the issues raised in the case and in its outcome?[33]

The Court hears only a tiny fraction of the thousands of petitions that come before it. When it declines to hear a case, the decision of the lower court stands as the final word on the case. The Court's caseload has been increasing steadily; today the Court has about 10,000 cases on the docket per term, and formal written opinions are delivered in 80 to 90 cases.[34]

Administration

The chief justice orders the business of the Supreme Court (a description of the chief justice's role is provided in Chapter 10) and administers the oath of office to the president and vice president upon their inauguration. According to Article I, Section 3, of the Constitution of the United States, the chief justice is also empowered to preside over the Senate in the event that it sits as a court to try an impeachment of the president.

The clerk of the Court serves as the Supreme Court's chief administrative officer, supervising a staff of 30 under the guidance of the chief justice. The marshal of the Court supervises all building operations. The reporter of decisions oversees the printing and publication of the Court's decisions. Other key personnel are the librarian and the public information officer. In addition, each justice is entitled to hire four law clerks, almost always recent top graduates of law schools, many of whom have served clerkships in a lower court the previous year.[35]

MAKING PREPARATIONS: PRETRIAL PROCESSES

In Chapter 1, we briefly discussed the sequence of major events that compose the U.S. criminal justice system, from the point of entry of the offender into the system and through the related police, courts, and corrections components. Here, we focus on the pretrial process, the events that occur prior to the trial itself. (We discuss judges as well as the roles and strategies of prosecution and defense attorneys later in Chapter 10.)

Booking, Initial Appearance, Bail, and Preliminary Hearing

As stated in Chapter 1, the criminal justice process is engaged when one is arrested. Following that, the accused will then proceed through the following steps:

- **Booking:** Basically a clerical function, booking usually involves taking the suspect to a police station or sheriff's office, where he or she may be fingerprinted, photographed, questioned, read his or her rights, and possibly be given a bail amount that must be paid in order to gain release until the next stage in the process. Meanwhile, the prosecutor will be sent a copy of the offense report written by the police, and will be considering whether or not enough probable cause (discussed in Chapter 8) exists to believe the suspect committed the offense.

- **Initial appearance:** Within a reasonable time after arrest, the suspect appears in court, where the judge gives the defendant formal notice of the charge(s), advises the suspect of his or her rights—including the right to a government-provided attorney if the

Standing: a legal doctrine requiring that one must not be a party to a lawsuit unless he or she has a personal stake in its outcome.

Booking: a clerical procedure for when an arrestee is taken to jail and a record is made of his or her name, address, charge(s), arresting officers, and time and place of arrest.

Initial appearance: a formal proceeding during which the accused is read his or her rights, informed of the charges, and given the amount of bail required to secure pretrial release.

defendant cannot afford one, and sets bail in appropriate cases. The judge also performs a cursory review of the evidence, and if he or she does not believe such evidence establishes probable cause that the defendant may have committed the crime charged, the case will be dismissed. Notice that defendants typically do not enter a plea at this stage because they have not yet been appointed an attorney, so they have not yet had a chance to consult anyone about their case.

• **Bail:** Bail is also known as "pretrial release," allowing defendants to remain out of jail while awaiting trial and affording them time to help with their defense and to maintain ties with family and their job. But bail is not a right, nor is it guaranteed under the U.S. Constitution. In fact, most state laws provide that bail cannot be granted in cases involving certain violent felonies. If a judge does grant bail, however, the Constitution's Eighth Amendment prohibits the bail amount from being "excessive." To ensure a fair decision-making process, a bail hearing is conducted (usually as part of the initial appearance), and the judge must consider a variety of factors, including:

✓ The risk that the defendant will flee before trial

✓ The defendant's criminal record

✓ The seriousness of the charges

✓ The safety of the community

Bail bonds operations are commonly located near county jails to serve criminal defendants seeking freedom on bail while their case is pending. Judges and bail bond agents use similar criteria in making decisions about bail.

There are several ways to make bail, all of which ensure that the accused will later appear in court and most of which require some financial commitment from the defendant or their family or friends. The court typically requires either cash or a bond, the latter of which is basically an insurance policy the defendant buys insuring his or her appearance. Defendants can "make bail" directly with some courts, but in other jurisdictions the defendant will have to get a bond through a bail bond company, which typically requires a nonrefundable payment of 10 percent of the bail amount. Either way, if the defendant fails to appear in court, the court issues a warrant for the defendant's arrest, and he or she loses any money posted with the court.

The bail decision can be critical for criminal defendants. Again, pretrial release affords defendants the chance to keep their jobs and maintain family and community ties, and to assist with their defense. Being denied bail—pretrial detention—can be devastating on all of these fronts, and it can provide prosecutors and police better access to the defendant for continued questioning and investigation (subject to certain *Miranda* limitations). So it is important to consider what types of defendants are detained and whether the process is truly fair. In 2015, researchers released findings showing that the bail decision is unfairly affecting the poor and racial minorities, with African American defendants being detained four times more often than whites.[36] The same study concluded that 75 percent of people held in pretrial detention are there for nonviolent offenses, but they simply cannot afford bail and so they are incarcerated in county jails until their cases are resolved. Indeed, 62 percent of jail populations are unconvicted

Bail: surety (e.g., cash or paper bond) provided by a defendant to guarantee his or her return to court to answer to criminal charges.

defendants awaiting trial.[37] As such, the bail decision affects not only defendants, but also our already-overcrowded jails and the criminal justice professionals tasked with keeping those populations secure.

- • **Preliminary hearing:** This hearing (which the defendant may choose to waive in some jurisdictions) allows a judge (no jury is present) to decide whether or not probable cause is sufficient against the person charged to proceed to trial. The prosecutor will offer physical evidence and testimony to try to get the accused "bound over" for trial while the defense offers counter-evidence. If the judge finds enough probable cause, he or she will order the accused to appear at trial to answer the state's formal charges, which the prosecutor will file in the form of an "information" (versus an "indictment," discussed in the next section). The preliminary hearing can help the accused and his or her counsel to prepare for trial, because they are able to hear much of the state's case. But as discussed in the next section, in some states, the prosecutor avoids this effect by presenting the case before a secretive grand jury.

Grand Juries

About half of all states use a **grand jury** to bring formal charges, rather than the prosecutor's doing so unilaterally (or after a preliminary hearing).[38] The prosecutor presents evidence to the grand jury, and, much like the judge in a preliminary hearing, the grand jury must find probable cause to charge the defendant with a crime (the functions of the grand jury are described in the next "Investigating Further" box). If so, the grand jury issues an "indictment"—a formal charge—and trial (or plea bargaining) will ensue.

The importance of the grand jury function cannot be overstated because, without an indictment, the state cannot move forward with criminal charges against a defendant.

Preliminary hearing: a stage in the criminal process conducted by a magistrate to determine whether a person charged with a crime should be held for trial based on probable cause; does not determine guilt or innocence.

Grand jury: a body that hears evidence and determines probable cause regarding crimes and can return formal charges against suspects; use, size, and functions vary among the states.

Michael Brown, left, was fatally shot by Officer Darren Wilson on August 9, 2014, in Ferguson, Missouri; the shooting sparked civil unrest and a national debate concerning police-minority relations, the militarization of the police, police use of force, and whether police should use body-worn cameras.

INVESTIGATING FURTHER

GRAND JURY POWERS

The primary function of the modern grand jury is to review the evidence presented by the prosecutor and to determine whether there is probable cause to return an indictment.

The Fifth Amendment to the U.S. Constitution requires that a grand jury indictment be brought to commence all federal criminal charges, so in virtually every federal jurisdiction, there is at least one grand jury sitting every day. Federal grand juries have extraordinary investigative power, which is the source of much of the criticism against grand juries: that they simply act as a rubber stamp for the prosecutor. And, unlike potential jurors in regular trials, grand jurors are not screened for biases or other improper factors.

For federal cases involving complex and long-term investigations (such as those involving organized crime, drug conspiracies, or political corruption), "long-term" grand juries will be impaneled. In most jurisdictions, grand jurors are drawn from the same pool of potential jurors as are any other jury panels, and in the same manner.

The Federal Rules of Criminal Procedure provide that the prosecutor, grand jurors, and the grand jury stenographer are prohibited from disclosing what happened before the grand jury, unless ordered to do so in a judicial proceeding. Secrecy prevents the escape of people whose indictment may be contemplated, ensures that the grand jury can deliberate without outside pressure, prevents witness tampering prior to trial, and encourages people with information about a crime to speak freely.

A prosecutor can obtain a subpoena to compel anyone to testify before a grand jury, without showing probable cause and, in most jurisdictions, without even showing that the person subpoenaed is likely to have relevant information.

In the federal system, a witness cannot have his or her lawyer present in the grand jury room, although witnesses may interrupt their testimony and leave the grand jury room to consult with their lawyer. A few states do allow a lawyer to accompany the witness. A witness who refuses to appear before the grand jury risks being held in contempt of the court.

If the grand jury refuses to return an indictment, the prosecutor can try again; double jeopardy does not apply to a grand jury proceeding. No judge is present in the grand jury room when testimony is being taken.

All states have some form of grand jury, but only about half the states now use grand juries routinely for bringing criminal charges.

Source: Adapted from the American Bar Association, "Frequently Asked Questions About the Grand Jury System," http://www.abanow.org/2010/03/faqs-about-the-grand-jury-system/.

Consider the 2014 case from Ferguson, Missouri (explored in more detail in Chapter 5), where a white Ferguson police officer, Darren Wilson, shot and killed unarmed, 18-year-old Michael Brown during an encounter in the street. The case sparked intense media coverage and debate over police-citizen race relations and the appropriate use of police force in encounters with unarmed suspects, with many people assuming Wilson had acted criminally because Brown was unarmed. The case against Wilson went to a St. Louis County grand jury, which—after 25 days of hearing testimony and reviewing evidence—determined there was not enough probable cause to conclude that Wilson acted criminally. But the Brown-Wilson proceedings were different from a typical grand jury review in several ways: The prosecutor did not recommend charges against Wilson, more than 60 witnesses testified (versus the typical three or four), and officer Wilson himself testified for more than four hours.[39] Some observers believe that, in cases like Wilson's, the state effectively "tries" the case but without the public oversight of a typical criminal trial, and, in that way, the grand jury role can be significant.

Arraignment

After being formally charged, the accused will again be advised of his or her rights, and is asked to enter a formal plea. A defendant may plead "not guilty," "guilty," or "no contest" (also known as *nolo contendere*). A "not guilty" plea means the defendant claims innocence and is forcing the state to prove its case at trial, whereas a "guilty" plea relieves the state of that burden and the defendant is convicted without trial. The *nolo* plea is unique in that it allows a defendant to plead guilty for purposes of avoiding trial, but the plea cannot be used against him or her later in a civil case (because technically he has not admitted guilt). The court must always approve a plea of *nolo contendere*.

If the plea at this **arraignment** is "not guilty," a trial must occur (unless plea bargaining takes place).

Plea Negotiation

When defendants enter a "guilty" or "no contest" plea, they often do so through a **plea negotiation**, or **plea bargaining**. In fact, the great majority of criminal convictions— up to 90 percent—are obtained through plea deals, without any courtroom fact-finding. In essence, in exchange for the defendant's plea of guilty, the government is willing to give the defendant certain concessions.

There are several forms of plea bargaining. The accused can engage in *charge bargaining* (offering to plead guilty to a lesser offense than the one charged, thus hoping for a lighter sentence), *count bargaining* (pleading guilty to, say, three of the charged counts and having the remaining six counts thrown out), or negotiating how he or she will serve an imposed sentence (e.g., two five-year terms to be served concurrently, as opposed to consecutively).

As the defendant benefits from plea bargaining, so does the government. First, criminal court dockets in most jurisdictions are seriously overburdened and the state simply cannot take every case to trial, so there is great pressure to resolve cases out of court. Further, the prosecutor "wins" a conviction while reducing the time, money, and uncertainty involved in taking the case to trial, where a jury may acquit because the defense produces unanticipated evidence or witnesses. The process also eases the burden on witnesses and prospective jurors, and can reduce the overcrowding of jails by more quickly funneling offenders out of pretrial detention and into prison or some form of community corrections (discussed in Chapter 14). Certainly there are many reasons why a high percentage of cases are bargained out of the system, and one can only imagine the havoc that would be caused in the court system if 9 of 10 cases that are plea bargained had to be tried. However, by signing the deal and pleading guilty, the defendant waives a number of constitutional protections (see the next "Investigating Further" box). But consider the realities of a typical barroom killing. There might be evidence of premeditation and malice that is sufficient enough to justify a jury verdict of murder in the first degree. Or, the defendant's long-time status as an alcoholic might convince the jury that he was unable to form the necessary intent to be heavily punished. Perhaps the defendant may indicate that he acted in "heat of passion," pointing to a verdict of manslaughter, or even that he acted in self-defense. When such cases are given to the jury to decide, a variety of outcomes is possible. Therefore, plea negotiations allow the prosecutor and the defense to arrive at some middle ground of what experience has shown to be "justice," without the defense running the risk of heavy punishment for the defendant, and the government not having to devote many days in trial—with the risk of the defendant's being acquitted.[40]

Video: The plea

Student on the Street Video: Trial versus plea-bargained cases

Arraignment: a criminal court proceeding during which a formally charged defendant is informed of the charges and asked to enter a plea of guilty or not guilty.

Plea negotiation (or bargaining): a preconviction process between the prosecutor and the accused in which a plea of guilty is given by the defendant, with certain specified considerations in return—for example, having several charges or counts tossed out, and a plea by the prosecutor to the court for leniency or shorter sentence.

The Michael Vick Case: Vick's case garnered extensive media coverage and commentary, but it followed the path of most criminal cases, as outlined in this chapter. The U.S. government took the lead in prosecuting Vick first. He was granted bail with certain conditions, including drug testing. He was indicted by a federal grand jury, meaning the government could proceed with formal charges against him. Facing such charges and the prospect of extensive evidence of his illegal activities and brutality against the dogs used in his fighting operations, Vick and his attorneys bargained with federal prosecutors to avoid a trial. During this time, Vick tested positive for marijuana, in violation of his bail conditions, so the federal judge ordered stricter home-confinement conditions. Vick ultimately pleaded guilty to a variety of charges and was sentenced to, among other penalties, 21 months in federal prison at Leavenworth, Kansas, and extensive community service in the interest of stopping animal cruelty. While Vick was serving time there, Virginia authorities moved forward with their case, using Vick's guilty pleas in the federal case to bolster the state's evidence. Again, Vick pleaded guilty and struck a bargain for a suspended sentence conditioned on the successful serving of his federal sentence. Vick was released from prison in 2009 and ultimately returned to play in the NFL while devoting significant time to speaking out against animal cruelty.[41]

INVESTIGATING FURTHER

PLEA BARGAINING

Some authors believe plea bargaining reduces the courthouse to something akin to a Turkish bazaar, where people barter over the price of copper jugs. They see it as justice on the cheap. Others believe that plea bargaining works to make the job of the judge, the prosecutor, and the defense attorney much easier, while sparing the criminal justice system the expense and time needed to conduct many more trials.

No matter where one stands on the issue, however, it is ironic that both police and civil libertarians oppose plea bargaining. Police and others in the crime control camp view plea bargaining as undesirable because defendants can avoid conviction and responsibility for crimes they actually committed when allowed to plead guilty to (and be sentenced for) lesser and/or fewer charges; police, in the crime control camp, would prefer to see the defendant convicted for the crime actually committed.

Civil libertarians and other supporters of the due process model also oppose plea bargaining, but for different reasons: When agreeing to negotiate a plea, the accused forfeits a long list of legal protections afforded under the Bill of Rights: the presumption of innocence; the government's burden of proof (beyond a reasonable doubt); and the right to face one's accuser, testify, and present witnesses in one's defense, the right to have an attorney and a trial by jury (except for lesser offenses), and the right to an appeal if convicted. Another concern is that an innocent defendant might be forced to enter a plea of guilty because of the threat of trial or police and prosecutorial coercion.

1. In your opinion, does plea bargaining sacrifice too many of the defendant's rights?

2. Or, does justice suffer by giving too many benefits to guilty persons?[42]

Jury Trials

Most civilizations—even the most primitive in nature—have used some means to get at the truth: to tell right from wrong, guilt from innocence, and so forth. In Burma, each suspected party to a crime had to light a candle, and the person whose candle burned the longest was not punished.[43] In Borneo, suspects poured lime juice on a shellfish; whoever's shellfish squirmed first was the guilty party.[44] The "trial by ordeal" method was also used around the world, with people's guilt or innocence determined by subjecting them to a painful task (often using fire and water); the idea was that God would intercede and help the innocent by performing a miracle on their behalf.[45]

The Sixth Amendment to the U.S. Constitution ensures that our method is more civilized, guaranteeing the defendant a trial by an impartial jury of his or her peers. Many people view the jury as the most sacred aspect of our criminal justice system, because it is where common citizens determine the truth and assess punishment. Not all criminal defendants are guaranteed a right to trial by jury (i.e., if charged with a *lesser misdemeanor*—one that has a penalty of less than six months in jail); furthermore, the defendant may waive the right to jury trial and be tried by a judge alone (known as

Criminal trials in the United States often involve a jury of one's peers to hear the evidence; then, if rendering a conviction, the same jury may be used to determine the proper form and extent of punishment.

a *bench trial*). There are advantages and disadvantages to each, and a wise defendant will want to discuss them with an attorney.

The method of selecting citizen *peers* to hear the evidence is important. First, in most states a questionnaire is mailed to people (whose names were obtained from voter, taxpayer, driver, or other lists) to determine who is qualified to serve, with certain exemptions given to specific groups. Those who are qualified to serve are then sent a *summons* to appear and form a jury pool, from which a smaller number of prospective jurors is selected for a process known as *voir dire* ("to speak the truth"), where the prosecutor and defense attorney question and screen pool members to determine whether they can be fair and impartial and decide the case based on the evidence presented. With the judge overseeing the selection process, both the prosecution and the defense can challenge and have removed an unlimited number of jurors *for cause*, meaning for some reason one

Pretrial motions/ processes: any number of motions filed by prosecutors and defense attorneys prior to trial, to include quashing of evidence, change of venue, discovery, to challenge a search or seizure, to raise doubts about expert witnesses, or to exclude a defendant's confession.

is prejudiced against their side. But both the prosecution and the defense also receive a limited number of *peremptory challenges* (usually set by statute), which allow them to remove jurors without any reason or explanation.

Generally, 12 jurors and 2 alternates are selected for a criminal trial, but that number is not required by the Constitution. In *Williams v. Florida*, the U.S. Supreme Court observed that the decision to fix the size of a jury at 12 "appears to have been a historical accident" and that a 6-member jury satisfied the constitutional requirement.[46] Nor is a unanimous verdict by the jury required by either the U.S. Constitution or the U.S. Supreme Court, so in some states a majority of "votes" from the jurors will support a verdict.[47]

Figure 9.4 shows several aspects of jury service and trials in the United States as reported by the Center for Jury Studies: the estimated number of jury trials, the percentage of actual trials by case type, and the estimated number of adults involved in jury service each year.

Pretrial Motions

Prior to the trial, either the defendant or the prosecutor may file **pretrial motions/processes** with the court in order to be better positioned for trial. Defense motions include requests to suppress evidence (e.g., the defense believes that a police search, physical evidence, or a confession was obtained illegally), to reduce bail (if the accused is still in jail awaiting trial), to conduct discovery (discussed in the next section), to change venue (to move the trial to another city, if a highly publicized or emotional crime is charged), and to delay trial (known as a "continuance").

FIGURE 9.4 Jury Trials and Service in United States

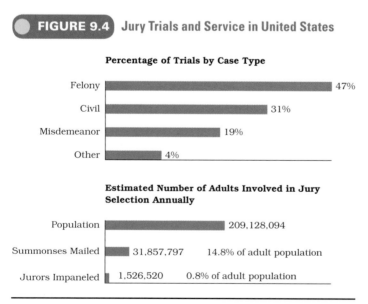

Percentage of Trials by Case Type

Felony — 47%
Civil — 31%
Misdemeanor — 19%
Other — 4%

Estimated Number of Adults Involved in Jury Selection Annually

Population — 209,128,094
Summonses Mailed — 31,857,797   14.8% of adult population
Jurors Impaneled — 1,526,520   0.8% of adult population

*This estimate was extrapolated using survey results for 1,546 counties representing 70 percent of the U.S. population.

Source: Reprinted with permission from The National Center for State Courts, Center for Jury Studies.

Discovery

No member of the court work group—including judges, prosecutors, and defense attorneys—likes major surprises or "bombshell" evidence coming to light in the courtroom. **Discovery** is simply the exchange of information between prosecution and defense, in order to promote a fair adversarial contest between the two sides and help the truth come to light. Essentially, each side is entitled to learn the other's strengths and weaknesses as well as the evidence and theories on which each will rely.

Discovery has become quite controversial in recent years, with prosecutors often being accused of withholding evidence that should have been provided to the defense, to the point that many jurisdictions have individuals—typically attorneys, skilled in the laws of evidence—serving as "discovery masters" to ensure fair exchange of information by both sides.

Amanda Nagel hugs her nine-month-old daughter, Alexis, while waiting to appear in drug court in Placer County, CA. Nagel, who had been arrested on a methanphetamine charge, told the judge she wants to go straight and stay out of jail to take care of her daughter. Drug courts, mental health courts, and veterans courts are just a few of the "speciality courts" operating across the country to divert low-risk offenders out of the criminal justice system.

Generally, the prosecution has a higher burden of providing "exculpatory" evidence (that which tends to support the defendant's innocence).[48] However, because the U.S. Supreme Court has required the prosecution to disclose only that evidence which is both material and exculpatory, this has become a confusing area of law and formal/informal policy—with some states adopting conservative, others liberal, and still others "middle ground" rules of discovery[49]—so that the question of what is to be exchanged is not always clear-cut.

Diversion Programs/Problem-Solving Courts

The increasing number of criminal cases in our already-overburdened courts, together with the high recidivism (reoffending) rate, has spawned a number of alternative courts and **diversion programs** around the country, including drug courts, mental health courts, veterans courts, and even some courts dedicated to offenders with gambling addictions. By 2012, more than 2,700 drug courts were operating in every U.S. state and territory,[50] and today more than 300 mental health courts operate in most U.S. jurisdictions.[51] These "problem-solving" courts allow eligible defendants—typically first-time, nonviolent offenders—to move their cases to a court where specialized court professionals (prosecutors, defense attorneys, judges, social workers, physicians, and treatment professionals) can better address the unique features of these defendants and their cases.

The model for these specialty courts is fairly similar across jurisdictions, utilizing either a pre-plea or post-plea process. In the former instance, a defendant demonstrates eligibility for the court's services and is not required to plead guilty but is diverted to the specialty court's program. In the latter instance, the defendant is diverted to the court's program after an initial guilty plea. In both models, defendants are then given the opportunity to complete a program to treat the problems that landed them in criminal trouble in the first place: drug rehabilitation for the drug offender; mental health counseling/medication for the mentally ill offender; and specialized debriefing/counseling for military veterans, most of whom are suffering from posttraumatic stress

Discovery: a procedure wherein both the prosecution and the defense exchange and share information as to witnesses to be used, results of tests, recorded statements by defendants, or psychiatric reports, so that there are no major surprises at trial

Diversion program: removing a case from the criminal justice system, typically to move a defendant into another treatment program or modality.

disorder (PTSD) and other postcombat issues. If the defendant successfully completes the court-ordered "program," the charges are dropped (for a pre-plea case) or the guilty plea is vacated (in a post-plea case). If the defendant fails to carry out his or her end of the court agreement, the state can pursue the original criminal charges and the defendant will risk a conviction and a possible jail or prison sentence.

Research indicates that many of these courts, drug courts in particular, are succeeding in providing treatment and reducing recidivism. Many drug courts report an average of 8–26 percent lower recidivism rates than other justice system responses, with some of the best courts yielding a 45 percent lower rate. The long-term effects of such programs appear to be promising as well, with positive effects (nonrecidivism, or remaining "clean") lasting from 3 years to 14 years in some cases.[52]

THE TRIAL PROCESS

Video: 11 years
in Guantanamo

After all pretrial processes have been addressed, the next challenge is to get the case into the courtroom in a timely manner and then see that certain rules are followed and defendants' rights protected. This **trial process** is described in the sections that follow.

Right to a Speedy Trial: "Justice Delayed . . ."

Swift justice is a term that is fairly well emblazoned in our collective psyche—and has even been the title for a number of books, movies, and even some television series. Bringing offenders to justice in a timely manner is felt to be essential for sending a meaningful message to the offender, to convey a message of deterrence to the general public, to maintain public confidence in the judicial process, and generally to help the criminal justice system better do its job.

Similarly, the adage that "justice delayed is justice denied" says much about the long-standing goal of processing court cases with due deliberate speed. Charles Dickens condemned the practice of slow litigation in 19th-century England.[53] Dickens was considerably harsh toward England's Chancery Courts in his novel *Bleak House*,[54] and Shakespeare mentioned "the law's delay" in *Hamlet*.[55] Most important, even our founding fathers saw fit to hasten the movement of criminal matters into the courtroom: The Sixth Amendment to the Constitution states in part, "In all criminal prosecutions, the accused shall enjoy the right to a speedy and public trial." As a result, the consequences of **delay** to society are potentially severe. The U.S. Supreme Court has ruled that if the defendant's right to a speedy trial has been violated, then the indictment must be dismissed and/or the conviction overturned.[56]

Certainly some criminal defendants want their trial dates delayed (or "continued") as long as possible—giving time for the community's emotions surrounding the crime to subside, the memories of its victims and witnesses to fade, and the defense to uncover further evidence. Others, however—particularly those who cannot post bail and are awaiting trial in a jail, and/or have jobs and family to return to—want their "day in court" to arrive as soon as possible.

But what does a "speedy trial" mean in practice, and how does an appellate court know if the right has been denied? Those questions have been addressed at the *federal* level, with Congress enacting the **Speedy Trial Act of 1974**.[57] This act mandates a 30-day limit from the point of arrest to indictment and 70 days from indictment to trial. Thus, federal prosecutors have a total of 100 days from the time of arrest until trial.

However, there is very little in the way of fixed, enforced time limits at the *state* level, and the U.S. Supreme Court has refused to give the concept of a "speedy trial" any precise time frame.[58] Also, where they exist, most state laws fail to provide the courts with adequate and effective enforcement mechanisms; furthermore, if a prosecutor has

Trial process: all of the steps in the adjudicatory process, from indictment or charge to conviction or acquittal.

Delay (trial): an attempt (usually by defense counsel) to have a criminal trial continued until a later date.

Speedy Trial Act of 1974: later amended, a law originally enacted to ensure compliance with the Sixth Amendment's provision for a speedy trial by requiring that a federal case be brought to trial no more than 100 days following the arrest.

INVESTIGATING FURTHER

AN INSIDER'S VIEW OF A LOWER COURT

On his website, the Honorable Kevin Higgins, a lower court judge in Nevada, provided compelling realism and insight—as well as a bit of humor—in describing the workings and proper decorum of people and lawyers who are about to litigate cases in his courtroom:

> We tend to be the fast-food operators of the court system—high volumes of traffic for short visits with a base of loyal repeat customers. Don't plan on having a private conversation with your client or a witness amidst the throngs of other people trying to do the same thing. Prepared attorneys can be in and out in short order. Meeting your client for the first time after calling out his name in the lobby can take longer.
>
> Patience is a virtue and communication with the bailiffs and court staff will keep everyone happy. We coordinate the court's calendar, your calendar, and opposing counsel's calendar with the availability of the witnesses.
>
> Here are a few other "do's" and "don'ts" for successfully navigating this Court:
>
> - Everyone goes through the metal detector. Having to go back to your car to stow your Leatherman, linoleum cutting knife, stun gun, giant padlock or sword-cane (all items caught by security) can be annoying.
> - I once ruled against a very sweet elderly lady who reminded me of my own grandmother. She simply didn't have a case and I thought I had ruled fairly and gently. As she slowly walked by the front of the bench on the way out of the courtroom, she looked up and said, "Aw, go ---- yourself," and walked out the door. My mouth was hanging open; I just didn't know what to do. I'm fairly sure that this is the first and last time someone will get away with this, so even if the judge rules against you, smile on the way out. You can mutter to yourself all you want on the way back to the office rather than the holding cell in the back of the courthouse.
> - I once watched a gentleman in the back row feed his parrot peanuts while it was sitting on his shoulder. I assumed I had a parrot case in the pile somewhere, but after the last case was called, the parrot left without testifying. I asked the security officer why he let the man with the parrot come into court. I was told that the man had been there to watch a friend's case and that his sick parrot needed to be fed every 15 minutes. While admiring the logic of his decision, I have advised our new court security officers that unless an animal is actually a service animal, various beasts, fish, and fowl are not allowed in simply to watch court.
> - Expect the unexpected. Recent interesting events include a live pipe bomb being left at the front door by a concerned citizen; a gentleman dancing on top of his motor home in the parking lot while his laundry hung from the trees and his morning coffee perked on the propane stove he had set up in the next space; and the occasional ammonia discharges into the holding cell by one of the neighboring businesses.

Are you surprised by Judge Higgins's comments concerning the manner in which some people conduct themselves in a court of law?

Source: Adapted from Hon. Kevin Higgins, "An Insider's View of Justice Court," *Nevada Lawyer* 16, no. 8 (August 2008), p. 21. Reprinted with permission from Judge Kevin G. Higgins.

---

clearly taken an excessively long amount of time to bring a case to trial, existing time limits may be waived due to the court's own congested dockets. As a result, there are no "teeth" in state statutes concerning time limits, so state-level speedy trial laws are often not followed in practice.

The concern, then, is with *unnecessary* delay. Where a court must determine whether or not the defendant's right to a speedy trial was violated, the Supreme Court in *Barker v. Wingo* established the following test:[59]

1. *Length of delay*: A delay of a year or more from the date of arrest or indictment, whichever occurs first, was termed "presumptively prejudicial"; however, as noted earlier, the Supreme Court has never explicitly ruled that any absolute time limit applies.

2. *Reason for the delay*: The prosecution may not excessively delay the trial for its own advantage; however, a trial may be delayed for good reason, such as to secure the presence of a key witness.

3. *Time and manner in which the defendant has asserted his right*: If a defendant agrees to the delay when it works to his own benefit, he cannot later claim that he has been unduly delayed.

4. Degree of prejudice to the defendant which the delay has caused.[60]

Trial Protocols

After the judge has given the jury its preliminary instructions—emphasizing that the defendant is presumed innocent until proven guilty—and other pretrial issues have been settled, typically the pattern of the trial process is as follows:

1. *Opening statements*: The prosecutor goes first, as he or she has the burden of proof (and must prove every element of the crimes charged—beyond a reasonable doubt), followed by the defense (although in many jurisdictions the defense can opt to defer making its opening statements until later, when it presents its main case, or waive it altogether). The purpose of this step is to succinctly outline the facts they will try to prove during the trial—and it is *not* a time to argue with the other side.

2. *Prosecution's case*: The prosecution will present its side of the case, presenting and questioning its witnesses and admitting relevant evidence. The defense may cross-examine these prosecution witnesses. A "redirect" allows the prosecution to reexamine its witnesses. Once the prosecution has finished presenting its evidence, it will rest its case.

3. *Motion to dismiss*: As a formality, at this point during a criminal trial the defense will often make a motion to dismiss all charges, arguing that the state has not proved its case and, as such, there is no need for the defense to put on its case. This request is generally denied by the judge, opening the way for the defense case.

4. *Defense's case*: Next, the defense presents its main case through direct examination of their chosen witnesses. The prosecution is then given an opportunity to cross-examine the defense witnesses, and, during redirect, the defense may reexamine its witnesses. The defendant cannot be compelled to testify against himself or herself but has the right to testify in his or her own defense if so desired. The defense then rests. Because a defendant is presumed innocent until proven guilty, the defense is not required to put on a case at all. If the defense does not have good evidence or bases for cross-examination of the state's witnesses, the defense can simply rest and the jury or judge will have to decide if the state has proven its case beyond a reasonable doubt.

5. *Prosecution rebuttal*: The prosecution may offer evidence to refute the arguments made by the defense.

6. *Closing arguments*: This is a time for both sides to review the evidence so that it is clear to the jury before they begin their deliberations. The order of closing arguments varies by jurisdiction. In some jurisdictions, the state always argues first, but in others the defense does.[61] The prosecution will offer reasons why the evidence proves the defendant's guilt, and the defense will explain why the defendant should be acquitted. This is *not* the time for the prosecutor to offer

personal opinion, make inflammatory or discriminatory remarks, or comment on the defendant's failure to testify. Such misconduct may result in a reversal of a conviction on appeal.

7. *Jury instructions*: The judge's instructions to the jury are important and, if improper, may later be grounds for a reversal and new trial. Also known as "charging the jury," the judge will explain the law that is applicable to that particular criminal case and the possible verdicts, and will typically include general comments concerning the presumption of the defendant's innocence, that guilt be proved beyond a reasonable doubt, and that the jury may not draw inferences from the fact that the defendant did not testify in his or her own behalf.

Closing arguments are used by both prosecutors and defense attorneys to review the evidence and make it more understandable for the jurors.

8. *Jury deliberations and verdict*: The jury will deliberate for as long as it takes to reach a verdict. In most states, unanimous agreement must be met for a verdict to be reached (however, as noted earlier, a unanimous verdict is not required by the Constitution). Once the jury has determined its verdict, either guilty or not guilty for each crime in question, the verdict will be read to the court. Then, either side, or the judge, may "poll the jury," asking all jurors individually if the verdict as read is theirs; if not unanimous, the jury may be returned to its room to deliberate again, or be discharged. If the jury acquits the defendant, the case is over. The prosecutor cannot appeal an acquittal because of the Fifth Amendment protection against double jeopardy. The jury may, instead, convict the defendant of some charges while acquitting of others.

9. *Posttrial motions*: If the jury delivers a guilty verdict, the defense will usually ask the judge to override the jury's decision and acquit the defendant or grant him or her a new trial. This motion is almost always denied.

- *Sentencing*: If the defendant was convicted of the crime(s), sentencing will be determined by the judge immediately after the verdict is read or at a later court date. In arriving at a sentence, the judge generally orders a presentence investigation report (PSI) by probation or court services personnel, to look at the history of the person convicted, any extenuating circumstances, a review of his or her criminal record, and a review of the specific facts of the crime. The person or agency preparing the PSI makes a recommendation to the court about the type and severity of the sentence. The judge may, however, be limited by federal and state sentencing guidelines (discussed in Chapter 11); some crimes carry a mandatory minimum sentencing requirement, while other sentences may be based largely on the discretion of the judge.

- *Punishments*: After a conviction, and upon receiving the PSI or using sentencing guidelines, the judge may opt for one of the following punishments:

  ○ Incarceration

  ○ Probation

- o Fines
- o Restitution
- o Community service

10. *Appeal*: After conviction, the defendant may challenge the outcome. Potential grounds for appeal in a criminal case include legal error (e.g., improperly admitted evidence, improper jury instructions), juror misconduct, ineffective counsel, or lack of sufficient evidence to support a guilty verdict. If this error affected the outcome of the case, the appeal is granted—the conviction is overturned—and, in some instances, the case is remanded back to the trial court and a retrial is ordered (the prosecutor may choose to drop charges if facing a retrial without key evidence, for example). If the appeals court finds that the error(s) would not have affected the outcome, then the errors are considered harmless and the appeal is denied.[62] Note also that, for the *first* appeal, the U.S. Supreme Court has said that if the person convicted is indigent, then free, appointed counsel must be provided.[63] However, the Court later ruled that, after losing the initial appeal, the convicted person is *not* entitled to free appointed counsel for any subsequent appeals.[64]

TECHNOLOGIES IN THE COURTS

As with the police, the courts are unveiling new technologies that it is hoped will provide more efficient and effective operations. Some of those technologies are described in the sections that follow.

Achieving Paper on Demand

A major goal for all courts in the United States is to go "paper on demand" (POD)—denoting an environment in which the routine use of paper no longer exists in general. Rather, paper documents may be used for court business only rarely, and as a last resort. The ultimate goal is that there are no more lost files, all receipts are issued electronically, all police citations are issued electronically, all filing formats and forms are standardized, all judges use POD, and there are no more folders in the courtroom.

Toward that end, electronic case filing has been possible for many years and allows courts to realize dramatic increases in efficiency and reductions in related costs—in clerical staff alone. Electronic filing also enables some court services— such as the payment of fines and fees, collection of fines and penalties, provision of case information and documents to the public, and jury management—to be centralized or regionalized for improved efficiency and service. In addition, an electronic case file enables a court to better distribute its workload across the system.

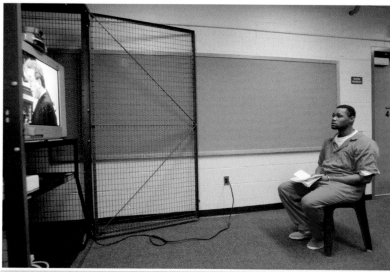

©AP Photo/Star Ledger, Pool

Raymond Dargan, 20, of New Brunswick, N.J., is arraigned on burglary and robbery charges at the Hunterdon County Jail via videoconference. Conducting initial appearances and arraignments via videoconference is increasingly common, especially in metropolitan areas where the courts and jails process record numbers of offenders.

INVESTIGATING FURTHER

HIGH-TECH COURTROOM CAPABILITIES

The National Judicial College in Reno, Nevada, has a state-of-the-art model courtroom—including a digital audio-video system, an evidence presentation system, and a convenient cable management system—that serves as a blueprint for other courtrooms. The 2,700-square-foot courtroom has a false floor allowing for a computer lab and hidden wires within. The audio-video system enables web conferencing and records everything going on in the courtroom; the system includes five voice-activated cameras and a tape backup system, which eliminates the need for a court reporter. Evidence can be digitally displayed to jurors so that it can be viewed more closely without having to be passed around.

As a safety feature, the judge's bench is fully armored; it not only deflects bullets, but also *catches* them, protecting everyone against bullet ricochets. Teleconferencing ability saves the attorneys and the court money; if a trial is not in session and the judge is deciding motions, attorneys can be in court without physically driving there.

Source: Adapted from Heather Singer, "Court Technology Partners," *Case in Point,* Winter/Spring 2005. Reprinted with permission from The National Judicial College. Copyright protected. www.judges.org.

Emerging Technologies

Following are two other areas in which court technologies are emerging or have already been put in place:

- *Digital recording:* Significant savings can be realized by replacing court stenographers with digital audio- or video-recording equipment. Many states have used digital recording extensively, and some states have used digital recording exclusively for many years without experiencing significant issues.

- *Conducting hearings via videoconferencing:* Videoconferencing has improved rapidly in both cost and quality over the past few years. Prices for basic capabilities have been reduced considerably, and the quality of the networks has steadily improved.

IN A
NUTSHELL

- As the population of the colonies grew, formal courts of law appeared based on the English system; however, fearing tyranny from this concentration of governmental power, a federal judiciary was created that was separate from the legislative branch of government. We now have the dual court system—one implemented by the state courts, the other created by Congress and entrusted to the federal courts.

- The policy decisions of the courts affect virtually all of us in our daily living. Perhaps nowhere have the nation's courts had more of an impact than in the prisons.

- The courts must *appear* to do justice—and provide rights that are embodied in the due process clause. Our court system relies on the adversarial system, using several means to get at the truth: Evidence is tested through cross-examination of witnesses, and power is lodged with several different people. This series of checks and balances is aimed at curbing misuse of the criminal courts.

- Each state has a court of last resort, all but 11 states have an appellate court, and there are trial courts of general jurisdiction that decide all matters not specifically delegated to lower courts.

- Lower state trial courts have limited jurisdiction, but after an arrest, the judge conducts the initial appearance, appoints counsel for indigents, and conducts the preliminary hearing.

- There are 94 U.S. district courts, which are trial courts of original jurisdiction for all major violations of federal criminal law.

- Federal judges are nominated by the president and confirmed by the Senate, and they serve for life. The Supreme Court has complete discretion to control the nature and number of the cases it reviews, and it hears only a tiny fraction of the thousands of petitions that come before it. The chief justice orders the business of the Supreme Court.

- There are 11 circuit courts of appeals plus the D.C. Circuit and the Federal Circuit; they hear appeals from the federal district courts located within their circuits, as well as appeals from decisions of federal administrative agencies.

- The criminal justice process is engaged when one is arrested. Following that, the accused will then proceed through a series of steps; at some point, the prosecutor will prepare an information setting forth the charge against the defendant; some jurisdictions use a grand jury to bring formal charges, rather than the prosecutor's doing so unilaterally.

- Discovery is the pretrial exchange of information between prosecution and defense, in order to promote a fair adversarial contest between the two sides and help the truth come to light.

- The Sixth Amendment gives defendants a trial by an impartial jury of his or her peers. The jury system is felt by many to be the most sacred aspect of our criminal justice system, because it is where common citizens sit as a forum to determine the truth and assess the punishment to be meted out.

- The Sixth Amendment guarantees the accused the right to a speedy and public trial. Although there are fixed, enforced time limits at the federal level, the Supreme Court has never defined a "speedy trial" with precise time frames at the state level. Rather, courts must use a test to determine whether or not the defendant's right to a speedy trial was violated.

- The courts are unveiling new technologies that it is hoped will provide more efficient and effective operations. These include paper on demand, digital recording, and videoconferencing.

KEY TERMS & CONCEPTS

▶ Review key terms with eFlashcards. ⑤SAGE edge™

Adversarial system, 217
Arraignment, 232
Bail, 229
Booking, 228
Causation, 223
Circuit courts, 226
Court of last resort, 222
Delay (trial), 236
Discovery, 235
District courts, 224

Diversion programs, 235
Dual court system, 217
Federal court system, 217
Grand jury, 230
Initial appearance, 228
Intermediate courts
   of appeal, 222
Jurisdiction, court, 219
Plea negotiation
   (or bargaining), 232

Policy making, 218
Preliminary hearing, 230
Pretrial motions/
   processes, 234
Speedy Trial Act of 1974, 236
Standing, 228
State court system, 217
Trial process, 236
U.S. Supreme Court, 226

REVIEW QUESTIONS

▶ Test your understanding of chapter content. Take the practice quiz. ⑤SAGE edge™

1. How is the adversarial system of justice related to the truth-seeking function of the courts?

2. How do the courts influence public policy making?

3. What are the types of, and reasons for, courts having a specific type(s) of jurisdiction?

4. What are the roles of the state court systems?

5. What is the structure and function of the trial courts of general and limited jurisdiction?

6. How does the U.S. Supreme Court decide to hear an appeal, and approximately how many cases does the Court hear per term?

7. What are some of the pretrial activities that occur?

8. Why does our jury system exist, and how is a jury formed?

9. What is meant by a right to a "speedy" trial? What are the ramifications of a defendant's being denied this right?

10. What are the major points of the trial process, from opening statements through appeal?

LEARN BY
DOING

1. Your local League of Women Voters is establishing a new study group to better understand the court system as it relates to political affairs. You are asked to explain the dual (federal and state) court system. You opt to use *Kibbe v. Henderson* as a good—and rare—example of a convicted offender's flow through both systems. Prepare your presentation.

2. You have been invited by a local civil rights group to discuss how the courts decide whether to grant someone bail or to order pretrial detention, and how those decisions have affected various racial and socioeconomic groups. Prepare your presentation with the most current data available.

3. Your criminal justice professor has assigned the class to debate the pros and cons of plea negotiation. What do you believe will be the prominent arguments presented by each side?

4. Assume you are a court administrator and your chief judge has tasked you to "bring the courtrooms into the new decade" by making recommendations concerning technologies that should be acquired. Using information and descriptions of the technologies presented in this chapter, select and prioritize which new technologies you would recommend be obtained, and why.

STUDY SITE

$SAGE edge™

Review → Practice → Improve

Sharpen your skills with **SAGE edge** at **edge.sagepub.com/peak2e**

SAGE edge for students provides a personalized approach to help you accomplish your coursework goals in an easy-to-use learning environment. Access the videos, audio clips, quizzes, and SAGE journal articles that are noted in this chapter.

LEARNING OBJECTIVES

As a result of reading this chapter, you will be able to:

1 Explain the five methods of judicial selection, and why the subject of judicial selection has come under scrutiny

2 List some of the benefits, training, and challenges of judges

3 Describe why courtroom civility is important, as well as the meaning of "good judging"

4 Relate the major duties of prosecutors and defense attorneys (to include their roles in plea negotiation)

ASSESS YOUR AWARENESS

Test your knowledge of the duties of judges, prosecutors, and defense attorneys by responding to the following six true-false items; check your answers after reading this chapter's materials.

1 Studies indicate that there is no difference in terms of how judges are selected; in all states, they are simply elected.

2 In recent years, people involved with courtroom matters have become much less friendly and less well-behaved.

3 The prosecutor may be fairly said to be the single most powerful person in the American criminal justice system.

4 A criminal defense attorney's primary role is to help the defendant escape punishment, even if the defendant is indeed guilty as charged.

5 A prosecutor's primary duty is not to convict, but to see that justice is done.

6 One's transition from public or private attorney to the role of judge can involve a number of psychological problems and issues.

Four things belong to a Judge:

To hear courteously,

To answer wisely,

To consider soberly, and

To decide impartially.

—Socrates

Fiat justitia ruat coelum [Let justice be done, though heaven should fall].

—Emperor Ferdinand I, 1563

<< Answers can be found on page 424.

Michael Morton (top, center) leaving a Texas courthouse in 1987 after being wrongfully convicted of murdering his wife and having been sentenced to life in prison. Twenty-five years later, Morton was freed after DNA evidence proved another man committed the crime.

When Michael Morton's wife was discovered brutally murdered in their Texas home in 1986, investigators did what they typically do in such cases—they focused on the husband as the prime suspect. Several people would later testify that Morton was at work at the time, but he'd left a note for his wife early that morning when he left home, expressing disappointment that she had not had sex with him the night before, his birthday. Police thought they had their motive, and they arrested Morton for first-degree murder.

Morton's attorneys tried to defend him, but they did so without critical evidence that could have proved his innocence. Police had recovered a bloody bandana near the Morton home, but the defense never had access to it for forensic testing. Morton's mother-in-law told police that the couple's three-year-old son, Eric, stated that he witnessed the murder and it wasn't Morton, but a "monster," and that "daddy" was not there. Neighbors also told police that a green van was parked near the Morton's house that day, and later, San Antonio police reported that they recovered the wife's Visa card in a San Antonio jewelry store days after the murder.

Morton's defense attorneys never had this evidence, and Morton was convicted and sentenced to life in prison. He maintained his innocence throughout the entire ordeal.

Twenty-five years after he was convicted, and after enduring what can only be described as a legal gauntlet run, forensic tests on the bandana yielded DNA from a convicted felon who was tied to a similar murder of another Texas woman. Morton's post-conviction team also finally obtained documents from the state's file that the prosecutor had not turned over at trial. After serving a quarter of a century in prison, Michael Morton walked free in October 2011.

A judge ultimately granted Morton his freedom, and we often think of judges as all-powerful players in the criminal justice system. As you will learn in this chapter, however, the prosecutor is responsible for most of the decisions that affect people, cases, and the system. In Morton's case, an extreme example to be sure, the prosecutor made the decision to charge Morton, and that decision would set in motion the events that changed Morton's life for 25 years and beyond.

As you read this chapter, think about how our justice system can properly check the power and discretion of its court players. What are the risks of trying to control discretion and authority of professionals like prosecutors and judges when we want those players to aggressively seek justice? Also consider how you would punish the prosecutor in Morton's case, if at all.

INTRODUCTION

Having looked at the general nature of courts and judges in the previous chapter, this chapter expands that discussion, focusing more on judges and other key personnel who are involved in the courts and their operation.

It is a part of our human nature that we hate losing. Therefore, even though in theory attorneys in a criminal courtroom are engaged in a truth-seeking process, make no mistake: They are *competing* from beginning to end—trying to convince the judge to include or exclude evidence or witnesses, to persuade the judge or jury of the guilt or innocence of the defendant, to sway the judge or jury that the convicted person should or should not be severely punished, and so on. This adversarial legal process is what drives our criminal justice system. Indeed, renowned defense attorney Percy Foreman is said to have remarked, "The best defense in a murder case is that the deceased should have been killed."[1] In a murder case where a woman was charged with shooting her husband, Foreman so slandered the victim that "the jury was ready to dig up the deceased and shoot him all over again."[2]

As will be seen in this chapter, the challenges (and criticisms) facing today's judges are several. They must successfully serve many masters and occupy many roles; as one person noted:

> The "grand tradition" judge, the aloof brooding charismatic figure in the Old Testament tradition, is hardly a real figure. The reality is the working judge who must be politician, administrator, bureaucrat, and lawyer in order to cope with a crushing calendar of cases.[3]

The chapter opens by considering the means by which judges ascend to the bench. This once-simple task has come under intense scrutiny—particularly in relation to the partisan election of judges, for which they must often solicit campaign contributions. Then we discuss the benefits and problems that occur when one becomes a judge; following that is an examination of the need for courtroom civility and a look at judicial misconduct. The roles and strategies of two other very important court figures—prosecutors and defense attorneys—are also reviewed.

THOSE WHO WOULD BE JUDGES: SELECTION METHODS AND ISSUES

The manner in which state and local court judges assume the bench matters—and it differs widely from state to state. The method used to select judges is important for at least four reasons: The type of judicial selection system affects judges' experience level; it determines the ability of qualified, but less politically connected, individuals to serve; it affects the gender and racial diversity of the judiciary; and it affects the public's perception of judicial impartiality and independence.[4] Across the United States at least five methods of **judicial selection** are used, but note that no two states use exactly the same selection method. In many states, more than one method of selection is used—for judges at different levels of the court system and even among judges serving at the same level. And when the same method is used, there are still variations in how the process works in practice.

Methods of Selection in State Courts

As noted in Chapter 9, all federal judges are nominated by the president and confirmed by the Senate, and they serve for life (unless they resign or are impeached).

$SAGE edge™

Get the edge on your studies. edge.sagepub .com/peak2e

- Take a quiz to find out what you've learned.
- Review key terms with eFlashcards.
- Watch videos that enhance chapter content.

Judicial selection (methods of): means by which judges are selected for the bench, to include election, a nominating commission, or a hybrid of these methods.

When a vacancy (due to death, retirement, or resignation of a judge)[5] occurs at the state level, however, candidates are as likely as not to face an election as part of their selection process. This becomes particularly important given that 97 percent of the cases heard in the United States are handled by state judges. Furthermore, every year, millions of Americans find themselves in state courts, whether called for jury service, to address a minor traffic offense, as a crime victim, or in a small claims case.[6]

The following five methods of selection used in state courts[7] are also depicted in Figure 10.1.

1. *Commission-based appointment* (also known as **merit selection** or the **Missouri Plan**): Judicial applicants are evaluated by a nominating commission, which then sends the names of the best-qualified candidates to the governor, who appoints one of those nominees. In most commission-based appointment systems, judges run unopposed in periodic retention elections, where voters are asked whether the judge should remain on the bench.

2. *Partisan election*: In a partisan election, multiple candidates may seek the same judicial position. Voters cast ballots for judicial candidates as they do for other public officials, and candidates run with the official endorsement of a political party. The candidate's party affiliation is listed on the ballot.

3. *Nonpartisan election*: In a nonpartisan election, a judicial candidate's party affiliation, if any, is not designated on the ballot.

4. *Gubernatorial appointment*: A judge is appointed by the governor (without a judicial nominating commission). The appointment may require confirmation by the legislature or an executive council.

5. *Legislative appointment/election*: This is the process by which judges are nominated and appointed or elected by legislative vote only.

Debating Judges and Politics

"They're awful. I hate them." Thus spoke former U.S. Supreme Court justice Sandra Day O'Connor concerning her views of judicial elections in May 2009 at an American Bar Association summit.[8] O'Connor added that the public is growing increasingly skeptical of elected judges in particular, with surveys showing that more than 70 percent of the public are considerably more distrustful of their judges than they have been in the past. At risk, O'Connor said, is the perception by the public that judges are "just politicians in robes."[9] O'Connor also said in November 2007 that "if I could wave a magic wand, I would wave it to secure some kind of merit selection of judges across the country."[10]

Our courts make decisions every day that affect nearly every aspect of our lives. Therefore, to a large extent, the quality of justice Americans receive depends on the quality of the judges who dispense it. The debate over how America chooses its judges has escalated in the 21st century. Consider this: In March 2009, the U.S. Supreme Court considered a case concerning a newly elected West Virginia Supreme Court of Appeals justice, Brent Benjamin, who voted on a mining company dispute; the mining company contributed $3 million in an election campaign to help Benjamin get elected. Instead of removing himself from the vote (known in the courts as *recusal*), Benjamin instead possibly cast the deciding vote in the 3–2 case—in favor of the mining company. There was no law in West Virginia saying a judge can't hear a case involving someone who financed his or her campaign. During oral arguments in the case, former justice David Souter said, "The system . . . is not working well."[11] The U.S. Supreme Court

Merit selection: a means of selecting judges whereby names of interested candidates are considered by a committee and recommendations are then made to the governor, who then makes the appointment; known also as the Missouri Plan.

FIGURE 10.1 Initial Selection of State Judges (Trial Courts of General Jurisdiction)

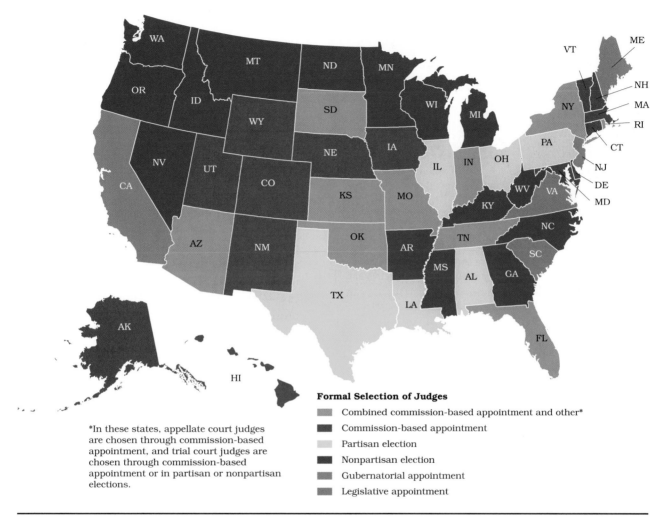

Formal Selection of Judges

- Combined commission-based appointment and other*
- Commission-based appointment
- Partisan election
- Nonpartisan election
- Gubernatorial appointment
- Legislative appointment

*In these states, appellate court judges are chosen through commission-based appointment, and trial court judges are chosen through commission-based appointment or in partisan or nonpartisan elections.

Source: Reprinted with permission from Institute for the Advancement of the American Legal System and American Judicature Society.

ruled in June 2009 that Benjamin's failure to recuse himself violated the Fourteenth Amendment's due process clause.[12]

Several states are now evaluating their judicial selection systems with a view to altering their current processes. And, by ruling in the West Virginia case, the Supreme Court certainly put a spotlight on this issue—one that has already been settled in about two dozen states by eliminating political fund-raising by their judicial candidates through the use of various merit selection systems.[13]

"Investing" in Judges?

Certainly adding fuel to the controversy over judicial selection is the amount of money now being spent to fund judges' elections, which has skyrocketed in state supreme courts since 1990, rising from $6.2 million then to $56.4 million in the 2011–2012 election cycle.[14] Furthermore, special interest groups have ramped up their efforts to influence the composition of state courts, making contributions to candidates, funding television ads, and pressuring candidates to speak publicly about their political views. In state supreme court elections in 2011–2012, special interest group spending represented 27 percent of the total dollars spent in such races.[15]

Judges are elected in many U.S. jurisdictions but their campaigns and the money used to fund them are under increasing scrutiny amid questions of how judges can possibly remain objective and resist influence on the bench.

© Jill Ann Spaulding/Moment Mobile/Getty Images

JUDGES' BENEFITS, TRAINING, AND CHALLENGES

Judges enjoy several distinct benefits of office, including life terms for federal positions and in some states. Ascending to the bench can be the capstone of a successful legal career for a lawyer, even though a judge's salary can be less than that of a lawyer in private practice. Judges certainly warrant a high degree of respect and prestige as well; from arrest to final disposition, the accused face judges at every juncture involving important decisions about their future: bail, pretrial motions, evidence presentation, trial, and punishment.

Although it would seem that judges are the primary decision makers in the courts, such is not always the case. Judges often accept recommendations from others who are more familiar with the case—for example, bail recommendations from prosecutors, plea negotiations struck by prosecuting and defense counsels, and sentence recommendations from probation officers. Such input is frequently accepted by judges in the kind of informal courtroom network that exists. Although judges run the court, if they deviate from the consensus of the courtroom work group, they may be sanctioned: Attorneys can make court dockets go awry by requesting continuances or by not having witnesses appear on time.

Newly elected judges are not simply "thrown to the wolves" and expected to immediately begin to conduct trials, listen to arguments, understand rules of evidence, render verdicts and sentences, and possibly write opinions, without the benefit of training or education. Many states mandate judicial education for new judges, sometimes even prior to assuming the role, as well as mandatory in-service or continuing education thereafter.

Other challenges can await a new jurist-elect or appointee. Judges who are new to the bench commonly face three general problems:

- *Mastering the breadth of law they must know and apply.* New judges would be wise, at least early in their career, to depend on other court staff, lawyers who appear before them, and experienced judges for invaluable information on procedural and substantive aspects of the law and local court procedures. Through informal discussions and formal meetings, judges learn how to deal with common problems. Judicial training schools and seminars have also been developed to ease the transition into the judiciary.

- *Administering the court and the docket while supervising court staff.* One of the most frustrating aspects of being a presiding judge is the heavy caseload and corresponding administrative problems. Instead of having time to reflect on challenging legal questions or to consider the proper sentence for a convicted felon, trial judges must move cases. They can seldom act like a judge in the "grand tradition."[16] Judges are required to be competent administrators, a fact of judicial life that comes as a surprise to many new judges. One survey of 30 federal judges found that three-fourths had major administrative difficulties on first assuming the bench, while half complained of heavy caseloads. One judge maintained that it takes about four years to "get a full feel of a docket."[17]

- *Coping with the psychological discomfort that accompanies the new position.* Most trial judges experience psychological discomfort on assuming the bench. Three-fourths of new

INVESTIGATING FURTHER

THE NATIONAL JUDICIAL COLLEGE

At the National Judicial College (NJC) in Reno, Nevada, the underlying message rings loud: Wearing a black robe alone does not a judge make. At the judicial college, the goal is not only to coach lawyers on how to be judges, but to teach veteran judges how to be better arbiters of justice. For many lawyers, the move to the other side of the bench is an awesome transition. "Judges aren't born judges," said former U.S. Supreme Court justice Sandra Day O'Connor. She recalled her anxieties the first time she assumed the bench: "It was frightening, really. There was so much to think about and to learn." Justice Anthony M. Kennedy, who is on the judicial college's faculty, states that

> judicial independence cannot exist unless you have skilled, dedicated, and principled judges. This leads to so many different areas—judicial demeanor, how to control a courtroom, basic rules of civility, how to control attorneys. These

are difficult skills for judges to learn. They're not something judges innately have. Judges have to acquire these skills.

The NJC offers about 65 onsite and online courses each year, ranging from a few days' duration to several weeks. The regular curriculum includes courses on courtroom technology; dealing with jurors; courtroom disruptions; domestic violence; managing complex cases; death penalty issues; traffic cases; ethics; mediation; family law; forensic, medical, and scientific evidence; and opinion writing. Certificates, extension programs, as well as specialized programs in administrative law, courts and media, international law, and other areas are also offered.

Source: The National Judicial College, "Course Planner," http://www.judges.org/planner.html; information also taken from Sandra Chereb, "Judges Must Train to Take the Bench," *Reno Gazette-Journal,* May 28, 1996, pp. 1B, 5B. Used with permission.

federal judges acknowledged having psychological problems in at least one of five areas: maintaining a judicial bearing both on and off the bench, dealing with the loneliness of the judicial office, sentencing criminals, forgetting the adversary role, and handling local pressure. One judge remembers his first day in court: "I'll never forget going into my courtroom for the first time with the robes and all, and the crier tells everyone to rise. You sit down and realize that it's all different, that everyone is looking at you and you're supposed to do something."[18] Like police officers and probation and parole workers, judges complain that they "can't go to the places you used to. You always have to be careful about what you talk about. When you go to a party, you have to be careful not to drink too much so you won't make a fool of yourself."[19] And the position can be a lonely one:

> After you become a . . . judge some people tend to avoid you. For instance, you lose all your lawyer friends and generally have to begin to make new friends. I guess the lawyers are afraid that they will someday have a case before you and it would be awkward for them if they were on too close terms with you.[20]

Judges frequently describe sentencing criminals as the most difficult aspect of their job: "This is the hardest part of being a judge. You see so many pathetic people and you're never sure of what is a right or a fair sentence."[21]

THE ART OF JUDGING, COURTROOM CIVILITY, AND JUDICIAL MISCONDUCT

To fully understand judges' role in the criminal justice system, one must consider some of the less obvious facets of their work on and off the bench—the art and craft of judging, maintaining civility among the many courtroom players, and the critical issue of judicial misconduct.

The Model Code of Judicial Conduct requires judges to be "patient, dignified, and courteous" to all persons engaged in court business.

"Good Judging"

What traits make for "good judging"? Obviously, judges should treat each case and all parties before them in court with absolute impartiality and dignity while providing leadership for court operations. But judging requires more than just those activities and roles. For example, a retired jurist with 20 years on the Wisconsin Supreme Court stated that the following qualities define the art and craft of judging:

- Judges are keenly aware that they occupy a special place in a democratic society. They exercise their power in the most undemocratic of institutions with great restraint.

- They are aware of the necessity for intellectual humility—an awareness that what we think we know might well be incorrect.

- They do not allow the law to become their entire life; they get out of the courtroom, mingle with the public, and remain knowledgeable of current events.[22]

Student on the Street Video: Courtroom civility

Other writers believe that judges should remember that the robe does not confer omniscience or omnipotence; as one trial attorney put it, "Your name is now 'Your Honor,' but you are still the same person you used to be, warts and all."[23]

Courtroom Civility

As if it weren't difficult enough to strive for and maintain humility, civility, and balance in their personal lives, judges must also enforce courtroom civility. Many persons have observed that we are becoming an increasingly uncivil society; the courts are certainly not immune to acts involving misconduct.

Author Video: Bias

Personal character attacks by lawyers, directed at judges, attorneys, interested parties, clerks, jurors, and witnesses, both inside and outside the courtroom, in criminal and civil actions have increased at an alarming rate in the past 15 years.[24] For example, an attorney stated that opposing and other attorneys were "a bunch of starving slobs," "incompetents," and "stooges."[25] Such behavior clearly does not enhance the dignity or appearance of justice and propriety that is so important to the courts' public image and function. The **Model Code of Judicial Conduct** addresses these kinds of behaviors; Canon 3B(4) requires judges to be "patient, dignified, and courteous to litigants, jurors, witnesses, lawyers, and others with whom the judge deals in an official capacity," and requires judges to demand "similar conduct of lawyers, and of staff, court officials, and others subject to the judge's direction and control."[26]

Model Code of Judicial Conduct: adopted by the House of Delegates of the American Bar Association in 1990, it provides a set of ethical principles and guidelines for judges.

At a minimum, judges need to attempt to prevent such behavior and discipline offenders when it occurs. Among the means that judges have at their disposal to control errant counsel are attorney disqualifications, new trials, and reporting of attorneys to disciplinary boards.[27]

Judicial Misconduct

Judicial misconduct: inappropriate behavior by a judge.

What types of **judicial misconduct** must the judiciary confront? Sometimes medications may affect a judge's cognitive process or emotional temperament, causing him or her to treat parties, witnesses, jurors, lawyers, and staff poorly. Some stay on the bench too long; such judges will ideally have colleagues who can approach them, suggest retirement, and explain why this would be to their benefit. And sometimes, according to one author, judicial arrogance (sometimes termed "black robe disease" or "robe-itis") is the primary problem. This is seen when judges "do not know when to close their mouths, do not treat people with dignity and compassion, do not arrive on time, or do not issue timely decisions."[28]

Some bar associations or judicial circuits perform an anonymous survey of a sample of local attorneys who have recently argued a case before a particular judge and then share the results with the judge. Sometimes these surveys are popularity contests, but a pattern of negative responses can have a sobering effect on the judge and encourage him or her to correct bad habits. Many judges will be reluctant to acknowledge they have such problems as those described here. In such cases, the chief judge may have to scold or correct a subordinate judge. Although difficult, it may be imperative to do so in

Prosecutors at trial must thoroughly question witnesses — not, the Supreme Court has said, to win a case, but to "see that justice shall be done."

trying to maintain good relations with bar associations, individual lawyers, and the public. A single judge's blunders and behaviors can affect the reputation of the entire judiciary as well as the workloads of the other judges in his or her judicial district. Chief judges must therefore step forward to address such problems formally or informally.[29]

THE ATTORNEYS

Next we look at the roles and strategies of attorneys who serve on both sides of the courtroom aisle—as prosecutors and defense attorneys.

"Gatekeeper" of the Justice System: Prosecutor

The prosecutor may be fairly said to be the single most powerful person in the American criminal justice system—and to have tremendous discretion in what he or she does. As described by the Southern Poverty Law Center, "Prosecutorial discretion is a necessary and important part of our system of justice—it allocates sparse prosecutorial resources, provides the basis for plea-bargaining and allows for leniency and mercy in a criminal justice system that is frequently harsh and impersonal. They literally have unchecked power to decide who will stand trial for crimes."[30] Indeed, prosecutors have the authority and power to make all of the following decisions, at their sole discretion, all of which affect criminal defendants and the criminal justice system in general:

Student on the Street Video: Most powerful person in the criminal justice system

- ✓ The decision to charge

- ✓ Type of charge(s)

- ✓ Whether to recommend granting or denying bail

- ✓ Plea agreements—whether to entertain such agreements and if so, the terms

- ✓ Sentencing recommendations

SAGE Journal Article: Negotiation tactics

Prosecutors represent the people, the victims in particular, and investigate crimes—often out in the field, having been called to the scene of a particularly heinous crime by the police. Still, remember that the primary role of the **prosecuting attorney**, as set forth by the U.S. Supreme Court (and as noted in Chapter 4), is "not that he shall win a case, but that justice shall be done."[31]

Once the police have completed a preliminary investigation, the prosecutor evaluates the arrest report and other documents to determine whether there is sufficient evidence to bring charges. Prosecutors also have the ability to scold officers who have not done their work properly—perhaps failing to have the requisite probable cause prior to making a search or an arrest—and can quash the arrest report. They have contact with the person suspected of the crime, the victim and witnesses, and the police. For them, the overarching question is, "Can I prove that a defendant committed a particular criminal act beyond a reasonable doubt?" If so, the prosecutor's office files charges and handles the case through pretrial negotiations (if any) and ultimately takes the case to trial. Other determining factors concerning how to handle a case are:

Prosecuting attorney: one who brings prosecutions, representing the people of the jurisdiction.

- The type of crime charged (personal or property crime)
- The prior criminal record of the person accused

INVESTIGATING FURTHER

VICTIM ADVOCATES

Michelle Cruz, the state of Connecticut's victim advocate, confers with Hakima Bey-Coon, an office attorney, during a hearing at New Britain Superior Court concerning grand jury testimony involving a missing person.

A relatively new member of the courtroom workgroup is the victim advocate. In our adversarial system of justice, the prosecutor represents the people of his or her state/county and seeks justice for them and the victim, but the prosecutor is not the victim's personal representative. Despite best efforts, victims can often feel lost in the dizzying process that is a criminal case. Victim advocates seek to remedy that problem,

providing victims with information about the criminal justice process, resources for recovery and counseling (especially for victims of violent crimes), legal rights, and a host of other services to help the victim navigate the uncertainties of post-victimization life.

The victim advocate role can be a paid or volunteer position and, in either instance, can be an opportunity for students with degrees in criminal justice, social work, or psychology, for example. Advocates get specialized training to work with victims, but these social science backgrounds are all excellent starting points to work with this unique population.

Not surprisingly, these advocates work in a variety of places along the criminal justice spectrum, often being called to crime scenes to comfort victims immediately after a crime. They also work at police stations and hospitals and are often in or around the court, to accompany victims who have been asked to testify, to work with prosecutors and defense attorneys as they negotiate plea deals or case outcomes, and to monitor the court process so that they can better inform the victim about what to expect. They also accompany victims' families to the morgue to claim personal effects.

Source: National Center for Victims of Crime, "What Is a Victim Advocate?" https://www.victimsofcrime.org/help-for-crime-victims/get-help-bulletins-for-crime-victims/what-is-a-victim-advocate-

- The number of counts in the complaint (the more counts there are, the stiffer the sentence sought)

- Whether there are aggravating or mitigating circumstances in the case

- The victim's attitude—what he or she wants done with the case (this is particularly important in crimes of violence)

Good prosecutors will also try to establish a good rapport with the victim prior to trial, to personalize the justice system. If possible, the prosecutor might take the victim to the court and show him or her the courtroom and witness stand and where the offender will be seated, explaining the process along the way.

Prosecutorial Immunity and Misconduct

Not only do prosecutors have nearly unfettered discretion and power, but also they are immune from prosecution for actions taken in their official capacity. In other words, defendants cannot sue prosecutors for civil damages for how they handled a case.[32] This "civil immunity" is unique in our system of justice. In fact, it's unique in the professional realm in general. Doctors, other lawyers, and most professionals (except judges) are subject to civil prosecution if they fail to maintain standards of conduct and performance that apply to their field. Probably the most dramatic contrasting example is that of police officers, who are not granted such immunity and yet are tasked with making a multitude of professional decisions in the field, many of them in split-seconds and in dynamic and dangerous situations.

Some scholars and observers believe prosecutorial immunity goes too far and unfairly insulates the most powerful player in the criminal justice system.[33] Proponents of this long-standing immunity counter that prosecutors, in serving the people and in seeking to do justice on behalf of communities, cannot be looking over their shoulders or second-guessing their decisions because they fear civil suits. As the U.S. Supreme Court has put it, prosecutorial immunity represents a "balance of evils," and that it is better "to leave unredressed the wrongs done by dishonest officers than to subject those who try to do their duty to the constant dread of retaliation."[34] The debate is ongoing, and cases like Michael Morton's in Texas, outlined at the beginning of this chapter, highlight the perils of entrusting such extensive power to one criminal justice player.

Texas district attorney Ken Anderson (left)—who convicted Michael Morton (right) for the 1986 killing of Morton's wife—was the first district attorney in the U.S. to be convicted on criminal charges (and disbarred) for withholding evidence in a criminal trial. Despite Anderson's criminal conviction, prosecutorial immunity shielded him from a civil suit, triggering more debate about whether prosecutorial immunity serves the quest for truth and justice.

The Michael Morton Case: Morton's case was a brutal example of prosecutorial misconduct, and the Texas Supreme Court ordered a review of Williamson County District Attorney Ken Anderson's conduct during the trial. In March 2013, the man whose DNA was found on the bloody bandana was convicted of Christine Morton's murder. In November 2013, facing possibly 10 years in prison for a charge of tampering with evidence, Anderson pleaded guilty to contempt (for withholding evidence) and was sentenced to 10 days in jail, assessed a $500 fine, and ordered to perform 500 hours of community service. He was also disbarred, so that he can never practice law again. He was the first district attorney in the United States to be found in criminal contempt for withholding evidence.[35]

"Guiding Hand of Counsel": Defense Attorney

In many countries, a person mired in some stage of a legal proceeding might also find himself or herself standing alone in the courtroom, overwhelmed by fear and befuddled by the activities swirling around him or her. Not so in the United States, where the fundamental principles of liberty and justice require that all Americans, even the poorest among us, will be given the "guiding hand of counsel" at all critical stages of a criminal proceeding.

Duties and Strategies

As noted in Chapter 8, many people believe that the Sixth Amendment's provision for effective counsel is the most important right we enjoy in a democracy. The law is complicated, and by requiring the state to prove its case and helping defendants understand their options in the criminal justice system, **defense attorneys** can help ensure that the state does not commit innocent people to jail or prison. Furthermore, defendants have the right to counsel during all "critical stages" of the proceedings—those in which rights could be lost—which include interrogation, jury selection, arraignment, trial, sentencing, and first appeal of conviction (but not the initial appearance, where the judge simply informs the defendant of his or her charges and rights), as well as pretrial testing of fingerprints, blood samples, clothing, hair, and so on.[36]

What does "ineffective" counsel mean in practice? Basically it means the attorney was deficient in his or her performance, and in being so, the resulting prejudice to the defendant was so serious as to bring the outcome of the proceeding into question.[37] Examples would include one's failures to investigate an alibi defense, investigate prosecution witnesses, obtain experts to challenge the prosecution's physical evidence, or even attend or stay awake for hearings.[38] The burden of proving ineffective counsel is high, and is on the defendant to show that "a reasonable probability" exists that, but for counsel's unprofessional errors, the result of the proceeding would have been different.[39] But it is possible to do so: In one Texas case, a defense attorney claimed he did not believe he needed to go into "sleazy bars to look for witnesses"; the appeals court essentially informed him that that's precisely what he would do, if doing so was required to locate witnesses for the defendant, persons to confirm the defendant's alibi, and so on.[40]

When one is charged with a crime, a defense lawyer, either hired or court-appointed, should:

- Explain the offense the accused is charged with, including the possible punishments and probation options

- Advise the accused of his or her rights, ensure those rights are upheld, and inform the accused of what to expect during the different stages of the criminal process

Defense attorney: one whose responsibility is to see that the rights of the accused are upheld prior to, during, and after trial; the Sixth Amendment provides for "effective" counsel, among other constitutionally enumerated rights that defense attorneys must see are upheld.

- Investigate the facts of the case

- Explain what is likely to happen if the case goes to trial

- If beneficial for the accused, attempt to negotiate a plea bargain with the prosecutor (bear in mind that more than 90 percent of criminal convictions come from negotiated pleas of guilty, which must be approved by the judge; therefore, less than 10 percent of criminal cases go to trial)[41]—this can involve arranging for reduced charges, a shorter sentence, sentences for different crimes to be served consecutively instead of concurrently, probation or a disposition that avoids certain imprisonment, and/or other consideration, in exchange for entering a plea of guilty

- If the case goes to trial, cross-examine government witnesses, object to improper questions and evidence, and present applicable legal defenses[42]

A defense lawyer with Brooklyn's Legal Aid reviews his client's arrest record at their first meeting in a jail cell behind the courtroom. The Sixth Amendment guarantees the assistance of counsel to all indigent criminal defendants at key stages throughout the criminal justice process.

Other defense strategies might include:

- Trying to make the victim appear to be the aggressor, or someone who "deserved" what happened to him or her (the general rule is that the defense attorney wants to try to overlook the victim's story, while the victim wishes to punish the defendant, and will also try to engender sympathy; particularly if the victim appears to have precipitated or participated in the crime, the defense will attack his or her faults at trial (within legal bounds)

- Coming up with ways to compensate the victim (for example, determining whether he or she will accept restitution or be satisfied if the defendant attends counseling)

- Getting continuances (which might mean that key witnesses move away, emotions and local publicity surrounding the crime diminish, and so forth).

Indigent Services

In *Griffin v. Illinois* (1956), the U.S. Supreme Court observed that "there can be no equal justice where the kind of trial a man gets depends on the amount of money he has."[43] There are basically three systems for providing legal representation to indigent persons in criminal prosecutions: the public defender system, the assigned counsel system, and the contract system.[44]

Public defenders, like prosecutors, are paid government employees—most commonly found in larger jurisdictions—whose sole function is to represent indigent defendants. Public defenders perform many of the duties of prosecutors, described earlier in this chapter. They provide representation to people, who not only are indigent but also may be illiterate, uneducated, and uncooperative, while managing a large caseload. Public defenders might also represent juveniles charged with acts of delinquency (offenses that would be a felony if committed by an adult) as well as children in child abuse and neglect cases.

Public defender: an attorney whose full-time job is to represent indigent defendants.

PRACTITIONER'S PERSPECTIVE

CRIMINAL DEFENSE ATTORNEY

Name: Michelle E. Beck

Current Position: Criminal Defense Attorney

City, State: Houston, Texas

College Attended/Academic Major: Bachelor of arts in political science from Rice University; Juris Doctorate (J.D.) from Thurgood Marshall School of Law, Texas Southern University

How long have you been a practitioner in this criminal justice position? 8 years; prior to that, 10 years as an assistant district attorney in Harris County, Texas

My primary duties and responsibilities as a practitioner in this position: To represent clients charged with felony and misdemeanor criminal offenses; to appear in court to advocate on behalf of defendants in court with the judge, prosecutor, and jury; and to explain to my clients the procedures of the criminal justice system and their constitutional rights.

The qualities/characteristics that are most helpful in this career: A desire to advocate on behalf of another; written and verbal communication skills; a passion for justice; empathy for those being accused of very serious offenses—which could possibly lead to loss of freedom; patience; ability to think quickly; tenacity; and knowledge of criminal law and procedure.

In general, this is what a *typical day* looks like for a practitioner in this career: Making court appearances for several clients in felony and misdemeanor courts where I review the contents of the state's file to see what evidence the state has to attempt to prove my client's guilt; communicate plea bargain offers between client and the prosecutor; file necessary motions with the court; interview witnesses, along with the investigator, relevant to the offense; research case law and relevant topics pertinent to the alleged offense; examine physical evidence collected in the case; visit clients who are incarcerated in jail; and prepare for trial if that becomes necessary.

If in trial, duties include representing the client in court/jury trial, cross-examining the state's witnesses and questioning defense witnesses if necessary; ensuring that the state meets its burden of proving my client guilty beyond a reasonable doubt; and objecting to violations of the rules of evidence and procedure by the court and the prosecutors during such proceedings.

My advice to someone either wishing to study, or now studying, criminal justice and wanting to become a practitioner in this career: Have a complete knowledge of criminal law and the code of criminal procedure; attend law school and pass the state bar exam; observe other defense attorneys in court, especially during trials; develop a passion and empathy for the accused and their right to have a fair trial and effective legal representation, no matter how heinous the alleged offense; shore up on oratory, communication, and people skills; and expose yourself to other socioeconomic and cultural experiences and perspectives (so that you can relate to potential witnesses and experiences that you may otherwise not be familiar with).

The assigned counsel system uses private attorneys appointed on an as-needed basis by the court. A primary problem with assigned counsel is that the attorney may have little or no experience handling the criminal matter at hand; indeed, it may have been long ago that the assigned counsel studied subjects such as criminal law, criminal procedure, rules of evidence, and so on, and such attorneys may have limited knowledge about their state's criminal statutes.

The contract system is one whereby an attorney, a law firm, or a nonprofit organization contracts for a certain dollar amount—often after engaging in competitive bidding—with a unit of government to represent its indigent defendants. Advantages of this system can include reduced and predictable costs, streamlining of the counsel appointment process, and greater expertise of the attorneys. A major disadvantage is that obtaining legal counsel from the "lowest bidder" may result in inadequate or ineffective legal services—which may, of course, interfere with the defendant's Sixth Amendment right to effective counsel and be the basis for appealing a conviction.

As with many things in life, it is said that with regard to legal representation, "You get what you pay for." Obviously, people with financial means to do so will typically "go to the marketplace" and hire the best-trained legal counsel they can afford to represent them for their particular criminal matter. Conversely, at the opposite end of this continuum is the *pro se* defendant who chooses instead to represent himself or herself. In such cases, there is an old adage: "He who represents himself at trial has a fool for a client."

IN A NUTSHELL

- The debate over how we select our judges has escalated in the 21st century. Certainly adding fuel to the controversy over judicial selection is the amount of money now being spent by judges to fund their elections; across the nation, states use five basic methods of judicial selection. One of the more common methods is the merit plan (or "Missouri Plan").

- Judges enjoy several distinct benefits of office, including life terms for federal positions and a high degree of respect and prestige. But problems can await new judges as well: mastering the breadth of law they must know and apply; administering the court and the docket; supervising court staff; and coping with the psychological discomfort and loneliness that accompanies the new position.

- The prosecutor is probably the most powerful person in our criminal justice system, controlling the floodgates in determining whether or not to file charges (and these attorneys also have the ability to scold officers who fail to do their work properly). The prosecutor also interacts with the person suspected of the crime, the victim, and witnesses.

- Defense attorneys require the state to prove its case, help defendants understand their options in the criminal justice system, and attempt to ensure that the entire slate of rights owed to the defendant is upheld. As with prosecutors, defense attorneys have a number of strategies at their disposal.

$SAGE edge™   Review key terms with eFlashcards. ◄

KEY TERMS & CONCEPTS

Defense attorney, 256
Judicial misconduct, 252
Judicial selection
(methods of), 247

Merit selection, 248
Model Code of Judicial
Conduct, 252

Prosecuting
attorney, 254
Public defender, 257

$SAGE edge™   Test your understanding of chapter content. Take the practice quiz. ◄

REVIEW QUESTIONS

1. What are the five methods by which judges are selected?

2. Why is the partisan election method of selecting judges currently under severe criticism?

3. What are the key points of the merit selection plan for selecting judges?

4. What is meant by "good judging," and why is courtroom civility so important?

5. Why is the prosecutor believed to occupy the most powerful position in the criminal justice system?

6. What is prosecutorial immunity, and why is it both important and potentially dangerous in our adversarial system?

7. What is a defense attorney's primary responsibility under the Sixth Amendment?

1. Your local League of Women Voters is establishing a new study group to better understand merit selection, or the so-called Missouri Plan for selecting judges, so as to be better informed when the matter comes up for a referendum. You are asked to explain this system of selecting judges, including its pros and cons when compared with, say, judges running for election on a partisan ticket. Develop your presentation.

2. Some countries do not subscribe to the adversarial process as part of their court system, believing that it is too combative, slow, and cumbersome, and can lead to a "win at all cost" mentality among the lawyers. Rather, they use a nonadversarial or inquisitorial system, where the court or a part of the court is actively involved in determining the facts of the case (as opposed to the court's being primarily an impartial referee in the adversarial system). Your instructor asks you to participate in a pro-con group project concerning the adversarial process. Choose a side and make your defense.

3. You have been asked by your criminal justice department chairperson to participate in the annual "Career Day" program that the faculty conducts; the focus is on different careers in law enforcement, courts, and corrections. Because the faculty members know you recently completed an internship with your local prosecutor's office, they ask you to make a presentation on the functions and challenges that exist for a prosecutor. Develop and organize into a 20-minute speech what you will say in your comprehensive presentation.

⑤SAGE edge™

Review → Practice → Improve

Sharpen your skills with **SAGE edge** at **edge.sagepub.com/peak2e**

SAGE edge for students provides a personalized approach to help you accomplish your coursework goals in an easy-to-use learning environment. Access the videos, audio clips, quizzes, and SAGE journal articles that are noted in this chapter.

COURT METHODS AND CHALLENGES
Sentencing and Punishment

LEARNING OBJECTIVES

As a result of reading this chapter, you will be able to:

1 Delineate the four goals of punishment and explain the factors that influence the type of punishment that a convicted person will receive

2 Describe the historical development of, and different philosophies regarding, crime and punishment from the colonial era to today, and how different types of prisons were built accordingly

3 Describe the differences between, and purposes of, both determinate and indeterminate sentences

4 Review the federal sentencing guidelines

5 Explain the law and purposes surrounding the use of victim impact statements

6 Describe the fundamental arguments for and against capital punishment, including key Supreme Court decisions concerning its existence and application, methods of execution, and DNA exonerations from death sentences

7 Describe aggravating and mitigating circumstances as they apply to sentencing decisions

8 Explain the right to appeals by those who are convicted

ASSESS YOUR AWARENESS

Test your knowledge of criminal sentencing and punishment by responding to the following seven true-false items; check your answers after reading this chapter's materials.

1 Historically, people have been punished for one purpose only: retribution.

2 A small number of offenders commit a disproportionately large number of offenses.

3 Today, American society adheres to the "rehabilitation model," which states that criminals have been failed by society and emphasizes offender treatment.

4 Offenders' sentences can be served in determinate or indeterminate and concurrent or consecutive configurations.

5 Prosecutors and defense attorneys can influence judges' sentencing decisions.

6 Victims' families are not allowed to present impact statements in court at the time of sentencing.

7 Federal sentencing guidelines are to be merely advisory and not mandatory.

If you are going to punish a man retributively, you must injure him. If you are going to reform him, you must improve him. And men are not improved by injuries.

—George Bernard Shaw[1]

<< Answers can be found on page 424.

©Reuters/CORBIS

Serial killer Jeffrey Dahmer was found guilty of brutally murdering and dismembering 15 young men. The judge sentenced Dahmer to 15 consecutive life sentences, providing both a legal and symbolic punishment to bring Dahmer to justice, and to bring justice to his victims and their families. The sentencing phase of criminal trials is often the most important in terms of "justice being done."

Few cases in the crime annals trigger as much horror and disbelief as that of Jeffrey Dahmer, convicted in 1992 in Milwaukee for killing at least 15 young men, having sex with their corpses, dismembering their bodies, and, in some cases, eating their remains. The world could not stop watching when his story first broke as investigators removed from his apartment acid-filled barrels containing body parts and other evidence of his unspeakable crimes. The media coverage of his trial was intense, with each day revealing new details of his serial killing, his necrophilia, and his attorneys' desperate bid to prove him insane, arguing that his bizarre sexual urges were irresistible impulses he could not control. A jury took less than a day to convict Dahmer, returning guilty verdicts on all counts. But the drama of Dahmer's case did not stop there. The court then moved to the sentencing phase and the world again watched what has increasingly become a critically important part of our criminal justice process.[2]

As you read this chapter and learn about the history and theories of punishment and sentencing in the United States, think about the moment when a court hands down a sentence to a criminal offender. What are we trying to achieve through the process? How can we best offer redress to victims and communities, if at all, through punishment and sentencing? Should victims be allowed to testify, or is such testimony too inflammatory to juries? Similarly, should defendants be allowed to make statements about their crime and punishment? Finally, how can we possibly find an appropriate punishment for someone like Dahmer, or, perhaps more important (and certainly more commonly), for the thousands of repeat offenders moving through our criminal justice system every year?

INTRODUCTION

For what reasons and purposes are people punished? Do punishments always fit the crimes committed? Does capital punishment work? Certainly punishing those who violate the right to life, liberty, and property of their fellow human beings is one of the primary functions of the American criminal justice system. However, many questions concerning the "how" and "how much" need to be addressed. As the preceding quotation by George Bernard Shaw might indicate, an enigma for our time is what might best be done with people who must be punished for their transgressions. As will be seen in this chapter, sentencing and punishment are complicated issues, with both having financial and societal factors that must be included in these discussions.

Although violent crime rates have been declining in the new millennium, people are increasingly being victimized by intelligent white-collar criminals, identity thieves, and cybercriminals. How should our society deal with these new types of offenders? Into this complicated mix might also be added the adage that "it is better to let a hundred guilty people go free than to convict one innocent person." The federal and state sentencing guidelines discussed in this chapter indicate how much concern and effort have recently gone into sentencing and punishment. This chapter approaches sentencing and punishment from several perspectives, including their purposes, types, and methods, as well as the recent influence of DNA evidence. Also examined are capital punishment and criminal appeals.

PURPOSES OF PUNISHMENT

The need to punish some of our fellow citizens has existed since the beginning of time—at least since biblical times, and likely much earlier. It would seem there have always been attempts—by a variety of methods and for a variety of reasons—to convince people that they should change their behavior and either obey the customs and laws of their society or suffer the consequences. Very often those attempts at changing behaviors meant that—by one means or another, such as imprisonment, banishment, or death—offenders would be removed from society in such a way that they were no longer in a position to do further harm to their fellow citizens. Here, we discuss the four goals of punishment—some or all of which are hoped to be achieved by all societies, even the most primitive. Furthermore, we will see that throughout history, crimes and criminals have been viewed and punished differently, depending on several factors. Some of those factors that determine punishment today were described in Chapter 1, in the discussions of the wedding cake and crime control/due process models of crime.

Placing people in stocks was used internationally and during medieval, Renaissance, and colonial American times as a form of physical punishment as well as for public humiliation.

Four Goals

Following are the historical reasons and goals for **punishment** of our fellow citizens—what is hoped will be achieved (note that all of these goals and justifications may also be achieved by methods employed in community-based corrections, discussed in Chapter 14):

SAGE Journal Article: American punishment

- *Retribution:* **Retribution** has its roots in Old Testament law where, in Exodus 21:24, the phrase "eye for eye, tooth for tooth, hand for hand, foot for foot" appears for the first time—labeled *lex talionis*, the law of equitable retribution. Death penalty supporters also quote this phrase often as justification for their position. However, neither the phrase "eye for eye" nor the verse itself is a complete sentence, and the death penalty is not mentioned. For many people, "eye for eye" dictates that offenders should be punished in a manner that reflects their crime: It is instinctive for people to want to get even when wronged by another, and it is deeply engrained within ourselves and our society that punishment should be meted out when someone breaks the law.

- *Deterrence:* **Deterrence** probably makes more sense than retribution in terms of betterment of society because it is not grounded on our primal human emotions and instincts. In essence, because people will typically avoid unpleasant things, they are much less likely to commit a crime if they know that punishment will occur if they get caught. Deterrence therefore has two components: general and specific. By seeing others being punished for their crimes, the public experiences a *general* deterrent effect because they can see what will befall them should they engage in similar behavior. *Specific* deterrence involves using punishment against specific offenders for their criminal acts in order to discourage them from committing such acts again in the future.

Punishment (and its purposes): penalties imposed for committing criminal acts, to accomplish deterrence, retribution, incapacitation, and/or rehabilitation.

Retribution: punishment that fits the crime, that is "equitable" for the offense

Deterrence: the effect of punishments and other actions to deter people from committing crimes.

Judges consider a variety of factors in deciding how to sentence criminal offenders. Despite competing arguments from defense attorneys and prosecutors, fundamental factors like a prior criminal record and the seriousness of the offense tyipcally guide judges' discretion in handing down punishments.

Student on the Street Video: Parole versus probation

Incapacitation: rendering someone as unable to act or move about, either through incarceration or by court order.

Rehabilitation: attempts to reform an offender through vocational and educational programming, counseling, and so forth, so that he or she is not a recidivist and does not return to crime/prison.

- *Incapacitation:* **Incapacitation**, by its very meaning, is beneficial in that it prevents criminals from victimizing others by placing them in a situation where they are physically unable to commit crimes. The best examples, of course, are incarceration in jails and prisons as well as execution. Bear in mind, however, that one can still commit crimes while in a state of incarceration. The methods of community corrections—probation and parole and other alternatives to incarceration—are forms of incapacitation, which also aims to prevent offenders from committing new crimes.

- *Rehabilitation:* Almost since its beginning, the modern criminal justice system has had as a primary goal—indeed a responsibility—to change criminals so that they become law-abiding citizens, in other words, to rehabilitate them. In fact, for most of the 20th century, **rehabilitation** was the system's primary goal in terms of how it was to function and be organized. During the past half-century, however, that ideology has been modified to the point that it is hardly recognizable.[3] The reasons for this ideological change are several, and include changing governmental priorities, other concerns of the public (as revealed in national polls), and institutional and political resistance to change.[4] Furthermore, politicians can point to the "nothing works" idea put forth by Robert Martinson, who studied prison programs (discussed in Chapter 12). Still, a wide array of correctional programs (i.e., vocational, educational, counseling) continues to be offered in prisons and jails, and with marked success. One cost-benefit analysis of 14 correctional treatment programs found that, in all but one of the programs, program benefits outweighed program costs. Such programs can be crucial for assisting offenders to reenter society and not recidivate (commit more crimes).[5]

Sentencing and punishment must accomplish one or more of these goals if the public is to be supportive of them. If increases in prison and jail sentences do not provide effective means of preventing crime, then a more cost-effective strategy must be found that will target the offenders most likely to commit serious crimes at high rates. As a federal report noted:

> It is frequently observed that a small number of offenders commit a disproportionately large number of offenses. If prison resources can be effectively targeted to high-rated offenders, it should be possible to achieve . . . levels of crime control. The key to such a policy rests on an ability to identify high-rate offenders . . . and at relatively early stages in their careers.[6]

Factors Influencing Punishment

As noted earlier, sentencing and punishment involve issues concerning their financial and societal benefit. For example, on average it costs about $31,000 per year to house an inmate in prison.[7] For that amount of money, society expects to be able to accomplish one or more of the four goals described earlier. Regarding the cost-benefit effect of prisons, some researchers argue that prisons should be used to greater advantage, believing it is at least twice as costly to let a prisoner be loose in society than it is to lock him or her up. For example, comparing the cost of incarceration with the human and financial toll of crime, prison expert John DiIulio Jr. believes that prisons are a "real bargain."[8]

In addition to victims making their wishes known early on to the prosecution concerning punishment, as well as victim impact statements and aggravating or mitigating circumstances involved in a crime (discussed later in this chapter), there are other factors that influence sentencing and punishment. First, the U.S. Constitution speaks briefly but forcefully regarding the use of punishment. The Eighth Amendment provides that incarceration will not involve "cruel and unusual punishment," and that fines will not be excessive. Furthermore, the Thirteenth Amendment states that U.S. citizens have a right against involuntary servitude.

Video: Cruel and unusual punishment

Prosecutors can influence the sentencing decision by agreeing to engage in plea negotiation in terms of the number of charges filed or the maximum penalty the judge may impose, or by explaining to the sentencing judge that the offender was particularly cruel in his or her crime or, alternatively, was very cooperative with the police and/or remorseful for the crime; in many states, prosecutors can also make a specific sentencing recommendation to the court that has been agreed upon with the defense.

Defense attorneys probably have less influence over sentencing decisions than prosecutors. Nonetheless, they can seek to obtain the lightest sentence possible, including probation or other alternatives to sentencing, as well as emphasize prior to sentencing such things as the defendant's minor involvement in the crime, the victim's participation, and so on.

Certainly the seriousness of the offense is the most important factor in determining the sentencing one receives for his or her offense. For instance, a violent crime against a person warrants a harsher penalty than an offense against one's property, and the judge, jury, prosecutor, and defense attorney must take into account the victim's suffering when carrying out their roles in arriving at a proper punishment.

Where sentencing is concerned, next in importance is the defendant's prior criminal record. The existence of a lengthy criminal record—particularly a record of violence, or even habitual crimes against property, such as home invasion—can weigh heavily in

You Be the... JUDGE

A habitual offender is essentially one who has been convicted of a crime several times (either a misdemeanor or a felony, and typically at least twice). Habitual offender laws usually impose additional punishments on such offenders. Such laws can even address traffic violations. For example, a first-time driving under the influence (DUI) offense is usually a misdemeanor that results in a fine and jail time of less than one year. However, upon being arrested for a second or third DUI, the offender may be charged with a felony (depending on state law). Being classified as a habitual offender can thus result in higher criminal fines, longer jail or prison sentences, and loss of various rights and privileges (e.g., the right to own a firearm or to possess a driver's license).

An example is a Florida law stating that

if you receive three (3) or more convictions of serious offenses on separate occasions you

will be deemed a habitual offender. Examples of serious traffic offense include voluntary manslaughter while driving, involuntary manslaughter while driving, [and] felony while driving. Other serious traffic offenses include not stopping at an accident with a personal injury or death, or driving with a suspended or revoked license. Three convictions of these offenses and you will be considered a habitual traffic offender.

1. Do you agree with the spirit and intent of such laws?

2. Are such laws too harsh or too lenient?

Source: See LegalMatch, "What Is a Habitual Offender," http://www.legalmatch.com/law-library/article/what-is-a-habitual-offender.html; see also Florida Drivers Association, "How to Get a Hardship License for Habitual Offenders," http://www.123driving.com/habitual-offender.shtml.

terms of sentencing and punishment. Many states have habitual offender laws (see the "You Be the Judge" box), which are related to and often viewed the same as three-strikes laws (discussed in Chapter 1). These laws vary widely from state to state but typically apply only to felonies and require third-time felons to serve a mandatory 25 years to life. Furthermore, many police departments have repeat offender units dedicated solely to surveilling known offenders.

Punishment Models, Methods, and Reforms

Philosophies of crime and punishment have changed significantly since the late 1700s, when American society was relatively sparsely populated and predominantly rural. However, with the Industrial Revolution came a new concept of criminal punishment embracing various correctional methods, including the following:[9]

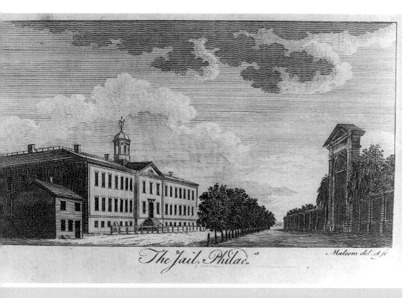

What is often termed the "first American penitentiary," if not the first in the world, was established in Philadelphia, in 1790: the Walnut Street Jail.

Built in 1829, Eastern State Penitentiary, a huge fortress near Philadelphia, emphasized complete solitary confinement.

Mike Graham

• *The colonial model (1600s–1790s):* During the colonial period most Americans lived under laws that were transferred from England. Puritans rigorously punished violations of religious laws, and banishment from the community, fines, death, and other punishments were the norm. Use of the death penalty was common.

• *The penitentiary model (1790s–1860s):* With the Industrial Revolution—and increasing populations—came a new concept of criminal punishment. Criminal offenders were to be isolated from the bad influences of society and from one another so that, while engaged in productive labor, they might reflect on their past misdeeds, and be "penitent" or remorseful for their crimes. As a result, what has been termed "the first American penitentiary, if not the first one in the world," was established in Philadelphia, in 1790, in the Walnut Street Jail. This penitentiary introduced the institutional pattern of outside cells with a central corridor and the use of solitary confinement as the central method of reforming inmates to "the good life." Inmates were also segregated according to "age, sex, and the type of the offenses charged against them."[10] Auburn Prison, built in New York in 1821, reflected this shift, emphasizing individual cell-block architecture to create an environment to rehabilitate and reform, separate criminals from all contact with corruption, and teach them moral habits, by means of severe discipline. Inmates worked as contract convict labor 10 hours per day, 6 days per week. The Auburn model influenced the emergence of reform schools and workhouses in the 1820s. Then, Eastern State Penitentiary, a huge fortress with thick walls near Philadelphia, was built in 1829, emphasizing complete solitary confinement rather than Auburn's contract labor. New inmates wore hoods when marched to their cells so that they would not see other prisoners. Regimentation included use of the lockstep (marching everywhere in single file), shuffling with the head turned right, practices that continued into the 1930s. No visitors, mail, or newspapers were allowed. The design of this prison became the most influential in U.S. history.

- *The reformatory model (1870s–1890s):* By the middle of the 1800s, reformers became disillusioned with the results of the penitentiary movement, and soon a new generation of reform came to the fore, motivated by humanitarian concerns. This new approach to penology emphasized inmate change and indeterminate sentences. Fixed sentences, lockstep, silence, and isolation were seen as destructive to inmate initiative. This wave of prison reform began with the founding of today's American Correctional Association in 1879 and the building of Elmira Reformatory in 1876. At Elmira, Zebulon Brockway began classification and segregation of prisoners, as well as providing vocational training, and rewards for good behavior—including early release for good behavior and parole. Brockway's "New Penology" included the creation of specialized institutions to care for the young, females, and the mentally impaired. The juvenile court system, created in Chicago in 1899, gave wide discretionary powers to judges, and Indiana's Female Prison and Reformatory Institution for Girls and Women was opened in Indianapolis in 1873. Inmates began producing license plates, constructing public highways, and working at prison farms and factories that produced food and items for internal consumption. In 1927, the first federal prison for women opened in Alderson, West Virginia; the minimum-security campus-like prison used residential cottages for inmates. Elsewhere, the camps that housed inmates working on roads became models for minimum-security prisons that emerged in the 1930s. Then, with Congress recognizing the need to build federal penitentiaries, the Three Prisons Act of 1891 authorized the first federal penitentiaries. The old army prison at Fort Leavenworth, Kansas, became the first U.S. penitentiary in 1895; the second opened in 1902 at Atlanta, Georgia; and the third was located at the old territorial prison on McNeil Island in Puget Sound, Washington.

Student on the
Street Video: Punish
or rehabilitate?

- *The progressive model (1890s–1930s):* The first two decades of the 20th century saw the Progressives coming from upper-socioeconomic-status backgrounds, being benevolent and philanthropic, and wanting to understand and cure crime—first by improving social conditions that appeared to breed crime, and second by treating criminals so that they would lead crime-free lives. Treatment would be focused on the individual and his or her specific problem. Probation was launched as an alternative to incarceration, allowing offenders to be treated in the community under supervision, and indeterminate sentences came into being.

- *The medical model (1930s–1960s):* This model generally included the idea that criminals are mentally ill, and the emphasis of corrections shifted to treatment. Criminals were seen as persons whose social, psychological, or biological deficiencies had caused them to engage in illegal activity and who should be treated. Rehabilitation took on national legitimacy and became the primary purpose of incarceration. The Federal Bureau of Prisons (discussed in Chapter 12) was established in 1930 to oversee the 11 federal prisons then in existence. In 1933, Alcatraz was acquired from the U.S. Army for a federal prison. The gangster era was in full swing, and national Prohibition wrought violent crime waves. Alcatraz was the ideal solution—serving the dual purpose of holding public enemies and being a visible icon to warn this new brand of criminal. Under Warden James A. Johnston, Alcatraz's rules of conduct were

AP Photo

In 1941 James V. Bennett, director of the Federal Bureau of Prisons, oversaw construction of the Federal Correctional Institution at Seagoville, Texas, a prison without walls.

among the most rigid in the correctional system, and harsh punishments were delivered to inmates who defied prison regulations. Then, more in keeping with the medical model was the appointment in 1937 of James V. Bennett as director of the Federal Bureau of Prisons. In 1941, he built the Federal Correctional Institution at Seagoville, Texas, a prison without walls. Similar prisons became widespread in the 1960s. Different treatment programs were offered to prisoners, and the Federal Prison Industries program began in 1934, allowing inmates to be furloughed out of prison for work and other purposes.

• *The community model (1960s–1970s):* Following the inmate riot and hostage taking at New York state's Attica Correctional Facility in 1971, prisons were seen as artificial institutions that interfered with the offender's ability to develop a crime-free lifestyle. Community reintegration was the dominant idea until the 1970s, when it gave way to a new punitive stance in criminal justice.

Video: Attica Correctional Facility

• *The crime control model (1970s–2000s):* The pendulum swung again, with the public during the late 20th century—and still today—being concerned about rapidly rising crime rates and studies of inmate treatment programs challenging their success and worth. Critics attacked the indeterminate sentence and parole, calling for longer sentences for career criminals and violent offenders. Legislators, judges, and officials responded with determinate sentencing laws, "three-strikes laws," mandatory sentencing laws (e.g., doubling one's sentence for a crime committed with a weapons), and so forth. (Regarding the accompanying changes in prisons, in 1961 Texas prison system director George Beto, in opposition to the medical model, began emphasizing strict discipline; in 1972, David Ruiz sued the Texas prison system, claiming that the system constituted "cruel and unusual punishment" prohibited by the Eighth Amendment to the U.S. Constitution; his class action suit was settled in 1980, the longest-running prisoners' lawsuit in U.S. history.)

FIGURE 11.1   A Timeline of Correctional Models

1600s–1790s	The Colonial Model
1790s–1860s	The Penitentiary Model
1870s–1890s	The Reformatory Model
1890s–1930s	The Progressive Model
1930s–1960s	The Medical Model
1960s–1970s	The Community Model
1970s–2000s	The Crime Control Model

PRACTITIONER'S PERSPECTIVE

JUDGE

Name: Diana L. Sullivan

Current Position: Justice of the Peace, Las Vegas Justice Court

City, State: Las Vegas, Nevada

College Attended/Academic Major: Bachelor of arts in criminal justice from University of Nevada, Reno; Juris Doctorate (J.D.) degree from University of San Diego School of Law

How long have you been a practitioner in this career? Four years

The primary duties and responsibilities of a limited-jurisdiction court judge: For misdemeanor cases, making the ultimate determination of guilt or innocence. For an offender who is found guilty of a misdemeanor, the magistrate also determines the punishment within the range allowed by law. Justice Court justices also oversee preliminary proceedings in felony cases.

In most sentences, I include jail time that is suspended while the offender satisfies his or her other sentencing requirements. Once the offender satisfies other sentencing requirements and stays out of trouble, the suspended jail sentence is vacated and the case is closed. If, on the other hand, the offender fails to successfully complete the other sentencing requirements or fails to stay out of trouble, the offender's suspended jail sentence is imposed. In felony cases, a retributive-based sentence by a district court or jury is often appropriate and warranted. My philosophy in sentencing misdemeanor offenders, however, is not one of retribution but one aimed at deterrence and rehabilitation. I am mindful of the harsh reality that even a short jail sentence of 30 days can drastically affect an offender's life circumstances, such as employment, residence, or visitation rights with children. Hence, based on the offender's charge, criminal history, family dynamics, employment status, and remorse (if any), my goal is to sentence the offender to just enough punishment to hopefully prevent future criminal activity. My sentences often include requirements alternative to—and hopefully in lieu of—any jail time, such as monetary fines, community service, counseling programs, and informal probation orders.

Our pretrial detention decisions are some of our most important roles in the entire criminal process. Decisions on an accused's custody status or bail setting while he or she awaits trial on serious charges are difficult because the magistrate must consider and weigh various factors in determining whether to release an accused person pending trial. Factors to be considered in making pretrial custody determinations include the accused's length of residence in the community; his or her employment status and criminal history; the serious nature of the charged offense; the likelihood of conviction and range of punishment if convicted; the likelihood of reoffending while awaiting trial; and the risk that the accused will fail to appear for future court appearances. These decisions must be made promptly after arrest and with very limited and sometimes unsupported information, always keeping in mind the constitutional presumption of innocence. Even though these initial custody decisions are made quickly, an accused's custody status can be revisited at any stage of the criminal case.

The qualities/characteristics that are most helpful in this career: The study and practice of criminal justice, which is, simply put, fascinating. Each and every day something occurs that makes today different from yesterday. In general, a typical day for a judge in a limited-jurisdiction court would include handling my caseload, which at any given time surpasses 8,000 nontraffic criminal cases. Thus, it is typical for me to have anywhere from 50 to 80 cases on my court docket each morning. I handle the majority of these tasks quickly and summarily, such as initial arraignments and postsentencing compliance hearings. Other types of daily hearings, such as misdemeanor trials and felony preliminary evidentiary hearings, can take several hours. When not handling my court docket, other daily tasks include reviewing probable cause reports for recent and future arrests, and researching and ruling on motions filed by parties. I also handle administrative duties, such as overseeing certain personnel and serving on committees for the improvement of local court rules and procedural processes. Lastly, as a public official I volunteer my time to the community, focusing on our local youth. I mentor at-risk high school students, participate in career fairs, and judge high school mock trial competitions.

My advice to someone either wishing to study, or now studying, criminal justice and wanting to become a practitioner in this career: Have at least a minimal understanding of psychology, sociology, cultural differences, and generational indigence. Anyone who wants to litigate either criminal or civil cases should also acquire training in public speaking, debate, and eventually trial advocacy.

Making Punishment Fit the Crime

Video: Global punishment

We might consider punishment from this perspective: A recent report by Amnesty International discusses capital punishment around the world, including beheadings in Saudi Arabia; hangings in Japan, Iraq, Singapore, and Sudan; firing squads in Afghanistan, Belarus, and Vietnam; stonings in Iran; and "the only country in the Americas that regularly executes: the United States." Amnesty reports that in the 58 countries retaining the death penalty around the world, at least 18,750 people are now under sentence of death, and at least 680 people were executed worldwide in 2011, excluding China (which does not release its figures).[11] The death penalty is administered to about 55 people each year in the United States (and that number has been declining since 2000).[12]

The concept of "justice" and acts deserving of punishment vary across nations. Consider that in many other countries people are executed for their political thoughts, apostasy (improper religious beliefs), and "highway robbery"—or people are flogged 80 times for possessing alcohol, or, as in Singapore, flogged with a rattan cane for vandalism.[13] Although the crime rates in these venues are likely to be relatively low, the question to be asked is this: Given a choice, would you opt to *live* in any of those places?

As you will learn in Chapter 12, for many offenders in the United States, being sentenced to prison is a "step up," partly because there they receive "three hots and a cot" without having to support a family, and they might even be surrounded by their family members, "homies," and gang-banger friends. If that sad commentary on American life is true, then one is left to wonder how our society can allow that to happen—or, perhaps, why we devote the time, effort, and money—$53.5 billion annually for state corrections expenditures prisons alone[14]—to basically "warehouse" 1.3 million people.[15]

Some observers might say we should abandon the warehousing approach and make every effort to try to identify those individuals for whom the prison experience can be beneficial. Then, while those individuals are a "captive audience" in prison, we should make all manner of rehabilitative educational and vocational programming available to them. But others might argue that those inmates for whom prison is a "step up" should be put to work at hard labor, to make prison life less attractive and thus discourage them from repeat offending. But which way should the pendulum swing?

The next "You Be the Judge" box poses some thought-provoking questions regarding punishment options. As you read them, consider the four goals of punishment discussed earlier, as well as your own philosophy concerning punishment.

TYPES OF SENTENCES TO BE SERVED

SAGE Journal Article: Determinate and indeterminate sentencing

How offenders serve their sentences—in a determinate or indeterminate, as well as a concurrent or consecutive, fashion—is a crucial distinction, particularly in terms of how long an offender must remain in prison and where parole is concerned. Next we distinguish between these types.

Determinate and Indeterminate Sentences

Determinate sentencing: a scheme whereby a specific, fixed-period sentence is ordered by a court.

Determinate sentencing is either legislatively determined or judicially determined. In states using a determinate sentencing structure, convicted offenders are sentenced for a fixed term, such as 10 years. There is no opportunity for a paroling authority to make adjustments in time served when making release decisions. Offenders are released at the expiration of their term, minus any good-time credits. Under a legislatively determined structure, the legislature fixes by law the penalty for specific offenses or offense categories. In a judicially determined system, the judge has broad discretion to choose a sanction, but once imposed, it is not subject to change.

You Be the... JUDGE

Given that many people have philosophical and practical disagreements with the four stated goals of punishment, consider the following questions and determine where you stand on these issues:

1. Do you support corporal punishment—the deliberate infliction of pain against someone through spanking? Would you alter your opinion if you knew that corporal punishment is legal in schools in 22 states? Does the end justify the means?

2. Would your opinion be changed if you were told that the U.S. Supreme Court refused to hear a case arguing that beating students is constitutionally impermissible? Does it change your thinking to know that the student in the case was an 18-year-old adult?

3. Does punishment generally fail to stop, or even increase, the problem behavior?

4. Does punishment typically arouse strong emotional responses, including anxiety, apprehension, and guilt?

5. Does punishment teach people to have and use internal controls at all times, or only when other people are present?

6. Does the infliction of pain arouse aggression toward the source of the pain?

7. Can punishment be effective when it is used sporadically, or must it be practiced regularly?

8. Can punishment ever become abuse?

Source: Adapted from "The School Law Blog," *Education Week,* http://blogs.edweek.org/edweek/school_law/2008/06/the_supreme_court_and_corporal.html.

Conversely, in an indeterminate sentencing format, the convicted individual will be sentenced for a set range of time, such as 5–10 years, so that his or her conduct inside the prison system, amenability to rehabilitative efforts (e.g., educational and vocational programs, counseling), apparent remorsefulness, and so forth can be taken into account in deciding a release date. The legislature sets a broad range of time, expressed as minimum and maximum sentences, for a particular offense or category of offenses, and the responsibility for determining the actual term of incarceration is divided between the judge and the parole board. The judge's sentence is also made in terms of a minimum and a maximum term.

The authority of a parole board to grant discretionary release to a prisoner before the expiration date of the maximum term varies from state to state. The parole board determines the actual release date, typically using a formula for determining earliest parole eligibility, which may occur after a percentage of the minimum, after a percentage of the maximum, or after the entire minimum has been served, depending on the state.[16]

Those persons supporting the rehabilitative ideal for offenders will obviously be more in favor of indeterminate sentencing, which allows for the length of sentence to be adjusted in response to the offender's positive responses to treatment and programs.[17]

Inmates often appear before their parole board to express remorse for their crimes, to explain how they have progressed while in prison, and to offer reasons why they should be released and placed on parole.

Consecutive and Concurrent Sentences

Assume that a man is convicted for committing three separate offenses as part of a night's crime spree: He unlawfully entered a couple's home (burglary), stole several valuable items (a felony theft), and violently assaulted the husband in making his escape. He is sentenced to 15 years, 3 years, and 20 years for each of these crimes. Depending on the sentencing court's decision, the offender will serve his three sentences for those crimes either concurrently or consecutively.

A *concurrent* sentence means he will serve all three sentences *at the same time*, with each sentence running along the same timeline, along parallel tracks as follows:

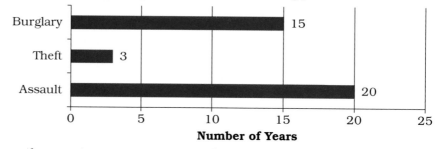

Because these sentences are running at the same time, the maximum amount of time the man will do is 20 years—his sentences of 3 and 15 years will have already run during the 20-year sentence.

If, instead, the offender is to serve the three sentences *consecutively*, each sentence will be served separately—in other words, when he finishes serving the sentence for the first crime, he immediately begins serving the sentence for the second crime, and so on. This approach is often referred to as "stacking" the sentences—one after the other—to maximize the sentence length, as follows:

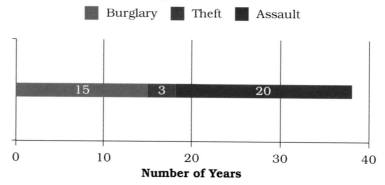

In this sentencing approach, the offender would serve a total (subject to reductions for good behavior and parole eligibility) of approximately 38 years (15 + 3 + 20).

The Jeffrey Dahmer Case: The judge sentenced Jeffrey Dahmer to 15 life terms without the possibility of parole, and ordered Dahmer to serve those terms consecutively— meaning the 15 sentences would be served one at a time, one after the other, making the sentence at least 936 years.[18]

Many people often wonder why courts hand down sentences that, in reality, no offender can ever serve. For example, in 2013 a federal judge sentenced organized crime boss Whitey Bulger to two consecutive life terms, plus five years,[19] and in 2014, an Ohio judge sentenced convicted kidnapper and rapist Ariel Castro to life plus 1,000 years.[20] But sentences like these and Dahmer's are partly symbolic, a way of expressing society's abhorrence of such criminal activity and the notion that we must truly "lock up and throw away the key" for these offenders. In some cases, with indeterminate sentences and parole possibilities, such sentences are handed down to ensure the offender can never realistically be released. Whatever the case, the moment when a judge hands down a sentence is one of the final phases in the criminal justice process (except for the convicted offender's appeals, discussed later in this chapter).

SENTENCING GUIDELINES

The growing complexity and importance of the **sentencing guidelines** now found in criminal justice pose a bit of a dilemma for this introductory course textbook: On the one hand, they are too complicated to discuss comprehensively or in great detail; on the other hand, they are far too important to ignore. Therefore, this chapter section strives to achieve an appropriate balance by looking at the guidelines in summary form.

Background: Legislation and Court Decisions

In the mid- to late 1970s and early 1980s, many people were becoming discontented with the indeterminate sentencing process; they witnessed inmates often being released after serving only a fraction of their sentences (some jurisdictions even allowed 30 days of "good-time" reduction of a sentence for each 30 days served). That, coupled with renewed concern about the rising crime rate throughout the nation, resulted in wide experimentation with sentencing systems by many states and the creation of sentencing guidelines at the federal level.

Federal Sentencing Guidelines

After more than a decade of research and debate, Congress decided that (1) the sentencing discretion given federal trial judges needed to be structured; (2) the administration of punishment needed to be more certain; and (3) specific offenders (e.g., white-collar and violent, repeat offenders) needed to be targeted for more serious penalties.[21] As a result, Congress abolished indeterminate sentencing at the federal level and created a determinate sentencing structure through the federal sentencing guidelines. The Sentencing Reform Act[22] was enacted to ensure that similarly situated defendants were sentenced in a more uniform fashion rather than depending on the judge to which they happened to be assigned.[23] The federal sentencing system was thus reformed by

- Dropping rehabilitation as one of the goals of punishment

- Creating the U.S. Sentencing Commission and charging it with establishing sentencing guidelines

- Making all federal sentences determinate

- Authorizing appellate review of sentences[24]

A long line of legal challenges ensued involving these sentencing guidelines. The first such challenge came from the state of Washington, where the petitioner had pleaded guilty to kidnapping. Under Washington's law, the maximum penalty for that offense is 10 years. A separate range-of-sentence provision limited the maximum allowable sentence to 53 months, but it authorized an upward departure for "exceptional" judge-determined factors. The trial judge increased the sentence to 90 months because the crime was committed with deliberate cruelty. Because the facts supporting the enhanced penalty were neither admitted by the petitioner nor found by a jury, the U.S. Supreme Court held in *Blakely v. Washington* (2004) that the sentence violated the Sixth Amendment right to trial by jury.[25] This decision, however, applied only to Washington.

Then, six months later, the Supreme Court decided *United States v. Booker*, this time addressing sentencing guidelines nationally.[26] The defendant, Booker, was found guilty by a jury of possessing at least 50 grams of crack cocaine (he actually had 92.5 grams). Under those facts, the guidelines required a possible 210- to 262-month sentence. Although the jury never heard any such evidence, the judge, finding by a preponderance

Sentencing guidelines: an instrument developed by the federal government that uses a grid system to chart the seriousness of offense, criminal history, and so forth and thus allows the court to arrive at a more consistent sentence for everyone.

of the evidence that Booker possessed the much larger amount of cocaine, rendered a sentence that was almost 10 years longer than what the guidelines prescribed. By a vote of 5 to 4, the U.S. Supreme Court found that the U.S. sentencing guidelines violated the Sixth Amendment by allowing judicial, rather than jury, fact-finding to form the basis for the sentencing; in other words, letting in these judge-made facts is unconstitutional. The guidelines also allowed judges to make such determinations with a lesser standard of proof than the jury's "beyond a reasonable doubt" and to rely on hearsay evidence that would not be admissible at trial.[27]

The Court did not discard the guidelines entirely. The guidelines, the Court said, are to be merely advisory and not mandatory. Thus, the guidelines are a resource a judge can look at but may choose to ignore. Although courts still must "consider" the guidelines, they need not follow them. In addition, sentences for federal crimes will become subject to appellate review for "unreasonableness," allowing appeals courts to clamp down on particular sentences that seem far too harsh.

Finally, in late 2007, the U.S. Supreme Court went further and explained what it meant in 2005 by "advisory" and "reasonableness," deciding two cases that together restored federal judges to their traditional central role in criminal sentencing. The Court found that district court judges do not have to justify their deviations from the federal sentencing guidelines, and have broad discretion to disagree with the guidelines and to impose what they believe are reasonable sentences—even if the guidelines call for different sentences. Both cases—*Gall v. United States*[28] and *Kimbrough v. United States*[29]—were decided by the same 7–2 margin and chided federal appeals courts for failing to give district judges sufficient leeway.

State-Level Sentencing Guidelines

Several states have enacted sentencing guidelines. As an example, Table 11.1 shows the sentencing grid used by the state of Washington, which has developed a sophisticated and objective sentencing tool called *The Adult Sentencing Guidelines Manual*.[30] This manual provides comprehensive information on adult felony sentencing as set forth under state law, identifying the seriousness level of the offense and "scoring" the offender's criminal history. The seriousness of crimes ranges from Level I (which includes offenses such as simple theft, malicious mischief, attempting to elude a pursuing police vehicle, and possessing stolen property) to Level XVI (aggravated murder, which includes first-degree murder with one or more of a number of aggravating circumstances).

©P/Corbis

Victim impact statements are increasingly common in the sentencing phase of criminal cases, where the focus has traditionally been on the offender rather than the victims and their loved ones. These statements help judges and juries to more fully understand the impact of a crime and what punishment is appropriate.

Victim impact statements: information provided prior to sentencing by the victims of a crime (or, in cases of murder, the surviving family members) about the impact the crime had on their lives; allowed by the U.S. Supreme Court.

VICTIM IMPACT STATEMENTS

Victim impact statements are written or oral information provided in court—most commonly at sentencing—and at offenders' parole hearings concerning the impact of the crime on the victim and the victim's family. These statements generally inform the court of the crime's financial, emotional, psychological, and/or physical impact on their lives. They provide a means for the court to refocus its attention on the human cost of the crime, as well as for the victim to participate in the criminal justice process. The

TABLE 11.1   State of Washington Sentencing Grid

SERIOUSNESS LEVEL	OFFENDER SCORE									
	0	**1**	**2**	**3**	**4**	**5**	**6**	**7**	**8**	**9+**
LEVEL XVI	LIFE SENTENCE WITHOUT PAROLE/DEATH PENALTY									
LEVEL XV	180-240	187.5-249.75	195.75-260.25	203.25-270.75	210.75-280.5	218.25-291	234-312	253.5-337.5	277.5-369.75	308.25-411
LEVEL XIV	92.25-165	100.5-175.5	108-183	115.5-190.5	123.75-198.75	131.25-206.25	146.25-221.25	162-237	192.75-267.75	223.5-297.75
LEVEL XIII	92.25-123	100.5-133.5	108-144	115.5-153.75	123.75-164.25	131.25-174.75	146.25-195	162-216	192.75-256.5	223.5-297.75
LEVEL XII	69.75-92.25	76.5-102	83.25-110.25	90-120	96.75-128.25	103.5-138	121.5-162	133.5-177	156.75-207.75	180-238.5
LEVEL XI	58.5-76.5	64.5-85.5	71.25-93.75	76.5-102	83.25-110.25	90-118.5	109.5-145.5	119.25-158.25	138.75-183.75	157.5-210
LEVEL X	38.25-51	42.75-56.25	46.5-61.5	50.25-66.75	54-72	57.75-76.5	73.5-97.5	81-108	96.75-128.25	111.75-148.5
LEVEL IX	23.25-30.75	27-36	30.75-40.5	34.5-45.75	38.25-51	42.75-56.25	57.75-76.5	65.25-87	81-108	96.75-128.25
LEVEL VIII	15.75-20.25	19.5-25.5	23.25-30.75	27-36	30.75-40.5	34.54-5.75	50.25-66.75	57.75-76.5	65.25-87	81-108
LEVEL VII	11.25-15	15.75-20.25	19.5-25.5	23.25-30.75	27-36	30.75-40.5	42.75-56.25	50.25-66.75	57.75-76.5	65.25-87
LEVEL VI	9-10.5	11.25-15	15.75-20.25	19.5-25.5	23.25-30.75	27-36	34.5-45.75	42.75-56.25	50.25-66.75	57.75-76.5
LEVEL V	4.5-9	9-10.5	9.75-12.75	11.25-15	16.5-21.75	24.75-32.25	30.75-40.5	38.25-51	46.5-61.5	54-72
LEVEL IV	2.25-6.75	4.59	9-10.5	9.75-12.75	11.25-15	16.5-21.75	24.75-32.25	32.25-42.75	39.75-52.5	47.25-63
LEVEL III	0.75-2.25	2.25-6	3-9	6.75-9	9-12	12.75-16.5	16.5-21.75	24.75-32.25	32.25-42.75	38.25-51
LEVEL II	0-67.5 days	1.5-4.5	2.25-6.75	3-9	9-10.5	10.5-13.5	12.75-16.5	16.5-21.75	24.75-32.25	32.25-42.75
LEVEL I	0-45 days	0-67.5 days	1.5-3.75	1.5-4.5	2.25-6	3-9	9-10.5	10.5-13.5	12.75-16.5	16.5-21.75

Source: Reprinted with permission, copyright © 2012 State of Washington/John C. Steiger, PhD.

right to make an impact statement is generally available not only to the victim, but also to homicide survivors, the parent or guardian of a minor victim, and a person representing an incompetent or incapacitated victim. A recent survey by the National Center for Victims of Crime found that 80 percent of all victims rated their ability to make a victim impact statement at sentencing and at parole hearings as "very important."[31]

Victim impact statements were upheld in 1991 by the U.S. Supreme Court, in *Payne v. Tennessee.*[32] Payne was convicted of two counts of murder for stabbing to death a mother and her two-year-old daughter and also wounding her three-year-old son. During the sentencing hearing, the boy's grandmother described how the killings affected the surviving grandson. On appeal, the Supreme Court held 72 that the victim has a right to be heard, and quoted from a 1934 opinion by Justice Benjamin Cardozo: "Justice, though due to the accused, is due to the accuser also."[33] See the next "Investigating Further" box for more discussion and examples of such statements.

Video: Victim impact statements

Author Video: Victim impact statements

INVESTIGATING FURTHER

VICTIM IMPACT STATEMENTS IN THE JEFFREY DAHMER CASE

Family members of nine of Jeffrey Dahmer's victims gave heart-wrenching victim impact statements, addressing Dahmer directly in court. Victims' families told of their pain and the life-changing impact Dahmer's crimes had on their lives.

- "I would like to say to Jeffrey Dahmer that he don't know the pain, the hurt, the loss, and the mental state that he had put our family in." —Shirley Hughes, Anthony Hughes's mother

- "You took my 17-year-old son away from me. I'll never get a chance to tell him that I loved him, have a chance to tell him that I loved him the last time I saw him, which will be a year tomorrow. You took my mother's oldest grandchild from her and for that I can never forgive you." —Dorothy Straughter, Curtis Straughter's mother

- "I don't understand how a person could really harm a person and to say that I did this because he isn't my type…. [T]his man should never be able to walk the face of the earth or to be able to harm anyone else again." —Inez Thomas, David Thomas's mother.

- Rita Isbell, sister of victim Errol Lindsey, called Dahmer "Satan," and screamed "Jeffrey, I hate you" before being led away, overcome with emotion.

Finally, Dahmer addressed the court to give a statement of his own, and the world was again riveted to hear from the serial killer for the first time since his arrest: "I know the families of the victims will never be able to forgive me for what I have done. I promise I will pray each day to ask for their forgiveness when the hurt goes away, if ever. I have seen their tears, and if I could give my life right now to bring their loved ones back, I would do it."

1. Should victim impact statements be allowed in court? Why or why not?

2. Should convicted offenders be allowed to offer statements during their sentencing phase? Why or why not?

Source: Jeffrey Dahmer Trial Victim Impact Statements Highlights, https://www.youtube.com/watch?v=yrTGCUkGiU0; "15 Life Terms and No Parole for Dahmer," *New York Times*, February 18, 1992, http://www.nytimes.com/1992/02/18/us/15-life-terms-and-no-parole-for-dahmer.html.

CAPITAL PUNISHMENT

Because of its finality, debate concerning the death penalty has always been emotionally charged. Certainly there are strong arguments put forth by those who favor and are opposed to **capital punishment**.

Arguments For and Against

For a politician or political entity to try to fashion a state or national policy on the death penalty that would definitively appeal to most Americans would be nearly impossible. The U.S. Supreme Court has halted death sentences and then approved them, and several states have done likewise (largely because many convicted murderers on death row have been found to be innocent). Some studies indicate that the death penalty works to prevent crimes of murder, and other studies show the opposite. Americans themselves seem fickle in their views of whether or not killers should be put to death.

Figure 11.2 shows the percentage of Americans who favor and are opposed to the death penalty. The percentages of people in favor of the death penalty rose steadily for the most part from about 1967 to 1995; from that point, however, there has been an overall decline in such support, dropping from about 80 percent to about 65 percent. Meanwhile, the percentage of people saying they are in opposition to the death penalty has remained fairly stable since 1937, ranging from about 31 percent to 38 percent (excluding a spike in 1967 to 42 percent).

Capital punishment: a sentence of death, or carrying out same via execution of the offender.

FIGURE 11.2 Percentage of Americans Favoring and Opposing the Death Penalty

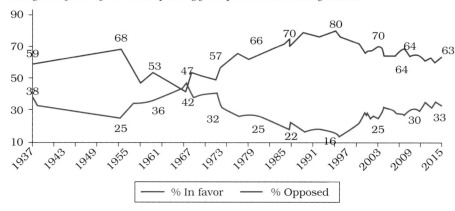

Are you in favor of the death penalty for a person convicted of murder?

Arguments in Favor

People who support the death penalty often believe that it deters other people from committing murder, while others base their stand on theological grounds—the commandment "Thou shalt not kill." Others favor capital punishment because of the retribution it provides to family members and friends of the victim; "getting even" is a proper punishment in the eyes of many people, rather than some "rehabilitative" ideal. It is society's nod to *lex talionis*—"eye for eye": "If you kill one of us, we will kill you." One thing the death penalty most certainly accomplishes, however, is the prevention of future murders by that particular offender. As James Q. Wilson noted, "Whatever else may be said about the death penalty, it is certain that it incapacitates."[34]

Does the existence of a death penalty deter individuals from committing murder? That is an important question, and one that is at the tip of the spear in this debate. The answer, unfortunately, is elusive, and it depends largely on which set of studies one looks at and gives credence to. Beginning in 2003, a number of studies were published that reportedly demonstrated the death penalty saves lives by acting as a deterrent to murder. One study that garnered a large amount of attention, conducted by Mocan and Gittings, analyzed 6,143 death sentences imposed in the United States between 1977 and 1997. Results indicated that each execution resulted in five fewer murders, and each commutation of a death sentence to a long or life prison term resulted in five additional homicides. Further, each additional removal from death row when one's sentence is vacated resulted in one additional homicide.[35]

Another study, by professors at Emory University, using a panel data set of over 3,000 counties from 1977 to 1996, found that each execution resulted in 18 fewer murders and that the implementation of state moratoria was associated with an increased incidence of murders.[36] Then, two studies by a Federal Communications Commission economist also supported the deterrent effect of capital punishment, finding that each additional execution, on average, resulted in 14 fewer murders[37] and that executions conducted by electrocution were the most effective at providing deterrence.[38] However, the findings of these studies were challenged by other criminologists.

Arguments in Opposition

Arguments against the death penalty include that it does not have any deterrent value, that it is discriminatory against minorities, that retribution is unfitting for a civilized society, and that it can (and does) claim the lives of innocent people.

Many people oppose capital punishment and express their disapproval by protesting against it – especially when someone is about to be executed.

At least two criminologists have found serious flaws in the Mocan-Gittings study, which found that each execution resulted in five fewer murders. Richard Berk, using Mocan and Gittings's original data set, removed the Texas data, ran the model exactly as the original authors did for the other 49 states, and found that the deterrent effect disappeared.[39]

A second reexamination of the Mocan-Gittings study was conducted by Jeffrey Fagan, who, by modifying their measure of deterrence, also found that all the deterrent effects disappeared. Rather than prove that Mocan and Gittings erred in their assumptions, Fagan showed that small changes in their assumptions could produce wild fluctuations in their deterrence estimates.[40] Regarding the contention that the death penalty is discriminatory, many people would agree with a finding by the U.S. Government Accountability Office that there is "a pattern of evidence indicating racial disparities in the charging, sentencing, and imposition of the death penalty."[41] Amnesty International argues, furthermore, that "from initial charging decisions to plea bargaining to jury sentencing, African-Americans are treated more harshly when they are defendants, and their lives are accorded less value when they are victims. All-white or virtually all-white juries are still commonplace in many localities."[42] Following are other findings regarding the death penalty discrimination thesis:

• A report sponsored by the American Bar Association concluded that one-third of African American death row inmates in Philadelphia would have received sentences of life imprisonment if they had not been African American.

• A study of death sentences in Connecticut conducted by Yale University School of Law revealed that African American defendants receive the death penalty at three times the rate of white defendants in cases where the victims are white. In addition, killers of white victims are treated more severely than people who kill minorities, when it comes to deciding what charges to bring.

• A study released by the University of Maryland concluded that race and geography are major factors in death penalty decisions. Specifically, prosecutors are more likely to seek a death sentence when the race of the victim is white and are less likely to seek a death sentence when the victim is African American.[43]

Finally, of course, is the argument that innocent people can be—and have been—executed for crimes they never committed, which is discussed in the "Wrongful Convictions" section.

Key Supreme Court Decisions

In *Furman v. Georgia* (1972), by vote of 5 to 4, the U.S. Supreme Court, for the first time, struck down the death penalty under the cruel and unusual punishment clause of the Eighth Amendment. The decision involved not only Furman, convicted for murder, but also two other men (in Georgia and Texas) convicted for rape; juries at the trials of all three men had imposed the death penalty without any specific guides or limits on their discretion. The justices for the majority found this lack of guidelines or limits on jury discretion to be unconstitutional, as it resulted in a random pattern among those receiving the death penalty; one justice also felt that death was disproportionately applied to the poor and socially disadvantaged, and felt those groups were denied equal protection under the law.[44]

Four years after *Furman*, the Supreme Court rendered another major death penalty decision. A Georgia jury had found Troy Gregg guilty of armed robbery and murder and sentenced him to death. Gregg challenged his death sentence, claiming that it was, *per se*, a "cruel and unusual" punishment that violated the Eighth and Fourteenth Amendments. In a 72 decision, the Court held that a punishment of death did not violate the Constitution. Where a defendant has been convicted of deliberately killing another person, the careful and judicious use of the death penalty may be appropriate if carefully employed. The Court noted that Georgia's death penalty statute required a bifurcated proceeding (where the trial and sentencing are conducted separately), as well as specific jury findings as to the severity of the crime and the nature of the defendant and a comparison of aggravating and mitigating circumstances.[45]

Another significant decision was rendered by the Supreme Court in 2005, in *Roper v. Simmons*, holding that the Eighth and Fourteenth Amendments forbid the execution of offenders who were under the age of 18 when their crimes were committed.[46] In addition, the Supreme Court has held that

- The Eighth Amendment prohibits the execution of persons who are mentally incompetent at the time of their execution.[47]

- The death penalty cannot be applied to adults who rape children (and, more broadly, that a state cannot impose the death penalty for a crime that did not result in the death of the victim, except for crimes committed against the state—i.e., espionage, treason).[48]

- In order to show their legal counsel was ineffective, defendants in capital cases must prove that the attorney's performance was less than reasonable (e.g., counsel did not present mitigating circumstances), and that there is a reasonable likelihood that this substandard performance changed the outcome of the trial.[49]

- People who are opposed to the death penalty cannot be automatically excluded from serving on juries in capital cases; however, people whose opposition is so strong as to "prevent or substantially impair the performance of their duties" (*Witherspoon v. Illinois*, 1968) may be removed from the jury pool during *voir dire* (preliminary examination).[50]

Methods of Execution

Here we discuss the methods of execution that are in use today in the United States. Those methods of execution by state are shown in Figure 11.3.

Although death by lethal injection has been widely thought to be much more humane than other methods, several challenges to this method of execution have been raised in the U.S. Supreme Court in recent years (and recent botched executions have ignited the out-of-court debate; see the next "Invesigating Further" box). Such challenges typically claim that the drugs used in the executions cause extreme and unnecessary pain, while masking the pain being experienced by the inmate, and thus violate the Eighth Amendment's ban on cruel and unusual punishment. Most recently, in *Baze v. Rees* (2008), the U.S. Supreme Court held that the three-drug "cocktail" used by

FIGURE 11.3 Method of Execution, by State, 2015

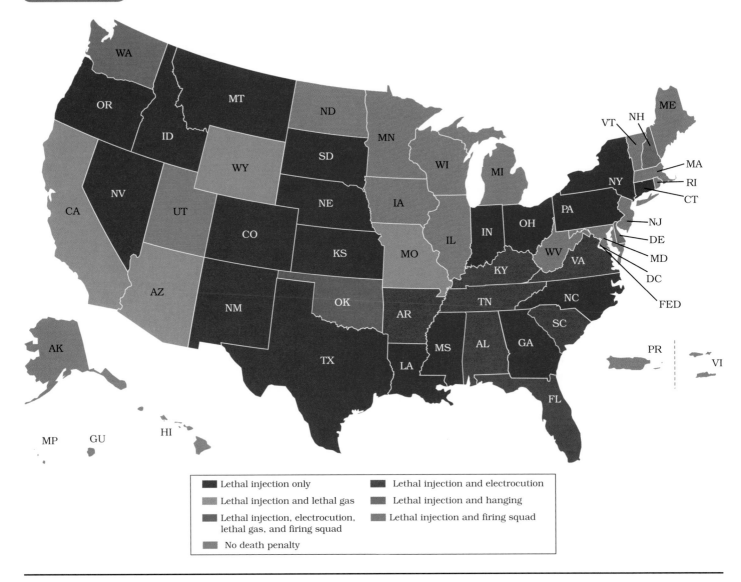

Lethal injection only

Lethal injection and lethal gas

Lethal injection, electrocution, lethal gas, and firing squad

No death penalty

Lethal injection and electrocution

Lethal injection and hanging

Lethal injection and firing squad

Source: U.S. Department of Justice, Bureau of Justice Statistics, Capital Punishment Series; http://www.bjs.gov/content/pub/pdf/cp13st.pdf and http://www.deathpenaltyinfo.org/methods-execution.

35 states and the federal government did not violate the Eighth Amendment.[51] Chief Justice John G. Roberts observed that a method of execution would violate the Constitution only if it was "deliberately designed to inflict pain." Two years earlier, Clarence Hill, an inmate on Florida's death row, challenged the use of lethal injection, *per se*, as causing unnecessary pain contrary to contemporary standards of decency; however, by a vote of 5 to 4, the U.S. Supreme Court denied a stay of execution (Justice Antonin Scalia noted that "lethal injection is much less painful than hanging"), and Hill was executed in September 2006.[52]

Wrongful Convictions: Rethinking the Death Penalty

Video:
Innocence Project

Being convicted of a crime is no guarantee that one is actually guilty as charged. It means simply that a jury or judge was persuaded by the state's case against the defendant or, in the case of plea bargaining, the defendant was persuaded to plead guilty to avoid trial. Today, we know that many innocent people have nonetheless been convicted and, in

INVESTIGATING FURTHER

THE REALITY OF DEATH BY LETHAL INJECTION

A series of botched executions in recent years have stirred the death penalty debate anew and refocused criticisms on the perceived "humane" method of lethal injection. In four cases from Georgia and Ohio between 2007 and 2010, prison officials struggled for significant periods of time to find a suitable vein for the intravenous delivery of lethal drugs used in executions in those states:

- Georgia (2007): John Hightower: 40 min. to find a vein; 59 total min. for execution.
- Georgia (2008): Curtis Osborne: 35 min. to find a vein; 14 min. for Osborne to die after the lethal drugs began flowing.
- Ohio (2009): Romell Broom: more than 2 hours to find a suitable vein in arms and legs; execution was stopped after Broom appeared to be in agonizing pain.
- Georgia (2010): Brandon Rhode: 40 min. to find a vein; 14 min. for Rhode to die.

In more recent cases, from 2014, it took exceedingly long periods of time for condemned prisoners to die, calling into further question the efficacy of the three-drug method and the death penalty in general.

- Ohio (2014): Dennis McGuire: 25 min. for McGuire to die, and witnesses reported that he snorted, gasped, and heaved in pain during that time.
- Oklahoma (2014): Clayton Lockett: 1 hour to find a suitable vein; 20 min. of Lockett in apparent pain—writhing, clenching, trying to lift his head off the pillow—before the execution was halted. Lockett's attorneys sought and won a two-week stay, but 43 min. after the execution had begun, Lockett died of a heart attack while still in the execution chamber.
- Arizona (2014): Joseph Wood: 1 hour and 40 min. to die after drugs were administered.

Source: Death Penalty Information Center, "Examples of Post-*Furman* Botched Executions," http://www.deathpenaltyinfo.org/some-examples-post-furman-botched-executions.

---

some cases, sentenced to death, until their names were cleared—they were exonerated—by DNA evidence (see "Investigating Further" box). The Death Penalty Information Center reports that 153 death row inmates in the United States have been exonerated since 1973, including 20 people facing death whose innocence was proven through DNA evidence.[53]

Exoneration: to absolve someone of criminal blame, or find someone not guilty.

These **exonerations** and problems with executions have not gone unnoticed. Since 2000, 16 states either issued formal moratoria on capital punishment—stopped executions—or they are under *de facto* moratoria (because they are not scheduling any further executions) while officials review questionable convictions, lethal injection issues, and the evolving legal questions.[54] Further, 30 states have not carried out an execution in the past five years, and 7 states have abolished the death penalty since 2004.[55] The U.S. Supreme Court held in 2002 that the execution of the intellectually disabled was unconstitutional[56] and that the finding of an aggravating factor justifying a death sentence must be made by a jury, not merely by the sentencing judge.[57] Then, in 2005, the Court limited the death penalty even further, ruling that executing offenders who were juveniles at the time of their crimes is cruel and unusual punishment.[58] More recently, on May 20, 2015, the Nebraska legislature voted to repeal its death penalty and replace it with life without parole. Nebraska governor Pete Ricketts vetoed the legislation, but the legislature voted to override, making Nebraska the 19th state to end the practice of capital punishment.

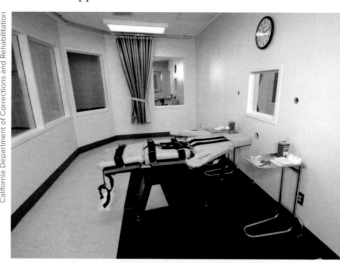

Lethal injection is the most commonly used method of execution in the United States. Shown here is the lethal execution chamber at San Quentin prison in California.

California Department of Corrections and Rehabilitation

INVESTIGATING FURTHER

DNA EXONERATIONS

Henry James served nearly 30 years in Lousiana's infamous Angola Prison for a sexual assault he did not commit. He was convicted in 1982 largely on the basis of an incorrect eyewitness identification—the cause of approximately 75 percent of all wrongful convictions. James was exonerated through DNA testing and finally released from Angola in 2011.

Henry James was 20 years old and poor when he was arrested and charged with aggravated sexual assault of his next door neighbor's wife. His public defender failed to introduce key evidence that would have proved James innocent, and he was quickly convicted and sentenced to life without parole at arguably one of the worst prisons in the world—Louisiana's Angola State Prison. Thirteen years into James's sentence, the detective who worked his case was fired when an FBI task force discovered the detective had coached

witnesses and destroyed evidence. Ten years later, the Innocence Project started searching for evidence in James's case. But the box on the police evidence shelf designated for his case was empty. Without the DNA evidence, James would die in Angola. Somewhat miraculously, five years later a lab technician stumbled on a DNA slide from James's case while working on evidence in another case. The sample was viable, and it proved James did not commit the sexual assault. Nearly 30 years after Angola's gates slammed shut on his life, Henry James walked out of prison a free man.

Henry James's case is extraordinary because such chance circumstances led to the discovery of DNA evidence that proved his innocence. But the fact that he was wrongfully imprisoned in the first place is not so unique. His case is classic and highlights some of the issues that typically lead to wrongful convictions: faulty eyewitness identifications, ineffective assistance of counsel, and exclusion of exculpatory DNA evidence at trial.

James is one of more than 1,600 people who have been exonerated in the United States since 1989, and he is one of 329 people in that group who were exonerated using DNA evidence. Because of these cases, it is hoped that reforms in place or under way throughout the criminal justice system (regarding reformed lineup/eyewitness identification procedures, evidence collection and preservation, and videotaping of police interrogations, for example) will give professionals and offenders alike more confidence in the system.

Source: The Innocence Project, May 2015, http://www.innocenceproject.org; National Registry of Exonerations, University of Michigan, May 2015, https://www.law.umich.edu/special/exoneration/Pages/about.aspx.

AGGRAVATING AND MITIGATING CIRCUMSTANCES

In passing sentence, judges (and, in death penalty cases, the jury) will look at factors other than the crime itself. They consider the manner in which the crime was committed, in order to determine whether or not they should increase or decrease the severity of the punishment. In other words, the judge or jury might "look behind" the crime to see if, for example, the victim was tortured prior to being killed or if the defendant played a minor role in the offense. These are termed aggravating and mitigating circumstances or factors.

Aggravating circumstances can include use of a weapon, committing other felonies, committing murder for hire, or where the offender is a peace officer engaged in official duties.[59] Mitigating circumstances include little or no prior criminal history, where the offender was acting under duress or under the influence of mental illness or extreme emotional disturbance, or where the offender was young.[60]

Under the Supreme Court's decision in *Gregg v. Georgia*, discussed earlier, the judge will also instruct the jury members that they may not impose the death penalty unless they first determine the existence of one or more statutory aggravating circumstances beyond a reasonable doubt, as well as determine that the aggravating circumstances outweigh the mitigating circumstances beyond a reasonable doubt.

CRIMINAL APPEALS

In an appeal, one who has been convicted for a crime attempts to show that the trial court made a legal error that affected the decision in the case, or that he or she had ineffective counsel or that due process was violated in some other way. The defendant now asks a higher (appellate) court to review the transcript of the case for such errors—and possibly have the conviction overturned or be granted a retrial. In addition, the defendant may contest the trial court's sentencing decision without challenging the underlying conviction. Then, if the appellate court grants the appeal, it may reverse the lower court's decision in whole or in part. However, if the appellate court denies the appeal, the lower court's decision stands.[61]

Article I, Section 9, of the Constitution speaks only briefly and indirectly to criminal appeals, saying that the privilege of the writ of *habeas corpus* (discussed in Chapter 9 in the case of *Kibbe v. Henderson*) shall not be suspended, "unless when in Cases of Rebellion or Invasion the public Safety may require it." The name of this writ, often referred to as "the great writ," is Latin for "you have the body." Habeas corpus is the inmate's means of asking a court to grant a hearing to determine whether or not he or she is being held illegally.

Convicted persons who are indigent (poor) are entitled to free legal counsel for their initial appeal,[62] and a free copy of their trial transcript.[63] (However, the Supreme Court has held that prison inmates are not entitled to free legal counsel for subsequent "discretionary" appeals.[64]) Furthermore, as is noted in Chapter 12, prison inmates also have a right to access to law libraries, and many law schools have defender clinics in which law students represent state and federal prisoners in appellate and postconviction litigation in state and federal courts. This is in addition to prison "writ-writers"—inmates who over time develop considerable expertise in constitutional law and means of filing writs and petitions.

Not only are inmates able to challenge their criminal conviction on a variety of grounds (the evidence introduced against them; the police arrest, search, and seizure of their person and property; the judge's instructions to the jury; and so on), but after being incarcerated they may attempt to obtain what are called postconviction remedies—making what are termed "collateral attacks." These lawsuits are civil in nature (unlike the original appeal of their conviction) and challenge, for example, the conditions of their confinement. Such cases often list the prison warden as the respondent and can involve the inmate's filing a *writ of habeas corpus*, typically in a federal court having jurisdiction over his or her place of incarceration.

IN A NUTSHELL

- Historically, we have punished people for the following reasons: retribution, deterrence, incapacitation, and rehabilitation. The U.S. Constitution speaks only briefly but forcefully regarding the use of punishment. The Eighth Amendment provides that incarceration will not involve "cruel and unusual punishment" and that fines will not be excessive.

- Prosecutors can influence the sentencing decision by agreeing to engage in plea negotiation concerning the number of charges filed or the maximum penalty the judge may impose, by explaining that the accused was very cooperative with the police and/or remorseful for the crime, and so on. Defense attorneys can seek to obtain the lightest possible sentence, or other alternatives to sentencing, or they can emphasize such things as the defendant's minor involvement in the crime.

• The seriousness of the offense is the most important factor in determining the sentencing one receives for his or her offense, followed by the defendant's prior criminal record.

• Philosophies of crime and punishment have changed significantly since the late 1700s; today people are calling for longer sentences for career criminals and violent offenders. Legislators, judges, and officials have responded with determinate sentencing laws, "three-strikes laws," mandatory sentencing laws (e.g., doubling one's sentence for a crime committed with a weapon), and so forth.

• Under *determinate* sentencing, convicted offenders are sentenced for a fixed term, such as 10 years, with no opportunity for a paroling authority to make adjustments in time served. Conversely, in an *indeterminate* sentencing format, the convicted individual will be sentenced for a set range of time, such as 5–10 years, allowing for the length of sentence to be adjusted in response to the offender's positive responses to treatment and programs.

• Becoming discontented with the sentencing process and the rising crime rate throughout the nation, Congress abolished indeterminate sentencing at the federal level and created a determinate sentencing structure through the federal Sentencing Reform Act. The U.S. Supreme Court found that the guidelines violated the Constitution by allowing judicial, rather than jury, fact-finding to form the basis for the sentencing. The Court said the guidelines are to be merely advisory and not mandatory. Thus, the guidelines are a resource a judge can look at but may choose to ignore.

• Victim impact statements are written or oral information provided in court—most commonly at sentencing—and at offenders' parole hearings, concerning the impact of the crime on the victim and the victim's family. These statements generally inform the court of the crime's financial, emotional, psychological, and/or physical impact on their lives.

• Supporters of the death penalty often believe that it deters other people from committing murder, while others base their stand on theological grounds. Others favor capital punishment because of the retribution it provides to family members and friends of the victim. Arguments against the death penalty include that it does not have any deterrent value, that it is discriminatory against minorities, that retribution is unfitting for a civilized society, and that it can (and does) claim the lives of innocent people. There is some, but not unanimous, research in support of the deterrence argument.

• In 1972, the U.S. Supreme Court struck down all death penalty laws as being cruel and unusual punishment, due to the manner in which the sanction was being administered. The Court later approved the death sentence in concept. Today, lethal injection is the method of execution authorized in a majority of the states.

• Since 1973, there have been 153 persons exonerated on death row in the United States. According to the Death Penalty Information Center, DNA led to 20 of those death row exonerations. Such exonerations resulted in several states placing a moratorium on their executions until capital punishment studies could be completed.

• Convicted, indigent persons are entitled to free legal counsel for their initial appeal as well as a free copy of their trial transcript. However, the Court later held that prison inmates are not entitled to free legal counsel for subsequent "discretionary" appeals.

KEY TERMS & CONCEPTS

▶ Review key terms with eFlashcards. ⑤SAGE edge™

⑤SAGE edge™ Test your understanding of chapter content. Take the practice quiz. ◀

REVIEW QUESTIONS **?**

1. How would you describe the four goals of punishment? Which one of them do you believe works the best? Which goal or function is now predominant in our society?

2. What are the factors that influence the degree—and harshness—of the punishment that a convicted person will receive?

3. How would you delineate the different philosophies regarding crime and punishment that evolved from the colonial era to today? How did prison construction change in accordance with those changes in punishment models?

4. What forms of punishment used around the world would you point to that are clearly excessive in terms of the offenses committed? Explain your answer.

5. What are the differences between, and purposes of, both determinate and indeterminate sentences? Which is likely used when the crime control model or due process model is more predominant in a community?

6. How would you explain the rationale for, and operation of, the federal sentencing guidelines?

7. What is the interesting legal history of victim impact statements? How do such statements work, and for what purpose?

8. What are the fundamental arguments for and against capital punishment? What did the Supreme Court say about capital punishment in *Furman* and *Gregg*?

9. What are the prevailing methods of execution in use today?

10. What changes have been brought by DNA with regard to the death penalty?

11. What are examples of both aggravating and mitigating circumstances, and how do they apply to sentencing decisions? To the death penalty?

12. What rights are possessed by a convicted person regarding access to legal counsel, trial transcripts, and law libraries?

LEARN BY DOING

1. Your state's governor is considering a moratorium on all executions because of DNA and death row exonerations. Knowing you are a criminal justice student, you are asked by a state senator to prepare a pro-con paper concerning the benefits and issues involved with doing so, and of DNA in general. How would you respond? Include in your response an assessment of the deterrent effects of capital punishment laws.

2. Assume your criminal justice instructor has assigned you to go to www.uwsp.edu/psych/s/389/landy69.pdf. There you will find a journal article by Landy and Aronson titled "The Influence of the Character of the

Criminal and His Victim on the Decisions of Simulated Jurors," published in the *Journal of Experimental Social Psychology* 5 (1969), pages 141–152. Read Experiment II, including the instructions and case study (involving an incident with both an attractive victim and an unattractive victim) as given to university sophomores, as well as the experiment's results and discussion, on pages 146–151. Summarize and explain the above in written form.

3. Your criminal justice class is to debate the following: "RESOLVED: Deterrence is lost for the general public when an inmate remains on death row a dozen or more years." Plan how you would respond on both the pro and con sides of the debate.

STUDY SITE

⑤SAGE edge™

Review → Practice → Improve

Sharpen your skills with **SAGE edge** at **edge.sagepub.com/peak2e**

SAGE edge for students provides a personalized approach to help you accomplish your coursework goals in an easy-to-use learning environment. Access the videos, audio clips, quizzes, and SAGE journal articles that are noted in this chapter.

PART IV

CORRECTIONS

This part includes three chapters and examines many aspects of correctional organizations and operations.

Chapter 12 examines federal and state prisons and local jails in terms of their evolution and organization, inmate population trends and classification, and some technologies.

Chapter 13 considers the "lives inside the walls" of both the correctional personnel and the inmates; included are selected court decisions concerning inmates' legal rights; administrative

challenges with overseeing executions, inmate litigation, drugs, and gangs; and the work of personnel in local jails.

Chapter 14 reviews community corrections and alternatives to incarceration: probation, parole, and several other diversionary approaches. Included are discussions of the origins of probation and parole, functions of probation and parole offices, and several intermediate sanctions (e.g., house arrest, electronic monitoring).

CHAPTER 12

PRISONS AND JAILS
Structure and Function

LEARNING OBJECTIVES

As a result of reading this chapter, you will be able to:

1 Explain correctional organizations in terms of the factors that affect prison and jail populations and the resources they require (e.g., employment and expenditures)

2 Explain the basic structure and function of state prisons

3 Explain the basic structure and function of the federal prison system

4 Describe how supermax prisons function, how they differ from other prisons, and critics' views concerning their effects on inmates and their constitutionality

5 Review how jails are organized and constructed, including the new generation jail

6 Describe some of the technologies now in use in corrections

ASSESS YOUR AWARENESS

Test your basic knowledge of prisons and jails by responding to the following seven true-false items; check your answers after reading this chapter's materials.

1 Factors influencing prison and jail populations include the nation's drug problem, violence on film and television, and a general deterioration of family and morals.

2 If one is convicted of committing a murder, he or she will likely be forced to serve a lengthy sentence in a local jail.

3 The general mission of correctional institutions is to securely hold criminals while providing them with opportunities to become productive and law-abiding citizens.

4 There are basically two custody levels of prisons: maximum and minimum.

5 Supermax prisons are so named because they offer the maximum amount of freedom and programming permitted by the courts.

6 Today, very few prison inmates, and no jail inmates, are involved in productive work programs.

7 Robots and devices to quell riots are not used in prisons.

The founders of a new colony . . . recognized it among their earliest practical necessities to allot a portion of the virgin soil as a cemetery, and another portion as the site of a prison.

—Nathaniel Hawthorne

I can think of nothing, not even war, that has brought so much misery to the human race as prisons.

—Clarence Darrow, 1936

<< Answers can be found on page 424.

Jasmine Barclay of Brooklyn, New York, believes that being an innocent victim of mass incarceration has affected her for her entire life. Although she has never broken the law, her mother was arrested when Jasmine was one year old, and it took 18 years to establish a relationship with her. Her father was in and out of prison as well. She cannot recall much of her childhood, except remembering that she lived in nine different homes since the age of two. She just wanted to find a place that was hers, rather than relying on family, friends, and others for help. She carried the stress of loneliness and of having both parents in prison. For her, the United States' tough-on-crime policies hurt a lot of people who didn't do anything wrong.[1]

What "works" with prisons and jails? We know that two-thirds of released prisoners are rearrested for at least one serious new crime. Put a different way, thousands of Americans are victimized every year by criminals who have already served time but derived no "correction" from the experience.[2] Yet, for many prison inmates who have been incarcerated for an extended period of time, life inside the institution is far easier than it is outside. After release, demands are placed on them in many domains of their lives. A job is needed (with the inmate possibly having little education and few if any skills for today's job market, as well as a felony record), and housing must be found. There will be a period of culture shock—coping with the many ways the free world has changed since they left it. Even the most mundane tasks— renewing a driver's license, purchasing groceries or subway tokens, using a computer or a cell phone—can cause anxiety. Ties with family members and old friends may have been severed and need to be reconnected.[3] Given all of these challenges, it is probably amazing if one does not return to a life of crime and to prison.

As you read this chapter's discussion of the general mission and function of prisons and jails and the effects of mass incarceration on society, consider whether or not we need new crime-control policies and if the harsh sentencing policies of the past should be reconsidered.

INTRODUCTION

What are the differences in definitions, missions, structures, and functions of prisons and jails and in the duties of persons working in them? How are decisions made concerning the type of institution to which one is sent? Are more people being incarcerated today due to the recent downturn in the economy? Certainly these are valid questions to ask, particularly given the expense associated with institutionalizing offenders rather than having them remain in the community.

In his classic 1961 book, *Asylums*, Erving Goffman described life inside what he termed "total institutions," or those places "organized to protect the community against what are felt to be intentional dangers to it: jail, penitentiaries, POW camps, and concentration camps."[4] Goffman said that total institutions share the following features:

- All aspects of life are conducted in the same place and under the same single authority.

- Each phase of the member's daily activity is carried on in the immediate company of a large batch of others.

- All phases of the day's activities are tightly scheduled.

- The various enforced activities are brought together in a single rational plan . . . to fulfill the official aims of the institution.[5]

Goffman appears to have captured the essence of our correctional organizations, which are typically viewed as the end result of one's movement through the criminal justice system (as described and illustrated in Chapter 1). However, it might well be argued that the correctional process begins at the point of one's *arrest*, when he or she is incarcerated in jail awaiting trial and official attempts are initiated to identify and change his or her criminal tendencies.

SAGE edge™

Get the edge on your studies. edge.sagepub .com/peak2e

- Take a quiz to find out what you've learned.
- Review key terms with eFlashcards.
- Watch videos that enhance chapter content.

In any case, corrections is composed of agencies and programs that are responsible for carrying out the sentences and punishment that the courts have administered to those who have been accused, tried, and convicted for their criminal acts. Keep in mind that most of the work of corrections is accomplished not by locking people away, but in the community, where offenders serve terms of probation or parole (see Chapter 14).

Unfortunately, most of what the public "knows" about prisons and jails is probably based on Hollywood's stylized portrayal—in movies such as *The Shawshank Redemption*, *The Green Mile*, *Escape From Alcatraz*, *Cool Hand Luke*, *The Longest Yard*, and *The Great Escape*. These and other such portrayals of prison and jail life typically show the administrators and their staff being cruel, bigoted, corrupt, and morally base.

The truth, however, is probably far different from Hollywood's depictions. In fact, the point is made early in this chapter that, for many members of our society, incarceration is anything but punishing and instead offers a reward and lifestyle improvement.

Although correctional populations began to decline slightly in 2011, corrections remains a boom industry. First, some considerations are presented regarding reasons for these substantial correctional populations, and then the focus shifts to correctional agencies as organizations, including some demographic and cost information, their mission, and purposes of inmate classification systems. After examining local jails, we look next at the state prison organization, supermax prisons, and the federal prison system.

Inmates in the Knox County Jail in Knoxville, Tennessee. Jails differ from prisons in that they are typically used as a short-term, temporary holding facility for persons recently arrested and awaiting trial.

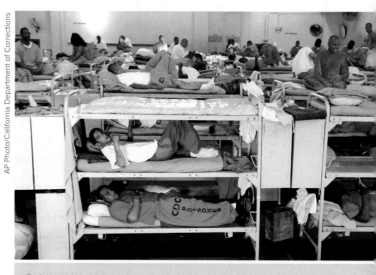

Being under court order to reduce its crowded prisons, the state of California has done so significantly since May 2011.

CORRECTIONAL FACILITIES AS ORGANIZATIONS

Like police and courts organizations, the correctional component of the U.S. criminal justice system also represents organizations—agencies composed of elements that are made up of collective functions and that contribute to their overall mission.

Defining Jails and Prisons

The words *jail* and *prison* are often used interchangeably, but there are major differences between the two. The major difference between whether someone is sentenced to jail or prison concerns the nature of the crime and the length of the sentence to be served. A **jail** is a short-term, often temporary holding facility for persons recently arrested and awaiting trial, and who often are unable to pay bond or bail for their release; or they might be serving short sentences for misdemeanors, generally one year's duration or less.

Conversely, **prisons** are designed for longer confinement. The majority of convicted felons serve their sentences in a prison. People convicted of committing federal crimes are typically sentenced to federal prisons, and those who break state laws go to state prisons.

Jail: a facility that holds persons who have been arrested for crimes and are awaiting trial, persons who have been convicted for misdemeanors and are serving a sentence (up to a year in jail), federal offenders, and others.

Prison: a state or federal facility housing long-term offenders, typically felons, for a period greater than one year.

Video:
Jail versus prison

Another important distinction concerns who administers the facility. Jails are generally run by a county sheriff's department, whereas prisons are operated by state or federal governments.[6]

Inmates, Employment, Expenditures

As shown in Figure 12.1, about 2.3 million Americans are now held in state and federal prisons and local jails; this overall population has generally been increasing since 2000.[7] Furthermore, prisons hold about 3,000 persons on death rows in the jurisdictions allowing capital punishment (35 states and the federal government).[8] Nearly $50 billion is spent per year by the states on corrections alone—as much as 3 percent of total state budgets, which may not appear to be significant, but which also includes expenditures for education, public welfare, highways, and health/hospitals.[9]

Factors Contributing to Correctional Populations

Student on the
Street Video: What
is the difference
between jails
and prisons?

Several factors affect prison and jail populations. First is the nation's drug problem. Indeed, nearly half (48 percent) of the 216,000 inmates in federal prisons are incarcerated for drug offenses, whereas only 17 percent of state prisoners are serving time for such offenses.[10] Other commonly cited factors include truth-in-sentencing laws, violence on television and in the movies, and a general deterioration of morals and of the family. In sum, the nation has become more punitive in nature.

Truth in sentencing for prison inmates began in 1984 in Washington state. The concept, which involves restriction or elimination of parole eligibility and good-time credits, spread quickly to other states after a determination in 1996 that prisoners were serving on average about 44 percent of their court sentences. To ensure that offenders serve larger portions of their sentence, Congress authorized funding for

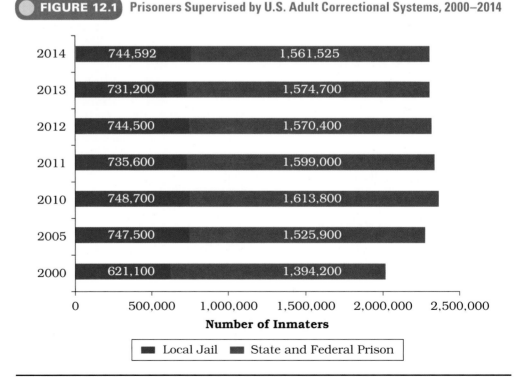

FIGURE 12.1 Prisoners Supervised by U.S. Adult Correctional Systems, 2000–2014

Source: U.S. Department of Justice, Bureau of Justice Statistics. *Correctional Populations in the United States,* 2014.

additional state prisons and jails if states met eligibility criteria for truth-in-sentencing programs.[11] To qualify, states must require violent offenders to serve at least 85 percent of their prison sentences. By 1998, 27 states and the District of Columbia qualified; 14 states have abolished early parole board release for all offenders.[12]

A philosophical shift in the purpose of incarceration also contributed to prison crowding. In response to the apparent failure of **rehabilitation** policies, the now prevailing philosophy sees prisons as places to incarcerate and punish inmates in an effort to deter crime. This philosophy has resulted in get-tough sentencing practices (including mandatory sentencing laws), which contribute to rising prison populations. Legislators have essentially removed the word *rehabilitation* from the penal code while focusing on fixed sentences. This shift from rehabilitating inmates to "just deserts" is based on the view that offenders make "free will" decisions to commit crimes and, therefore, no longer deserve compassion and "correction." U.S.

AP Photo/Nick de la Torre

Many people believe that, rather than using punishment alone, it is also important to try to rehabilitate offenders—that is, providing treatment programs to help them to recover from a criminal lifestyle or personality, substance abuse or addiction, and so on, in order to become productive citizens.

citizens, however, may be leaning more toward rehabilitative efforts. One survey found that about 72 percent of Americans "completely agree" or "mostly agree" that it is more important to try to rehabilitate people who are in prison than merely to punish them.[13]

Robert Martinson, who studied more than 200 correctional treatment programs and reported in 1973 that "almost nothing works," ignited a firestorm of debate that lasted nearly two decades.[14] Although Martinson's methodology was brought into serious question, and he later attempted to recant his findings, his assessment clearly had a major impact. Legislators and correctional administrators became unwilling to fund treatment programs from dwindling budgets, whereas academics and policy makers claimed that the medical model of correctional treatment programs failed to accomplish its goals. Paul Louis and Jerry Sparger noted that "perhaps the most lasting effect of the **'nothing works' philosophy** is the spread of cynicism and hopelessness" among prison administrators and staff members.[15]

An even greater widening between the rehabilitation and "just deserts" approaches occurred in the 1980s. Ted Palmer identified these modified positions as the "skeptical" and "sanguine" camps.[16] The skeptics believed that relatively few prison programs work and that successful ones account for only negligible reductions in recidivism. Furthermore, they believed that rehabilitation programs had not been given an adequate chance in correctional settings because they were either poorly designed or badly implemented. The sanguine perspective is that although the existing rehabilitation programs have not been very effective to date, evidence indicates that many programs provide positive treatment for selected portions of the offender population. A reassessment of Martinson's "nothing works" statement by Palmer and others has given new hope for rehabilitation. Palmer rejected Martinson's critical finding and demonstrated that many of the programs initially reviewed by Martinson were actually quite successful.[17] Other research has supported Palmer's position.[18] Still, the rehabilitative philosophy is not expected to see a resurgence in the foreseeable future.

Some observers, however, also believe that the "just deserts" logic is defeated by a combination of demography and justice system inefficiency. Each year, a new crop of youths in their upper teens constitutes the majority of those arrested for serious crimes. As these offenders are arrested and removed from the crime scene, a new crop replaces

Rehabilitation: attempts to reform an offender through vocational and educational programming, counseling, and so forth, so that he or she is not a recidivist and does not return to crime/prison.

"Nothing works" philosophy: Robert Martinson's belief, published in the 1970s, that correctional treatment programs generally do not rehabilitate offenders or significantly reduce recidivism.

them: "The justice system is eating its young. It imprisons them, paroles them, and rearrests them with no rehabilitation in between," according to prison researcher Dale Secrest.[19] Still, large-scale, long-term imprisonment unquestionably keeps truly serious offenders behind bars, preventing them from committing more crimes.

Mass Incarceration in America: Time to Rethink and Reform?

Student on the Street Video: Which country imprisons the most people?

Given the high costs of building and operating prisons and jails—as well as rising health and other related costs for inmates—it is probably difficult to hear a politician or policy maker arguing that U.S. state and federal prison or local jail populations should be expanded. Yet, we know that since the late 1970s the number of prison inmates in the United States has quadrupled. With 716 prison inmates per 100,000 population, the United States has the highest imprisonment rate in the world (the rest of the world averages about 155 inmates per 100,000). As shown in Figure 12.1, about 2.3 million persons are incarcerated in the United States, in state and federal prisons and local jails. Thirty-six U.S. states have higher incarceration rates than Cuba, the country with the second highest prison rate.[20]

Colette Monahan awaits release from Utah State Prison, where the state department of corrections and the driver's license division have set up an office for eligible offenders to obtain employment on the day of their release.

David Garland, a sociologist at New York University, coined the term **mass incarceration** in 2001, to characterize the extraordinarily high incarceration rates in the United States.[21] Together, the incarcerated population would constitute the fourth largest city in the nation (and if offenders on probation and parole were included, the population would be second only to New York City). There is no reason to doubt that such populations will continue to climb.

Michelle Alexander, Ohio State University law professor and civil rights advocate, wrote in *The New Jim Crow* (which spent 70 weeks on the *New York Times* best-seller list)[22] that mass incarceration "emerged as a stunningly comprehensive and well-disguised system of racialized social control." Alexander asserts that no other country imprisons as many of its racial or ethnic minorities. Alexander emphasizes that "nothing has contributed more to the systematic mass incarceration of people of color . . . than the War on Drugs." (*Note:* A prize-winning documentary film, *The House I Live In*, also explores the effects of U.S. drug policy on the nation's poor and minority communities.) Alexander predicts that, given current trends, one in three young African Americans will serve time in prison, and in some cities, more than half of all such men are currently under some form of correctional control.[23]

Mass incarceration: A term generally referring to what is perceived as America's disproportionately high rates of imprisonment of young, African American men; some believe it deters crime and incapacitates offenders, while others say that it weakens poor families and keep them socially marginalized.

In addition to the negative effects of one's coming out of prison with a felony record and typically few job skills, the additional effects of mass incarceration on such individuals include that for the rest of their lives, they can be denied the right to vote, automatically excluded from juries, and legally discriminated against in employment, housing, and access to education and public benefits.[24] Furthermore, mass incarceration is said to cripple families (causing home instability and food insecurity) and communities, perpetuate poverty, and institutionalize a form of racial control.[25] Many people today—like U.S. Circuit Court Judge Gerard E. Lynch—believe that we have a "vastly overinflated system of incarceration that is excessively punitive, disproportionate in its impact on the poor and minorities, exceedingly expensive, and largely irrelevant to reducing predatory crime."[26]

Video: Michelle Alexander lecture: Mass incarceration in the age of colorblindness

Should the inmate population be reduced dramatically by releasing individuals who are being held for nonviolent and drug-related crimes? Law professor and noted criminal justice expert Michael Tonry believes that no good purpose is served by sending drug-selling youths to prison for decades for being "stupid, impulsive, greedy, or unduly swayed by peers."[27] Tonry argues that "the way forward is clear": three-strikes and truth-in-sentencing laws should be repealed; mandatory minimum sentences should be narrowed in scope and severity; life-without-possibility-of-parole sentences should be repealed or substantially narrowed; every state should establish sentencing and paroling guidelines; and every state and the federal government should reduce their jail and prison populations by half by 2020.[28]

General Mission and Features

Correctional organizations are complex, hybrid organizations that utilize two distinct yet related management subsystems to achieve their goals: One is concerned primarily with managing correctional employees, and the other is concerned primarily with delivering correctional services to a designated offender population. The correctional organization, therefore, employs one group of people—correctional personnel—to work with and control another group—offenders.

The mission of correctional agencies has changed little over time. It is as follows: to protect the citizens from crime by safely and securely handling criminal offenders while providing offenders some opportunities for self-improvement and increasing the chance that they will become productive and law-abiding citizens.[29]

Video: Solitary nation

An interesting feature of the correctional organization is that *every* correctional employee who exercises legal authority over offenders is a supervisor, even if the person is the lowest-ranking member in the agency or institution. Another feature of the correctional organization is that—as with the police—everything a correctional supervisor does may have civil or criminal ramifications, both for himself or herself and for the agency or institution. Therefore, the legal and ethical responsibility for the correctional (and police) supervisor is greater than it is for supervisors in other types of organizations.

Finally, it is probably fair to say there are two different philosophies concerning what a correctional organization should be: (1) a custodial organization, which emphasizes the caretaker functions of controlling and observing inmates, and (2) a treatment organization, which emphasizes rehabilitation of inmates. These different philosophies contain potential conflict for correctional personnel.

Punishment for Some, a "Step Up" for Others

Most Americans probably assume that sending offenders to prisons and jails—depriving them of their freedom of movement and many amenities while living under an oppressive set of rules—serves a useful purpose, will bring them to the "good life," and instill in them a desire to obey the laws and avoid returning to prison after their release. In fact, experts have said that such punishments will work only under the following two conditions: (1) if they injure the offender's "social standing by the punishment," and (2) if they make "the individual feel a danger of being excluded from the group."[30]

PRACTITIONER'S PERSPECTIVE

PRISON WARDEN

Name: Robert Bayer

Current Position: Former director of corrections and prison warden; currently an adjunct professor and prison consultant

City, State: Reno, Nevada

College Attended/Academic Major: Bachelor of arts in liberal arts and master of arts in English literature from State University of New York, College at Oswego; master of public administration and PhD in political science/public administration from University of Nevada, Reno

How long have you been a practitioner in this criminal justice position? 39 years

The primary duties and responsibilities as a practitioner in this position: First, being responsible for one facility in a much larger network of facilities. To some degree, a warden can be considered as the mayor of a city and the director/commissioner is the governor of the state in which the city resides, ensuring that facility policies, procedures, and general orders are fine-tuned for that specific facility within the guidelines of the department. Additionally, the warden is usually responsible for the human resources, safety and security operations, budget development and implementation, and the institution's physical plant. He/she must manage critical incidents that arise, and has the overall responsibility to ensure a positive work and living culture exists within that facility. To accomplish all of these tasks, the warden typically will bring extensive experience to the job. A warden is one of the highest-level management positions in a prison system and represents the "boots on the ground" administrator for the entire system.

The qualities/characteristics that are most helpful in this career: The ability to be both an administrator and a leader, with a very thorough knowledge of how a prison functions and the laws, policies, and procedures promulgated by the system; the ability to see the overall big picture of corrections and how the facility functions within that picture; a comprehension of the budget process and calendar; and the ability to be politically

sensitive, personable, approachable, intelligent, hard-working, decisive, yet thoughtful. As a leader, the warden must act in a way that reflects the best traditions of the agency and be completely ethical in his or her decisions and actions. The warden should reflect all of the attributes prized in the front-line employee—loyalty, dedication, honesty, and reliability—and should instill confidence in all levels of staff and inmates. Staff wants a warden who is steady under pressure and not prone to swings in mood or behavior. Ultimately, though staff may perform an infinite variety of jobs in the facility itself, they look to the warden to ensure they have the proper orders and resources needed to keep them safe day in and day out. Finally, the warden must be a skilled communicator at all levels, with good writing and verbal skills as well as being an effective listener.

In general, this is what a _typical day_ looks like for a practitioner in this career: Various functions, but the day should cover all three shifts to foster good communication. One should be at the facility during each shift change to ensure access to staff as they leave and enter the next shift, personally greeting or chatting with the support staff before the workday begins. An early morning staff meeting with the associate wardens and the maintenance supervisor is essential, to review the last 24 hours of shift activities and develop a priority list of operational issues that need resolution. Next, items on the in-basket are reviewed, delegated, or responded to, and it is important to physically "walk the yard" (for about two hours) on a daily basis to make upper management accessible to staff and inmates and to provide the opportunity for personal observation of any issues. This is also a time to obtain firsthand feedback as to the morale, conditions, and security of the yard. Next are formally scheduled meetings with inmate families, employee group representatives, other agency representatives, etc. Time is also spent reviewing new policies, reading inmate appeals and requests, responding to correspondence, and conducting any necessary interviews of staff. Work continues after 5:00 p.m., to complete paperwork, prepare court testimony, work on difficult personnel issues, and handle budget execution and construction matters. Once a week, do a facility inspection, looking at sanitation and security compliance, while focusing on a different aspect of facility operations each week (such as fire suppression readiness).

My advice to someone either wishing to study, or now studying, criminal justice and wanting to become a practitioner in this career: Become a "triple threat" in the field, which includes a solid understanding of operations, programs, and budget; know where you are going; and study leadership, and become a leader. Try to find a competent mentor in the field who will take an interest in your career and guide you on a path of experience and education that will facilitate achieving your goals. The best administrators become leaders in our field, and to succeed one needs experience, training, and education.

Unfortunately, however, this view overlooks two very important facts—facts that are perhaps a sad commentary on the kinds of lives being led by many people in the United States:

 Video: The Interrupters

- Most serious offenders neither accept nor abide by those norms.

- Most incarcerated people today come from communities where conditions fall far below the living standards that most Americans would accept.[31]

As stated by corrections researcher Joan Petersilia, the grim fact and national shame is that for many people who go to prison, the conditions inside are not all that different from (and might even be better than) the conditions outside.[32] For some members of our society, going to prison or jail—and obtaining "three hots and a cot" (three meals and a bed)—may actually represent an *increased* standard of living. Obviously, for those individuals, the threat of imprisonment no longer represents a horrible punishment and therefore has lost much of its deterrent power. When such people go to prison, they seldom feel isolated but are likely to find friends, if not family, already there.[33]

Furthermore, it appears that prison life is not perceived as being as difficult as it once was. Inmates' actions speak loudly in this respect: More than 50 percent of today's inmates have served a prior prison term—and evidently believe the "benefits" of committing a new crime outweigh the costs of being in prison.[34]

Finally, the stigma of having a prison record is not the same as in the past, because so many of the offenders' peers and family members also have done time. Imprisonment also confers status in some neighborhoods. To many people, serving a prison term is a badge of courage. It also is their source of food, clothing, and shelter.[35]

Any discussion of jails and prisons should be prefaced with these facts concerning the inmates' world.

Classification of Inmates: A Cornerstone of Corrections

If the prison or jail experience is to carry any benefit, classifying inmates into the proper levels of housing, programming, and other aspects of their incarceration must be accomplished so as to have an influence on their behavior, treatment, and progress while in custody—as well as for the general safety of inmates and staff. Correctional staff must make **classification** decisions in at least two areas: the inmate's level of *physical restraint* or "security level," and the inmate's level of supervision or *custody grade*. These two concepts are not well understood and are often confused, but they significantly impact a prisoner's housing and program assignments,[36] as well as an institution's overall security level.

Classification (of inmates): inmate security and treatment plan based on one's security, social, vocational, psychological, and educational needs while incarcerated.

AP Photo/Rich Pedroncelli

Although there are safety and security concerns, several factors argue in favor of allowing inmates to engage in physical exercise: to teach them discipline and goal-setting, to reduce boredom, to burn off tension, and to improve their overall health and self-esteem.

The most recent development in classification is unit management, in which a large prison population is subdivided into several mini-institutions analogous to a city and its neighborhoods. Each unit has specified decision-making authority and is run by a staff of six, whose offices are on the living unit; this enables classification decisions to be made by personnel who are in daily contact with their inmates and know them fairly well.[37]

Robert Levinson delineated four categories into which correctional officials classify new inmates: security, custody, housing, and program:[38]

- *Security* needs are classified in terms of the number and types of architectural barriers that must be placed between the inmates and the outside world to ensure they will not escape and can be controlled. Most correctional systems have four security levels: supermax (highest), maximum (high), medium (low), and minimum (lowest).

- *Custody* assignments determine the level of supervision and types of privileges an inmate will have. A basic consideration is whether or not an inmate will be allowed to go outside the facility's secure perimeter, so some systems have adopted a fourfold array of custody grades—two inside the fence (one more restrictive than the other) and two outside the fence (one more closely supervised than the other).

- *Housing* needs were historically determined by an "assign to the next empty bed" system, which could place the new, weak inmate in the same cell with the most hardened inmate. A more sophisticated approach is known as internal classification, in which inmates are assigned to live with prisoners who are similar to themselves. This approach can involve the grouping of inmates into three broad categories: heavy—victimizers; light—victims; and moderate— neither intimidated by the first group nor abusers of the second.

- *Program* classification involves using interview and testing data to determine where the newly arrived inmate should be placed in work, training, and treatment programs. These programs are designed to help the prisoner make a successful return to society.

In the past, most prison systems used a highly subjective system of classifying inmates that involved a review of records pertaining to the inmate's prior social and criminal history, test scores, school and work performance, and staff impressions developed from interviews. Today, however, administrators employ a much-preferred objective system that is more rational, efficient, and equitable. Factors used in making classification decisions are measurable and valid, and are applied to all inmates in the same way. Criteria most often used are escape history, any detainers (requests filed with the institution holding an inmate asking that the jurisdiction hold the prisoner for that agency, or notify the agency when release of the prisoner is about to occur), prior commitments, criminal history, prior institutional adjustment, history of violence, and length of sentence.[39]

STATE PRISONS AS ORGANIZATIONS

As noted earlier in this chapter, the mission of most prisons is to provide a safe and secure environment for staff and inmates, as well as programs for offenders that can assist them after release.[40] This section describes how **state prisons** are organized to accomplish this mission. First is a look at the larger picture—the typical organization of the central office within the state government that oversees *all* prisons within its jurisdiction—and then a look at the characteristic organization of an individual prison.

Over time, prison organizational structures (see Figure 12.2) have changed considerably. Until the beginning of the 20th century, prisons were administered by state boards of charities, boards composed of citizens, boards of inspectors, state prison commissions, or individual prison keepers. Most prisons were individual provinces; wardens, who were given absolute control over their domain, were appointed by governors through a system of political patronage. Individuals were attracted to the position of **warden** because it carried many fringe benefits, such as a lavish residence, unlimited inmate servants, food and supplies from institutional farms and warehouses, furnishings, and a personal automobile. Now most wardens or superintendents are civil service employees who have earned their position through seniority and merit.[41] We discuss the warden's position more later in this chapter.

Video: Prison state

State prison: a correctional facility that houses convicted felons.

Warden: the chief administrator of a federal penitentiary or state prison.

● **FIGURE 12.2** **Organizational Structure for a Maximum-Security Prison**

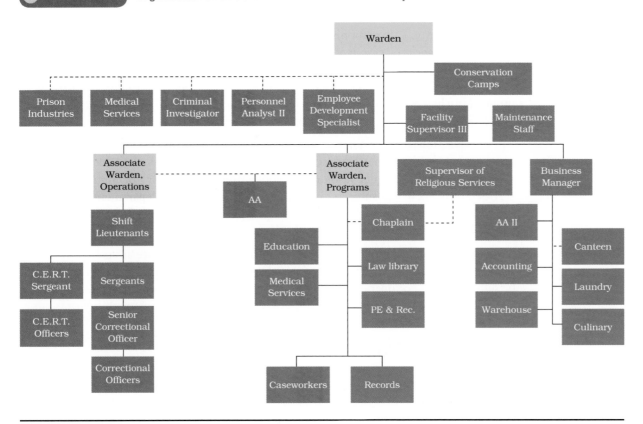

Notes: AA = administrative aide; C.E.R.T. = correctional emergency response team; PE & Rec. = physical education and recreation.

Reporting to the warden are deputy or associate wardens, each of whom supervises a department within the prison. The deputy warden for operations will typically oversee correctional security, unit management, the inmate disciplinary committee, and recreation. The deputy warden for special services will typically be responsible for the library, mental health services, drug and alcohol recovery services, education, prison job assignments, religious services, and prison industries. The deputy warden for administration will manage the business office, prison maintenance, laundry, food service, medical services, prison farms, and the issuance of clothing.[42]

We now discuss correctional security, unit management, education, and penal industries in greater detail:

Author Video: Prisons and jails as productive places

- The correctional security department is usually the largest department in a prison, with 50 to 70 percent of all staff. It supervises all of the security activities within a prison, including any special housing units, inmate transportation, and the inmate disciplinary process. Security staff wear military-style uniforms; a captain typically runs each 8-hour shift, lieutenants often are responsible for an area of the prison, and sergeants oversee the rank-and-file correctional staff.

- The unit management concept was originated by the federal prison system in the 1970s and now is used in nearly every state to control prisons by providing a "small, self-contained, inmate living and staff office area that operates semi-autonomously within the larger institution."[43] The purpose of unit management is twofold: to decentralize the administration of the prison and to enhance communication among staff and between staff and inmates. Unit management breaks the prison into more manageable sections based on housing assignments; assignment of staff to a particular unit; and staff authority to make decisions, manage the unit, and deal directly with inmates. Units are usually composed of 200 to 300 inmates; staff members are assigned to specific units, and their offices are located in the housing area, making them more accessible to inmates and better able to monitor inmate activities and behavior. Directly reporting to the unit manager are "case managers," or social workers, who develop the program of work and rehabilitation for each inmate and write progress reports for parole authorities, classification, or transfer to another prison. Correctional counselors also work with inmates in the units on daily issues, such as finding a prison job, working with their prison finances, and creating a visiting and telephone list.[44]

- Education departments operate the academic teaching, vocational training, library services, and sometimes recreation programs for inmates. An education department is managed in similar fashion to a conventional elementary or high school, with certified teachers for all subjects that are required by the state department of education or are part of the General Educational Development (GED) test. Vocational training can include carpentry, landscaping or horticulture, food service, and office skills.

- **Prison industries** are legislatively chartered as separate government corporations and report directly to the warden because there is often a requirement that the industry be self-supporting or operate from funds generated from the sale of products. Generally, no tax dollars are used to run the programs, and there is strict accountability of funds.

FEDERAL PRISONS

Prison industries: use of prison and jail inmates to produce goods or provide services for a public agency or private corporation.

The Federal Bureau of Prisons (BOP) was established in 1930 to provide care for federal inmates. Today, the BOP has more than 36,000 employees and consists of 119 institutions and nearly 220,000 federal offenders.[45] Approximately 80 percent of these inmates are confined in BOP-operated facilities, while the remainder are confined in privately managed or community-based facilities and local jails.[46]

Prison Types and General Information

The BOP operates institutions at five different security levels in order to confine offenders in an appropriate manner. Security levels are based on such features as the presence of external patrols, towers, security barriers, or detection devices; the type of housing within the institution; internal security features; and the staff-to-inmate ratio. Each facility is designated as minimum, low, medium, high, or correctional complex.

Minimum Security

Minimum-security institutions, also known as federal prison camps, have dormitory housing, a relatively low staff-to-inmate ratio, and limited or no perimeter fencing. These institutions are work and program oriented, and many are located adjacent to larger institutions or on military bases, where inmates help serve the labor needs of the larger institution or base.

Low Security

Low-security federal correctional institutions have double-fenced perimeters, mostly dormitory or cubicle housing, and strong work and program components. The staff-to-inmate ratio in these institutions is higher than in minimum-security facilities.

Medium Security

Medium-security correctional institutions and penitentiaries designated to house medium-security inmates have strengthened perimeters (often double fences with electronic detection systems), mostly cell-type housing, a wide variety of work and treatment programs, an even higher staff-to-inmate ratio than low-security federal correctional institutions, and even greater internal controls.

High Security

High-security institutions, also known as U.S. penitentiaries, have highly secured perimeters (featuring walls or reinforced fences), multiple- and single-occupant cell housing, the highest staff-to-inmate ratio, and close control of inmate movement.

Correctional Complexes

A number of BOP institutions belong to federal correctional complexes, where institutions with different missions and security levels are located in proximity to one another. Examples would include administrative facilities such as for the detention of pretrial offenders; the treatment of inmates with serious or chronic medical problems; or the containment of extremely dangerous, violent, or escape-prone inmates.

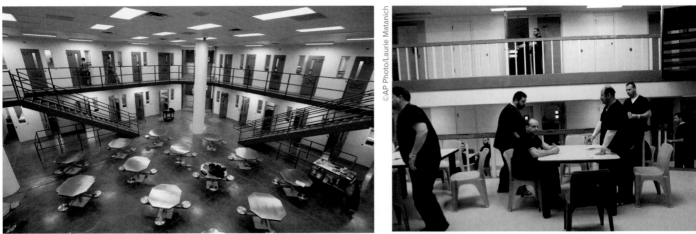

Prison housing units vary, but they usually consist of 200–300 inmates and place staff members in the housing area, to be more accessible to inmates and better able to monitor their activities and behavior.

In addition, a number of BOP institutions have a small, minimum-security camp adjacent to the main facility. These camps, often referred to as satellite camps, provide inmate labor to the main institution and to off-site work programs.

A Career With BOP

Probably differing from the majority of local jails and state prisons, the BOP has exceptionally high standards one must meet in order to obtain a position. For consideration at the federal civil service GS-05 level, possession of a bachelor's degree from an accredited college or university is required; or, one may be hired if in possession of at least three years of full-time related experience. To be considered for a GS-06 level position, the candidate must possess 9 semester hours or 14 quarter hours of graduate study, from an accredited school, in criminal justice, criminology, social science, or another related field such as law; or, one must possess one year of specialized experience equivalent in difficulty and complexity to the next lower grade level in federal service.[47]

©Lizzie Himmel/Sygma/Corbis

The "Administrative Maximum" prison, or ADX, located in Florence, Colorado, is the only federal supermax in the nation.

Community Corrections in the Federal System

Parole was abolished in the federal prison system in 1987, when the federal sentencing guidelines went into effect (discussed in Chapter 11). Since then, inmates can have no more than 54 days a year subtracted from a federal sentence, commencing after the person has served 12 months; this policy was upheld in 2010 by the U.S. Supreme Court.[48] Nonetheless, the BOP is actively supporting and using community-corrections techniques.

SUPERMAX PRISONS

Super-maximum—or "supermax"—prisons represent the most secure form of incarceration now in existence in the United States and abroad (although they are given different names in other countries). They began to proliferate in the United States in the mid-1980s as a means of holding extremely disruptive or violent inmates. Such prisons have not been without controversy, however, and this chapter section includes a brief history, some research findings on effects on inmates, and some constitutional questions that have been raised.

Origin and Operation

Supermax prisons exist in both state and federal prison systems and effectively originated in 1983 in Marion, Illinois, when two correctional officers were murdered by inmates on the same day and the warden put the prison in "permanent lockdown." Thus began 23-hour-a-day cell isolation and no communal yard time for inmates, who were also not permitted to work, attend educational programs, or eat in a cafeteria.[49]

Today 40 states operate supermax prisons in the United States.[50] To understand what supermax prisons are and how they operate, one can look at the "Administrative Maximum" prison, or ADX, located in Florence, Colorado, 90 miles south of Denver.

ADX is the only federal supermax in the country (the others are state prisons). It is home to a "who's who" of criminals: "Unabomber" Ted Kaczynski; "Shoe Bomber"

Supermax prison: a penal institution that, for security purposes, affords inmates very few if any amenities and a great amount of isolation.

Richard Reid; Ramzi Yousef, who plotted the 1993 World Trade Center attack; Oklahoma City bomber Terry Nichols; and Olympic Park bomber Eric Rudolph. Ninety-five percent of the prisoners at ADX, known as the "Alcatraz of the Rockies," are the most violent, disruptive, and escape-prone inmates from other federal prisons. Upon viewing its external aspect for the first time, one immediately sees that this is not the usual prison: Large cables are strung above the basketball courts and track; they are helicopter deterrents.[51]

Video: Life in a supermax prison

Supermax inmates rarely leave their cells; in most such prisons, an hour a day of out-of-cell time is the norm. Inmates eat all of their meals alone in the cells, and typically no group or social activity of any kind is permitted. They are also typically denied access to vocational or educational training programs. Inmates can exist for many years separated from the natural world around them.[52]

Clearly, as shown in Table 12.1, wardens themselves believe that supermax prisons provide a high degree of safety for staff and inmates.

Effects on Inmates

Given the high degree of isolation and lack of activities in supermax prisons, a major concern voiced by critics of these facilities is their "social pathology" and potential effect on inmates' mental health. Although there is very little research to date concerning the effects of supermax confinement,[53] some authors point to previous isolation research that shows greater levels of deprivation lead to psychological, emotional, and physical problems. For example, studies show that as inmates face greater restrictions and social deprivations, their levels of social withdrawal increase; limiting human contact, autonomy, goods, or services is detrimental to inmates' health and rehabilitative prognoses, and tends to result in depression, hostility, severe anger, sleep disturbances, and anxiety. Women living in a high-security unit have been found to experience claustrophobia, chronic rage reactions, depression, hallucinatory symptoms, withdrawal, and apathy.[54]

TABLE 12.1 Wardens' Views of Supermax Prisons

SUPERMAX PRISONS . . .	SOUTH (%)	NORTHEAST (%)	WEST (%)	MIDWEST (%)	TOTAL (%)
Increase safety throughout prison system	99.1	97.7	97.7	97.5	98.4
Increase order throughout prison system	98.1	100.0	96.6	96.7	97.7
Increase control over prison system	97.5	100.0	98.9	95.9	97.6
Incapacitate violent/disruptive inmates	95.3	100.0	94.2	95.0	95.4
Improve inmate behavior in prison system	86.2	86.4	77.9	80.3	83.7
Decrease prison riots	86.1	81.4	79.3	75.2	82.4
Decrease influence of gangs in prisons	80.4	90.9	84.9	68.6	79.4
Reduce prison escapes	81.1	74.4	57.5	55.7	71.6
Punish violent and disruptive inmates	49.7	54.5	42.5	52.1	49.5
Reduce recidivism of violent/disruptive inmates	47.2	38.6	48.8	42.1	45.7
Rehabilitate violent/disruptive inmates	37.0	36.4	38.4	34.7	36.7
Deter crime in society	28.3	18.6	24.7	15.6	24.3

Note: *N*s for each question ranged from 567 to 575. In the total sample (*N* = 601), the distribution of wardens across regions was as follows: 45 in the Northeast, 130 in the Midwest, 335 in the South, and 91 in the West.

Source: From Daniel P. Mears, "A Critical Look at Supermax Prisons," *Corrections Compendium* (published by the American Corrections Assn.), September /October 2005, p. 46. Reprinted with permission of the American Correctional Association, Alexandria, VA.

THE WORLD'S WORST PRISONS

Certainly any attempt to catalog the worst prisons in the world will be open to serious debate, and the list provided here of five such prisons is no exception. However, as will be seen, these are included (in no particular order) for very good reasons:

- *La Santé, France:* This institution, the last remaining prison in Paris, was established in 1867. Its mattresses are infested with lice; because prisoners can take only two cold showers per week, skin diseases are common. Overcrowded cells, infestation of vermin, and inmate rape are also common. Its rate of suicide attempts each year is estimated to be almost five times higher than that of California's prison system. Its conditions have been condemned by the United Nations Human Rights Committee and the country's own minister of justice.

- *Black Beach, Equatorial Guinea:* Amnesty International has described life in this prison as a slow, lingering death sentence. Torture, burning, beatings, and rape are systematic and brutal. Because food rations are minimal, with prisoners sometimes going up to six days without food, starving to death is common. Amnesty also reports that inmates are routinely denied access to medical treatment.

- *Vladimir Central Prison, Russia:* Constructed by Catherine the Great to house political prisoners, during the Soviet era the prison became synonymous with persecution of political dissidents. Today the prison also functions as a museum for the public. Visitors are not allowed into the penitentiary, where cells often contain

six prisoners and reports of abuse by guards are common. HIV and tuberculosis are also rampant.

- *Camp 1391, Israel:* Officially, this prison does not exist, but descriptions of its conditions have been validated. Even the Red Cross is banned from visiting, and prisoners typically have no idea where they are being kept or when they might be released—a fact that former inmates say is the worst torture of all. Sexual humiliation and even rape are reportedly used as interrogation techniques.

- *The North Korean Gulag:* Up to 200,000 prisoners are held in these detention centers, and one houses more than 50,000 inmates. Entire families and even neighborhoods are sent here as punishment for the infraction of one member. In some camps, up to 25 percent of the prisoners die every year, only to be replaced by new inmates. Most of the camps are located along the North Korean border with China and Russia; thus, prisoners are forced to endure harsh weather conditions as well as inhumane treatment.

Again, any such list is debatable given harsh prison conditions in many places around the world; prisons and/or labor camps in China, Thailand, Cuba, Venezuela, Syria, Africa, and other venues could easily have been included.[58]

Source: Greg Shtraks, "The List: The World's Most Notorious Prisons," *Foreign Policy*, January 21, 2009, http://www.foreignpolicy.com/articles/2009/01/20/the_list_the_worlds_most_notorious_prisons.

Some researchers argue that supermax facilities are not effective management tools for controlling violence and disturbances within prisons, nor are they effective in reducing violence or disturbances within the general population; they conclude that supermax prisons should not be used for their current purpose.[55]

Constitutionality

Because of the relatively recent origin of supermax prisons, their constitutionality has been tested in only a few cases. The first, *Madrid v. Gomez* (1995), addressed conditions of confinement in California's Pelican Bay Security Housing Unit.[56] The judge observed that its image was "hauntingly similar to that of caged felines pacing in a zoo"; however, the judge concluded that he lacked any constitutional basis to close the prison. In the most recent case, *Jones-El v. Berge* (2004), a federal district court in Wisconsin concluded that "extremely isolating conditions . . . cause SHU [Security Housing Unit] syndrome in relatively healthy prisoners . . . Supermax is not appropriate for seriously mentally ill inmates."[57] The judge ordered several prisoners to be removed from the supermax facility.

JAILS AS ORGANIZATIONS

Across the United States, approximately 3,316 jails are administered locally.[59] As indicated in Figure 12.1 earlier in the chapter, these institutions hold over 740,000 prisoners. The primary purposes of local jails are (1) to hold accused law violators who cannot post bond so as to ensure their appearance at trial, and (2) to hold those persons convicted of lesser offenses until they complete their court-ordered sentences.

The incarceration of persons charged with crimes and awaiting trial, as well as some persons serving sentences for lesser offenses, distinguishes local jails from state and federal prisons. Whereas prisons house persons convicted of more serious offenses—usually felons with sentences of a year or more—jails generally hold persons charged with misdemeanors for up to a year.[60] Jail organization and hierarchical levels are determined by several factors: size, budget, level of crowding, local views toward punishment and treatment, and even the levels of training and education of the jail administrator. An organizational structure for a jail serving a population of about 250,000 is suggested in Figure 12.3.

The New Generation/Direct Supervision Jail

Federal courts have at times abandoned their traditional hands-off doctrine toward prison and jail administration, largely in response to the deplorable conditions and inappropriate treatment of inmates (discussed in more detail in Chapter 13). The courts became more willing to hear inmate allegations of constitutional violations ranging from inadequate heating, lighting, and ventilation to the censorship of mail.[61]

In response to lawsuits and to improve conditions, many local jurisdictions explored new ideas and designed new jail facilities. The first **new generation/direct supervision jail** opened in the 1970s in Contra Costa County, California. This facility quickly became a success, was deemed cost-effective to build and safer for inmates and staff, and carried several advantages: Officers "live" with the inmates and are encouraged to mingle with them and to provide them privileges and activities (thus increasing good behavior and reducing idleness) while being better able to control inmate movement. As a result, there is a low level of tension in the unit, as fights are broken up quickly, weapons are not involved, and sexual assaults are almost nonexistent. Bathroom and shower areas are monitored closely, and noise levels are low due to the architecture and close supervision.[62] To the extent possible, symbols of incarceration are removed in these new jails, which have no bars in the living units; windows are generally provided in every prisoner's room; and padded carpets, movable furniture, and colorful wall coverings are used to reduce the facility's institutional atmosphere. Inmates are to be divided into small groups of approximately 40 to 50 for housing purposes. All of these facility features were designed to reduce the "trauma" of incarceration.[63] Figure 12.4 provides three views of how new generation/direct supervision jails are configured.

SAGE Journal Article: New generation jails

New generation/direct supervision jail: jails that, by their architecture and design, eliminate many of the traditional features of a jail, allowing staff members greater interaction and control.

FIGURE 12.3 Organization Structure for Jail Serving County of 250,000 Population

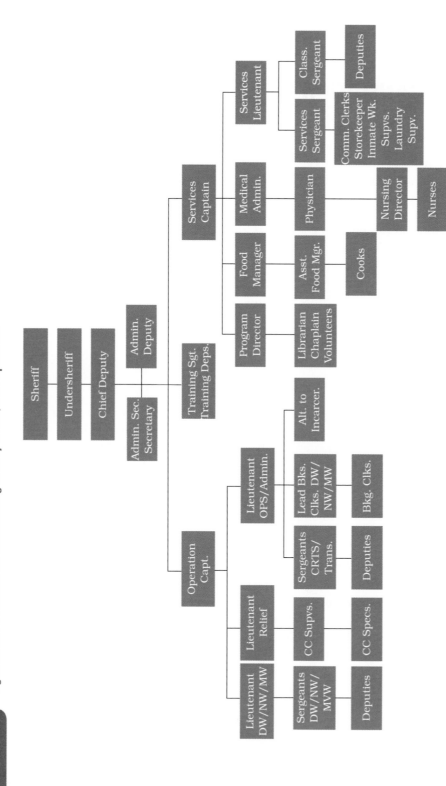

Note: DW = day watch; NW = night watch; MW = mid watch; CC = conservation camps; CRTS/Trans = court transportation; OPS/Admin = operation/administration; Comm. Clerks = commissary clerks.

FIGURE 12.4 Direct Supervision Jails

Jails can have a combination of design styles – Jails that are not predominantly direct supervision in design or management can have an addition or section of inmate housing that uses direct supervision.

- **Podular/direct supervision jails** – Inmates' cells are arranged around a common area, usually called a "dayroom." An officer is stationed in the pod with the inmates. The officer moves about the pod and interacts with the inmates to manage their behavior. There is no secure control booth for the supervising officer, and there are no physical barriers between the officer and the inmates. The officer may have a desk or table for paperwork, but it is in the open dayroom area.

- **Linear/intermittent supervision jails** – Includes jails with cells arranged along the sides of a cell block. Officers come into the housing unit on scheduled rounds or as needed to interact with the inmates.

- **Podular/remote supervision jails** – Includes jails that have a podular design with cells around a dayroom, but no officer is permanently stationed inside the pod. Indirect supervision is provided through remote monitoring at a console.

Source: U.S. Department of Justice, National Institute of Corrections, *Direct Supervision Jails: 2006 Yearbook*, p. vii, http://nicic.org/Downloads/PDF/Library/021968.pdf.

Jail Programs

Rehabilitation and reintegration are considered secondary goals of local jails; however, many of them provide a wide array of programs for inmates, such as the following that are provided by the Washington County, Oregon, Sheriff's Office:[64]

- Religious services and life-based skills

- Drug and alcohol prevention groups

- Substance abuse classes

- Cognitive and behavioral groups targeting violence prevention, personal control, and problem solving skills

- Women's groups on anger management and domestic violence prevention

- Life skills classes in parenting, computer skills, and finding and keeping employment

- GED testing preparation

- GED completion

- Individual tutoring

- Credit recovery

- High school completion

- English-as-a-second-language (ESL) classes

Making Jails Productive Through Labor

The 1984 Justice Assistance Act removed some of the long-standing restrictions on interstate commerce of prisoner-made goods. By 1987, private-sector work programs were under way in 14 state correctional institutions and two county jails.[65] Today, many inmates in U.S. jails are involved in productive work. Some simply work to earn privileges, and others earn wages applied to their custodial costs and compensation to crime victims. Some hone new job skills, improving their chances for success following release. At one end of the continuum is the "trusty" (an inmate requiring a low security level) who mows the grass in front of the jail and thereby earns privileges; at the other end are jail inmates working for private industry for real dollars.[66] Some

©Rick Loomis/Los Angeles Times/Getty Images

Jail and prison inmate work programs can afford several benefits, such as earning privileges and wages (including restitution to their victims), honing new job skills, and improving their chances for success following release. These Washington state inmates make mini frozen pizzas.

jails have work programs involving training in dog grooming, auto detailing, food service, book mending, mailing service, painting, printing, carpet installation, and upholstering.

TECHNOLOGIES IN CORRECTIONAL FACILITIES: THE GOOD AND THE BAD

As with police and court systems, technologies are used in jails and prisons to provide a greater degree of safety for both officers and inmates, and thus to improve efficiency and effectiveness of correctional practices.

Video: High-tech jail in the 21st century

Coping With Riots

Since the beginning of institutional confinement there has been a need for correctional officers to possess tactics and equipment to handle outbreaks of violence among inmates. Although full-scale riots are rare in American prisons, potentially violent situations (such as inmates' refusing to leave their cells) can occur almost daily.

Today there are wall-climbing reconnaissance robots and "sound cannons" designed to sweep rioters into a corner or stun them with a blast of noise. Also in use are a Hydro-Force fogger (a cross between a fire extinguisher and a can of Mace); a rolling barrier with wheels and side shields that prevents officers from being struck by thrown objects;[67] and a "stinger" grenade that explodes and emits dozens of hard rubber pellets and is particularly useful in a cafeteria or yard riot.

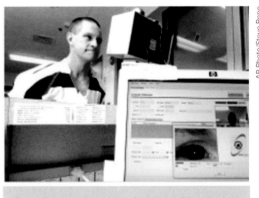

Retinal eye scanners are being used in prisons to ensure that inmates do not swap identities in order to escape.

AP Photo/Steve Pope

You Be the... WARDEN

Both adults and juvenile offenders in correctional institutions in several states are required to wear Global Positioning System (GPS) devices on their wrists to track their locations at all times. Following are some of the anticipated benefits:

- An alarm will sound if an inmate enters an off-limits area or tries to escape.
- In the case of a prison brawl, the devices will show the correctional staff who was in the area where the fight occurred.
- If an inmate claims to have been assaulted by a prison guard, there will be a record of whether the inmate was at the correctional officer's post.
- It is also expected that the devices will substantially increase the level of control without increasing staff.

Some civil libertarians and youth advocates have concerns about the bracelets, however, because the

technology is far from flawless. In many jurisdictions, false alarms have strained personnel and called into question the effectiveness of the tracking tool. One state found more than 35,000 false alerts by 140 subjects wearing the GPS devices. Another concern is that the tool could be used as evidence against persons who are not involved in crimes. However, supporters say the program represents one piece of a broader crime-prevention strategy that includes a bike patrol to monitor gang hot spots and funding to support people who want to escape gang life.

1. What do you believe? Does the need for security justify adults and youths in prisons being monitored so closely via these bracelets?

2. Or, conversely, do privacy issues—and the technical problems involved—override the institutions' security interests?

Source: Adapted from Associated Press, "Prison Inmates to Wear GPS Tracking Bracelets," *Reno Gazette Journal*, June 13, 2006, p. C6.

Correctional officers often train with such devices in full view of the inmates to demonstrate the kinds of tools that can be employed. According to one prison administrator, what separates prison professionals from inmates is constant training as well as measured, unflappable control.[68]

Offender Programming and Management

Technology is changing the methods of offender management through the use of web-based systems that provide educational programs to prisoners, treat prisoners who are addicted to drugs or are sex offenders, and provide vocational training. Prison administrators now keep accurate records of inmates' purchases for items in the prison store, payments to victims and their families, and other reasons for which money flows in and out of prisoners' bank accounts.[69] Automated systems also control access gates and doors, individual cell doors, and the climate in cells and other areas of the prison. Correctional agencies have also used computers to conduct presentence investigations, supervise offenders in the community, and train correctional personnel. With computer assistance, jail administrators receive daily reports on court schedules, inmate rosters, time served, statistical reports, maintenance costs, and other data.

The "You Be the Warden" box describes how offenders are now being tracked using GPS bracelets.

"Virtual Visits" to Hospitals and Courtrooms

Prison and jail inmates make frequent visits to hospitals and courtrooms, which creates public safety concerns. In Ohio alone, 40,000 inmate trips to and from medical facilities were eliminated because videoconferencing technology—virtual visits—made medical consultations available from within the institution. An onsite prison physician or nurse assists with the physical part of the examination, taking cues from the offsite specialist via video and relaying information such as electrocardiogram and blood pressure data.[70]

INVESTIGATING FURTHER

A BAD COMBINATION: CELL PHONES AND DRONES

Although prisons are now more high-tech than ever before—able to employ video monitoring, GPS devices worn on wrists, biometric entry points that scan an inmate's iris or fingerprints, and even remote medical tools so that inmates receive virtual checkups from doctors—the benefits provided by these enhancements can be overcome when technologies are used for illegitimate purposes. For example, since drones have become cheaper and thus more widespread, their use to smuggle contraband into prisons has become a worldwide problem. Drugs, cell phones, SIM cards, batteries, and small LCD screens have been dropped into prisons in Thailand, Canada, Russia, Brazil, and England, among other locations.[71] In late 2013, four persons were arrested and face 20 years in prison for using a drone to drop tobacco products into Calhoun State Prison in Morgan, Georgia.[72]

The increased smuggling of cell phones into prisons now poses serious problems. Inmates contact people outside of prison to organize crimes and escapes, retaliate against other inmates, threaten witnesses, transmit photographs, and bribe prison officers.[73] Following are some examples:

- In South Carolina, a prisoner ordered a hit on a prison guard (he was shot at his home but survived).[74]

- A Kansas inmate allegedly used a phone smuggled in by an accomplice to escape.[75]

- A Texas death row inmate allegedly used a phone inside the prison to threaten a state senator and his family[76]

The problem is not insignificant: A sweep in a Vacaville, California, prison resulted in more than 2,000 cell phones being confiscated.[77] In some prisons, cell phones are even more valuable than drugs, with undercover officers being offered much more money to bring in phones than for heroin.

Prisons are trying to fight back with full body scanners to detect cell phones carried on inmates' bodies. However, their bigger goal—using equipment to jam the wireless cell phone signals—has been frustrated by legal impediments. In 2009, the U.S. Senate passed the Safe Prisons Communications Act, which would have allowed prison officials to jam wireless telephone communication signals; however, the bill died in the House of Representatives. Although the Federal Communications Commission has finally agreed to consider changing its rules to address the serious problem, the wireless industry and some public safety groups have opposed jamming for fear it would interfere with commercial and public safety wireless services.[78] For the present time, the legality of prisons being able to jam prisoner cell phones remains in doubt.

IN A
NUTSHELL

- Erving Goffman described the characteristics of "total institutions." His definition seems to capture the essence of correctional organizations. Unfortunately, most of what the public "knows" about prisons and jails is probably obtained through Hollywood's fictional versions.

- Sending people to prisons and jails is intended to serve a useful purpose. However, for many inmates, the conditions inside are not all that different from (and might even be better than) the conditions outside. Indeed, for some members of society, going to prison or jail may represent an increased standard of living.

- Several factors affect prison and jail populations. First is the nation's drug problem. Other commonly cited factors include truth-in-sentencing laws, violence on television and in the movies, and a general deterioration of morals and of the family. The nation has simply become more punitive in nature. Robert Martinson's well-publicized finding in 1973 that "almost nothing works" in correctional treatment programs also spelled the demise of the rehabilitative era.

- Mass incarceration is said to be a form of racialized social control, primarily affecting people of color, resulting in the imprisonment of large numbers of minorities for nonviolent drug offenses, and taking a huge toll on such individuals (in terms of rights lost) as well as minority families.

- Correctional organizations are complex, hybrid organizations that utilize two related management subsystems to achieve their goals: One is managing correctional employees, and the other is concerned primarily with delivering correctional services to a designated offender population.

- The mission of correctional agencies has changed little over time. It is to protect the citizens from crime by safely and securely handling criminal offenders while providing offenders some opportunities for self-improvement and increasing the chance that they will become productive and law-abiding citizens.

- Today, many inmates in U.S. jails are involved in productive work. Some simply work to earn privileges, and others earn wages applied to their custodial costs and compensation to crime victims. Some hone new job skills, improving their chances for success following release.

- The correctional security department is typically the largest department in a prison, with 50 to 70 percent of all staff. It supervises all of the security activities within a prison.

- The unit management concept was originated by the federal prison system in the 1970s, to control prisons by providing a "small, self-contained, inmate living and staff office area that operates semi-autonomously within the larger institution." Unit management breaks the prison into more manageable sections based on housing assignments.

- Education departments operate the academic teaching, vocational training, library services, and sometimes recreation programs for inmates.

- Prison industries are separate government corporations that provide meaningful, productive employment that helps to reduce inmate idleness and supplies companies with a readily available and dependable source of labor.

- Correctional staff must make classification decisions in at least two areas: the inmate's level of *physical restraint* or "security level," and the inmate's level of supervision or *custody grade.*

- The Federal Bureau of Prisons operates institutions at five different security levels in order to confine offenders in an appropriate manner. Security levels are based on such features as the presence of external patrols, towers, security barriers, or detection devices; the type of housing within the institution; internal security features; and the staff-to-inmate ratio. Each facility is designated as minimum, low, medium, high, or correctional complexes.

- Supermax prison operations are quite different from traditional prisons. Inmates rarely leave their cells; they eat all of their meals alone in the cells, and typically no group or social activity of any kind is permitted; and they are typically denied access to vocational or educational training programs. Although little research has examined the effects of supermax confinement, some authors point to previous isolation research that shows greater levels of deprivation lead to psychological, emotional, and physical problems.

- Technological developments have improved the operations and safety of correctional institutions, while also raising some privacy concerns.

- The primary purpose of jails is to hold accused law violators who cannot post bond to ensure their appearance at trial, and to hold those persons convicted of lesser offenses until they complete their court-ordered sentences.

- The term *new generation jail* refers to a style of architecture and inmate management that is totally new and unique to local detention facilities. There is a greater level of personal safety for both staff and inmates, greater staff satisfaction, more orderly and relaxed inmate housing areas, and a better maintained physical plant; these facilities are also cost-effective to construct and to operate.

- A wide array of rehabilitative and reintegrative programs are in use for jail inmates.

KEY TERMS & CONCEPTS

▶ Review key terms with eFlashcards. $SAGE edge™

Classification (of inmates), 299
Jail, 293
Mass incarceration, 296
New generation/direct supervision jail, 307

"Nothing works" philosophy, 295
Prison, 293
Prison industries, 302
Rehabilitation, 295

State prison, 301
Supermax prison, 304
Warden, 301

REVIEW QUESTIONS

▶ Test your understanding of chapter content. Take the practice quiz. $SAGE edge™

1. What factors affect prison and jail populations?

2. What is meant by mass incarceration, and what are its causes?

3. What prison reform efforts have occurred in the past?

4. What is the general mission of a correctional organization?

5. How is it that, for many members of our society, being incarcerated is not "punishment" but rather an improved lifestyle?

6. What is the basic purpose underlying prison inmate classification?

7. What are the basic elements of the federal prison system?

8. How would you describe supermax prisons and how they differ from conventional prisons?

9. How do jails differ in structure and functions from prisons, what programs are provided for inmate rehabilitation, and how does the new generation jail differ from the traditional model?

1. Assume you are on a high school recruiting trip for your university's criminal justice department, and a member of a student group mentions that he wishes to major in criminal justice. He is motivated to do so by an uncle who is "serving a three- to five-year *jail* sentence for *robbing* people's homes while they were away at work." Because he is overheard by the group, you wish to tactfully correct his misuse of the terms *jail* and *robbery*. What will you say?

2. You are assigned as part of a "Current Correctional Practices" class project to explain the differences between supermax prisons and traditional prisons. What will be your response?

3. Your criminal justice professor assigns the class to prepare a paper on the major differences between state prisons and local jails, including their structure and function. How will you delineate the differences between them?

STUDY
SITE

⑤SAGE edge™

Review → Practice → Improve

Sharpen your skills with **SAGE edge** at **edge.sagepub.com/peak2e**

SAGE edge for students provides a personalized approach to help you accomplish your coursework goals in an easy-to-use learning environment. Access the videos, audio clips, quizzes, and SAGE journal articles that are noted in this chapter.

THE INMATES' WORLD
The "Keepers" and the "Kept"

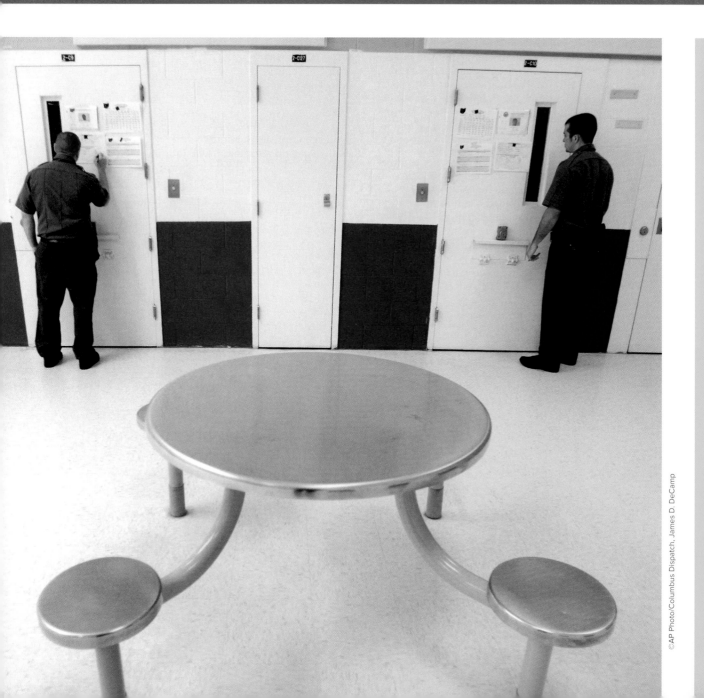

LEARNING OBJECTIVES

As a result of reading this chapter, you will be able to:

1 Describe the deprivations, effects, and prisonization caused by places of confinement

2 Explain the conditions of regular and solitary confinement, and the underground economy that inmates use to make their detention less unpleasant

3 Review the general duties of prison and jail staff members, including some sage advice for institutional governance

4 Illustrate the unique challenges posed for prison governance by litigation, drugs, and gangs, as well as by female, mentally ill, geriatric, and death row inmates

5 Describe some important measures that can be taken to assist with inmates' reentry and aftercare

6 Describe several major federal court decisions that greatly expanded prisoners' rights

ASSESS YOUR AWARENESS

Test your knowledge of prison inmates and employees by responding to the following seven true-false items; check your answers after reading this chapter's materials.

1 Under our system of justice, it may be said that incarcerated persons are not to suffer pains beyond the deprivation of liberty; confinement itself is the punishment.

2 The warden's philosophies regarding security and treatment will have a major impact on prison inmates and staff.

3 Today, the courts generally follow a hands-off policy regarding prison and jail administration, allowing them to run their institutions as they see fit.

4 Supreme Court decisions support the notion that there exists an "iron curtain" between the U.S. Constitution and the prisons—that is, inmates have no rights.

5 Federal legislation has greatly reduced litigation by inmates.

6 Prisonization, a process whereby an inmate takes on the value system of the prison and its culture, actually helps to rehabilitate the offender.

7 As with the police, prisons subscribe to the paramilitary system, having ranks, division of labor, and so on.

[Correctional administrators] undoubtedly must take into account the very real threat unrest presents to inmates and officials alike, in addition to the possible harm to inmates. To resolve a disturbance . . . we think the question whether the measure taken inflicted unnecessary and wanton pain and suffering ultimately turns on whether force was applied in a good-faith effort to maintain or restore discipline or maliciously and sadistically for the very purpose of causing harm.

—*Whitley v. Albers* (1986)[1]

Boredom is beautiful.

—Former Nevada prison warden

<< Answers can be found on page 424.

Ohio inmate Whitney Lee had undergone continuous hormone therapy for a dozen years, but the prison abruptly halted the treatments in 2012. Lee sued, saying she suffered a medical setback and depression when the treatments stopped. After a two-day hearing, Judge Algenon Marbley ordered the state on Friday to permanently continue the treatments.

Antione Lee, who began dressing as a woman as a teenager and had been living as a woman since age 18, was housed with men at Ohio's Mansfield Correctional Institution, serving three years for forgery and theft. Lee, who goes by the name Whitney, had undergone continuous hormone therapy since 1999—at home, in jail, and in federal prison—until the Department of Rehabilitation and Correction abruptly halted the treatments in February 2012. Without the treatments, Lee argued, she lost breast tissue, her voice deepened, facial hair began growing, and she became irritable and angry (eventually being placed on suicide watch). However, the prisons department argued that it halted the therapy because Lee didn't exhaust the prison grievance procedures and thus the case should be dismissed. As you read this chapter, consider the legal (inmate's) and practical (prison's) issues presented in this case, and which side should prevail: the prison's legitimate security interests or the inmate's liberty and First Amendment rights. The outcome of the inmate's appeal is given in the Notes section.[2]

INTRODUCTION

In 1971, Stanford University researcher Philip Zimbardo set up a mock prison experiment he hoped would explain the abusive behaviors that had been going on in prisons. He paid 24 undergraduate student volunteers to assume the roles of "prisoners" and "guards" and run the prison as they saw fit. The experiment lasted only six days; volunteers internalized their roles to the extent that the guards began using authoritarian measures and ultimately subjected some of the prisoners to psychological torture. Within 36 hours, prison revolts broke out.[3] More than four decades later, this study is still widely discussed in academia and often cited as one of the most influential studies in human behavior. Indeed, in early 2015 a film based on the study had its world premiere at the Sundance Film Festival in Park City, Utah.[4]

As indicated in Chapter 12, prisons and the lives of their inhabitants have always fascinated us, as can be attested by the number of related movies in our popular culture. We wonder what life is like for those who live and work in a prison. What are the challenges faced by female, elderly, and mentally ill inmates? How are gangs, drugs, and capital punishment dealt with administratively? What constitutional rights do inmates possess? This chapter addresses those questions as it attempts to bare the lives of those Americans who spend their time in what is a very restrictive environment.

Presented first is a look at the perilous nature of these jails and prisons, which can be "mean and brutish" places. Next is a look at the local jails: their purpose, environment, and personnel. Following that is a discussion of the role of prison correctional officers, and next are reviews of several challenges to prison administrators, including inmate litigation and drug use, special-needs inmates (e.g., women, the mentally ill, and gangs), and the administration of capital punishment. Then an examination of prison life is presented, followed by a review of prisoners' constitutional rights based on selected federal court decisions.

When examining what correctional personnel do, it would be good to remember two basic principles put forth by prison expert John DiIulio Jr.: First, incarcerated persons are not to suffer pains beyond the deprivation of liberty; confinement itself is the punishment. Second, regardless of the crime, even the most heinous offender is to be treated with respect and dignity.[5] The analysis of correctional institutions that follows is predicated on these two principles.

THE NATURE OF INCARCERATION

As mentioned in Chapter 12, approximately 2.3 million Americans (716 per 100,000 population) are now living in federal and state prisons and in local jails. When viewed in relation to other countries' prison populations (see Table 13.1), it is evident that the United States has had (since 2002) the highest imprisonment rate in the world.[6] There are about 9 million prisoners worldwide.[7]

In this chapter section, we briefly examine the deprivations and conditions of confinement, as well as some of the means (mostly illegitimate) employed by inmates to try to ease their discomfort. Included are findings on the effects of solitary confinement.

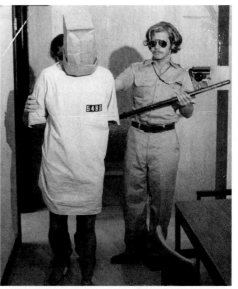

Dr. Philip Zimbardo's Stanford Prison Experiment examined the psychological effects of becoming a prison guard or inmate. Shown are two of the university students who were assigned roles as guard and prisoner.

Deprivations and Effects

Prisons vary in their environments and practices. Most prisons are said to "expose prisoners to severe levels of deprivation, degradation, and danger."[8] The extreme stress that can arise due to these circumstances can adversely affect inmates' physical and mental health. Emotional numbing, anxiety, isolation, and hypervigilance—not unlike that which is experienced by military veterans with posttraumatic stress disorder (PTSD)—can occur in prisoners as much as 10 times more often than in the general population.[9] Furthermore, these pains of imprisonment can produce long-lasting effects that persist long after a prisoner is released.

Jack Henry Abbott, a violent convict who spent more than 30 years in prison, gained literary celebrity from his book *In the Belly of the Beast: Letters From Prison*, and was once supported for parole by Norman Mailer, wrote that

> Men who had been in prison as much as five years still knew next to nothing on the subject. It probably took a decade behind bars for any real perception on the matter to permeate your psychology and your flesh.[10]

Research has made it possible to understand the lives led by inmates without our having to actually live in a prison for 10 years.

Although many people—and certainly many crime victims—would argue that prison life today is too "soft" for inmates, Gresham Sykes described the following "pains of imprisonment":

- *Deprivation of liberty:* The inmate's loss of freedom is the most obvious aspect of incarceration; however, not only does this restriction of movement include living in a small space such as a prison cell, but it also includes doing so

TABLE 13.1 World Prison Populations

COUNTRY	PRISON POPULATION	POPULATION PER 100,000	JAIL OCCUPANCY LEVEL (%)	UN-SENTENCED PRISONERS (%)	WOMEN PRISONERS (%)
China	1,548,498	118	N/A	N/A	4.6
Russia	874,161	615	79.5	16.9	6.8
Brazil	371,482	193	150.9	33.1	5.4
India	332,112	30	139	70.1	3.7
Mexico	214,450	196	133.9	43.2	5
Ukraine	162,602	350	101.3	19.5	6.1
South Africa	158,501	334	138.6	27.5	2.1
Poland	89,546	235	124.4	16.8	3
England/ Wales	80,002	148	112.7	16.4	5.5
Japan	79,052	62	105.9	14.7	5.9
Kenya	47,036	130	284.3	45.6	4.2
Turkey	65,458	91	77.4	47.7	3.3
Nigeria	40,444	30	101.5	64.3	1.9
Australia	25,790	125	105.9	21.6	7.1
Scotland	6,872	134	107.5	21	4.4
Northern Ireland	1,375	79	91.5	37.4	2.2

Source: BBC News, "World Prison Populations," http://news.bbc.co.uk/2/shared/spl/hi/uk/06/prisons/html/nn2page1.stm. Data compiled from International Centre for Prison Studies website.

involuntarily. Friends and family are prohibited from visiting except at limited times, causing relationships to fray. Sykes said this pain of imprisonment is the most acute, because it represents a "deliberate, moral rejection of the criminal by free society."[11]

- *Deprivation of goods and services:* Inmates do not have access to the wide array of food, entertainment, and services that free people enjoy. For some inmates, this is a relative loss, because prison life is a "step up," and having room and board provided to them each day is an improvement in lifestyle (as discussed in Chapter 12). Sykes, however, felt that some inmates view this impoverishment as the prison's acting as a tyrant to deprive them of the kinds of goods and services they deserve.[12]

- *Deprivation of heterosexual relationships:* Inmates do not leave their sexuality at the front gate while incarcerated. This is certainly an area of prison life that represents a source of major stress and violence. In men's prisons, Sykes contended, where one's self-concept is tied to his sexuality, by depriving men of female company their "self-image is in danger of becoming half complete, fractured," and, as described later, with often-violent results.[13]

- *Deprivation of autonomy:* Inmates cannot make decisions for themselves about the most basic tasks, such as walking from one room to another, when they will eat and sleep, and so forth, and they must ask for everything. Bureaucratic rules and staff control their lives, and finding ways to cope with this deprivation can lead to stress.

- *Deprivation of security:* Perhaps the most stressful pain of imprisonment, there are few places in the institution where the inmate can feel secure, and he or she is confined with people who are brutish and violent. Having to "watch one's back" and cope with people who constantly test each other and seek out weaknesses in others will lead to internal power struggles, development of gangs, and other forms of "protection."

AP Photo/Fort Worth Star-Telegram, Ron Jenkins

Among the deprivations of incarceration are those involving goods and services; inmates do not have access to the wide array of food, entertainment, and services that free people enjoy.

Becoming "Prisonized"

Prisoners differ in their ability to adapt, cope, and adjust to the pains of imprisonment. The process of socialization—legitimizing, adjusting to, and accommodating the prison subculture's norms and values—is termed **prisonization**. According to prison expert Jeanne Stinchcomb, inmates conform to the norms and values considered socially acceptable by other inmates—"for example, disdain for the system and those in authority, use of vulgar language, name calling, distrust of fellow prisoners and staff, and acceptance of the status quo."[14] Stinchcomb compares the institutional adaptation of an inmate to

> breaking the spirit of a wild horse to shape its response to the commands of the rider. Like horse and rider—who develop a working accommodation with each other—the subsequent relationship is characterized by routines of dominance, surrender, and behavior on cue. Among inmates, this conformity creates a façade of courtesy toward authority figures and promotes flat, non-committal responses to others, which are devoid of any emotional investment.[15]

Furthermore, every correctional institution has informal and unwritten norms, the violation of which can quickly bring the wrath of other inmates, ranging from ostracism to physical violence or death. These informal rules, as originally set down by Gresham Sykes and Sheldon Messinger, are as follows:[16]

- Don't interfere with the interests of other inmates. This means that inmates "never rat on an inmate" or betray each other; don't be nosy, don't have loose lips, and never put an inmate on the spot. There is no justification for not complying with these rules.

- Don't quarrel or feud with fellow inmates: This is expressed in the directives "Play it cool" and "Do your own time."

Prisonization: the process whereby an inmate becomes socialized into the culture and social life of prison society so that adjusting to the norms of outside society becomes difficult.

- Don't exploit other inmates: In inmate culture, this means "Don't break your word," "Don't steal from other inmates," and "Don't go back on bets."

- Don't weaken; withstand frustration or threat without complaint: This means "Be tough," and "Be a man."

- Don't trust the custodians or the things they stand for: This translates to "Don't be a sucker" and "The officials are wrong and the prisoners are right."

Inmates living in a poorly run prison may face a stark choice: become either a victim or a victimizer. A study of a maximum-security prison in the South found that three-fourths of the inmates had been forced to "get tough" with other inmates to avoid victimization, and more than one-fourth kept a "shank" (some object fashioned into a makeshift knife) for self-defense.[17] Fear is equated with weakness, and weakness invites aggression.[18]

Overcrowding can exacerbate all of the other pains of imprisonment. Not only is crowding a major source of administrative problems, but also it can adversely affect inmates' health, behavior, and morale. Crowding has been shown to elevate inmates' blood pressure, lead to increased illness complaints, and cause high levels of stress.[19]

Conditions of Confinement

What constitutional requirements of confinement must be met with persons who are incarcerated? (Specific rights such as access to courts and legal materials, religion, and due process are discussed below.) To begin, in *Price v. Johnston* (1948), the Supreme Court observed that "lawful incarceration brings about the necessary withdrawal or limitation of many privileges and rights."[20] More recently, in 1981, the Court stated that routine discomfort is "part of the penalty that criminal offenders pay for their offenses against society"; therefore, only those deprivations that deny "the minimal civilized measure of life's necessities" are sufficient to be considered in violation of the Eighth Amendment (i.e., constitute cruel and unusual punishment).[21]

However, the courts have said that conditions in prison must not involve the wanton and unnecessary infliction of pain, nor be grossly disproportionate to the severity of the crime for which one is imprisoned. Even in the case of emergency actions or critical incidents, only malicious or sadistic acts by prison officials will be deemed unconstitutional. When an inmate alleges that excessive force was used, the standard used is whether or not the force was applied in good faith so as to maintain or restore discipline.[22]

Finally, in *Whitley v. Albers* (1986), the Court held that correctional officers in Oregon did not violate the Eighth Amendment when using potentially deadly force rather than tear gas to quell a prison riot (the plaintiff was shot in the knee during the riot).[23] The Court said that the use of such force to quell a disturbance is unconstitutional only if it is done "sadistically or maliciously." Thus, the court continued its trend of allowing prison officials broad discretion to preserve order and discipline, while restricting inmate rights where necessary.

Making Prison Less Disagreeable: The Underground Economy

In the mid-1990s, state prisons (and local jails) began enacting no-smoking policies for inmates; in 2004, the Federal Bureau of Prisons joined the no-smoking movement for its 105 prisons and 180,000 inmates. Today, at least some if not all correctional facilities in the 50 states are either smoke-free or have partial smoking bans.[24]

It is no surprise, then, that an **underground economy** will develop, given that some prison inmates still crave—and trade—prohibited (contraband) items such as tobacco and alcohol (in prison jargon, known as "pruno," made from yeast and sugar from fruit). Even at Pelican Bay State Prison, a maximum-security facility in California where 80 percent of the inmates are serving a life sentence, alcohol (in addition to tobacco) has been a highly sought after commodity.[25]

But other black-market goods are also highly sought after—and obtained. For example, prison inmates trade goods and services in the form of currency they call "mack"—small tins or pouches of preserved mackerel. If the tin containing the oily fish is not opened, it never spoils.[26] Also desirable are so-called "Green Dot" cards, which are prepaid MasterCard and Visa cards such as those sold at retail stores nationwide. The cards allow inmates the opportunity to transfer money, both within and outside of their prison.[27] In 2010, the Drug Enforcement Administration raided a female correctional officer's home and uncovered numerous cards that were being smuggled for the Black Guerilla Family prison gang; she was later indicted by a federal grand jury in Baltimore, Maryland.[28] Then, any number of items available in the prison canteen may be used for barter, including sugary snacks and "soups" such as Top Ramen.

The most widely used prison currency, however, is postage stamps, which offer a few major advantages over other forms of payment. First, inmates are allowed to possess them, up to three books of first-class postage stamps (but inmates often stockpile many, many more). Inmates can typically expect 70 percent of a stamp's face value when bartering.[29]

A legitimate question to be posed is "How do inmates obtain drugs, Green Dot cards, tobacco, and other forms of illegal contraband?" The answer rests with people on the outside who bring the goods inside. Visitors bring narcotics and tobacco to inmates in the general population by hiding contraband in anal and vaginal cavities. Legitimate mail from outside can be intercepted and used to send narcotics to inmates. And, as indicated earlier, correctional staff have been bribed into bringing in the goods. Once such items are smuggled inside, their prices become very steep when sold by the "entrepreneur" who comes into their possession.

Solitary Confinement: Use and Effects

Today, tens of thousands of individuals in the United States are incarcerated alone in small, spare, concrete, windowless cells for about 23 hours per day. The number of inmates serving time in **solitary confinement** has grown tremendously, coinciding with the supermax prison concept (discussed in Chapter 12) that began to proliferate in the mid-1980s. The solitary cells typically have a toilet and a shower, a slot in the door large enough for a guard to slip a food tray through, and little else. Prisoners in solitary confinement are generally not allowed to make telephone calls or have contact visits, and their recreational regimen often involves being taken to another solitary area where they pace alone for an hour before being returned to their cell.[30]

©AP Photo/Rich Pedroncelli

In addition to obtaining drugs, tobacco products, and homemade alcohol, inmates also manage to obtain such contraband as cellphones—2,000 of which were confiscated from inmates in California's state prison in Solano.

Underground economy: forms of currency or commodities that inmates use for trading and bartering, such as tobacco products, prisoner-made wine, fish, and instant coffee.

Solitary confinement: a form of imprisonment in which an inmate is isolated from any human contact (except for members of prison staff).

PRACTITIONER'S PERSPECTIVE

AN INMATE'S PERSPECTIVE ON PRISON

Name: David Milner

Current Residence: Warm Springs Correctional Center (a medium-security institution)

City, State: Carson City, Nevada

Educational Background: Two associate degrees, one in general studies and one in business (the latter was earned while incarcerated).

How long have you been an inmate in this institution? Since December 2011 (originally incarcerated in 1999).

The circumstances that resulted in your being here: Poor judgment, attempted murder, robbery.

In general, a *typical day* would include: Waking up at 4:30 a.m., working out until 5:15 a.m., participating in the dog training program until 6:00 a.m., having breakfast, working in the prison laundry; then, engaging in the dog training program again until 11 a.m., working out again, continuing working with dogs until 1 p.m.; then, writing letters, playing games, talking to family.

The programs in which I am involved here include: Dog training program, anger and aggression management, Sierra Arts art classes, sports.

The greatest challenges I face in my current position include: Getting ready to reenter society. I've been locked up for a *long* time. . . . I will be released in the next couple of years. I am trying to better myself in every way I can until then.

My longevity and experiences in prison have taught me: The world does *not* revolve around me. It's okay to ask for help. And, above all, I am responsible for my actions.

My suggestions for improvement in correctional institutions: More vocational training. Give people other options, rather than falling into old patterns.

My suggestions for students wishing to work in a correctional institutional setting: Be fair, honest, and consistent. Everyone has bad days. . . . Don't take it out on others.

My plans upon reentry into society: Getting another degree (preferably a technical degree) and training for a job which I can be suited for. I want to reconnect with my family and restart my life. I came to prison when I was 18. . . . I've alienated or hurt so many of my family. They have stood by me through this whole ordeal. I NEED to be there for them at any opportunity. I have so much catching up to do. . . . I committed a crime, but I've never considered myself a "criminal." It's time for me to live the life I was meant to.

(Authors' note: By mid-2015, Milner had trained 58 dogs in a variety of obedience techniques. Warm Springs Correctional Center [WSCC] warden Gregory Smith brought the program to WSCC and believes it has two institutional benefits: Inmates in the program are very well-mannered and cause no problems, and the program has created a very good relationship between the Department of Corrections and the community. More than 200 dogs are adopted by community members each year.)

Contrary to what the general public might believe, there is no limit on the length of time an inmate might serve in solitary confinement; the courts' primary concern is that the constitutional requirements for care and custody that apply to all inmates be met. Indeed, many such cases involve inmates who have spent decades in such confinement. One notable case involved the so-called Angola Three, prison inmates Robert H. King, Albert Woodfox, and Herman Wallace, three Black Panthers who were put in solitary confinement in Louisiana's Angola Prison after the 1972 killing of a prison guard. The three were held in their cells for 23 hours a day. In their one hour of freedom, they were allowed to shower and walk up and down the corridor or, weather permitting, to have an isolated walk in the exercise yard. King spent 29 years in solitary confinement before his conviction was overturned and he was released. Wallace and Woodfox both spent 40 years of solitary confinement. The prisoners have been the subject of two documentary films and international attention.[31]

INVESTIGATING FURTHER

GONE AND FORGOTTEN: TWO YEARS IN SOLITARY CONFINEMENT

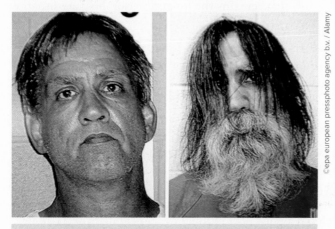

Stephen Slevin, who spent nearly two years in solitary confinement awaiting trial for a DUI arrest in New Mexico, was awarded $15.5 million for his mental and physical ordeal.

©epa european pressphoto agency b.v. / Alamy

Stephen Slevin's 22 months in solitary confinement in a New Mexico county jail left him traumatized and physically weak, but he was awarded $15.5 million for his suffering. After being put in jail for a drunk-driving charge, Slevin was isolated from other inmates and essentially forgotten for nearly two years.

Slevin, 59, went into jail as a well-nourished, physically healthy individual, but he emerged from jail with a long beard and bad teeth and weighing only 133 pounds. He had also developed bedsores and a fungus, and he was not aware of his situation or surroundings.

Jailers initially separated Slevin from other inmates because of his history of mental illness. The charges of driving while intoxicated and receiving a stolen vehicle were never prosecuted.[36]

A large number of studies—dating back to the 19th century—have indicated that solitary confinement profoundly affects inmates' psychological and physical health.[32] As a result, many researchers and civil rights organizations have long called for it to be banned. Most of the damage done to an inmate is psychological and can include psychosis and paranoia; anxiety; depression, varying from low mood to clinical depression; anger; cognitive disturbances; and perceptual distortions. Physiological effects of solitary confinement, owing largely to lack of access to fresh air and sunlight and long periods of inactivity, include gastrointestinal, cardiovascular, and genitourinary problems; migraine headaches; and profound fatigue. Insomnia; back and other joint pains; deterioration of eyesight; poor appetite and weight loss are often observed.[33]

Although the U.S. Supreme Court has taken notice of the negative effects of solitary confinement for more than 125 years (see *In re Medley* [1890]),[34] the federal courts, according to Sharon Shalev, have been "examining the issue anew as if the accumulated experience that the judge referred to in [*Medley*] had not existed.[35] In sum, the courts have generally not intervened unless the conditions of confinement were so inadequate as to be tantamount to cruel and unusual punishment.

POTENTIALLY HAZARDOUS WORK

As perilous as places of confinement are for the inmates, so too are they perilous for the correctional staff—all of whom are unarmed, and most of whom are outnumbered. It is probably a tribute and great credit to both prison and jail administrators and staff across the nation that so few institutional riots and other serious incidents occur in the United States, especially when one considers that staff is so outnumbered. Following are some noteworthy incidents where inmates have taken control of their institutions:

- At the Morey Unit of the Lewis Prison Complex in Buckeye, Arizona, two inmates took two correctional officers hostage and seized the unit's tower, triggering a 15-day standoff that remains the longest prison hostage situation in this nation's history.[37]

- Approximately 450 prisoners at the Southern Ohio Correctional Facility in Lucasville engaged in a riot, resulting in the deaths of nine inmates and one officer during the 10-day siege.[38]

- Federal detainees in a Louisiana parish jail held hostage the warden and two correctional officers, demanding a helicopter to escape.[39]

- A sheriff's negotiator won the release of three employees before a SWAT team stormed the Bay County Jail in Florida. Inmates had threatened to rape and cut off the body parts of a fourth hostage, a nurse. They had taken over the jail's infirmary, and one was holding a scalpel to the nurse's neck when the SWAT team and armed correctional officers ended the 11-hour standoff.[40]

- At the U.S. Penitentiary in Atlanta, Georgia, the U.S. Department of State reinstated an accord that permitted the repatriation of about 2,500 Cuban nationals. Three days later, the detainees seized control of the penitentiary, demanding that they not be repatriated. The uprising lasted 11 days and involved more than 100 hostages.[41]

- Permanently seared in the annals of corrections rioting are the horrific incidents at the Attica Correctional Facility in New York in 1971 (39 inmates and employees killed) and at the New Mexico State Prison in Santa Fe in 1980 (33 inmates dead).[42]

As may be seen with these tragic events, jail and prison rioting and hostage taking are potentially explosive and perilous situations from beginning to end. Hostages always are directly in harm's way, and their jeopardy is continuous and uninterrupted until they are released and safely in the hands of authorities.[43] Some inmate-involved riots and hostage situations come as a complete surprise, whereas others flow from a precipitating event or some type of a "spark."

Corrections hostage-taking events can involve any individuals, employees, visitors, or prisoners held against their will by an inmate seeking to escape, gain concessions, or achieve other goals, such as publicizing a particular cause. They can be planned or impulsive acts,[44] and they can involve one hostage or hundreds.[45]

It is critical that both prisons and jails have a coordinated plan to address such incidents, not

AP Photo/Michael Conroy

Prisons and jails must have a coordinated plan to address riot and hostage incidents, not only to keep a small disturbance from escalating into a full-fledged riot but also to protect staff and inmates from harm. This Emergency Response Team from the Indiana Department of Corrections at New Castle Correctional Facility stands down following a riot.

only to keep a small disturbance from escalating into a full-fledged riot, but, more important, to prevent unnecessary deaths.[46]

JAIL PERSONNEL

Jail employees, like other public servants, have serious responsibilities and must conduct themselves in an exemplary manner at all times while ensuring the care, custody, and control of inmates as per agency policies and procedures.

Today, about 730,000 adults are incarcerated in city and county jails in the United States, either awaiting trial or serving a sentence.[47] Whereas prisons hold persons who have committed felonies and have been sentenced to at least one year of incarceration, as noted earlier, jails hold persons who are arrested and are waiting for a court appearance if they cannot arrange bail, as well as inmates who are serving sentences of up to one year for misdemeanors.

Jail administrators and employees need to be thoroughly trained in all aspects of their jobs. Jail workers have been criticized for being untrained and apathetic, although most are highly effective and dedicated. One observer wrote that

> personnel is still the number one problem of jails. Start paying decent salaries and developing decent training and you can start to attract bright young people to jobs in jails. If you don't do this, you'll continue to see the issue of personnel as the number one problem for the next 100 years.[48]

Training should be provided on the booking process, inmate management and security, general liability issues, policies related to AIDS, problems of inmates addicted to alcohol and other drugs, communication and security technology, and issues concerning suicide, mental health problems, and medication.

Prison Correctional Officers

As with employees of local jails, prison **correctional officers** have serious responsibilities, must conduct themselves in an exemplary manner at all times, and ensure the care, custody, and control of inmates as per agency policies and procedures.

A Job Description

Subordinate to the prison administrators and other supervisors are the correctional staff members—those who, in the words of Gordon Hawkins, are "the other prisoners."[49] Their role is particularly important, given that they provide the front-line supervision and control of inmates and constitute the level from which correctional administrators may be chosen. Prison expert Jess Maghan described the task of the correctional officers as follows:

> Correctional officers are generally charged with overseeing individuals who have been arrested, are awaiting trial or other hearing, or who have been convicted of a crime and sentenced to serve time in a jail, reformatory, or penitentiary. They maintain security and observe inmate conduct and behavior to prevent disturbances and escapes. They manage and communicate with inmates, peers and supervisors, direct inmate movement, maintain key, tool, and equipment control, distribute authorized items to inmates, as well as maintain health, safety, and sanitation.[50]

Correctional officer: one who works in a jail or prison and supervises correctional inmates.

Author Video:
Prison administrators

Clearly the job of a correctional officer is challenging and stressful. In many if not most assignments, correctional officers experience stimulus overload, assailed with the sounds of "doors clanging, inmates talking or shouting, radios and televisions playing, and food trays banging . . . [and odors] representing an institutional blend of food, urine, paint, disinfectant, and sweat."[51] According to a federal report, sources of stress for correctional officers include organization-related conditions, such as understaffing, overtime, shift work, and unreasonable supervisor demands; work-related sources of stress, including the threat of inmate violence, actual inmate violence, inmate demands and manipulation, and problems with coworkers; and a poor public image and low pay.[52] Due process rights for prisoners and the constant threat of lawsuits have also made corrections jobs even more difficult,[53] leading to what Richard Hawkins and Geoffrey Alpert referred to as "the big bitch" of correctional officers: They are losing power and influence while inmates are gaining them.[54] This frustration can be vented in physical ways.[55]

Changes Wrought by the Attica Revolt

The core responsibilities of the correctional officer have remained essentially the same for the past 150 years: care, custody, and control. The preferred ways of performing this job, however, have undergone considerable change over time.

The civil rights movement, which began in the 1960s and continued into the 1970s, also led to more prison uprisings—an impetus to the prisoners' rights movement. With that came a point where correctional officers became the focus of considerable scholarly research and discussion, including David Fogel's *We Are the Living Proof*; Leo Carroll's *Hacks, Blacks, and Cons*; James B. Jacobs's *Stateville: The Penitentiary in Mass Society*; Lucien Lombardo's *Guards Imprisoned: Correctional Officers at Work*; Robert Johnson and Shelley Price's "The Complete Correctional Officer, Human Service and the Human Environment of Prison"; and Lynn Zimmer's *Women Guarding Men*.[56]

The aforementioned brutal prison uprising in Attica, New York, in September 1971, made clear that the correctional officers and staff of the nation's state and local correctional facilities were not being appropriately selected and trained[57] and that relations between the correctional officers and inmates of those facilities were akin to a lit powder keg. Over half the town of Attica's nearly 2,800 residents worked at the facility, with white rural guards watching over a largely black and Latino urban population. This situation was an incubator of resentment and fear. As one person stated, for at least four years it was a "seething cauldron of discontent that was about to erupt."[58] Indeed, following the uprising, in which 43 hostages were held for four days and 39 people lay dead after state troopers stormed the institution, the revenge the prisoners feared was meted out as the guards retook the prison, forcing inmates to strip, beating them, and threatening to castrate them. Only a few wounded prisoners were allowed out; the others were treated in an 8- by 10-foot cell soaked in blood. A physician told the press, "It was the worst thing I've ever seen."[59]

Evolving Roles, Selection, and Training

As a result of the above examination of their roles, today prison correctional officers are viewed and used much differently than in pre-Attica times. First, the term *correctional officer* was adopted during the 1970s (replacing *guard*) as the official occupational reference term used by the U.S. Department of Labor. The position of correctional officer became available to both men and women. Other changes included closer screening and hiring by civil service exams. Likewise, the entry-level salary, overtime and hazardous duty pay, pension plans, and recognition as public safety "peace officer" status by state law also served to enhance the recruitment pool and long-term retention of correctional personnel. Staff training programs were also improved, to include topics such as constitutional law and cultural awareness, inmate behavior, contraband control, custody and security procedures, fire and safety, inmate legal rights, written and oral communication, use of force, first aid including cardiopulmonary resuscitation (CPR), and physical fitness training.[60]

Custodial staff members at most prisons are typically divided into four ranks: captain, lieutenant, sergeant, and officer. Captains typically work closely with the prison administration in policy-making and disciplinary matters; lieutenants are even more closely involved with the security and disciplinary aspects of the institution; and sergeants oversee a specified number of rank-and-file correctional officers who work in their assigned cell blocks or workplaces.

Perhaps the most difficult position of all within this hierarchy is that of the front-line officer, who is in close contact each day (and greatly outnumbered, as a rule) with the prison population. Following is a more specific listing of duties of the correctional officers:

The aftermath of the inmate riot at Attica State Prison in September 1971, in which 10 hostages and 29 inmates were killed and 89 other persons were seriously injured.

- *Cell block officers:* Officers supervise the daily activities and the general "well-being" of the inmates in the cell blocks, to ensure that inmates follow institutional rules and routines, to ensure that inmates do not harm themselves or others, and to assist inmates who are experiencing problems of a personal nature.

- *Work detail supervisors:* Many prisons have inmates working in various positions, such as the prison cafeteria, laundry, and other such locations; officers must supervise them during such activities.

- *Industrial shop and educational programs:* Prison industries have inmates producing everything from license plates, state-use paint, and mattresses to computer parts; correctional officers ensure that inmates do not create any problems during their work day and do not misappropriate any related tools that may be fashioned into weapons.

- *Yard officers:* While inmates are outdoors and engaged in physical exercise and socialization, there is the potential for problems, such as fights between different racial or ethnic groups; officers must be alert for breaches of security and order.

- *Tower guards:* Officers observe inmates who are in the prison yard while encased in an isolated, silent post high above the prison property, being vigilant for any outbreaks of violence or attempts to escape while inmates are outdoors.

- *Administrative building assignments:* Officers are responsible for providing security at all prison gates, places where inmates' families come to visit, clerical work that involves inmate transfer, and so on.[61]

PRACTITIONER'S PERSPECTIVE

PRISON CORRECTIONAL OFFICER

Name: Keith McKeehan

Current Position: Correctional lieutenant, Nevada Department of Corrections

Previous Positions: Jailer/deputy sheriff, Esmeralda County (NV) Sheriff's Office; police officer, West Wendover (NV) Police Department

City, State: Indian Springs, NV

College attended/academic major: Associate of applied science in criminal justice-law enforcement from the College of Southern Nevada; bachelor of public administration in law enforcement from Nevada State College; and master of justice management from the University of Nevada, Reno.

How long have you been a practitioner in this criminal justice position? I have been in corrections for eight years total, starting as a correctional officer and working through the ranks of senior officer, sergeant, and currently lieutenant. I am also on the eligibility lists for associate warden.

My primary duties and responsibilities as a practitioner in this position: First, as a lieutenant, to train subordinate supervisors and manage a shift or major division of the prison institution. My overall mission is to ensure that my staff goes home safe and unharmed at the end of their shift. I do this by ensuring the line officers have the tools and resources needed to be safe in the performance of their duties. As a correctional officer, my primary duty is to ensure safety and security of the inmates, staff, and institution. I am responsible for identifying possible or potential breaches in security, monitoring inmate activities to include gang activities, and investigating disturbances to learn their cause and attempt to correct the problem. I am also responsible for the detection and control of

the movement of contraband, to include weapons, drugs, and other unauthorized items.

The qualities/characteristics that are most helpful in this career: Open-mindedness, adaptability to change (both professionally and in your surroundings), alertness, ability to read behaviors, and integrity. Also, one must be firm, fair, and consistent.

In general, a *typical day* for a practitioner in this career would include: Monitoring the movement of inmates and their activities, while also keeping in mind that danger is lurking in every corner, walkway, tier, shower, and cell. You will be searching cells and common areas for contraband to ensure safety and security of the staff, inmates, and institution. You will be correcting unwanted inmate behaviors and preparing written reports of violations. You also must be prepared for emergency response inside the institution.

My advice to someone either wishing to study, or now studying, criminal justice and to become a practitioner in this career: Get your degree! Education promotes professionalism. Also, do not take this job personally. You are a professional and inmates are acting like inmates, as they should. You will be held to the higher standard by your peers, your supervisors, the public, and the inmates. You will see things that are not normal (such as six-on-one gang-related assaults where the victim is stabbed multiple times and doesn't want to report it, or staff being sexually assaulted by inmates), and you won't want to speak of them. You have to learn to find the humor in the darkest of places and laugh at it all. If you take it all personally, you will not survive! So, do not bring work home! Your personal life has enough challenges without adding your work stress to the mix. You must also be firm, fair, and consistent at all times. And, keep in mind that your conduct on- and off-duty are a reflection of the department and the criminal justice profession. Be guided accordingly.

A Warden's Wisdom

Ultimately, all topics discussed in this chapter are the responsibility of those who govern the prisons—directors and wardens. However, their challenges also include such daunting responsibilities as addressing prison litigation, administering capital punishment, attempting to prevent institutional problems relating to drugs and gangs, and addressing all manner of staffing needs and problems.

Prison administration is now more challenging than ever—made much more so because of the recent fiscal crises that have faced all states as well as the federal government. Two former prison wardens from a western state have provided solid advice for administering prisons in general, and specifically in times of fiscal exigency.

First, the wise prison warden will recognize that there is simply never enough money to accomplish all four goals of punishment: to *incapacitate* and *rehabilitate* offenders, and to provide *deterrence* to crime and *retribution*. Different states have different correctional philosophies, and that will affect how they budget and spend their prison monies. One must make choices—bearing in mind that the warden must, first and foremost, provide for incapacitation—while providing society, staff, and inmates a safe facility. Therefore, it is very important to focus on operations, programs, and finances.[62]

The warden's philosophies regarding security and treatment will have a major impact on both the prison inmates and staff. In addition to providing inmates with a variety of vocational training programs (including manufacturing items such as limousines and outdoor furniture, and training wild horses) and to a wide variety of physical fitness equipment, some prisons have allowed inmates to ride and repair their motorcycles inside the walls,[63] have an inmate band, and engage in unlimited planting of gardens, sunflowers, and fruit trees to occupy their time.

Other wardens take a more hard-line approach and even discontinue those amenities that were initiated by their predecessors. For example, one warden recently halted the planting of sunflowers because inmates were planting them close to the fence line, and when the night breeze caused the sunflowers to stir from side to side, officers in the gun towers were lulled into a state of complacency—becoming conditioned to ignore the movement in the area, which posed a security risk. Another prison director recently disallowed inmate bands and the planting of gardens and flowers in the prison yard on grounds of institutional security (inmates were concealing weapons and other contraband in the gardens and flowers).[64] Note also that once such privileges are given to inmates, it is very difficult to take them away without generating considerable angst.

Today's prison wardens and other correctional staff members (and jail personnel as well) need to be as aware as possible of their surroundings and the general goings-on within the institution. As with police officers, whose academy training was discussed in Chapter 6, these correctional workers must also nurture a "sixth sense": a suspicion that something may be wrong.

A former western prison warden termed this ability **JDLR**—knowing when things "just don't look right."[65] To maintain a sense of what's going on with the inmates—"reading the yard"—some wardens recommend that they and their staff walk the yard at least two times each day. Following are some aspects of the yard that should be noted and may portend trouble:

- Inmates banding together in groups—in political associations (i.e., by race, ethnicity, gang affiliation, and so forth)

Warden Esther Torres walks through one of the dormitories at the Willard-Cybulski Correctional Institution in Connecticut; Torres oversees a staff of 234 people and 1,160 prisoners.

JDLR: in prison jargon, the sense that things "just don't look right."

- Loud music playing (possibly to conceal conversations and activities from the staff)

- Unusually high canteen spending, with inmates purchasing long-term items, such as canned goods (which might indicate that a riot is being planned)[66]

ISSUES OF PRISON GOVERNANCE

The Prison Litigation Reform Act

SAGE Journal Article:
Inmates and courts

As discussed in Chapter 11, prison inmates not only can appeal their criminal convictions but may also attempt to challenge their conditions of confinement and file other writs, typically listing the prison warden as the respondent.

The volume of **inmate litigation** increased significantly following the *Cooper v. Pate* decision in 1964, discussed later in this chapter. In 1980, inmates in state and federal correctional institutions filed 23,287 petitions alleging both civil and criminal violations and seeking compensatory damages, injunctions, and property claims.[67] By 1996, the number of such petitions had grown to more than 64,000.[68]

Then, in April 1996, the Prison Litigation Reform Act (PLRA) was enacted[69] "to provide for appropriate remedies for prison condition lawsuits, to discourage frivolous and abusive prison lawsuits, and for other purposes."[70] The PLRA requires that inmates must try to resolve their complaint through the prison's grievance procedure, pay court filing fees in full (indigent prisoners pay less), and show physical injury prior to filing a lawsuit for mental or emotional injury. Clearly PLRA served its purpose: In 1997, the first year following implementation of the act, there were 62,966 inmate petitions; by 2009, there were 10,566—an 83 percent decrease.[71]

Prison administrators often conduct surprise inspections (shakedowns) of inmates' cells to search for weapons and other contraband items.

AP Photo/Southern Illinoisan, Joe Jines

Drug Interdiction and Treatment

Every adult in our society is aware of the problems wrought by drug abuse. Certainly that problem is reflected within state prison populations, where 17 percent of male inmates and 25 percent of female inmates are incarcerated for drug crimes.[72] Furthermore, offenders still manage to obtain illicit drugs during their incarceration, threatening the safety of inmates and staff while undermining the authority of correctional administrators, contradicting rehabilitative goals, and reducing public confidence.[73]

What can be done about drug abuse in prisons and jails? The state of Pennsylvania realized that drug use was pervasive in several of its prisons. Six inmates had died from overdoses in a two-year period, and assaults on correctional officers and inmates had become more common. To combat the problem, the state first adopted a zero-tolerance drug policy, the so-called Pennsylvania plan: Inmates caught with drugs were to be criminally prosecuted, and those testing positive (using hair testing) were to serve disciplinary custody time. Highly sensitive drug detection equipment was employed

Inmate litigation: lawsuits filed by prison and jail inmates challenging their conditions of confinement.

INVESTIGATING FURTHER

INMATE LITIGATION

Of course, legitimate lawsuits are filed by inmates against prison administrators concerning living conditions and treatment. However, many such petitions are clearly questionable if not outright frivolous, such as the following:

- A prisoner sued 66 defendants alleging that unidentified physicians implanted mind control devices in his head.
- A prisoner suit demanded L.A. Gear or Reebok "Pumps" instead of Converse shoes.
- An inmate claimed his rights were violated because he was forced to send packages via UPS rather than U.S. mail.

- An inmate sued because he was served chunky instead of smooth peanut butter.
- An inmate claimed it was cruel and unusual punishment that he was forced to listen to his unit manager's country and western music.
- An inmate claimed $1 million in damages because his ice cream melted (the judge ruled that the "right to eat ice cream . . . was clearly not within the contemplation" of our nation's forefathers).

Source: Jennifer A. Puplava, "Peanut Butter and the Prison Litigation Reform Act," http://www.law.indiana.edu/ilj/volumes/v73/no1/puplava.html.

to detect drugs that visitors might try to smuggle into the prison, to inspect packages arriving in the mail, and to detect drugs that correctional staff might try to bring in. New policies were issued for inmate movement and visitation, and a new phone system was installed to randomly monitor inmates' calls.[74] The results were impressive. The state's 24 prisons became 99 percent drug free, the number of drug finds during cell searches dropped 41 percent, assaults on staff decreased 57 percent, inmate-on-inmate assaults declined 70 percent, and the number of weapons seized during searches dropped from 220 to 76.[75]

Women in Prison: Selected Rights and Challenges

Chapter 3 discussed theories of how and why the role of women in crime has expanded since the 1970s. Here, it might be said, the punitive *effects* of their increased criminality are discussed.

Certainly the numbers speak to how large a role women now occupy in the nation's crime picture: About 1.9 million women are arrested each year in the United States,[76] about 200,000 women are in jails or prison, and more than 1 million are on probation or parole.[77]

The major area of difference between male inmates and female inmates concerns their children, because child rearing tends to fall on a mother's shoulders. Added to the "pains" of imprisonment for women, therefore, is the further frustration, conflict, and guilt that arises when women are removed from their homes and are unable to care for their children.[78] Only seven states allow women who are pregnant at the time of sentencing to keep their infants with them inside a correctional facility after the baby's birth, and in most prisons the length of the child's stay with the mother depends on the length of the mother's sentence.[79]

About one-fourth (approximately 22,000 inmates of 89,000 total) of all women in state prisons are incarcerated for either possessing or trafficking drugs—a proportion that is higher than for males, and almost as high as the percentage of women serving time in state prisons for property crime.[80] Therefore, it is desirable that women in prisons for such offenses receive drug treatment programs, to include detoxification, counseling, education, vocational courses, and group therapy.

Women who are incarcerated in state and federal prisons have other unique challenges—and constitutional rights, such as the following:

- Female prisoners have different, and often more severe, health problems than male prisoners. Many women prisoners suffer from chronic and complex health conditions resulting from lives of poverty, drug use, family violence, sexual assault, adolescent pregnancy, malnutrition, and poor health care. Women have a constitutional right to receive adequate medical care for serious medical needs.[81]

- About 6 percent of female prisoners report being pregnant at the time of their incarceration.[82] Many prisons thus assess the diet and nutrition, prenatal care, and work assignments for such inmates. In a related vein, although federal prisons and some state prisons prohibit the use of shackles or leg irons on pregnant women while being transported to the hospital or during labor, in some states it is still common to shackle women while on the way to the hospital, or even while they are in labor.[83]

- Under the Constitution, women have the right to be free from unreasonable searches and seizures of their property. However, the Supreme Court has found that this right is severely limited in prison because of the security concerns of prison and incarceration. An exception, however, was in *Jordan v. Gardner*, where female prisoners protested the prison policy of random full-body pat-down searches by male guards (see "You Be the Judge" box). Many of these female prisoners had been severely sexually and physically abused by men in the past, and experienced severe trauma and revictimization during these searches.

Student on the Street Video: Women and men corrections officers

A conundrum has occurred where male correctional officers observe women inmates while in various states of undress: in bed, showering, or using toilet facilities. The U.S. Supreme Court stated in *Turner v. Safley* (1987) that prison regulations that restrict the rights of prisoners must be substantially related to some legitimate concern of the prison.[84] Beyond that, however, the lower federal courts differ on what expectation of privacy women enjoy in prison. Some courts believe that all prisoners have a right to be free from unnecessary viewing by correctional officers of the opposite sex while nude or performing private bodily functions in their cells, requiring that women thus be allowed to cover their windows as needed when undressing or using the toilet. Other courts, however, have merely suggested that prisons should allow women to cover their windows while dressing or using the toilet,[85] or have suggested that these prisoners be allowed to cover the window of their cells for privacy for brief time intervals.

The U.S. Constitution guarantees the right to be free from unreasonable searches and seizures of one's property. However, the Supreme

A corrections officer keeps watch on female inmates in an indoor room at the Maricopa County tent jail.

©Jim West / Alamy

You Be the... JUDGE

"[U]se a flat hand and pushing motion across the [inmate's] crotch area. . . . [P]ush inward and upward when searching the crotch area and upper thighs of the inmate." All seams in the leg and the crotch area are to be "squeezed and kneaded." Using the back of the hand, the guard also is to search the breast area in a sweeping motion, so that the breasts will be "flattened."

Thus read the training instructions as given to male prison guards at the Washington Corrections Center for Women in 1989, when the superintendent of the women's correctional facility instituted a pat-frisk policy permitting male guards to randomly search the clothed bodies of female inmates.

1. When challenged by female inmates, will this policy be allowed to stand on the ground of institutional security?
2. Alternatively, do you believe it will be struck down by the courts as too intrusive?

The facts of this case, and its outcome, are provided in the Notes section.[86]

Court has found that this right is severely limited in prison, again, because of security concerns. Prisons may conduct a visual body cavity search (where the prisoner's ears, nose, mouth, anus, or vagina are inspected for contraband); the prison's interest in maintaining a secure facility is deemed to outweigh the prisoner's need for privacy. This interest includes body frisks, cell searches, and strip searches. However, the test for when a digital body cavity search may be performed is stricter because of its intrusive nature—a guard places his or her fingers into a prisoner's ears, nose, mouth, anus, or vagina. Here, prison officials must have a reasonable suspicion that is specific to the individual prisoner, such as a suspicion that a prisoner has a weapon.[87]

Female prisoners also have a right to be free from unwanted sexual activity. Any unwanted sexual attention that a female inmate experiences, like leering, pinching, patting, verbal comments, and pressure to engage in sexual activity, can be considered sexual assault or harassment.[88]

Mentally Ill Inmates

It is estimated that about 13 percent of all state prison inmates are receiving therapy and/or counseling, and about 10 percent of them are also taking psychotropic medications.[89] Clearly many inmates have mental health issues. As an example, while in solitary confinement in a Massachusetts prison, an inmate cut his legs and arms, tried to hang himself with tubing from a breathing machine, smashed the machine to get a sharp fragment to slice his neck, and ate pieces of it, hoping to cause internal bleeding; he eventually hanged himself.[90] In prison, such individuals pose a dual dilemma for administrators. They are often violent and may be serving long sentences. Therefore, they require a high level of security and are housed with other offenders who have committed equally serious offenses and who are serving equally long sentences. The presence of potentially violent, mentally ill prisoners in high-security and probably overcrowded institutions is a dangerous situation. The challenge for correctional administrators is to maintain a viable program to treat and control a difficult group of offenders. The treatment of this group requires resources, trained staff, and appropriate facilities.

Video: The released

Prison Gangs

Certainly an element of prisonization and a highly negative aspect of prison life is the widespread existence of prison gangs, which develop in prison for several reasons:

INVESTIGATING FURTHER

GERIATRIC INMATES

As the general population is aging due to improved medical care, and criminals receive longer prison terms—due to mandatory sentencing, life without parole, and "three-strikes" laws—the number of inmates who are geriatric (defined as over 60 or even over 50) is increasing. Such inmates have chronic health problems (e.g., arthritis, diabetes, cardiovascular diseases, failing eyesight and hearing, and other problems), memory and cognitive problems, mental health issues, and substance abuse and other criminal histories. A unique program at the Northern Nevada Correctional Center in Carson City, called the Senior Structured Living Program (SSLP), is designed to work with such inmates. The program provides physical fitness, diversion therapy (arts, crafts, games, reading, poetry), music (a choir and band), wellness and life skills training, individual and group therapy, and community involvement (involving area social services, veterans' groups, Alcoholics

Anonymous, and other groups). Volunteers also provide psychological, spiritual, and social support to the men. To enter the program, inmates must sign a contract obligating them to maintain certain standards of conduct, be at least 60 years of age (one inmate in the program is 90), and not be engaged in a full-time job or educational program. Today, 120 men are enrolled in the program. Although an extensive evaluation of the program is under way, it is known that the prison medical department has witnessed a significant reduction in the men's overall medical complaints, overutilization of medical care, and use of psychotropic medications.

Source: Mary Harrison, *True Grit Notes* 5, no. 3 (Summer 2009); Terence P. Hubert, Mary T. Harrison, and William O. Harrison, *"True Grit": An Innovative Humanistic Living Program for a Geriatric Population* (Carson City, Nev.: Nevada Department of Corrections, n.d.).

©Ted Soqui/Corbis

A heavily tattooed inmate in California State Prison, Lancaster.

solidarity, protection, and power. They often continue their operations outside of the penal system.

Typically, a prison gang consists of a select group of inmates who have an organized hierarchy and who are governed by an established code of conduct. They vary from highly structured to loosely structured associations, generally have fewer members than street gangs, are structured along racial or ethnic lines, and typically are more powerful in state correctional facilities than in the federal penal system.[91]

Furthermore, gang members returning to the community from prison often adversely affect neighborhoods and foment notable increases in crime, violence, and drug trafficking.[92] Prison gangs have also made it more difficult for prison officials to maintain order and discipline[93] and have wrought a rapid increase in inmate violence—often related to increases in drug trafficking, extortion, prostitution, protection, gambling, and contract inmate murders.[94] One study of prison gangs reported that they account for half or more of all prison problems.[95]

Gang members have a belligerent attitude toward all authority and its institutions when they enter prison; members are preoccupied with status and gang rivalry. They plan boycotts, strikes, and even riots. Despite administrative attempts to accommodate gangs in some prisons, they continue to pursue "loot, sex, respect, revenge, [and] will attack any outsider."[96]

Wardens and superintendents have been brought into gang-ridden prison systems specifically to "do something" with the gang problem. By transferring gang leaders and using other methods to segregate and isolate members, some prison administrators have managed to greatly diminish the gangs' power.

Death Work: Administering Capital Punishment

One of the major responsibilities of prison administrators, currently in 31 states and in federal prisons,[97] is to carry out the death penalty, or capital punishment. By law, the warden or a representative presides over the execution.

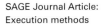

SAGE Journal Article: Execution methods

To minimize the possibility of error, executions are carried out by highly trained teams. The mechanics of the process have been broken down into several discrete tasks and are practiced repeatedly. During the actual death watch—the 24-hour period that ends with the prisoner's execution—a member of the execution team is with the prisoner at all times. During the last 5 or 6 hours, two officers are assigned to guard the prisoner. The prisoner then showers, dons a fresh set of clothes, and is placed in an empty, tomb-like death cell. The warden reads the court order, or death warrant. Meanwhile, official witnesses—typically 6 to 12 citizens—are prepared for their role. The steps that are taken from this point to perform the execution depend on the method of execution that is used.[98]

Approximately 3,000 prisoners are now under sentence of death in the United States; 56 percent are white, 42 percent are black, and 2 percent are of other races; 60 (about 2 percent) are women.[99] As discussed in Chapter 11, when executions are performed, lethal injection is the predominant method in all 31 states and in federal prisons; 9 states still authorize electrocution; 3 states, lethal gas; 3 states, hanging; and 2 states, firing squad (a number of states authorize more than one method).[100]

WORLDWIDE EXECUTIONS

Although 58 countries now have death penalty laws, only about 20 countries actually perform executions in a given year—executing about 700 people. Of the nations where death penalty data are released, four—Iraq (at least 68 executions), Iran (at least 360), Saudi Arabia (at least 82), and Yemen (at least 41)—accounted for 99 percent of all recorded executions in the Middle East and North Africa.[101] The United States, meanwhile, has executed an average of 56 persons per year since 2000—the highest number being 85 in 2000.[102]

In the majority of countries where people were sentenced to death or executed, Amnesty International asserts that the trials of the accused did not meet international fair trial standards—specifically, that many people were executed after supposedly "confessing" through torture or other forms of duress, particularly in China, Iran, Iraq, North Korea, and Saudi Arabia.[103]

But these figures do not include the thousands of executions that Amnesty International believes were carried out in China, where the numbers are suppressed. Thousands of people were executed in China in 2011, more than in the rest of the world put together. Figures on the death penalty are a state secret. Amnesty International has stopped publishing figures it collects from public sources in China as these are likely to grossly underestimate the true number.[104]

Each year Amnesty renews its challenge to the Chinese authorities to publish data on those executed and sentenced to death, in order to confirm their claims that various changes in law and practice have led to a significant reduction in the use of the death penalty in the country since 2000.[105]

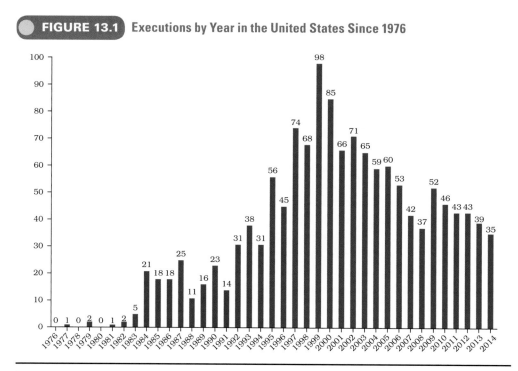

FIGURE 13.1 Executions by Year in the United States Since 1976

Source: Reprinted with permission of the Death Penalty Information Center.

During the early 2000s the U.S. Supreme Court rendered two significant decisions concerning the death penalty: First, in *Roper v. Simmons* (2005), the Supreme Court abolished the death penalty for convicted murderers who were less than 18 years of age when they committed their crimes (affecting about 70 such persons);[106] and second, in *Atkins v. Virginia* (2002), the Court held that the execution of mentally retarded persons—which was permissible in 20 states—constituted cruel and unusual punishment.[107]

Figure 13.1 depicts executions performed in the United States since 1976.

PREPARATION FOR REENTRY AND AFTERCARE

Like one who is returning home after a long hospital stay for serious illness, individuals who return to their homes after release from prison will be faced with many challenges. This process, known as **reentry and aftercare**, involves providing services to, and supervision for, paroled inmates who are about to reintegrate into the community. This population often may have multiple deficiencies and problems: little education, poor work record and thus few job prospects, substance abuse or drug dependency, mental and physical health issues, few positive role models, and so on. It is no surprise, then, that reoffending rates upon release are high: Nearly two-thirds of all released prisons will be rearrested within three years. Thus, it is imperative that prison be viewed as an opportunity to improve the inmates' skills, treat their addictions, improve their job skills and education, and so on.[108] Evidence suggests that correctional programming should include adult drug courts, prison therapeutic communities, drug treatment, behavioral treatment, industry programs, basic adult education, and employment and vocational training.[109]

Then, as the parolee reenters the community, a comprehensive program should be in effect to monitor and assist the individual with finding housing and employment,

Reentry and aftercare: providing services to, and supervision for, paroled inmates who are about to reintegrate into the community.

reconnecting with family and friends, addressing any drug and alcohol problems, avoiding reoffending, and so on. Some halfway houses assist with these activities—as do reentry courts, which review the prisoner's plans and progress, oversee the prisoner's reentry, and see that he or she participates in the individualized array of transitional programs that are to be attended.[110] Studies have shown that parolees who have completed both the prison-based and the ensuing aftercare programs have fewer substance abuse problems and rearrests, compared with an untreated comparison group.[111]

PRISONERS' CONSTITUTIONAL RIGHTS

As will be seen in the following discussion, the rights and remedies available to prisoners have been expanded greatly over the past 150 years. Certainly prison and jail administrators must know—and apply—the law in order to be in compliance with the Constitution and federal court decisions.

Demise of the "Hands-Off" Doctrine

Historically, the courts followed a **hands-off doctrine** regarding prison administration and **prisoners' rights**, deeming prisoners to be "slaves of the state." The judiciary, recognizing that it was not trained or knowledgeable in penology, allowed wardens the freedom and discretion to operate their institutions without outside interference, while being fearful of undermining the structure and discipline of the prison.

All that has changed, and the era of the **hands-on doctrine**, beginning in the mid-1960s, brought about a change of philosophy in the courts regarding prisoners' rights; prison inmates now retain all the rights of free citizens except those restrictions necessary for their orderly confinement or to provide safety in the prison community.

Selected Court Decisions

Following is a brief discussion of selected major U.S. Supreme Court decisions that spelled the demise of the hands-off era, while also vastly improving the everyday lives of prison and jail inmates and reforming correctional administration.

A "Slave of the State"

The 1871 case of Woody Ruffin serves as an excellent beginning point for an overview of significant court decisions concerning inmates' rights. Ruffin, an inmate in Virginia, killed a correctional officer while attempting to escape, and later challenged his conviction; the Virginia Supreme Court stated that Ruffin, like other prisoners, had "not only forfeited his liberty, but all his personal rights." The court added that inmates were **"slaves of the state,"** losing all their citizenship rights, including the right to complain about living conditions (*Ruffin v. Commonwealth*, 1871).[112]

Legal Remedy and Access to the Courts

In *Cooper v. Pate* (1964),[113] the Supreme Court first recognized the use of Title 42 of U.S. Code Section 1983 (discussed in Chapter 7) as a legal remedy for inmates. An Illinois state penitentiary inmate sued prison officials claiming that he was unconstitutionally punished by being placed in solitary confinement and being denied permission to purchase certain religious materials. The Supreme Court decided that he was entitled to purchase the articles—and that he could use Section 1983 to sue the prison administration.

Another significant case involved the right of access to the courts. Here, a Tennessee prisoner was disciplined for assisting other prisoners in preparing their legal writs, which violated a prison regulation. The Court acknowledged that "writ writers"

Student on the Street Video: Hands-off doctrine today

SAGE Journal Article: Hands-off doctrine

Hands-off doctrine: the notion by courts that prison administrators should be given free rein to run their prisons as they deem best.

Prisoners' rights: the collective body of rights given to inmates by the courts, in such areas as conditions of confinement, communications (mail and letters), access to law library and medical facilities, and so on.

Hands-on doctrine: the belief by courts that inmates have certain constitutional rights that the courts must see are upheld and also be obeyed by prison administrators.

"Slave of the state": an early philosophy toward prison inmates essentially stating that inmates had no legal rights that had to be observed by prison administrators.

are sometimes a menace to prison discipline, and their petitions are often a burden on the courts. However, because the state provided no "reasonable alternative" for illiterate or poorly educated inmates to prepare appeals, the Supreme Court said inmates could not be prevented from giving such assistance to other prisoners (*Johnson v. Avery*, 1969).[114]

In 1977, in another court-access decision, the Court said prisoners have a constitutional right to adequate law libraries or assistance from persons trained in the law. Alternative methods for providing such access included training inmates as paralegals; using paraprofessionals and law students to advise inmates; hiring lawyers on a part-time consultant basis; and having voluntary programs through bar associations, where lawyers make visits to the prisons to consult with inmates (*Bounds v. Smith*, 1977).[115]

First Amendment: Freedom of Religion

A landmark 1972 case clarified the right of inmates to exercise their religious beliefs. The plaintiff, a Buddhist, was not allowed to use the prison chapel and was placed in solitary confinement on a diet of bread and water for sharing his religious material with other prisoners. The Supreme Court held that inmates with unconventional religious beliefs must be given a reasonable opportunity to exercise those beliefs (*Cruz v. Beto*, 1972).[116]

The Supreme Court has also looked at prison mail censorship regulations that permitted authorities to hold back or to censor mail to and from prisoners. The Court based its ruling not on the rights of the prisoner, but instead on the *free-world* recipient's right to communicate with the prisoner, either by sending or by receiving mail. The court said mail censorship, if it is to be done, must be shown to enhance security, order, and rehabilitation; it must not be used simply to censor opinions or other expressions (*Procunier v. Martinez*, 1974).[117]

Fourth Amendment: Search and Seizure

Estelle v. Gamble (1976)[118] was the first major prison medical treatment case decided by the Supreme Court. Here, the Court coined the phrase "deliberate indifference," which is where the serious medical needs of prisoners involve the unnecessary and wanton infliction of pain. A Texas inmate claimed that he received cruel and unusual punishment due to inadequate treatment of a back injury sustained while he was engaged in prison work. The Court found that, because medical personnel saw him on 17 occasions during a three-month period, and failed to treat his injury and related problems, such deliberate indifference to his medical needs constituted the "unnecessary and wanton infliction of pain."

©Andrew Lichtenstein/Corbis

The U.S. Supreme Court has required that inmates must be given a reasonable opportunity to exercise their religious beliefs.

Fourteenth Amendment: Due Process

The Supreme Court's decision in *Wolff v. McDonnell* (1974)[119] is significant because, for the first time, the court acknowledged that inmates are entitled to certain due process rights during prison disciplinary proceedings. McDonnell and other inmates at a Nebraska prison alleged, among other things, that disciplinary proceedings at the prison violated due process. The Court said that "there is no iron curtain drawn between the Constitution and the prisons of this country," that "a prisoner is not wholly stripped of constitutional protections." This statement has become known as the Court's **"iron curtain" speech**. Prisoners were given several due process rights:

- Advance written notice of charges

- A written statement as to the evidence being relied on for the disciplinary action

- Ability to call witnesses and to present documentary evidence in the inmate's defense

- Use of counsel substitutes (e.g., a friend or staff member) if the inmate is illiterate or when complex issues require such assistance

- An impartial prison disciplinary board

"Iron curtain" speech: in *Wolff v. McDonnell* (1973), the Supreme Court stated that there is no iron curtain between the Constitution and the prisons of the United States; in sum, inmates have rights.

You Be the... CRIMINAL JUSTICE POLICY MAKER

Multiple murderer Charles Manson led a "family" who became notorious in 1969 after killing seven people, including pregnant actress Sharon Tate. Manson has been turned down for parole 12 times, and is eligible for parole next in 2027.

Now an octogenarian, Manson was issued a marriage license in late 2014 to wed 26-year-old Afton Burton (nicknamed "Star"), who says she loves Manson and even left her Illinois home nine years ago in order to live near Manson's place of incarceration, the California State Prison, Corcoron.[120] Manson later cancelled the wedding plans after learning that Star planned to put his corpse on display after his death and charge people money for the right to look at it.[121]

Noted criminologist James Alan Fox of Northeastern University characterizes such individuals as Star as "killer groupies," and notes that there is even a clinical label for them: hybristophilia, where someone is sexually aroused or attracted to a person who has committed a particularly violent crime.[122] Some such groupies, Fox believes, are attracted to their idol's controlling, manipulative personalities, or attempt to prove that their lover is innocent or a victim of injustice. Others wish to break through their lover's vicious façade with warm feelings, while still others merely wish to acquire the glamour and celebrity status that killer groupies find exciting.[123]

1. Should persons such as Manson who are in prison for heinous, capital crimes be allowed to marry?

2. If you believe not, then should nonviolent inmates (i.e., those convicted of property or drug offenses) be allowed to do so?

Note: Manson's photo is shown and his parole status discussed in Chapter 14.

IN A NUTSHELL

- Prison expert John Dilulio Jr. stated that incarcerated persons are not to suffer pains beyond the deprivation of liberty; confinement itself is the punishment. Furthermore, regardless of the crime, even the most heinous offender is to be treated with respect and dignity.

- Gresham Sykes described the "pains of imprisonment" as deprivations of liberty, goods and services, heterosexual relationships, autonomy, and security.

- Even with certain constitutional protections in place, there are a number of deprivations

and ill-effects of living in confinement, especially in solitary confinement; prisoners use an underground economy to make their incarceration less unpleasant. In addition, inmates can become "prisonized," where they adopt the morals and values of the prison culture.

- Prisons and jails are dangerous settings, and rioting and hostage taking are potentially explosive and perilous situations. It is critical that both prisons and jails have a coordinated plan to address such incidents.

- Some wardens believe there is simply never enough money to accomplish all four goals of punishment: to *incapacitate* and *rehabilitate* offenders, and to provide *deterrence* to crime and *retribution*. One must make choices—bearing in mind that the warden must, first and foremost, provide for incapacitation.

- Astute prison leadership will develop a JDLR mentality—knowing when things "just don't look right." It refers to having a sense of what's going on with the inmates—"reading the yard"—and thus knowing when problems are about to erupt.

- Historically, the courts followed a hands-off policy regarding prisons and prisoners' rights; that has changed, and the hands-on era, beginning in the mid-1960s, brought about a change of philosophy in the courts regarding prisoners' rights. Prison inmates now retain all the rights of free citizens except those restrictions necessary for their orderly confinement or to provide safety in the prison community.

- Women who are in prison pose unique problems: They often are in poor health, they are likely to have substance abuse problems, and they have special needs in terms of the right to privacy and the Fourth Amendment (i.e., the need to be searched).

- It is essential that correctional programs exist to assist inmates with their job skills, substance abuse issues, and so on prior to their reintegration into the community. Such programming should include adult drug courts, prison therapeutic communities, drug treatment, behavioral treatment, industry programs, basic adult education, and employment and vocational training.

- Prison administrators must know and understand the constitutional rights and privileges that exist for inmates under the U.S. Constitution as well as those established by federal court decisions.

▶ Review key terms with eFlashcards. ⑤SAGE edge™

KEY TERMS & CONCEPTS

Correctional officer, 327
Hands-off doctrine, 339
Hands-on doctrine, 339
Inmate litigation, 332

"Iron curtain" speech, 341
JDLR, 331
Prisoners' rights, 339
Prisonization, 321

Reentry and aftercare, 338
"Slave of the state," 339
Solitary confinement, 323
Underground economy, 323

REVIEW QUESTIONS

▶ Test your understanding of chapter content. Take the practice quiz. ⑤SAGE edge™

1. What did Philip Zimbardo set out to prove in his mock prison experiment? What was the outcome?

2. What are the constitutional conditions of confinement, and what are the deprivations of prison life that are said to be the "pains" of imprisonment?

3. How does an inmate become "prisonized"?

4. What kinds of factors make prisons and jails dangerous in nature, and what indicators or conditions might exist that would foreshadow a riot or another major incident?

5. How do jails differ from prisons in terms of purpose and environment?

6. What are the duties of correctional officers?

7. What are some of the unique aspects of women being in prison in terms of their deprivations and adjustment? Of older (geriatric), mentally ill, drug-addicted, and gang-affiliated inmates?

8. How would you describe the administrative duties involved in carrying out executions?

9. What major federal court decisions have been rendered concerning prisoners' rights?

10. What is the nature and extent of litigation by prison and jail inmates? How has the PLRA affected such litigation?

11. What kinds of correctional programming can assist with inmate reintegration into the community?

1. Running a "take back the streets" anticrime campaign, a newly elected governor sends all prison wardens a letter stating in effect that prisons should not be a "Hotel Ritz" operation and that he is considering a new policy that would end all "useless educational programs beyond a GED," and "end all weight-lifting and such programs as Alcoholics Anonymous, the prison band, and gardening." The governor asks you as a warden for your viewpoint concerning these changes, particularly the following:

   a. Do such prison programs have positive benefits for the inmates? Negative aspects for the institution?

   b. Where might you try to negotiate with the governor?

2. The prison warden's associate director for security has been directed to prepare an immediate plan for dealing with the following situation:

   Inmates in the local prison are stocking up on long-term items (e.g., canned goods) in the commissary and banding together more throughout the institution by racial groupings; furthermore, inmates tend to be seen standing in or near doorways, as if preparing for a quick exit. Over the past several months, the inmates have become increasingly unhappy with their conditions of confinement—not only concerning the food, but also with the increasing numbers of assaults and gang attacks. The staff members, for their part, have also become increasingly unhappy, particularly with their low salaries and benefits, perceived unsafe working conditions and attacks on officers, prison overcrowding, and a trend toward greater amounts of contraband being found in the cell blocks. They demand that the prison administration ask the parole board to grant more early releases and the courts to give more consideration to house arrest and electronic monitoring to ease the situation.

   What sort of plan will the associate warden prepare? Include in your response the critical issues that should be dealt with immediately, what steps you would take to defuse the potential for a riot, and measures that might be adopted later, in the long term, concerning staff morale and demands.

$SAGE edge™

Review → Practice → Improve

Sharpen your skills with **SAGE edge** at **edge.sagepub.com/peak2e**

SAGE edge for students provides a personalized approach to help you accomplish your coursework goals in an easy-to-use learning environment. Access the videos, audio clips, quizzes, and SAGE journal articles that are noted in this chapter.

CHAPTER 14

CORRECTIONS IN THE COMMUNITY

Probation, Parole, and Other Alternatives to Incarceration

LEARNING OBJECTIVES

As a result of reading this chapter, you will be able to:

1 Describe what is meant by community corrections

2 Explain why the criminal justice system uses alternatives to incarceration

3 Describe the definitions and origins of probation and parole, as well as the differences between them

4 Identify the eligibility and rights accorded to people serving terms of probation or parole

5 Explain the functions of probation and parole officers—and the impact of high caseloads

6 Explain the purposes and functions of intermediate sanctions, including intensive supervision, house arrest, electronic monitoring, shock incarceration/boot camps, and day reporting centers

7 Provide an overview of the risk-needs-responsivity (RNR) model for addressing reoffending

8 Explain the rationale that underlies the use of restorative justice

ASSESS YOUR AWARENESS

Test your knowledge of probation and parole by responding to the following seven true-false items; check your answers after reading this chapter's materials.

1 Probation began with the voluntary work of a simple Boston shoe cobbler.

2 Probation, because it is more costly than prison, is used sparingly in the United States.

3 Being placed on parole allows the offender to remain in the community and thus avoid the "pains" of imprisonment.

4 A person may have his or her probation revoked and then be sent to prison for behaviors such as use of alcohol, curfew violations, and associating with other known criminals.

5 Persons whose probation or parole status might be revoked and who thus might be sent to prison enjoy no legal rights or benefits.

6 In addition to probation and parole, other alternatives to prison that have been attempted include house arrest, electronic monitoring, and boot camps.

7 Restorative justice places stronger emphasis on involving the community and focusing on the victim.

The mood and temper of the public in regard to the treatment of crime and criminals is one of the most unfailing tests of the civilization of any country.

—Winston Churchill

<< Answers can be found on page 424.

United States Federal Bureau of Investigation

In 1981, 25-year-old John Hinckley Jr. fired six shots, striking President Ronald Reagan, press secretary James Brady, and two Secret Service agents, in a highly irrational attempt to gain the attention of actress Jodie Foster. Since 1982, Hinckley has been confined to St. Elizabeth's Hospital in Washington, D.C., having been found not guilty by reason of insanity. Since 1999, federal judges have gradually expanded the time he is allowed off-campus. In December 2013, he was allowed to visit his mother in Williamsburg, Virginia, for 17 days. Federal prosecutors are unhappy, however, with Hinckley's increasing freedom, arguing that he has a history of deceptiveness and that the concerns of the Reagan and Brady families were not given enough weight in the decision. Furthermore, while institutionalized, Hinckley has corresponded with notorious serial killer Ted Bundy and tried to write to Charles Manson (discussed later in this chapter). Not only do Hinckley's psychiatrists believe that he does not pose a danger to himself or others and should be granted an unconditional, permanent release, but a judge has allowed him to spend up to 17 days a month in Virginia, where he even drives himself up to a 50-mile radius to visit friends and family.[1] As you read about probation and parole in this chapter, consider the goals of each as well as whether or not violent offenders such as Hinckley can ever be safely released back into the community.

John Hinckley Jr., who attempted to assassinate President Ronald Reagan in March 1981, was found not guilty by reason of insanity.

INTRODUCTION

"I would like to use my college degree to help people who have gotten into trouble. Should I work in probation or parole? Should I work with adults or juveniles? And what kind of work would I be doing?" These questions have a ring of familiarity to most if not all criminal justice professors, as many students today seek to make their contributions to society by working with and trying to reform criminal offenders.

The word *probation* is probably familiar to most college and university students. If they don't "make the grades," they can be placed on academic probation; if their athletic programs fail to adhere to the rules of the National Collegiate Athletic Association (NCAA), the institution and its athletic program(s) can be placed on probationary status. The common thread here is that each group or individual is served warning that it had better change its behavior, or there will be more severe penalties.

And so it is with our criminal offenders—most of whom are sentenced to a *community-based* form of punishment, with probation being one form that is quite often used. This chapter examines **community corrections**—probation, parole, and a variety of other measures that constitute a broad array of alternatives to incarceration. It begins by looking at arguments for having alternatives to incarcerations, both philosophical and economic in nature. Following that are discussions of the origins and contemporary aspects of probation and parole. Included here are the rights that probationers and parolees have when the state wishes to remove their freedom and send them to prison, as well as the functions of probation and parole officers—including the impact of high caseloads and the debate concerning whether or not these officers should be armed.

Then intermediate sanctions are discussed. These alternatives to incarceration may be lesser known but are still quite beneficial to offenders and help to decrease prison and

Community corrections: probation, parole, and a variety of other measures that offer convicted offenders an alternative(s) to incarceration

jail populations; they include intensive supervision (of probation), house arrest, electronic monitoring, shock incarceration/boot camps, and day reporting centers. Following a review of the risk-needs-responsivity (RNR) model, which is used to assess what programs to use with offenders to stop the cycle of reoffending and reincarceration, is a discussion of a relatively new movement in criminal justice: restorative justice.

Several topics relating closely to this chapter—for example, issues facing offenders concerning release, reentry, and aftercare—are discussed in Chapter 13.

Video: Community corrections

WHY ALTERNATIVES TO INCARCERATION?

The leading alternative to incarceration is probation, which was discussed briefly in Chapter 1 and is defined as the court's allowing a convicted person to remain at liberty in the community, while being subject to certain conditions and restrictions on his or her activities. The United States is not soft on crime, but there are several valid reasons for using **alternatives to incarceration**:

Student on the Street Video: Probation versus prison costs

- It allows the offender to remain in the community, which has a greater rehabilitative effect than incarceration, thereby reducing recidivism.

- It allows the offender to take greater advantage of treatment or counseling options.

- It allows the offender to avoid the "pains" of imprisonment (as discussed in Chapter 13).

- It is far less expensive.

- It permits ongoing ties with family, employment, and other social networks.

However, to be effective, a real alternative to incarceration needs to have three elements: It must incapacitate offenders enough so that it is possible to interfere with their lives and activities to make committing a new offense extremely difficult; it must be unpleasant enough to deter offenders from wanting to commit new crimes; and it has to provide real and credible protection for the community.[2]

Nearly a half-century ago, the President's Commission on Law Enforcement and Administration of Justice (1967) endorsed community-based corrections—the use of probation and parole—as a humane, logical, and effective approach for working with and changing criminal offenders. According to the commission, that includes

> building or rebuilding solid ties between the offender and the community, obtaining employment and education, securing in the large sense a place for the offender in the routine functioning of society. This requires . . . efforts directed towards changing the individual offender (and) mobilization and change of the community and its institutions.[3]

The demand for prison space has created a reaction throughout corrections.[4] With the cost of prison construction now exceeding a quarter of a million dollars per cell in maximum-security institutions, cost-saving alternatives are becoming more attractive, if not essential.

The realities of prison construction and overcrowding have led to a search for intermediate punishments.[5] This in turn has brought about the emergence of a new generation of programs, making community-based corrections, according to Barry Nidorf, a "strong, full partner in the fight against crime and a leader in confronting the crowding

Alternatives to incarceration: a sentence imposed by a judge other than incarceration, such as probation, parole, shock probation, or house arrest.

crisis."[6] Economic reality dictates that cost-effective measures be developed, and this is motivating the development of intermediate sanctions.[7]

ORIGINS OF PROBATION AND PAROLE

The concepts of probation and parole have long and interesting histories.

Probation Begins: The Humble Shoe Cobbler

Although contemporary **probation** has roots dating to biblical times,[8] its history in the United States dates to the 19th century. "Judicial reprieve" was used in English courts to serve as a temporary suspension of sentence to allow the defendant to appeal to the Crown for a pardon. In the United States, the suspended sentence was used as early as 1830 in Boston and became widespread in American courts, even though there was no statutory provision for it. By the mid-19th century, though, many courts were using a judicial reprieve to suspend sentences.[9] This posed a legal question: Could judges suspend sentences wholesale, after trials that were scrupulously fair, simply to give the defendant a second chance?[10]

In 1916, the U.S. Supreme Court, in a decision affecting only the federal courts, held that judges did not have the discretionary authority to suspend sentences. However, the Court ruled that Congress could authorize the temporary or indefinite suspension of sentences; this led to the development of probation statutes.[11]

John Augustus, a Boston shoe cobbler, is credited as being the "father of probation." In 1841 Augustus appeared in court on behalf of a drunkard; as Augustus later explained, "I was in court one morning . . . in which the man was charged with being a common drunkard. He told me that if he could be saved from the House of Correction, he never again would taste intoxicating liquors; I bailed him, by permission of the court."[12] During his first year of service as an unpaid, volunteer probation officer, Augustus assisted 10 drunkards. By Augustus's own account, he eventually bailed "eleven hundred persons, both male and female."

Augustus performed several tasks that are reminiscent of modern probation. He investigated each case—inquiring into the offender's character, age, and influences—and kept careful records of each person's progress. His probation work soon caused him to fall into financial difficulties, however, requiring his friends' monetary assistance. Augustus died in 1859.

By 1869, the Massachusetts legislature had required that a state agent be present if court actions might result in the placement of a child in a reformatory (the forerunner of today's caseworkers). Then, in 1878, Massachusetts passed the first probation statute, mandating an official state probation system with salaried probation officers. Other states quickly followed suit:

- By 1900, Vermont, Rhode Island, New Jersey, New York, Minnesota, and Illinois passed probation laws.

- By 1910, 32 more states passed legislation establishing juvenile probation.

- By 1930, juvenile probation was legislated in every state except Wyoming.[13]

Parole Origins: Alexander Maconochie

The word *parole* stems from the French *parol*, or "word of honor," which was a means of releasing prisoners of war who promised not to resume arms in a current conflict.[14]

Probation: an alternative to incarceration in which the convict remains out of jail or prison and in the community and thus on the job, with family, and so on, while subject to conditions and supervision of the probation authority.

One writer cited the year 1840 as one in which "one of the most remarkable experiments in the history of penology was initiated."[15]

In that year, Alexander Maconochie became superintendent of the British penal colony on Norfolk Island, about 930 miles northeast of Sydney, Australia. He began a philosophy of punishment based on reforming offenders: The convict was to be punished for the past while being trained for the future. Maconochie advocated open-ended ("indeterminate") sentences. His system worked, although it was harshly ridiculed by some Australians as "coddling criminals."

Returning to England in 1844, Maconochie began writing and speaking of his experiment. One of those impressed by Maconochie was Walter Crofton, who in 1854 became director of the renowned Irish system of penal management. Crofton implemented, among many other things, a "ticket of leave" system, allowing inmates to be conditionally released from prison, to be supervised by the police. Crofton recommended a similar system for the United States.

Inmates on parade in Elmira's yard.

In 1876, when Zebulon Brockway was appointed superintendent of the Elmira Reformatory in New York, he drafted a statute providing for indeterminate sentences. Continued good behavior by inmates resulted in early release—America's first parole system. Paroled inmates remained under the jurisdiction of reformatory authorities for an additional six months, during which the parolee was required to report on the first day of every month to his appointed guardian and provide an account of his conduct and situation (a decade after Elmira began operations, New York opened three women's reformatories). This system was copied by other states; it was expanded further by the Great Depression, which abolished economic exploitation of convict labor.[16]

Once introduced in the United States, parole spread fairly rapidly. In doing so, it survived an early series of constitutional challenges.[17] A 1939 survey reported that, by 1922, parole existed in 44 states, the federal system, and Hawaii.[18] Mississippi adopted a parole law in 1944, becoming the last state to do so.

Many reasons have been offered for the relatively rapid spread of parole legislation:

- There was general dissatisfaction with the determinate sentencing provisions of the time, and parole was seen as a response to some of the criticisms: Parole would promote reformation of prisoners by providing an incentive to change; at the same time, it would serve as a means of equalizing disparate judicial sentences.[19]

- Release before sentence expiration was already an aspect of most prison systems—through "good-time" deductions, which began in New York in 1817, and through gubernatorial clemency, which was used far more extensively than today.

- Parole was believed useful for enforcing prison discipline and for controlling prison population levels.[20]

PROBATION AND PAROLE TODAY

Probation and parole—together termed "community corrections"—is the status of a majority of persons who are under correctional supervision. Today about 4.8 million adults are under correctional supervision in the community in the United States; about 4 million of these adults are on probation, and the remainder are serving parole.[21] Regarding offenses, about half (53 percent) of the persons on *probation* were convicted for committing a felony; furthermore, about one-fourth of them committed a drug offense, while another one-fourth committed a property offense.[22]

Probation: Eligibility and Rights

Student on the
Street Video: Serving
full prison terms

Judges consider a number of factors when evaluating the eligibility of an offender for probation:

- The nature and seriousness of the current offense

- Whether a weapon was used and the degree of physical or emotional injury, if any, to the victim

- Whether the victim was an active or a passive participant in the crime

- The length and seriousness of the offender's prior record

- The offender's previous success or failure on probation

- The offender's prior incarcerations and success or failure on parole[23]

Technical violation: in probation and parole, when one violates certain conditions that must be obeyed to remain out of prison, such as curfew violation, drug or alcohol use, or not maintaining a job.

Although a decision is made for the offender to remain free and avoid incarceration, the probationer must still abide by certain conditions that the court and probation officers will put in place to govern his or her behavior. If the probationer does not comply with those conditions, there are two possible types of violations that might be committed:

- **Technical violations:** These may include failing to pay court costs or fines, missing a probation meeting, using alcohol, violating curfew, associating with

You Be the... JUDGE

After a jury acquitted 25-year-old Casey Anthony in July 2011 on charges of first-degree murder, aggravated child abuse, and aggravated manslaughter of her 2-year-old daughter Caylee, the only convictions that remained were for lying to detectives seeking to find out what happened to the child. The task then facing Orlando, Florida, judge Belvin Perry was to determine whether and how Anthony would serve a term of probation. Complicating Judge Perry's decision was a survey that found Anthony was the most hated person in America—and a high probability that many people would like to do her harm. Anthony's attorneys argued that she had already served her probation while in jail awaiting the murder trial. On the other side, prosecutors maintained that probation should be continued, because the purpose of probation is to

help offenders after they are released back into the community. Meanwhile, Anthony's parents stated that she would not be returning to their home (wishing to avoid media and traffic problems there). Other possibilities included having her serve probation out of state or giving her administrative probation—being able to travel anywhere but contacting her probation officer each month.

1. Should the judge order Casey Anthony to serve probation?
2. If so, where, how, and for what length of time would you recommend it be served?

The judge's decision is provided in the Notes section at the end of the book.[24]

other known criminals, failing to submit to a mandatory drug test, failing a drug test, failing to complete community service, and engaging in out-of-state travel or changing address without permission.

- **Substantive violations:** These occur when the probationer commits a new criminal offense.

Following are several factors that the judge and prosecutor may take into account when considering a probation violation:

- The seriousness and nature of the probation violation

- The history of previous probation violations

- New criminal activity surrounding the probation violation

- Aggravating and mitigating circumstances of the probation violation

Substantive violation: an allegation that one was arrested for a new criminal offense while serving probation.

INVESTIGATING FURTHER

TERMS AND CONDITIONS OF PROBATION

Rules of the Superior Court of the State of New Hampshire Applicable in Criminal Cases Filed in Superior Court

Sec.107. The probationer shall:

(a) Report to the probation or parole officer at such times and places as directed, comply with the probation or parole officer's instructions, and respond truthfully to all inquiries from the probation or parole (P&P) officer;

(b) Comply with all orders, including orders for payment of money;

(c) Obtain permission before changing residence, employment, or traveling out of State;

(d) Notify the P&P officer immediately of any arrest or questioning by a law enforcement officer;

(e) Diligently seek and maintain lawful employment, notify employer of legal status, and support dependents to the best of your ability;

(f) Not receive, possess, control or transport any weapon, explosive or firearm, or simulated weapon, explosive, or firearm;

(g) Be of good conduct, obey all laws, and be arrest-free;

(h) Submit to reasonable searches of person, property and possessions as requested by the P&P officer and permit same to visit the residence at reasonable times, to examine and inspect conditions of probation or parole;

(i) Not associate with any person having a criminal record or with other individuals;

(j) Not indulge in the illegal use, sale, possession, distribution, or transportation, or be in the presence, of controlled drugs, or use alcoholic beverages to excess;

(k) Agree to waive extradition to the State from any State in the U.S. if directed by the P&P officer; and

(l) Comply with the following, or any other special conditions as may be imposed by the Court or the P&P board or officer:

(1) Participate regularly in Alcoholics Anonymous;

(2) Secure written permission prior to purchasing and/or operating a motor vehicle;

(3) Participate in and satisfactorily complete a specific designated program;

(4) Enroll and participate in mental health counseling on a regular basis;

(5) Not be in the unsupervised company of minors of one or the other sex at any time;

(6) Not leave the county without permission of the probation or parole officer;

(7) Refrain totally from the use of alcoholic beverages;

(8) Submit to breath, blood or urine testing for abuse substances as directed; and

(9) Comply with designated house arrest provisions.

Source: For the purpose of brevity, this list is adapted and condensed from the original; for the complete listing of rules, see http://www.courts.state.nh.us/rules/sror/sror-h3-107.htm.

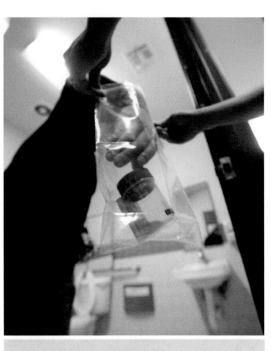

One of the typical conditions placed on a probationer is that he or she submit to mandatory drug tests.

- The probation officer and/or probation department's view of the probation violation

- The probation violation with respect to the probation term (whether it occurred at the beginning, middle, or end of the probationary term)

About 30 percent of probationers exit probation supervision each year because they are incarcerated for a new crime, violate a condition of supervision, or abscond, or for some other reason (see Table 14.1).[25] The violation of probation is a serious offense, can be a felony, and can result in a judge's revoking probation. As soon as a probation violation occurs, an arrest may soon follow, and the defendant may be ordered to appear in court for a probation violation hearing. If a judge revokes probation, state laws often allow the judge to impose the maximum penalty for the charge.

Certain rights have been afforded probationers who are about to undergo a probation **revocation** hearing. First, in *Mempa v. Rhay* (1967), the U.S. Supreme Court held that such hearings are a "critical stage" where substantive rights could be lost, and that the Sixth Amendment therefore required the presence of counsel to help in "marshaling facts."[27] Later, in 1973, the Supreme Court decided *Gagnon v. Scarpelli*, in which a probationer had his probation revoked without a hearing; the court determined that probationers had certain due process rights, including the following:[28]

Video:
Probation officers

- Notice of the alleged violation

- A preliminary hearing to determine probable cause

- The right to present evidence

- The right to confront adverse witnesses

- A written report of the hearing

- A final revocation hearing

Parole: Eligibility and Rights

About one-third of all *parolees* were incarcerated for a drug offense, and one-fourth had committed a property offense.[29]

Similar to probation decision making, the following general criteria will be taken into account when considering whether or not an inmate should be granted parole:

- The nature and seriousness of the current offense, including aggravating and mitigating circumstances

- Statements made in court concerning the sentence

- The length and seriousness of the offender's prior record

- The inmate's attitude toward the offense, family members, the victim, and authority in general

- The attitude of the victim or victim's family regarding the inmate's release

Revocation: the court's revoking probation/parole status for the purpose of returning an offender to prison (usually for not following the conditions of probation/parole or for committing a new offense).

TABLE 14.1 Probationers Who Exited Supervision, by Type of Exit, 2008–2013[26]

TYPE OF EXIT	2008	2009	2010	2011	2012	2013
Completion	63%	65%	65%	66%	68%	66%
Incarceration[a]	17	16	16	16	15	15
Absconder	4	3	3	2	3	3
Discharged to custody, detainer, or warrant	1	1	1	1	1	–
Other unsatisfactory[b]	10	10	11	9	9	11
Transferred to another probation agency	1	*	1	1	1	1
Death	1	1	1	1	1	1
Other[c]	4	4	4	4	4	3
Estimated number[d]	2,320,100	2,327,800	2,261,300	2,189,100	2,089,800	2,131,300

Note: Details may not sum to total due to rounding. Distributions are based on probationers for which type of exit was known.

* = Less than 0.5%.

[a]Includes probationers who were incarcerated for a new offense or those who had their current probation sentence revoked (e.g., violating a condition of their supervision).

[b]Includes probationers discharged from supervision who did not meet all conditions of supervision, including some with financial conditions remaining, some who had their probation sentence invoked but were not incarcerated because their sentence was immediately reinstated, and other types of unsatisfactory exits. May include some early terminations and expirations of sentence reported as unsatisfactory exits.

[c]Includes probationers discharged from supervision through legislative mandate because they were deported or transferred to the jurisdiction of Immigration and Customs Enforcement (ICE); they were transferred to another state through an interstate compact agreement; their sentence was dismissed or overturned by the court through an appeal; their sentence was closed administratively, deferred, or terminated by the court; they were awaiting a hearing; they were released on bond; and other types of exits.

[d]Estimates rounded to the nearest hundred. Includes estimates for nonreporting agencies. Estimates are based on most recent data available and may differ from published Bureau of Justice Statistics reports.

- The inmate's insight into causes of past criminal conduct

- The inmate's adjustment to previous probation, parole, or incarceration

- The inmate's participation in institutional programs

- The adequacy of the inmate's parole plan, including residence and employment[30]

As with probationers, the parolee must still abide by certain conditions that the court and parole officers will put in place. If the parolee does not comply with those conditions, there are two possible types of violations that might be committed:

Author Video:
Probation officers
and challenges

- Technical violations: These may include failing to report regularly to the parole officer (PO), not keeping the PO advised of changes in address, not providing notice of change in employment, not reporting any new arrest, associating with other felons, traveling in violation of time or distance constraints, possessing weapons, using alcohol or drugs, wearing electronic monitoring device improperly, or contacting a partner who was victimized in a domestic violence case.

- Substantive violations: These occur when the parolee commits a new criminal offense.

If either or a combination of these conditions occurs, charges of parole violation may be initiated by a parole officer.

PRACTITIONER'S PERSPECTIVE

PROBATION AND PAROLE OFFICER

Name: Dori Ege

Current Position: Arizona Deputy Compact Administrator for Adult Probation, Arizona Compact Commissioner for Parole and Probation

City, State: Phoenix, Arizona

College Attended/Academic Major: Bachelor of arts in criminal justice from St. Cloud State University, Minnesota

How long have you been a practitioner in a career relating to probation and parole? 13 years, 3 months.

The primary duties and responsibilities of a probation and parole officer: To ensure offender compliance with the conditions of supervision imposed by the court or paroling authority through required face-to-face contacts, reports from treatment providers, drug testing, residence searches, and providing or referring the offender to other resources as needed (e.g., employment skills training). In addition, officers must update the court or paroling authority regarding the offender's compliance with the conditions of supervision through official memos, emails, or petitions to either modify the term of supervision for compliant behavior or revoke the offender's supervision and return him or her to a custody status. Probation and parole officers are often required to testify at status or official hearings regarding the offender's compliance with conditions and terms. These can range from hearings to determine early termination of supervision or hearings to revoke supervision and return the offender to custody. In many, officers are also required to update victims who are associated with an offender's case in accordance with local victim notification requirements.

The qualities/characteristics that are most helpful in this career: Resilience, integrity, confidence, reliability, excellent writing skills, excellent communication skills, leadership skills, and fairness and consistency.

In general, this is what a *typical day* looks like for a practitioner in this career: Conducting office and field visits with offenders to monitor compliance with conditions imposed by a court or paroling authority; writing reports regarding compliance or noncompliance of conditions; testifying at or attending court hearings regarding assigned offenders; and fielding phone calls and email correspondence from offenders, their families, employers, treatment providers, attorneys, and other members of the criminal justice system regarding cases assigned to the officer's caseload.

My advice to someone either wishing to study, or now studying, criminal justice and wanting to become a practitioner in this career: If you possess a passion for working in the criminal justice system, remember that passion and always remain fair and consistent. Complacency has no place in this field, and it can be detrimental. This is a rewarding field of study and an incredible field for a career for those who want to effect change in others, while also promoting public safety.

Until 1972, decisions to revoke one's parole and return him or her to prison could be made arbitrarily by individual parole officers. However, the U.S. Supreme Court, in *Morrissey v. Brewer*, held in that year that parolees who faced the possibility of losing their freedom possessed certain rights under the Fourteenth Amendment:[31]

- Written notice of the alleged violation(s)
- A preliminary hearing to establish whether there is probable cause that the parolee violated the conditions of parole
- Disclosure of the evidence against the parolee
- The opportunity to be heard in person and to present witnesses and documentary evidence

- The right to confront and cross-examine adverse witnesses
- A neutral and detached body to hear the evidence
- A written statement by the fact-finders concerning the evidence relied upon for any revocation decision

If the hearing officer (not necessarily a judge) finds that probable cause exists to believe that a violation has occurred, the hearing will move to the adjustment phase, which is where the information is introduced about why the individual should or should not be continued on supervision.

One of the most important groups of individuals that parole board members come in contact with is victims of crime. At one time, victims were not typically involved with the parole process in this country, but that has changed. Through strong victim advocacy, crime victims have begun to be recognized as key stakeholders in the criminal justice process. Today, paroling authorities typically provide victims with information concerning any activity in their offender's case, provide opportunities for input to the board—in person and/or in writing—and take into account the needs and dangers to victims as part of their decision-making procedures. A number of states now appoint victims of crime or victim advocates as members of their paroling authorities.[32]

Figure 14.1 shows the parole decision-making guidelines employed by the Pennsylvania Board of Probation and Parole.

You Be the... PAROLE BOARD

California Department of Corrections and Rehabilitation

Charles Manson, born in 1934, is serving a life sentence for leading a 1969 killing spree in Los Angeles that ended the lives of seven people. Manson has not been a model inmate. Should he ever be paroled?

Assume you are serving on the state parole board in the following matter: Charles Manson, age 77, is serving a life sentence for a 1969 killing spree in Los Angeles (his "family" brutally murdered seven people). Manson has not been a model inmate, recently possessing a weapon, threatening a peace officer, and being caught twice with contraband cell phones. Given his age, this could be Manson's final appearance before the state parole board. Debra Tate, a victim's sister (murdered actress Sharon Tate), is attending the hearing, and attorneys from both sides are prepared to give presentations, read documents by victims' relatives or other interested parties, and examine Manson's prison records. Manson, as is his custom, is not attending the parole hearing.

1. Will you vote to grant or deny Manson's parole at this time?

2. If not, do you believe there are programs or redeeming actions or qualities Manson might undertake or possess to secure his freedom in the future?

The outcome of his 2012 parole hearing is provided in the Notes section at the end of the book.[33]

FIGURE 14.1   Pennsylvania Board of Probation and Parole, Parole Decision-Making Guidelines

**PENNSYLVANIA BOARD
OF PROBATION AND PAROLE**

PAROLE DECISION MAKING GUIDELINES

Name _____

Parole No. _____ SID No. _____ Institution No. _____

Date of Interview _____ Institution _____

Interview Type ___ Minimum ___ Review ___ Reparole Review ___ Parole Application

---

Violence Indicator

1. Instant Offense

Violent ▢ +3
Non-Violent ▢ +1

(1) Murder, Voluntary Manslaughter, Aggravated Assault, Robbery, Arson, Burglary (Residential), Assault by Prisoner, Assault by Life Prisoner, Kidnapping, Extortion Accompanied by Threats of Violence, all Sex Crimes, and criminal attempt, criminal conspiracy, and/or criminal solicitation to commit any of the above-noted offenses.

Risk/Needs Assessment

2. Level of Service Inventory - Revised

Raw Score: _____

High Risk ▢ +3
Medium Risk ▢ +2
Low Risk ▢ +1

Sex Offender Risk Assessment (Static 99)

Raw Score: _____

High Risk ▢ +3
Medium Risk ▢ +2
Low Risk ▢ +1

(All offenders considered for parole shall be assessed using the Level of Service Inventory - Revised ("LSI-R"). Offenders convicted of a sex offense shall be assessed using the LSI-R as well as the Sex Offender Risk Assessment Instrument. **The higher level of risk shall be used for all sex offenders.***

Institution Adjustment

3. Institutional Programming

Unacceptable Program Compliance ▢ +3
Reasonable Efforts (2) ▢ +2
Currently Involved ▢ +1
Completion of Required Programs (3) ▢ +0

(2) No access or on waiting list.
(3) Includes offenders who are currently involved and will complete prior to release

---

Source: Peggy B. Burke, *A Handbook for New Parole Board Members* (Washington, D.C.: U.S. Department of Justice, National Institute of Corrections, and Association of Paroling Authorities International, April 2003), pp. 41–42, http://www.apaintl.org/documents/CEPPParoleHandbook.pdf.

Note: The Level of Service Inventory—Revised (LSI-R) mentioned in the figure includes both criminal history items and measures of offender needs, such as substance abuse, employment, and special-needs accommodations. The tool is administered during a standardized, one-hour interview, and it evaluates indicators of program success (e.g., residence, family ties, employment) and predictors of program failure (e.g., prior convictions, prior failures to appear, prior violations of sentence). It includes 54 items, and responses are totaled to give a risk-needs score. *Source:* Joan Petersilia, *When Prisoners Come Home* (New York: Oxford University Press, 2003), pp. 72–73.

DO PROBATION AND PAROLE WORK?

Do probation and parole work by reducing arrests? An ambitious 2013 study by California's Council of State Governments (CSG) Justice Center attempted to learn the answer, examining more than 2.5 million adult arrest, probation, and parole supervision records from 11 agencies in four cities—Los Angeles, Redlands, Sacramento, and San Francisco—over a 42-month period.[34] The CSG wanted to determine (1) the extent to which people on probation and parole contribute to crime, as measured by arrests, and (2) the types of crimes these people are most likely to commit.[35]

The findings were a bit surprising. First, people under probation or parole supervision accounted for 22 percent of total arrests—which means that nearly 8 of 10 arrestees were not supervised, certainly a respectable finding. However, one in three arrests for *drug* crimes involved someone who was on probation or parole—in fact, people under supervision were more likely to be arrested on drug offenses than for violent, property, or other types of crimes.[36] During the study period, the number of total arrests declined by 18 percent, while the number of arrests of people who were under supervision declined by *40 percent*—61 percent for persons on parole and 26 percent for individuals under probation supervision.[37] It seems, therefore, that supervision generally works, but more work remains to be done in terms of keeping parolees and probationers from reoffending for drug abuse. Figure 14.2 displays some of the findings.

FUNCTIONS OF PROBATION AND PAROLE OFFICERS

Both probation and parole officers perform similar functions; in fact, in some states, the jobs of parole and probation officers are combined. Both must possess important skills, such as good interpersonal communication, decision-making, and writing skills. They operate independently, with less supervision than most prison staff experience. Both are trained in the techniques for supervising offenders and then assigned a caseload. They may be on call 24 hours a day to supervise and assist offenders at any time.[38]

Probation and "Front-End" Duties

Probation officers supervise offenders at the *front* end of the sentencing continuum—those offenders with a suspended prison sentence—monitoring their behavior in the community and their compliance with the conditions of probation. Probation officers usually work with either adults or juveniles exclusively. Only in small, usually rural, jurisdictions do probation officers counsel both adults and juveniles.

Probation officers have a number of duties, including

- Report to the court any violations of probation

- As officers of the courts, perform presentence investigations (as discussed in Chapter 9) and prepare reports concerning the clients on their caseload

- Enforce court orders, such as arresting those who violate the terms of their probation

- Perform searches, seize evidence, and arrange for drug testing

- Attend hearings to update the court on offenders' efforts at rehabilitation and compliance with the terms of their sentences

SAGE Journal Article: Probation and parole training

Probation officer: one who supervises the activities of persons on probation.

FIGURE 14.2 Do Probation and Parole Work?

RESEARCH FINDINGS

Approximately one in five arrests involved an individual under probation or parole supervision; the majority of total arrests involved people who were not under supervision.

A key objective of this study was to determine to what extent people under correctional supervision drove arrest activity. To make that determination, researchers matched arrest data with parole and probation supervision data.

Supervision Status Among All Adult Arrestees:

Total Adult Arrests

🧍 = Probationers

🧍 = Parolees

🧍 = Not on Supervision

DESIGNATION	ADULT ARRESTS	% OF TOTAL
Total	476,054	100%
Parolees	40,476	8.5%
Probationers	66,251	13.9%
Not Supervised	369,327	77.6%

Source: Council of State Governments Justice Center, *The Impact of Probation and Parole Populations on Arrests in Four California Cities* (January 2013), p. 14, http://www.cdcr.ca.gov/Reports/docs/External-Reports/CAL-CHIEFS-REPORT.pdf.

- Utilize technologies as required, including electronic monitoring devices and drug screening

- Seek the assistance of community organizations, such as religious institutions, neighborhood groups, and local residents, to monitor the behavior of many offenders[39]

Probation officers—as well as parole officers—often experience role conflict, which is brought about by what they perceive as a discrepancy between their two main functions: On the one hand, their job is to "enforce" lawful behavior of their clients, and sometimes revoke probation and parole, which is obviously more law enforcement oriented in nature; on the other hand, they must also be empathetic and understanding, and provide guidance and counseling to their clients, which is more of a social worker role.[40] These seemingly contradictory roles can contribute to job stress.

Parole and "Back-End" Duties

Parole officers perform *back*-end duties of the sentencing continuum, supervising offenders who have been released from prison. Parole officers are most often employed by the state department of corrections; the state criminal justice department; or a youth authority/juvenile corrections, county, or federal justice department. Like probation officers, parole officers supervise offenders through personal contact with the offenders and their families; this can be quite dangerous (and lead to role conflict, discussed previously), as parole officers work with paroled convicts, their friends, and their family. As with probationers, some parolees are required to wear an electronic device so that probation officers can monitor their location and movements. Parole officers

Probation officers monitor offenders' behavior in order to check their compliance with the conditions of their probation. These probation officers are performing a compliance sweep at a probationer's home.

- Help parolees adjust back into society, as well as avert any actions that would jeopardize their parole status

- Develop a plan for the parolee before he or she is released from prison

- Plan the employment, housing, health care, education, drug screening, and other activities that help the parolee's rehabilitation and functioning in a community environment

- Arrange for offenders to get substance abuse rehabilitation or job training

- Attend parole hearings and make recommendations based on their interviews with and surveillance of parolees[41]

The Burden of Large Caseloads

Caseload refers to the average number of cases supervised by a probation or parole officer in a given period. Each case represents an offender on probation and parole supervised by an individual officer. As John Conrad observed,

> There is much that a good probation/parole officer can do for the people on his or her caseload. A parole officer who makes it clear that, "fellow, if you don't watch your step I'm gonna run your ass right back to the joint," is not in a position to be helpful as a counselor or facilitator. With the best intentions, a[n] officer struggling with the standard unwieldy caseload of 100 or more will deal with emergencies only, and sometime will not be able to do that very well.[42]

As noted earlier, about 4.8 million persons are either on probation or parole in the United States. Is there a precise number of offenders that can be supervised effectively by an officer? The answer is no, because the number of offenders an officer can supervise effectively is a function of the type of offenders being supervised by certain officers; all offenders and officers are unique and bring different knowledge, skills,

Parole officer: one who supervises those who are on parole.

Caseload: the number of cases awaiting disposition by a court, or the number of active cases or clients maintained by a probation or parole officer.

capacities, and competencies. The American Probation and Parole Association (APPA) asks the question, rhetorically,

> How many patients can a surgeon operate on in a given day? How many cars can a mechanic fix each week? How many haircuts can a barber complete in a month? It does not take an expert in any of these fields to realize the answer normally is that *it depends*.[43]

Video: System failure in Jaycee Dugard case

Of course, caseload size can affect the quality of supervision that an officer is able to provide—and can also bring the glare of the media when something goes horribly wrong. An example is where a newspaper in Detroit published an exposé titled "Felons on Probation Often Go Unwatched." This county had roughly 30,000 probationers and approximately 250 officers to supervise them—an average of nearly 120 offenders per officer. In one case, an officer was fired after a probationer was arrested for attempted murder and engaging in a shootout with police. The probationer was a fugitive, missing several office visits, but he was never reported as an absconder, nor was he listed as a fugitive at the time of the shooting. According to the article, the probation officer "was so overworked that she failed to get an arrest warrant for [the probationer] when he became a fugitive for missing his monthly probation office appointment. [The officer] still hadn't done so by March 28 when he was arrested."[44]

The APPA points out that caseload sizes have long been too large, and for several identifiable reasons:

> For at least the past four decades it has been well-known to professional insiders that probation and parole officer workloads exceed realistic potential for accomplishing the numerous tasks required to supervise offenders. The point here is that many departments are increasing caseloads to well over 200 offenders per officer, making it virtually impossible for offenders to receive adequate attention and interaction from officers to have any substantial rehabilitative effect. Compounding these issues is the current trend of concentrating on sex-offenders, the infusion of electronic monitoring technologies, and increasing the use of probation for higher-risk offenders as well as widening the justice net to low risk offenders.[45]

To Arm or Not to Arm

SAGE Journal Article: Armed, private probation

Whether probation and parole officers should be armed has also been debated. Traditionalists believe that carrying a firearm contributes to an atmosphere of distrust between the client and the officer; they argue that if officers carry weapons they are perceived differently than as counselors or advisors, whose purpose is to guide offenders into treatment and self-help programs. Conversely, some people view a firearm for these officers as an essential for protecting them from the risks associated with confronting violent, serious, or high-risk offenders.[46] Officers must make visits to the homes and places of employment in the neighborhoods in which offenders live; some of these areas are not safe. Equally or more dangerous is when officers must revoke parole or probation, which could result in the offender's imprisonment.

There is no national or standard policy regarding weapons, and officers themselves are not in agreement about being armed. Some states classify probation and parole officers as peace officers and grant them the authority to carry a firearm both on and off duty.[47] In sum, it would seem that the prudent decision concerning arming should be based on the need, officer safety, and local laws and policies.

OTHER ALTERNATIVES: INTERMEDIATE SANCTIONS

There are additional corrections programs—**intermediate sanctions**—that are less restrictive than total confinement but more restrictive than probation. A survey by the federal Bureau of Justice Statistics found that, of about 63,000 persons being supervised outside a jail facility, about 19 percent were under electronic monitoring, 19 percent were involved in some form of community service, and about 28 percent were undergoing home detention without electronic monitoring.[48] These and other forms of supervision are discussed in the sections that follow.

SAGE Journal
Article: Intermediate
sanctions

Intensive Supervision Probation and Parole

Since their beginning, **intensive supervision probation and parole** have been based on the premise that increased client contact would enhance rehabilitation while affording greater client control. Current programs are largely a means of easing the burden of prison overcrowding.[49]

Intensive supervision can be classified into two types: those stressing diversion and those stressing enhancement. A *diversion program* is commonly known as a "front door" program because its goal is to limit the number of generally low-risk offenders who enter prison. An *enhancement program* generally selects already-sentenced probationers and parolees and subjects them to closer supervision in the community than they receive under regular probation or parole.[50]

As of 1990, jurisdictions in all 50 states had instituted *intensive supervision probation* (ISP). Persons placed on ISP are supposed to be those offenders who, in the absence of intensive supervision, would have been sentenced to imprisonment. Although ISP is invariably more costly than regular supervision, the costs "are compared not with the costs of normal supervision but rather with the costs of incarceration."[51]

ISP is demanding for probationers and parolees and does not represent freedom; in fact, it may stress and isolate repeat offenders more than imprisonment does. Given the option of serving prison terms or participating in ISPs, many offenders have chosen prison.[52] Consider the alternatives now facing offenders in one western state:

Intensive supervision probation and parole are premised on the idea that increased client contact enhances rehabilitation while affording greater client control.

- *ISP.* The offender serves two years under this alternative. During that time, a probation officer visits the offender two or three times per week and phones on the other days. The offender is subject to unannounced searches of his or her home for drugs and has his or her urine tested regularly for alcohol and drugs. The offender must strictly abide by other conditions as set by the court: not carrying a weapon, not socializing with certain persons, performing community service, and being employed or participating in training or education. In addition, he or she will be strongly encouraged to attend counseling and/or other treatment, particularly if he or she is a drug offender.

Intermediate sanctions: forms of punishment that are between freedom and prison, such as home confinement and day reporting.

Intensive supervision probation and parole: ISP usually includes much closer and stricter supervision, more contact with offenders, more frequent drug tests, and other such measures.

- ***Prison.*** The alternative is a sentence of two-four years, of which the offender will serve only about three-six months. During this term, the offender is not required to work or to participate in any training or treatment but may do so voluntarily. Once released, the offender is placed on a two-year routine parole supervision and must visit his or her parole officer about once a month.[53]

Although evidence of the effectiveness of this program is lacking, it has been deemed a public relations success.[54] Intensive supervision is usually accomplished by severely reducing caseload size per probation or parole officer, leading to increased contact between officers and clients or their significant others (such as spouse or parents).[55]

AP Photo/Suchat Pederson

Electronic monitoring systems are particularly useful for high-risk offenders, especially sex offenders for whom use of a Global Positioning System (GPS) is desirable.

House Arrest

Since the late 1980s, **house arrest** (also known as **home confinement**) has become increasingly common. With house arrest, offenders receive a "sentence" of detention in their own homes, and their compliance is often monitored electronically. The primary motivation for using this intermediate sanction is a financial one: the conservation of scarce resources.

Many people apparently feel that house arrest is not effective or punitive enough for offenders. Indeed, one study reported that nearly half (44 percent) of the public feels that house arrest is not very effective or not effective at all.[56]

Does house arrest work? Looking at a sample of 528 adult felony offenders who had been released from house arrest, Jeffery Ulmer found that the sentence combination associated with the least likelihood of rearrest was house arrest/probation.[57] The combinations of house arrest/work release and house arrest/incarceration were also significantly associated with decreased chances of rearrest compared to traditional probation. Furthermore, whenever any other sentence option was paired with house arrest, that sentence combination significantly reduced chances and severity of rearrest.[58] House arrest puts the offender in touch with opportunities and resources for rehabilitative services (substance abuse or sex offender counseling, anger management classes, and so on), which supports the contention that for intermediate sanctions of any type to reduce recidivism, they must include a rehabilitative emphasis.[59]

Electronic Monitoring

House arrest/home confinement offenders are detained in their own homes; compliance is often monitored electronically.

Electronic monitoring: use of electronic devices (bracelets or anklets) to emit signals when a convicted offender (usually on house arrest) leaves the environment in which he or she is to remain.

Electronic monitoring or supervision can be used for a variety of offenders, but it is particularly useful for high-risk offenders, especially sex offenders for whom use of a Global Positioning System (GPS) is desirable.[60] Electronic monitoring generally costs between $4 and $9 per day to administer (the cost is often paid by the offender) and is thus a particularly attractive alternative in many jurisdictions that are spending up to $80 per day to house a person in jail.[61]

Two basic types of electronic monitoring devices are available: active and passive. Active forms are continuous signaling devices attached to the offender that constantly monitor his or her presence at a particular location. A central computer accepts reports from the receiver-dialer over telephone lines, compares them with the offender's curfew schedule, and alerts correctional officials to unauthorized absences.[62] Simpler systems consist of only two basic components: a transmitter and a portable receiver. The transmitter, which is strapped to the offender's ankle or wrist or worn around the neck, emits a radio signal that travels about one city block. By driving past the offender's residence, his or her place of employment, or wherever he or she is supposed to be, the officer can verify the offender's presence with the handheld portable receiver.[63]

The passive type of electronic monitoring involves the use of programmed contact devices that contact the offender periodically to verify his or her presence. One system uses voice verification technology. Another system uses satellite technology; the subject wears an ankle bracelet and carries or wears a portable tracking device about the size of a small lunchbox and weighing 3.5 pounds. A GPS satellite constellation is able to establish an offender's whereabouts within 150 feet of his or her location 24 hours a day.[64]

Correctional boot camps, also called shock incarceration, have been used in jails and prisons to place offenders in a quasi-military program to instill discipline and thus reduce recidivism, prison and jail populations, and operating costs.

Shock Probation/Parole

Shock probation/parole is another less costly intermediate alternative to incarceration that is supported by many correctional administrators. This form of corrections combines a brief exposure to incarceration with subsequent release. It allows sentencing judges to reconsider the original sentence to prison and, upon motion, to recall the inmate after a few months in prison and place him or her on probation, under conditions deemed appropriate. The idea is that the "shock" of a short stay in prison will give the offender a taste of institutional life and will make such an indelible impression that he or she will be deterred from future crime and will avoid the negative effects of lengthy confinement.[65]

Boot Camps/Shock Incarceration

Correctional **boot camps**, also called shock incarceration, were first implemented as an intermediate sanction in 1983.[66] Early versions of boot camps placed offenders in a quasi-military program of 36 months' duration similar to a military basic training program. The goal was to reduce recidivism, prison and jail populations, and operating costs. Offenders generally served a short institutional sentence and then were put through a rigorous regimen of drills, strenuous workouts, marching, and hard physical labor. To be eligible, inmates generally had to be young, nonviolent offenders.

Unfortunately, early evaluations of boot camps generally found that participants did no better than other offenders without this experience.[67] Only boot camps that were carefully designed, targeted the right offenders, and provided rehabilitative services and aftercare were deemed likely to save the state money and reduce recidivism.[68] As a result of these findings, the number of boot camps declined; by the year 2000, only 51 prison boot camps remained.[69] Boot camps have evolved over time, however, and have added components such as alcohol and drug treatment and social skills training (some even include postrelease electronic monitoring, house arrest, and random urine tests); some boot camps have substituted an emphasis on educational and vocational skills for the military components.[70]

Day Reporting Centers

Another intermediate sanction that has recently gained popularity among correctional administrators and policy makers is the **day reporting center** (DRC). DRCs are places

Shock probation/parole: a situation in which individuals are sentenced to jail or prison for a brief period, to give them a taste or "shock" of incarceration and, it is hoped, turn them into more law-abiding citizens.

Boot camp: a short-term jail or prison program that puts offenders through a rigorous physical and mental regimen designed to instill discipline and respect for authority.

Day reporting center: a structured corrections program requiring offenders to check in at a community site on a regular basis for supervision, sanctions, and services.

where offenders report with some frequency (usually once or twice a day); treatment services (job training and placement, counseling, and education) are usually provided at the DRCs, either by the agency running the program or by other human services agencies.[71]

The purposes of DRCs are to heighten control and surveillance of offenders placed on community supervision, increase offender access to treatment programs, give offenders more proportional and certain sanctions, and reduce prison or jail crowding. One study of the effect of day reporting centers on recidivism, however, found no significant reduction in the rate of rearrest.[72]

CONFRONTING RECIDIVISTS: THE RISK-NEEDS-RESPONSIVITY (RNR) MODEL

How can the cycle of reoffending and reincarceration be stopped? Should an offender be confined in prison, placed on community supervision, or both? Several decades of research and experience have provided specific programs—practices and principles—that, when implemented, can answer this age-old question.

First, it is imperative that an offender's future risk for reoffending be assessed and that it be possible to do so. As an example, in 2009 the Washington state legislature required its department of corrections to develop and use an instrument that has the "highest degree of predictive accuracy" for assessing an offender's risk of reoffense. After considering a number of such instruments, five assessment tools were selected and used for this purpose.[73]

Next, what kinds of programs should be used with these offenders who are in jails and prisons, and on probation and parole? Such approaches are known collectively as the risk-need-responsivity (RNR) model. In short, they operate on the assumption that using trained personnel to identify individual offenders' risks and needs—and then responding to those needs with the best combination of services and supervision—can lead to a significant reduction in recidivism (repeat offending).[74]

Offenders' risk levels are determined by certain factors or characteristics that can be changed through intervention: one's antisocial behavior, close association with known offenders, poor family and/or marital relationships, bad school/work relationships, and substance abuse. Once these risks are identified, specific treatment interventions can be put in place to reduce offenders' likelihood of continuing criminality.[75] Screening and assessment instruments are used for these purposes within the corrections field. Dozens of studies have shown, unequivocally, that using RNR principles of offender rehabilitation significantly reduces recidivism.[76] Figure 14.3 shows the kinds of questions used in an RNR assessment tool.

RESTORATIVE JUSTICE

SAGE Journal Article: Restorative justice in prison

For some time, many people who have experienced the criminal justice system have grown dissatisfied—specifically, as participants, they feel disconnected; as victims, dissatisfied; and as people working in the system, frustrated. Policy makers are increasingly concerned about the burgeoning cost of justice in the face of this discontent and the high rates of recidivism that exist.

There has been growing interest in new approaches to justice that involve the community and focus on the victim. The current system, in which crime is considered an act against the state, works on a premise that largely ignores the victim and the community that is hurt most by crime. Instead, it focuses on punishing offenders without forcing them to face the impact of their crimes.

FIGURE 14.3 Center for Advancing Correctional Excellence Criminal Cognitions Scale, RNR Simulation Tool

Please indicate how well each statement describes your current thinking.

Externalization of Blame

Please indicate how well each statement describes your current thinking.			
	Strongly Disagree	Disagree	Agree	Strongly Agree
Bad childhood experiences are partly to blame for my current situation.	O	O	O	O
I feel like what happens in my life is mostly determined by powerful people.	O	O	O	O
Because of my history I get blamed for a lot of things I did not do.	O	O	O	O
Sometimes I cannot control myself.	O	O	O	O
I am just a "born criminal."	O	O	O	O

Notions of Entitlement

Please indicate how well each statement describes your current thinking.			
	Strongly Disagree	Disagree	Agree	Strongly Agree
When I want something, I expect people to deliver.	O	O	O	O
I will never be satisfied until I get all that I deserve.	O	O	O	O
I expect people to treat me better than other people.	O	O	O	O
I insist on getting the respect that is due me.	O	O	O	O
I deserve more than other people.	O	O	O	O

Devaluing Authority

Please indicate how well each statement describes your current thinking.			
	Strongly Disagree	Disagree	Agree	Strongly Agree
Most of the laws are good.	O	O	O	O
Most police officers/guards abuse their power.	O	O	O	O
People in authority are usually looking out for my best interest.	O	O	O	O
If a police officer/guard tells me to do something, there's usually a good reason for it.	O	O	O	O
People in positions of authority generally take advantage of others.	O	O	O	O

Immediate Gratification

Please indicate how well each statement describes your current thinking.			
	Strongly Disagree	Disagree	Agree	Strongly Agree
The future is unpredictable and there is no point planning for it.	O	O	O	O
Even though I got caught, it was still worth the risk.	O	O	O	O
Why plan to save for something if you can have it now.	O	O	O	O
I think it is better to enjoy today than worry about tomorrow.	O	O	O	O
I do not like to be tied down to a regular work schedule.	O	O	O	O

Insensitivity to Impact of Crime

Please indicate how well each statement describes your current thinking.			
	Strongly Disagree	Disagree	Agree	Strongly Agree
My crime(s) did not really harm anyone.	O	O	O	O
A theft is all right as long as the victim is not physically injured.	O	O	O	O
Victims of crime usually get over it with time.	O	O	O	O
When you commit a crime the only one affected is the victim.	O	O	O	O
Society makes too big of a deal about my crime(s).	O	O	O	O

Source: Adapted from Jeffrey Stuewig, Emi Furukawa, Sarah Kopelo, June Price Tangney, Sarah Kopelovich, Patrick J. Meyer, and Brandon Cosby, "Reliability, Validity, and Predictive Utility of the 25-Item Criminogenic Cognitions Scale (CCS)," *Criminal Justice and Behavior 39* (October 2012): pp. 1340–1360.

©REUTERS/Lucy Nicholson

Restorative justice maintains that crime affects not only the victim but the entire community as well, so it involves meetings including the offender, the victim, and members of the community in order to devise a rehabilitative plan to make them whole again.

Restorative justice: the view that crime affects the entire community, which must be healed and made whole again through the offender's remorse, community service, restitution to the victim, and other such activities.

Restorative justice has been finding a receptive audience, along with its guiding principles:

- Crime is an offense against human relationships.
- Victims and the community are central to justice processes.
- The first priority of justice processes is to assist victims.
- The second priority is to restore the community, to the degree possible.
- The offender has personal responsibility to victims and to the community for crimes committed.
- The offender will develop improved competency and understanding as a result of the restorative justice experience.[77]

A fundamental precept of restorative justice is as follows: "Violations create obligations and liabilities."[78] More specifically,

- Offenders' obligations are to make things right as much as possible.
- The community's obligations are to victims and to offenders and for the general welfare of its members.
- The community has a responsibility to support and help victims of crime to meet their needs.[79]

INVESTIGATING FURTHER

THE MINNESOTA RESTORATIVE JUSTICE INITIATIVE

The Minnesota Department of Corrections (DOC) has as its purpose repairing the harm of crime and strengthening communities in all jurisdictions around the state.

The Minnesota initiative has been implemented in numerous schools, law enforcement agencies, community corrections departments, juvenile facilities, adult institutions, and neighborhoods.

In the Schools: Restorative practices are used in response to discipline problems, particularly as an alternative to expulsion. Practices include peer mediation, classroom circles to resolve problems, and family group conferencing—all of which involve face-to-face resolution in which the multiple impacts of the offending behavior are identified and addressed.

In Law Enforcement: The major new restorative practice in law enforcement, piloted by about a dozen police departments in Minnesota, is the use of family group conferencing as a diversion process for juveniles.

In Community Corrections: Community corrections departments and DOC offices have implemented victim-offender meeting programs, family group conferencing, a crime repair crew of supervised offenders, increased emphasis on paying restitution, community panels that meet with offenders, multidisciplinary case management with juveniles and their families, and victim awareness education for staff.

In Prisons: Several adult institutions have begun to apply restorative principles, implementing a victim empathy curriculum for all new inmates entering the facility and encouraging community volunteer involvement in the facility.

Source: Adapted from Kay Pranis, in "The Minnesota Restorative Justice Initiative: A Model Experience," *The Crime Victims Report* (U.S. Department of Justice, National Institute of Justice, May/June 1997), http://www.ojp.usdoj .gov/nij/topics/courts/restorative-justice/perspectives/The%20Minnesota%20 Restorative%20Justice%20Initiative:%20A%20Model%20Experience.htm.

- Probation involves a court allowing a convicted person to remain at liberty in the community, subject to certain conditions and restrictions; similarly, parole is the conditional release of a prisoner but before the prisoner's full sentence has been served. Both allow the offender to remain in the community to take advantage of treatment or counseling, maintain family and employment ties, and so on.

- If one is allowed to be placed on probation, the probationer must still abide by certain conditions. A technical violation occurs when, for example, the probationer fails to pay court costs or fines, misses a probation meeting, uses alcohol, or violates curfew. A substantive violation occurs when a new crime is committed by the probationer.

- Because they may lose their freedom, probationers are allowed to have counsel present at the probation revocation hearing; other due process rights are afforded as well.

- Parolees must also abide by certain conditions that the court and parole officers put in place. If they do not comply, parole may be revoked and the parolee returned to prison. Parolees also have certain due process rights prior to revocation.

- Probation officers perform duties such as reporting to the court any violations of probation, performing presentence investigations, arresting those who violate the terms of their probation, performing searches, seizing evidence, and arranging for drug testing.

- Parole officers supervise offenders who have been released from prison through personal contact with offenders and their families. They help parolees adjust back into society, developing a plan for employment, housing, health care, education, drug screening, and other activities.

- Whether probation and parole officers should be armed has been a debated topic in corrections; there is no national or standard policy for these personnel regarding weapons, and officers themselves are not in agreement about being armed.

- Intensive supervision probation/parole can be classified into two types: those stressing diversion and those stressing enhancement. ISP is very demanding for probationers and parolees and may stress and isolate repeat offenders more than imprisonment does.

- With house arrest, offenders receive a "sentence" of detention in their own homes, and their compliance is often monitored electronically.

- Shock probation combines a brief exposure to incarceration with subsequent release.

- Only boot camps that are carefully designed, target the right offenders, and provide rehabilitative services and aftercare are deemed likely to save the state money and reduce recidivism.

- Day centers provide treatment services (job training and placement, counseling, and education) onsite, either by the agency running the program or by other human services agencies.

- To avoid reincarceration, offenders' future risk for reoffending must be assessed; approaches used are known as the risk-need-responsivity (RNR) model.

- Restorative justice holds that the first priority of justice processes is to assist victims whereas the second priority is to restore the community.

$SAGE edge™ Review key terms with eFlashcards. ◀

REVIEW QUESTIONS ?

▶ Test your understanding of chapter content. Take the practice quiz. **⑤SAGE** edge™

1. What is meant by the term *community corrections*?

2. What historical events led to modern-day probation? Parole?

3. What are the rights granted by the U.S. Supreme Court to people who are on probation and parole in general? When the state wishes to revoke their probation/parole status and send them to prison?

4. What are some examples of technical and substantive conditions that correctional agencies commonly apply to probationers and parolees?

5. Why does the criminal justice system use alternatives to incarceration?

6. How would you describe the primary functions of probation and parole officers, and the impact of high caseloads in terms of how these officers are able to achieve their goals?

7. How would you describe the arguments for and against arming probation and parole officers?

8. What are the purposes and functions of intermediate sanctions, including intensive supervision, house arrest, electronic monitoring, shock incarceration/boot camps, and day reporting centers?

9. How does the risk-needs-responsivity model work with offenders to stop the cycle of reoffending and reincarceration?

10. What is restorative justice, and what are the rationales underlying it?

LEARN BY DOING

1. You graduated recently with a criminal justice degree and are now employed as a state probation and parole officer. You are asked by a criminal justice professor at a nearby college to guest lecture in an introduction to criminal justice course concerning the primary challenges of working in probation and parole. Develop what would be your presentation for the class.

2. Assume it is your first day working as a state probation and parole officer, and your new training officer says the following:

   "Hi, nice to meet you. I'm Chuck, the training advisor. Here's what I tell everyone on their first day. First, the real world is different from what you've been told in college classes. Politicians promise the public that they will get tough on crime, so first off they spend money for more police officers. No one gets elected by promising to build more courts, or add more probation and parole officers. Eventually having more police means the courts get backlogged, which in turn crowds the prisons and the jails, puts more people on probation, and forces the parole board to grant more early releases. Meanwhile, our average caseload increases by 50 percent. We also have more drug and sex offenders than we know what to do with. We spend too much time bailing water out of the boat, with no one steering, so we are just drifting in circles. To vent the frustrations, about once a week the gang and I hold 'choir practice' at a bar down the street. After about five or six beers and some carousing and loud singing, then this job looks a lot better."

   a. Should Chuck be retained as a training officer? Why or why not?

   b. How would changes in politics affect the corrections system directly and indirectly?

   c. Do you believe Chuck's comments are accurate concerning the police getting so much new funding—and the subsequent impacts on courts and corrections?

   d. Why do crowded jails and prisons make the job of parole officers more difficult?

   e. If you were Chuck's supervisor and heard others discussing their frequent "choir practices" at the bar, would you attempt to discontinue such gatherings or leave the situation alone?

3. Your criminal justice instructor has assigned a class debate concerning the use of incarceration versus alternatives to incarceration (e.g., intensive probation and parole, house arrest, shock probation). What will be your argument?

PRACTICE AND APPLY WHAT YOU'VE LEARNED

▶ edge.sagepub.com/peak2e

HEAR IT FROM THE PROFESSIONALS

Head to the study site where you'll find:

- Chapter-related insights and perspectives directly from the authors Kenneth J. Peak and Pamela M. Everett
- Interviews with Los Angeles County Lieutenant Brian D. Fitch
- Student interviews highlighting misconceptions on key CJ concepts with author responses

15 Juvenile Justice: Philosophy, Law, and Practices

16 On the Crime Policy and Prevention Agenda: Terrorism, the Mentally Ill in the Criminal Justice System, and the Changing War on Drugs

PART V

SPANNING THE SYSTEM
Methods and Issues

This part is composed of two chapters. **Chapter 15** examines juvenile justice—an area where the legal and criminal justice processes are quite different from those of adults. Included are the history and extent of juvenile crime, the case flow of juvenile courts, and juvenile rights.

Chapter 16 provides an in-depth view of three selected problems that—because of their nature and/or extent—plague society and pose serious questions for the future concerning criminal justice policy and practices.

LEARNING OBJECTIVES

As a result of reading this chapter, you will be able to:

1 Describe the early treatment of juveniles and history of our juvenile justice system, which includes houses of refuge, reformatories, and the first juvenile court, created in Illinois

2 Explain the unique philosophy, principles, and goals underlying the treatment of youthful offenders by the juvenile court system

3 Discuss the extent of, and theories underlying, juvenile criminality today

4 Review the process and flow of cases through the juvenile justice system

5 Discuss whether or not there exists a school-to-prison pipeline and, if so, reasons for and possible solutions to it

6 Describe the types of secure and nonsecure custodial options that are available to juvenile court judges

7 Elaborate on the problem of—and possible solutions to—youth gangs

8 Survey the reasons for, and approaches to, providing formal aftercare and reentry services for juveniles who are exiting a facility and returning to their homes and neighborhoods

9 Delineate the due process and other major rights of juveniles as set forth by the U.S. Supreme Court

ASSESS YOUR AWARENESS

Test your knowledge of juvenile rights and the justice system by responding to the following nine true-false items; check your answers after reading this chapter's materials.

1 The prevailing philosophy toward all juveniles is that there should be as much involvement as possible by the state, through the juvenile justice system.

2 The overall juvenile justice philosophy, process, and terminology are essentially the same as those of adult offenders.

3 It is generally best to place some type of label on juvenile offenders, to assist with their classification and treatment.

4 Paramilitary juvenile boot camps have been proven to be an ineffective means of treating delinquency.

5 A juvenile who commits a heinous crime, and is thus not felt to be suited to the philosophy of the juvenile court, may be transferred to the jurisdiction of an adult court.

6 Procedural safeguards in the juvenile court system include the right to counsel, the right to confront and cross-examine witnesses, and the privilege against self-incrimination.

7 Juvenile offenders who are under the age of 18 when committing a murder may be executed.

8 Police do not need to read the *Miranda* warning to juveniles being questioned while in custody.

9 Juveniles may be sentenced to life without parole.

There are three ways of trying to win the young. You can preach at them, that is a hook without a worm. You can say, "You must volunteer," that is the devil; and you can tell them, "You are needed." That appeal hardly ever fails.

—Kurt Hahn

<< Answers can be found on page 424.

The home where Gina Grant murdered her mother, Dorothy Mayfield.

Fourteen-year-old Gina Grant gave several conflicting accounts of how her abusive, alcoholic mother came to her death in South Carolina: She was killed by intruders, she stabbed herself, she fell down the stairs to the first floor, her boyfriend committed the murder. In the end, however, Grant—a straight-A student and school cheerleader—admitted that she had committed the murder herself, bludgeoning her mother 13 times with a candlestick. Charged with murder, she later pleaded guilty to voluntary manslaughter and served one year in detention. Five years later, she applied to Harvard University and was accepted. Later, Harvard rescinded her admission, which it said is common if students lie on their application or if they behave in ways that "bring into question honesty, maturity or moral character" (Grant had never told Harvard about her role in her mother's death). Although Grant received strong public support before, during, and after her trial—her attorney stated that "the guiding principle of the juvenile justice system is redemption"—her prosecutor argued that "there can hardly be any excuse for what was done to that woman."[1]

As you read this chapter, consider the generally nonpunitive, rehabilitative goals of the juvenile justice system, as well as the point at which juveniles who commit particularly heinous crimes should lose the juvenile court's "protective shroud" and be transferred to the adult courts for processing.

INTRODUCTION

What rights does one possess as a juvenile? What are the differences in law and criminal justice treatment of juveniles? These are important questions, because as an old adage states, crime is primarily a "young person's game."

As indicated in Chapter 1, the criminal justice system's philosophy toward juveniles is very different from its philosophy toward adults. Consequently, police officers and others whose occupations put them in frequent contact with juvenile offenders must know and apply a different standard of treatment in these situations. The philosophical approach toward juvenile offenders overall is that society—through poor parenting, poverty, environment, and so forth—is primarily responsible for their criminal behavior.

As is also emphasized in this chapter, the juvenile justice system seeks to protect the child—to rehabilitate, not punish; therefore, the juvenile justice process is generally amiable, not adversarial. However, many of today's juvenile offenders are also quite violent. When a juvenile commits an act that is so heinous and violent that the juvenile court philosophy is not tenable in the matter, the protective shroud extended by the juvenile justice process can disappear. In such cases, the youthful offender may be transferred to the jurisdiction of the adult court to be processed as an adult.

This chapter begins with a discussion of the origins of juvenile justice, including houses of refuge and the creation of the juvenile court. Next is a look at the unique philosophy, principles, and goals that underlie today's juvenile justice system. Following is a review of the general flow of juvenile cases through the juvenile justice process. Several related methods and challenges are then discussed: the problem of labeling offenders, the school-to-prison pipeline, various custodial options available to judges, youth gangs, and the need for aftercare and reentry services for juveniles returning home from custody. The chapter concludes with an examination of several major U.S. Supreme Court decisions granting juveniles legal rights.

HISTORY OF JUVENILE JUSTICE

The U.S. juvenile justice system has a rich and, at times, painful history. Here, we discuss the early treatment of juveniles, and how the system developed from one that was very harsh and dangerous to that of today, which is much more protective and rehabilitative in philosophy and practice.

Early Treatment: Houses of Refuge, Reformatories

In the early part of the 19th century, to the chagrin of prosecutors and many citizens, juries were acquitting children who were charged with crimes—not wishing to see children incarcerated with adults in ramshackle facilities. Quakers in New York City sought to establish a balance between those two camps—people wanting to see justice done with child offenders, and those not wanting them to be incarcerated—and founded the first **house of refuge** in 1825 to "receive and take . . . all such children as shall be taken up or committed as vagrants, or convicted of criminal offenses." The children worked an eight-hour day at various trades in addition to attending school for another four hours. Many of them had not committed any criminal act, and a number were probably status offenders (breaking criminal laws that apply only to minors, described later in this chapter).[2]

At about the middle of the 19th century, the house of refuge movement evolved into the slightly more punitive reform school, or **reformatory**, approach,[3] to segregate young offenders from adult criminals; imprison the young and remove them from adverse home environments until the youths were reformed; help youth avoid idleness through military drills, physical exercise, and supervision; focus on education—preferably vocational and religious; and teach sobriety, thrift, industry, and prudence.

Later in the 19th century, an occasional legal attack on the incarceration of children in such youth prisons was successful. In an 1870 case, the Illinois Supreme Court held it unconstitutional to confine in a Chicago reform school a youth who had not been convicted of criminal conduct or afforded legal due process.[4] It was against this backdrop in the last quarter of the 19th century that the juvenile court movement began.

Quakers in New York City founded the House of Refuge in 1825 to provide an alternative to children being housed with adult offenders. This picture depicts some of the work- and school-related daily activities at the House.

Houses of refuge: workhouses established in the early 1800s as a means of separating juvenile offenders from adult offenders.

Reformatory: a detention facility designed to reform individuals—historically juveniles.

Illinois Juvenile Court Act (1899): legislation that established the first juvenile court in the United States.

Juvenile court: a court that has original jurisdiction to hear juvenile crime matters.

A Movement Begins: Illinois Legislation

In 1899, the Illinois legislature enacted the **Illinois Juvenile Court Act**,[5] creating the first separate **juvenile court**. At that time in the United States, juveniles were tried along with adults in criminal courts and sometimes sentenced to prison and occasionally to death. Prior to 1900, at least 10 children were executed in the United States for crimes committed before their 14th birthdays.[6]

Other children died in adult prisons. Virginia penitentiary records from 1876 reflect that a 10-year-old prisoner died from being scalded accidentally in a tub of boiling coffee. These deaths shocked the public conscience. Accordingly, Americans in the 20th century sought more pervasive reform than the infancy defense to address the distinctive nature of children and youth.[7]

Author Video: Juvenile offenders

Although the Illinois act did not fundamentally change procedures in the existing courts that now were sitting as juvenile courts to adjudicate cases involving children, it did emphasize the *parens patriae* philosophy (discussed later in this chapter) to govern such cases. In addition to giving the courts jurisdiction over children charged with crimes, the act gave them jurisdiction over a variety of behaviors and conditions, including

> any child who for any reason is destitute or homeless or abandoned; or dependent on the public for support; or has not proper parental care or guardianship; or who habitually begs or receives alms; or who is living in any house of ill fame or with any vicious or disreputable person; or whose home, by reason of neglect, cruelty or depravity on the part of its parents, guardian or other person in whose care it may be, is an unfit place for such a child; and any child under the age of 8 who is found peddling or selling any article or singing or playing a musical instrument upon the street or giving any public entertainment.[8]

Student on the Street Video: Juvenile offenders and the death penalty

The act was unique in that it created a special court for neglected, dependent, or delinquent children under age 16; defined a rehabilitative rather than punishment purpose for that court; established the confidentiality of juveniles' court records to minimize stigma; required that juveniles be separated from adults when placed in the same institution in addition to barring altogether the detention of children under age 12 in jails; and provided for the informality of procedures within the court.[9]

In its initial year, the Chicago judge presiding over the first juvenile court, the Honorable Richard S. Tuthill, sent 37 boys to the grand jury for adult handling, deeming them unsuitable for the juvenile court's treatment orientation. His successor, Judge Julian Mack, described the court's goals as follows:

An eight-year-old boy charged with stealing a bicycle appears in juvenile court in 1910.

Library of Congress Prints and Photographs Division Washington

> The child who must be brought into court should, of course, be made to know that he is face to face with the power of the state, but he should at the same time, and more emphatically, be made to feel that he is the object of its care and solicitude. The ordinary trappings of the courtroom are out of place in such hearings. The judge on a bench, looking down upon the boy standing at the bar, can never evoke a proper sympathetic spirit. Seated at a desk, with the child at his side, where he can on occasion put his arm around his shoulder and draw the lad to him, the judge, while losing none of his judicial dignity, will gain immensely in the effectiveness of his work.[10]

Status Offenses

The post–World War II period witnessed further development, as the **status offense** became a separate category. New York created a new jurisdictional category for persons in need of supervision (**PINS**): runaways, truants, and other youths who committed acts that would not be criminal if committed by an adult. Other states followed New York's lead. Then came the enactment of the very powerful and far-reaching Juvenile Justice and Delinquency Prevention Act of 1974,[11] which

- removed status offenders from secure detention and correctional facilities; and more significant, perhaps,

- prevented the placement of any juveniles in any institutions where they would have regular contact with adults convicted of criminal charges.

UNIQUE PHILOSOPHY, PRINCIPLES, AND GOALS

This chapter section examines the philosophical underpinnings of the juvenile justice system as well as a number of contrasts (in both terminology and court proceedings) between these and the adult criminal courts.

Parens Patriae and *In Loco Parentis*

The prevailing doctrine or philosophy guiding our treatment of juveniles is ***parens patriae***, meaning that the "state is the ultimate parent" of the child. In effect, this means that as long as we as parents adequately care for and provide at least the basic amenities for our children as required under the law, they are ours to keep. But when our children are physically or emotionally neglected or abused, the juvenile court and police may intervene and remove the children from that environment. Then the doctrine of ***in loco parentis*** takes hold, meaning that the state will act in place of the parent.

For police and other criminal justice personnel, there is perhaps no greater or more somber duty than having to testify under subpoena in juvenile court that a woman is an unfit mother (and that her parental ties should be legally severed). However, when a parent or guardian's actions indicate a pattern of neglect and/or abuse toward a child, it is clearly better that the state assume responsibility for the child's care and custody.

Table 15.1 shows the **idealistic contrast** between the juvenile court process and the adult criminal justice process. Note that this is the *ideal* process for juveniles, in keeping with the more nurturing and forgiving juvenile justice philosophy; however, that can easily go away when a juvenile commits a crime(s) that is so heinous that he or she is deemed to not be amenable to the more lenient philosophy and jurisdiction of the juvenile courts, and will thus be remanded to the custody of the appropriate adult court. Also note that much of the difference between the philosophies of juvenile and adult courts is found in the terminology used.

Children from poor, disadvantaged backgrounds are much more likely to engage in delinquent behavior.

Status offense: a crime committed by a juvenile that would not be a crime if committed by an adult; examples would be purchasing alcohol and tobacco products, truancy, and violating curfew.

PINS (person in need of supervision): usually a juvenile thought to be on the verge of becoming a delinquent.

Parens patriae: a doctrine in which the state is the ultimate parent of the child (and will step in to provide and care for the child if parents neglect those duties).

In loco parentis: a doctrine in which the state will act in place of the parents if they fail in their duties to protect and provide for the child.

Idealistic contrast: the differences between juvenile and adult criminal justice processes, to include treatment and terminology.

TABLE 15.1 The Idealistic Contrast Between Juvenile and Adult Criminal Justice Processes

ADULT	JUVENILE
Adversarial procedure	Relatively amiable procedure
Individual responsibility for crime	Societal/family factors involved
Punishment is typically the goal	Rehabilitation is the goal
Arrest process	Petition
Trial—public	Hearing—private
Guilt or innocence	Guilt not the sole issue
Public record	Confidential record
Verdict	Decision
Sentence	Disposition

Underlying Principles of the Juvenile Court

Most states' juvenile court decisions and legislation contain three underlying principles:[12]

Video: Juvenile status offenses

- The presumption of innocence
- The presumption of the least amount of involvement with the system
- The presumption of the best interest of the minor

The decision maker—whether the police deciding to take a minor into custody, an intake worker deciding to detain a child, or a juvenile court judge presiding at a hearing—must apply these three principles unless evidence exists to the contrary. The amount of evidence may vary depending on the decision maker; for example, although police or detention intake may hold a minor if reasonable or probable cause exists to believe that the minor has committed an offense, a judge must be satisfied beyond a reasonable doubt that an offense has been committed.

Presumption of Innocence

The **presumption of innocence** is one of the hallmarks of our criminal justice system. It places the burden on the state to prove that the accused has committed an offense. The state cannot force accused persons to testify against themselves, cannot use illegally seized evidence, and must use a process consistent with due process standards to establish guilt.

Least Involvement With the System

The principle of least involvement assumes that minors, like adults, have liberty interests that include the right to be left alone or the right to live in a family situation without state interference. The state has the burden of showing that intervention is necessary for the protection of either the minor or society. Diversion should be considered before a formal petition is filed, and probation should be considered before commitment to an institution. In the detention situation, many codes require that a child not be held unless a probable cause exists to believe that he or she has committed a crime and an immediate and urgent necessity exists to admit the child. Detention is discussed more later in this chapter.

Presumption of innocence: the premise that a defendant is assumed to be innocent until guilt is established beyond a reasonable doubt.

Best Interest of the Child

The primary purpose of juvenile justice is to operate in the best interest of the child; this interest must be balanced against the interests of society. Society benefits by programs that help minors mature into law-abiding citizens, and children benefit by being held accountable and developing responsibility.

Goals of the Juvenile Justice System

The four primary goals of the juvenile justice system are as follows:

• *Separation from adults*: This is clearly the most important goal of the juvenile justice system. Reformers argued that children and families needed (1) a different form of justice, (2) separate courtrooms, (3) separate detention centers and institutions to avoid corruption of juveniles by adult criminals, and (4) separate sentencing guidelines to avoid the harsh penalties of adult sentencing. Furthermore, there is a separate group of professionals, judges, probation officers, and detention staff with specialized training who are dedicated to working with youths and their families.

Society benefits by programs that help young offenders mature into law-abiding citizens, be held accountable, and develop responsibility. These youths are attending a class while in juvenile corrections.

• *Youth confidentiality*: Confidentiality of court proceedings and services for youths reinforces the belief that they will mature beyond a criminal lifestyle if given proper guidance and alternatives. Because of their immaturity, youths lack sound judgment and should not be held fully accountable. Consequently, no criminal record should hinder adult advancement. From a developmental standpoint, confidentiality minimizes stigma and labeling and helps them to maintain a positive self-image, thereby reducing the likelihood that they will perceive themselves as criminals.

• *Community-based corrections*: Reformers strongly believed that young people should learn and grow in their own communities. Offering probation as a method for monitoring youth behavior in the community, while providing services that allow youths to grow to adulthood, is seen as the primary dispositional alternative.

• *Individualized justice of minors*: Each case is to be viewed separately. A social history that explores the total social circumstances of the youth and his or her family, and a casework plan that encourages appropriate development and reduced future criminality, is developed. Probation staff members are to look into the social situation early in the process and be involved in the decision to file a case. Whenever possible, the case is not filed formally, and an informal outcome is encouraged.[13]

JUVENILE OFFENDING TODAY

There is good news in terms of the numbers of juveniles who are arrested for all offenses in the United States. The juvenile arrest rate for all offenses climbed to and reached its highest level about two decades ago (in 1996) and has been declining since (see Figure 15.1). However, ample room remains for concern with juvenile crime. According to arrest data from the Federal Bureau of Investigation, juveniles (under age 18) commit about 11 percent of all violent crimes and about 16 percent of all property crimes in the United States (see Figure 15.2).

PRACTITIONER'S PERSPECTIVE

JUVENILE PROBATION OFFICER

Name: David Medina

Current Position: Juvenile Probation Officer

City, State: Orlando, Florida

College attended/academic major: Bachelor of science in criminal justice with an emphasis on homeland security from Florida Technical College

How long have you been a practitioner in this criminal justice position? Two years

My primary duties and responsibilities as a practitioner in this position: To prepare and present reports to the court, to commitment programs, and to other service providers. I provide and document the supervision and case management of clients who are placed on supervision as required by state statute as well as department policies and procedures, as relate to probation, commitment, and conditional release. I maintain and update case files on all delinquent youth per Florida Department of Juvenile Justice standards, policies, and procedures, and make recommendations to the State Attorney's Office within statutory time frames. I also provide necessary services after initiating an ongoing assessment of the youth. Also included are coordinating services, multidisciplinary staffing (for commitment conferences), and assessments as needed. I provide information for Interstate Compact on Juveniles (ICJ), and appear in court in order to provide the necessary reports and information. [*Authors' note*: ICJ involves the transfer and supervision of juveniles who are on probation and parole supervision across state lines, to ensure accountability of the juvenile and community safety.] Finally, I gather information as directed by statute, policy, and procedures, while ensuring that updated information is reflected in the Juvenile Justice Information System or other designated computer database information systems.

The qualities/characteristics that are most helpful in this career: Possessing excellent communication skills, especially with regard to listening. Probation officers must listen to and understand court orders as they relate to monitoring offenders' activities, while also listening to offenders, their employers, and others involved in their lives to find out whether they are in compliance with all conditions of probation. A probation officer must also possess the ability to help offenders understand what is expected of them during probation. In court, the probation officer must be able to communicate to the judge recommendations concerning terms of probation for the offender. Having the ability to motivate others definitely provides an advantage in this career field. Some offenders enter into probation feeling depressed about their situation and uncertain about what is to come. For example, someone convicted of robbery in a small community might feel ashamed about returning to that community; in such cases, the probation officer must assist the offender in setting goals for improvement and provide encouragement to take the steps necessary to achieve those goals. Positive thoughts and behavioral strategies are often the best tools a probation officer has for preventing new crime problems.

In general, a this is what a *typical day* looks like for a practitioner in this career: Generally checking on offenders who are on my caseload. Specifically, I must ensure that they are attending school (if that is a condition of probation; and if so, checking on their grades), keeping their jobs, and/or attending all court-ordered classes or meetings as part of their probation orders. I also perform random drug tests and home curfew checks.

My advice to someone either wishing to study, or now studying, criminal justice and wanting to become a practitioner in this career: Have the mind and heart to want to help people to make necessary changes in their lives. Probation, like government work in general, can be a relatively thankless job, so don't get discouraged if you don't receive positive reinforcement for your efforts. Probation officers need to make logical decisions and think out of the box, often in a timely manner. When interacting with an offender, you must be able to assess whether the offender is being genuine and truly fulfilling the terms of his or her probation, or is basically trying to be manipulative. In some cases, the officer must contact the courts and recommend either stricter or more lenient probationary terms, depending on how things are going for the offender. Therefore, you must also be prepared to, in effect, act as a judge in terms of making a recommendation concerning probationers' sentencing. In making those recommendations, you must diligently consider the facts of the case, the criminal background, and other life experiences of offenders, as well as the likelihood of additional crimes in making suggestions.

FIGURE 15.1 Arrest Rates for Juveniles

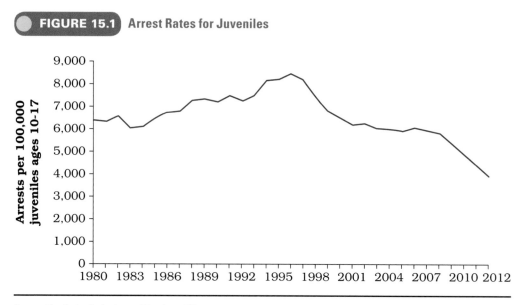

Source: Abadinsky, Probation and Parole, p. 143.

Many theories have been offered by experts to explain juvenile crime; however, no single theory has been universally accepted. Nevertheless, experts agree that a correlation exists between juvenile crime and the following factors:

• *Family dysfunction*: Family background is one of the most potent influences on juvenile development. Dysfunctional families transfer dysfunctional norms to their children. Juveniles who live in unstable homes and social environments are deemed to be *at-risk* children because of their vulnerability to detrimental influences. Such environments can contribute to antisocial behavior in children, often resulting in criminally deviant behavior later in life.

• *Drug use and deviance*: Alcohol and tobacco are the drugs of choice for many juveniles.

• *Socioeconomic class*: Children from poor and working-class backgrounds are much more likely to engage in delinquent behavior. Studies of the inner-city underclass have found that large numbers of the urban poor are caught in a chronic generational cycle of poverty, low educational achievement, teenage parenthood, unemployment, and welfare dependence.

• *Educational experiences*: Academic achievement is considered to be one of the principal stepping stones toward success in American society. Ideally, opportunities for education, mentoring, and encouragement to excel would be equally available for all children. Unfortunately, that is not the situation. Socioeconomic and demographic factors can also have an impact on educational opportunities and performance. Poor children often experience a very different educational environment in comparison to middle-class children, such as in inner-city, underclass environments, where educational achievement is frequently not commonly encouraged—or achieved.[14]

CASE FLOW OF THE JUVENILE JUSTICE PROCESS

This section describes the youthful offender's flow through the juvenile justice process, using as a guide the diagram shown in Figure 15.3.[15]

FIGURE 15.2 Percentage of Arrests, by Crime and Age, 2013

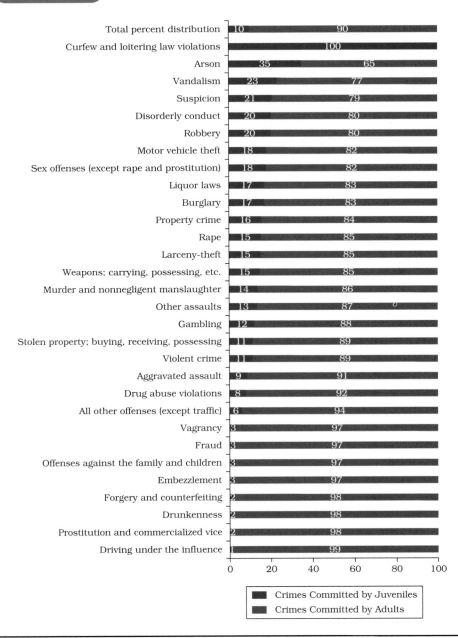

Note: Percentages may not add to 100.0 due to rounding.

Video:
Juvenile prisons

Note that each state's processing of law violators is unique, depending on local practice and tradition; therefore, any description of juvenile justice processing must be general, outlining a common series of decision points.

1. *Law enforcement diverts many juvenile offenders out of the justice system:* Young law violators generally enter the juvenile justice system through police contacts, but school officials, social services agencies, neighbors, and even parents provide information about a juvenile's crime that commences the process. At arrest, a decision is made either to send the matter further into the justice system or to divert the case out of the system, often into alternative programs. Usually the police make this decision after talking to the victim, the juvenile, and the parents, and after reviewing the juvenile's

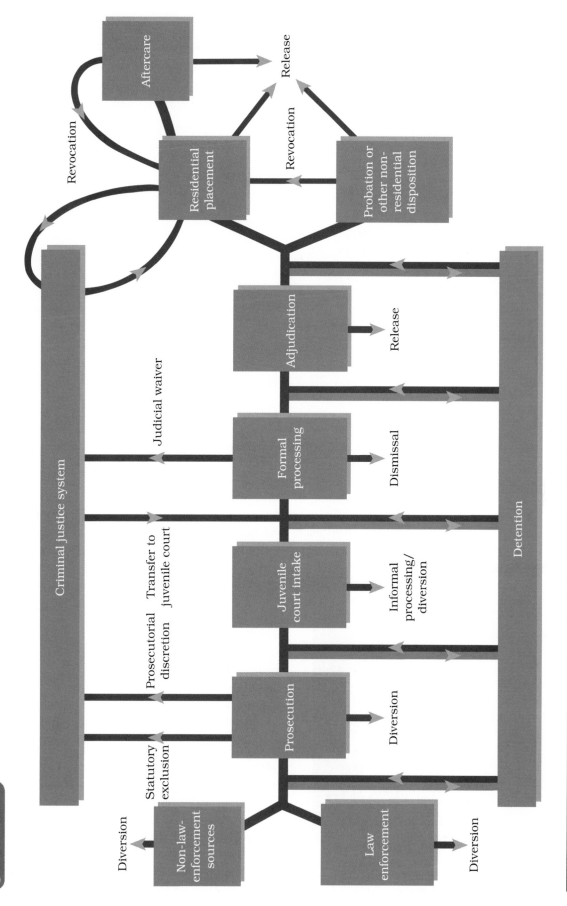

FIGURE 15.3 Case Flow Diagram of the Juvenile Justice Process

You Be the... PROSECUTOR

Should juveniles be prosecuted as adults? A number of states have said yes, responding to public perceptions that violent juvenile crime is a growing menace by making it easier to transfer juveniles from the relatively protective shroud of juvenile court to the jurisdiction of adult courts, thus trying juveniles as adults (also known as "certification" or "waiver"). States are also lowering the age and increasing the list of crimes for which juveniles can be transferred. Today, at least 24 states have laws sending violent juveniles to adult courts. Concerns regarding due process include the worry that this approach carries the possibility of juveniles being incarcerated with adult offenders and possibly being raped or assaulted by the older inmates. Advocates of restorative justice emphasize that juveniles are the prime example of where efforts at reconciliation are likely to yield more positive results than punitive measures.

1. Assume a juvenile is charged with committing a serious offense. Does prosecuting this case in an adult court mean that society has given up on the possibility of reform?

2. Is reform worth attempting (in terms of time, effort, cost, and other resources) for certain serious juvenile offenders?

Source: Adapted from R. E. Redding and J. C. Howell, "Blended Sentencing in American Juvenile Courts," *The Changing Borders of Juvenile Justice: Waiver of Adolescents to the Criminal Court,* ed. J. Fagan and F. E. Zimring (Chicago: University of Chicago Press, 2002), pp. 145–180; also see David Neubauer, *America's Courts and the Criminal Justice System,* 9th ed. (Belmont, Calif.: Thomson Wadsworth, 2010), pp. 449–453.

prior contacts with the juvenile justice system. Examples of alternative programs include drug treatment, individual or group counseling, or referral to educational and recreational programs.

2.   *A non-law-enforcement agency may divert juvenile offenders out of the justice system:* The court intake function is generally the responsibility of the juvenile probation department and/or the prosecutor's office. At this point, intake must decide to dismiss the case, handle the matter informally, or request formal intervention by the juvenile court. To make this decision, an intake officer first reviews the facts of the case to determine if there is sufficient evidence to prove the allegation. If there is not, the case is dismissed. If there is sufficient evidence, intake will then determine if formal intervention is necessary. About half of all cases referred to juvenile court intake are handled informally. Most informally processed cases are dismissed. In the other informally processed cases, the juvenile voluntarily agrees to specific conditions for a specific time period. Conditions may include victim restitution, school attendance, drug counseling, or a curfew. If the juvenile successfully complies with the informal disposition, the case is dismissed. If, however, the juvenile fails to meet the conditions, the intake decision may be to formally prosecute the case.

3.   *During the processing of a case, a juvenile may be held in a secure detention facility:* Juvenile courts may hold delinquents in a secure detention facility if the court believes it is in the best interest of the community or the child. After arrest, a youth is often brought to the local juvenile detention facility by the police. Juvenile probation officers or detention workers review the case and decide if the juvenile should be held pending a hearing by a judge. In all states, a

A youth shakes hands with a police captain in front of a Baltimore Police Department stationhouse during a protest against police-custody death of Freddie Gray, in Baltimore April 23, 2015.

©REUTERS/Sait Serkan Gurbuz

detention hearing must be held within a time period defined by statute, generally within 24 hours. At the detention hearing, a judge reviews the case and determines if continued detention is warranted. As a result of the detention hearing, the youth may be released or detention continued. Detention may extend beyond further hearings.

4.   *Cases may be filed in either juvenile or criminal court:* In many states, the legislature excludes certain (usually serious) offenses from the jurisdiction of the juvenile court regardless of the age of the accused. In other states and at the federal level under certain circumstances, prosecutors have the discretion to either file criminal charges against juveniles directly in criminal courts or proceed through the juvenile justice process. The juvenile court's intake department or the prosecutor may petition the juvenile court to **transfer** (also termed **remand**) jurisdiction to criminal court. The juvenile court also may order referral to criminal court for trial as adults. In some jurisdictions, juveniles processed as adults may upon conviction be sentenced to either an adult or a juvenile facility.

Residential commitment may provide juveniles with either a secure prison-like environment or a more open, even home-like setting. These teens lives in a small, home-like setting that stresses group therapy and personal development over isolation and punishment.

5.   *A **disposition** is reached in the case:* At the disposition hearing, recommendations are presented to the judge. The prosecutor and the youth (usually through his or her guardian ad litem) may also present dispositional recommendations. After considering options presented, the judge orders a disposition in the case. Most juvenile dispositions are multifaceted. In disposing of cases, juvenile courts usually have far more discretion than adult courts. In addition to such options as probation, commitment to a residential facility, restitution, and fines, state laws grant juvenile courts the power to order removal of children from their homes to foster homes or treatment facilities. Juvenile courts also may order participation in special programs aimed at shoplifting prevention, drug counseling, or driver education. Once a juvenile is under juvenile court disposition, the court may retain jurisdiction until the juvenile legally becomes an adult (at age 21 in most states). In some jurisdictions, juvenile offenders may be classified as youthful offenders, which can lead to extended sentences.

6.   *The judge may order the juvenile committed to a residential placement:* Residential commitment may be for a specific or indeterminate ordered time period. The facility may be publicly or privately operated and may have a secure prison-like environment or a more open, even home-like setting. In many states, when the judge commits a juvenile to the state department of juvenile corrections, the department determines where the juvenile will be placed and when the juvenile will be released. In other instances, the judge controls the type and length of stay. In these situations, review hearings are held to assess the juvenile's progress.

7.   *The juvenile receives aftercare, similar to adult parole:* Following release from an institution, the juvenile is often ordered to a period of aftercare or parole. During this period, the juvenile is under supervision of the court or the juvenile corrections department. If the juvenile does not follow the conditions of aftercare, he or she may be recommitted to the same facility or to another facility.[16]

Transfer (remand): the movement or assigning of a juvenile offender to an adult court, because the youth's behavior is such that he or she is not amenable to the juvenile court's rehabilitative philosophy.

Disposition: an outcome of a criminal or juvenile court process signifying that the matter is completed.

THE PROBLEM OF LABELING

Video: The wire and labeling

Looking at steps 1 through 7 above—after the youth has been apprehended, adjudicated, and placed—there is a concern that he or she will be officially labeled as deviant. A consequence of labeling in our society is that the individual may never be redeemed in the eyes of the community. Cox et al. stated that when labeling offenders, "John Q. Convict does not become John Q. Citizen. Instead, he becomes John Q. Ex-Convict."[17] Being labeled can thus make it extremely difficult for one who is a former deviant to find employment and succeed in society. Furthermore, labeling can change the delinquent's self-image to one that is negative. This "disintegrative shaming" (negative stigmatization) morally condemns and isolates the individual and does not attempt to reintegrate the youth into the larger society. Conversely, a better approach is to practice "reintegrative shaming," where there is an attempt to reconnect the stigmatized person to the larger society.[18]

Is There a "School-to-Prison Pipeline"?

Some authors believe there is a **school-to-prison pipeline**—often perceived as grounded in racial discrimination—that is an epidemic that plagues our schools. In sum, students who are expelled from school for disruptive behavior are then compelled to live in the homes and neighborhoods of negative influences where their problems began, causing them to become stigmatized, more hardened and embittered, and often more engaged in criminality.

Video: School-to-prison pipeline

Regarding the possible link of racial discrimination with this "pipeline," according to Rocque and Paternoster, African American youth fare worse in schools than whites in several areas: They show less interest in school activities, have lower grades, are more likely to be held back and to be in special education, and have higher rates of incarceration.[19] Added to those factors is their lower-socioeconomic-status background and environment, in which academic success may be dismissed and ridiculed by one's peers, as well as the increased likelihood that they will be singled out for punishment in school—and a school-to-prison pipeline trajectory for minorities is present.

What can be done about this pipeline or trajectory? First, according to some educators, is the need to realize that suspensions do not really work—they merely get the individual out of the classroom. Next is the need to examine existing discipline structures to ensure that they help, rather than hurt, students. Examples of the need to reassess discipline policies include the youth who spent 21 days in a juvenile detention center for talking back in class, the seven-year-old who was suspended for chewing his Pop-Tart into the shape of a gun, the senior expelled for forgetting the pocketknife in her purse, and seven teenagers who were arrested and charged with disorderly conduct for an end-of-the-year water balloon fight.[20] Some districts have signed "memorandums of understanding" with local law enforcement agencies that keep minor offenders out of criminal courts.[21] Others have attempted something called "restorative practices," which entails more adult involvement in letting youths know that their behavior is detrimental to the needs of the community and also to themselves. It involves getting to the root cause of the problem so that it does not recur, through the use of restorative justice circles; in this way, adults show children that they care about them and do not wish to suspend them from the classroom.[22]

Custodial Options

School-to-prison pipeline: the notion that certain policies and practices push schoolchildren, particularly those who are most at risk, out of classrooms and into the juvenile and adult criminal justice and prison systems.

Several options are available to juvenile judges who feel that some sort of custodial living arrangement in a residential or institutional facility is warranted for a particular youth. Generally, they fall into two categories: nonsecure and secure.

Nonsecure confinement facilities are those that afford the youth some movement within the community. They include foster home placement, shelter care facilities, group homes, halfway houses, and camps or ranches. Foster homes provide youths with a substitute family in cases where their own homes lack consistent adult supervision or the youths are unruly. More than a half-million youths are estimated to live in foster homes in the United States.[23] The typical stay is short, averaging about 26 months, and the majority of foster children are returned to their parents.[24]

Shelter care facilities provide youths with a home-like environment on a short-term basis; house parents provide the children care and safety for a few hours up to a few weeks. Youths in shelter care are nonviolent and are awaiting placement in a foster home or group home. There are about 175 such facilities in the United States.[25] Group homes are an intermediate alternative available to the judge; community-based, they have counselors or residents who act as parental figures for youths in groups of 10 to 20. They are able to offer residential community placement, treatment, and supervision. There are about 750 group homes in the United States, with about 8,200 youths in residence.[26]

Halfway houses, often used by adult parolees as they transition from prison into the community, also serve a valuable purpose for juveniles who are in transition. These youths have often spent a period of time in a secure residential facility because of delinquent acts, and halfway houses assist as they transition into the community. Camps and ranches experience wilderness projects that typically deal with less serious offenders and strive to improve their self-worth, pride, and trust in others. They are most likely to be operated by private agencies rather than state or local units of government.[27]

Secure confinement is generally used as a last resort and includes placing youths in shock probation, boot camps, and industrial schools or other institutions. In shock probation (or, more accurately, parole), a judge sends the offender to an institution providing secure placement; after a period of usually 60 to 90 days, the youth is brought back for a hearing and is placed on probation. The youth does not know he or she will soon be released from custody, so the idea is to "shock" the youth into displaying good behavior after getting a taste of institutionalization.[28]

As mentioned in Chapter 14, boot camps are highly structured, paramilitary, short-term correctional program that last from 90 to 180 days and strive to impart physical fitness and teach youths strict discipline. By 2007, there were more than 100 residential boot camps operating in 35 states.[29] However, no evaluation of juvenile boot camps has found this type of program to reduce recidivism.[30] Others problems have been uncovered: The U.S. Government Accountability Office conducted an investigation of juvenile boot camps in the mid-2000s and identified 1,619 incidents of child abuse in 33 states.[31]

Finally, a number of states operate an industrial or training school or other program that emphasizes vocational training, coping skills, education, and substance abuse and mental health counseling. There are about 200 such schools in the United States, housing some 34,000 youths. Nearly all such facilities are operated by some unit of government. As with boot camps, evaluations have not shown them to be effective in reducing recidivism; in fact, they are generally believed to increase reoffending.[32]

YOUTH GANGS: AN OVERVIEW

What Defines a Youth Gang and Its Members?

Although it is difficult to arrive at a common definition of a youth gang—because state and local jurisdictions often devise their own definitions—it is generally defined as a group or association of peers sharing a gang name, recognizable symbols, and identifiable leadership; having an identified geographic territory; holding regular meetings;

Halfway house: a community center or home staffed by professionals or volunteers designed to provide counseling to ex-prisoners as they transition from prison to the community.

PANAMA'S "CRUEL, INHUMAN" JUVENILE DETENTION

The U.S government has donated $3.5 million to provide vocational training as well as religious and educational workshops to juvenile inmates, as part of a three-year pilot rehabilitation project organized by the Panamanian and the U.S. government.

In early 2011, a team of researchers from the International Human Rights Clinic at Harvard Law School visited four juvenile detention centers in Panama. At that time, these detention centers housed 268 juvenile detainees, approximately 82 percent of the total population of the juvenile detention system.

The team learned that Panamanian authorities routinely subject juveniles in these centers to cruel, inhuman, and degrading treatment, occasionally rising to the level of torture. In one such incident, police stood by while juveniles locked in a cell slowly burned to death. The police officers were filmed laughing while the boys screamed and begged for help; one officer told the boys to die. Authorities were also found to have routinely beaten and used tear gas on detainees, and guards and police shot them with rubber bullets and threatened them with rifles. One director reported that, in the past, it was standard policy to inflict physical punishment for infractions such as fighting; the policy involved guards hitting detainees on the buttocks with a paddle and then sending them to the punishment cell.

One detainee was beaten for turning up the volume on a communal television set. Several others were beaten for pleading with the guards to give them water. The guards shouted obscenities at the detainees and refused to bring them water. When one juvenile threw a container of urine at a guard, as many as five guards entered the cell and beat him, continuing to do so even after they had him handcuffed.

Detainees described incidents in which guards beat them, shot at them with rubber bullets, and punched, kicked, and beat one juvenile with police batons for attempting to escape. They have also been sprayed with tear gas, which is especially egregious given the crowded conditions and poor ventilation in the detention centers. The team confirmed that detention center authorities also send detainees who commit infractions to maximum-security cells, where conditions also constitute cruel, inhuman, and degrading treatment.[33]

All such treatment is in violation of the United Nations' Convention on the Rights of the Child.[34]

and being collectively engaged in illegal activities. Second, the age range given for youth gang members is wide—about 12 to 24 years—with gang membership being more common at the top of the age range.[35]

How and Where They Proliferate

The latest National Youth Gang Survey estimates that there are approximately 30,000 gangs and 850,000 gang members across the United States; the estimated number of gangs has increased by 8 percent, and the number of gang members by 11 percent since 2010.[36] There is some good news in the survey findings, however. First, a common misconception concerning gangs is that once a person joins, he or she stays in the gang for many years. Studies have found repeatedly that most youths who join a gang do not remain in it for an extended period of time. Most youths who join a gang remain active members for only about 12 years. Another positive finding is that even in the most gang-ridden areas of the United States, most youths do not join a gang.[37]

Finally, a positive finding is that gangs were active in slightly less than 30 percent of the U.S. jurisdictions (cities and counties) surveyed, a slight decline over the preceding four years. This drop is attributable largely to the decline of gangs in smaller cities, where about 25 percent of cities report gang activity.

SAGE Journal
Article: Youth gangs

What Works With Youth Gangs?

As seen in Table 15.2, targeted patrols or a dedicated gang unit (or officer) were the measures used most frequently to combat gangs, followed by participation in a multi-agency gang task force and coordinated probation searches. Less frequently reported across all agencies were civil gang ordinances or injunctions (civil gang injunction is a court order issued in a civil case against a criminal street gang and its members to prohibit certain behavior within a defined Safety Zone—which may include associating together in public, and violating trespass and curfew laws).[38]

Finally, as with other crime and disorder problems, arrests alone do not solve problems in the long term. A comprehensive, multifaceted approach to the gang problem is needed, to include fundamental changes in the way schools operate (acting as community centers involved in teaching, providing services, and serving as locations for activities before and after the school day); job skills development; a range of services provided to families (parental training, child care, health care, and crisis intervention); changes in the way the criminal justice system—particularly policing—responds generally to problems, by increasing their understanding of the communities they serve; and intervention and control of known gang members—either by diverting peripheral members from gang involvement and criminal activity or by arresting and incapacitating hard-core gang members, thus sending a message that the community will not tolerate intimidating, violent, and/or criminal gang activity.[39]

TABLE 15.2 Antigang Measures Used by Police Agencies

	AGENCIES REPORTING USE (PERCENT)
Targeted patrols	76
Dedicated gang unit/Officer	64
Participation in multiagency gang task force	52
Coordinated probation searches	51
Curfew ordinance	47
Participation in a multiagency community-based anti-gang strategy	30
Targeted firearms initiative	26
Gang member call-ins	15
Participation in a multiagency reentry initiative	15
Civil gang injunction	8
Other civil gang ordinance	6

Source: Arlen Egley Jr., James C. Howell, and Meena Harris, Highlights of the 2012 National Youth Gang Survey (December 2014), U.S. Department of Justice, Office of Juvenile Justie and Delinquency Prevention, http://www.ojjdp.gov/pubs/248025.pdf.

INVESTIGATING FURTHER

HOMEBOY INDUSTRIES

Homeboy Industries teamed up with the East Side Spirit and Pride club to offer a class called Bridge to College on a routine basis. Youths are taken on tours to East Los Angeles College and other colleges; as a result, many youths have enrolled there and at other community colleges in the greater Los Angeles area.

In the 1980s, Father Greg Boyle realized that a need existed to provide jobs and education as alternatives to the gangs and the senseless violence they created. So, he began a mission in 1988, which became Homeboy Industries in 2001. The program has since grown to become one of the largest, most comprehensive, and successful gang intervention, rehabilitation, and reentry programs in the United States. Since the beginning, it has sought alternatives to violence, given second chances, and provided jobs and education. It is a therapeutic community, a place of healing, and a place to discover resilience. Since moving to its current location in Downtown Los Angeles, the program has grown exponentially. Now, each month more than 1,000 people walk through its doors seeking job placement, free services, and referrals; there are more than 800 tattoo removal sessions; more than 400 students are tutored and mentored; and nearly 400 people receive legal and mental health counseling.[40]

Homeboy Industries offers

- *Case management:* multidisciplinary method of monitoring trainees' 18-month plan of action as they establish and attain personal, educational, and vocational goals
- *Tattoo removal*
- *Employment services:* job preparation and placement
- *Mental health services:* individual therapy, substance abuse counseling, and group classes
- *Legal services*
- *Curriculum and education:* a GED program, Charter High School, life skills and enrichment classes[41]

AFTERCARE AND REENTRY

Although no program evaluations have shown a conclusive means of doing so, as with adult offenders (discussed in Chapter 13), a youth who is about to reenter the community after being in a custodial facility sorely needs aftercare services. Given that up to two-thirds of all youths will be rearrested and one-third will be reincarcerated within a few years after release, it is imperative that support services be in place to facilitate this reentry. This should include wraparound support services that are collaborations between family members and a transition specialist to ensure that the transition is a successful one. Many of these youths have depression, schizophrenia, other mental disorders, or learning disabilities, so it is important that aftercare includes helping them to develop skills for participating in the work force, school, and/or independent living; interacting appropriately with others; and developing a positive self-image and the ability to set personal goals.[42]

SIGNIFICANT COURT DECISIONS

Between 1960 and 1970, several important decisions by the U.S. Supreme Court addressed and expanded the legal rights of juveniles. Then, from 2010 to 2012, there was another spate of decisions.

You Be the... YOUTH AFTERCARE SPECIALIST

Very little is known about the best way to transition youths from a custodial facility back into the community. This lack of knowledge presents several hurdles to ensuring that reentry and aftercare are successful.

After a several-terms confinement in California Youth Authority facilities, a 20-year-old youth was asked about the most difficult challenge that he faced during reentry. The youth said, "It's the way people look at you." He related how the police and others simply assumed that he was the same person he'd been earlier and could not be trusted. He thus struggled to find work, support his family, get into schools,

and even avoid the influence of drug dealers in his community. In short, he was stigmatized and expected to fail, which only made his reentry all the more difficult.[43]

1. What do you believe should be done to end this cycle, especially with young people who spend a substantial amount of their adolescent years in secure confinement?

2. To end this cycle, are changes in laws required or merely a change in attitude and approach by the offender?

Right to Counsel

Kent v. United States (1966) involved a 16-year-old boy who was arrested in the District of Columbia for robbery, rape, and burglary.[44] The juvenile court, without conducting a formal hearing, transferred the matter to a criminal court, and Kent was tried and convicted as an adult. Kent appealed, arguing that the transfer to adult court without a hearing violated his right to due process. The Supreme Court agreed, and also decided that there must be a meaningful right to representation by counsel—who must be given access to the documents being considered by the juvenile court in making its decision—and that the court must also provide reasons for transfer.[45]

Video: Stickup kid

The Centerpiece: *In Re Gault*

Gerald Gault, age 15, was accused of making an obscene call to a neighbor. The police picked up Gault and took him to the juvenile detention center while his parents were at work. His parents were told later that a hearing would be held the next day, but the charges against Gault were not explained. The complaining neighbor did not show up at the hearing; rather, a police officer testified to what the neighbor had said. Gault, who had no attorney present, denied making the obscene calls. No record was made of the court testimony, and there was no jury present; only a judge heard the case, who declared Gault to be a delinquent and ordered him to be sent to a state reform school—until he was released or turned 21 years old,[46] whichever came first. Ultimately, Gault filed a *writ of habeas corpus* (discussed in Chapter 9), claiming that he had been denied due process rights at his hearing; this writ was denied, and state courts offered him no relief; the case was eventually taken up by the U.S. Supreme Court.[47] The Court noted the historically different treatment of juveniles, including their often being committed to an institution for several years, where "his world is peopled by guards, custodians, state employees, and 'delinquents' confined with him for anything from waywardness to rape and homicide." Finding that the Fourteenth Amendment is not "for adults alone,"[48] the Court held that juveniles were entitled to the same basic procedural safeguards afforded therein, including advance notice of charges; right to counsel and to confront and cross-examine witnesses; and the privilege against self-incrimination.

Student on the Street Video: Questioning a juvenile

The U.S. Supreme Court has decided that juveniles have the right to be represented by counsel as well as several other procedural rights prior to and during their involvement with the juvenile justice process.

Burden of Proof Standard

In 1970, *In re Winship* involved a 12-year-old boy convicted of larceny in New York.[49] At trial, the court relied on the "preponderance of the evidence" standard of proof against him rather than the more demanding "beyond a reasonable doubt" standard used in adult courts. The U.S. Supreme Court reversed Winship's conviction on grounds that the "beyond a reasonable doubt" standard had not been used.

Trial by Jury, Double Jeopardy, Executions

In *McKeiver v. Pennsylvania* (1971), the Supreme Court said that juveniles do not have an absolute right to trial by jury; whether or not a juvenile receives a trial by jury is left to the discretion of state and local authorities.[50] Then, in *Breed v. Jones* (1975), the Court concluded that the Fifth Amendment protected juveniles from double jeopardy, or being tried twice for the same offense.[51] (Breed had been tried both in California Juvenile Court and later in Superior Court for the same offenses.) Finally, as noted in Chapter 11, in 2005 the U.S. Supreme Court held that the Eighth and Fourteenth Amendments forbid the execution of offenders who were under the age of 18 when their crimes were committed.[52]

Right to the *Miranda* Warning

In 2011, the U.S. Supreme Court expanded the *Miranda* warning for suspects to include children questioned by police in school. In *J. D. B. v. North Carolina*, a 13-year-old North Carolina boy was taken from his classroom by a police officer and questioned, without an attorney or guardian present, in a conference room (where a police investigator and three school officials were present) concerning a string of burglaries. The boy eventually confessed, and his attorney lost his state appeal in trying to have the confession thrown out due to the boy's age and lack of *Miranda* warning (the state had argued that the boy should have felt free to leave the room and, therefore, was not in custody). The Supreme Court agreed with his attorney, saying for the first time that age must be considered in determining whether a suspect is aware of his or her rights.[53] This decision tells police they cannot avoid giving a youth the *Miranda* warning simply by questioning the youth at school, away from his or her parents or guardians; it is thus expected to force police to adopt a "when in doubt, give the *Miranda* warnings" approach with juveniles.

Serving Sentences of Life Without Parole

Life without parole: a penalty or sentence imposed, according to which the inmate is to serve a life sentence without parole eligibility.

In 2012, the U.S. Supreme Court, combining two cases, ruled that the Eighth Amendment's ban on cruel and unusual punishment prohibits sentencing any juvenile offender who commits a murder to serve a term of **life without parole** (LWOP) (see *Miller v. Alabama* and *Jackson v. Hobbs*).[54] The Court had already (in 2010) rejected life sentences for juveniles who had committed a *nonhomicidal* offense,[55] noting that such sentences had been "rejected the world over." The Court's reasoning was that such sentences do not take into account the possibility that an adolescent's personality and judgment are still developing, and that criminal tendencies can be outgrown.

You Be the... OFFICER

It is about 10:00 on a warm summer's night. A municipal police officer is dispatched to a residence to take a theft report. Upon arrival, she is informed by the residents that a very expensive bicycle has been stolen from their front porch. The victims further inform the officer that earlier that afternoon they observed a juvenile—whom they know by name, because he lives a few blocks up the street—walking on the sidewalk across the street and looking furtively at the bicycle. The officer recognizes the youth's name by reputation (i.e., prior involvement with police).

She drives her patrol car by the youth's home and, through the open front door, observes that the living room is dark but the television is turned on. She goes to the front door, and the juvenile is alone watching television; he comes to the door and tells the officer that his parents are sleeping. The officer knows that if she wakes the parents and (in their presence) asks the boy if he knows anything about the stolen bicycle, he will deny any such knowledge.

1. How should the officer proceed?
2. Is there an option available that will have a positive outcome for the juvenile, the victims, and the police officer?

Note: This relatively simple case study represents police work as it often occurs on the streets, where there is little opportunity for patrol officers to immediately seek a search warrant. It also involves the Fourth Amendment (probable cause, arrest, search and seizure); the police being aware of someone's history with and reputation for committing certain types of offenses; police policy and procedures (regarding treatment of juveniles); and, of course, police ethics. Also implicated are the informal nature of police work, use of discretion, Wilson's "watchman," order mainenance role of police (see Chapter 6), and Packer's crime control/due process dichotomy (discussed in Chapter 1).

IN A NUTSHELL

- Quakers in New York City in 1825 sought to establish a balance between two camps—people wanting to see justice done with child offenders, and those not wanting them to be incarcerated; they founded the first house of refuge.

- At about the middle of the 19th century, the house of refuge movement evolved into the slightly more punitive reform school, or reformatory, approach, to segregate young offenders from adult criminals, remove the young from adverse home environments, minimize court proceedings, and provide indeterminate sentences.

- In 1870, the Illinois Supreme Court held it unconstitutional to confine in a Chicago reform school a youth who had not been convicted of criminal conduct or afforded legal due process; thus, the juvenile court movement began.

- In 1899, the Illinois legislature enacted the Illinois Juvenile Court Act, creating the first separate juvenile court.

- In the post–World War II period, *status offenses* became a separate category: acts that would not be criminal if committed by an adult.

- Although juvenile arrests have been declining since 1996, juveniles still commit about 11 percent of all violent crimes and about 16 percent of all property crimes.

- Experts agree that a correlation exists between juvenile crime and family dysfunction, drug use and deviance, socioeconomic class, and educational experiences.

- The prevailing philosophy of the treatment of juveniles is *parens patriae*, meaning that the "state is the ultimate parent" of the child; the doctrine of *in loco parentis* means the state will act in place of the parent.

- There is an idealistic contrast between the juvenile court process and adults' criminal procedure, involving different terminology and court processes.

- Most states' juvenile court decisions and legislation contain three underlying principles: the presumption of innocence, the presumption of the least amount of involvement with the system, and the presumption of the best interest of the minor.

- The primary goals of the juvenile justice system are separation from adults, youth confidentiality, community-based corrections, and individualized justice of minors.

- Each state's processing of law violators is unique, depending on local practice and tradition.

- A consequence of labeling juveniles is that they may never be redeemed in the eyes of the community.

- Some authors believe there is a school-to-prison pipeline, whereby students who are expelled from school, being in their neighborhoods with negative influences, stigmatized, and more hardened, will then become more engaged in criminality.

- Several options exist—both custodial and noncustodial—for judges who feel that some sort of living arrangement in a residential or institutional facility is warranted for a particular youth.

- Although the number of youth gangs and their members has been increasing, the good news is that youths do not remain in gangs forever, and fewer communities now see gang problems. There are successful programs that work to help get youths out of gangs.

- As with adult offenders, a youth who is about to reenter the community after being in a custodial facility sorely needs aftercare services, to reduce his or her chances of being rearrested and reincarcerated.

- Several important rights have been granted to juveniles by the courts in the areas of due process, representation by counsel, advance notice of charges, confronting and cross-examining witnesses, the privilege against self-incrimination, burden-of-proof standard, having *Miranda* warnings given, and serving sentences of life without parole.

KEY TERMS & CONCEPTS

▶ Review key terms with eFlashcards. $SAGE edge™

Disposition, 385
Halfway house, 387
Houses of refuge, 375
Idealistic contrast, 377
Illinois Juvenile Court Act (1899), 375

In loco parentis, 377
Juvenile court, 375
Life without parole, 392
Parens patriae, 377
PINS (person in need of supervision), 377

Presumption of innocence, 378
Reformatory, 375
School-to-prison pipeline, 386
Status offenses, 377
Transfer (remand), 385

REVIEW QUESTIONS

▶ Test your understanding of chapter content. Take the practice quiz. $SAGE edge™

1. How would you describe the early treatment of juveniles, including houses of refuge and reformatories?

2. What contributions were made by the Illinois legislation that created the first juvenile justice/court system?

3. What are the major differences in philosophy and treatment between juvenile and adult offenders?

4. What is the definition of a status offense?

5. What are the prevailing theories underlying juvenile criminality causation?

6. What is the "idealistic contrast" between the juvenile and adult justice systems?

7. How would you explain the process and flow of cases through the juvenile justice system?

8. For what reason(s) might a juvenile offender be transferred to the jurisdiction of an adult criminal court?

9. What concerns exist with labeling of juvenile offenders?

10. Is there evidence that a school-to-prison pipeline exists? If so, what are some reasons for and possible solutions to it?

11. How would you describe the types of secure and nonsecure custodial options that are available to juvenile court judges?

12. What are some reasons for, and approaches to, providing formal aftercare and reentry services for juveniles as they leave custodial confinement and return to their homes and neighborhoods?

13. What due process rights were given to juveniles in *In re Gault?*

14. Aside from the rights secured in *Gault,* what other rights do juveniles now enjoy in their justice system?

1. Your criminal justice class has been assigned a group project, with each group citing what it believes are the major factors contributing to juvenile delinquency and related policy implications. Develop your argument using the following: Terence P. Thornberry, David Huizinga, and Rolf Loeber, "The Causes and Correlates Studies: Findings and Policy Implications," *Juvenile Justice* 9, no. 1 (September 2004), www.ncjrs.gov/html/ojjdp/203555/jj2.html.

2. A number of potential interview topics are presented in this chapter regarding the treatment of juveniles in your area or region. As examples, you can inquire of area juvenile judges, facility staff, probation officers, and police officers concerning their work generally, as well as the use of secure and nonsecure confinement facilities in the area, whether or not they believe there exists a school-to-prison pipeline, how often juvenile offenders are transferred to the adult courts, and the aftercare/reentry services that are provided.

$SAGE edge™

Review → Practice → Improve

Sharpen your skills with **SAGE edge** at **edge.sagepub.com/peak2e**

SAGE edge for students provides a personalized approach to help you accomplish your coursework goals in an easy-to-use learning environment. Access the videos, audio clips, quizzes, and SAGE journal articles that are noted in this chapter.

CHAPTER 16

ON THE CRIME POLICY AND PREVENTION AGENDA
Terrorism, the Mentally Ill in the Criminal Justice System, and the Changing War on Drugs

MARIJUANA IS SAFER THAN ALCOHOL

NO JAIL 4 POT

HOW CAN A PLANT BE A CRIME?

STOP ARRESTING ADULTS FOR MARIJUANA

PRO-CHOICE TAX & REGULATE

TAX

Not a Criminal

Matthew Micah Wright/Lonely Planet Images/Getty Images

LEARNING OBJECTIVES

As a result of reading this chapter, you will be able to:

1 Delineate the types of terrorism, including the cybercrime threat posed by China and bioterrorism, and some law enforcement and legislative approaches enacted for combating these threats

2 Identify major issues facing the criminal justice system relating to handling the mentally ill, to include current programs and proposals to address those challenges

3 Explain the movement to legalize marijuana as part of the broader, changing policy of the war on drugs and sentencing, and some of the legal, political, and technical questions involved

4 Comprehend the problem that now constitutes a national epidemic: the abuse of prescription painkillers

ASSESS YOUR AWARENESS

Test your knowledge of selected criminal justice policy issues by responding to the following seven true-false items; check your answers after reading this chapter's materials.

1 Currently, terrorist attacks in the United States and abroad involve well-organized groups and sophisticated weaponry.

2 The greatest threat of cyberterrorism against U.S. military and business establishments is now posed by Iran.

3 The U.S. Constitution unquestionably supports the government's use of drones against its citizens who fit the profile of a terrorist, both here and abroad.

4 Our nation's mental health system handles the majority of mentally ill persons, so only the worst and most violent offenders end up in the criminal justice system.

5 Most police officers today receive mandatory special training to deal with mentally ill persons.

6 U.S. laws regarding marijuana have changed little in the past, in terms of either its recreational use or its medical use.

7 Federal law currently prohibits the possession, growing, distributing, and legalization of marijuana.

We worry about the potential domestic-based, home-grown terrorist threat that may be lurking in our own society—the independent actor or "lone wolf"—those who did not train at a terrorist camp or join the ranks of a terrorist organization overseas, but who are inspired at home by a group's social media, literature or extremist ideology.

—Jeh Johnson, Secretary, Department of Homeland Security[1]

America's prisons have become warehouses for the mentally ill. Mass incarceration has been largely fueled by misguided drug policy and excessive sentencing. But the internment of hundreds of thousands of poor and mentally ill people has been a driving force in achieving our record levels of imprisonment. It has created unprecedented problems.

—Bryan Stevenson, Executive Director, Equal Justice Initiative[2]

<< **Answers can be found on page 424.**

Handout /Handout /Getty Images

Aaron Alexis killed 12 people at the Washington Navy Yard in 2013, refocusing attention on the mentally ill, their interactions with police and their access to guns.

Aaron Alexis had no trouble getting into Building 197 of the Washington Navy Yard on a September morning in 2013. He used the civilian contractor pass he had been using for several weeks, but on this particular day, he brought with him a backpack containing a disassembled shotgun and ammunition and a plan to kill multiple people. In less than 90 minutes, Alexis had shot and killed 12 and injured 3, committing the second deadliest shooting in history at a U.S. military base. He then hid in an office cubicle area, where a Washington, D.C., police tactical team tracked him down and killed him. That a civilian contractor could breach such a secure facility shocked military officials and civilians alike and called into question screening and access clearances for bases around the country.

But as the story unfolded in the days after the shooting, another disturbing question entered the nation's collective mind: Was Alexis mentally ill, and could police or medical professionals have stopped him months, even years, before that deadly morning in 2013?

During Alexis's four years in the U.S. Navy (2007–2011), he was cited eight times for misconduct and arrested three times for mischief and disorderly conduct, with two of his arrests stemming from shooting-related incidents. Later, just a month before the Navy Yard shooting, Alexis reported hearing voices and believed low-frequency electromagnetic waves were controlling him. Also in August 2013, naval police responded to a call at Alexis's hotel, where he had torn apart his bed trying to find someone he believed was hiding under it. Officers also discovered that Alexis had taped a microphone to the ceiling of his hotel room in hopes of recording the voices of people he believed were following him. Later that month, he twice sought help at hospital emergency rooms for insomnia, and after reporting to health professionals that he was not in danger of harming anyone, he was prescribed antidepressants. Whatever was tormenting Alexis, it apparently pushed him into his murderous rage. Law enforcement officials reported that Alexis had etched the words "End to the Torment!" and "My ELF weapon!" (referring to electronic low-frequency [ELF]) onto his shotgun, along with the message "Better off this way!" Perhaps most revealing, investigators also reported that they found a document in which Alexis wrote, "Ultra low frequency attack is what I've been subject to for the last 3 months, and to be perfectly honest that is what has driven me to this."

Because Alexis was killed, we will never fully understand what caused him to commit this horrific crime. To most mental health and law enforcement professionals, these symptoms— voices, delusions, and attention-seeking behaviors—are all hallmarks of potentially serious mental illness, such as schizophrenia, paranoia, or schizoaffective disorder. Although most mentally ill persons do not commit violent crimes like Alexis did that fateful morning, these brain diseases bring the mentally ill into increasing contact with the police and the criminal justice system, which has become the nation's de facto mental health system. But being mentally ill is not a crime and, as you have learned throughout this book, the rule of law and due process mean that we cannot prosecute persons for mere status or for behaving oddly unless they are indeed breaking the criminal law. At what point should police officers and other criminal justice professionals see trouble brewing, and what legal tools are available to them to help the mentally ill? Why was someone like Alexis able to buy the gun he used to commit this mass shooting? What happens to ill offenders if they are processed in the system, and perhaps more important, what happens to them when they get out?

These questions about the mentally ill in our criminal justice system—along with the issues of terrorism and the war on drugs—are just some of the cutting-edge issues we explore in this final chapter.

INTRODUCTION

What should be done about terrorists who now attack using little help and with inexpensive, widely available weapons and explosives made from everyday ingredients—and, increasingly, computers?[3] How should our justice system deal with the mentally ill who populate our jails and prisons in record numbers? Should marijuana be legalized nationwide?

The U.S. criminal justice system is affected, directly or indirectly, by nearly every public crime and policy issue that is raised (such as those mentioned above), because the system reflects the broader society and its changing times. And, like any other academic discipline or occupational environment, the system's priorities and trends are constantly in flux as to what is considered a crime and what methods of punishment are appropriate.

Certainly there is no shortage of additional policy challenges: How should Congress and the nation deal with human trafficking? What should be done with repeat sex offenders, and those who abuse children, in particular? What should be done about prison and jail overcrowding? Nonviolent drug offenders? Repeat offenders? These are all issues that have been, or must be, confronted in our nation and the international community.

This chapter briefly examines three such "hot-button" issues—specifically, the nature of terrorism, challenges to the criminal justice system posed by mentally ill persons, and the war on drugs in our society. Each has been at the forefront of our collective consciousness—and media reports—to some extent in recent times, and these issues give no sign of abating in the foreseeable future.

TERRORISM

New Challenges and Concerns

Life in the United States, indeed the world, changed forever on September 11, 2001, when al-Qaeda terrorists flew hijacked jetliners into the twin towers of the World Trade Center in New York City, the Pentagon in Virginia, and a field in rural Pennsylvania, killing nearly 3,000 people and bringing international terrorism to the American homeland.[4] More recently, two "lone wolf" brothers, inspired by online radical Islamic material and bomb-making instructions, detonated two bombs at the Boston Marathon in April 2013, killing 3 and injuring 264.[5]

Even since before the 9/11 attacks, our nation has been vulnerable to both "homegrown" and international terrorists. In 1993, radical Islamic terrorists linked to al-Qaeda bombed the World Trade Center by parking a rental truck packed with explosives in the underground parking garage, killing 6 and injuring 1,000.[6] Then in 1995, Americans Timothy McVeigh and Terry Nichols, using an eerily similar method—a rental truck packed with explosives—bombed the Alfred P. Murrah federal building in Oklahoma City, killing 168 and injuring more than 500.[7]

Meanwhile, terrorism is on the rise around the world, as international terrorist groups become more adept at recruiting "foot soldiers" through the Internet and other means. These attacks have become increasingly focused on civilian targets, with terrorists using more traditional methods of violence such as guns and hostage-taking rather than large-scale bombings:

• In Paris in January 2015, two masked gunmen attacked the offices of the satirical newspaper *Charlie Hebdo*. They killed 12 people and then escaped but were killed in a standoff with police several days later. When the attackers were still at large, another man linked to them took hostages at a Jewish grocery store near Paris, ultimately killing

Several attacks on American soil have demonstrated this nation's vulnerability to terrorism. But perhaps the most shocking were those occurring in September 2001 when hijacked jetliners crashed into the World Trade Center complex in New York City and the Pentagon in Virginia.

four hostages before police were able to kill him. Al-Qaeda in the Arabian Peninsula claimed responsibility for the attacks.[8]

• In Nairobi, Kenya, in September 2013, gunmen attacked an upscale shopping mall, terrorizing shoppers and ultimately killing 67. Investigators learned that the gunmen had rented a store in the mall for a time, allowing them to observe security and to stockpile weapons before the attack. The Islamist group Al-Shabaab (which is known to recruit from a large Somali population in Minnesota) claimed responsibility for the attack.[9]

• In Norway in July 2011, lone wolf terrorist Anders Breivik detonated a car bomb in downtown Oslo, killing 8 and injuring more than 200. Two hours later, Breivik arrived at an island summer camp dressed as a police officer. He opened fire and killed 69 people—many of them children and teenagers—and injured more than 100.[10]

These and other attacks have called the nation's law enforcement agencies to action, to learn more about terrorists' methods here and abroad, how to predict and possibly prevent future attacks, and how to respond when terrorists do strike. In addition, they have had to adopt a broader view of protecting the homeland (the organization and functions of the Department of Homeland Security were discussed in Chapter 5). Table 16.1 delineates terrorist attacks in the United States since 9/11. At least three dozen additional attempts to attack targets were thwarted by law enforcement agencies before they could be carried out.

The Federal Bureau of Investigation (FBI) defines **terrorism** as the "unlawful use of force against persons or property to intimidate or coerce a government, the civilian population, or any segment thereof, in furtherance of political or social objectives."[11] Terrorism can take many forms, however, and does not always involve bombs and guns; as examples, environmental and animal activists seek to further their agendas by burning greenhouses, tree farms, logging sites, ski resorts, and mink farms.[12] Cyberterrorism is another form of terrorism, and because it is carried out in the ether of cyberspace, it has posed unique challenges for lawmakers and law enforcement officials.

According to Michael Morell, twice an acting director of the Central Intelligence Agency, there is now a compelling threat from the Islamic State (ISIS) on U.S. soil: 3,500 to 5,000 "jihadist wannabes" have traveled from the United States, Western Europe, Canada, and other countries to Syria and Iraq to gain battlefield experience and have easy access to the U.S. homeland (part of at least 20,000 foreign nationals from about 90 countries who have joined ISIS). Morell states that while an attack in the United States from such fighters at the direction of ISIS has not yet occurred, "it will." Indeed, in November 2014, an individual sympathetic to ISIS attacked two New York City police officers with a hatchet.[13]

Cyberterrorism—and the Asian Threat

According to INTERPOL, **cybercrime/cyberterrorism** is one of the fastest growing areas of crime and includes attacks against computer hardware and software, financial crimes and corruption, and abuse, in the form of grooming or "sexploitation," especially crimes against children.[14] Unquestionably, many people around the world are now working full time trying to hack into online data and perpetrate related crimes. Not only are these cyberattacks becoming more frequent, but also they are becoming more expensive to address. A recent study found that, on average, about 28,000 records are hacked in each data breach in the United States.[15] These incidents are estimated to cost American businesses millions of dollars each year—$8.6 million per store for retail outlets, $20.8 million for financial services companies, $14.5 million in the technology sector, and $12.7 million in communications industries.[16]

Student on the Street Video: Cyberterrorism

Video: Cyber warfare

Terrorism: acts that are intended to intimidate or coerce a civilian population or government, usually for some political purpose or objective.

Cybercrime/cyberterrorism: using computers to commit crimes, such as embezzlement, diversion of bank monies to other accounts, and hacking personal information; making use of high technology, typically the Internet, to plan and carry out acts of terrorism.

TABLE 16.1   Selected Terrorist Attacks in the United States, 2001–2015

DATE	LOCATION	KILLED	INJURED	DESCRIPTION
Sept. 11, 2001	New York City, New York	2,759	8,700	Two hijacked planes crash into World Trade Center towers.
	Alexandria, Virginia	189	200	Crashing of hijacked plane into Pentagon.
	Somerset County, Pennsylvania	45	0	Crashing of hijacked plane into rural area of Pennsylvania.
Sept. 18, 2001	West Palm Beach, Florida	1	10	Anthrax-laced letters mailed to West Palm Beach, Florida, and New York City.
Oct. 9, 2001	Washington, D.C.	4	7	Anthrax-laced letters mailed to Washington, D.C.
July 4, 2002	Los Angeles, California	2	4	Egyptian gunman kills two Israelis at Los Angeles International Airport.
Oct. 2–23, 2002	Maryland, Virginia, D.C.	0	1	Two Beltway snipers kill at least 10 people, aiming to extort money and recruit more shooters.*
Nov. 29, 2005	Santa Cruz, California	0	4	Four injured via incendiary attacks by suspected animal rights activists.
March 5, 2006	Chapel Hill, North Carolina	0	9	Man drives vehicle into pedestrians at the University of North Carolina.
July 28, 2006	Seattle, Washington	1	5	Gunman fires on women at the Jewish Federation of Greater Seattle.
Feb. 24, 2008	Los Angeles, California	0	1	Animal rights activists attempt home invasion of biomedical researcher, injuring the researcher's husband.
July 27, 2008	Knoxville, Tennessee	2	7	Gunman fires on congregation at a church.
May 31, 2009	Wichita, Kansas	1	0	One doctor killed in shooting attack at Reformation Lutheran Church.
June 1, 2009	Little Rock, Arkansas	1	1	One army private killed, another injured in shooting attack at Army Navy Career Center.
June 10, 2009	Washington, D.C.	1	1	One guard killed in shooting attack at the Holocaust Museum.
Nov. 5, 2009	Foot Hood, Texas	13	44	Shooting attack at Soldier Readiness Center at Foot Hood.
Dec. 25, 2009	Michigan	0	3	Yemeni terrorist attempts to detonate bomb on flight from Amsterdam to Detroit; passengers and crew subdue the terrorist.
March 4, 2010	Alexandria, Virginia	1	2	Shooting at gate outside Pentagon; gunman killed.
Jan. 8, 2011	Tucson, Arizona	6	13	Shooting attack at political event at a supermarket; a federal judge is killed, a congresswoman injured.
Aug. 5, 2012	Oak Creek, Wisconsin	7	4	Seven killed, four injured in shooting attack at a Sikh temple.
Aug. 14, 2012	LaPlace, Louisiana	2	4	Two police officers killed, four injured while investigating attack; shooters had ties to the sovereign citizen movement.
April 15, 2013	Boston, Massachusetts	3	264	Two bombings at Boston Marathon kill 3, injure 264.

(Continued)

(Continued)

April 18–19, 2013	Watertown, Massachusetts	2	2	One police officer killed, one injured during manhunt for the Boston Marathon bombers; one terrorist killed and one injured and captured.
Nov. 1, 2013	Los Angeles, CA	1	7	Shooting attack at Los Angeles International Airport; one TSA officer killed, two TSA officers and several civilians injured.
April 2, 2014	Fort Hood, Texas	4	16	Shooting attack on Fort Hood; gunman killed himself.
Nov. 18, 2014	Austin, Texas	1	0	Shots fired at Mexican consulate, U.S. courthouse, and police station; failed attempt at arson at consulate; attacker was shot at by police.
Dec. 20, 2014	New York City	3	0	Shooting attack killed two police officers; gunman shot and killed himself.
June 17, 2015	Charleston, South Carolina	9	1	Gunman kills nine in attack at Emanuel African Methodist Episcopal Church; one injured.
July 16, 2015	Chattanooga, Tennessee	6	2	Gunman kills five Marines and one police officer at two locations; gunman shot and killed by police.

Source: Adapted from Wm. Robert Johnston, "Terrorist Attacks and Related Incidents in the United States," http://www.johnstonsarchive.net/terrorism/wrjp255a.html.

*Regarding the Beltway Snipers case, see Crime Museum, "The DC Sniper: *The Beltway Sniper Attacks,*" http://www.crimemuseum.org/Washington_DC_Sniper.

Without question the most challenging and potentially disastrous type of cyber-crime—actually, cyberespionage—now being perpetrated against the United States is by Chinese hackers, who are estimated to be responsible for the theft of 50 to 80 percent of all American intellectual property and have compromised many of the nation's most sensitive advanced weapons systems, including missile defense technology and combat aircraft.[17] It is believed that Chinese hackers have accessed designs for more than two dozen of the U.S. military's most important and expensive weapon systems (the cost to develop plans for one aircraft alone—the F-35 Joint Strike Fighter—was $1.4 trillion). Doing so enables China to understand those systems and be able to jam or otherwise disable them. The Pentagon recently concluded that another country's computer sabotage can constitute an act of war, which could eventually lead to U.S. use of military force.[18]

Of course, China's computer hacking does not stop with the U.S. military complex; corporate and business secrets are also prime targets of hackers. Estimates are that hundreds of private companies, research institutions, and Internet service providers have already been hacked, and there are also concerns about threats posed to U.S. nuclear reactors, banks, subways, and pipeline companies.[19] The specter of electricity going out for days and perhaps weeks, the gates of a major dam opening suddenly and flooding complete cities, or pipes in a chemical plant rupturing and releasing deadly gas are nightmare scenarios that keep homeland security professionals awake at night.

©REUTERS/Reuters Photographer

Counterterrorism experts believe it is only a matter of time before terrorists use chemical/biological weapons to attack the U.S. Local police and fire officials across the country train to respond to such incidents.

PRACTITIONER'S PERSPECTIVE

CYBERSECURITY CONSULTANT

Name: Mitchell Bezzina

Position: Cybersecurity Consultant, Guidance Software, Inc.

City, State: Pasadena, California

College Attended/Academic Major: Currently enrolled in a master of business administration program

How long have you been a practitioner in this criminal justice position? More than 15 years' experience in information security, digital forensics, and e-discovery

My primary duties and responsibilities as a practitioner in this position: Designing, developing, and implementing operational and procedural policies for digital forensics, e-discovery, and engineering departments to gain production efficiencies and comply with business requirements; managing forensic and e-discovery services and staff in support of investigations centered on intellectual property theft, employee misconduct, fraud investigations, cross-border investigations, court orders, and regulatory inquiries.

The qualities/characteristics that are most helpful in this career: Constant curiosity; an ability to spot details and map disparate facts to find anomalies—a fact could be anything, an out-of-character activity or process that appears to be out of place; an understanding of the need to "verify, verify, verify," never to assume any information is correct unless you have performed your own research; an understanding that tools and websites are out there to assist—whether open source or licensed, each plays an active role in accessing or interpreting data and reducing time; an ability to write clearly and concisely and to communicate technical terminology into terms and phrases that nontechnical people can understand; and the desire to continue learning and evolving.

In general, this is what a *typical day* looks like for a practitioner in this career: Checking for fires and overnight changes to cases/projects; checking international news for information on breaches or reports; checking forums for new information and findings in the field of interest; using handles to gain access to black sites and forums that may reveal attacks before they occur; updating intelligence database and reference lists with new findings and references; reviewing current cases/projects logs and verifying processes to meet imposed deadlines; communicating current case/project timeline to stakeholders; conducting investigation work; analyzing and researching to identify the anomaly; logging and reporting results.

My advice to someone either wishing to study, or now studying, criminal justice and wanting to become a practitioner in this career: Regardless of intended position, whether a lawyer or investigator, a solid understanding of computers is a must. Computer forensics is the foundation for three career paths: digital forensics, e-discovery, and incident response/threat intelligence. From there, your path is defined by your interests as you will be investing more than 40 hours per week doing what you love. The astute technical engineer is greatly sought after, but we must all be able to have business-level conversations; they are not mutually exclusive in every role. You will never stop learning. Seek out additional information and build your own referenceable knowledge base that can grow with you throughout your career.

Bioterrorism

Another means of attack by terrorists involves the use of chemical/biological agents, or **bioterrorism**. We know that poisons have been used for several millennia; recent attacks using chemical/biological agents including toxins, viruses, or bacteria such as anthrax, ricin, and sarin have underscored their potential dangers and uses by terrorists today. Chemical weapons—including several types of gases—suffocate the victim immediately or cause massive burning. Biological weapons are slower acting, spreading a disease such as anthrax or smallpox through a population before the first signs are noticed. Many experts believe it is only a matter of time before chemical/biological

Bioterrorism: the use of biological material, such as anthrax or botulin, to commit an act of terrorism.

weapons are used like explosives have been to date.[20] All that is required is for a toxin to be cultured and put into a spray form that can be weaponized and disseminated into the population. Fortunately, such bioterrorism agents are extremely difficult for all but specially trained individuals to make in large quantities and in the correct dosage; they are also difficult to transport because live organisms are delicate.

Law Enforcement Measures

Police have several possible means of addressing terrorism. On a broad level, four major aspects are involved in dealing with terrorist organizations:[21]

1. Gathering raw intelligence on the organization's structure, its members, and its plans (or potential for the use of violence)

2. Determining what measures can be taken to counter or thwart terrorist activities

3. Assessing how the damage caused by terrorists can be minimized through rapid response and containment of the damage

4. Apprehending and convicting individual terrorists and dismantling their organizations

Another means of addressing domestic terrorism is through military support of law enforcement. The Posse Comitatus Act of 1878 prohibits using the military to execute the laws domestically; the military may be called on, however, to provide personnel and equipment for certain special support activities, such as domestic terrorist events involving weapons of mass destruction.[22]

Furthermore, President George W. Bush directed the Department of Homeland Security secretary to develop and administer a National Incident Management System (NIMS). This system provides a consistent nationwide approach for federal, state, and local governments to work effectively together to prepare for, prevent, respond to, and recover from domestic incidents. This directive required all federal departments and agencies to adopt the NIMS and to use it—and to make its adoption and use by state and local agencies a condition for federal preparedness assistance beginning in fiscal year 2005.[23]

Finally, each FBI field office has established a Field Intelligence Group (FIG), composed of agents, analysts, linguists, and surveillance specialists. Their mantra is "Know Your Domain." As the FIGs have evolved, each office has developed its own model for intelligence gathering and operations. Furthermore, the FBI developed a Strategic Execution Team (SET) to assess the intelligence program, evaluate best practices, and decide what works and what does not work. This intelligence is regularly shared with police around the nation.[24]

Legislative Measures

In the immediate wake of the 9/11 attacks, Congress passed the USA PATRIOT Act (Uniting and Strengthening America by Providing Appropriate Tools Required to Intercept and Obstruct Terrorism Act of 2001). The act dramatically expanded the federal government's ability to investigate Americans without establishing probable cause for "intelligence purposes" and to conduct searches if there are "reasonable grounds to believe" there may be national security threats. Federal agencies such as the FBI and others are given access to financial, mental health, medical, library, and other records.[25] The act was reauthorized in March 2006, providing additional tools for protecting mass transportation systems and seaports from attack: the "roving wiretap" portion and the "sneak and peek" section. The first allows the government to get a wiretap on every phone a suspect uses, while the second allows federal investigators to get access to library, business, and medical records without a court order.[26] In June 2015, Congress extended the Act through 2019, but amended it to stop the National Security Agency from continuing its mass phone data collection program.[27]

The fight against terrorism was also aided and expanded in October 2006, when President George W. Bush signed Public Law 109-366, the Military Commissions Act (MCA).[28] Under the MCA, the president is authorized to establish military commissions to try unlawful enemy combatants, the commissions are authorized to sentence defendants to death, and defendants are prevented from invoking the Geneva Conventions as a source of rights during commission proceedings. The law contains a provision stripping detainees of the right to file *habeas corpus* petitions in federal court and also allows hearsay evidence to be admitted during proceedings, so long as the presiding officer determines it to be reliable. This law allows the Central Intelligence Agency to continue its program for questioning key terrorist leaders and operatives—a program felt by many to be one of the most successful intelligence efforts in U.S. history. The MCA excludes all statements obtained by use of torture, makes U.S. interrogators subject to only a limited range of "grave breaches," and clarifies what actions would subject interrogators to liability under the existing federal War Crimes Act.[29]

Balancing Security and Privacy: Use of Unmanned Aerial Vehicles

Because of the aforementioned PATRIOT Act and related legislation, Americans have had to give up much of their privacy since 9/11, and for some, the sacrifice has been worth it to catch would-be terrorists. But in 2013, National Security Administration employee Edward Snowden leaked classified documents to the press showing that the government was using provisions of the PATRIOT Act to access extensive telephone, computer, travel, financial, and other personal information.[30] Many Americans took notice and began questioning the delicate balance between security and privacy. The result was congressional enactment of the USA Freedom Act (Uniting and Strengthening American by Fulfilling Rights and Ensuring Effective Discipline of Monitoring Act) of June 2015. The Freedom Act replaced key provisions of the PATRIOT Act by allowing the government to continue certain surveillance methods but also halted the National Security Agency's controversial bulk collection of mass phone data from millions of Americans who had no ties to terrorism.[31]

AP Photo/U.S. Customs and Border Protection

Unmanned aerial vehicles (UAVs), or drones, are powered aerial vehicles that have many capabilities and beneficial uses. However, their increasing use has raised security and privacy concerns as well.

Another rapidly emerging issue in the fight against terrorism is the use—by government and private parties—of drones, also known as **unmanned aerial vehicles** (UAVs). These powered aerial vehicles are directed by a ground or airborne controller, do not carry human operators, and are designed to carry nonlethal payloads for reconnaissance, command and control, and deception. UAVs have rapidly become available in a variety of shapes, sizes, and capabilities, from one that is about the size and appearance of a hummingbird and carrying a tiny camera, to another the size of a jumbo airplane.[32]

Unmanned aerial vehicles: also termed "drones," aircraft without a human pilot that are controlled by computers and used for a variety of purposes by military and civilian police agencies.

Drones would seem to be tailor-made for seeking out and surveilling persons who are planning or involved in terroristic activities. However, the issue concerning use of drones came to the forefront in early 2013 during Senate confirmation hearings for President Obama's nominee to head the Central Intelligence Agency, John Brennan. A U.S. Department of Justice (DOJ) memo came to light in which the DOJ supported Obama's legal authority to use drones as mentioned above—to target American citizens whose behavior conforms to a particular profile and who are working with al-Qaeda—but with little or no oversight by Congress or the judicial system.[33] What is evident from the hearings is that Americans are very suspicious of—and may demand that legal criteria be established for—the overflights of drones in this country as we have deployed them over Pakistan and other countries. Clearly these are vexing security and privacy issues that our government and society must resolve, and each day the U.S. criminal justice system is closer and closer to the day when it will likewise be embroiled in those same issues.

You Be the... JUDGE

POLICE USE OF DRONES

More local law enforcement agencies are using drones, and only 14 states have passed privacy legislation regulating how such agencies can use them (including requiring officers to obtain a search warrant before using drones for surveillance). Some observers describe the relative lawless time in which drone technology is emerging as a "wild west" for law enforcement.[34] Assume you are an advisor to a presidential panel that is to make recommendations for *police* use of UAVs/drones, and respond to the following questions:

1. Would you support police use of drones for surveillance purposes involving serious offenses? If so, for what crime-related purposes?

2. Would you allow the police to use drones for Fourth Amendment (search and seizure) types of operations, if legal conditions have been met?

3. Do you endorse using drones for lower-level functions, such as catching traffic speeders?

4. Would your panel be in favor of arming the drones with bullets or tear gas?

5. Do you believe drones should be used, without prior consent from any courts or other oversight body, for killing persons whose "profile" indicates they are a dangerous threat to security?

THE "NEW ASYLUMS": THE MENTALLY ILL IN THE CRIMINAL JUSTICE SYSTEM

Police on the Front Lines

In September 2012, when Mohamad Bah's mother became concerned about his erratic behavior as he holed up in his apartment, she called 9-1-1 and asked for help for her mentally ill son. New to the country, she expected medical professionals to arrive, but instead NYPD officers responded. When Bah opened the door to officers, he was naked and holding a knife. Officers pulled the door shut and called for an Emergency Services Unit (ESU) because Bah was apparently "emotionally disturbed." When Bah refused to open the door to ESU officers, the team forced its way in and Bah lunged at them with the knife. Officers deployed an electronic control device and shot him with a rubber bullet, but Bah continued to come at them, eventually stabbing two officers. Police then fatally shot Bah, which unleashed a firestorm of criticism against the NYPD for not having an effective training program for officers to deal with the mentally ill.[35]

Bah's case may seem extreme, but Bah's mother did what most people do when confronted with a mentally ill person, whether it is a family member wielding a knife or a homeless person screaming on a street corner: They call 9-1-1 for help. And so begins the criminal justice system's role as the primary mental health system in this country.

At the front end, an estimated 20 to 40 percent of police calls for service involve mentally ill persons.[36] On the back end, America's jails and prisons have been termed by the Treatment Advocacy Center[37] as the "new asylums" because they house more mentally ill persons than any psychiatric hospital in the country. Researchers reported in 2015 that more than half the inmates in jails and state prisons were mentally ill, particularly with depressive disorder, schizophrenia and bipolar disorder.[38] Further, inmates diagnosed with mental illness are often serving time for drug-related offenses because one-third of the mentally ill (and nearly one-half of those with severe mental illness such as schizophrenia or bipolar disorder) have a "dual diagnosis," of mental illness and substance abuse.[39] A dual diagnosis only increases the chances that a mentally ill person will come in contact with police.

The crisis—for both the mental health and criminal justice systems—began in the 1960s and 1970s, when most large, state psychiatric hospitals were closed after investigations revealed their poor treatment of patients. The federal government provided funding for smaller, community facilities, but these centers simply could not absorb the tens of thousands of mentally ill people who flooded America's streets and who became part of the growing homeless population we know today.[40] Police officers became first responders, and the criminal justice system became America's mental health system. With that responsibility came significant challenges at every juncture. Today's criminal justice professionals can expect to deal with the mentally ill in record numbers, as they return again and again, as through a revolving door.[41]

Police officers are very often the first responders for the mentally ill. They make critical decisions about how to handle a variety of situations—violent and nonviolent—and most officers today are specially trained to do so.

Crisis Intervention Training

In 1988, a Memphis, Tennessee, police officer—much like the NYPD officers in the Bah case—responded to a call involving a man wielding a knife. The man would not comply with the officer's demands to disarm, and the officer had to resort to deadly force. Investigators later learned that the man suffered from schizophrenia and likely could not separate fact from fiction when dealing with the officer. The tragedy gave way to reforms and what we know today as the "Memphis Model," a program to train officers to deal with mentally ill individuals.

Known as crisis intervention training (CIT), officers learn to approach mentally ill suspects differently, using body language and voice commands to deescalate situations and to ease emotionally disturbed persons into compliance and safety for all. Officers are also trained to know the various diversion options in their jurisdiction, options for delivering such people to mental health/medical professionals rather than the local jail. CIT is critical for the modern officer. But to date, only about 2,700 agencies nationwide use the programs; advocates call for such programs to be standard police training everywhere.[42]

INVESTIGATING FURTHER

THE MENTALLY ILL AND GUNS

Despite a prior brush with the law and the mental health system, Seung Hui Cho was able to legally purchase the guns he used to carry out the deadliest mass shooting in American history when he killed 32 and injured 17 at Virginia Tech in 2007.

In Blacksburg, Virginia, in April 2007, Virginia Tech student Seung Hui Cho carried out the deadliest mass shooting in American history, killing 32 and wounding 17. More than a year earlier, he had sent suicidal text messages to a female classmate. Campus police officers then delivered him to the local mental health facility, where a physician determined that Cho was an "imminent danger to himself or others." The finding was not altogether surprising given that Cho had been diagnosed earlier with a severe anxiety disorder and major depressive disorder.

Upon a review of the diagnosis by a court, a judge found Cho was a possible danger to himself and ordered him to seek outpatient treatment, a ruling that disqualified him from buying guns under federal law. Despite the

court order, Cho never sought treatment and in February 2007, because of gun laws in Virginia at the time, Cho was able to purchase guns and ammunition that he would eventually use in the massacre.

Cho's case touched off a national debate about the intersection of mental health and gun laws, debates that would be renewed after the Sandy Hook Elementary shootings in Connecticut in 2012 and again in 2013 after the Aurora, Colorado, movie theater shootings. Today, after these mass shootings and others, the problem continues. Police in most jurisdictions are able to confiscate weapons from apparently mentally ill persons, but state and federal laws allow people in most cases to reclaim their guns. Unless a court has determined that someone is mentally ill/incompetent, or if an individual has been involuntarily committed to a psychiatric hospital, he or she is free to buy guns. Those results typically do not happen in all but the most serious cases, so severely mentally disturbed persons like Cho slip under the radar.

Critics of these legal loopholes argue for stricter gun-buying controls on the mentally ill, especially after police officers have confiscated weapons. Gun rights advocates consistently argue that Second Amendment rights should be limited in only those extreme cases where the potential for violence is more certain. Indeed, most mentally ill persons are not violent, but as these high-profile cases illustrate, very often we discover the capacity for violence only after it is too late.

Sources: Michael Luo, "U.S. Rules Made Killer Ineligible to Buy Guns," *New York Times,* April 21, 2007, http://www.nytimes.com/2007/04/21/us/21guns.html; Michael Luo and Michael McIntire, "When the Right To Bear Arms Includes the Mentally Ill," *New York Times,* December 21, 2013, http://www.nytimes.com/2013/12/22/us/when-the-right-to-bear-arms-includes-the-mentally-ill.html?action=click&contentCollection=Opinion&module=RelatedCoverage&region=Marginalia&pgtype=article.

Problems in Prisons and Jails

The nation's correctional systems bear the brunt of the mental illness problem, with record numbers of inmates in jails and prisons.[43] The mentally ill are difficult to house, requiring extra monitoring and medical treatment. And when medications fail or something illness-related goes wrong, these inmates can be exceedingly destructive and dangerous to themselves and officers.[44]

Mental health courts have helped lighten this burden, but they can handle only a limited number of cases. Recall from Chapter 9 that mental health courts are a problem-solving court, where court officials work with mental health professionals to get treatment—rather than incarceration—for eligible (typically first-time, nonviolent) offenders. The large numbers of ineligible offenders who end up in jails and prisons face potential abuse and mistreatment while incarcerated and almost certain failure upon release.

Video: The released

For example, a 2014 *New York Times* investigation revealed widespread abuse of the mentally ill at the country's second-largest jail, Riker's Island, with inmates being beaten while in handcuffs, for example.[45] Other cases have revealed more extreme misconduct, like the dehydration death of Timothy Souders at a Michigan prison in 2006 and a similar death in a North Carolina prison in 2014. Both mentally ill inmates were in solitary confinement.[46] Reformers recommend CIT for correctional officials to deal with mentally ill inmates, and many institutions across the country have implemented such programs, resulting in significant reductions of the use of force and inmate-officer assaults.[47]

Reentry is also a major issue. These offenders return to the streets with little medication and even less ability to arrange for medical care, so they unravel quickly and end up back in the system. The answer has been reentry programs that allow mental health professionals to "reach-in" and work with correctional officials while offenders are still in prison. The professionals prepare the offenders for release, and then follow them afterward with intensive supervision or "care management," with parole and mental health specialists working together. In Oklahoma, officials using this approach reported a 41 percent reduction in recidivism.[48]

America's prisons and jails have become the nation's "new asylums," housing more mentally ill persons than mental health facilities and creating increasing challenges for corrections officials, who must try to balance the need to treat these inmates with the priority of maintaining security.

THE CHANGING WAR ON DRUGS

As discussed in Chapter 12, the United States now imprisons about 2.3 million persons, and the majority of those incarcerated are in prison or jail for drug violations[49] (a related concept, mass incarceration, was also discussed in that chapter). Many of those violations involve marijuana, a drug relegated by law and much social opinion to the "lesser evil" end of the drug spectrum. Nonetheless, enforcement of U.S. marijuana laws consumes tremendous criminal justice resources: A Harvard University economist estimated that legalizing marijuana would save $13.7 billion per year in government expenditures on enforcement of prohibition by eliminating arrests for trafficking and possession as well as costs for related court and jail/prison activities. Others, of course, believe the enforcement of marijuana laws has been successful and balanced, and has contributed to reductions in the rate of marijuana use in the nation.[50] Whatever the case, social and political opinion on the **war on drugs**, and in particular marijuana laws, is changing, as evidenced by state legalization and the federal government's response.

SAGE Journal
Article: Legalize it?

A Sea Change in State Laws

In November 2012, voters in Colorado and Washington approved marijuana use for recreational purposes. Such enactments represent a significant "chink in the armor" of the nation's marijuana laws. Furthermore, 23 states and the District of Columbia have enacted laws to legalize use of marijuana for medical purposes.[51] This sea change in marijuana laws is gaining more support than ever before (see below).

First, as indicated earlier, proponents of legalization point to the fact that the enforcement of marijuana laws in the United States exerts a financial strain on societal as well as

War on drugs: a federal and state initiative to control the distribution and use of illegal drugs in the United States.

INVESTIGATING FURTHER

MENTAL ILLNESS AND SUICIDES IN PRISONS AND JAILS

Armando Cruz, who suffered from psychosis and schizophrenia, hanged himself in his solitary confinement cell at a California prison in 2011. Suicide is just one of the many risks corrections officials face with mentally ill inmates.

Armando Cruz hanged himself from the ceiling of his prison cell in California State Prison, Sacramento.

The note he left simply said "Remember me." Cruz's suicide in September 2011, after a long history of mental illness, is an example of how the criminal justice system is ill-equipped to handle people with mental health issues.

Cruz spent several years in solitary confinement; in fact, he died while locked in a tiny solitary cell. As a teenager he began to experiment with drugs and alcohol. Upon being arrested for stealing tools from his neighbor's garage at age 15, he admitted that he heard voices in his head. He would later be diagnosed with psychosis and schizophrenia. His mother tried for years to obtain treatment for her son, but doctors attributed his legal troubles to drugs and criminal associates. Eventually he was prescribed medications, but those that worked left him nearly catatonic.

At age 17, Cruz attacked a police officer from behind, cutting his throat. The officer survived. Although Cruz's mother attributed the attack to the voices in his head, Cruz was convicted of attempted murder of a police officer and sentenced to life in prison.[52]

According to the Bureau of Justice Statistics, suicide is the number one cause of death among inmates in local jails and in the top five causes for state prisons.[53]

criminal justice system resources. About half of all drug arrests are for marijuana, which equates to one marijuana arrest every 42 seconds.[54] Proponents also argue that legalizing marijuana would result in reduced prices and better quality control, reductions in related street crimes, benefits for cancer patients, additional tax revenues, and freeing up criminal justice resources for more serious crimes.[55] Table 16.2 shows annual marijuana arrests as a percentage of total drug arrests for manufacturing, sale, and possession.

Indeed, public support for legalizing adult use of marijuana has been increasing since the early 1990s.[56] Even some law enforcement officials—few of whom spoke out against marijuana laws in past decades—are now banding together in a national (and rapidly growing) organization whose name defines its purpose: Law Enforcement Against Prohibition (LEAP). This organization, launched in 2002, now boasts as members more than a thousand police, judges, prosecutors, prison wardens, and FBI and Drug Enforcement Administration agents, as well as about 70,000 civilian supporters.[57] LEAP, through its website, bemoans that

> for four decades the US has fueled its policy of a "war on drugs" with over a trillion tax dollars and increasingly punitive policies. More than 39 million arrests for nonviolent drug offenses have been made. The incarcerated population quadrupled over a 20-year period, making building prisons the nation's fastest growing industry. Each year this war costs the US another 70 billion dollars. Despite all the lives destroyed and all the money so ill spent, today illicit drugs are cheaper, more potent, and much easier to access than they were at the beginning of the war on drugs, 40 years ago.[58]

TABLE 16.1   Marijuana Arrests as a Percentage of Total Drug Arrests for Manufacturing, Sale, and Possession

YEAR	% TOTAL DRUG ARRESTS	% TOTAL MANUFACTURING AND SALE ARRESTS	% TOTAL POSSESSION ARRESTS
2014	44.9	5.2	39.7
2013	46.2	5.6	40.6
2012	48.3	5.9	42.4
2011	49.5	6.2	43.3
2010	52.1	6.3	45.8
2009	51.6	6.0	45.6
2008	49.8	5.5	44.3
2007	47.4	5.3	42.1
2006	43.9	4.8	39.1
2005	42.6	4.9	37.7
2004	44.3	5.0	39.3
2003	45.0	5.5	39.5
2002	45.3	5.4	39.9
2001	45.6	5.2	40.4
2000	46.5	5.6	40.9
1999	46.0	5.5	40.5
1998	43.8	5.4	38.4
1997	43.9	5.6	38.3
1996	42.6	6.3	36.3
1995	39.9	5.8	34.1

Source: DrugWarFacts.org, "Marijuana," http://www.drugwarfacts.org/cms/Marijuana#Share.

Opponents, conversely, argue that marijuana legalization can serve as a stepping-stone to harder drugs, result in people driving while "stoned" and thus pose a danger, increase the chances of the drug being used by kids, cause physical damage to users, and lead to the possible legalization of harder drugs.[59]

But these new state laws will not offer future marijuana aficionados unfettered use of or access to pot. As an example, in May 2013 Colorado governor John Hickenlooper, while acknowledging that the state is in "uncharted territory" in this area of law, signed bills that

- Require markings on labels stating the potency of the marijuana sold, as well as childproof packaging

- Place blood limits for driving under the influence of marijuana, placed at 5 nanograms per milliliter

- Require placing of marijuana-related magazines behind the counters of stores, sold only to customers 21 or older

- Require that no more than six plants be grown, and no more than an ounce of marijuana be possessed, by adults 21 and older[60]

©STEVE DIPAOLA/Reuters/Corbis

As more and more states legalize marijuana for both medicinal and recreational use, the debate about the war on drugs and law enforcement actions continues.

- Prohibit smoking of marijuana outdoors in public, in public parks, on sidewalks, in schools or on school grounds, or in privately owned buildings and apartments where the owner prohibits its use[61]

Conflicting Federal Law

A glaring aspect of legalization is that such laws are wholly in violation of federal law. Specifically, since 1970 the Code of Federal Regulations, Title 21, Section 1308.11, has listed marijuana as a Schedule I controlled substance,[62] meaning that it has no medical value and that the potential for abuse is high.[63]

Furthermore, for more than four decades, prohibitions on marijuana possession and use have been a major prop in the so-called war on drugs, initiated by President Richard Nixon in 1971. Following the Washington and Colorado votes to legalize marijuana, the *New York Times* reported that the Obama administration was holding "high-level meetings" to debate the response of federal law enforcement agencies.[69] Ultimately, the U.S. Department of Justice decided it would not challenge the Washington or Colorado laws and would focus instead on enforcing serious trafficking cases and keeping the drug away from schools and children.[70]

"Unintended Consequences" and Lawsuits

In 2015, news of "unintended consequences" of the new laws surfaced, when sheriffs from Nebraska and Oklahoma filed a federal lawsuit challenging Colorado's legalization, claiming that federal law should take precedence over the state law and that Colorado's new law was overburdening their departments with an influx of Colorado pot into their states.[71] Then in 2015, twelve sheriffs from three states—Colorado, Nebraska, and Kansas—filed a similar federal suit arguing that Colorado's marijuana laws put them in the untenable position of having to enforce state law in violation of federal law.[72] These suits are pending, but Colorado's attorney general in March 2015 asked the U.S. Supreme Court to throw out the Nebraska/Oklahoma suit, so the issue remains controversial among the many states affected.[73]

going GLOBAL

FOREIGN VENUES SUPPORT MARIJUANA LEGALIZATION

Following are recent actions taken in five selected foreign venues regarding the enforcement, legalization, and/or possession of marijuana under their laws.

1. In August 2013, Uruguay became the world's first nation to legalize marijuana; the new law allows the government to control the cultivation, trade, and sale of the crop.[64]

2. In Colombia, President Juan Manuel Santos called drugs a "matter of national security" due to the related cartels and their heinous crimes. He supports legalization, and in July 2012, the country's highest court ruled that minor possession of the drug was not a jailable offense.[65]

3. The Czech Republic decriminalized minor possession of marijuana for private use in 2010 and enacted a law legalizing medical use (however, local growth is restricted to registered firms).[66]

4. Argentina's Supreme Court deemed it unconstitutional in 2009 to punish people for private marijuana use as long as no one else was harmed, thus effectively authorizing personal use of pot.[67]

5. In Mexico, where marijuana users can possess up to 5 grams legally, two former presidents have advocated for decriminalization in order to curb cartel violence; the current president, Enrique Peña Nieto, is open to considering such a measure.[68]

The federal government has retreated somewhat even in its treatment of cocaine offenders. In 2010, Congress passed the Fair Sentencing Act, reducing the disparity between sentences for crack cocaine offenses versus powder cocaine offenses. Before the act, the disparity was 100:1, meaning those sentenced for certain amounts of crack cocaine would face penalties 100 times more severe than those sentenced for powder cocaine offenses. The act reduced that disparity to 18:1. Then in 2011, the Federal Sentencing Commission went a step further and made the new sentences retroactive to persons sentenced before the act was passed.[74]

The marijuana and cocaine examples illustrate how state and federal lawmakers will likely always make incremental changes to our nation's drug laws. To do otherwise would be risky in terms of social policy and political futures. But with mounting evidence of the failed drug war and its extraordinary burdens on the criminal justice system, further changes seem inevitable and those changes will impact criminal law policy makers, law enforcement officials, attorneys and judges, and our correctional system.

When Jails Become Rehab Clinics: The "National Epidemic" of Prescription Drug Abuse

Another problem that is increasingly confronting our society and the criminal justice system is the abuse of prescription painkillers. An estimated 100 million Americans suffer from chronic pain. As new painkillers have been developed and increasingly prescribed by health professionals to provide extended relief, it is no surprise that about 219 million opioid prescriptions are now written each year in the United States. This amounts to enough painkillers for every U.S. adult to be medicated around the clock for a month.[75]

Video: Prescription painkiller abuse

This national epidemic—so termed by the Centers for Disease Control and Prevention (CDC)—has resulted in many problems for both society at large as well as the criminal justice system. First, the longer a person is on such a drug, the better the chance that he or she will become addicted or develop a resistance to the drug's effects. Indeed, of the 9.4 million Americans who take opioids for long-term pain, about 2.1 million are

You Be the... JUDGE

Both sides of the marijuana controversy have the same goal: putting an end to the U.S. drug problem. However, each side makes arguments that should be examined prior to making public policy.

Those who are opposed to marijuana legalization argue that punishing its users with fines and jail time will deter other people from using the drug (however, that has not been the case). Furthermore, many if not most such users are nonviolent, petty offenders whose incarceration is expensive and who may well come out of jail or prison more dangerous and hardened than before. The relative success of drug courts (see Chapter 9) suggests these "offenders" need treatment rather than punishment.

In the other camp are those who believe marijuana is a part of our culture, has medical value, and should be legalized and that its users should go unpunished. Potential problems with this latter view are that legalization may well substantially increase the use of marijuana (including by motor vehicle operators),

and that there is no evidence to support the notions that legalization will result in close regulation and the cessation of illegal sales.

1. More arguments can certainly be made on both sides, but which faction's arguments wins your support? Why?

2. Should states that have either legalized or are considering legalization of marijuana be allowed to do so, given that they would be in conflict with federal laws?

3. Several attorneys general in neighboring states where marijuana remains illegal have filed suit against marijuana-legalization states. They allege that the flow of legal marijuana into their jurisdictions has injured their ability to enforce marijuana laws, increased their drug arrests, overburdened police and courts, and cost them money in overtime. Do they have a legal argument? If so, what is the solution?

estimated to be addicted. Some people have addictions so severe that they dissolve their pills and inject them with a syringe as often as 20 times per day, often sharing the same needles. Also, in many such cases, people who otherwise would never have engaged in illicit drug abuse then turn to the black market to obtain their higher dose. Then they are at risk of experiencing an overdose, and about 50 Americans die every day from prescription-opioid overdoses.[76]

Many addicted individuals—and related businesses—run afoul of the law and come to the attention of law enforcement. For example, the federal Drug Enforcement Administration fined Walgreens $80 million recently for allowing opioids to be possessed by criminals, and two CVS stores had their pharmaceutical licenses revoked for lax oversight of opioids. In Scott County, Kentucky, a common means of getting rid of one's addiction is by going cold turkey in jail. The sheriff has stated that the local jail is in fact the county's rehab and counseling clinic; with 65 beds and a 120-inmate capacity, about 90 percent of the jail's inmates are incarcerated for prescription-drug-related crimes. And, because of the aforementioned needle sharing, a related problem has been a fast-spreading outbreak of HIV. Indeed, in April 2015 the CDC issued a national health advisory in an effort to halt the 50,000 new HIV infections in the United States each year.[77] In Scott County, the problem became so prevalent (with nearly 90 new cases of HIV in the first three months of 2015) that the sheriff convinced the state's governor to issue an emergency order overriding the state's law against needle-sharing in order to allow syringe-swapping in the area.[78] Figure 16.1 shows the increases in rates of prescription painkiller sales, deaths, and hospital admissions over time.

FIGURE 16.1 Rates of Prescription Painkiller Sales, Deaths, and Substance Abuse Treatment Admissions, 1999–2010

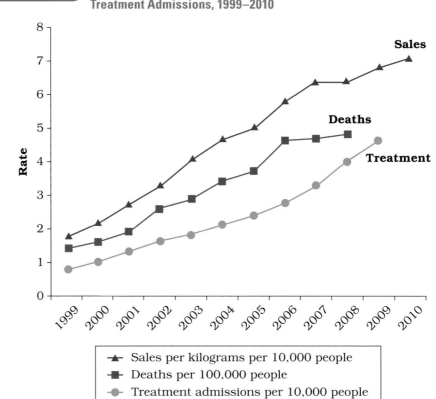

Sales per kilograms per 10,000 people
Deaths per 100,000 people
Treatment admissions per 10,000 people

Sources: Centers for Disease Control and Prevention. National Vital Statistics System, 1999–2008, Automation of Reports and Consolidated Orders System (ARCOS) of the Drug Enforcement Administration (DEA), 1999–2010; Treatment Episode Data Set, 19992009; http://www.cdc.gov/vitalsigns/painkilleroverdoses/infographic.html.

- There are a number of policy and prevention issues facing the criminal justice system today, including terrorism, state legalization of marijuana sales and use, human trafficking, and treating and punishing sex offenders.

- Terrorists are both foreign and domestic, and they use a variety of methods of attack for achieving their political and social objectives.

- Today China appears to pose the greatest threat to U.S. security through its cybercrimes.

- A number of law enforcement and legislative approaches have been developed for addressing terrorism and preventing such attacks.

- The expanding use of unmanned aerial vehicles (UAVs) or drones poses significant issues from both legal and political perspectives. As the technology—size, safety, capability, expanded use—changes with the use of UAVs, so do problems and policy issues involved—one being the use of drones by the federal government against U.S. citizens here and abroad who fit the profile of a terrorist.

- The criminal justice system has become the nation's *de facto* mental health system, handling and incarcerating more mentally ill persons than the country's psychiatric hospitals and mental facilities.

- Police are often the first responders to mental illness, and specialized crisis intervention training (CIT) has become standard practice in many agencies to deal with this ever-growing population.

- The nation's jails and prisons are the "new asylums" and have had to adapt to handling increasing numbers of mentally ill inmates with special training for correctional officers, more professional/medical staff, and protective custody for many of these disturbed offenders.

- A sea change in long-standing marijuana laws may be occurring, in terms of both its recreational and its medical use.

- State and federal lawmakers are also looking more broadly at the war on drugs and its impact, particularly the impact of sentencing laws, on nonviolent drug offenders, racial minorities, and the criminal justice system in general.

- The use and abuse of prescription painkillers (opioids) is at an all-time high, leading many typically law-abiding Americans to turn to the black market to obtain illegal drugs to address their pain, as well as a surge in HIV cases due to needle-sharing. Criminal justice agencies become involved not only by making arrests but also by supporting changes in related laws and attempting to rehabilitate addicted persons in local jails.

$SAGE edge™ Review key terms with eFlashcards. ◀

Bioterrorism, 403
Cybercrime/cyberterrorism, 400

Terrorism, 400
Unmanned aerial vehicles, 405

War on drugs, 409

$SAGE edge™ Test your understanding of chapter content. Take the practice quiz. ◀

1. What are two types of terrorism, and what are examples of each?

2. What law enforcement and legislative approaches have been used to combat terrorism?

3. What kinds of threats do cyberterrorists—particularly hackers in China—pose to U.S. security?

4. How do unmanned aerial vehicles—drones—fit into the overall discussion of terrorism, and what are some attendant legal considerations?

5. Why has the criminal justice system become the nation's *de facto* mental health system, and what are specific ways the system is dealing with the problem of the mentally ill?

7. What are some examples of how the war on drugs is changing in light of evidence showing sentencing disparities and the problem with mass incarceration?

8. What are some legal, technical, and policy issues that are at the heart of the marijuana-legalization question?

9. How do prescription painkillers now impact U.S. society and its criminal justice system?

1. Terrorists target critical landmarks—those having symbolic, economic, or public value (e.g., buses, restaurants)—to get public attention and change public behavior. You are to assume the role of someone working in a local police organization or disaster planning agency and then identify all such locations in your area. Then, for each location, consider the priority responses (i.e., measures taken by police, fire, medical, media, and so on) that would need to occur in the event such an attack took place.

2. A state legislative subcommittee contacts your criminal justice professor seeking input concerning privacy concerns with unmanned aerial vehicles. As your professor's research assistant, what kinds of questions would you recommend be included in the survey?

3. Your state lawmakers are debating a bill to provide funding for increased mental health care for the state's poor and mentally ill. Your professor is asked to testify about the impacts of the mentally ill on the state's criminal justice system, and she asks you to write a policy brief on the issue. How will you summarize the impacts/reforms regarding the criminal law, policing, the courts, and corrections?

4. Assume that your state legislator asks you to have lunch and discuss the status of marijuana legalization in the United States. What will you say?

$SAGE edge™

Review → Practice → Improve

Sharpen your skills with **SAGE edge** at **edge.sagepub.com/peak2e**

SAGE edge for students provides a personalized approach to help you accomplish your coursework goals in an easy-to-use learning environment. Access the videos, audio clips, quizzes, and SAGE journal articles that are noted in this chapter.

APPENDIX

CONSTITUTION OF THE UNITED STATES

The United States Constitution was written at a convention that Congress called on February 21, 1787, for the purpose of recommending amendments to the Articles of Confederation. Every state but Rhode Island sent delegates to Philadelphia, where the convention met that summer. The delegates decided to write an entirely new constitution, completing their labors on September 17. Nine states (the number the Constitution itself stipulated as sufficient) ratified by June 21, 1788.

The framers of the Constitution included only six paragraphs on the Supreme Court. Article III, Section 1, created the Supreme Court and the federal system of courts. It provided that "[t]he judicial power of the United States, shall be vested in one supreme Court," and whatever inferior courts Congress "from time to time" saw fit to establish. Article III, Section 2, delineated the types of cases and controversies that should be considered by a federal—rather than a state—court. But beyond this, the Constitution left many of the particulars of the Supreme Court and the federal court system for Congress to decide in later years in judiciary acts.

We the People of the United States, in Order to form a more perfect Union, establish Justice, insure domestic Tranquility, provide for the common defence, promote the general Welfare, and secure the Blessings of Liberty to ourselves and our Posterity, do ordain and establish this Constitution for the United States of America.

ARTICLE I

Section 1. All legislative Powers herein granted shall be vested in a Congress of the United States, which shall consist of a Senate and House of Representatives.

Section 2. The House of Representatives shall be composed of Members chosen every second Year by the People of the several States, and the Electors in each State shall have the Qualifications requisite for Electors of the most numerous Branch of the State Legislature.

No Person shall be a Representative who shall not have attained to the age of twenty five Years, and been seven Years a Citizen of the United States, and who shall not, when elected, be an Inhabitant of that State in which he shall be chosen.

[Representatives and direct Taxes shall be apportioned among the several States which may be included within this Union, according to their respective Numbers, which shall be determined by adding to the whole Number of free Persons, including those bound to Service for a Term of Years, and excluding Indians not taxed, three fifths of all other Persons.][1] The actual Enumeration shall be made within three Years after the first Meeting of the Congress of the United States, and within every subsequent Term of ten Years, in such Manner as they shall by Law direct. The Number of Representatives shall not exceed one for every thirty Thousand, but each State shall have at Least one Representative; and until such enumeration shall be made, the State of New Hampshire shall be entitled to chuse three, Massachusetts eight, Rhode-Island and Providence Plantations one, Connecticut five, New-York six, New Jersey four, Pennsylvania eight, Delaware one, Maryland six, Virginia ten, North Carolina five, South Carolina five, and Georgia three.

When vacancies happen in the Representation from any State, the Executive Authority thereof shall issue Writs of Election to fill such Vacancies.

The House of Representatives shall chuse their Speaker and other Officers; and shall have the sole Power of Impeachment.

Section 3. The Senate of the United States shall be composed of two Senators from each State, [chosen by the Legislature thereof,][2] for six Years; and each Senator shall have one Vote.

Immediately after they shall be assembled in Consequence of the first Election, they shall be divided as equally as may be into three Classes. The Seats of the Senators of the first Class shall be vacated at the Expiration of the second Year, of the second Class at the Expiration of the fourth Year, and of the third Class at the Expiration of the sixth Year, so that one third may be chosen every second Year; [and if Vacancies happen by Resignation, or otherwise, during the Recess of the Legislature of any State, the Executive thereof may make temporary Appointments until the next Meeting of the Legislature, which shall then fill such Vacancies.][3]

No Person shall be a Senator who shall not have attained to the Age of thirty Years, and been nine Years a Citizen of the United States, and who shall not, when elected, be an Inhabitant of that State for which he shall be chosen.

The Vice President of the United States shall be President of the Senate, but shall have no Vote, unless they be equally divided.

The Senate shall chuse their other Officers, and also a President pro tempore, in the Absence of the Vice President, or when he shall exercise the Office of President of the United States.

The Senate shall have the sole Power to try all Impeachments. When sitting for that Purpose, they shall be on Oath or Affirmation. When the President of the United States is tried, the Chief Justice shall preside: And no Person shall be convicted without the Concurrence of two thirds of the Members present.

Judgment in Cases of Impeachment shall not extend further than to removal from Office, and disqualification to hold and enjoy any Office of honor, Trust or Profit under the United States: but the Party convicted shall nevertheless be liable and subject to Indictment, Trial, Judgment and Punishment, according to Law.

Section 4. The Times, Places and Manner of holding Elections for Senators and Representatives, shall be prescribed in each State by the Legislature thereof; but the Congress may at any time by Law make or alter such Regulations, except as to the Places of chusing Senators.

The Congress shall assemble at least once in every Year, and such Meeting shall [be on the first Monday in December],[4] unless they shall by Law appoint a different Day.

Section 5. Each House shall be the Judge of the Elections, Returns and Qualifications of its own Members, and a Majority of each shall constitute a Quorum to do Business; but a smaller Number may adjourn from day to day, and may be authorized to compel the Attendance of absent Members, in such Manner, and under such Penalties as each House may provide.

Each House may determine the Rules of its Proceedings, punish its Members for disorderly Behaviour, and, with the Concurrence of two thirds, expel a Member.

Each House shall keep a Journal of its Proceedings, and from time to time publish the same, excepting such Parts as may in their Judgment require Secrecy; and the Yeas and Nays of the Members of either House on any question shall, at the Desire of one fifth of those Present, be entered on the Journal.

Neither House, during the Session of Congress, shall, without the Consent of the other, adjourn for more than three days, nor to any other Place than that in which the two Houses shall be sitting.

Section 6. The Senators and Representatives shall receive a Compensation for their Services, to be ascertained by Law, and paid out of the Treasury of the United States. They shall in all Cases, except Treason, Felony and Breach of the Peace, be privileged from Arrest during their Attendance at the Session of their respective Houses, and in going to and returning from the same; and for any Speech or Debate in either House, they shall not be questioned in any other Place.

No Senator or Representative shall, during the Time for which he was elected, be appointed to any civil Office under the Authority of the United States, which shall have been created, or the Emoluments whereof shall have been encreased during such time; and no Person holding any Office under the United States, shall be a Member of either House during his Continuance in Office.

Section 7. All Bills for raising Revenue shall originate in the House of Representatives; but the Senate may propose or concur with Amendments as on other Bills.

Every Bill which shall have passed the House of Representatives and the Senate, shall, before it become a Law, be presented to the President of the United States; If he approve he shall sign it, but if not he shall return it, with his Objections to that House in which it shall have originated, who shall enter the Objections at large on their Journal, and proceed to reconsider it. If after such Reconsideration two thirds of that House shall agree to pass the Bill, it shall be sent, together with the Objections, to the other House, by which it shall likewise be reconsidered, and if approved by two thirds of that House, it shall become a Law. But in all such Cases the Votes of both Houses shall be determined by yeas and Nays, and the Names of the Persons voting for and against the Bill shall be entered on the Journal of each House respectively. If any Bill shall not be returned by the President within ten Days (Sundays excepted) after it shall have been presented to him, the Same shall be a Law, in like Manner as if he had signed it, unless the Congress by their Adjournment prevent its Return, in which Case it shall not be a Law.

Every Order, Resolution, or Vote to which the Concurrence of the Senate and House of Representatives may be necessary (except on a question of Adjournment) shall be presented to the President of the United States; and before the Same shall take Effect, shall be approved by him, or being disapproved by him, shall be repassed by two thirds of the Senate and House of Representatives, according to the Rules and Limitations prescribed in the Case of a Bill.

Section 8. The Congress shall have Power To lay and collect Taxes, Duties, Imposts and Excises, to pay the Debts and provide for the common Defence and general Welfare of the United States; but all Duties, Imposts and Excises shall be uniform throughout the United States;

To borrow Money on the credit of the United States;

To regulate Commerce with foreign Nations, and among the several States, and with the Indian Tribes;

To establish an uniform Rule of Naturalization, and uniform Laws on the subject of Bankruptcies throughout the United States;

To coin Money, regulate the Value thereof, and of foreign Coin, and fix the Standard of Weights and Measures;

To provide for the Punishment of counterfeiting the Securities and current Coin of the United States;

To establish Post Offices and post Roads;

To promote the Progress of Science and useful Arts, by securing for limited Times to Authors and Inventors the exclusive Right to their respective Writings and Discoveries;

To constitute Tribunals inferior to the supreme Court;

To define and punish Piracies and Felonies committed on the high Seas, and Offences against the Law of Nations;

To declare War, grant Letters of Marque and Reprisal, and make Rules concerning Captures on Land and Water;

To raise and support Armies, but no Appropriation of Money to that Use shall be for a longer Term than two Years;

To provide and maintain a Navy;

To make Rules for the Government and Regulation of the land and naval Forces;

To provide for calling forth the Militia to execute the Laws of the Union, suppress Insurrections and repel Invasions;

To provide for organizing, arming, and disciplining, the Militia, and for governing such Part of them as may be employed in the Service of the United States, reserving to the States respectively, the Appointment of the Officers, and the Authority of training the Militia according to the discipline prescribed by Congress;

To exercise exclusive Legislation in all Cases whatsoever, over such District (not exceeding ten Miles square) as may, by Cession of particular States, and the Acceptance of Congress, become the Seat of the Government of the United States, and to exercise like Authority over all Places purchased by the Consent of the Legislature of the State in which the Same shall be, for the Erection of Forts, Magazines, Arsenals, dock-Yards, and other needful Buildings;— And

To make all Laws which shall be necessary and proper for carrying into Execution the foregoing Powers, and all other Powers vested by this Constitution in the Government of the United States, or in any Department or Officer thereof.

Section 9. The Migration or Importation of such Persons as any of the States now existing shall think proper to admit, shall not be prohibited by the Congress prior to the Year one thousand eight hundred and eight, but a Tax or duty may be imposed on such Importation, not exceeding ten dollars for each Person.

The Privilege of the Writ of Habeas Corpus shall not be suspended, unless when in Cases of Rebellion or Invasion the public Safety may require it.

No Bill of Attainder or ex post facto Law shall be passed.

No Capitation, or other direct, Tax shall be laid, unless in Proportion to the Census or Enumeration herein before directed to be taken.[5]

No Tax or Duty shall be laid on Articles exported from any State.

No Preference shall be given by any Regulation of Commerce or Revenue to the Ports of one State over those of another; nor shall Vessels bound to, or from, one State, be obliged to enter, clear, or pay Duties in another.

No Money shall be drawn from the Treasury, but in Consequence of Appropriations made by Law; and a regular Statement and Account of the Receipts and Expenditures of all public Money shall be published from time to time.

No Title of Nobility shall be granted by the United States: And no Person holding any Office of Profit or Trust under them, shall, without the Consent of the Congress, accept of any present, Emolument, Office, or Title, of any kind whatever, from any King, Prince, or foreign State.

Section 10. No State shall enter into any Treaty, Alliance, or Confederation; grant Letters of Marque and Reprisal; coin Money; emit Bills of Credit; make any Thing but gold and silver Coin a Tender in Payment of Debts; pass any Bill of Attainder, ex post facto Law, or Law impairing the Obligation of Contracts, or grant any Title of Nobility.

No State shall, without the Consent of the Congress, lay any Imposts or Duties on Imports or Exports, except what may be absolutely necessary for executing its inspection Laws: and the net Produce of all Duties and Imposts, laid by any State on Imports or Exports, shall be for the Use of the Treasury of the United States; and all such Laws shall be subject to the Revision and Controul of the Congress.

No State shall, without the Consent of Congress, lay any Duty of Tonnage, keep Troops, or Ships of War in time of Peace, enter into any Agreement or Compact with another State, or with a foreign Power, or engage in War, unless actually invaded, or in such imminent Danger as will not admit of delay.

ARTICLE II

Section 1. The executive Power shall be vested in a President of the United States of America. He shall hold his Office during the Term of four Years, and, together with the Vice President, chosen for the same Term, be elected, as follows:

Each State shall appoint, in such Manner as the Legislature thereof may direct, a Number of Electors, equal to the whole

Number of Senators and Representatives to which the State may be entitled in the Congress: but no Senator or Representative, or Person holding an Office of Trust or Profit under the United States, shall be appointed an Elector.

[The Electors shall meet in their respective States, and vote by Ballot for two Persons, of whom one at least shall not be an Inhabitant of the same State with themselves. And they shall make a List of all the Persons voted for, and of the Number of Votes for each; which List they shall sign and certify, and transmit sealed to the Seat of the Government of the United States, directed to the President of the Senate. The President of the Senate shall, in the Presence of the Senate and House of Representatives, open all the Certificates, and the Votes shall then be counted. The Person having the greatest Number of Votes shall be the President, if such Number be a Majority of the whole Number of Electors appointed; and if there be more than one who have such Majority, and have an equal Number of Votes, then the House of Representatives shall immediately chuse by Ballot one of them for President; and if no Person have a Majority, then from the five highest on the list the said House shall in like Manner chuse the President. But in chusing the President, the Votes shall be taken by States, the Representation from each State having one Vote; A quorum for this Purpose shall consist of a Member or Members from two thirds of the States, and a Majority of all the States shall be necessary to a Choice. In every Case, after the Choice of the President, the Person having the greatest Number of Votes of the Electors shall be the Vice President. But if there should remain two or more who have equal Votes, the Senate shall chuse from them by Ballot the Vice President.][6]

The Congress may determine the Time of chusing the Electors, and the Day on which they shall give their Votes; which Day shall be the same throughout the United States.

No Person except a natural born Citizen, or a Citizen of the United States, at the time of the Adoption of this Constitution, shall be eligible to the Office of President; neither shall any Person be eligible to that Office who shall not have attained to the Age of thirty five Years, and been fourteen Years a Resident within the United States.

In Case of the Removal of the President from Office, or of his Death, Resignation, or Inability to discharge the Powers and Duties of the said Office,[7] the Same shall devolve on the Vice President, and the Congress may by Law provide for the Case of Removal, Death, Resignation or Inability, both of the President and Vice President, declaring what Officer shall then act as President, and such Officer shall act accordingly, until the Disability be removed, or a President shall be elected.

The President shall, at stated Times, receive for his Services, a Compensation, which shall neither be increased nor diminished during the Period for which he shall have been elected, and he shall not receive within that Period any other Emolument from the United States, or any of them.

Before he enter on the Execution of his Office, he shall take the following Oath or Affirmation:—"I do solemnly swear (or affirm) that I will faithfully execute the Office of President of the United States, and will to the best of my Ability, preserve, protect and defend the Constitution of the United States."

Section 2. The President shall be Commander in Chief of the Army and Navy of the United States, and of the Militia of the several States, when called into the actual Service of the United States; he may require the Opinion, in writing, of the principal Officer in each of the executive Departments, upon any Subject relating to the Duties of their respective Offices, and he shall have Power to grant Reprieves and Pardons for Offences against the United States, except in Cases of Impeachment.

He shall have Power, by and with the Advice and Consent of the Senate, to make Treaties, provided two thirds of the Senators present concur; and he shall nominate, and by and with the Advice and Consent of the Senate, shall appoint Ambassadors, other public Ministers and Consuls, Judges of the supreme Court, and all other Officers of the United States, whose Appointments are not herein otherwise provided for, and which shall be established by Law: but the Congress may by Law vest the Appointment of such inferior Officers, as they think proper, in the President alone, in the Courts of Law, or in the Heads of Departments.

The President shall have Power to fill up all Vacancies that may happen during the Recess of the Senate, by granting Commissions which shall expire at the End of their next Session.

Section 3. He shall from time to time give to the Congress Information of the State of the Union, and recommend to their Consideration such Measures as he shall judge necessary and expedient; he may, on extraordinary Occasions, convene both Houses, or either of them, and in Case of Disagreement between them, with Respect to the Time of Adjournment, he may adjourn them to such Time as he shall think proper; he shall receive Ambassadors and other public Ministers; he shall take Care that the Laws be faithfully executed, and shall Commission all the Officers of the United States.

Section 4. The President, Vice President and all civil Officers of the United States, shall be removed from Office on Impeachment for, and Conviction of, Treason, Bribery, or other high Crimes and Misdemeanors.

ARTICLE III

Section 1. The judicial Power of the United States, shall be vested in one supreme Court, and in such inferior Courts as the Congress may from time to time ordain and establish. The Judges, both of the supreme and inferior Courts, shall hold their Offices during good Behaviour, and shall, at stated Times, receive for their Services, a Compensation, which shall not be diminished during their Continuance in Office.

Section 2. The judicial Power shall extend to all Cases, in Law and Equity, arising under this Constitution, the Laws of the United States, and Treaties made, or which shall be made, under their Authority; —to all Cases affecting Ambassadors, other public Ministers and Consuls; —to all Cases of admiralty and maritime Jurisdiction; —to Controversies to which the United States shall be a Party; —to Controversies between two or more States; —between a State and Citizens of another State;[8] —between Citizens of different States; —between Citizens of the same State claiming Lands under Grants of different States, and between a State, or the Citizens thereof, and foreign States, Citizens or Subjects.

In all Cases affecting Ambassadors, other public Ministers and Consuls, and those in which a State shall be Party, the supreme Court shall have original Jurisdiction. In all the other Cases before mentioned, the supreme Court shall have appellate Jurisdiction, both as to Law and Fact, with such Exceptions, and under such Regulations as the Congress shall make.

The Trial of all Crimes, except in Cases of Impeachment, shall be by Jury; and such Trial shall be held in the State where the said Crimes shall have been committed; but when not committed within any State, the Trial shall be at such Place or Places as the Congress may by Law have directed.

Section 3. Treason against the United States, shall consist only in levying War against them, or in adhering to their Enemies, giving them Aid and Comfort. No Person shall be convicted of Treason unless on the Testimony of two Witnesses to the same overt Act, or on Confession in open Court.

The Congress shall have Power to declare the Punishment of Treason, but no Attainder of Treason shall work Corruption of Blood, or Forfeiture except during the Life of the Person attainted.

ARTICLE IV

Section 1. Full Faith and Credit shall be given in each State to the public Acts, Records, and judicial Proceedings of every other State. And the Congress may by general Laws prescribe the Manner in which such Acts, Records and Proceedings shall be proved, and the Effect thereof.

Section 2. The Citizens of each State shall be entitled to all Privileges and Immunities of Citizens in the several States.

A Person charged in any State with Treason, Felony, or other Crime, who shall flee from Justice, and be found in another State, shall on Demand of the executive Authority of the State from which he fled, be delivered up, to be removed to the State having Jurisdiction of the Crime.

[No Person held to Service or Labour in one State, under the Laws thereof, escaping into another, shall, in Consequence of any Law or Regulation therein, be discharged from such Service or Labour, but shall be delivered up on Claim of the Party to whom such Service or Labour may be due.][9]

Section 3. New States may be admitted by the Congress into this Union; but no new State shall be formed or erected within the Jurisdiction of any other State; nor any State be formed by the Junction of two or more States, or Parts of States, without the Consent of the Legislatures of the States concerned as well as of the Congress.

The Congress shall have Power to dispose of and make all needful Rules and Regulations respecting the Territory or other Property belonging to the United States; and nothing in this Constitution shall be so construed as to Prejudice any Claims of the United States, or of any particular State.

Section 4. The United States shall guarantee to every State in this Union a Republican Form of Government, and shall protect each of them against Invasion; and on Application of the Legislature, or of the Executive (when the Legislature cannot be convened) against domestic Violence.

ARTICLE V

The Congress, whenever two thirds of both Houses shall deem it necessary, shall propose Amendments to this Constitution, or, on the Application of the Legislatures of two thirds of the several States, shall call a Convention for proposing Amendments, which, in either Case, shall be valid to all Intents and Purposes, as Part of this Constitution, when ratified by the Legislatures of three fourths of the several States, or by Conventions in three fourths thereof, as the one or the other Mode of Ratification may be proposed by the Congress; Provided [that no Amendment which may be made prior to the Year One thousand eight hundred and eight shall in any Manner affect the first and fourth Clauses in the Ninth Section of the first Article; and][10] that no State, without its Consent, shall be deprived of its equal Suffrage in the Senate.

ARTICLE VI

All Debts contracted and Engagements entered into, before the Adoption of this Constitution, shall be as valid against the United States under this Constitution, as under the Confederation.

This Constitution, and the Laws of the United States which shall be made in Pursuance thereof; and all Treaties made, or which shall be made, under the Authority of the United States, shall be the supreme Law of the Land; and the Judges in every State shall be bound thereby, any Thing in the Constitution or Laws of any State to the Contrary notwithstanding.

The Senators and Representatives before mentioned, and the Members of the several State Legislatures, and all executive and judicial Officers, both of the United States and of the several States, shall be bound by Oath or Affirmation, to support this Constitution; but no religious Test shall ever be required as a Qualification to any Office or public Trust under the United States.

ARTICLE VII

The Ratification of the Conventions of nine States, shall be sufficient
for the Establishment of this Constitution between the States so ratifying the Same.

Done in Convention by the Unanimous Consent of the States present the Seventeenth Day of September in the Year of our Lord one thousand seven hundred and Eighty seven and of the Independence of the United States of America the Twelfth. IN WITNESS whereof We have hereunto subscribed our Names,

George Washington, President and deputy from Virginia, and thirty-eight other delegates.

[The language of the original Constitution, not including the Amendments, was adopted by a convention of the states on September 17, 1787, and was subsequently ratified by the states on the following dates: Delaware, December 7, 1787; Pennsylvania, December 12, 1787; New Jersey, December 18, 1787; Georgia, January 2, 1788; Connecticut, January 9, 1788; Massachusetts, February 6, 1788; Maryland, April 28, 1788; South Carolina, May 23, 1788; New Hampshire, June 21, 1788.

Ratification was completed on June 21, 1788.

The Constitution subsequently was ratified by Virginia, June 25, 1788; New York, July 26, 1788; North Carolina, November 21, 1789; Rhode Island, May 29, 1790; and Vermont, January 10, 1791.]

AMENDMENTS

Amendment I

(First ten amendments ratified December 15, 1791.)

Congress shall make no law respecting an establishment of religion, or prohibiting the free exercise thereof; or abridging the freedom of speech, or of the press; or the right of the people peaceably to assemble, and to petition the Government for a redress of grievances.

Amendment II

A well regulated Militia, being necessary to the security of a free State, the right of the people to keep and bear Arms, shall not be infringed.

Amendment III

No Soldier shall, in time of peace be quartered in any house, without the consent of the Owner, nor in time of war, but in a manner to be prescribed by law.

Amendment IV

The right of the people to be secure in their persons, houses, papers, and effects, against unreasonable searches and seizures, shall not be violated, and no Warrants shall issue, but upon probable cause, supported by Oath or affirmation, and particularly describing the place to be searched, and the persons or things to be seized.

Amendment V

No person shall be held to answer for a capital, or otherwise infamous crime, unless on a presentment or indictment of a Grand Jury, except in cases arising in the land or naval forces, or in the Militia, when in actual service in time of War or public danger; nor shall any person be subject for the same offence to be twice put in jeopardy of life or limb; nor shall be compelled in any criminal case to be a witness against himself, nor be deprived of life, liberty, or property, without due process of law; nor shall private property be taken for public use, without just compensation.

Amendment VI

In all criminal prosecutions, the accused shall enjoy the right to a speedy and public trial, by an impartial jury of the State and district wherein the crime shall have been committed, which district shall have been previously ascertained by law, and to be informed of the nature and cause of the accusation; to be confronted with the witnesses against him; to have compulsory process for obtaining witnesses in his favor, and to have the Assistance of Counsel for his defence.

Amendment VII

In Suits at common law, where the value in controversy shall exceed twenty dollars, the right of trial by jury shall be preserved, and no fact tried by a jury, shall be otherwise re-examined in any Court of the United States, than according to the rules of the common law.

Amendment VIII

Excessive bail shall not be required, nor excessive fines imposed, nor cruel and unusual punishments inflicted.

Amendment IX

The enumeration in the Constitution, of certain rights, shall not be construed to deny or disparage others retained by the people.

Amendment X

The powers not delegated to the United States by the Constitution, nor prohibited by it to the States, are reserved to the States respectively, or to the people.

Amendment XI *(Ratified February 7, 1795)*

The Judicial power of the United States shall not be construed to extend to any suit in law or equity, commenced or prosecuted against one of the United States by Citizens of another State, or by Citizens or Subjects of any Foreign State.

Amendment XII *(Ratified June 15, 1804)*

The Electors shall meet in their respective states and vote by ballot for President and Vice-President, one of whom, at least, shall not be an inhabitant of the same state with themselves; they shall name in their ballots the person voted for as President, and in distinct ballots the person voted for as Vice-President, and they shall make distinct lists of all persons voted for as President, and of all persons voted for as Vice-President, and of the number of votes for each, which lists they shall sign and certify, and transmit sealed to the seat of the government of the United States, directed to the President of the Senate; — The President of the Senate shall, in the presence of the Senate and House of Representatives, open all the certificates and the votes shall then be counted; — The person having the greatest number of votes for President, shall be the President, if such number be a majority of the whole number of Electors appointed; and if no person have such majority, then from the persons having the highest numbers not exceeding three on the list of those voted for as President, the House of Representatives shall choose immediately, by ballot, the President. But in choosing the President, the votes shall be taken by states, the representation from each state having one vote; a quorum for this purpose shall consist of a member or members from two-thirds of the states, and a majority of all the states shall be necessary to a choice. [And if the House of Representatives shall not choose a President whenever the right of choice shall devolve upon them, before the fourth day of March next following, then the Vice-President shall act as President, as in the case of the death or other constitutional disability of the President. —][11]
The person having the greatest number of votes as Vice-President, shall be the Vice-President, if such number be a majority of the whole number of Electors appointed, and if no person have a majority, then from the two highest numbers on the list, the Senate shall choose the Vice-President; a quorum for the purpose shall consist of two-thirds of the whole number of Senators, and a majority of the whole number shall be necessary to a choice. But no person constitutionally ineligible to the office of President shall be eligible to that of Vice-President of the United States.

Amendment XIII *(Ratified December 6, 1865)*

Section 1. Neither slavery nor involuntary servitude, except as a punishment for crime whereof the party shall have been duly convicted, shall exist within the United States, or any place subject to their jurisdiction.

Section 2. Congress shall have power to enforce this article by appropriate legislation.

Amendment XIV *(Ratified July 9, 1868)*

Section 1. All persons born or naturalized in the United States, and subject to the jurisdiction thereof, are citizens of the United States and of the State wherein they reside. No State shall make or enforce any law which shall abridge the privileges or immunities of citizens of the United States; nor shall any State deprive any person of life, liberty, or property, without due process of law; nor deny to any person within its jurisdiction the equal protection of the laws.

Section 2. Representatives shall be apportioned among the several States according to their respective numbers, counting the whole number of persons in each State, excluding Indians not taxed. But when the right to vote at any election for the choice of electors for President and Vice President of the United States, Representatives in Congress, the Executive and Judicial officers of a State, or the members of the Legislature thereof, is denied to any of the male inhabitants of such State, being twenty-one years of age,[12] and citizens of the United States, or in any way abridged, except for participation in rebellion, or other crime, the basis of representation therein shall be reduced in the proportion which the number of such male citizens shall bear to the whole number of male citizens twenty-one years of age in such State.

Section 3. No person shall be a Senator or Representative in Congress, or elector of President and Vice President, or hold any Office, civil or military, under the United States, or under any State, who, having previously taken an oath, as a member of Congress, or as an officer of the United States, or as a member of any State legislature, or as an executive or judicial officer of any State, to support the Constitution of the United States, shall have engaged in insurrection or rebellion against the same, or given aid or comfort to the enemies thereof. But Congress may by a vote of two-thirds of each House, remove such disability.

Section 4. The validity of the public debt of the United States, authorized by law, including debts incurred for payment of pensions and bounties for services in suppressing insurrection or rebellion, shall not be questioned. But neither the United States nor any State shall assume or pay any debt or obligation incurred in aid of insurrection or rebellion against the United States, or any claim for the loss or emancipation of any slave; but all such debts, obligations and claims shall be held illegal and void.

Section 5. The Congress shall have power to enforce, by appropriate legislation, the provisions of this article.

Amendment XV *(Ratified February 3, 1870)*

Section 1. The right of citizens of the United States to vote shall not be denied or abridged by the United States or by any State on account of race, color, or previous condition of servitude.

Section 2. The Congress shall have power to enforce this article by appropriate legislation.

Amendment XVI *(Ratified February 3, 1913)*

The Congress shall have power to lay and collect taxes on incomes, from whatever source derived, without apportionment among the several States, and without regard to any census or enumeration.

Amendment XVII *(Ratified April 8, 1913)*

The Senate of the United States shall be composed of two Senators from each State, elected by the people thereof, for six years; and each Senator shall have one vote. The electors in each State shall have the qualifications requisite for electors of the most numerous branch of the State legislatures.

When vacancies happen in the representation of any State in the Senate, the executive authority of such State shall issue writs of election to fill such vacancies: Provided, That the legislature of any State may empower the executive thereof to make temporary appointments until the people fill the vacancies by election as the legislature may direct.

This amendment shall not be so construed as to affect the election or term of any Senator chosen before it becomes valid as part of the Constitution.

Amendment XVIII *(Ratified January 16, 1919)*

Section 1. After one year from the ratification of this article the manufacture, sale, or transportation of intoxicating liquors within, the importation thereof into, or the exportation thereof from the United States and all territory subject to the jurisdiction thereof for beverage purposes is hereby prohibited.

Section 2. The Congress and the several States shall have concurrent power to enforce this article by appropriate legislation.

Section 3. This article shall be inoperative unless it shall have been ratified as an amendment to the Constitution by the legislatures of the several States, as provided in the Constitution, within seven years from the date of the submission hereof to the States by the Congress.[13]

Amendment XIX *(Ratified August 18, 1920)*

The right of citizens of the United States to vote shall not be denied or abridged by the United States or by any State on account of sex.

Congress shall have power to enforce this article by appropriate legislation.

Amendment XX *(Ratified January 23, 1933)*

Section 1. The terms of the President and Vice President shall end at noon on the 20th day of January, and the terms of Senators and Representatives at noon on the 3d day of January, of the years in which such terms would have ended if this article had not been ratified; and the terms of their successors shall then begin.

Section 2. The Congress shall assemble at least once in every year, and such meeting shall begin at noon on the 3d day of January, unless they shall by law appoint a different day.

Section 3.[14] If, at the time fixed for the beginning of the term of the President, the President elect shall have died, the Vice President elect shall become President. If a President shall not have been chosen before the time fixed for the beginning of his term, or if the President elect shall have failed to qualify, then the Vice President elect shall act as President until a President shall have qualified; and the Congress may by law provide for the case wherein neither a President elect nor a Vice President elect shall have qualified, declaring who shall then act as President, or the manner in which one who is to act shall be selected, and such

person shall act accordingly until a President or Vice President shall have qualified.

Section 4. The Congress may by law provide for the case of the death of any of the persons from whom the House of Representatives may choose a President whenever the right of choice shall have devolved upon them, and for the case of the death of any of the persons from whom the Senate may choose a Vice President whenever the right of choice shall have devolved upon them.

Section 5. Sections 1 and 2 shall take effect on the 15th day of October following the ratification of this article.

Section 6. This article shall be inoperative unless it shall have been ratified as an amendment to the Constitution by the legislatures of three-fourths of the several States within seven years from the date of its submission.

Amendment XXI *(Ratified December 5, 1933)*

Section 1. The eighteenth article of amendment to the Constitution of the United States is hereby repealed.

Section 2. The transportation or importation into any State, Territory, or possession of the United States for delivery or use therein of intoxicating liquors, in violation of the laws thereof, is hereby prohibited.

Section 3. This article shall be inoperative unless it shall have been ratified as an amendment to the Constitution by conventions in the several States, as provided in the Constitution, within seven years from the date of the submission hereof to the States by the Congress.

Amendment XXII *(Ratified February 27, 1951)*

Section 1. No person shall be elected to the office of the President more than twice, and no person who has held the office of President, or acted as President, for more than two years of a term to which some other person was elected President shall be elected to the office of the President more than once. But this Article shall not apply to any person holding the office of President when this Article was proposed by the Congress, and shall not prevent any person who may be holding the office of President, or acting as President, during the term within which this Article becomes operative from holding the office of President or acting as President during the remainder of such term.

Section 2. This article shall be inoperative unless it shall have been ratified as an amendment to the Constitution by the legislatures of three-fourths of the several States within seven years from the date of its submission to the States by the Congress.

Amendment XXIII *(Ratified March 29, 1961)*

Section 1. The District constituting the seat of Government of the United States shall appoint in such manner as the Congress may direct:

A number of electors of President and Vice President equal to the whole number of Senators and Representatives in Congress to which the District would be entitled if it were a State, but in no event more than the least populous State; they shall be in addition to those appointed by the States, but they shall be considered, for the purposes of the election of President and Vice President, to be electors appointed by a State; and they shall meet in the District and perform such duties as provided by the twelfth article of amendment.

Section 2. The Congress shall have power to enforce this article by appropriate legislation.

Amendment XXIV *(Ratified January 23, 1964)*

Section 1. The right of citizens of the United States to vote in any primary or other election for President or Vice President, for electors for President or Vice President, or for Senator or Representative in Congress, shall not be denied or abridged by the United States or any State by reason of failure to pay any poll tax or other tax.

Section 2. The Congress shall have power to enforce this article by appropriate legislation.

Amendment XXV *(Ratified February 10, 1967)*

Section 1. In case of the removal of the President from office or of his death or resignation, the Vice President shall become President.

Section 2. Whenever there is a vacancy in the office of the Vice President, the President shall nominate a Vice President who shall take office upon confirmation by a majority vote of both Houses of Congress.

Section 3. Whenever the President transmits to the President pro tempore of the Senate and the Speaker of the House of Representatives his written declaration that he is unable to discharge the powers and duties of his office, and until he transmits to them a written declaration to the contrary, such powers and duties shall be discharged by the Vice President as Acting President.

Section 4. Whenever the Vice President and a majority of either the principal officers of the executive departments or of such other body as Congress may by law provide, transmit to the President pro tempore of the Senate and the Speaker of the House of Representatives their written declaration that the President is unable to discharge the powers and duties of his office, the Vice President shall immediately assume the powers and duties of the office as Acting President.

Thereafter, when the President transmits to the President pro tempore of the Senate and the Speaker of the House of Representatives his written declaration that no inability exists, he shall resume the powers and duties of his office unless the Vice President and a majority of either the principal officers of the executive departments or of such other body as Congress may by law provide, transmit within four days to the President pro tempore of the Senate and the Speaker of the House of Representatives their written declaration that the President is unable to discharge the powers and duties of his office. Thereupon Congress shall decide the issue, assembling within forty-eight hours for that purpose if not in session. If the Congress, within twenty-one days after receipt of the latter written declaration, or, if Congress is not in session, within twenty-one days after Congress is required to assemble, determines by two-thirds vote of both Houses that the President is unable to discharge the powers and duties of his office, the Vice President shall continue to discharge the same as Acting President; otherwise, the President shall resume the powers and duties of his office.

Amendment XXVI

(Ratified July 1, 1971)

Section 1. The right of citizens of the United States, who are eighteen years of age or older, to vote shall not be denied or abridged by the United States or by any State on account of age.

Section 2. The Congress shall have power to enforce this article by appropriate legislation.

Amendment XXVII *(Ratified May 7, 1992)*

No law varying the compensation for the services of the Senators and Representatives shall take effect, until an election of Representatives shall have intervened.

Source: U.S. Congress, House, Committee on the Judiciary, The Constitution of the United States of America, as Amended, 100th Cong., 1st sess., 1987, H Doc 100–94.

Notes:

1. The part in brackets was changed by section 2 of the Fourteenth Amendment.
2. The part in brackets was changed by the first paragraph of the Seventeenth Amendment.
3. The part in brackets was changed by the second paragraph of the Seventeenth Amendment.
4. The part in brackets was changed by section 2 of the Twentieth Amendment.
5. The Sixteenth Amendment gave Congress the power to tax incomes.
6. The material in brackets was superseded by the Twelfth Amendment.
7. This provision was affected by the Twenty-fifth Amendment.
8. These clauses were affected by the Eleventh Amendment.
9. This paragraph was superseded by the Thirteenth Amendment.
10. Obsolete.
11. The part in brackets was superseded by Section 3 of the Twentieth Amendment.
12. See the Nineteenth and Twenty-sixth Amendments.
13. This amendment was repealed by Section 1 of the Twenty-first Amendment.
14. See the Twenty-fifth Amendment.

Answers

Chapter 1   1. t; 2. f; 3. f; 4. f; 5. t; 6. f   3

Chapter 2   1. t; 2. f; 3. f; 4. t; 5. t; 6. t; 7. f   23

Chapter 3   1. f; 2. f; 3. t; 4. t; 5. f; 6. t; 7. t; 8. f   49

Chapter 4   1. t; 2. f; 3. t; 4. f; 5. f; 6. f; 7. f   79

Chapter 5   1. t; 2. f.; 3. t; 4. f; 5. t; 6. f; 7. t; 8. t; 9. f   107

Chapter 6   1. f; 2. t; 3. f; 4. f; 5. f; 6. t; 7. f   133

Chapter 7   1. t; 2. f; 3. f; 4. f; 5. f; 6. t; 7. f; 8. t   163

Chapter 8   1. t; 2. t; 3. t; 4. t; 5. f; 6. t; 7. t   189

Chapter 9   1. t; 2. t; 3. t; 4. f; 5. f; 6. f   215

Chapter 10   1. f; 2. t; 3. t; 4. f; 5. t; 6. t   245

Chapter 11   1. f; 2. t; 3. f; 4. t; 5. t; 6. f; 7. t   263

Chapter 12   1. t; 2. f; 3. t; 4. f; 5. f; 6. f; 7. f   291

Chapter 13   1. t; 2. t; 3. f; 4. f; 5. t; 6. f; 7. t   317

Chapter 14   1. t; 2. f; 3. f; 4. t; 5. f; 6. t; 7. t   345

Chapter 15   1. f; 2. f; 3. f; 4. t; 5. t; 6. t; 7. f; 8. f; 9. f   373

Chapter 16   1. f; 2. f; 3. f; 4. f; 5. f; 6. f; 7. t   397

Glossary

Absolute ethics: the type of ethics where there are only two sides—good or bad, black or white; some examples would be unethical behaviors such as bribery, extortion, excessive force, and perjury, which nearly everyone would agree are unacceptable for criminal justice personnel.

Academy training: where police and corrections personnel are trained in the basic functions, laws, and skills required for their positions.

Accepted lying: police activities intended to apprehend or entrap suspects. This type of lying is generally considered to be trickery.

Acquittal: a court or jury's judgment or verdict of not guilty of the offenses charged.

Actus reus: "guilty deed" (Latin)—an act that accompanies one's intent to commit a crime, such as pulling out a knife and then stabbing someone.

Adjudication: the legal resolution of a dispute—for example, when one is declared guilty, or a juvenile is declared to be dependent and neglected—by a judge or jury.

Adoption studies: criminological research that looks at whether adopted children share criminal tendencies with their natural or adoptive parents.

Adversarial system: a legal system wherein there is a contest between two opposing sides, with a judge (and possibly jury) sitting as an impartial arbiter, seeking truth.

Affidavit: any written document in which the signer swears under oath that the statements in the document are true.

Affirmative defense: the defendant admits he or she committed the act charged but argues that for some mitigating reason he or she should not be held criminally responsible under the law.

Aggravating circumstances: elements of a crime that enhance its seriousness, such as the infliction of torture, killing of a police or corrections officer, and so on.

Alternatives to incarceration: a sentence imposed by a judge other than incarceration, such as probation, parole, shock probation, or house arrest.

Arraignment: a criminal court proceeding during which a formally charged defendant is informed of the charges and asked to enter a plea of guilty or not guilty.

Arrest: the taking into custody or detaining of one who is suspected of committing a crime, to answer the charges against him or her.

Bail: surety (e.g., cash or paper bond) provided by a defendant to guarantee his or her return to court to answer to criminal charges.

Bioterrorism: the use of biological material, such as anthrax or botulin, to commit an act of terrorism.

Booking: a clerical procedure for when an arrestee is taken to jail and a record is made of his or her name, address, charge(s), arresting officers, and time and place of arrest.

Boot camp: a short-term jail or prison program that puts offenders through a rigorous physical and mental regimen designed to instill discipline and respect for authority.

Burden of proof: the requirement that the state must meet to introduce evidence or establish facts.

Capital punishment: a sentence of death, or carrying out same via execution of the offender.

Caseload: the number of cases awaiting disposition by a court, or the number of active cases or clients maintained by a probation or parole officer.

Causation: a link between one's act and the injurious act or crime, such as one tossing a match in a forest and igniting a deadly fire.

Chain of command: vertical and horizontal power relations within an organization, showing how one position relates to others.

Circuit courts: originally courts wherein judges traveled a circuit to hear appeals, now courts with several counties or districts in their jurisdiction; the federal court system contains 11 circuit courts of appeals (plus the District of Columbia and territories), which hear appeals from district courts.

Civil law: a generic term for all noncriminal law, usually related to settling disputes between private citizens, governmental, and/or business entities.

Civil liability: in tort law, the basis for which a cause of action (e.g., fine) is made to recover damages; in criminal justice, where a police or corrections officer, for example, violates someone's civil rights.

Classical school (of criminology): a perspective indicating that people have free will to choose between criminal and lawful behavior, and that crime can be controlled by sanctions and should be proportionate to the offense.

Classification (of inmates): inmate security and treatment plan based on one's security, social, vocational, psychological, and educational needs while incarcerated.

Community corrections: locally operated services that offer minimum-security, work-release alternatives to prisoners about to be paroled.

Community era: beginning in about 1980, a time when the police retrained to work with the community to solve problems by looking at their underlying causes and developing tailored responses to them.

Conflict theory: said to exist in societies where the worker class is exploited by the ruling class, which owns and controls the means of production and thus maintains a constant state of conflict between the two classes.

Consensus theory: said to exist where a society functions as a result of a group's common interests and values, which have been developed largely because the people have experienced similar socialization.

Constable: in England, favored noblemen who were forerunners of modern-day U.S. criminal justice functionaries; largely disappearing in the United States by the 1970s.

Contract services: a for-profit firm or individuals hired by an individual or company to provide security services.

Conviction: the legal finding, by a jury or judge, or through a guilty plea, that a criminal defendant is guilty.

Coroner: an early English court officer; today one (usually a physician) in the United States whose duty it is to determine cause of death.

Corporate crime: crimes committed by wealthy or powerful individuals in the course of their professions or occupations; includes price-fixing, insider trading, and other white-collar crimes.

Correctional officer: one who works in a jail or prison and supervises correctional inmates.

Court of last resort: the last court that may hear a case at the state or federal level.

Crime against persons: a violent crime, to include murder, rape, robbery, and assault.

Crime against property: a crime during which no violence is perpetrated against a person, such as burglary, theft, and arson.

Crime control model: a model by Packer that emphasizes law and order and argues that every effort must be made to suppress crime, and to try, convict, and incarcerate offenders.

Crime mapping: plotting of crimes on maps so as to show patterns of location, time, day, and so on.

Crime rate: the number of reported crimes divided by the population of the jurisdiction, and multiplied by 100,000 persons; developed and used by the FBI *Uniform Crime Reports*.

Criminal intent: a necessary element of a crime; the evil intent, or *mens rea*.

Criminal justice flow and process: the horizontal movement of defendants and cases through the criminal justice process, beginning with the commission of a crime, investigation, arrest, initial appearance, arraignment, trial, verdict, sentencing, and appeal (to include vertical movement, as when a case is dropped or leaves the system for some other reason).

Criminal law: the body of law that defines criminal offenses and prescribes punishments for their infractions.

Criminalistics: the interdisciplinary study of physical evidence related to crime; drawing on mathematics, physics, chemistry, biology, anthropology, and many other scientific fields.

Critical theory: a school of thought in criminology arguing that crime is largely a product of capitalism, that laws are created to separate haves and have-nots and are wielded by those in power.

Cybercrime/cyberterrorism: using computers to commit crimes, such as embezzlement, diversion of bank monies to other accounts, and hacking personal information; making use of high technology, typically the Internet, to plan and carry out acts of terrorism.

Day reporting center: a structured corrections program requiring offenders to check in at a community site on a regular basis for supervision, sanctions, and services.

Defendant: a person against whom a criminal charge is pending; one charged with a crime.

Defense: the response by a defendant to a criminal charge, to include denial of the criminal allegations in an attempt to negate or overcome the charges.

Defense attorney: one whose responsibility is to see that the rights of the accused are upheld prior to, during, and after trial; the Sixth Amendment provides for "effective" counsel, among other constitutionally enumerated rights that defense attorneys must see are upheld.

Delay (trial): an attempt (usually by defense counsel) to have a criminal trial continued until a later date.

Deontological ethics: one's duty to act.

Detective/investigator: a police officer who is assigned to investigate reported crimes, to include gathering evidence, completing case reports, testifying in court, and so on.

Determinate sentence: a specific, fixed-period sentence ordered by a court.

Deterrence: the effect of punishments and other actions to deter people from committing crimes.

Deviant lying: occasions when officers commit perjury to convict suspects or are deceptive about some activity that is illegal or unacceptable to the department or public in general.

Discovery: a procedure wherein both the prosecution and the defense exchange and share information as to witnesses to be used, results of tests, recorded statements by defendants, or psychiatric reports, so that there are no major surprises at trial.

Discretion: authority to make decisions in enforcing the law based on one's observations and judgment ("spirit of the law") rather than the letter of the law.

Disposition: an outcome of a criminal or juvenile court process signifying that the matter is completed.

District courts: trial courts at the county, state, or federal level with general and original jurisdiction.

Diversion program: removing a case from the criminal justice system, typically to move a defendant into another treatment program or modality.

DNA: deoxyribonucleic acid, which is found in all cells; used in forensics to match evidence (hair, semen) left at a crime scene with a particular perpetrator.

Double jeopardy: subjecting an accused person to be tried twice for the same offense; prohibited by the Fifth Amendment.

Dual court system: the state and federal court systems of the United States.

Due process model: Packer's view that criminal defendants should be presumed innocent, courts must protect suspects' rights, and some limits must be placed on police powers.

Duty of care: a legal obligation imposed on someone; in the case of the police, they have a legal responsibility to see that persons in their custody are free from harm, given necessary medical assistance when necessary, and treated humanely.

Electronic control devices: less-lethal tools used by police to incapacitate noncompliant suspects by stimulating the motor neurons, thus causing temporary motor skill dysfunction.

Electronic monitoring: use of electronic devices (bracelets or anklets) to emit signals when a convicted offender (usually on house arrest) leaves the environment in which he or she is to remain.

Entrapment: police tactics that unduly encourage or induce an individual to commit a crime he or she typically would not commit.

Ethical decision-making process: a series of steps for addressing an ethical dilemma; includes looking at alternatives, considering stakeholders and consequences, and explaining the decision to others.

Ethics: a set of rules or values that spell out appropriate human conduct.

Exclusionary rule: the rule (see *Mapp v. Ohio*, 1961) providing that evidence obtained improperly cannot be used against the accused at trial.

Exigent circumstance: an instance where quick, emergency action is required, such as searching for drugs before they are removed or destroyed.

Exoneration: to absolve someone of criminal blame, or find someone not guilty.

Failure to protect: a situation where police place someone in jeopardy, such as giving out the location of a battered spouse or names of victims or witnesses.

False arrest: unlawful physical restraint by a police officer, for no valid reason.

Federal court system: the four-tiered federal system that includes supreme courts, circuit courts of appeal, district courts, and magistrate courts.

Federal law enforcement agencies: federal organizations that, for example, are charged with protecting the homeland (DHS); investigating crimes (DOJ, FBI) and enforcing particular laws, such as those pertaining to drugs (DEA) or alcohol/tobacco/firearms/explosives (ATF); and guarding the courts and transporting prisoners (USMS).

Felony: a serious offense with a possible sentence of more than a year in prison.

Felony-murder rule: the legal doctrine that says that, if a death occurs during the commission of a felony, the perpetrator of the crime may be charged with murder in the first degree.

Feminist theory: emphasizes gender involvement in crime.

Field training officer (FTO): one who is to oversee and evaluate the new police officer's performance as he or she transitions from the training academy to patrolling the streets.

Fifth Amendment: in the Bill of Rights, among other protections, it guards against self-incrimination and double jeopardy.

Forensic science: the study of causes of crimes, deaths, and crime scenes.

Fourth Amendment: in the Bill of Rights, it contains the protection against unreasonable searches and seizures and protects people's homes, property, and effects.

Grand jury: a body that hears evidence and determines probable cause regarding crimes and can return formal charges against suspects; use, size, and functions vary among the states.

Gratuities: the receipt of some benefit (a meal, gift, or some other favor) either for free or for a reduced price.

Halfway house: a community center or home staffed by professionals or volunteers designed to provide counseling to ex-prisoners as they transition from prison to the community.

Hands-off doctrine: the notion by courts that prison administrators should be given free rein to run their prisons as they deem best.

Hands-on doctrine: the belief by courts that inmates have certain constitutional rights that the courts must see are upheld and also be obeyed by prison administrators.

Hierarchy rule: in the FBI *Uniform Crime Reports* reporting scheme, the practice whereby only the most serious offense of several that are committed during a criminal act is reported by the police.

Homeland security (police role in): local police working with federal agencies to obtain the tools, information, and resources necessary for understanding tactics, behaviors, and other indicators of terrorist activity.

House arrest/home confinement (see *Electronic monitoring*).

Houses of refuge: workhouses established in the early 1800s as a means of separating juvenile offenders from adult offenders.

Idealistic contrast: the differences between juvenile and adult criminal justice processes, to include treatment and terminology.

Illinois Juvenile Court Act (1899): legislation that established the first juvenile court in the United States.

In loco parentis: a doctrine in which the state will act in place of the parents if they fail in their duties to protect and provide for the child.

Incapacitation: rendering someone as unable to act or move about, either through incarceration or by court order.

Indeterminate sentence: a scheme whereby one is sentenced for a flexible time period (e.g., 5–10 years) so as to be released when rehabilitated or when the opportunity for rehabilitation is presented.

Initial appearance: a formal proceeding during which the accused is read his or her rights, informed of the charges, and given the amount of bail required to secure pretrial release.

Inmate litigation: lawsuits filed by prison and jail inmates challenging their conditions of confinement.

Institutionalization: a process that occurs with long-term inmates, whereby they take on the values and mores of the inmate culture and thus are more likely unable to succeed in the free world.

Intensive supervision probation and parole: ISP usually includes much closer and stricter supervision, more contact with offenders, more frequent drug tests, and other such measures.

Intent, specific: a purposeful act or state of mind to commit a crime.

Intermediate courts of appeal: a level of courts in state courts that stand between trial courts and courts of last resort; they typically have appellate jurisdiction only.

Intermediate sanctions: forms of punishment that are between freedom and prison, such as home confinement and day reporting.

INTERPOL: the only international crime-fighting organization, it collects intelligence information, issues alerts, and assists in capturing world criminals; it has nearly 200 member countries.

Interrogation: police questioning of a suspect about a particular crime(s); the suspect may have an attorney present if he or she desires (see *Escobedo v. Illinois,* 1964).

"Iron curtain" speech: in *Wolff v. McDonnell* (1973), the Supreme Court stated that there is no iron curtain between the Constitution and the prisons of the United States; in sum, inmates have rights.

Jail: a facility that holds persons who have been arrested for crimes and are awaiting trial, persons who have been convicted for misdemeanors and are serving a sentence (up to a year in jail), federal offenders, and others.

JDLR: in prison jargon, the sense that things "just don't look right."

Judicial misconduct: inappropriate behavior by a judge.

Judicial selection (methods of): means by which judges are selected for the bench, to include election, a nominating commission, or a hybrid of these methods.

Jurisdiction, court: the authority of a court to hear a particular type of case, based on geography (city, state, or federal) and subject matter (e.g., criminal, civil, probate).

Justice of the peace (JP): a minor justice official who oversees lesser criminal trials; one of the early English judicial functionaries.

Juvenile court: a court that has original jurisdiction to hear juvenile crime matters.

Kansas City Preventive Patrol Experiment: in the early 1970s, a study of the effects of different types of patrolling on crime—patrolling as usual in one area, saturated patrol in another, and very limited patrol in a third area; the results showed no significant differences.

Labeling theory (of crime): holds that persons acquire labels or defined characteristics that are deviant or criminal; thus, perceiving themselves as criminals, they follow through and commit crimes.

Learning theory (of crime): any school of thought that suggests criminal behaviors are learned from associating with others and from social interactions and social experiences.

Lex talionis: "eye for eye, tooth for tooth"; retaliation or revenge that dates back to the Bible and Middle Ages.

Life without parole: a penalty or sentence imposed, according to which the inmate is to serve a life sentence without parole eligibility.

Lineup: a procedure in which police ask suspects to submit to a viewing by witnesses to determine the guilty party, based on personal and physical characteristics; information obtained may be used later in court.

Locard's exchange principle: the notion that offenders both leave something at the crime scene and take something from it; the crime scene analyst or investigator's job is to locate that evidence and use it in the investigation.

Mass incarceration: A term generally referring to what is perceived as America's disproportionately high rates of imprisonment of young, African American men; some believe it deters crime and incapacitates offenders, while others say that it weakens poor families and keep them socially marginalized.

Mens rea (see *Criminal intent*).

Merit selection: a means of selecting judges whereby names of interested candidates are considered by a committee and recommendations are then made to the governor, who then makes the appointment; known also as the Missouri Plan.

Militarization: the use of military equipment and tactics by local police.

Misdemeanor: a lesser offense, typically punishable by a fine or up to one year in a local jail.

Mitigating circumstances: circumstances that would tend to lessen the severity of the sentence, such as one's youthfulness, mental instability, not having a prior criminal record, and so on.

Model Code of Judicial Conduct: adopted by the House of Delegates of the American Bar Association in 1990, it provides a set of ethical principles and guidelines for judges.

Motive: the reason for committing a crime.

Municipal police department: a police force that enforces laws and maintains peace within a specified city or municipality.

National Crime Victimization Survey: a random survey of households that measures crimes committed against victims; includes crimes not reported to police.

National Incident-Based Reporting System: a crime reporting system in which police describe each offense in a crime as well as describing the offender.

Negligence: failure to perform a duty owed.

Neoclassical criminology: views the accused as exempted from conviction if circumstances prevented the exercise of free will.

New generation/direct supervision jail: jails that, by their architecture and design, eliminate many of the traditional features of a jail, allowing staff members greater interaction and control.

Noble cause corruption: a situation in which one commits an unethical act but for the greater good; for example, a police officer violates the Constitution in order to capture a serious offender.

"Nothing works" philosophy: Robert Martinson's belief, published in the 1970s, that correctional treatment programs generally do not rehabilitate offenders or significantly reduce recidivism.

Organization: an entity of two or more people who cooperate to achieve an objective(s).

Organizational structure or chart: a diagram of the vertical and horizontal parts of an organization, showing its chain of command, lines of communication, division of labor, and so on.

Parens patriae: a doctrine in which the state is the ultimate parent of the child (and will step in to provide and care for the child if parents neglect those duties).

Parole: early release from prison, with conditions attached and under supervision of a parole agency.

Parole officer: one who supervises those who are on parole.

PINS (person in need of supervision): usually a juvenile thought to be on the verge of becoming a delinquent.

Plaintiff: the party bringing a lawsuit or initiating a legal action against someone else.

Plea negotiation (or bargaining): a preconviction process between the prosecutor and the accused in which a plea of guilty is given by the defendant, with certain specified considerations in return—for example, having several charges or counts tossed out, and a plea by the prosecutor to the court for leniency or shorter sentence.

Police brutality: unnecessary use of force by police against citizens, resulting in injury.

Police corruption: misconduct by police officers that can involve but is not limited to illegal activities for economic gain, gratuities, favors, and so on.

Policing styles: James Q. Wilson argued that there are three styles of policing: watchman, legalistic, and service.

Policy making: the act of creating laws or setting standards to govern the activities of government; the U.S. Supreme Court, for example, has engaged in policy making in several areas, such as affirmative action, voting, and freedom of communication and expression.

Political era: from the 1840s to the 1930s, the period of time when police were tied closely to politics and politicians, dependent on them for being hired, promoted, and assignments—all of which raised the potential for corruption.

Political influence: matters taken into account for developing public policies, allocating funds and other resources, and choosing among preferred alternatives.

Positivist school: a school of thought arguing that science can be used to discover the true causes of crime, which are a result of social, biological, psychological, and economic factors.

Preliminary hearing: a stage in the criminal process conducted by a magistrate to determine whether a person charged with a crime should be held for trial based on probable cause; does not determine guilt or innocence.

Presumption of innocence: the premise that a defendant is assumed to be innocent until guilt is established beyond a reasonable doubt.

Pretrial motions/processes: any number of motions filed by prosecutors and defense attorneys prior to trial, to include quashing of evidence, change of venue, discovery, to challenge a search or seizure, to raise doubts about expert witnesses, or to exclude a defendant's confession.

Prison: a state or federal facility housing long-term offenders, typically felons, for a period greater than one year.

Prison industries: use of prison and jail inmates to produce goods or provide services for a public agency or private corporation.

Prisoners' rights: the collective body of rights given to inmates by the courts, in such areas as conditions of confinement, communications (mail and letters), access to law library and medical facilities, and so on.

Prisonization: the process whereby an inmate becomes socialized into the culture and social life of prison society so that adjusting to the norms of outside society becomes difficult.

Private police/security: all nonpublic officers, including guards, watchmen, private detectives, and investigators; they have limited powers and only the same arrest powers as regular citizens.

Probable cause: a reasonable basis to believe that a crime has been, or is about to be, committed by a particular person.

Probation: an alternative to incarceration in which the convict remains out of jail or prison and in the community and thus on the job, with family, and so on, while subject to conditions and supervision of the probation authority.

Probation officer: one who supervises the activities of persons on probation.

Procedural law: rules that set forth how substantive laws are to be enforced, such as those covering arrest, search, and seizure.

Proprietary services: in-house security services, whose personnel are hired, trained, and supervised by the company or organization.

Prosecuting attorney: a federal, state, or local prosecutor who represents the people, particularly victims.

Prosecution: the bringing of charges against an individual, based on probable cause, so as to cause the matter to go to court.

Proximate cause: a factor that contributed heavily to an event, such as an auto crash or death.

Psychological rationales for crime: explanations of crime that link it to mental states or antisocial personality.

Public defender: an attorney whose full-time job is to represent indigent defendants.

Punishment (and its purposes): penalties imposed for committing criminal acts, to accomplish deterrence, retribution, incapacitation, and/or rehabilitation.

Reasonable doubt: the standard used by jurors to arrive at a verdict—whether or not the government (prosecutor) has established guilt beyond a reasonable doubt.

Reasonable suspicion: suspicion that is less than probable cause but more than a mere hunch that a person may be involved in criminal activity.

Reentry and aftercare: providing services to, and supervision for, paroled inmates who are about to reintegrate into the community.

Reform era: also the professional era, from the 1930s to 1980s, when police sought to extricate themselves from the shackles of politicians, and leading to the crime-fighter era—with greater emphases being placed on *numbers*—arrests, citations, response times, and so on.

Reformatory: a detention facility designed to reform individuals—historically juveniles.

Rehabilitation: attempts to reform an offender through vocational and educational programming, counseling, and so forth, so that he or she is not a recidivist and does not return to crime/prison.

Relative ethics: the gray area of ethics that is not so clear-cut, such as releasing a serious offender in order to use him later as an informant.

Respondeat superior: "let the master answer" (Latin)—a doctrine in liability that establishes a duty of supervisors to control their employees and be considered liable for their actions.

Restorative justice: the view that crime affects the entire community, which must be healed and made whole again through the offender's remorse, community service, restitution to the victim, and other such activities.

Retribution: a goal of punishment that states the offender ought to be made to experience revenge for his actions.

Revocation: the court's revoking probation/parole status for the purpose of returning an offender to prison (usually for not following the conditions of probation/parole or for committing a new offense).

Right-wrong test: the test of legal insanity, asking whether the defendant understood the nature and quality of his or her act and, if so, if he or she understood it was wrong.

Robotics: technology for designing, building, and operating robots.

Sanction: a penalty or punishment.

School-to-prison pipeline: the notion that certain policies and practices push schoolchildren, particularly those who are most at risk, out of classrooms and into the juvenile and adult criminal justice and prison systems.

Search and seizure: in the Fourth Amendment, the term refers to an officer's searching for and taking away evidence of a crime.

Section 1983: a portion of the U.S. Code that allows a legal action to be brought against a police officer or other person in position of authority who, it is believed, used his or her position ("acted under color of law") to violate one's civil rights.

Sentencing guidelines: an instrument developed by the federal government that uses a grid system to chart the seriousness of offense, criminal history, and so forth and thus allows the court to arrive at a more consistent sentence for everyone.

Sheriff: the chief law enforcement officer of a county, typically elected and frequently operating the jail as well as law enforcement functions.

Shock probation/parole: a situation in which individuals are sentenced to jail or prison for a brief period, to give them a taste or "shock" of incarceration and, it is hoped, turn them into more law-abiding citizens.

Sixth Amendment: in the Bill of Rights, it guarantees the right to a speedy and public trial by an impartial jury, the right to effective counsel at trial, and other protections.

"Sixth sense": in policing, the notion that an officer can "sense" or feel when something is not right, as in the way a person acts, talks, and so on.

"Slave of the state": an early philosophy toward prison inmates essentially stating that inmates had no legal rights that had to be observed by prison administrators.

"Slippery slope": the idea that a small first step can lead to more serious behaviors, such as the receipt of minor gratuities by police officers believed to eventually cause them to desire or demand receipt of items of greater value.

Social control theory: argues that deviant behavior results when social controls are weakened or break down, so that people are not motivated to conform to them.

Social process theory: argues that criminality is a normal behavior and that everyone has the potential to commit crime, depending on the influences that compel them toward or away from crime and on how they are viewed by others.

Social structure theory: generally attempts to explain criminality as a result of the creation of a lower-class culture based on poverty and deprivations, and the subsequent response of the poor to the situation.

Solitary confinement: a form of imprisonment in which an inmate is isolated from any human contact (except for members of prison staff).

Special-purpose state agencies: specially trained units for particular investigative needs, such as those for violations of alcoholic beverage laws, fish and game laws, organized crime, and so on.

Speedy Trial Act of 1974: later amended, a law originally enacted to ensure compliance with the Sixth Amendment's provision for a speedy trial by requiring that a federal case be brought to trial no more than 100 days following the arrest.

Standing: a legal doctrine requiring that one must not be a party to a lawsuit unless he or she has a personal stake in its outcome.

Stare decisis: "to stand by a decision" (Latin)—a doctrine referring to court precedent, whereby lower courts must follow (and render the same) decisions of higher courts when the same legal issues and questions come before them, thereby not disturbing settled points of law.

State bureau of investigation: a state agency that is responsible for enforcing state highway laws and investigating crimes involving state statutes; they may also be called in to assist police agencies in serious criminal matters, and often publish state crime reports.

State court system: civil or criminal courts in which cases are decided through an adversarial process; typically including a court of last resort, an appellate court, trial courts, and lower courts.

State police: a state agency responsible for highway patrol and other duties as delineated in the state's statutes; some states require their police to investigate crimes against persons and property.

State prison: a correctional facility that houses convicted felons.

Status offense: a crime committed by a juvenile that would not be a crime if committed by an adult; examples would be purchasing alcohol and tobacco products, truancy, and violating curfew.

Stored Communications Act: an act allowing law enforcement access to electronic messages greater than 180 days old without a warrant (but with a court order or subpoena, such access may be obtained for messages less than 180 days old).

Substantive law: the body of law that spells out the elements of criminal acts.

Substantive violation: an allegation that one was arrested for a new criminal offense while serving probation.

Supermax prison: a penal institution that, for security purposes, affords inmates very few if any amenities and a great amount of isolation.

Tasks of policing (four basic): enforce the law, prevent crime, protect the innocent, and perform welfare tasks.

Technical violation: in probation and parole, when one violates certain conditions that must be obeyed to remain out of prison, such as curfew violation, drug or alcohol use, or not maintaining a job.

Terrorism: acts that are intended to intimidate or coerce a civilian population or government, usually for some political purpose or objective.

Terry Stop: also known as a "stop and frisk"; when a police officer briefly detains a person for questioning and then frisks ("pats down") the person if the officer reasonably believes he or she is carrying a weapon.

Three-strikes law: a crime control strategy whereby an offender who commits three or more violent offenses will be sentenced to a lengthy term in prison, usually 25 years to life.

Tort: a civil wrong or infraction; the remedy will be damages awarded in civil trial.

Traffic function: the aggregate of motor vehicles, pedestrians, streets, and highways, for which police must investigate and apply laws to provide safe travels for citizens in their jurisdictions.

Transfer (remand): the movement or assigning of a juvenile offender to an adult court, because the youth's behavior is such that he or she is not amenable to the juvenile court's rehabilitative philosophy.

Trial process: all of the steps in the adjudicatory process, from indictment or charge to conviction or acquittal.

U.S. Supreme Court: the court of last resort in the United States, also the highest appellate court; it consists of nine justices who are appointed for life.

Underground economy: forms of currency or commodities that inmates use for trading and bartering, such as tobacco products, prisoner-made wine, fish, and instant coffee.

Uniform Crime Reports: published annually by the FBI, each report describes the nature of crime as reported by law enforcement agencies; includes analyses of Part I crimes.

Unmanned aerial vehicles: also termed "drones," aircraft without a human pilot that are controlled by computers and used for a variety of purposes by military and civilian police agencies.

Use of force: the type and amount of effort required to compel compliance by an unwilling suspect.

Utilitarianism: in ethics, as articulated by John Stuart Mill, a belief that the proper course of action is that which maximizes utility—usually defined as that which maximizes happiness and minimizes suffering.

Vicarious liability: a legal doctrine whereby a person is responsible for the actions of another and is to exercise reasonable and prudent care in supervising that person.

Victim impact statements: information provided prior to sentencing by the victims of a crime (or, in cases of murder, the surviving family members) about the impact the crime had on their lives; allowed by the U.S. Supreme Court.

War on drugs: a federal and state initiative to control the distribution and use of illegal drugs in the United States.

Warden: the chief administrator of a federal penitentiary or state prison.

Warrant, arrest: a document issued by a judge directing police to immediately arrest a person accused of a crime.

Warrant, search: a document issued by a judge, based on probable cause, directing police to immediately search a person, a premises, an automobile, or a building for the purpose of finding illegal contraband felt to be located therein and as stated in the warrant.

Wedding cake model of criminal justice: a model of the criminal justice process whereby a four-tiered hierarchy exists, with a few celebrated cases at the top, and lower tiers increasing in size as the severity of cases become less (serious felonies, felonies, and misdemeanors).

Whistleblower Protection Act: a federal law prohibiting reprisal against employees who reveal information concerning a violation of law, rules, or regulations; gross mismanagement or waste of funds; an abuse of authority; and so on.

XYY chromosome: the so-called criminal chromosome, where criminal behavior is felt to be caused in some offenders who possess an extra Y chromosome—believed to cause agitation, aggression, and greater criminal tendencies—as opposed to the "passive" X chromosome.

Notes

Chapter 1

1. Federal Bureau of Investigation, "Table 2. Crime in the United States by Community Type, 2013," *Crime in the United States—2013* (Washington, D.C.: Uniform Crime Reporting Program), http://www.fbi.gov/about-us/cjis/ucr/crime-in-the-u.s/2013/crime-in-the-u.s.-2013/tables/2tabledatadecoverviewpdf/table_2_crime_in_the_united_states_by_community_type_2013.xls.

2. Tracey Kyckelhahn, "Justice Expenditures and Employment, FY 1982–2007," *Statistical Tables* (Washington, D.C.: U.S. Department of Justice, Office of Justice Systems, Bureau of Justice Statistics, December 2011), p. 1, http://bjs.ojp.usdoj.gov/content/pub/pdf/jee8207st.pdf.

3. YourDictionary, "Justice Quotes," *Webster's New World Dictionary of Quotations* (Hoboken, N.J.: Wiley, 2010), http://www.yourdictionary.com/quotes/justice.

4. James Austin, "'Three Strikes and You're Out': The Likely Consequences on the Courts, Prisons, and Crime in California and Washington State," *St. Louis University Public Law Review* 14, no. 1 (1994): 239–257.

5. See, for example, Joe Domanick, *Cruel Justice: Three Strikes and the Politics of Crime in America's Golden State* (Berkeley: University of California Press, 2004).

6. Austin, "'Three Strikes and You're Out'," pp. 239–257.

7. Scott Ehlers, Vincent Schiraldi, and Jason Ziedenberg, *Still Striking Out: Ten Years of California's Three Strikes* (Washington, D.C.: Justice Policy Institute, 2004), http://www.justicepolicy.org/research/2028.

8. Brent Staples, "California Horror Stories and the 3-Strikes Law," *New York Times,* November 24, 2012, http://www.nytimes.com/2012/11/25/opinion/sunday/california-horror-stories-and-the-3-strikes-law.html.

9. Ehlers et al., *Still Striking Out.*

10. Ibid.

11. Staples, "California Horror Stories and the 3-Strikes Law."

12. Ibid.

13. Alexander B. Smith and Harriet Pollack, *Criminal Justice: An Overview* (New York: Holt, Rinehart and Winston, 1980), p. 9.

14. Ibid., p. 10.

15. Ibid., p. 366.

16. Thomas J. Bernard, *The Consensus–Conflict Debate: Form and Content in Social Theories* (New York: Columbia University Press, 1983), p. 78.

17. William D'Urso, "'Sovereign Citizen' Gets 8 Years in Money Laundering Case," *Las Vegas Sun,* March 20, 2013, http://www.lasvegassun.com/news/2013/mar/20/sovereign-citizen-gets-8-years-money-laundering-ca/.

18. Nadine Maeser, "Special Report: A Closer Look at Sovereign Citizens," *WECT 6,* February 22, 2013, http://www.wect.com/story/21237082/special-report-sovereign-citizens.

19. Ibid.

20. See Federal Bureau of Investigation's Counterterrorism Analysis Section, "Sovereign Citizens: A Growing Domestic Threat to Law Enforcement," *Law Enforcement Bulletin* (September 2011), http://www.fbi.gov/stats-services/publications/law-enforcement-bulletin/september-2011/sovereign-citizens.

21. Thomas Hobbes, *Leviathan* (New York: E. P. Dutton, 1950), pp. 290–291.

22. Jean-Jacques Rousseau, "A Discourse on the Origin of Inequality," in G. D. H. Cole (ed.), *The Social Contract and Discourses* (New York: E. P. Dutton, 1946), p. 240.

23. Bernard, *Consensus–Conflict Debate,* pp. 83, 85.

24. Frank Schmalleger, *Criminal Justice Today,* 8th ed. (Upper Saddle River, N.J.: Prentice Hall, 2005), p. 18.

25. One of the first publications to express the nonsystems approach was the American Bar Association, *New Perspective on Urban Crime* (Washington, D.C.: ABA Special Committee on Crime Prevention and Control, 1972).

26. Norm Stamper, *Breaking Rank: A Top Cop's Exposé of the Dark Side of American Policing* (New York: Nation Books, 2005), p. 185.

27. Herbert L. Packer, *The Limits of the Criminal Sanction* (Stanford, Calif.: Stanford University Press, 1968).

28. Herbert L. Packer, *Two Models of the Criminal Process,* 113 U. PA. L. Rev. 1, 2 (1964).

29. The President's Commission on Law Enforcement and Administration of Justice, *The Challenge of Crime in a Free Society* (Washington, D.C.: U.S. Government Printing Office, 1967), p. 5.

30. See Office of Juvenile Justice and Delinquency Prevention, "Upper Age of Original Juvenile Court Jurisdiction," *Statistical Briefing Book: Juvenile Justice System Structure and Process* (Washington, D.C.: U.S. Department of Justice, 2012), http://www.ojjdp.gov/ojstatbb/structure_process/qa04101.asp.

31. Samuel Walker, *Sense and Nonsense About Crime and Drugs,* 4th ed. (Belmont, Calif.: Wadsworth, 1997), p. 15.

32. Adapted from Mike Broemmel, *The Wedding Cake Model Theory of Criminal Justice* (Bellevue, Wash.: eHow, n.d.), http://www.ehow.com/about_5143074_wedding-model-theory-criminal-justice.html.

33. Timothy J. Flanagan and Kathleen Maguire, eds., *Sourcebook of Criminal Justice Statistics 1991* (Washington, D.C.: U.S. Government Printing Office, 1992), p. 555.

34. Benjamin S. Bloom (ed.), Max D. Englehart, Edward J. Furst, Walker H. Hill, and David R. Krathwohl, *Taxonomy of Educational Objectives: The Classification of Educational Goals. Handbook I: Cognitive Domain* (New York: Longman, 1956).

Chapter 2

1. Brian P. Block and John Hostettler, *Famous Cases: Nine Trials That Changed the Law* (Hook, Hampshire: Waterside Press, 2002), pp. 9–12.

2. Henry Campbell Black, *Black's Law Dictionary,* 4th ed. (St. Paul, Minn.: West, 1951).

3. Law Library of Congress, "Case Law (or Common Law)," *American Memory,* http://memory.loc.gov/ammem/awhhtml/awlaw3/common_law.html.

4. Texas Politics, "State Constitutions," *The Texas Constitution Today,* http://texaspolitics.laits.utexas.edu/7_3_1.html.

5. Carissa Byrne Hessick, "Motive's Role in Criminal Punishment," *Southern California Law Review, 80,* no. 89 (2006): p. 89.

6. See Arizona Criminal Code, generally, at http://www.azleg.gov/arizonarevisedstatutes.asp?title=13.

7. Ibid.

8. *People v. Anderson,* 70 Cal.2d 15 (1968).

9. *U.S. v. Brown,* 518 F.2d 821 (1975).

10. See, for example, James R. Elkins, "Depraved Heart Murder," *West Virginia Homicide Jury Instructions Project* (Morgantown: West Virginia University

College of Law, Spring 2006), http://myweb.wvnet.edu/~jelkins/adcrimlaw/depraved_heart_murder.html.

11. In August 2012, Huguely was convicted of second-degree murder and sentenced to 23 years in prison. In March 2014, the Virginia Court of Appeals affirmed Huguely's conviction; the Virginia Supreme Court later declined to hear his appeal. *See* "Ex U.Va Lacrosse Player's Murder Conviction Affirmed," CBS News, March 5, 2014, http://www.cbsnews.com/news/former-university-of-virginia-lacrosse-players-murder-conviction-affirmed/. Huguely is attempting to appeal his case to the U.S. Supreme Court. See Matt Bonesteel, "George Huguely V Appeals Murder Conviction to the U.S. Supreme Court," *Washington Post,* June 17, 2015, http://www.washingtonpost.com/blogs/early-lead/wp/2015/06/17/george-huguely-v-appeals-murder-conviction-to-u-s-supreme-court/.

12. See *People v. Heidgen*, 22 NY 3d 259 (2013); Justia Opinion Summary, http://law.justia.com/cases/new-york/court-of-appeals/2013/174-1.html; Bob Simon, "DWI Deaths: Is It Murder?" *60 Minutes,* January 4, 2009, http://www.cbsnews.com/news/dwi-deaths-is-it-murder/.

13 Sofi Sinozich and Lynn Langton, *Rape and Sexual Assault Among College-age Females, 1995–2013.* Bureau of Justice Statistics, December 11, 2014, http://www.bjs.gov/content/pub/pdf/rsavcaf9513.pdf.

14. See California Senate Bill 967, https://leginfo.legislature.ca.gov/faces/billNavClient.xhtml?bill_id=201320140SB967; Ian Urbina, "The Challenge of Defining Rape," *New York Times,* October 12, 2014, http://www.nytimes.com/2014/10/12/sunday-review/being-clear-about-rape.html?_r=0; Sinozich and Langton.

15. Federal Bureau of Investigation, *Crime in the United States—2011* (Washington, D.C.: Uniform Crime Reporting Program), http://www.fbi.gov/about-us/cjis/ucr/crime-in-the-u.s/2010/crime-in-the-u.s.-2010/violent-crime/robberymain.

16. Federal Bureau of Investigation, *Crime in the United States—2011* (Washington, D.C.: Uniform Crime Reporting Program), http://www.fbi.gov/about-us/cjis/ucr/crime-in-the-u.s/2010/crime-in-the-u.s.-2010/violent-crime/aggravatedassaultmain.

17. Federal Bureau of Investigation, *Crime in the United States—2011* (Washington, D.C.: Uniform Crime Reporting Program), http://www.fbi.gov/about-us/cjis/ucr/crime-in-the-u.s/2010/crime-in-the-u.s.-2010/property-crime/burglarymain.

18. For Nevada's larceny-theft statute, see *Nevada Revised Statutes,* Chapter 205.220; for Iowa's larceny statutes, see *Iowa Code,* Chapter 714.2, "Degrees of Theft," http://coolice.legis.iowa.gov/Cool-ICE/default.asp?category=billinfo&service=Iowa Code&input=714.2.

19. Federal Bureau of Investigation, "Property Crime," *Crime in the United States—2011* (Washington, D.C.: Uniform Crime Reporting Program), http://www.fbi.gov/about-us/cjis/ucr/crime-in-the-u.s/2011/crime-in-the-u.s.-2011/property-crime/property-crime.

20. Federal Bureau of Investigation, "Arson," *Crime in the United States—2011* (Washington, D.C.: Uniform Crime Reporting Program), http://www.fbi.gov/about-us/cjis/ucr/crime-in-the-u.s/2011/crime-in-the-u.s.-2011/property-crime/arson.

21. *Sherman v. U.S.*, 356 U.S. 369 (1958).

22. *U.S. v. Russell*, 411 U.S. 423 (1973).

23 Leo Katz, "Excuse: Duress—The Nature of the Threat, the Nature of the Crime, the Mistaken Defendant, the Semiculpable Defendant—Superior Orders: Husbands and Wives," *Law Library: American Law and Legal Information—Crime and Criminal Law,* http://law.jrank.org/pages/1128/Excuse-Duress.html.

24. *Spakes v. State*, 913 S.W.2d 597 (Tex. Crim. App. 1996).

25. PBS, "Biography: John Hinckley, Jr.," *American Experience,* http://www.pbs.org/wgbh/americanexperience/features/biography/reagan-hinckley/.

26. David Gates, "Everybody Has Scars," *Newsweek*, October 13, 1986, p. 10; also see "Man Given 5-to-15-Year Term in Model's Slashing," *New York Times,* May 12, 1987, http://www.nytimes.com/1987/05/12/nyregion/man-given-5-to-15-year-term-in-model-s-slashing.html.

27. Carol Pogash, "Myth of the 'Twinkie Defense': The Verdict in the Dan White Case Wasn't Based on His Ingestion of Junk Food," *San Francisco Chronicle,* November 23, 2003, http://www.sfgate.com/health/article/Myth-of-the-Twinkie-defense-The-verdict-in-2511152.php.

28. Michael Perlin, *The Jurisprudence of the Insanity Defense* (Durham, N.C.: Carolina Academic Press, 1994), p. 108.

29. *M'Naghten's Case*, 8 Eng. Rep. 718 (H.L. 1843).

30. *Parsons v. State*, 2 So. 854 (Ala. 1887).

31. See, generally, James F. Hooper and Alix M. McLearen, "Does the Insanity Defense Have a Legitimate Role?" *Psychiatric Times*, April 1, 2002, http://www.psychiatrictimes.com/display/article/10168/54196.

32. Dirk Johnson, "Milwaukee Jury Says Dahmer Was Sane," *New York Times*, February 16, 1992, http://www.nytimes.com/1992/02/16/us/milwaukee-jury-says-dahmer-was-sane.html.

33 PBS, "Other Notorious Insanity Cases," *Frontline,* http://www.pbs.org/wgbh/pages/frontline/shows/crime/trial/other.html.

34. Ibid.

35. *See "If I Did It"—The Quasi-Confession of OJ Simpson,* http://law2.umkc.edu/faculty/projects/ftrials/Simpson/ifididit.html.

36. *See State v. Thompson*, 865 p.2d 1125 (Mont. 1993) and Mont. Code. Ann. §§45-501-1-3. The principal was acquitted of sexual assault because the statute did not contemplate purely psychological force. The Montana legislature later amended the statute to clarify this issue in anticipation of future cases.

37. This is the Florida case of Marissa Alexander from 2010. Her defense failed because she took the time to go to the garage and get the gun, which the prosecution successfully argued meant she also had time to call the police and escape the "immediate" danger she feared. The state argued that she acted/fired out of anger and not fear, imperiling both her husband and children. She was convicted and sentenced to 20 years in prison (under a mandatory sentencing scheme triggered in part by her use of the gun). In the wake of the George Zimmerman acquittal, Alexander's case garnered renewed attention. In 2013, she won a new trial based on an error at her original trial: The burden of proving the self-defense issue had been improperly shifted to Alexander and not to the prosecution. She was released from prison in November 2013 and ordered to remain on house arrest. The Florida prosecutor—the same prosecutor from the Zimmerman trial—vowed she would retry Alexander and seek 60 years (the maximum sentence allowed on such a retrial). In November 2014, Alexander pleaded guilty in exchange for time served, to avoid retrial and the potential 60-year sentence. She was sentenced in January 2015 to two years of house arrest. See Irin Carmon, "Marissa Alexander Released From Jail," MSNBC, January 27, 2015, http://www.msnbc.com/msnbc/marissa-alexander-may-be-released.

38. Defendant Peterson was charged with manslaughter. At trial, the judge instructed the jury that self-defense is *not* available as a defense when someone acts as the aggressor, stands one's ground when other options are available, and actually provokes a conflict. Peterson was convicted; he appealed on the grounds that his shooting the driver should be excused because he acted in self-defense. The appellate court agreed with the trial judge: One cannot claim to have acted in "self-defense" by a *self-generated necessity to kill* another

person. The evidence demonstrated that Peterson instigated the confrontation, and his failure to retreat was also a factor that the jury could take into account. *U.S. v. Peterson*, 483 F. 2d 1222 (D.C. Cir. 1973).

Chapter 3

1. Janet Reitman, "Jahar's World," *Rolling Stone,* July 17, 2013.

2. Meghan Hoyer and Brad Heath, "Mass Killings Occur in USA Once Every Two Weeks," *USA TODAY*, December 19, 2012, http://www.usatoday.com/story/news/nation/2012/12/18/mass-killings-common/1778303/.

3 The Rosetta Stone, found in the Nile River delta in 1799, furnished Egyptologists with the key to deciphering hieroglyphics. E. A. Wallis Budge, *Rosetta Stone in the British Museum* (London: Harrison and Sons, 1929).

4. Cesare Beccaria, *On Crimes and Punishments,* trans. H. Paolucci (Indianapolis, Ind.: Bobbs-Merrill, 1963; original work published 1764).

5. Frank E. Hagan, *Introduction to Criminology: Theories, Methods, and Criminal Behavior,* 8th ed. (Los Angeles, Calif.: Sage, 2013), p. 115.

6. Adapted from George F. Cole and Christopher E. Smith, *Criminal Justice in America,* 6th ed. (Belmont, Calif.: Wadsworth, 2011), p. 56.

7. Hagan, *Introduction to Criminology,* p. 129.

8. Ibid.

9. Ibid.

10. Mary Gibson, *Born to Crime: Cesare Lombroso and the Origins of Biological Criminology* (Westport, Conn.: Praeger, 2002); David G. Horn, *The Criminal Body: Lombroso and the Anatomy of Deviance* (New York: Routledge, 2003).

11. Ibid.

12. Hagan, *Introduction to Criminology,* pp. 132–133.

13 R. G. Fox, "The XYY Offender: A Modern Myth?" *Journal of Criminal Law, Criminology, and Police Science* 62 (March 1971): 59–73.

14. Ibid.

15. William H. Sheldon, *Varieties of Delinquent Youth: An Introduction to Constitutional Psychiatry* (New York: Harper, 1949); William H. Sheldon, *The Varieties of Human Physique: An Introduction to Constitutional Psychology* (New York: Harper, 1940).

16. John Glatt, *Evil Twins: Chilling True Stories of Twins, Killing and Insanity* (New York: St. Martin's, 1999).

17. Ibid.

18. See *Skinner v. State of Oklahoma, ex. rel. Williamson*, 316 U.S. 535 (1942).

19. Policy implications that flow from studies showing that criminals are biologically inferior include *selective incapacitation*—either imprisoning or executing people who have been adopted and whose natural fathers had a criminal record—which is of course repugnant to our sense of justice and values unless one has in fact committed a heinous crime. Some people may argue instead that neurological defects may be identified through CT scan, and that medications can suppress violent tendencies. There may be help in the future in this regard, however, as scientists come closer to being able to identify and remove or alter defective genes through genetic engineering; furthermore, one could argue that persons with learning disabilities may be helped by receiving special education and counseling.

20. Jason Fletcher and Barbara Wolfe, "Long Term Consequences of Childhood ADHD on Criminal Activities," *Journal of Mental Health Policy Economics,* 12, no. 3 (September 2009), 119–138.

21. Hagan, *Introduction to Criminology,* p. 143.

22. Sigmund Freud, *The Complete Works of Sigmund Freud,* Vol. 19 (London: Hogarth, 1961).

23 Edwin H. Sutherland, "Mental Deficiency and Crime," in *Social Attitudes,* ed. Kimball Young (New York: Holt, Rinehart and Wilson, 1931), pp. 357–375.

24. Robert Gordon, "Prevalence: The Rare Datum in Delinquency Measurement and Its Implications for the Theory of Delinquency," in *The Juvenile Justice System,* ed. Malcolm W. Klein, (Beverly Hills, Calif.: Sage, 1976); Travis Hirschi and Michael J. Hindelang, "Intelligence and Delinquency: A Revisionist Review," *American Sociological Review* 42 (1977): 572–587.

25. D. Black, T. Gunter, P. Loveless, J. Allen, and B. Sieleni, "Antisocial Personality Disorder in Incarcerated Offenders: Psychiatric Comorbidity and Quality of Life," *Annals of Clinical Psychiatry* 22, no. 2 (May 2010): 113–120. Policy implications for the psychological theories—if indeed found to be solid predictors of criminality—might include treatments such as psychotherapy and counseling, as well as individual and group therapies to target specific disorders.

26. Robert K. Merton, "Social Structure and Anomie," *American Sociological Review* 3, no. 5 (October 1938): 672–682.

27. Ibid.

28. Ibid., pp. 675–676.

29. Lois M. Davis, *Education and Vocational Training in Prisons Reduces Recidivism and Improves Job Outlook,* August 2013, http://www.rand.org/news/press/2013/08/22.html. Social structure theory certainly has strong policy implications if decision makers believe it is a solid explanation of criminality. If crime is indeed grounded in a number of social conditions that serve to breed crime (e.g., poverty, unemployment, and discrimination), then those conditions might well be addressed by educational (including vocational) programs and governmental programs that will enhance living conditions in terms of housing, health care, and employment opportunities.

30. E. D. Sutherland, D. Cressey and D. Luckenbill, *Principles of Criminology* (New York: General Hall, 1992).

31. Travis Hirschi, *Causes of Delinquency* (Berkeley: University of California Press, 1969).

32. Howard S. Becker, *Outsiders: Studies in the Sociology of Deviance* (New York: Free Press, 1963), p. 9.

33 Bald Eagle Protection Act of 1940, as amended, Public Law 95-616 (92 Stat. 3114), November 8, 1978.

34. Social process theory is obviously broad in its reach and includes a number of possible explanations for crime. Policy makers need to focus on the various means by which crime is learned, and address the aforementioned problems of control, association, and labeling by striving to provide programs that have positive role models and will reinforce the proper value system and norms. See A. Matz, "Do Youth Mentoring Programs Work? A Review of the Empirical Literature," *Journal of Juvenile Justice* (Spring 2014), http://www.journalofjuvjustice.org/JOJJ0302/article06.htm.

35. Otwin Marenin, "Parking Tickets and Class Repression: The Concept of Policing in Critical Theories of Criminal Justice," *Contemporary Crises,* 6 (1982): 241–266.

36. George Vold, *Theoretical Criminology* (New York: Oxford University Press, 1958).

37. Thorsten Sellin, *Culture and Conflict in Crime* (New York: Social Science Research Council, 1938); Austin Turk, *Criminality and Legal Order* (Chicago: Rand McNally, 1969); also see Vold, *Theoretical Criminology.*

38. See Stephen B. Bright and Sia M. Sanneh, *Fifty Years of Defiance and Resistance After Gideon v. Wainright,* 122 Yale L.J. 2150 (2013).

39. See The Sentencing Project, "It's Not Fair, It's Not Working," http://www.sentencingproject.org/crackreform/. Policy implications for the critical theory of crime—where the system itself foments crime—are certainly challenging. Decision makers must attempt to provide minorities with programs that will lessen or alleviate the injustices of the criminal justice system that might be found at the hands of the police, courts, or corrections system—while also making the system more

equitable by meting out punishment more equally among upper-class as well as lower-class offenders.

40. See, for example, Mark Kleiman, "Smart on Crime," *Democracy: A Journal of Ideas* 28 (Spring 2013), http://www.democracyjournal.org/28/smart-on-crime.php?page=all.

41. Freda Adler, *Sisters in Crime: The Rise of the New Female Criminal* (New York: McGraw-Hill, 1975), p. 12.

42. Equal Employment Opportunity Act, Public Law 92–261.

43 Pregnancy Discrimination Act of 1978, 42 U.S.C. Sec. 2000e (k).

44. Family and Medical Leave Act (FMLA), Public Law 103-3, 5 U.S.C. 6381-6387, 5 CFR part 630.

45. Robert Witt and Ann Dryden Witte, "Crime, Imprisonment, and Female Labor Force Participation: A Time-Series Approach," *Social Science Research Network,* November 1998, http://papers.ssrn.com/sol3/papers.cfm?abstract_id=226386.

46. Adler, *Sisters in Crime*, p. 3.

47. B. Brown, "Women and Crime: The Dark Figures of Criminology," *Economy and Society* 15, no. 3 (1986): 355.

48. Adler, *Sisters in Crime*, pp. 83–84.

49. B. Brown, "Women and Crime," p. 355.

50. Rita Simon, *Women and Crime* (Lexington, Mass.: Lexington Books, 1975).

51. M. Chesney-Lind and L. Pasko, *The Female Offender*, 2nd ed. (Thousand Oaks, Calif.: Sage, 2004).

52. See, for example, Sandra Walklate, *Gender, Crime, and Criminal Justice,* 2nd ed. (Cullompton, Devon, England: Willan Publishing, 2004); Drew Humphries, ed., *Women, Violence, and the Media: Readings in Feminist Criminology,* Northeastern Series on Gender, Crime, and Law (Lebanon, N.H.: Northeastern University Press, 2009); Lynne M. Vieraitis, Tomislav V. Kovandzic, and Sarah Britto, "Women's Status and Risk of Homicide Victimization: An Analysis With Data Disaggregated by Victim-Offender Relationship," *Homicide Studies* 12, no. 2 (2008): 163–176; Matthew Makarios and Andrew Myer, "Gender, Race, and Marijuana Use: Testing the Generality of Traditional and Feminist Theories of Crime," paper presented at the ASC Annual Meeting, St. Louis Adam's Mark, St. Louis, Missouri, November 11, 2008.

53 Frank E. Hagan, *Introduction to Criminology: Theories, Methods, and Criminal Behavior,* 8th ed. (Los Angeles, Calif.: Sage Publications, 2013), p. 320.

54. Quoted in ibid., p. 284.

55. Edwin H. Sutherland, "White Collar Criminality," *American Sociological Review* 5 (February 1940): 1–12.

56. Hagan, *Introduction to Criminology*, p. 281.

57. Ibid., p. 288.

58. Robert Lenzner, "Bernie Madoff's $50 Billion Ponzi Scheme," *Forbes*, December 12, 2008, http://www.forbes.com/2008/12/12/madoff-ponzi-hedge-pf-ii-in_rl_1212croesus_inl.html.

59. "Martha Stewart's Conviction Upheld," February 11, 2009, http://www.cbsnews.com/2100-207_162-1183526.html.

60. Charles B. Fleddermann, "The Ford Pinto Exploding Gas Tank," in *Engineering Ethics*, 2nd ed. (Upper Saddle River, N.J.: Prentice Hall, 2004), pp. 72–73.

61. Adapted from Abigail Tracy, "Not All White-Collar Crime Sentences Are the Same Length," Vocativ, August 19, 2014, http://www.vocativ.com/underworld/crime/white-collar-crime/.

62. Hagan, *Introduction to Criminology*, p. 258.

63. Federal Bureau of Investigation, "Common Fraud Schemes," http://www.fbi.gov/scams-safety/fraud.

64. See, for example, Steven Pizzo, Mary Fricker, and Paul Muolo, *Inside Job: The Looting of America's Savings and Loans* (New York: McGraw-Hill, 1989); P. J. Benekos and Frank E. Hagan, "The Great Savings and Loan Scandal," *Journal of Security Administration* (July 14, 1991): 41–64.

65. Richard T. Wright and Scott H. Decker, "Creating the Illusion of Impending Death," in Paul Cromwell, *In Their Own Words: Criminals on Crime*, 5th ed. (Cary, N.C.: Oxford University Press, 2009), pp. 159–164.

66. Ibid., pp. 161–162.

67. Ibid., p. 162.

68. Ibid., p. 164.

69. Richard T. Wright and Scott H. Decker, "Deciding to Commit a Burglary," in Ibid., pp. 90–101.

70. Ibid., p. 100.

71. Volkan Topalli and Richard T. Wright, "Dubs and Dees, Beats and Rims," in Ibid., pp. 129–141.

72. See the Anti Car Theft Act of 1992, Public Law 102-519; the full text of the act may be viewed at http://www.ojp.usdoj.gov/BJA/pdf/Anti_Car_Theft_Act.pdf.

73 Topalli and Wright, "Dubs and Dees, Beats and Rims," p. 129.

74. Ibid., pp. 131, 140.

75. See "Statistics," http://www.twainquotes.com/Statistics.html.

76. Federal Bureau of Investigation, "Hate Crimes Accounting," *Hate Crime Statistics—2011*, December 10, 2012, http://www.fbi.gov/news/stories/2012/december/annual-hate-crimes-report-released/annual-hate-crimes-report-released.

77. Lynn Langton and Michael Planty, *Hate Crime, 2003–2009* (Washington, D.C.: U.S. Department of Justice, Office of Justice Programs, Bureau of Justice Statistics, June 2011), p. 2, http://bjs.ojp.usdoj.gov/content/pub/pdf/hc0309.pdf.

78. For access to the publications, see Federal Bureau of Investigation, *Uniform Crime Reports,* http://www.fbi.gov/ucr/ucr.htm.

79. Federal Bureau of Investigation, "Table 1," *Crime in the United States—2011* (Washington, D.C.: U.S. Department of Justice), http://www.fbi.gov/about-us/cjis/ucr/crime-in-the-u.s/2011/crime-in-the-u.s.-2011/tables/table-1.

80. Federal Bureau of Investigation, "Table 1. Crime in the United States by Volume and Rate per 100,000 Inhabitants, 1992–2011," *Crime in the United States—2011* (Washington, D.C.: Uniform Crime Reporting Program), http://www.fbi.gov/about-us/cjis/ucr/crime-in-the-u.s/2011/crime-in-the-u.s.-2011/tables/table-1.

81. Federal Bureau of Investigation, "Murder," *Crime in the United States—2011* (Washington, D.C.: Uniform Crime Reporting Program), http://www.fbi.gov/about-us/cjis/ucr/crime-in-the-u.s/2011/crime-in-the-u.s.-2011/violent-crime/murder.

82. Federal Bureau of Investigation, "Offense Definitions," *Crime in the United States—2011,* http://www.fbi.gov/about-us/cjis/ucr/crime-in-the-u.s/2011/crime-in-the-u.s.-2011/offense-definitions.

83 Federal Bureau of Investigation, "Caution Against Ranking: Variables Affecting Crime," *Crime in the United States—2011* (Washington, D.C.: U.S. Department of Justice), http://www.fbi.gov/about-us/cjis/ucr/crime-in-the-u.s/2011/crime-in-the-u.s.-2011/caution-against-ranking.

84. See, for example, Nathan James and Logan Rishard Council, "How Crime in the United States Is Measured," *Congressional Research Service Report for Congress* January 3, 2008, pp. 17–20, http://www.policyarchive.org/handle/10207/bitstreams/18912.pdf.

85. See Federal Bureau of Investigation, *Uniform Crime Reporting Handbook* (Washington, D.C.: U.S. Department of Justice), p. 10, http://www.fbi.gov/about-us/cjis/ucr/additional-ucr-publications/ucr_handbook.pdf/view.

86. Federal Bureau of Investigation, "NIBRS General Frequently Asked Questions," *Uniform Crime Reports* (Washington, D.C.: U.S. Department of Justice), http://www.fbi.gov/ucr/nibrs_general.html#basics.

87. Bureau of Justice Statistics, "Data Collection: National Crime Victimization Survey (NCVS)," http://bjs.ojp.usdoj.gov/index.cfm?ty=dcdetail&iid=245.

88. National Archive of Criminal Justice Data, "National Crime Victimization Survey Resource Guide," http://www

.icpsr.umich.edu/icpsrweb/NACJD/
NCVS/.

89. National Archive of Criminal Justice Data, "Accuracy of NCVS Estimates," http://www.icpsr.umich.edu/NACJD/NCVS/accuracy.html.

Chapter 4

1. In a unanimous 7–0 decision, the state supreme court court ruled that Judge Vincent Sicari's acting and comedy career "is incompatible" with judicial conduct codes. He opted to resign from the bench and continue his comedy career. See Abbott Koloff and Matthew McGrath, "Final Verdict: South Hackensack Judge Chooses a Life of Comedy," NorthJersey.com, September 19, 2013, http://www.northjersey.com/news/politics/final-verdict-south-hackensack-judge-chooses-a-life-of-comedy-1.608963.

2. Adapted from John R. Jones and Daniel P. Carlson, *Reputable Conduct: Ethical Issues in Policing and Corrections,* 2nd ed. (Upper Saddle River, N.J.: Prentice Hall, 2001), p. 14.

3. This scenario is based loosely on David Gelman, Susan Miller, and Bob Cohn, "The Strange Case of Judge Wachtler," *Newsweek,* November 23, 1992, pp. 34–35. Wachtler was later arraigned on charges of attempting to extort money from the woman and threatening her 14-year-old daughter (it was later determined that the judge had been having an affair with the woman, who had recently ended the relationship). After being placed under house arrest with an electronic monitoring bracelet, the judge resigned from the court, which he had served with distinction for two decades.

4. Adapted from Jones and Carlson, *Reputable Conduct,* pp. 162–163.

5. Immanuel Kant, "Foundations of the Metaphysics of Morals," *The German Library* 13 (New York: Continuum, 2006).

6. Richard Kania, "Police Acceptance of Gratuities," *Criminal Justice Ethics* 7 (1988): 37–49.

7. John Kleinig, *The Ethics of Policing* (New York: Cambridge University Press, 1996).

8. T. J. O'Malley, "Managing for Ethics: A Mandate for Administrators," *FBI Law Enforcement Bulletin* (April 1997): 20–25.

9. Thomas J. Martinelli, "Unconstitutional Policing: The Ethical Challenges in Dealing With Noble Cause Corruption," *The Police Chief* (October 2006): 150.

10. John P. Crank and Michael A. Caldero, *Police Ethics: The Corruption of Noble Cause* (Cincinnati, Ohio: Anderson, 2000), p. 75.

11. U.S. Department of Justice, National Institute of Justice, Office of Community Oriented Policing Services, *Police Integrity: Public Service with Honor* (Washington, D.C.: U.S. Government Printing Office, 1997), p. 62.

12. Ibid.

13 Lawrence W. Sherman, ed., *Police Corruption: A Sociological Perspective* (Garden City, N.Y.: Anchor, 1974), p. 1.

14. Herman Goldstein, *Policing a Free Society* (Cambridge, Mass.: Ballinger, 1977), p. 188.

15. Ibid.

16. William A. Westley, *Violence and the Police* (Cambridge, Mass.: MIT Press, 1970), pp. 113–114.

17. International Association of Chiefs of Police, "What Is the Law Enforcement Oath of Honor?" http://www.theiacp.org/PoliceServices/ExecutiveServices/ProfessionalAssistance/Ethics/WhatistheLawEnforcementOathofHonor/tabid/150/D efault.aspx.

18. Based on International Association of Chiefs of Police, "What Is the Law Enforcement Oath of Honor," www.theiacp.org/PoliceServices/ExecutiveServices/ProfessionalAssistance/Ethics/WhatistheLawEnforcementOathofHonor/tabid/150/Default.aspx.

19. "More Than 3,000 Mexican Federal Police Fired, Commissioner Says," *CNN World,* March 10, 2010, http://articles.cnn.com/2010-08-30/world/mexico.federal.police.fired_1_federal-police-officers-police-headquarters?_s=PM:WORLD.

20. Anne Barrowclough, "Hundreds of Mexican Police Officers Sacked over Corruption," *The Times: U.S. & Americas,* November 3, 2012, http://www.thetimes.co.uk/tto/news/world/americas/article3589373.ece.

21. Dudley Althaus, "Despite Millions in U.S. Aid, Police Corruption Plagues Mexico," *Houston Chronicle,* October 18, 2010, http://www.chron.com/news/houston-texas/article/Despite-millions-in-U-S-aid-police-corruption-1710872.php.

22. David Carter, "Theoretical Dimensions in the Abuse of Authority," in *Police Deviance,* ed. Thomas Barker and David Carter (Cincinnati, Ohio: Anderson, 1994), pp. 269–290; also see Thomas Barker and David Carter, "Fluffing Up the Evidence and 'Covering Your Ass': Some Conceptual Notes on Police Lying," *Deviant Behavior* 11 (1990): 61–73.

23 Gary T. Marx, "Who Really Gets Stung? Some Issues Raised by the New Police Undercover Work," *Crime & Delinquency* (1982): 165–193.

24. *Illinois v. Perkins,* 110 S. Ct. 2394 (1990).

25. Barker and Carter, *Police Deviance.*

26. Thomas Barker, "An Empirical Study of Police Deviance Other than Corruption," in *Police Deviance,* ed. Thomas Barker and David Carter (Cincinnati, Ohio: Anderson, 1994), pp. 123–138.

27. For an excellent analysis of how the acceptance of gratuities can become endemic to an organization and pose ethical dilemmas for new officers within, see Jim Ruiz and Christine Bono, "At What Price a 'Freebie'? The Real Cost of Police Gratuities," *Criminal Justice Ethics* (Winter/Spring 2004): 44–54. The authors also demonstrate through detailed calculations how the amount of gratuities accepted can reach up to 40 percent of an annual officer's income—and is therefore no minor or inconsequential infraction of rules that can be left ignored or unenforced.

28. "Police Aides Told to Rid Commands of All Dishonesty," *New York Times,* October 29, 1970.

29. Gail Saltz, "Why People Lie—and How to Tell If They Are," *Today Health,* January 31, 2004, http://www.today.com/id/4072816/ns/today-today_health/t/why-people-lie-how-tell-if-they-are/#.Ua-ko-Dn_cs).

30. Carl B. Klockars and Stephen D. Mastrofski, "Police Discretion: The Case of Selective Enforcement," in *Thinking About Police: Contemporary Readings,* 2nd ed., ed. Carl B. Klockars and Stephen D. Mastrofski (Boston: McGraw-Hill, 1991), p. 331.

31. Hugh Hartshorne and Mark A. May, *Studies in Deceit* (New York: Macmillan, 1928) and David P. Farrington and Barry J. Knight, "Stealing From a 'Lost' Letter," *Criminal Justice and Behavior* 7 (1980), pp. 423–436.

32. Edward Tully, "Misconduct, Corruption, Abuse of Power: What Can the Chief Do?" http://www.neiassociates.org/mis2.htm (Part I) and http://www.neiassociates.org/misconductII.htm (Part II).

33. Roscoe Pound, "The Causes of Popular Dissatisfaction With the Administration of Justice," address before the annual convention of the American Bar Association, August 29, 1906, in 14 AM. LAW. 445 (1996).

34. John P. MacKenzie, *The Appearance of Justice* (New York: Scribner, 1974).

35. Pierro Calamandrei, quoted in Frank Greenberg, "The Task of Judging the Judges," *Judicature* 59 (May 1976): 464.

36 For thorough discussions and examples of these areas of potential ethical shortcomings, see Jeffrey M. Shaman, Steven Lubet, and James J. Alfini, *Judicial Conduct and Ethics,* 3rd ed. (San Francisco: Matthew Bender, 2000).

37. Ibid.

38. Ibid., p. vi.

39. Tim Murphy, "Test Your Ethical Acumen," *Judges' Journal* 8 (1998): 34.

40. American Judicature Society, *Judicial Conduct Reporter* 16 (1994): 2–3.

41. Shaman, Lubet, and Alfini, *Judicial Conduct and Ethics,* p. viii.

42. Walter Pavlo, "Pennsylvania Judge Gets 'Life Sentence' for Prison Kickback

Scheme," http://www.forbes.com/sites/walterpavlo/2011/08/12/pennsylvania-judge-gets-life-sentence-for-prison-kickback-scheme/.

43. Ian Urbina and Sean D. Hamill, "Judges Plead Guilty in Scheme to Jail Youths for Profit," *New York Times*, February 12, 2009, http://www.nytimes.com/2009/02/13/us/13judge.html?pagewanted=all&_r=0.

44. Ibid.

45. See *In re Gault,* 387 U.S. 1 (1967).

46. Urbina and Hamill, "Judges Plead Guilty in Scheme to Jail Youths for Profit."

47. *Berger v. U.S.*, 295 U.S. 78 (1935).

48. See *Dunlop v. U.S.,* 165 U.S. 486 (1897), involving a prosecutor's inflammatory statements to the jury.

49. 386 U.S. 1 (1967). In this case, the Supreme Court overturned the defendant's conviction after determining that the prosecutor "deliberately misrepresented the truth."

50. Elliot D. Cohen, "Pure Legal Advocates and Moral Agents: Two Concepts of a Lawyer in an Adversary System," in *Justice, Crime and Ethics,* 2nd ed., ed. Michael C. Braswell, Belinda R. McCarthy, and Bernard J. McCarthy (Cincinnati, Ohio: Anderson, 1996), p. 168.

51. Ibid.

52. Ibid., pp. 131–167.

53. Cynthia Kelly Conlon and Lisa L. Milord, *The Ethics Fieldbook: Tools for Trainers* (Chicago: American Judicature Society, n.d.), pp. 23–25.

54. Ibid., p. 28.

55. Elizabeth L. Grossi and Bruce L. Berg, "Stress and Job Dissatisfaction Among Correctional Officers: An Unexpected Finding," *International Journal of Offender Therapy and Comparative Criminology* 35 (1991): 79.

56 Irving L. Janis, "Group Dynamics Under Conditions of External Danger," in *Group Dynamics: Research and Theory,* ed. Darwin Cartwright and Alvin Zander (New York: Harper & Row, 1968).

57. Ibid.

58. Ibid., p. 85.

59. CBS News, March 30, 1977; see Jones and Carlson, *Reputable Conduct,* p. 76.

60. Jones and Carlson, *Reputable Conduct,* p. 77.

61. Adapted from Florida Regional Community Policing Institute, *Ethical Issues and Decisions in Law Enforcement* (March 2005): 37–39, http://cop.spcollege.edu/Training/Ethics/EN/ethicsInstructorMarch2005.pdf.

62. Kleinig, *The Ethics of Policing.*

63. Ibid.

64. Adapted from Gail Diane Cox, "Judges Behaving Badly (Again)," *National Law Journal* 21 (May 3, 1999): 1–5.

Chapter 5

1. Executive Office of the President, *Review: Federal Support for Local Law Enforcement Equipment Acquisition*, The White House, December 2014, https://www.whitehouse.gov/sites/default/files/docs/federal_support_for_local_law_enforcement_equipment_acquisition.pdf; also see Josh Hicks, "White House Review Finds Lax Oversight of Police Military Equipment," *Washington Post*, December 3, 2015, http://www.washingtonpost.com/blogs/federal-eye/wp/2014/12/03/white-house-review-finds-lax-federal-oversight-of-police-military-gear/.

2. Bruce Smith, *Rural Crime Control* (New York: Columbia University, 1933), p. 40.

3. Ibid.

4. Ibid.

5. Ibid., pp. 182–184.

6. Ibid., pp. 188–189.

7. Ibid., pp. 218–222.

8. Ibid., pp. 245–246.

9. David R. Johnson, *American Law Enforcement History* (St. Louis, Mo.: Forum Press, 1981), pp. 18–19.

10. Leon Radzinowicz, *A History of English Criminal Law and Its Administration From 1750:* Volume IV. *Grappling for Control* (London: Stevens and Son, 1968), pp. 20–21.

11. C. Germann, Frank D. Day, and Robert R. J. Gallati, *Introduction to Law Enforcement and Criminal Justice* (Springfield, Ill.: Charles C. Thomas, 1962), p. 63.

12 Johnson, *American Law Enforcement History*, p. 26.

13. James F. Richardson, *Urban Police in the United States* (London: Kennikat Press, 1974), pp. 47–48.

14. Johnson, *American Law Enforcement History*, p. 26.

15. Herman Goldstein, *Policing a Free Society* (Cambridge, Mass.: Ballinger, 1977).

16. August Vollmer, "Police Progress in the Past Twenty-Five Years," *Journal of Criminal Law and Criminology* 24 (1933): 161–175.

17. Alfred E. Parker, *Crime Fighter: August Vollmer* (New York: Macmillan, 1961).

18. Nathan Douthit, "August Vollmer," in *Thinking About Police: Contemporary Readings*, ed. Carl B. Klockars (New York: McGraw-Hill, 1983), p. 102.

19. Ibid.

20. Ibid.

21. Richardson, *Urban Police in the United States*, pp. 139–143.

22 Herman Goldstein, *Policing a Free Society* (Cambridge, Mass.: Ballinger, 1977).

23. Kenneth J. Peak and Ronald W. Glensor, *Community Policing and Problem Solving: Strategies and Practices*, 5th ed. (Upper Saddle River, N.J.: Prentice Hall, 2008), pp. 15–16.

24. Elaine Cumming, Ian Cumming, and Laura Edell, "Policeman as Philosopher, Guide, and Friend," *Social Problems* 12 (1965), p. 285; T. Bercal, "Calls for Police Assistance," *American Behavioral Scientist* 13 (1970): 682; Albert J. Reiss Jr., *The Police and the Public* (New Haven, Conn.: Yale University Press, 1971).

25. FederalLawEnforcement.org, "The Scope and Mission of Federal Law Enforcement," http://www.federallawenforcement.org/what-is-federal-law-enforcement/.

26. For specific requirement for all agencies, see FederalLawEnforcement.org, "Preparing for a Job in Federal Law Enforcement"; also see FederalLawEnforcement.org, "Careers with Federal Law Enforcement Agencies."

27. Ibid.

28. U.S. Department of Homeland Security, "Creation of the Department of Homeland Security," http://www.dhs.gov/creation-department-homeland-security.

29. National Priorities Project, "U.S. Security Spending Since 9/11," February 28, 2013, https://www.nationalpriorities.org/analysis/2013/homeland-security-spending-since-911/.

30. U.S. Customs and Border Protection, "On a Typical Day," http://www.cbp.gov/linkhandler/cgov/about/accomplish/typical_day_fy11.ctt/typical_day_fy11.pdf.

31. Department of Homeland Security, "ICE: Enforcement and Removal Operations," http://www.ice.gov/about/offices/enforcement-removal-operations/.

32 ICE, "Homeland Security Investigations," http://www.ice.gov/hsi; also see ICE, "Become a Criminal Investigator," http://www.ice.gov/careers/occupation/investigator.

33. Department of Homeland Security, Transportation Security Administration, "TSA Workforce," http://www.tsa.gov/about-tsa.

34. See "Are TSA Screeners Really Law Enforcement 'Officers'?" November 4, 2013, http://kdvr.com/2013/11/04/are-tsa-screeners-really-law-enforcement-officers/.

35. See United States Coast Guard, Office of Law Enforcement, "Missions," http://www.uscg.mil/top/missions/MaritimeSecurity.asp.

36. United States Secret Service, "Frequently Asked Questions About the United States Secret Service," www.secretservice.gov/faq.shtml#employees.

37. FederalLawEnforcement.org, "Federal Protective Service Careers," http://www.federallawenforcement.org/federal-protective-service/.

38. Michael Fooner, *Interpol: Issues in World Crime and International Criminal Justice* (New York: Plenum Press, 1989), p. 179.

39. U.S. Department of Justice, Federal Bureau of Investigation, "About Us—Quick Facts," http://www.fbi.gov/about-us/quick-facts/quickfacts.

40. U.S. Department of Justice, Federal Bureau of Investigation, "What We Investigate," http://www.fbi.gov/about-us/investigate/what_we_investigate.

41. "FBI Seeks Sweeping New Powers," *The Nation*, August 22, 2008, www.thenation.com/article/fbi-seeks-sweeping-new-powers.

42. Bureau of Alcohol, Tobacco, Firearms and Explosives, "ATF's History," http://www.atf.gov/about/history/.

43. U.S. Department of Justice, Drug Enforcement Administration, "DEA History," http://www.justice.gov/dea/about/history.shtml.

44. U.S. Marshals Service, *The FY 1993 Report to the U.S. Marshals* (Washington, D.C.: U.S. Department of Justice, 1994), pp. 188–189; also see U.S. Marshals Service, "Fact Sheets: Facts and Figures," *Office of Public Affairs,* April 15, 2011 (Washington, D.C.: U.S. Department of Justice), http://www.usmarshals.gov/duties/factsheets/facts-2011.html.

45. Central Intelligence Agency, "CIA Vision, Mission, & Values," https://www.cia.gov/about-cia/cia-vision-mission-values/index.html; also see CIA, "About CIA," https://www.cia.gov/about-cia/index.html.

46. Internal Revenue Service, "Financial Investigations: Criminal Investigation (CI)," http://www.irs.gov/uac/Financial-Investigations—Criminal-Investigation-(CI).

47. Brian Reaves, *Census of State and Local Law Enforcement Agencies, 2008* (Washington, D.C.: U.S. Department of Justice, Bureau of Justice Statistics, July 2011), http://bjs.ojp.usdoj.gov/content/pub/pdf/csllea08.pdf.

48. Missouri State Highway Patrol, Career Recruitment Division, "Duties of a Trooper," http://www.mshp.dps.missouri.gov/MSHPWeb/PatrolDivisions/HRD/Trooper/troopCareer.html.

49. Ibid., p. 1.

50. Ibid.

51. See, for example, Ravikanth B. Lamani and G. S. Venumadhava, "Police Corruption in India*," International Journal of Criminology and Sociological Theory* 6, no. 4 (December 2013): 228–234.

52 Vrinda Bhandari, "On Trial: The Criminal Justice System," *The Indian Express*, September 18, 2014, http://indianexpress.com/article/opinion/columns/on-trial-the-criminal-justice-system/2/.

53. Ibid.

54. "Indians Say Criminal Justice System Cannot Cope With Rape Cases," *The Guardian*, April 22, 2014, http://indianexpress.com/article/opinion/columns/on-trial-the-criminal-justice-system/.

55. Tom DeCastella, "How Many Acid Attacks Are There?" BBC News, August 9, 2013, http://www.bbc.com/news/magazine-23631395.

56. Bureau of Justice Statistics, "Census of State and Local Law Enforcement Agencies, 2008" (Washington, D.C.: U.S. Department of Justice, July 2011), p. 1, http://bjs.ojp.usdoj.gov/content/pub/pdf/csllea08.pdf.

57. Bureau of Justice Statistics, *Local Police Departments, 2007* (Washington, D.C.: U.S. Department of Justice, December 2010), p. 6, http://bjs.ojp.usdoj.gov/content/pub/pdf/lpd07.pdf.

58. Bureau of Justice Statistics, *Sheriff's Offices, 2003* (Washington, D.C.: U.S. Department of Justice), http://bjs.ojp.usdoj.gov/index.cfm?ty=tp&tid=72.

59. Bureau of Justice Statistics, *Local Police* (Washington, D.C.: U.S. Department of Justice), http://www.bjs.gov/index.cfm?ty=tp&tid=71.

60. Andrea M. Burch, *Sheriff's Offices, 2007* (Washington, D.C.: U.S. Department of Justice, Bureau of Justice Statistics, December 6, 2012), http://www.bjs.gov/index.cfm?ty=pbdetail&iid=4555.

61. Saul D. Astor, "A Nation of Thieves," *Security World* 15 (September 1978).

62 Bureau of Justice Statistics, *Criminal Victimization—2011* (Washington, D.C.: U.S. Department of Justice, October 2012), http://bjs.ojp.usdoj.gov/index.cfm?ty=pbdetail&iid=4494; U.S. Department of Justice, Bureau of Justice Statistics, *Criminal Victimization, 2013* (September 2014), p. 1, http://www.bjs.gov/content/pub/pdf/cv13.pdf.

63. Ibid., p. 238.

64. Lawrence J. Fennelly, ed., *Handbook of Loss Prevention and Crime Prevention,* 2nd ed. (Boston: Butterworths, 1989), in foreword.

65. George F. Cole and Christopher E. Smith, *The American System of Criminal Justice,* 11th ed. (Belmont, Calif.: Thomson Wadsworth, 2007), p. 253.

66. National Advisory Commission on Criminal Justice Standards and Goals, *Private Security* (Washington, D.C.: U.S. Government Printing Office, 1976), p. 99.

Chapter 6

1. Albert Antony Pearsall III and Kim Kohlhepp, "Strategies to Improve Recruitment," *The Police Chief* (April 2010), http://www.policechiefmagazine.org/magazine/index.cfm?fuseaction=display_arch&article_id=2056&issue_id=42010.

2. Jeffrey Goldberg, "The Color of Suspicion," *New York Times Magazine*, June 20, 1999, http://www.nytimes.com/1999/06/20/magazine/the-color-of-suspicion.html?pagewanted=all&src=pm.

3 William A. Westley, *Violence and the Police* (Cambridge, Mass.: MIT Press, 1970).

4. Quoted in V. A. Leonard and Harry W. More, *Police Organization and Management*, 3rd ed. (Mineola, N.Y.: Foundation Press, 1971), p. 128.

5. Alan Gomez, "Police Departments Hiring Immigrants as Officers," *USA Today*, March 21, 2015, http://www.usatoday.com/story/news/nation/2015/03/21/immigrant-police-officers/70236828/.

6. U.S. Department of Justice, Bureau of Justice Statistics, *Local Police Departments, 2007* (December 2010), p. 11.

7. National Advisory Commission on Criminal Justice Standards and Goals, *Police* (Washington, D.C.: U.S. Government Printing Office, 1973), p. 369.

8. Gerald W. Lynch, "Why Officers Need a College Education," *Higher Education and National Affairs* (September 20, 1986): 11.

9. Victor E. Kappeler, Allen D. Sapp, and David L. Carter, "Police Officer Higher Education, Citizen Complaints and Departmental Rule Violations," *American Journal of Police* 11 (1992): 37–54.

10. Charles L. Weirman, "Variances of Ability Measurement Scores Obtained by College and Non-College Educated Troopers," *The Police Chief* 45 (August 1978): 34–36.

11. Ibid.

12. Robert Trojanowicz and T. Nicholson, "A Comparison of Behavioral Styles of College Graduate Police Officers v. Non-College Going Police Officers," *The Police Chief* 43 (August 1976): 56–59.

13 A. F. Dalley, "University and Non-University Graduated Policemen: A Study of Police Attitudes," *Journal of Police Science and Administration* 3 (1975): 458–468.

14. Wayne F. Cascio, "Formal Education and Police Officer Performance," *Journal of Police Science and Administration* 5 (1977): 89–96; Bernard Cohen and Jan M. Chaiken, *Police Background Characteristics and Performance* (New York: RAND, 1972); B. E. Sanderson, "Police Officers: The Relationship of College Education to Job Performance," *The Police Chief* (August 1977): 62–63.

15. James W. Sterling, "The College Level Entry Requirement: A Real or Imagined Cure-all?" *The Police Chief* 41 (April 1974): 28–31.

16. Gerald W. Lynch, "Cops and College," *America* (April 4, 1987): 274–275.

17. *Davis v. City of Dallas*, 777 F.2d 205 (5th Cir. 1985).

18. Norm Stamper, *Breaking Rank: A Top Cop's Expose of the Dark Side of American Policing* (New York: Nation Books, 2005, p. 178.

19. Lawrence S. Wrightsman, *Psychology and the Legal System* (Monterey, Calif.: Brooks/Cole, 1987), pp. 85–86.

20. Roger G. Dunham and Geoffrey P. Alpert, *Critical Issues in Policing: Contemporary*

Readings, 5th ed. (Long Grove, Ill.: Waveland, 2005), p. 12.

21. Ibid., p. 111.

22. Jerome Skolnick, "A Sketch of the Policeman's Working Personality," quoted in *The Police Community,* eds. Jack Goldsmith and Sharon S. Goldsmith (Pacific Palisades, Calif.: Palisades, 1974), p. 106.

23 Adapted from Dennis Nowicki, "Twelve Traits of Highly Effective Police Officers," *Law and Order* (October 1999): pp. 45–46.

24. Samuel Walker, *The Police in America: An Introduction,* 2nd ed. (New York: McGraw-Hill, 1992), p. 61.

25. Steven M. Cox, *Police: Practices, Perspectives, Problems* (Boston: Allyn and Bacon, 1996), p. 61.

26. See Albert Reiss, *The Police and the Public* (New Haven, Conn.: Yale University Press, 1971), p. 96.

27. Jerome H. Skolnick and David H. Bayley, *The New Blue Line: Police Innovation in Six American Cities* (New York: Free Press, 1986), p. 4.

28. James Q. Wilson, *Varieties of Police Behavior* (Cambridge, Mass.: Harvard University Press, 1968), pp. 140–226.

29. Sarah Korones, "The 10 Most Dangerous Jobs in America," *CBS News,* January 27, 2013, http://www.smartplanet.com/blog/bulletin/the-10-most-dangerous-jobs-in-america/11396.

30. Federal Bureau of Investigation, "FBI Releases 2013 Statistics on Law Enforcement Officers Killed and Assaulted" (November 24, 2014), http://www.fbi.gov/news/pressrel/press-releases/fbi-releases-2013-statistics-on-law-enforcement-officers-killed-and-assaulted.

31. U.S. citizen living in Saudi Arabia, personal communication, September 12, 1994.

32. Chris Hedges, "Everywhere in Saudi Arabia, Islam Is Watching," *New York Times,* January 6, 1993, p. A4(N), col. 3.

33 Quoted in Kevin Krajick, "Does Patrol Prevent Crime?" *Police Magazine* 1 (September 1978): pp. 4–16.

34. Quoted in J. Bartlett, ed., *Familiar Quotations,* 16th ed. (Boston: Little, Brown, 1992).

35. Merry Morash and Robin Haarr, "Gender, Workplace Problems, and Stress in Policing." Paper presented at the annual meeting of the Academy of Criminal Justice Sciences, Nashville, TN (March 12, 1991).

36. Bureau of Justice Statistics, *Characteristics of Drivers Stopped by Police, 2002* (Washington, D.C.: U.S. Department of Justice, 2006), pp. 1–2, 5.

37. See, for example, Terry C. Cox and Mervin F. White, "Traffic Citations and Student Attitudes Toward the Police: An Examination of Selected Interaction Dynamics," *Journal of Police Science and Administration* 16, no. 2 (Fall 1988): 105–121.

38. Herman Goldstein, "Police Discretion: The Ideal Versus the Real," *Public Administration Review* 23, no. 3 (1963): 140–148.

39. Carl B. Klockars and Stephen D. Mastrofski, "Police Discretion: The Case of Selective Enforcement," in *Thinking About Police: Contemporary Readings,* 2nd ed., ed. Carl B. Klockars and Stephen D. Mastrofski (Boston: McGraw-Hill, 1991), p. 330.

40. David H. Bayley and Egon Bittner, "Learning the Skills of Policing," in *Critical Issues in Policing: Contemporary Readings,* ed. Roger G. Dunham and Geoffrey P. Alpert (Prospect Heights, Ill.: Waveland, 1989), pp. 87–110.

41. Kenneth Culp Davis, *Police Discretion* (St. Paul, Minn.: West, 1975), p. 73.

42. Kenneth Culp Davis, *Discretionary Justice* (Urbana: University of Illinois Press, 1969), p. 222.

43 Klockars and Mastrofski, "Police Discretion," p. 331.

44. Quoted in Leonard Roy Frank, ed., *Random House Webster's Quotationary* (New York: Random House, 1999), p. 761.

45. Marc H. Caplan and Joe Holt Anderson, *Forensic: When Science Bears Witness* (Washington, D.C.: U.S. Government Printing Office, 1984), p. 2.

46. Charles R. Swanson, Neil C. Chamelin, Leonard Territo, and Robert W. Taylor, *Criminal Investigation,* 9th ed. (Boston: McGraw-Hill, 2006), p. 10.

47. Peter R. DeForest, R. E. Gaensslen, and Henry C. Lee, *Forensic Science: An Introduction to Criminalistics* (New York: McGraw-Hill, 1983), p. 29.

48. W. Jerry Chisum and Brent E. Turvey, "Evidence Dynamics: Locard's Exchange Principle & Crime Reconstruction," *Journal of Behavioral Profiling* 2, no. 1 (2000): 3.

49. President's Commission on Law Enforcement and the Administration of Justice, *Task Force Report: Science and Technology* (Washington, D.C.: U.S. Government Printing Office, 1967), pp. 7–18.

50. Paul B. Weston and Kenneth M. Wells, *Criminal Investigation: Basic Perspectives,* 4th ed. (Englewood Cliffs, N.J.: Prentice Hall, 1986), pp. 5–10.

51. Peter W. Greenwood and Joan Petersilia, *The Criminal Investigation Process:* Volume 1. *Summary and Policy Implications* (Santa Monica, Calif.: RAND, 1975). The entire report is found in Peter W. Greenwood, Jan M. Chaiken, and Joan Petersilia, *The Criminal Investigation Process* (Lexington, Mass.: D. C. Heath, 1977).

52. Ibid., p. 19.

53 Weston and Wells, *Criminal Investigation,* p. 5.

54. Thomas Hughes and Megan Magers, "The Perceived Impact of Crime Scene Investigation Shows on the Administration of Justice," *Journal of Criminal Justice and Popular Culture* 14, no. 3 (2007): 262, http://www.albany.edu/scj/jcjpc/vol14is3/HughesMagers.pdf.

55. Ibid., p. 265.

56. Kit Roane, "The CSI Effect," *U.S. News & World Report,* April, 17, 2005, http://www.usnews.com/usnews/culture/articles/050425/25csi.htm.

57. Solomon Moore, "Progress Is Minimal in Clearing DNA Cases," *New York Times,* October 24, 2008, http://www.nytimes.com/2008/10/25/us/25dna.html?pagewanted=all&_r=0.

58. DeForest et al., *Forensic Science,* p. 11.

59. John S. Dempsey and Linda S. Forst, *An Introduction to Policing,* 6th ed. (Independence, Ky.: Cengage, 2012), p. 470, http://books.google.com/books?id=PmUwsHp8m1wC&pg=PA470&dq=.

60. Richard Willing, "DNA to Clear 200th Person," *USA Today,* April 23, 2007, http://usatoday30.usatoday.com/news/nation/2007-04-22-dna-exoneration_N.htm.

Chapter 7

1. Tyler Kingkade, "Campus Police Have History of Excessive Force Against Protesters," *Huffington Post,* December 9, 2011, http://www.huffingtonpost.com/2011/12/09/california-campus-police-clash-with-protesters-ows_n_1125537.html.

2. Tyler Kingkade, "UC Davis Pepper Spraying Victims to Receive Nearly $1 Million Settlement," *Huffington Post,* September 16, 2012, http://www.huffingtonpost.com/2012/09/26/uc-davis-pepper-spraying-settlement_n_1916803.html.

3 President's Task Force on 21st Century Policing, 2015, *Interim Report of the President's Task Force on 21st Century Policing,* p. 1.

4. Michael Pearson, Steve Almasy, and Ben Brumfield, "Freddie Gray Death Ruled Homicide; Officers Charged," CNN, May 1, 2015, http://www.cnn.com/2015/05/01/us/freddie-gray-baltimore-death/.

5. See Rick Harmon, "Timeline: The Selma-to-Montgomery Marches," *USA Today,* March 6, 2015, http://www.usatoday.com/story/news/nation/2015/03/05/black-history-bloody-sunday-timeline/24463923/.

6. National Advisory Commission on Civil Disorders, Report Summary, http://www.eisenhowerfoundation.org/docs/kerner.pdf.

7. James Baldwin, *Nobody Knows My Name: More Notes of a Native Son* (New York, Dial Press, 1962), p. 98.

8. Office of Justice Programs, Department of Justice, "Police Stop White, Black, and Hispanic Drivers at Similar Rates According to Department of Justice Report," www.ojp.usdoj.gov/newsroom/pressreleases/2007/BJS07020.htm.

9. CBS News, "Families of Michael Brown, Eric Garner, Tamir Rice to March to Capitol," December 13, 2014, http://www.cbsnews.com/news/families-of-michael-brown-eric-garner-tamir-rice-to-march-to-capitol/.

10. Jamie Gumbrecht, "Dartmouth Launches #BlackLivesMatter course," CNN, February 4, 2015, http://www.cnn.com/2015/02/04/living/feat-dartmouth-black-lives-matter/.

11. John Bacon, "Peacefully, Madison Processes Police Shooting," *USA Today*, March 9, 2015, http://www.usatoday.com/story/news/nation/2015/03/08/madison-police-shooting-robinson/24612157/.

12. Dana Ford, "South Carolina Ex-Police Officer Indicted in Walter Scott Killing," CNN, June 18, 2015, http://www.cnn.com/2015/06/08/us/south-carolina-slager-indictment-walter-scott/.

13 Alan Scher Zagier, "Uneasy Calm in Ferguson After Shooting of Police Officers," *Associated Press*, March 13, 2015, http://www.msn.com/en-us/news/us/calm-prevails-in-ferguson-after-shooting-of-police-officers/ar-AA9G992.

14. See, for example, Tierney Sneed, "Ferguson Report Prompts Resignations, Court Takeover," *U.S. News*, March 11, 2015, http://www.usnews.com/news/articles/2015/03/11/doj-ferguson-report-prompts-resignations-court-takeover.

15. Yamiche Alcindor, "Unrelenting Ferguson Protests Pushed Year of National Change," *USA Today*, August 10, 2015, http://www.usatoday.com/story/news/2015/08/08/unrelenting-ferguson-protests-pushed-year-national-change/31075079/.

16. Brad Heath, "Racial Gap in U.S. Arrest Rates: 'Staggering Disparity'," *USA Today*, November 19, 2014, http://www.usatoday.com/story/news/nation/2014/11/18/ferguson-black-arrest-rates/19043207/.

17. President's Task Force on 21st Century Policing, *Interim Report of the President's Task Force on 21st Century Policing*, p. 9.

18. Ibid., p. 10.

19. Rick Hampson, Marisol Bello, and Kevin Johnson, "Nine Solutions to Fix Ferguson," *USA Today*, March 13, 2015, http://www.usatoday.com/story/news/2015/03/12/ferguson-how-to-fix-problems/70230164/.

20. "The Lessons of Ferguson," *The Economist*, August 23, 2014, http://www.economist.com/news/leaders/21613261-there-no-excuse-rioting-smarter-policing-would-make-it-less-likely-lessons.

21. The Leadership Conference, *Lessons From Ferguson, Missouri—The Need for Sensible Law Enforcement Reform*, December 2014, http://www.civilrights.org/publications/reports/civil-rights-act-report-december-2014/lessons-from-ferguson.html.

22. Amanda Yeager, "As Baltimore Grapples With Police-Community Relations, Columbia Pastor Returns to Ferguson. Columbia Reverend Discusses Baltimore Unrest," *Baltimore Sun*, May 5, 2015, http://www.baltimoresun.com/news/maryland/howard/columbia/ph-ho-cf-david-anderson-0507-20150504-story.html#page=1.

23 Quoted in "Do Cops Need College?" *Michigan State University Today*, February 15, 2015, http://msutoday.msu.edu/news/2015/do-cops-need-college/.

24. See Dallas Police Department, http://dallaspolice.net/ois/docs/narrative/2013/OIS_2013_311475A.pdf.

25. Kevin Johnson, Meghan Hoyer, and Brad Heath, "Local Police Involved in 400 Killings per Year," *USA Today*, August 15, 2014, http://www.usatoday.com/story/news/nation/2014/08/14/police-killings-data/14060357/.

26. President's Task Force on 21st Century Policing, 2015, *Interim Report of the President's Task Force on 21st Century Policing*, p. 22.

27. Kevin Johnson, "Panel to Consider Tracking of Civilians Killed by Police," *USA Today*, December 12, 2014, http://www.usatoday.com/story/news/nation/2014/12/11/tracking-cop-deaths/20104193/.

28. L. Morris, *Incredible New York* (New York: Bonanza, 1951).

29. James A. Inciardi, *Criminal Justice*, 5th ed. (Orlando, FL: Harcourt Brace, 1996).

30. Ibid.

31. Richard N. Holden, "The Technology Cycle and Contemporary Policing," paper presented at the annual meeting of the Academy of Criminal Justice Sciences, March 5, 2015, Orlando, Florida.

32. Steve Miletich and Jennifer Sullivan, "Costly Public-Records Requests May Threaten SPD Plan for Body Cameras," *Seattle Times*, November 20, 2014, http://www.seattletimes.com/seattle-news/costly-public-records-requests-may-threaten-spd-plan-for-body-cameras/.

33 Ibid.

34. Ibid.

35. Ibid.

36. See Peter H. Russell and David M. O'Brien, *Judicial Independence in the Age of Democracy: Critical Perspectives From Around the World* (Charlottesville, VA: University of Virginia Press, 2001), p. 306.

37. Chris Buckley and Michael Forsythe, "China Restricts Voting Reforms for Hong Kong," *New York Times*, August 31, 2014, http://www.nytimes.com/2014/09/01/world/asia/hong-kong-elections.html?_r=0.

38. "Hong Kong Protesters Agitating Against China's Volte-Face Arrested," *International Business Times*, September 2, 2014.

39. Calum MacLeod and Alia E. Dastagir, "Meet the 17-Year-Old Face of Hong Kong's Protests," *USA Today*, October 2, 2014, http://www.usatoday.com/story/news/world/2014/10/02/joshua-wong-hong-kong-protests/16597653/.

40. Michael Forsythe and Austin Ramzynov, "Officers Arrested in Beating of a Protester in Hong Kong," *New York Times*, November 26, 2014, http://www.nytimes.com/2014/11/27/world/asia/hong-kong-protests-mong-kok.html?ref=topics.

41. Anna Marie Roantree and Lisa Jucca, "Thousands Denounce HSBC Board Member's Likening of Hong Kong People to Freed Slaves," *Reuters*, October 31, 2014, http://www.reuters.com/article/2014/10/31/us-hongkong-china-idUSKBN0IK0DV20141031; David Harding, "HSBC's Laura Cha Sparks Outrage Comparing Wait for Hong Kong Voting Rights to That of U.S. Slaves," *New York Daily News*, November 1, 2014, http://www.nydailynews.com/news/world/hsbc-laura-cha-sparks-outrage-comparing-hong-kong-voting-rights-u-s-slaves-article-1.1995397.

42. See "'Umbrella Revolution' Brings Hong Kong to a Halt in Push for Democracy," *News Hong Kong*, September 29, 2014, https://newshongkong.wordpress.com/2014/09/29/umbrella-revolution-brings-hong-kong-to-a-halt/; "The End of Trust? Hong Kong Sees Police Force in a New Light," CNN, October 7, 2014, http://www.cnn.com/2014/10/07/world/asia/hong-kong-police-public-trust; "HKPF Report Card: Occupy Central Term," *Harbour Times*, October 9, 2014, http://harbourtimes.com/openpublish/article/hkpf-report-card-occupy-central-term-20141009.

43 "Protest Probe: Top Cop Speaks," *The Standard*, December 16, 2014, http://www.thestandard.com.hk/news_detail.asp?pp_cat=30&art_id=152398&sid=43546869&con_type=1.

44. Michael Forsythe, "U.N. Human Rights Panel Urges China to Allow Free

Elections in Hong Kong," *New York Times,* http://www.nytimes.com/2014/10/24/world/asia/un-urges-china-to-allow-free-elections-in-hong-kong.html?_r=1.

45. Ishaan Tharoor, "Hong Kong's Tense Protests Echo Around the World," *Washington Post,* October 2, 2014, http://www.washingtonpost.com/blogs/worldviews/wp/2014/10/02/hong-kongs-tense-protests-echo-around-the-world/; Rishi Iyengar, "Global Support Pours in for Hong Kong Democracy Protests," *Time,* September 29, 2014, http://time.com/3444225/hong-kong-democracy-protests-global-support/.

46. Kenneth J. Peak, *Policing America: Challenges and Best Practices,* 6th ed. (Upper Saddle River, N.J.: Prentice Hall, 2009), p. 263.

47. C. Germann, Frank D. Day, and Robert R. J. Gallati, *Introduction to Law Enforcement and Criminal Justice* (Springfield, Ill.: Charles C. Thomas, 1976), p. 225.

48. Scott Sonner and Ken Ritter, "FBI Probes Possible Case of Domestic Terrorism at KFC," *Reno Gazette Journal,* March 11, 2015, p. 3A.

49. Michael P. Downing, "Policing Terrorism in the United States: The Los Angeles Police Department's Convergence Strategy," *The Police Chief* (February 2009), http://www.policechiefmagazine.org/magazine/index.cfm?fuseaction=display_arch&article_id=1729&issue_id=22009.

50. For a more complete listing of terrorist attacks since 9/11, see William Robert Johnston, "Summary of Historical Attacks Using Chemical or Biological Weapons," October 2014, http://www.johnstonsarchive.net/terrorism/chembioattacks.html.

51. Graeme R. Newman and Ronald V. Clarke, *Policing Terrorism: An Executive's Guide* (Washington, D.C.: U.S. Department of Justice, Office of Community Oriented Policing Services, July 2008), http://www.popcenter.org/library/reading/pdfs/policingterrorism.pdf.

52. Ibid.

53. Ibid.

54. Ibid.

55. Adapted from Albert Sabaté, "6 Police Misconduct Settlements Worth Millions," ABC News, May 1, 2013, http://abcnews.go.com/ABC_Univision/News/police-misconduct-settlements-worth-millions/story?id=19077115#.

56. H. E. Barrineau III, *Civil Liability in Criminal Justice* (Cincinnati, Ohio: Pilgrimage, 1987), p. 58.

57. Ibid., p. 5.

58. Kenneth J. Peak, *Policing America: Methods, Issues, Challenges* (Englewood Cliffs, N.J.: Regents/Prentice Hall), 1992;

for a complete account of King's beating and its aftermath, see pp. 318–327.

59. Seth Mydans, "Punitive Damages Denied in Beating of Rodney King," *New York Times,* June 2, 1994, http://www.nytimes.com/1994/06/02/us/punitive-damages-denied-in-beating-of-rodney-king.html?sec=&spon=&page wanted=all.

60. See, for example, *Black v. Stephens,* 662 F.2d 181 (1991).

61. *Fielder v. Jenkins* (N.J. Super. A.D. 1993833 A.2d 906).

62. Kenneth J. Peak, Larry K. Gaines, and Ronald W. Glensor, *Police Supervision and Management: In an Era of Community Policing,* 3rd ed. (Upper Saddle River, N.J.: Prentice Hall, 2010).

63 *Thomas v. Williams,* 124 S.E.2d 409 (Ga. App. 1962).

64. *Guice v. Enfinger,* 389 So.2d 270 (Fla. App. 1980).

65. *Davis v. City of Detroit*, 386 N.W.2d 169 (Mich. App. 1986).

66. Ronald Palmer, chief of police, *Procedure Manual* (Tulsa, Okla.: Police Department, June 10, 1998), p. 1.

67. The U.S. Supreme Court said, in a 7–2 decision, that Gonzales could not sue the city and claim the police had violated her rights to due process. Furthermore, it held she had no constitutionally protected interest in the enforcement of the restraining order. The opinion also established that the holder of a restraining order is not entitled to any specific mandatory action by the police; rather, restraining orders only provide grounds for *arresting* the person restrained by order. See *Castle Rock v. Gonzales,* 545 U.S. 748 (2005).

68. See *County of Sacramento v. Lewis,* 118 S.Ct. 1708 (1998).

69. *Scott v. Harris,* 550 U.S. 372 (2007), at p. 13.

70. U.S. Department of Justice, Bureau of Justice Statistics, *Local Police Departments, 2007* (Washington, D.C.: Author, 2010), p. 14.

71. U.S. Department of Justice, Bureau of Justice Statistics, *Women in Law Enforcement, 1987–2008* (Washington, D.C.: Author, June 2010), p. 3; also see U.S. Department of Justice, Bureau of Justice Assistance, *Recruiting & Retaining Women: A Self-Assessment Guide for Law Enforcement* (June 2001), https://www.ncjrs.gov/pdffiles1/bja/188157.pdf.

72. Ibid., p. 2.

73 See Jon Felperin, "Women in Law Enforcement: Two Steps Forward, Three Steps Back," http://www.policeone.com/police-recruiting/articles/87017-Women-in-Law-Enforcement-Two-steps-forward-three-steps-back/.

74. Bureau of Justice Statistics, *Local Police Departments, 2013: Personnel, Policies, and Practices,* May 2015, pp. 1, 5, http://www.bjs.gov/content/pub/pdf/lpd13ppp.pdf.

75. Paulina Firozi, "5 Things to Know About Ferguson Police Department," *USA Today,* August 19, 2014, http://www.usatoday.com/story/news/nation-now/2014/08/14/ferguson-police-department-details/14064451/.

76. President's Task Force on 21st Century Policing, *Interim Report of the President's Task Force on 21st Century Policing,* p. 16.

77. Brad Heath, "New Police Radars Can 'See' Inside Homes," *USA Today,* January 19, 2015, http://www.usatoday.com/story/news/2015/01/19/police-radar-see-through-walls/22007615/.

78. Kaveh Ghaemian, "Small-Town Cops Wield Big-City Data," *Government Technology* 9 (September 1996): 38.

79. Lois Pilant, "Computerized Crime Mapping," *Police Chief* (December 1997): 58.

80. U.S. Department of Justice, National Institute of Justice, *Crime Mapping Research Conference,* http://www.nij.gov/events/maps/; the CMRC web address is www.ojp.usdoj.gov/nij/maps/welcome.htm.

81. Bill McGarigle, "Crime Profilers Gain New Weapons," *Government Technology* (December 1997): 28–29.

82. Ibid.

83 Lauren Katims, "Crime Scan," *Government Technology* (April 2011): 38.

84. U.S. Department of Justice, Bureau of Justice Statistics, *Local Police Departments, 2007* (Washington, D.C.: Author, 2010), p. 17; U.S. Department of Justice, Bureau of Justice Statistics, *Sheriff's Offices, 2003* (Washington, D.C.: Author, 2006), p. 26.

85. Kyle Malone, "The Fourth Amendment and the Stored Communications Act: Why the Warrantless Gathering of Historical Cell Site Location Information Poses No Threat to Privacy," *Pepperdine Law Review* 39, no. 3 (September 8, 2012), http://digitalcommons.pepperdine.edu/plr/vol39/iss3/4/.

86. Massimo Calabresi, "The Phone Knows All," *Time,* August 27, 2012, http://www.time.com/time/magazine/article/0,9171,2122241,00.html.

87. See 18 U.S.C. Chapter 121 §§ 2701–2712.

88. 18 U.S.C. § 2703(b) (2006).

89. Brian Huber, "Wis. Police Get Robo-Cop's Help," *PoliceOne.com,* November 14, 2006, www.policeone.com/police-technology/robots/articles/1190983.

90. Alison Bath, "Accident Scene Investigation Is High Tech," *Reno Gazette-Journal* (Sparks Today section), November 18, 2003, p. 4.

91. Ibid., p. 46.

Chapter 8

1. *McCulloch v. Maryland*, 17 U.S. 316 (1819).
2. John Adams, "Novanglus Papers," in *The Works of John Adams*, ed. Charles Francis Adams (Boston: Little Brown and Company, 1851), p. 106.
3 David Neubauer, *America's Courts and the Criminal Justice System*, 9th ed. (Belmont, Calif.: Wadsworth, 2008), pp. 294–300.
4. *Draper v. United States*, 358 U.S. 307 (1959).
5. *Illinois v. Gates*, 462 U.S. 213 (1983).
6. *U.S. v. Sokolow*, 109 S.Ct. 1581 (1989).
7. *People v. Defore*, 242 N.Y. 214, 150 N.E. 585 (1926).
8. *Weeks v. United States*, 232 U.S. 383 (1914).
9. *Mapp v. Ohio*, 367 U.S. 643 (1961).
10. *Payton v. New York*, 445 U.S. 573 (1980).
11. *Delaware v. Prouse*, 440 U.S. 648 (1979).
12. *Michigan Department of State Police v. Sitz*, 110 S.Ct. 2481, 110 L.Ed.2d 412 (1990).
13 *Pennsylvania v. Muniz*, 110 S.Ct. 2638, 110 L.Ed.2d 528 (1990).
14. *Maryland v. Pringle*, 124 S.Ct. 795 (2004).
15. *Illinois v. Lidster*, 124 S.Ct. 885 (2004).
16. *Kentucky v. King*, 131 S.Ct. 1849 (2011).
17. *California v. Greenwood*, 486 U.S. 35 (1988).
18. *Florida v. Bostick*, 59 LW 4708 (June 20, 1991).
19. *California v. Hodari D.*, 59 LW 4335 (April 23, 1991).
20. *Florida v. Jardines*, 569 U.S. ___ ; 133 S. Ct. 1409 (2013). Justice Antonin Scalia's opinion stated that "to find a visitor knocking on the door is routine (even if sometimes unwelcome); to spot that same visitor exploring the front path with a metal detector, or marching his bloodhound into the garden before saying hello and asking permission, would inspire most of us to—well, call the police." Scalia said using the dog was no different from using thermal imaging technology from afar to peer inside homes without a warrant.
21. *Florida v. Harris*, 568 U.S. ___ ; 133 S. Ct. 1050 (2013). In a unanimous decision, the Supreme Court gave police authority to use dogs to uncover illegal drugs at traffic stops, upholding a police Labrador retriever's search of a truck that uncovered methamphetamine ingredients inside.
22. *Chimel v. California*, 395 U.S. 752 (1969).
23 *Maryland v. Buie*, 58 LW 4281 (1990).
24. *Arizona v. Gant*, 07-542 (2009).
25. *Maryland v. King*, 569 U.S. 12 (2013).
26. *Riley v. California*, 573 U.S. ___ (2014).
27. *Terry v. Ohio*, 319 U.S. 1 (1968).
28. *Minnesota v. Dickerson*, 113 S.Ct. 2130 (1993).
29. *Maryland v. Wilson*, 117 S.Ct. 882 (1997).
30. Daniel Bergner, "Is Stop and Frisk Worth It?" *Atlantic Monthly* (April 2014), http://www.theatlantic.com/features/archive/2014/03/is-stop-and-frisk-worth-it/358644/; see also "The Hunted and the Hated," The *Nation*, https://www.youtube.com/watch?v=7rWtDMPaRD8 (originally posted October 9, 2012).
31. *Carroll v. United States*, 267 U.S. 132 (1925).
32. *Harris v. United States*, 390 U.S. 234 (1968).
33 *Florida v. Jimeno*, 59 LW 4471 (May 23, 1991).
34. *Wyoming v. Houghton*, 119 S.Ct. 1297 (1999).
35. *Illinois v. Caballes*, 543 U.S. 405 (2005).
36. World Justice Project, "Who We Are," http://worldjusticeproject.org/rule-law-index-map (accessed June 6, 2013).
37. *U.S. v. Jones*, 565 U.S. ___, 132 S.Ct. 945 (2012).
38. *Oliver v. United States*, 466 U.S. 170 (1984).
39. *California v. Ciraolo*, 476 U.S. 207 (1986).
40. *New York v. Class*, 54 LW 4178 (1986).
41. *Bumper v. North Carolina*, 391 U.S. 543 (1968).
42. *Stoner v. California*, 376 U.S. 483 (1964).
43 *Georgia v. Randolph*, 126 S.Ct. 1515 (2006).
44. *Fernandez v. California,* 571 U.S. ____ (2014).
45. *Katz v. United States*, 389 U.S. 347 (1967).
46. *Berger v. New York*, 388 U.S. 41 (1967).
47. *Lee v. United States*, 343 U.S. 747 (1952).
48. *Missouri v. McNeely*, 569 U.S. ____ (2013). The U.S. Supreme Court ruled in *Missouri v. McNeely* that police must obtain a warrant in order to subject a drunk driving suspect to a blood test. The Court found that the natural metabolism of alcohol in the bloodstream did not constitute an exigency that would justify a warrantless blood test.
49. John Kaplan, Jerome H. Skolnick, and Malcolm M. Feeley, *Criminal Justice: Introductory Cases and Materials*, 5th ed. (Westbury, N.Y.: Foundation Press, 1991), pp. 220–221.
50. *Edwards v. Arizona*, 451 U.S. 477 (1981).
51. *Arizona v. Roberson*, 486 U.S. 675 (1988).
52. *Berkemer v. McCarty*, 468 U.S. 420 (1984).
53 *Quarles v. New York*, 467 U.S. 649 (1984).
54. Adam Goodman, "How The Media Have Misunderstood Dzhokhar Tsarnaev's *Miranda* Rights," *The Atlantic,* April 22, 2013; http://www.theatlantic.com/national/archive/2013/04/how-the-media-have-misunderstood-dzhokhar-tsarnaevs-i-miranda-i-rights/275189/.
55. *Michigan v. Mosley*, 423 U.S. 93 (1975).
56. *Colorado v. Spring*, 479 U.S. 564 (1987).
57. *Connecticut v. Barrett*, 479 U.S. 523 (1987).
58. *Duckworth v. Eagan*, 109 S.Ct. 2875 (1989).
59. *Berghuis v. Thompkins*, 560 U.S. 370 (2010).
60. *U.S. v. Wade*, 388 U.S. 218 (1967).
61. *Kirby v. Illinois*, 406 U.S. 682 (1972).
62. *Foster v. California*, 394 U.S. 440 (1969).
63 E. F. Loftus, J. M. Doyle, and J. Dysert, *Eyewitness Testimony: Civil & Criminal*, 4th ed. (Charlottesville, Va: Lexis Law Publishing, 2008); E. F. Loftus, "The Malleability of Human Memory," *American Scientist* 67 (1979): 312–320; Gary L. Wells, et al., "Eyewitness Identification Procedures: Recommendations for Lineups and Photospreads," *Law and Human Behavior* 22, no. 6 (1998): 603–647; Gary L. Wells, "Eyewitness Identifications: Systemic Reforms," *Wisconsin Law Review* 615 (2006): 628–629.
64. *State v. Henderson*, 27 A.3rd 872 (2011).
65. *Powell v. Alabama*, 287 U.S. 45 (1932).
66. *Gideon v. Wainwright*, 372 U.S. 335 (1963).
67. *Argersinger v. Hamlin*, 407 U.S. 25 (1973).
68. *Escobedo v. Illinois*, 378 U.S. 478 (1964).

Chapter 9

1. CNN Library: *Michael Vick Fast Facts*, November 10, 2014, http://www.cnn.com/2013/06/24/us/michael-vick-fast-facts/.
2. Erwin C. Surrency, "The Courts in the American Colonies," *American Journal of Legal History* 11 (1967): 258.
3 Kermit Hall, *The Magic Mirror: Law in American History* (New York: Oxford University Press, 1989).
4. Surrency, "The Courts in the American Colonies," p. 258.
5. Freda Adler, Gerhard O. W. Mueller, and William S. Laufer, *Criminal Justice: An Introduction* (Boston: McGraw-Hill, 2006), pp. 325–326.
6. Stephen Whicher and R. Spiller, eds., *The Early Lectures of Ralph Waldo Emerson* (Philadelphia: University of Pennsylvania Press, 1953), p. 112.
7. *Tehan v. United States ex rel. Shott*, 382 U.S. 406 (1966), p. 416.
8. Howard Abadinsky, *Law and Justice: An Introduction to the American Legal System*, 4th ed. (Chicago: Nelson-Hall, 1999), p. 174.
9. Ibid., p. 170.
10. U.S. Department of Justice, "Table 5.65: Petitions Filed in U.S. District Courts by Federal and State Prisoners," *Sourcebook of Criminal Justice Statistics Online,* http://www.albany.edu/sourcebook/pdf/t5652010.pdf.
11. Malcolm M. Feeley and Edward L. Rubin, *Judicial Policy Making and the Modern State: How the Courts Reformed America's Prisons* (New York: Cambridge University Press, 1998).

12. Stephen L. Wasby, *The Supreme Court in the Federal System,* 3rd ed. (Chicago: Nelson-Hall, 1989), p. 5.

13 Abadinsky, *Law and Justice,* p. 171.

14. Ibid., p. 166.

15. Cassie Spohn and Craig Hemmens, *Courts: A Text/Reader* (Thousand Oaks, Calif.: Sage, 2008), p. 10.

16. David W. Neubauer, *America's Courts and the Criminal Justice System,* 8th ed. (Belmont, Calif.: Thomson Wadsworth, 2005), p. 81.

17. Ibid., pp. 402–403.

18. Ibid., p. 82.

19. Ibid., pp. 81, 83.

20. U.S. Department of Justice, Bureau of Justice Statistics, *State Court Organization, 2011* (Washington, D.C.: Author, November 2013); http://www.bjs .gov/content/pub/pdf/sco11.pdf.

21. Nevada Appellate Courts, http:// nvcourts.gov/CourtOfAppeals.aspx.

22. National Center for State Courts, *Examining the Work of the State Courts: An Analysis of 2012 State Court Caseloads,* http://www.courtstatistics .org/Appellate/2014Appellate.aspx .

23 Neubauer, *America's Courts and the Criminal Justice System,* 8th ed., p. 85.

24. Ibid.

25. Ibid., p. 87

26. The U.S. Supreme Court reversed the decision of the lower court (i.e., the circuit court), saying the lack of an instruction on causation by itself in this case was not a violation of due process rights. The Court also said, notably, that "a person who is aware of, and consciously disregards a risk, must foresee the ultimate harm involved." See *Kibbe v. Henderson,* 534 F.2d 493 (1976). Kibbe's adversary (the appellee) in this case, Henderson, was the superintendent at Auburn Correctional Facility in New York. The term *exhausting all possible state remedies* is a legal doctrine meaning that the *state*'s appeals courts are to be given the opportunity to correct any defects that occurred at trial before a party may pursue a case in federal court. This is basically the rule of comity, or courtesy—the federal courts defer to state courts to correct any defects prior to those claims being raised in a federal court. *Habeas corpus* (sometimes termed "the great writ") is a Latin term for "you have the body," and it is the inmate's means of asking a court to grant a hearing to determine whether or not he or she is being held illegally.

27. Federal Judicial Center, "The U.S. District Courts and the Federal Judiciary," http:// www.fjc.gov/history/home.nsf/page/ courts_district.html.

28. Federal Judicial Center, "The U.S. Courts of Appeals and the Federal Judiciary," http://www.fjc.gov/history/home.nsf.

29. Supreme Court of the United States, "A Brief Overview of the Supreme Court," http://www.supremecourt.gov/about/ briefoverview.aspx.

30. David W. Neubauer, *America's Courts and the Criminal Justice System,* 9th ed. (Belmont, Calif.: Thomson Wadsworth, 2008), p. 63.

31. Supreme Court of the United States, "Instructions for Admission to the Bar," http://www.supremecourtus.gov/bar/ barinstructions.pdf.

32. See U.S. Courts, "U.S. Supreme Court Procedures," http://www.uscourts.gov/ EducationalResources/Constitution Resources/SeparationOfPowers/ USSupremeCourtProcedures.aspx.

33 Ibid.

34. Supreme Court of the United States, "The Justices' Caseload," http:// www.supremecourt.gov/about/ justicecaseload.aspx; also see, as examples of written opinions, Supreme Court of the United States, "2011 Term Opinions of the Court," http://www .supremecourt.gov/opinions/slipopinions .aspx?Term=11.

35. Ibid.; see the *Rules of the Supreme Court of the United States*, generally, at http://www.supremecourt.gov/ ctrules/2010RulesoftheCourt.pdf.

36. Ram Subramanian et al., *Incarceration's Front Door: The Misuse of Jail in America* (New York: Vera Institute of Justice, 2015); Aimee Picchi, "Are America's Jails Used to Punish Poor People?" http:// www.cbsnews.com/news/how-jails-are- warehousing-those-too-poor-to-make- bail/.

37. Ibid.

38. American Bar Association, "FAQs About the Grand Jury System," http://www .abanow.org/2010/03/faqs-about-the- grand-jury-system/.

39. Larry Buchanan et al., "What Happened in Ferguson?" *New York Times,* November 25, 2014, http://www.nytimes.com/ interactive/2014/08/13/us/ferguson- missouri-town-under-siege-after-police- shooting.html?_r=0.

40. Arlen Specter, book review, 76 *Yale Law Journal* 604 (1967): pp. 606–607.

41. CNN Library, *Michael Vick Fast Facts.*

42. Alvin Rubin, "How We Can Improve Judicial Treatment of Individual Cases Without Sacrificing Individual Rights: The Problems of the Criminal Law," *Federal Rules Decisions* 70 (1976): p. 176.

43. John Nisbet, *Burma Under British Rule— and Before,* Vol. I (London: Archibald Constable, 1901), p. 177.

44. Cora L. Daniels and C. M. Stevans, eds., *Encyclopedia of Superstitions, Folklore, and the Occult Sciences of the World,* Vol. III (Milwaukee: J. H. Yewdale, 1903), p. 1243.

45. "Trial by Ordeal," http://www.absolute astronomy.com/topics/Trial_by_ordeal.

46. *Williams v. Florida,* 399 U.S. 78, 86 (1970).

47. *Apodaca v. Oregon,* 406 U.S. 404 (1972).

48. See *Brady v. Maryland,* 373 U.S. 83 (1963).

49. Neubauer, *America's Courts and the Criminal Justice System,* 9th ed., p. 263.

50. National Association of Drug Court Professionals, "What Are Drug Courts?" http://www.nadcp.org/learn/what-are- drug-courts/drug-court-history.

51. Council of State Governments Justice Center, "Mental Health Courts," May 2015, http://csgjusticecenter.org/mental- health-court-project/.

52. West Huddleston and Douglas B. Marlowe, *Painting the Picture: A National Report on Drug Courts and Other Problem- Solving Court Programs in the United States,* July 2011, National Drug Court Institute, http://www.ndci.org/sites/ default/files/nadcp/PCP%20Report%20 FINAL.PDF; see also Bureau of Justice Assistance, "What Are Problem- Solving Courts?" https://www.bja .gov/evaluation/program-adjudication/ problem-solving-courts.htm.

53 See Thomas Alexander Fyfe, *Charles Dickens and the Law* (London: Chapman and Hall, 1910), pp. 28–29.

54. Charles Dickens, *Bleak House* (London: Penguin Book, 1971; first published in 1853).

55. William Shakespeare, *Hamlet,* Act 3, Scene 1.

56. *Strunk v. United States,* 412 U.S. 434 (1973).

57. Speedy Trial Act of 1974, 18 U.S.C.S. §§ 3161–3174 (as amended, 1979).

58. *Barker v. Wingo,* 407 U.S. 514 (1972).

59. Ibid.

60. Ibid., p. 522.

61. American Prosecutors Research Institute, *Basic Trial Techniques for Prosecutors* (May 2005), http://www .ndaa.org/pdf/basic_trial_techniques_ 05.pdf.

62. Justia, "Criminal Appeals Overview," http://www.justia.com/criminal/criminal- appeals/.

63 *Douglas v. California,* 372 U.S. 353 (1963).

64. *Ross v. Moffitt,* 417 U.S. 600 (1974).

Chapter 10

1. Samuel J. Brakel and Alexander D. Brooks, *Law and Psychiatry in the Criminal Justice System* (Buffalo, N.Y.: William S. Hein, 2001), p. 130.

2. Quoted in David Landy and Elliott Aronson, "The Influence of the Character of the Criminal and His Victims on the Decisions of Simulated Jurors," *Journal of Experimental Social Psychology* 5 (1969), pp. 141–142.

3 Abraham Blumberg, *Criminal Justice* (Chicago: Quadrangle Books, 1967), p. 120.

4. See, for example, Pennsylvanians for Modern Courts, "Choosing Judges," http://www.pmconline.org/node/25.

5. U.S. Department of Justice, Bureau of Justice Statistics, *State Court Organization, 2004* (Washington, D.C.: Author, October 2006), p. 23.

6. American Judicature Society, *Judicial Selection in the States: How It Works, Why It Matters* (Des Moines, Iowa: Author, 2008), p. 4.

7. Ibid.

8. ABA Journal, "O'Connor on Judicial Elections: 'They're Awful. I Hate Them,'" http://www.abajournal.com/news/oconnor_chemerinsky_sound_warnings_at_aba_conference_about_the_dangers_of_s/.

9. Ibid.

10. Law.com, "O'Connor Says Judges Shouldn't Be Elected," http://www.law.com/jsp/law/LawArticleFriendly.jsp?id=1194429842107.

11. Martha Neil, "Top Court Hears Judicial Influence Case, Leans Toward Stricter Recusal Standard," *ABA Journal,* http://www.abajournal.com/news/top_court_hears_judicial_influence_case_leans_toward_stricter_recusal_stand.

12. *Caperton v. A.T. Massey Coal Co., Inc.,* 556 U.S. _____ (2009).

13. Jeff Cranson, *The Grand Rapids Press,* "The Price of Justice: High Court Wrestles With a Case That Should Spark Discussion in Michigan," March 3, 2009, http://blog.mlive.com/talkingpolitics/2009/03/the_price_of_justice_high_cour.html.

14. Alice Bannon, Eric Velasco, Linda Casey and Lianna Reagan, "The New Politics of Judicial Elections 20112012: How New Waves of Special Interest Spending Raised the Stakes for Fair Courts," Brennan Center for Justice (October 2013), http://newpoliticsreport.org/content/uploads/JAS-NewPolitics2012-Online.pdf.

15. Ibid.

16. Blumberg, *Criminal Justice,* p. 120.

17. Russell R. Wheeler and Howard R. Whitcomb, *Judicial Administration: Text and Readings* (Englewood Cliffs, N.J.: Prentice-Hall, 1977), p. 370.

18. Ibid., p. 372.

19. Ibid.

20. Ibid.

21. Ibid., p. 373.

22. William A. Batlitch, "Reflections on the Art and Craft of Judging," *The Judges Journal* 43, no. 4 (Fall 2003), pp. 7–8.

23. Charles E. Patterson, "The Good Judge: A Trial Lawyer's Perspective," *The Judges Journal* 43, no. 4 (Fall 2003), pp. 14–15.

24. See, for example, Allen K. Harris, "The Professionalism Crisis—The 'Z' Words and Other Rambo Tactics: The Conference of Chief Justices' Solution," 53 S.C. L. Rev. 549, 589 (2002).

25. *In re First City Bancorp of Tex., Inc.,* 282 F.3d 864 (5th Cir. 2002).

26. Marla N. Greenstein, "The Craft of Ethics," *The Judges Journal* 43, no. 4 (Fall 2003), p. 42.

27. Ty Tasker, "Sticks and Stones: Judicial Handling of Invective in Advocacy," *The Judges Journal* 43, no. 4 (Fall 2003), pp. 17–18.

28. Collins T. Fitzpatrick, "Building a Better Bench: Informally Addressing Instances of Judicial Misconduct," *The Judges Journal* 45, no. 2 (Winter 2005), pp. 16–20.

29. Ibid.

30. Southern Poverty Law Center, "Are There Limits to Prosecutorial Discretion?" http://www.splcenter.org/get-informed/intelligence-report/browse-all-issues/2007/summer/legal-brief#.UafrguDn_cs.

31. *Berger v. United States,* 295 U.S. 78 (1935).

32. *Connick v. Thompson,* 563 U.S. _____ (2011).

33. Radley Balko, "The Untouchables: America's Misbehaving Prosecutors, and the System that Protects Them," *Huffington Post,* August 1, 2013, http://www.huffingtonpost.com/2013/08/01/prosecutorial-misconduct-new-orleans-louisiana_n_3529891.html.

34. *Van De Kamp v. Goldstein,* 555 U.S. _____ (2009) quoting *Gregoire v. Biddle,* 177 F. 2d 579, 581 (2 Cir. 1949).

35. Pamela Koloff, "Jail Time May Be the Least of Ken Anderson's Problems," *Texas Monthly,* November 14, 2013, http://www.texasmonthly.com/story/jail-time-may-be-least-ken-anderson%E2%80%99s-problems; see also the film *An Unreal Dream: The Michael Morton Story* (2013).

36. *Maine v. Moulton,* 474 U.S. 159 (1985).

37. Legal Information Institute, "Effective Assistance of Counsel," http://www.law.cornell.edu/anncon/html/amdt6frag9_user.html.

38. See California Innocence Project, "Ineffective Assistance of Counsel," http://californiainnocenceproject.org/issues-we-face/ineffective-assistance-of-counsel/.

39. Ibid.; also see *Strickland v. Washington,* 466 U.S. 668 (1984).

40. William A. Mintz, "Lawyer Wouldn't Go to 'Sleazy Bar,' Client Wins Freedom From Life Term," *National Law Journal,* November 24, 1980, p. 7.

41. FindLaw, "Plea Bargaining Pros and Cons," http://criminal.findlaw.com/criminal-procedure/plea-bargain-pros-and-cons.html.

42. See, for example, Texas Fair Defense Project, "What Defense Lawyers Do," http://www.texasfairdefenseproject.org/info/right_to_counsel/defense_lawyers.

43. *Griffin v. Illinois,* 351 U.S. 12 (1956).

44. For more information about defense attorneys in general and indigent services specifically, see Cassia Spohn and Craig Hemmens, *Courts: A Text/Reader,* 2nd ed. (Los Angeles, Calif.: Sage, 2012), pp. 218–223.

Chapter 11

1. Quoted in Louis P. Carney, *Probation and Parole: Legal and Social Dimensions* (New York: McGraw-Hill, 1977), p. 75.

2. "15 Life Terms and No Parole for Dahmer," *New York Times,* February 18, 1992, http://www.nytimes.com/1992/02/18/us/15-life-terms-and-no-parole-for-dahmer.html.

3. Francis T. Cullen and Paul Gendreau, "Assessing Correctional Rehabilitation: Policy, Practice, and Prospects," *Criminal Justice 2000,* p. 111, https://www.ncjrs.gov/criminal_justice2000/vol_3/03d.pdf.

4. Brandon C. Welsh, "Monetary Costs and Benefits of Correctional Treatment Programs: Implications for Offender Reentry," *Federal Probation* (September 2004), p. 12, http://bcotn.org/subcommittees/csct/monetary_costs_and_benefits_of_correctional_treatment.pdf.

5. Ibid., pp. 9–12.

6. Jacqueline Cohen, *Incapacitating Criminals: Recent Research Findings I* (Washington, D.C.: National Institute of Justice, Research in Brief, 1983), p. 2.

7. CBS News, "The Cost of a Nation of Incarceration," http://www.cbsnews.com/8301-3445_162-57418495/the-cost-of-a-nation-of-incarceration/.

8. John J. Dilulio Jr., "Prisons Are a Bargain, by Any Measure," *New York Times,* January 16, 1996, p. A17.

9. The discussion of the corrections models is adapted from Todd R. Clear, George F. Cole, and Michael D. Reisig, *American Corrections,* 8th ed. (Belmont, Calif.: Thomson Wadsworth, 2009), pp. 40–64; the discussion of the accompanying prison design and operation is adapted from Steven E. Schoenherr, "Prison Reforms in American History," http://history.sandiego.edu/gen/soc/prison.html.

10. Quotes taken from the *Handbook of Correctional Institution Design and Construction* (U.S. Bureau of Prisons, 1949).

11. Amnesty International, "Death Sentences and Executions in 2011," http://www.amnesty.org/en/library/asset/ACT50/001/2012/en/241a8301-05b4-41c0-bfd9-2fe72899cda4/act500012012en.pdf; also see Amnesty International, *The Death*

Penalty in 2011, http://amnesty.org/en/death-penalty/death-sentences-and-executions-in-2011.

12. Tracy L. Snell, *Capital Punishment 2010* (Washington, D.C.: U.S. Department of Justice, Bureau of Justice Statistics, December 2011), http://www.bjs.gov/index.cfm?ty=pbdetail&iid=2236.

13. "U.S. Student Tells of Pain of His Caning in Singapore," *New York Times*, June 26, 1994, http://www.nytimes.com/1994/06/26/us/us-student-tells-of-pain-of-his-caning-in-singapore.html?pagewanted=1.

14. U.S. Department of Justice, Bureau of Justice Statistics, "Expenditures/Employment," http://www.bjs.gov/index.cfm?ty=tp&tid=16.

15. U.S. Department of Justice, Bureau of Justice Statistics, *State Corrections Expenditures, FY 1982–2010* (Washington, D.C.: Author, December 2011), http://bjs.ojp.usdoj.gov/content/pub/pdf/scefy8210.pdf.

16. Adapted from U.S. Department of Justice, National Institute of Corrections, and Association of Paroling Authorities International, *A Handbook for New Parole Board Members* (April 2003), p. 3, http://www.apaintl.org/documents/CEPPParoleHandbook.pdf.

17. Quoted by Sheldon G. Glueck in his "Foreword" to John V. Barry, *Alexander Maconochie of Norfolk Island* (Melbourne: Oxford University Press, 1958).

18. "15 Life Terms and No Parole for Dahmer."

19. Doug Stanglin and G. Jeffrey MacDonald, "Mobster 'Whitey' Bulger Gets Two Life Terms Plus 5 Years," *USA Today*, November 14, 2013, http://www.usatoday.com/story/news/2013/11/14/white-bulger-sentenced/3525087/.

20. Eliot McLauglin and Pamela Brown, "Judge Sentences Cleveland Kidnapper, Ariel Castro, to Life Plus 1,000 Years," August 1, 2013, http://www.cnn.com/2013/08/01/justice/ohio-castro/.

21. Mark Allenbaugh, "The Supreme Court's New Blockbuster U.S. Sentencing Guidelines Decision," http://writ.news.findlaw.com/allenbaugh/20050114.html.

22. At 18 U.S.C. Secs. 3551–3626 and 28 U.S.C. Secs. 991–998 (October 12, 1984).

23 Allenbaugh, "The Supreme Court's New Blockbuster U.S. Sentencing Guidelines Decision."

24. Lisa M. Seghetti and Alison M. Smith, *Federal Sentencing Guidelines: Background, Legal Analysis, and Policy Options* (Congressional Research Service Report for Congress, June 30, 2007), http://www.fas.org/sgp/crs/misc/RL32766.pdf.

25. *Blakely v. Washington,* 542 U.S. (2004).

26. *United States v. Booker,* 543 U.S. 125 (2005).

27. Allenbaugh, "The Supreme Court's New Blockbuster U.S. Sentencing Guidelines Decision," p. 2.

28. *Gall v. United States*, 552 U.S. 38 (2007).

29. *Kimbrough v. United States*, 552 U.S. 85 (2007).

30. *2011 Washington State Sentencing Guidelines Manual*, http://www.cfc.wa.gov/PublicationSentencing/SentencingManual/Adult_Sentencing_Manual_2011.pdf.

31. The National Center for Victims of Crime, "Victim Impact Statements," http://www.victimsofcrime.org/help-for-crime-victims/get-help-bulletins-for-crime-victims/victim-impact-statements.

32. *Payne v. Tennessee*, 501 U.S. 808 (1991).

33. *Snyder v. Massachusetts*, 291 U.S. 97 (1934), at 122.

34. James Q. Wilson, *Thinking About Crime* (New York: Vintage Books, 1985), p. 260.

35. H. Naci Mocan and R. Kaj Gittings, "Getting Off Death Row: Commuted Sentences and the Deterrent Effect of Capital Punishment," *Journal of Law and Economics* 46 (October 2003), pp. 453–478.

36. Hashem Dezhbakhsh, Paul H. Rubin, and Joanna M. Shepherd, "Does Capital Punishment Have a Deterrent Effect? New Evidence from Postmoratorium Panel Data," *American Law and Economics Review* 5, no. 2 (2003), pp. 344–376.

37. Paul R. Zimmerman, "State Executions, Deterrence, and the Incidence of Murder," *Journal of Applied Economics* 7, no. 1 (May 2004), pp. 163–193.

38. Paul R. Zimmerman, "Estimates of the Deterrent Effect of Alternative Execution Methods in the United States: 1978–2000," *American Journal of Economics and Sociology* 65, no. 4 (October 2006), pp. 909–941.

39. Richard Berk, "New Claims About Executions and General Deterrence: Déjà Vu All Over Again?" *Journal of Empirical Legal Studies* 2 (2005), pp. 303–330.

40. Jeffrey Fagan, "Death and Deterrence Redux: Science, Law and Causal Reasoning on Capital Punishment," *Ohio State Journal of Criminal Law* 4 (2006), pp. 255–320.

41. Quoted in Amnesty International, "Death Penalty and Race," http://www.amnestyusa.org/death-penalty/death-penalty-facts/death-penalty-and-race/page.do?id=1101091.

42. Ibid.

43 Ibid.

44. *Furman v. Georgia*, 408 U.S. 238 (1972).

45. *Gregg v. Georgia*, 428 U.S. 153 (1976).

46. *Roper v. Simmons,* 543 U.S. 551 (2005).

47. *Ford v. Wainwright*, 477 U.S. 399 (1986).

48. *Kennedy v. Louisiana*, 554 U.S. 407 (2008).

49. *Strickland v. Washington*, 466 U.S. 668 (1984)

50. *Witherspoon v. Illinois*, 391 U.S. 510 (1968).

51. *Baze v. Rees*, 553 U.S. 35 (2008).

52. *Hill v. Florida*, No. SC06-2 (2006).

53 Death Penalty Information Center, "The Innocence List," http://www.deathpenaltyinfo.org/innocence-list-those-freed-death-row.

54. Death Penalty Information Center: "The Death Penalty in Flux," May 2015, http://www.deathpenaltyinfo.org/death-penalty-flux.

55. National Coalition to Abolish the Death Penalty, "State by State Stats," May 2015, http://www.ncadp.org/map.

56. *Atkins v. Virginia,* 536 U.S. 304 (2002).

57. *Ring v. Arizona*, 536 U.S. 584 (2002).

58. *Roper v. Simmons*, 125 S.Ct. 1183 (2005)

59. Adapted from *Nevada Revised Statutes* 200.033.

60. Adapted from *Nevada Revised Statutes* 200.035.

61. "Criminal Appeals," http://www.justia.com/criminal/criminal-appeals/.

62. *Douglas v. California*, 372 U.S. 353 (1963).

63 *Griffin v. Illinois*, 351 U.S. 12 (1956).

64. *Ross v. Moffitt*, 417 U.S. 600 (1974).

Chapter 12

1. Jasmine Barclay, "Mass Incarceration Has Affected Me My Whole Life," *Huffington Post*, December 15, 2014, http://www.huffingtonpost.com/jasmine-barclay/mass-incarceration-has-af_b_6327872.html.

2. National Institute of Justice, "Beyond the Prison Bubble," November 3, 2011, http://www.nij.gov/journals/268/pages/prison-bubble.aspx.

3. See Brendan Kirby, "Adjusting to Freedom: Even the Mundane Can be Daunting for Mobile Ex-con," December 20, 2011, http://blog.al.com/live/2011/12/adjusting_to_freedom_even_the.html.

4. Erving Goffman, *Asylums* (Garden City, N.Y.: Anchor Books, 1961), p. 5.

5. Ibid., p. 6.

6. See, for example, Deanne Katz, "What's the Difference Between Jail and Prison?" *FindLaw,* December 10, 2012, http://blogs.findlaw.com/blotter/2012/12/whats-the-difference-between-jail-and-prison.html.

7. U.S. Department of Justice, Bureau of Justice Statistics, *Correctional Populations in the United States, 2013* (December 2014), p. 2, http://www.bjs.gov/content/pub/pdf/cpus13.pdf.

8. U.S. Department of Justice, Bureau of Justice Statistics, *Capital Punishment, 2013 – Statistical Tables* (December 2014),

http://www.bjs.gov/content/pub/pdf/cp13st.pdf.

9. U.S. Department of Justice, Bureau of Justice Statistics, *State Corrections Expenditures, FY 1982–2010* (Washington, D.C.: Author), p. 1, http://bjs.ojp.usdoj.gov/content/pub/pdf/scefy8210.pdf.

10. Ibid., pp. 1, 9.

11. See the Violent Offender Incarceration and Truth-in-Sentencing Incentive Grants program, Public Law 103–322, 108 Stat. 1796 (1994).

12. U.S. Department of Justice, Bureau of Justice Statistics Special Report: Truth in Sentencing in State Prisons (Washington, D.C.: Author, 1999), pp. 1–3.

13. "Attitudes Toward Whether the Criminal Justice System Should Try to Rehabilitate Criminals," *Sourcebook of Criminal Justice Statistics*, p. 139, http://www.albany.edu/sourcebook/pdf/t246.pdf.

14. T. Paul Louis and Jerry R. Sparger, "Treatment Modalities within Prison," *Are Prisons Any Better? Twenty Years of Correctional Reform*, ed. John W. Murphy and Jack E. Dison (Newbury Park, Calif.: Sage, 1990), p. 148; also see Francis T. Cullen, Paula Smith, Christopher T. Lowenkamp, and Edward J. Latessa, "Nothing Works Revisited: Deconstructing Farabee's *Rethinking Rehabilitation*," *Victims and Offenders* 4 (2009), pp. 101–123, http://www.uc.edu/content/dam/uc/ccjr/docs/articles/nothing_works_revisted.pdf.

15. Ibid., p. 149.

16. Ted Palmer, "The 'Effectiveness' Issue Today: An Overview," *Federal Probation* 42 (1983), pp. 3–10.

17. Ibid.

18. See D. A. Andrews, "Program Structure and Effective Correctional Practices: A Summary of the CAVIC Research," *Effective Correctional Treatment*, ed. Robert R. Ross and Paul Gendreau (Toronto, Canada: Butterworth, 1980); R. Peters, *Deviant Behavioral Contracting with Conduct Problem Youth* (Kingston, Canada: Queen's University, 1981).

19. Quoted in Andrews, "Program Structure and Effective Correctional Practices," p. 42.

20. Grace Wyler, "The Mass Incarceration Problem in America," July 26, 2014, https://news.vice.com/article/the-mass-incarceration-problem-in-america.

21. See David Garland, *Mass Imprisonment: Social Causes and Consequences* (Thousand Oaks, Calif.: SAGE), 2001.

22. Michelle Alexander, *The New Jim Crow* (New York: New Press, 2012), doi:10.1111/j.1743-4580.2012.00406.x.

23. Ibid.

24. Mark Karlin, "Michelle Alexander on the Irrational Race Bias of the Criminal Justice and Prison Systems," Truthout, http://truth-out.org/opinion/item/10629-truthout-interviews-michelle-alexander-on-the-irrational-race-bias-of-the-criminal-justice-and-prison-systems#.

25. Stephen Lurie, "The Only Man Who Can Fix Mass Incarceration Is Barack Obama," *The Atlantic,* November 12, 2014, http://www.theatlantic.com/politics/archive/2014/11/the-only-man-who-can-fix-mass-incarceration-is-barack-obama/382314/.

26. Gerard E. Lynch, "Ending Mass Incarceration," *Criminology & Public Policy* 13, no. 4 (November 2014), p. 561.

27. Michael Tonry, "Remodeling American Sentencing: A Ten-Step Blueprint for Moving Past Mass Incarceration," *Criminology & Public Policy* 13, no. 4 (November 2014), p. 503.

28. Ibid.

29. Richard P. Seiter, *Correctional Administration: Integrating Theory and Practice* (Upper Saddle River, N.J.: Prentice Hall, 2002), p. 11.

30. Franklin E. Zimring and Gordon J. Hawkins, *Deterrence: The Legal Threat in Crime Control* (Chicago: University of Chicago Press, 1973).

31. Joan Petersilia, "When Probation Becomes More Dreaded Than Prison," *Federal Probation* 54 (March 1990), pp. 27.

32. Ibid.

33 Ibid.

34. Ibid., p. 25.

35. Ibid.

36. Robert B. Levinson, "Classification: The Cornerstone of Corrections," *Prison and Jail Administration: Practice and Theory,* ed. Peter M. Carlson and Judith Simon Garrett (Boston: Jones and Bartlett, 2006), pp. 261–267.

37. Ibid., p. 262.

38. Ibid., pp. 262–263.

39. James Austin and Patricia L. Hardyman, *Objective Prison Classification: A Guide for Correctional Agencies* (Washington, D.C.: National Institute of Corrections, July 2004); also see R. Buchanan, "National Evaluation of Objective Prison Classification Systems: The Current State of the Art," *Crime & Delinquency* 32, no. 3 (1986), pp. 272–290.

40. Ibid., p. 192.

41. James A. Inciardi, *Criminal Justice,* 7th ed. (Fort Worth, Tex.: Harcourt Brace, 2001), p. 454.

42. Ibid., p. 194.

43 United States Bureau of Prisons, *Unit Management Manual* (Washington, D.C.: Author, 1977), p. 6.

44. Seiter, *Correctional Administration,* p. 196.

45. Federal Bureau of Prisons, "Prison Types & General Information," http://www.bop.gov/locations/institutions/index.jsp.

46. Federal Bureau of Prisons, "About the Bureau of Prisons," http://www.bop.gov/about/index.jsp.

47. Federal Bureau of Prisons, "Correctional Officer," http://www.bop.gov/jobs/positions/?p=Correctional%20Officer.

48. *Barber v. Thomas,* No. 09–5201. (9th Cir., 2010).; also see U.S. Department of Justice, United States Parole Commission, *History of the Federal Parole System,* http://www.usdoj.gov/uspc/history.pdf (accessed March 12, 2015).

49. Laura Sullivan, "Timeline: Solitary Confinement in U.S. Prisons," http://www.npr.org/templates/story/story.php?storyId=5579901.

50. Ibid.

51. Terry Frieden, "Reporters Get First Look Inside Mysterious Supermax Prison," *CNN.com/U.S.,* September 14, 2007, http://www.cnn.com.

52. Craig Haney, "Mental Health Issues in Long-Term Solitary and 'Supermax' Confinement," *Crime & Delinquency* 49, no. 1 (January 2003), pp. 124–156.

53 Ibid.

54. Jesenia Pizarro and Vanja M. K. Stenius, "Supermax Prisons: Their Rise, Current Practices, and Effect on Inmates," *The Prison Journal* 84, no. 2 (June 2004), pp. 248–264.

55. Ibid., p. 260.

56. *Madrid v. Gomez,* 889 F. Supp. 1146 (1995), at p. 1229.

57. *Jones-El v. Berge,* 374 F.3d 541 (7th Cir. 2004), at p. 1118.

58. "The Ten Worst Prisons in the World," http://www.thetoptenworld.com/violent_prisons.html.

59. U.S. Department of Justice, *Bureau of Justice Statistics Bulletin, Prison and Jail Inmates at Midyear 1998* (Washington, D.C.: U.S. Government Printing Office, 1999), pp. 1, 7.

60. U.S. Department of Justice, National Institute of Corrections, *Jail Resource Issues: What Every Funding Authority Needs to Know* (February 2012), https://s3.amazonaws.com/static.nicic.gov/Library/017372.pdf.

61. National Sheriffs' Association, *The State of Our Nation's Jails, 1982* (Washington, D.C.: Author, 1982), p. 55.

62. See a description of such a jail in use and its benefits, by the Corrections Center of Northwest Ohio, "The New Generation Direct Supervision Jail," http://www.ccnoregionaljail.org/newgenerationjail.htm.

63. Linda L. Zupan, *Jails: Reform and the New Generation Philosophy* (Cincinnati, Ohio: Anderson, 1991), p. 67.

64. Washington County (Oregon) Sheriff's Office, "Jail Programs for Inmates," http://www.co.washington.or.us/sheriff/jail/jailprograms/.

65. U.S. Department of Justice, National Institute of Justice Research in Brief, *Making Jails Productive* (Washington, D.C.: Author, 1987), p. 1.

66. Ibid., p. 16.

67. Thomas Hayden, "Putting Down a Riot," *U.S. News and World Report*, June 14, 2004, pp. 72–73.

68. Ibid.

69. Shane Peterson, "The Internet Moves Behind Bars," *Government Technology* (Supplement: *Crime and the Tech Effect*) (April 2001), p. 18.

70. Jim McKay, "Virtual Visits," *Government Technology* (October 2001), p. 46.

71. Nation of Change, "Prisoners Using Drones to Smuggle Contraband," August 18, 2014, http://www.nationofchange .org/prisoners-using-drones-smuggle-contraband-1408374489.

72. Douglas Ernst, "Special Delivery: Drone Drops Contraband into Georgia Prison Yard," *Washington Times*, November 27, 2013, http://www.washingtontimes .com/news/2013/nov/27/drone-drops-contraband-georgia-prison-yard/.

73. South University, "Prison Security Goes High-Tech," http://source .southuniversity.edu/prison-security-goes-hightech-24647.aspx.

74. "Start Jamming Prisoner Cell Phones," *The Post and Courier*, January 22, 2013, http://www .postandcourier.com/article/20130122/ PC1002/130129834/1268/start-jamming-prisoner-cell-phones& source=RSS.

75. Tod W. Burke, and Stephen S. Owen, "Cell Phones as Prison Contraband," FBI Law Enforcement Bulletin (July 2010), https://www2.fbi.gov/publications/ leb/2010/july2010/cell_feature.htm.

76. Ibid.

77. Tom McNichol, "Prison Cell-Phone Use a Growing Problem," *Time.com*, May 26, 2009, http://www.time.com/time/nation/ article/0,8599,1900859,00.html.

78. "Start Jamming Prisoner Cell Phones."

Chapter 13

1. *Whitley v. Albers,* 475 U.S. 312. (1986).

2. Judge Algenon Marbley found that the state's actions harmed and injured Lee and the prison must immediately resume her estrogen treatment. See *Lee v. Eller* (SD Ohio 2014); also see Andrew Welsh-Huggins, "Ohio Judge: Inmate Must Receive Requested Hormone Treatments," *Washington Time,* May 2, 2014, http://www.washingtontimes.com/ news/2014/may/2/hearing-continues-for-ohio-transgender-inmate-case/.

3. Diana Le, *The Stanford Daily*, "The Legacy of the Stanford Prison Experiment Lives on at Sundance," http://www. stanforddaily.com/2015/02/06/legacy-of-the-stanford-prison-experiment-lives-on-at-sundance/.

4. Justin Chang, "The Stanford Prison Experiment," *Variety*, http://variety .com/2015/film/reviews/sundance-film-review-the-stanford-prison-experiment-1201415952/.

5. John J. DiIulio Jr., *Governing Prisons: A Comparative Study of Correctional Management* (New York: Free Press, 1987), p. 167.

6. The Sentencing Project, " Incarceration," http://www.sentencingproject.org/ template/page.cfm?id=107.

7. BBC News, "World Prison Populations," http://news.bbc.co.uk/2/shared/spl/hi/ uk/06/prisons/html/nn2page1.stm.

8. Craig Haney, "Prison Effects in the Age of Mass Incarceration," *The Prison Journal* 20, no. 10 (2012), p. 3.

9. A. Goff, E. Rose, S. Rose, S., and D. Purves, "Does PTSD Occur in Sentenced Prison Populations? A Systematic Literature Review, *Criminal Behavior and Mental Health*, 17 (2007), pp. 152162; C. Heckman, K. Cropsey, and T. Olds-Davis, "Traumatic Stress Disorder Treatment in Correctional Settings: A Brief Review of the Empirical Literature and Suggestions for Future Research," *Psychotherapy: Theory, Research Practice, Training* 44 (2007), pp. 4653.

10. Jack Henry Abbott, *In the Belly of the Beast: Letters From Prison* (New York: Vintage Books, 1981), p. x.

11. Gresham Sykes, *The Society of Captives: A Study of Maximum Security Prison* (Princeton, N.J.: Princeton University Press, 1974), p. 65.

12. John Randolph Fuller, *Criminal Justice: Mainstream and Crosscurrents*, 2nd ed. (Upper Saddle River, N.J.: Prentice Hall, 2010), p. 396.

13. Sykes, *The Society of Captives*, p. 12.

14. Jeanne B. Stinchcomb, *Corrections: Past, Present, and Future* (Lanham, Md.: American Correctional Association, 2005), p. 307.

15. Ibid.

16. Gresham Sykes and Sheldon Messinger, "The Inmate Social Code," in *The Sociology of Punishment and Corrections*, eds. Normal Johnston, Leonard Savitz, and Marvin Wolfgang (New York: Wiley, 1970), pp. 401–408.

17. Craig Haney, "Prison Effects in the Age of Mass Incarceration," pp. 56.

18. H. Toch and K. Adams, *Acting Out: Maladaptive Behavior in Confinement* (Washington, D.C.: American Psychological Association, 2002).

19. P. Paulus, V. Cox, G. McCain, and J. Chandler, "Some Effects of Crowding in a Prison Environment," *Journal of Applied Social Psychology* 5 (1975), pp. 8691; G. McCain, V. Cox, and P. Paulus, "The Relationship Between Illness Complaints and Degree of Crowding in a Prison Environment," *Environment and Behavior*, 8 (1976), pp. 283290; D. D'Atri, "Psychophysiological Responses to Crowding," *Environment and Behavior* 7 (1975), pp. 237252.

20. *Price v. Johnston*, 334 U.S. 266, 144 F.2d 260 (1948).

21. *Rhodes v. Chapman*, 52 U.S. 347 (1981).

22. FindLaw for Legal Professionals, "Annotation 8: Eighth Amendment," http://constitution.findlaw.com/ amendment8/annotation08.html#f173.

23. *Whitley v. Albers*, 475 U.S. 312 (1986).

24. American Nonsmokers Rights Foundation, "100% Smokefree and Tobacco-Free Correctional Facilities," January 1, 2015, http://www.no-smoke .org/pdf/100smokefreeprisons.pdf.

25. Nicholas Grube, "Pelican Bay's Underground Economy," *Del Norte Triplicate,* March 31, 2007, http://www .triplicate.com/News/Local-News/ In-Focus-Pelican-Bays-underground-economy.

26. Matt Davis, "Five Surprising Things Inmates Use as Currency," March 16, 2014, http://www.therichest.com/ business/economy/five-surprising-things-prisoners-use-as-currency/4/.

27. Ibid.

28. U.S. Attorney's Office, District of Maryland, "Federal Racketeering Charges Filed Against Alleged Members and Associates of The 'Black Guerilla Family' Gang," http://www.justice. gov/usao/md/news/archive/Federal RacketeeringChargesFiledAgainst AllegedMembersandAssociatesofthe BlackGuerillaFamily.html.

29. Davis, "Five Surprising Things Inmates Use as Currency."

30. The Center for Constitutional Rights, "Torture: The Use of Solitary Confinement in U.S. Prisons," http:// ccrjustice.org/solitary-factsheet.

31. Ed Pilkington, "Angola Three Inmate in Longest Solitary Confinement Seeking Damages in Court," *The Guardian*, September 4, 2014, http://www .theguardian.com/world/2014/sep/04/ angola-three-albert-woodfox-lawsuit-louisiana-prison.

32. See, for example, Craig Haney, "Mental Health Issues in Long-Term Solitary and Supermax Confinement," *Crime and Delinquency* 49, no. 1 (2003): pp. 124125; Jeffrey L. Metzner and Jamie Fellner, "Solitary Confinement and Mental Illness in U.S. Prisons: A Challenge for Medical Ethics," *Journal of the American Academy of Psychiatry and the Law* 38 (2010), pp. 104108; Human Rights Watch, "Solitary Confinement and Mental Illness in U.S. Prisons: A Challenge for Medical Ethics," http://www.hrw.org/news/2010/03/22/ solitary-confinement-and-mental-

illness-us-prisonsas; Jason M. Breslow, "What Does Solitary Confinement Do to Your Mind?" PBS, April 22, 2014, http://www.pbs.org/wgbh/pages/frontline/criminal-justice/locked-up-in-america/what-does-solitary-confinement-do-to-your-mind/.

33. See, for example, Sharon Shalev, "Solitary Confinement and Supermax Prisons: A Human Rights and Ethical Analysis," *Journal of Forensic Psychology Practice* 11, no. 2/3 (2011), pp. 151183; American Public Health Association, "Solitary Confinement as a Public Health Issue," http://www.apha.org/policies-and-advocacy/public-health-policy-statements/policy-database/2014/07/14/13/30/solitary-confinement-as-a-public-health-issue; Stuart Grassian, "The Psychiatric Effects of Solitary Confinement," *Washington University Journal of Law and Policy* 22 (2006): pp. 325, 330.

34. *In re Medley*, 134 U.S. 160 (1890).

35. Shalev, "Solitary Confinement as a Public Health Issue" (see section entitled "From Re: Medley To Madrid: A Brief History of Legal Challenges to Solitary Confinement in the American Courts").

36. Bill Chappell, "County Will Pay $15.5 Million to Man Who Spent 22 Months in Solitary Confinement," NPR, March 7, 2013, http://www.npr.org/blogs/thetwo-way/2013/03/07/173761410/county-will-pay-15-5-million-to-man-who-spent-22-months-in-solitary-confinement.

37. State of Arizona, Office of the Governor, *The Morey Unit Hostage Incident: Preliminary Findings and Recommendations* (Phoenix, Ariz.: Author), p. 1.

38. Ohio History Central, "Lucasville Prison Riot," http://www.ohiohistorycentral.org/entry.php?rec=1634.

39. Tribune News Services, "Meet Captors' Demands, Hostages Urge," *Chicago Tribune News*, December 17, 1999, http://articles.chicagotribune.com/1999-12-17/news/9912170075_1_warden-todd-louvierre-jolie-sonnier-female-guard.

40. Associated Press, "Officials: Inmates Talked of Killing Jail Hostage," *St. Petersburg Times,* September 8, 2004, http://www.sptimes.com/2004/09/08/State/Officials__Inmates_ta.shtml.

41. National Institute of Justice, *Resolution of Prison Riots* (Washington, D.C.: U.S. Department of Justice, October 1995), pp. 1–2.

42. For an examination and comparison of these two extremely violent prison riots, see Sue Mahan, "An Orgy of Brutality at Attica and the Killing Ground at Santa Fe: A Comparison of Prison Riots," in *Prison Violence in America,* 2nd ed., ed. Michael

C. Braswell, Reid H. Montgomery Jr., and Lucien X. Lombardo (Cincinnati, Ohio: Anderson, 1994), pp. 253–264.

43. Thomas A. Zlaket, personal communication to Hon. Janet Napolitano, Governor of Arizona, October 25, 2004.

44. Kelly Taylor and Jilian Flight, *Hostage-Taking Incidents Involving Women Inmates: A Profile and Exploratory Investigation* (Ottawa, Ontario, Canada: Correctional Service of Canada, 2003), p. 5.

45. David Ensor, "U.S. Captures Mastermind of Achille Lauro Hijacking," CNN, http://www.cnn.com/2003/WORLD/meast/04/15/sprj.irq.abbas.arrested.

46. See, for example, Kenneth J. Peak, Eric Radli, Cecil Pearson, and Darin Balaam, "Hostage Situations in Detention Settings: Planning and Tactical Considerations," *FBI Law Enforcement Bulletin* 77, no. 10 (2008), pp. 1–14.

47. U.S. Department of Justice, Bureau of Justice Statistics, *Jail Inmates at Midyear 2013—Statistical Tables* (May 2014), p. 1, http://www.bjs.gov/content/pub/pdf/jim13st.pdf.

48. Quoted in Advisory Commission on Intergovernmental Relations, *Jails: Intergovernmental Dimensions of a Local Problem* (Washington, D.C.: Author, 1984), p. 1.

49. Gordon Hawkins, *The Prison* (Chicago: University of Chicago Press, 1976).

50. Jess Maghan, "Correctional Officers in a Changing Environment: 21st Century—USA," http://www.jmfcc.com/CorrOfficersChangingEnvirnmnt.pdf.

51. Ben M. Crouch, *The Keepers: Prison Guards and Contemporary Corrections* (Springfield, Ill.: Charles C Thomas, 1980), p. 73.

52. Peter Finn, *Addressing Correctional Officer Stress: Programs and Strategies* (Washington, D.C.: U.S. Department of Justice, National Institute of Justice, December 2000), p. 2, https://www.ncjrs.gov/pdffiles1/nij/183474.pdf.

53. Richard Hawkins and Geoffrey P. Alpert, *American Prison Systems: Punishment and Justice* (Upper Saddle River, N.J.: Prentice Hall, 1989), p. 340.

54. Ibid., p. 345.

55. See Lee H. Bowker, *Prison Victimization* (New York: Elsevier, 1980), Chapter 7.

56. Maghan, "Correctional Officers in a Changing Environment."

57. Ibid.

58. State Representative Bertram L. Podell, quoted in Linda Charlton, "Deaths Decried; Critics Disagree," *New York Times*, September 14, 1971, http://jfk.hood.edu/Collection/White%20%20Files/Attica/Attica%20050.pdf.

59. Ibid.

60. Ibid.

61. Adapted from Lucien X. Lombardo, *Guards Imprisoned: Correctional Officers*

at Work (Cincinnati, Ohio: Anderson, 1989), pp. 51–71.

62. Robert Bayer, personal communication, November 12, 2009.

63. John J. Dilulio Jr., *Governing Prisons: A Comparative Study of Correctional Management* (New York: Free Press, 1987), p. 37.

64. Bayer, personal communication.

65. John Slansky, personal communication, October 28, 1993.

66. Ibid.

67. Timothy J. Flanagan and Kathleen Maguire, eds., *Sourcebook of Criminal Justice Statistics 1991* (Washington, D.C.: U.S. Government Printing Office, 1992), p. 555.

68. Ibid.; also see Kathleen Maguire and Ann L. Pastore, eds., *Sourcebook of Criminal Justice Statistics 1995* (Washington, D.C.: U.S. Government Printing Office, 1996), p. 177.

69. Public Law No. 104-134, 110 Stat. 1321 [codified as amended in scattered sections of 18 U.S.C., 28 U.S.C., and 42 U.S.C.] (1996).

70. See 141 *Congressional Record* S14413 (daily ed., Sept. 27, 1995), Senator Robert Dole's statement in his introduction of the PLRA as a bill to the Senate. Senator Dole provided other examples of the frivolous litigation that he felt the PLRA was needed to cure: "insufficient storage locker space, a defective haircut by a prison barber, [and] the failure of prison officials to invite a prisoner to a pizza party for a departing prison employee."

71. U.S. Courts, "Caseload Statistics, 2009," Table C3, http://www.uscourts.gov/Statistics/FederalJudicial Case loadStatistics/Federal Judicial CaseloadStatistics2009.aspx.

72. U.S. Department of Justice, Bureau of Justice Statistics, *Prisoners in 2011* (Washington, D.C.: Author, December 2012), p. 9, http://bjs.ojp.usdoj.gov/content/pub/pdf/p11.pdf.

73. Thomas E. Feucht and Andrew Keyser, *Reducing Drug Use in Prisons: Pennsylvania's Approach* (Washington, D.C.: National Institute of Justice Journal, October 1999), p. 11.

74. Ibid., pp. 11–12.

75. Ibid., pp. 14–15.

76. Federal Bureau of Investigation, "Table 33. Ten-Year Arrest Trends by Sex, 2002–2011," *Crime in the United States—2011* (Washington, D.C.: U.S. Department of Justice), http://www.fbi.gov/about-us/cjis/ucr/crime-in-the-u.s/2011/crime-in-the-u.s.-2011/tables/table-33.

77. American Civil Liberties Union, "Women in Prison," http://www.aclu.org/prisoners-rights/women-prison.

78. Sandra Enos, *Mothering From the Inside: Parenting in a Women's Prison* (Albany: Sate University of New York Press, 2001).

79. Institute on Women and Criminal Justice, "Mothers, Infants and Imprisonment: A National Look at Prison Nurseries and Community-Based Alternatives" (May 2009), p. 9, http://www.wpaonline.org/pdf/Mothers%20Infants%20and%20Imprisonment%202009.pdf.

80. U.S. Department of Justice, Bureau of Justice Statistics, *Prisoners in 2013* (September 2014), pp. 1516.

81. See World Health Organization Europe, *Women's Health in Prison: Correcting Gender Inequities in Prison Health* (2009), http://www.euro.who.int/__data/assets/pdf_file/0004/76513/E92347.pdf.

82. Barbara A. Hotelling, "Perinatal Needs of Pregnant, Incarcerated Women," National Center for Biotechnology Information (Spring 2008), http://www.ncbi.nlm.nih.gov/pmc/articles/PMC2409166/.

83. ACLU Briefing Paper, "The Shackling of Pregnant Women & Girls in U.S. Prisons, Jails & Youth Detention Centers," https://www.aclu.org/files/assets/anti-shackling_briefing_paper_stand_alone.pdf.

84. *Turner v. Safley*, 482 U.S. 78, 89 (1987).

85. *Forts v. Ward*, 621 F.2d 1210, 1214 16 (2d Cir. 1980).

86. In *Jordan v. Gardner*, 986 F.2d 1521, 1523 (9th Cir. 1993), a male guard at the WCCW conducted (as per the policy) such a random, full-body, clothed search of a female prisoner. He squeezed her breasts and probed her crotch as well as the seams in her crotch area. While being searched, the female inmate, being distressed and shocked, grabbed ahold of nearby cell bars to the extent that later, her fingers had to be pried loose from them. The federal district court concluded that the cross-gender clothed body search policy constituted cruel and unusual punishment in violation of the Eighth Amendment.

87. For an excellent overview of incarcerated women's rights, see "A Jailhouse Lawyer's Manual, Chapter 41, Special Issues of Women Prisoners," *Columbia Human Rights Law Review* (9th ed., 2011), http://www3.law.columbia.edu/hrlr/jlm/chapter-41.pdf.

88. Ibid.

89. U.S. Department of Justice, Bureau of Justice Statistics, *Sourcebook of Criminal Justice Statistics Online* (Washington, D.C.: Author), p. 53, http://www.albany.edu/sourcebook/index.html.

90. Pam Belluck, "Mentally Ill Inmates Are at Risk Isolated, Suit Says," *New York Times*, March 9, 2007, p. A10.

91. U.S. Department of Justice, "About Violent Gangs," http://www.justice.gov/criminal/ocgs/gangs/.

92. National Gang Intelligence Center, *National Gang Threat Assessment 2011* (Washington, D.C.: U.S. Department of Justice), http://www.fbi.gov/stats-services/publications/2011-national-gang-threat-assessment/2011-national-gang-threat-assessment-emerging-trends, p. 11.

93 Joel Samaha, *Criminal Justice* (St. Paul, Minn.: West, 1988), p. 558.

94. James Jacobs, *Stateville: The Penitentiary in Mass Society* (Chicago: University of Chicago Press, 1977).

95. John Irwin, *Prisons in Turmoil* (Boston: Little, Brown, 1980).

96. George M. Camp and Camille G. Camp, *The Correctional Year Book* (South Salem, N.Y.: Criminal Justice Institute, 1987).

97. Death Penalty Information Center, "States With and Without the Death Penalty as of July 1, 2015," http://www.deathpenaltyinfo.org/states-and-without-death-penalty.

98. See Robert Johnson, *Death Work: A Study of the Modern Execution Process,* 2nd ed. (Belmont, Calif.: West/Wadsworth, 1998); Robert Johnson, "This Man Has Expired," *Commonweal* (January 13, 1989), pp. 9–15.

99. U.S Department of Justice, Bureau of Justice Statistics, *Capital Punishment, 2013—Statistical Tables* (December 2014), p. 1, http://www.bjs.gov/content/pub/pdf/cp13st.pdf.

100. U.S Department of Justice, Bureau of Justice Statistics, *Capital Punishment, 2010—Statistical Tables*, p. 6.

101. Amnesty International, "Figures on the Death Penalty," http://www.amnesty.org/en/death-penalty/numbers.

102. Death Penalty Information Center, "Executions by Year Since 1976," http://www.deathpenaltyinfo.org/executions-year.

103. Amnesty International, "Death Penalty 2011: Alarming Levels of Executions in the Few Countries That Kill," http://www.amnesty.org/en/news/death-penalty-2011-alarming-levels-executions-few-countries-kill-2012-03-27.

104. Ibid.

105. Ibid.

106. *Roper v. Simmons*, 543 U.S. 551 (2005).

107. *Atkins v. Virginia*, 536 U.S. 304 (2002).

108. Jeremy Travis, Amy L. Solomon, and Michelle Waul, *From Prison to Home—The Dimensions and Consequences of Prisoner Reentry* (Washington, D.C.: The Urban Institute, 2001), pp. 6, 9.

109. Pamela K. Lattimore, "The Challenges of Reentry," *Corrections Today* 69, no. 2 (April 2007), p. 90.

110. Richard P. Seiter, *Correctional Administration: Integrating Theory and Practice*, 2nd ed. (Upper Saddle River, NJ: Prentice Hall, 2012), pp. 451452.

111. Ibid.

112. *Ruffin v. Commonwealth*, 62 Va. 790 (1871).

113 *Cooper v. Pate*, 378 U.S. 546, 384 S Ct 1733 (1964).

114. *Johnson v. Avery*, 393 U.S. 483, 89 S.Ct. 747 (1969).

115. *Bounds v. Smith*, 430 U.S. 817, 97 S.Ct. 1491 (1977).

116. *Cruz v. Beto*, 405 U.S. 319, 92 S. Ct. 1079 (1972).

117. *Procunier v. Martinez*, 416 U.S. 396, 94 S. Ct. 1800 (1974).

118. *Estelle v. Gamble*, 429 U.S. 974, 97 S.Ct. 285 (1976).

119. *Wolff v. McDonnell*, 418 U.S. 539, 394 S. Ct. 296 (1974).

120. James Alan Fox, "Lovesick Over Charles Manson. Really?" *USA Today*, November 19, 2014, http://www.usatoday.com/story/opinion/2014/11/19/james-alan-fox-manson-nuptials/19279531/.

121. Brad Reed, "Charles Manson Calls Off Wedding After Learning His Fiance Is Too Evil Even for Him," BGR Media, http://bgr.com/2015/02/10/charles-manson-wedding-called-off/.

122. Fox, "Lovesick Over Charles Manson. Really?" http://www.usatoday.com/story/opinion/2014/11/19/james-alan-fox-manson-nuptials/19279531/.

123. Ibid.; also see NBCNews.com, "Charles Manson Marriage License to Expire Without a Wedding," http://www.nbcnews.com/news/us-news/charles-manson-marriage-license-expire-without-wedding-n298936.

Chapter 14

1. Spencer Hsu, "Hospital Joins Bid for Full Release of Reagan Shooter John W. Hinckley Jr.," *Washington Post*, April 22, 2015, http://www.washingtonpost.com/local/attorneys-for-john-hinckley-jr-argue-for-his-full-time-release/2015/04/22/f3bb01a6-e901-11e4-9a6a-c1ab95a0600b_story.html; also see Michael Winter, "John Hinckley: The Man Who Shot Brady, Reagan," *USA Today*, August 15, 2014, http://www.usatoday.com/story/news/nation/2014/08/04/james-brady-john-hinckley/13598699/.

2. Peter J. Benekos, "Beyond Reintegration: Community Corrections in a Retributive Era," *Federal Probation* 54 (March 1990), p. 53.

3 See the President's Commission on Law Enforcement and Administration of Justice, *Task Force Report: Corrections* (Washington, D.C.: U.S. Government Printing Office, 1967), p. 7.

4. Benekos, "Beyond Reintegration," p. 53.

5. Belinda R. McCarthy, *Intermediate Punishments: Intensive Supervision, Home Confinement, and Electronic Surveillance* (Monsey, N.Y.: Criminal Justice Press, 1987), p. 3.

6. Barry J. Nidorf, "Community Corrections: Turning the Crowding Crisis Into Opportunities," *Corrections Today* (October 1989), p. 85.

7. Benekos, "Beyond Reintegration," p. 54.

8. Although neither the word *probation* nor today's definition of it appear in the Bible, it was historically assumed that all mankind was under the sentence of eternal death—an endless life in misery during this life. However, humans could escape this sentence through repentance and faith in Christ; this was man's "probation," an opportunity to escape hell and secure heaven. If he failed to improve this opportunity, and died impenitent, the sentence was irrevocably executed and the man was eternally lost. See Tentmaker, "Probation," http://www.tentmaker.org/books/SpiritOfTheWord/014Probation.htm.

9. Howard Abadinsky, *Probation and Parole: Theory and Practice,* 3rd ed. (Englewood Cliffs, N.J.: Prentice Hall, 1987), p. 18.

10. Lawrence M. Friedman, *A History of American Law* (New York: Simon and Schuster, 1973), p. 518.

11. Paul F. Cromwell Jr., George C. Killinger, Hazel B. Kerper, and Charles Walker, *Probation and Parole in the Criminal Justice System,* 2nd ed. (St. Paul, Minn.: West, 1985).

12. John Augustus, *John Augustus, First Probation Officer* (Montclair, N.J.: Patterson Smith, 1972), pp. 4–5.

13. John Augustus, *A Report of the Labors of John Augustus* (Boston: Wright & Hasty, 1852) (republished in 1984 by the American Probation and Parole Association, Lexington, Ky., pp. 96–97).

14. Abadinsky, *Probation and Parole*, p. 143.

15. Torsten Eriksson, *The Reformers: An Historical Survey of Pioneer Experiments in the Treatment of Criminals* (New York: Elsevier, 1976), p. 81.

16. Abadinsky, *Probation and Parole*, pp. 146–147.

17. The issues concerned whether parole (1) infringed on the power of the judiciary to sentence, the governor to pardon, or the legislature to determine penalty levels; (2) denied prisoners due process; or (3) constituted cruel and unusual punishment.

18. U.S. Attorney General's Survey of Release Procedures, *Parole*, Vol. 4 (New York: Arno Press, 1974), p. 20.

19. Sheldon L. Messinger, "Introduction," *The Question of Parole: Retention, Reform, or Abolition?* ed. Andrew von Hirsch and Kathleen J. Hanrahan (Cambridge, Mass.: Ballinger, 1970), pp. xviii–xix.

20. U.S. Attorney General's Survey of Release Procedures, *Parole*, p. 20.

21. U.S. Department of Justice, Bureau of Justice Statistics, *Correctional Populations in the United States, 2013* (December 2014), http://www.bjs.gov/content/pub/pdf/cpus13.pdf.

22. Laura M. Maruschak and Erika Parks, *Probation and Parole in the United States, 2011*, p. 7, http://www.bjs.gov/content/pub/pdf/ppus11.pdf.

23. Robert M. Regoli and John D. Hewitt, *Exploring Criminal Justice: The Essentials* (Sudbury, Mass.: Jones and Bartlett, 2010), p. 316.

24. Adapted from Michael Muskal, "Two of Casey Anthony's Four Convictions Overturned by Appeals Court," *Los Angeles Times,* January 25, 2013, http://www.latimes.com/news/nation/nationnow/la-na-nn-casey-anthony-appeals-court-20130125,0,3022534.story; "Judge Perry Rules on Casey Probation," *WESH Orlando,* August 12, 2011, http://www.wesh.com/news/casey-anthony-extended-coverage/Judge-Perry-Rules-On-Casey-Probation/-/13479888/13130886/-/item/0/-/po7t4vz/-/index.html. Judge Perry ruled that Anthony must serve a year of supervised probation, with the Florida Department of Corrections to keep Anthony's residential information confidential. Perry said in the order that he did not want any information released that could lead to the discovery of her location.

25. Laura M. Maruschak and Erika Parks, *Probation and Parole in the United States, 2011* (Washington, D.C.: U.S. Department of Justice, Bureau of Justice Statistics, November 2012), p. 6, http://www.bjs.gov/content/pub/pdf/ppus11.pdf.

26. Ibid.; Erinn J. Herberman and Thomas P. Bonczar, *Probation and Parole in the United States, 2013* (Washington, D.C.: U.S. Department of Justice, Bureau of Justice Statistics, January 2015), http://www.bjs.gov/content/pub/pdf/ppus13.pdf.

27. *Mempa v. Rhay*, 389 U.S. 128 (1967).

28. *Gagnon v. Scarpelli*, 411 U.S. 778 (1973).

29. Maruschak and Parks, *Probation and Parole in the United States, 2011*, p. 20.

30. Park Dietz, "Hypothetical Criteria for the Prediction of Individual Criminality," *Dangerousness: Probability and Prediction, Psychiatry, and Public Policy*, ed. Christopher Webster, Mark Ben-Aron, and Stephen Hucker (Cambridge, UK: Cambridge University Press, 1985), p. 32.

31. *Morrissey v. Brewer*, 92 S.Ct. 2593 (1972).

32. Ibid.

33. Manson was denied parole for the 12th time in April 2012. The parole board duly noted that he had recently bragged to a prison psychologist, "I'm special. I'm not like the average inmate. I have spent my life in prison. I have put five people in the grave. I am a very dangerous man." The board stated: "This panel can find nothing good as far as suitability factors go." See Christina Ng, "Charles Manson Denied Parole After Saying He Is a 'Very Dangerous Man,'" *ABC News*, April 11, 2012, http://abcnews.go.com/US/charles-manson-denied-parole-dangerous-man/story?id=16111128.

34. Council of State Governments Justice Center, *The Impact of Probation and Parole Populations on Arrests in Four California Cities* (January 2013), p. 4, http://www.cdcr.ca.gov/Reports/docs/External-Reports/CAL-CHIEFS-REPORT.pdf.

35. Ibid., p. 1.

36. Ibid., p. 17.

37. Ibid., p. 6.

38. U.S. Bureau of Labor Statistics, "Occupational Outlook Handbook: Probation Officers and Correctional Treatment Specialists," http://www.bls.gov/ooh/Community-and-Social-Service/Probation-officers-and-correctional-treatment-specialists.htm#tab-2.

39. Ibid.

40. H. S. Ntuli, V. I. Khoza, J. M. Ras, and P. J. Potgieter, "Role Conflict in Correctional Supervision," *Acta Criminologica* 20, no. 4 (2007), pp. 85–95.

41. Ibid.

42. John Conrad, "The Pessimistic Reflections of a Chronic Optimist," *Federal Probation* 55 (June 1991), pp. 4–9.

43. Matthew T. DeMichele, *Probation and Parole's Growing Caseloads and Workload Allocation: Strategies for Managerial Decision Making* (Lexington, Ky.: American Probation and Parole Association), pp. 14–15, http://www.appa-net.org/eweb/docs/appa/pubs/SMDM.pdf.

44. M. Claxton, N. Sinclair, and R. Hanson, "Felons on Probation Often Go Unwatched," *Detroit News*, December 10, 2002, p. 2.

45. DeMichele, *Probation and Parole's Growing Caseloads and Workload Allocation*, pp. 13, 33.

46. Shawn E. Small and Sam Torres, "Arming Probation Officers: Enhancing Public Confidence and Officer Safety," *Federal Probation* 65, no. 3 (2001), pp. 24–28.

47. Richard P. Seiter, *Correctional Administration: Integrating Theory and Practice* (Upper Saddle River, N.J.: Prentice Hall, 2002), p. 387.

48. U.S. Department of Justice, Bureau of Justice Statistics, *U.S. Jail Population Declines for Third Consecutive Year* (Washington, D.C.: Author, April 25, 2012), http://bjs.ojp.usdoj.gov/content/pub/press/jim11stpr.cfm.

49. Howard Abadinsky, *Probation and Parole: Theory and Practice*, 7th ed. (Upper Saddle River, N.J.: Prentice Hall, 2000), p. 410.

50. Joan Petersilia and Susan Turner, *Evaluating Intensive Supervision Probation/Parole: Results of a Nationwide Experiment* (Washington, D.C.: National Institute of Justice, 1993).

51. Lawrence A. Bennett, "Practice in Search of a Theory: The Case of Intensive Supervision—An Extension of an Old Practice," *American Journal of Criminal Justice* 12 (1988), pp. 293–310.

52. Ibid., p. 293.

53. This information was compiled from ISP brochures and information from the Oregon Department of Corrections by Joan Petersilia.

54. Todd R. Clear and Patricia R. Hardyman, "The New Intensive Supervision Movement," *Crime & Delinquency* 36 (January 1990), pp. 42–60.

55. Ibid., p. 44.

56. Barbara A. Sims, "Questions of Corrections: Public Attitudes Toward Prison and Community-Based Programs," *Corrections Management Quarterly* 1, no. 1 (1997), p. 54.

57. Jeffery T. Ulmer, "Intermediate Sanctions: A Comparative Analysis of the Probability and Severity of Recidivism," *Sociological Inquiry* 71, no. 2 (Spring 2001), pp. 164–193.

58. Ibid., p. 184.

59. Ibid., p. 185.

60. Bureau of Justice Assistance, *Offender Supervision With Electronic Technology: Community Corrections Resource,* 2nd ed. (Washington, D.C.: U.S. Department of Justice, 2009), p. 16, http://www.appa-net.org/eweb/docs/APPA/pubs/OSET_2.pdf.

61. House Arrest Services, "Welcome to House Arrest Services," https://housearrest.com/.

62. Annesley K. Schmidt, "Electronic Monitors: Realistically, What Can Be Expected?" *Federal Probation* 59 (June 1991), pp. 47–53.

63. Abadinsky, *Probation and Parole,* 7th ed., p. 428.

64. David Brauer, "Satellite 'Big Brother' Tracks Ex-Inmates," *Chicago Tribune,* December 18, 1998, p. 31.

65. Jeanne B. Stinchcomb and Vernon B. Fox, *Introduction to Corrections*, 5th ed. (Upper Saddle River, N.J.: Prentice Hall, 1999), p. 165.

66. Gaylene Styve Armstrong, Angela R. Gover, and Doris Layton MacKenzie, "The Development and Diversity of Correctional Boot Camps," *Turnstile Justice: Issues in American Corrections,* ed. Rosemary L. Gido and Ted Alleman (Upper Saddle River, N.J.: Prentice Hall, 2002), pp. 115–130.

67. Doris Layton MacKenzie, "Boot Camp Prisons and Recidivism in Eight States," *Criminology* 33, no. 3 (1995), pp. 327–358.

68. Doris Layton MacKenzie and Alex Piquero, "The Impact of Shock Incarceration Programs on Prison Crowding," *Crime & Delinquency* 40, no. 2 (April 1994), pp. 222–249.

69. John Ashcroft, Deborah J. Daniels, and Sarah V. Hart, *Correctional Boot Camps: Lessons from a Decade of Research* (Washington, D.C.: U.S. Department of Justice, Office of Justice Programs, June 2003), p. 2.

70. Ibid.

71. Dale G. Parent, "Day Reporting Centers: An Evolving Intermediate Sanction," *Federal Probation* 60 (December 1996), pp. 51–54.

72. Liz Marie Marciniak, "The Addition of Day Reporting to Intensive Supervision Probation: A Comparison of Recidivism Rates," *Federal Probation* 64 (June 2000), pp. 34–39.

73 See Washington State Institute for Public Policy, *Predicting Criminal Recidivism: A Systematic Review of Offender Risk Assessments in Washington State* (February 2014), http://www.wsipp.wa.gov/ReportFile/1554/Wsipp_Predicting-Criminal-Recidivism-A-Systematic-Review-of-Offender-Risk-Assessments-in-Washington-State_Final-Report.pdf.

74. Bureau of Justice Assistance and the Council of State Governments, *Integrated Reentry and Employment Strategies: Reducing Recidivism and Promoting Job Readiness* (September 2013), p. 10, https://www.bja.gov/Publications/CSG-Reentry-and-Employment.pdf.

75. Ibid., p. 12.

76. Jan Looman and Jeffrey Abracen, "The Risk Need Responsivity Model of Offender Rehabilitation: Is There Really a Need for a Paradigm Shift," *International Journal of Behavioral Consultation and Therapy* 8 (34) (2013), p. 32.

77. U.S. Department of Justice, National Institute of Justice, "Restorative Justice, http://www.ojp.usdoj.gov/nij/topics/courts/restorative-justice/welcome.htm.

78. U.S. Department of Justice, National Institute of Justice, "Fundamental Concepts of Restorative Justice," http://www.ojp.usdoj.gov/nij/topics/courts/restorative-justice/fundamental-concepts.htm.

79. Ibid.

Chapter 15

1. Fox Butterfield, "Woman Who Killed Mother Denied Harvard Admission," *New York Times*, April 8, 1995, http://www.nytimes.com/1995/04/08/us/woman-who-killed-mother-denied-harvard-admission.html.

2. R. Pickett, *House of Refuge: Origins of Juvenile Reform in New York State 1815–1857* (Syracuse, N.Y.: Syracuse University Press, 1969), p. 21.

3 M. Platt, *The Child Savers: The Invention of Delinquency,* 2nd ed. (Chicago, Ill.: University of Chicago Press, 1977).

4. *People ex rel O'Connell* v. *Turner,* 55 Ill. 280, 283-84, 287 (1870).

5. 1899 Ill. Laws 132 *et seq.*

6. Victor L. Streib, *Death Penalty for Juveniles* (Bloomington: Indiana University Press, 1987).

7. Robert E. Shepherd Jr., "The Juvenile Court at 100 Years: A Look Back," *Juvenile Justice* 6, no. 2 (December 1999), http://www.ncjrs.gov/html/ojjdp/jjjournal1299/2.html.

8. Ibid.

9. Ibid.

10. Julian Mack, "The Juvenile Court," *Harvard Law Review* 23 (1909), pp. 104–122.

11. P.L. 93-415, 42 U.S.C. 5601 *et seq.*

12. David W. Roush, *A Desktop Guide to Good Juvenile Detention Practice* (Washington, D.C.: Office of Juvenile Justice and Delinquency Prevention, 1996), pp. 26–27.

13 Ibid., pp. 23–24.

14. Adapted from Gus Martin, *Juvenile Justice: Process and Systems* (Thousand Oaks, Calif.: Sage, 2005), pp. 64–67.

15. Both the text and the diagram are from U.S. Department of Justice, Office of Juvenile Justice and Delinquency Prevention Programs, *Juvenile Justice Structure and Process: Case Flow Diagram,* http://www.ojjdp.gov/ojstatbb/structure_process/case.html.

16. Adapted from U.S. Department of Justice, Bureau of Justice Statistics, "The Juvenile Justice System," http://www.ojp.usdoj.gov/bjs/justsys.htm#sentencing.

17. Steven M. Cox, Jennifer M. Allen, Robert D. Hanser, and John J. Conrad, *Juvenile Justice: A Guide to Theory, Policy, and Practice* (Boston: Pearson, 2014), p. 104.

18. See John Braithwaite, *Crime, Shame and Reintegration* (Cambridge, UK: Cambridge University Press, 1989).

19. Michael Rocque and Raymond Paternoster, "Understanding the Antecedents of the 'School-to Jail' Link: The Relationship Between Race and School Discipline," *Journal of Criminal Law & Criminology* 101, no. 2 (2011), pp. 633643; see also Carla Amurao, "Fact Sheet: How Bad Is the School-to-Prison Pipeline?" *Tavis Smiley Reports,* http://www.pbs.org/wnet/tavissmiley/tsr/education-under-arrest/school-to-prison-pipeline-fact-sheet/.

20. Mary Ellen Flannery, "The School-to-Prison Pipeline: Time to Shut It Down,"

NEA Today, January 5, 2015, http://neatoday.org/2015/01/05/school-prison-pipeline-time-shut/.

21. Ibid.

22. Stephanie Francis Ward, "How Do We Fix the School-to-Prison Pipeline?" *American Bar Association Journal,* August 4, 2014, http://www.abajournal.com/news/article/podcast_monthly_episode_53.

23. Pew Charitable Trusts, *Commission on Children in Foster Care, 2009,* http://www.pewtrusts.org/en/archived-projects/commission-on-children-in-foster-care.

24. Dean John Champion, Alida V. Merlo, and Peter J. Benekos, *The Juvenile Justice System: Delinquency, Processing, and the Law,* 6th ed. (New York: Prentice Hall, 2009), p. 435.

25. Ibid., p. 436.

26. Ibid., p. 437.

27. Ibid., pp. 438–439.

28. Ibid., pp. 440–441.

29. Ibid., p. 442.

30. American Bar Association, "Abuse and Inefficiency in Juvenile Offender Boot Camps: Is Regulation the Answer?" http://www.americanbar.org/content/dam/aba/publishing/criminal_justice_section_newsletter/crimjust_juvjust_newsletterjune09_june09_pdfs_bootcamps.authcheckdam.pdf.

31. Testimony Before the Committee on Education and Labor, House of Representatives, "Residential Treatment Programs: Concerns Regarding Abuse and Death in Certain Programs for Troubled Youth," 110th Cong. (2007) (statement of Gregory D. Kutz, Managing Director of Forensic Audits and Special Investigations).

32. Cox et al., *Juvenile Justice,* p. 446.

33. Harvard Law School, International Human Rights Clinic, Human Rights Program, *Preventable Tragedy in Panama: Unnecessary Deaths and Rights Violations in Juvenile Detention Centers* (May 2011), pp. 48, http://hrp.law.harvard.edu/wp-content/uploads/2011/06/panama-juvenile-detention-alianza-asamblea-harvard-6-20.pdf. International standards of treatment for juveniles are promulgated by the United Nations; see United Nations, the Convention on the Rights of the Child, http://www.ohchr.org/en/professionalinterest/pages/crc.aspx.

34. For a full description of the standards of treatment for juveniles under the Convention on the Rights of the Child, see United Nations, http://www.ohchr.org/en/professionalinterest/pages/crc.aspx.

35. U.S. Department of Justice, Office of Juvenile Justice and Delinquency Prevention, *Youth Gangs* (December 1997), p. 1, file:///C:/Users/Ken/AppData/Local/Microsoft/Windows/Temporary%20Internet%20Files/Content.IE5/2KMZTFCP/youthgangs.pdf.

36. National Gang Center, "Frequently Asked Questions About Gangs," http://www.nationalgangcenter.gov/About/FAQ#q1.

37. Ibid.

38. See U.S. Department of Justice, Office of Juvenile Justice and Delinquency Prevention, *NGC Newsletter* (Winter 2013), p. 1.

39. Catherine H. Conly, Patricia Kelly, Paul Mahanna, and Lynn Warner, *Street Gangs: Current Knowledge and Strategies* (Washington, D.C.: U.S. Department of Justice, National Institute of Justice, 1993).

40. See Homeboy Industries, http://www.homeboyindustries.org/.

41. Homeboy Industries, "What We Do," http://www.homeboyindustries.org/what-we-do/faq/.

42. Daniel P. Mears and Jeremy Travis, "Youth Development and Reentry," *Youth Violence and Juvenile Justice* 2, no. 1 (January 2004), pp. 320; also see David Altschuler and Shay Bilchik, "Critical Elements of Juvenile Reentry in Research and Practice," April 21, 2014, http://csgjusticecenter.org/youth/posts/critical-elements-of-juvenile-reentry-in-research-and-practice/.

43. Adapted from ibid., p. 8.

44. *Kent v. United States,* 383 U.S. 541 (1966).

45. American Bar Association, "Still Seeking the Promise of *Gault*: Juveniles and the Right to Counsel," http://www.abanet.org/crimjust/juvjus/cjmag/18-2shep.html.

46. American Bar Association, "For Schools: Lessons," http://www.abanet.org/publiced/lawday/schools/lessons/handout_gault.html.

47. *Gault v. Arizona,* 387 US 1 (1967).

48. Ibid., p. 14.

49. *In Re Winship,* 397 U.S. 358 (1970).

50. *McKeiver v. Pennsylvania,* 403 U.S. 528 (1971).

51. *Breed v. Jones,* 421 U.S. 519 (1975).

52. *Roper v. Simmons,* 543 U.S. 551 (2005).

53. *J. D. B. v. North Carolina,* No. 09–11121 (2011).

54. *Miller v. Alabama,* 132 S. Ct. 2455 (2012); *Jackson v. Hobbs,* No. 10–9647 (2012).

55. See *Graham v. Florida,* 130 S. Ct. (2010).

Chapter 16

1. Jerry Markon, "Amid Threats Abroad, Homeland Security Chief Keeps Eye on Homegrown Terrorism," *Washington Post,* October 1, 2014, http://www.washingtonpost.com/blogs/federal-eye/wp/2014/10/01/amid-threats-abroad-homeland-security-chief-keeps-eye-on-homegrown-terrorism/.

2. Ibid.

3. See, for example, a discussion of the "lone wolf model" of terrorism now in use here and abroad—and discussed in al-Qaeda publications—in Lori Hinnant, "Intel Dilemma in Boston, London, Paris Attacks," *Associated Press,* May 31, 2013, http://abcnews.go.com/International/wireStory/intel-dilemma-boston-london-paris-attacks-19294987#.UazbZuDn_cs.

4. See Kenneth J. Peak, *Policing America: Challenges and Best Practices,* 8th ed. (Columbus, Ohio: Pearson Education, in press).

5. See, for example, "Reconstructing the Scene of the Boston Marathon Bombing," *New York Times,* April 23, 2013, http://www.nytimes.com/interactive/2013/04/17/us/caught-in-the-blast-at-the-boston-marathon.html?ref=bostonmarathon.

6. See Kenneth J. Peak, *Policing America: Challenges and Best Practices,* 8th ed. (Columbus, OH: Pearson Education, 2014), pp. 312–314.

7. Ibid.

8. "Terror in Paris: A Timeline," CNN, January 2015, http://www.cnn.com/2015/01/09/europe/charlie-hebdo-paris-shooting/.

9. Daniel Howden, "Terror in Westgate Mall," *Guardian,* October 4, 2013, http://www.cnn.com/2015/01/09/europe/charlie-hebdo-paris-shooting/; see also Joyce Hackel, "In Minnesota, ISIS May Be Building on the Recruiting Networks Once Used by Other Terror Groups," PRI, March 27, 2015, http://www.pri.org/stories/2015-03-27/minnesota-isis-may-be-building-recruiting-networks-once-used-other-terror-groups.

10. Elisa Mala and J. David Goodman, "At Least 80 Dead in Norway Shooting," *New York Times,* July 22, 2011, http://www.nytimes.com/2011/07/23/world/europe/23oslo.html.

11. Quoted in M. K. Rehm and W. R. Rehm, "Terrorism Preparedness Calls for Proactive Approach," *The Police Chief* (December 2000), pp. 38–43.

12. D. Westneat, "Terrorists Go Green," *U.S. News and World Report,* June 4, 2001, p. 28; see also "SUVs Torched in Pennsylvania," *Reno Gazette Journal,* January 5, 2003, p. 4A.

13. Michael Morell, "The Gathering Threat," *Time,* May 25, 2015, pp. 2021.

14. INTERPOL, "Cybercrime," http://www.interpol.int/Crime-areas/Cybercrime/Cybercrime.

15. "The World's Most Hacked," *Time,* June 8, 2015, p. 10.

16. Riley Waters, "Cyber Attacks on U.S. Companies in 2014," The Heritage Foundation, Issue Brief #4289 on National Security and Defense, October 27, 2014, http://www.heritage.org/research/

reports/2014/10/cyber-attacks-on-us-companies-in-2014.

17. "Admit Nothing and Deny Everything," *Economist*, June 8, 2013, http://www.economist.com/news/china/21579044-barack-obama-says-he-ready-talk-xi-jinping-about-chinese-cyber-attacks-makes-one.

18. Siobhan Gorman and Julian E. Barnes, "Cyber Combat: Act of War," *Wall Street Journal*, May 30, 2011, http://online.wsj.com/article/SB10001424052702304563104576355623135782718.html.

19. Michael Riley and John Walcott, "China-Based Hacking of 760 Companies Shows Cyber Cold War," December 14, 2011, http://www.bloomberg.com/news/2011-12-13/china-based-hacking-of-760-companies-reflects-undeclared-global-cyber-war.html.

20. Dana A. Shea and Frank Gottron, *Small-Scale Terrorist Attacks Using Chemical and Biological Agents: An Assessment Framework and Preliminary Comparisons*, Congressional Research Service, Report for Congress, May 20, 2004, http://www.fas.org/irp/crs/RL32391.pdf.

21. Edward J. Tully and E. L. Willoughby, "Terrorism: The Role of Local and State Police Agencies," National Executive Institute Associates, May 2002, http://www.neiassociates.org/terrorism-role-local-state-pol/.

22. D. G. Bolgiano, "Military Support of Domestic Law Enforcement Operations: Working Within Posse Comitatus," *FBI Law Enforcement Bulletin* (December 2001), pp. 16–24.

23. U.S. Department of Homeland Security, *National Incident Management System* (Washington, D.C.: Author, March 2004), pp. viii, ix.

24. Robert S. Mueller III, "Statement Before the Senate Judiciary Committee," September 17, 2008, http://www.fbi.gov/news/testimony/preparing-for-the-challenges-of-the-future.

25. Gary Peck and Laura Mijanovich, "Give Us Security While Retaining Freedoms," *Reno Gazette Journal,* August 28, 2003, p. 9A.

26. "House Approves Patriot Act Renewal," http://www.cnn.com/2006/POLITICS/03/07/patriot.act/.

27. Julien Hattam, "Obama signs NSA bill, renewing Patriot Act powers," *The Hill,* June 2, 2015; http://thehill.com/policy/national-security/243850-obama-signs-nsa-bill-renewing-patriot-act-powers

28. Jurist: Legal News and Research, "Bush Signs Military Commissions Act," http://jurist.law.pitt.edu/paperchase/2006/10/bush-signs-military-commissions-act.php.

29. Ibid.

30. Seana Beaghly, "The USA Freedom Act: The Definition of a Compromise," *The Hill,* May 29, 2015, http://thehill.com/blogs/congress-blog/homeland-security/243333-the-usa-freedom-act-the-definition-of-a-compromise.

31. Erin Kelly, "Senate Approves USA Freedom Act," *USA Today*, June 2, 2015, http://www.usatoday.com/story/news/politics/2015/06/02/patriot-act-usa-freedom-act-senate-vote/28345747/.

32. Lev Grossman, "Drone Home," *Time*, February 11, 2013, pp. 26–33.

33. See "White House, Justice Officials Defend Drone Program After Release of Memo," *Associated Press* and *Fox News*, February 5, 2013, http://www.foxnews.com/politics/2013/02/05/senators-threaten-confrontation-with-obama-nominees-over-drone-concerns/.

34. Kaveh Waddell, "Few Privacy Limitations Exist on How Police Use Drones," *National Journal*, February 5, 2015, http://www.nationaljournal.com/tech/few-privacy-limitations-exist-on-how-police-use-drones-20150205.

35. Agnes Radomski, "It's Time for the NYPD to Stop Treating Mentally Ill New Yorkers Like Criminals," *Nation*, October 9, 2014, http://www.thenation.com/article/181926/its-time-nypd-stop-treating-mentally-ill-new-yorkers-criminals#.

36. Kevin Johnson, "Memphis Program Offers Example for Police and Mentally Ill," *USA Today*, October 2, 2013, http://www.usatoday.com/story/news/nation/2013/10/02/police-navy-yard-mental-illness-alexis-shooting/2910763/.

37. Treatment Advocacy Center, *The Treatment of Persons With Mental Illness in Prisons and Jails: A State Survey (abridged)*, April 8, 2014, p. 4, http://tacreports.org/treatment-behind-bars/executive-summary.

38. Sam P. K. Collins, "Introducing Mental Health Courts," ThinkProgress, April 10, 2015, http://thinkprogress.org/health/2015/04/10/3645289/mental-health-prison-report/. *Note:* "Mental illness" refers generally to diagnosable diseases of the brain recognized in the American Psychiatric Association's *Diagnostic and Statistical Manual,* such as schizophrenia, psychosis, bipolar disorder, and schizoaffective disorder.

39. Ken Duckworth and Jacob Freedman, "Dual Diagnosis Fact Sheet," National Alliance on Mental Illness, February 2013, http://www2.nami.org/factsheets/dualdiagnosis_factsheet.pdf.

40. Rick Jervis, "Mental Disorders Keeps Thousands of Homeless on Streets," *USA Today*, August 27, 2014, http://www.usatoday.com/story/news/nation/2014/08/27/mental-health-homeless-series/14255283/.

41. Joseph Galanek, "The 'Revolving Door' for the Justice-Involved Mentally Ill," Justice Center—The Council for State Governments, April 21, 2015, http://csgjusticecenter.org/mental-health/media-clips/the-revolving-door-for-the-justice-involved-mentally-ill/.

42. Kevin Johnson, "Memphis Program Offers Example for Police and Mentally Ill," *USA Today*, October 2, 2013, http://www.usatoday.com/story/news/nation/2013/10/02/police-navy-yard-mental-illness-alexis-shooting/2910763/.

43. See generally Stanford Law School, Three Strikes Project, *When Did Prisons Become Acceptable Mental Healthcare Facilities?* May 2014, https://www.law.stanford.edu/organizations/programs-and-centers/stanford-three-strikes-project/report-when-did-prisons-become-acceptable-mental-healthcare-fa.

44. "The New Asylums," PBS Frontline, May 10, 2005, http://www.pbs.org/wgbh/pages/frontline/shows/asylums/.

45. Michael Winerip and Michael Schwirtz, "Rikers: Where Mental Illness Meets Brutality in Jail," *New York Times*, July 14, 2014, http://www.nytimes.com/2014/07/14/nyregion/rikers-study-finds-prisoners-injured-by-employees.html?_r=0.

46. "The Death of Timothy Souders," *60 Minutes*, July 17, 2007, http://www.cbsnews.com/news/the-death-of-timothy-souders/; Tyler Dukes, "One Year Later, Inmate's Death Looms Over State Prison Mental Health Debate," WRAL.com, March 12, 2014, http://www.wral.com/one-year-later-inmate-s-death-looms-over-prison-mental-health-debate/14506834/.

47. Erin Hicks, "Crisis Intervention in a Correctional Setting," Corrections One, August 10, 2011, http://www.correctionsone.com/jail-management/articles/4206236-Crisis-intervention-in-a-correctional-setting/.

48. NCJA Center for Justice Planning, "Addressing the Intersection: The Oklahoma Collaborative Mental Health Reentry Program," http://www.ncjp.org/index.php?q=content/addressing-intersection-oklahoma-collaborative-mental-health-reentry-program.

49. "The Drug War, Mass Incarceration and Race," Drug Policy Alliance Fact Sheet, January 2015, http://www.drugpolicy.org/sites/default/files/DPA_Fact_Sheet_Drug_War_Mass_Incarceration_and_Race_Jan2015.pdf.

50. Rob Reuteman, "The Cost-and-Benefit Arguments Around Enforcement," CNBC, April 20, 2010, http://www.cnbc.com/id/36600923.

51. ProCon.org, "23 Legal Medical Marijuana States and DC," May 5, 2015, http://medicalmarijuana.procon.org/view.resource.php?resourceID=000881.

52. Alan Horowitz, "Mental Illness Soars in Prisons, Jails While Inmates Suffer," *Huffington Post*, February 4, 2014, http://www.huffingtonpost.com/2013/02/04/mental-illness-prisons-jails-inmates_n_2610062.html.

53. U.S. Department of Justice, Bureau of Justice Statistics, *Mortality in Local Jails and State Prisons, 20002010: Statistical Tables* (December 2012), p. 2, http://www.bjs.gov/content/pub/pdf/mljsp0010st.pdf.

54. Matt Ferner, "One Marijuana Arrest Occurs Every 42 Seconds in U.S.: FBI Report," *Huffington Post,* October 29, 2012, http://www.huffingtonpost.com/2012/10/29/one-marijuana-arrest-occu_n_2041236.html.

55. BalancedPolitics.org, "Should Marijuana Be Legalized Under Any Circumstances?" http://www.balancedpolitics.org/marijuana_legalization.htm.

56. Micah Cohen, "Marijuana Legalization and States Rights," *New York Times*, December 8, 2012, http://fivethirtyeight.blogs.nytimes.com/2012/12/08/marijuana-legalization-and-states-rights/?pagewanted=print.

57. Law Enforcement Against Prohibition, "Who We Are," http://www.leap.cc/about/who-we-are/.

58. Ibid.

59. BalancedPolitics.org, "Should Marijuana Be Legalized Under Any Circumstances?"

60. Raven Clabough, "Colorado Governor Signs Marijuana Regulations Into Law," *New American,* May 31, 2013, http://www.thenewamerican.com/usnews/politics/item/15578-colorado-governor-signs-marijuana-regulations-into-law.

61. John Ingold, "Colorado Pot Legalization: 30 Questions (and Answers)," *Denver Post,* December 12, 2012, http://www.denverpost.com/breakingnews/ci_22184944/colorado-pot-legalization-30-questions-and-answers.

62. See U.S. Department of Justice, Drug Enforcement Administration, "Title 21 CFR, Part 1300-1399," http://www.deadiversion.usdoj.gov/21cfr/cfr/index.html.

63. "Medical Marijuana: Research, Not Fear," *Los Angeles Times*, July 13, 2011, http://articles.latimes.com/2011/jul/13/opinion/la-ed-marijuana-20110713.

64. Lizette Borelli, "Uruguay to Legalize Marijuana for Entire Country: Will the Bill Save Money and Lives?" *Medical Daily*, August 13, 2013, http://www.medicaldaily.com/uruguay-legalize-marijuana-entire-country-will-bill-save-money-and-lives-248250.

65. Natalie Dalton, "Marijuana Should Be Legalized Worldwide: Santos," *Colombia Reports*, October 25, 2011, http://colombiareports.com/marijuana-should-be-globally-legalized-santos/.

66. "Czech Republic Legalizes Medical Marijuana Use," *Huffington Post*, February 15, 2013, http://www.huffingtonpost.com/2013/02/15/czech-republic-medical-marijuana_n_2693657.html.

67. Arthur Brice, "Argentina Court Ruling Would Allow Personal Use of Pot," CNN.com/World, August 25, 2009, http://www.cnn.com/2009/WORLD/americas/08/25/argentina.drug.decriminalization/.

68. *Washington Post*, "Time to Legalize Marijuana in Mexico City" (editorial appearing in TicoTimes.net, July 27, 2013), http://www.ticotimes.net/More-news/News-Briefs/Time-to-legalize-marijuana-in-Mexico-City_Sunday-July-28-2013.

69. Charlie Savage, "Administration Weighs Legal Action Against States That Legalized Marijuana Use," *New York Times*, December 6, 2012, http://www.nytimes.com/2012/12/07/us/marijuana-initiatives-in-2-states-set-federal-officials-scrambling.html?_r=1&.

70. Evan Perez, "No Federal Challenge to Pot Legalization in Two States," CNN Justice, August 30, 2013, http://www.cnn.com/2013/08/29/politics/holder-marijuana-laws/.

71. Matt Ferner, "Nebraska, Oklahoma File Federal Suit Against Colorado Over Marijuana Legalization," *Huffington Post,* December 29, 2014, http://www.huffingtonpost.com/2014/12/18/lawsuit-colorado-marijuana_n_6350162.html.

72. Samantha Lochman, "Sheriffs From 3 States Join Forces to Take Aim at Colorado's Marijuana Laws," *Huffington Post,* March 5, 2015, http://www.huffingtonpost.com/2015/03/05/colorado-marijuana-lawsuit_n_6808358.html.

73. Matt Ferner, "Colorado Asks Supreme Court to Toss Marijuana Lawsuit Filed by Nebraska, Oklahoma," *Huffington Post,* March 27, 2015, http://www.huffingtonpost.com/2015/03/27/colorado-marijuana-lawsuit_n_6958336.html.

74. American Civil Liberties Union, "Fair Sentencing Act," May 2015, https://www.aclu.org/node/17576.

75. Massimo Calabresi, "The Price of Relief," *Time,* June 15, 2015, pp. 2533.

76. Ibid.

77. Centers for Disease Control and Prevention, "Outbreak of Recent HIV and HCV Infections Among Persons Who Inject Drugs," April 24, 2015, http://www.bt.cdc.gov/han/han00377.asp.

78. Calabresi, "The Price of Relief," p. 33.

Index

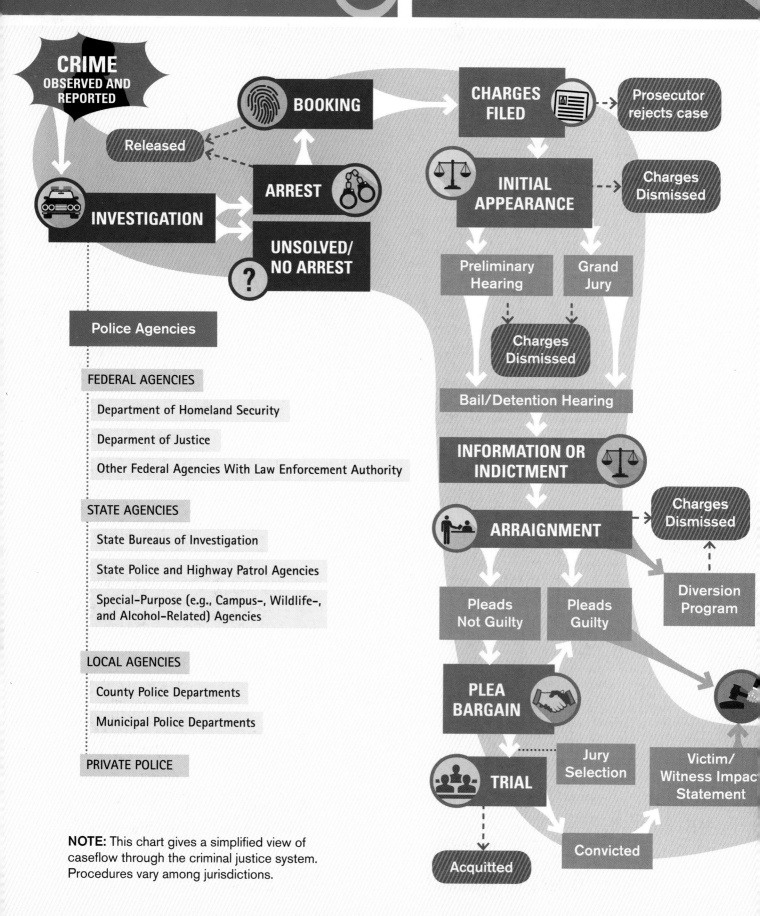

POLICING

COURTS

CRIME OBSERVED AND REPORTED

BOOKING

Released

ARREST

INVESTIGATION

UNSOLVED/ NO ARREST

?

CHARGES FILED

Prosecutor rejects case

INITIAL APPEARANCE

Charges Dismissed

Preliminary Hearing

Grand Jury

Charges Dismissed

Bail/Detention Hearing

INFORMATION OR INDICTMENT

ARRAIGNMENT

Charges Dismissed

Pleads Not Guilty

Pleads Guilty

Diversion Program

PLEA BARGAIN

Jury Selection

Victim/ Witness Impact Statement

TRIAL

Convicted

Acquitted

Police Agencies

FEDERAL AGENCIES

Department of Homeland Security

Deparment of Justice

Other Federal Agencies With Law Enforcement Authority

STATE AGENCIES

State Bureaus of Investigation

State Police and Highway Patrol Agencies

Special-Purpose (e.g., Campus-, Wildlife-, and Alcohol-Related) Agencies

LOCAL AGENCIES

County Police Departments

Municipal Police Departments

PRIVATE POLICE

NOTE: This chart gives a simplified view of caseflow through the criminal justice system. Procedures vary among jurisdictions.